£1·99

CHAMBERS

REFERENCE
ATLAS

CHAMBERS

REFERENCE ATLAS

CHAMBERS

For the English-language edition:

Consultant

Dr David Munro, Director,
Royal Scottish Geographical Society

Cartographers

Ruth Hall
Belinda Kane

Editor

Camilla Rockwood

Publishing manager

Patrick White

Prepress

Vienna Leigh

Prepress manager

Sharon McTeir

Translator

Sheila Hardie

Proofreaders

Harry Campbell
Ruth Hall

Originally published by Larousse as *Atlas Petit Larousse des pays du monde*

© Larousse/VUEF 2003

English-language edition
© Chambers Harrap Publishers Ltd 2005

ISBN 0550 10163 2

Cover image: Getty Images

Typeset by Chambers Harrap Publishers Ltd, Edinburgh
Printed in Singapore by Tien Wah Press (PTE.) Ltd

CONTENTS

5

NATIONS OF
THE WORLD

7

276 OCEANIA

Endpapers:

European Union
Antarctica
Arctic

GLOSSARY

Annual inflation rate

A measurement of the change in consumer prices from one year to the next.

Area

The total surface area of a country's national territory, excluding any dependencies. In most countries this includes inland waters but excludes territorial waters. The data for Cyprus correspond to the whole island.

Armed forces

The total number of regular members and conscripts of the army, navy, air force and strategic army, as well as administrative and support staff and army police forces. Reservists are not counted.

Average daily calorie intake

The equivalent in calories of the net national food supply (local production plus imports and less exports), divided by the total number of inhabitants in the country.

Birth rate

The gross birth rate, which is the ratio (for one year or a given period) between the number of births and the total population, expressed per 1,000 inhabitants.

Cars

The number of cars in service per 1,000 inhabitants in a given country for a given year. Bearing in mind that different means of calculation are used in different countries, comparisons between countries should be made with caution.

Death rate

The gross mortality rate, which is the ratio (for one year or a given period) between the number of deaths and the total population, expressed per 1,000 inhabitants.

Defence budget

The amount of money in a country's national budget allocated to military expenditure. This is expressed as a percentage of the country's GDP (Gross Domestic Product).

Density

The average density, which is the figure obtained by dividing the total population of a country by its total surface area. Locally, this figure can often differ greatly from the country's overall average density (suburbs, deserts, etc).

Exports

The value of all commodities sold by a country. The figures given do not take into account insurance (CIF: Cost, Insurance and Freight) and are calculated free on board (FOB). The percentage of a country's exports in relation to its GDP (Gross Domestic Product) is a good indicator of the extent to which the country is involved in the world economy.

GDP annual growth rate

The variation in the GDP (Gross Domestic Product) over two successive years, assuming prices to be constant.

GNP

The Gross National Product (GNP) is the sum of all goods and services produced in a given year within a country (the GDP, or gross domestic product) plus the income from property held in foreign countries and incomes of domestic residents received from abroad, minus similar payments made to residents of other countries. The GNP is given in US dollars.

GNP per capita

The Gross National Product (GNP) per capita is the GNP of a given country, as defined above, divided by the total population of the country. The GNP per capita is given in US dollars.

GNP per capita PPP

The Gross National Product (GNP) per capita expressed in purchasing power parity. The purchasing power parity is established by defining the number of monetary units of a given country that are required to purchase a representative 'basket' of goods and services. The results are compared with the same purchases made in the USA and expressed in US dollars; this is then compared to a fictitious dollar known as the 'international dollar'. The GNP per capita measured in purchasing power parity provides values that can allow us to compare directly the relative purchasing power of different countries' currencies to purchase the same goods and services.

Gross public debt

The public finances deficit/surplus is the sum of a country's financial commitments with regard to its public administration. The financial commitments of central government, local government and the social security system are all included in this figure.

HDI (Human Development Index)

The Human Development Index was created in 1990 by the United Nations Development Programme in order to provide a more realistic statistical measure of human development than GNP (Gross National Product) per capita. This index takes equal account of three elements: life expectancy, education and standard of living. This is achieved by studying the following factors: life expectancy at birth, the level of school attendance, the adult literacy rate/educational attainment and the GDP per capita PPP (purchasing power parity). A country with high human development will have an HDI equal to or over 0.800. A country with a moderate level of human development will have an HDI between 0.500 and 0.799, and a country with a low level of human development will have an HDI of under 0.500. These statistics cover most UN member countries.

Imports

The value of all commodities bought by a country. As in the case of exports, the figures are calculated free on board (FOB).

Infant mortality rate

The ratio between the annual number of deaths of children under one year old and the total number of births, expressed per 1,000 live births.

Inhabitants per doctor

This number is obtained by dividing the total population of a country by the total number of doctors in that country. The total number of doctors includes practising doctors and all graduates of medical schools and faculties employed in the field of medicine (practical work, teaching, administration and research).

Labour force by occupation

The distribution by occupation of all the economically active persons in a country above a certain age (usually 15 years old).

Life expectancy at birth

The average life expectancy for men or women at birth. The figures are calculated for a given year and apply to that year's generation of men and women (ie to all children born that year), taking into account all deaths during that year across all generations.

Percentage of population in urban areas

The proportion of the total population living in zones that are defined as urban in each country. This definition can vary considerably from one country to the next.

Population

The total population is the total number of inhabitants of a country on a given date. The data (provided by the United Nations) are forecasts for 2002, based on estimates from 2000 and determined by applying an average fertility rate. These estimates are themselves based on data from national demographic institutes, which carry out fairly regular censuses and propose estimates. The estimate of a population size in the middle of a year includes all the country's residents, irrespective of their legal status or citizenship. Refugees who have not become permanently established in the country where they have found asylum are counted in their countries of origin. The estimates provided by the UN sometimes differ considerably from those provided by the countries themselves. This is because different means of calculation have been used, in particular with regard to the fertility rate.

Televisions

The number of televisions in service per 1,000 inhabitants in a given country for a given year.

Tourism revenue

The total amount of money spent by international tourists whilst visiting a given country. This includes international transport costs paid to national transport companies, and all prepayments for goods and services in the host country.

Unemployment rate

The percentage of the economically active population that is unemployed, available for work and capable of working.

MAIN SOURCES

2002 World Development Indicators, The World Bank, Washington, 2002.

FAO Statistical Databases, United Nations Food and Agricultural Organization, Rome, 2002.

Human Development Report 2002, United Nations Development Programme, Oxford University Press, Oxford, 2002.

International Financial Statistics, International Monetary Fund, Washington, January 2003.

Population Division, Databases of Population, Estimates and Projections, Population Division, United Nations Organization, New York, 2000.

The Military Balance 2001–2002, The International Institute for Strategic Studies, Oxford University Press, London, 2002.

GENERAL DATA

Average life expectancy at birth: the top ten countries for the period 2000–5 (in years)	
Japan	81.6
Sweden	80.1
Iceland	79.8
Spain	79.3
Canada	79.3
Israel	79.2
Australia	79.2
Switzerland	79.1
France	79
Norway	78.9

Gross National Product: the top ten countries in 2002 (in billions of US dollars)	
USA	10 207
Japan	4 324
Germany	1 876
United Kingdom	1 511
France	1 362
China	1 234
Italy	1 101
Canada	702
Mexico	597
Spain	596

Oil: the top ten producing countries in 2002 (in thousands of tonnes)	
Saudi Arabia	418 100
Russia	379 600
USA	346 816
Mexico	177 999
China	168 900
Iran	166 800
Norway	156 381
Venezuela	151 400
Canada	123 347
United Kingdom	116 205
World	3 556 800

Average life expectancy at birth: the bottom ten countries for the period 2000–5 (in years)	
Zambia	32.4
Zimbabwe	33.1
Sierra Leone	34.2
Swaziland	34.4
Lesotho	35.1
Malawi	37.5
Mozambique	38.1
Rwanda	39.3
Central African Republic	39.5
Botswana	39.7

Gross National Product per capita expressed in purchasing power parity: the top ten countries in 2002 (in international dollars)	
Luxembourg	53 290
Norway	36 690
USA	36 110
Switzerland	31 840
Denmark	30 600
Ireland	29 570
Iceland	29 240
Canada	28 930
Austria	28 910
The Netherlands	28 350

Gas: the top ten producing countries in 2002 (in millions of m³)	
Russia	554 900
USA	547 700
Canada	187 574
United Kingdom	108 435
Algeria	80 400
The Netherlands	75 555
Indonesia	70 600
Norway	67 627
Iran	64 500
Saudi Arabia	56 400
World	2 527 600

Fertility rate: the ten highest rates for the period 2000–5 (in number of children per woman)	
Niger	8
Somalia	7.25
Angola	7.2
Guinea-Bissau	7.1
Uganda	7.1
Yemen	7.01
Mali	7
Afghanistan	6.8
Burundi	6.8
Liberia	6.8

Gross National Product per capita expressed in purchasing power parity: the bottom ten countries in 2002 (in international dollars)	
Sierra Leone	500
Malawi	570
Tanzania	580
Burundi	630
Congo (Dem. Rep. of the)	630
Guinea-Bissau	680
Congo (Republic of)	710
Madagascar	730
Ethiopia	780
Yemen	800

Coal: the top ten producing countries in 2001 (in thousands of tonnes)	
China	1 032 201
USA	937 435
India	284 870
Australia	257 264
South Africa	225 573
Russia	155 689
Poland	102 490
Indonesia	90 370
Kazakhstan	77 584
Czech Republic	65 640
World	3 833 000

Fertility rate: the ten lowest rates for the period 2000–5 (in number of children per woman)	
Bulgaria	1.1
Latvia	1.1
Russia	1.14
Slovenia	1.14
Armenia	1.15
Spain	1.15
Ukraine	1.15
Czech Republic	1.16
Belarus	1.2
Hungary	1.2

Gross Domestic Product: the top ten countries in 2002 (in billions of US dollars)	
USA	10 383
Japan	3 993
Germany	1 984
United Kingdom	1 566
France	1 431
China	1 266
Italy	1 184
Canada	714
Spain	653
Mexico	637

Electricity: the top ten producing countries in 2001 (in millions of kWh)	
USA	3 719 485
China	1 420 349
Japan	1 036 798
Russia	846 455
Canada	566 310
Germany	544 828
India	533 335
France	520 149
United Kingdom	360 926
Brazil	321 165
World	14 732 800

Wheat: the top ten producing countries in 2002 (in thousands of tonnes)	
China	90 290
India	71 814
Russia	50 609
USA	44 062
France	38 934
Germany	20 818
Ukraine	20 556
Turkey	19 500
Pakistan	18 227
Canada	16 198
World	572 666

Soya beans: the top ten producing countries in 2002 (in thousands of tonnes)	
USA	74 825
Brazil	42 027
Argentina	30 000
China	16 900
India	4 270
Paraguay	3 300
Canada	2 335
Bolivia	1 167
Indonesia	653
Italy	566
World	180 552

Sorghum: the top ten producing countries in 2002 (in thousands of tonnes)	
USA	9 392
Nigeria	7 704
India	6 920
Mexico	5 206
China	3 347
Argentina	2 847
Sudan	2 800
Ethiopia	1 566
Burkina	1 373
Mali	951
World	52 191

Rice: the top ten producing countries in 2002 (in thousands of tonnes)	
China	176 342
India	113 580
Indonesia	51 579
Bangladesh	37 851
Vietnam	34 447
Thailand	25 611
Myanmar (Burma)	22 780
Philippines	13 271
Japan	11 111
Brazil	10 472
World	575 429

Citrus fruits: the top ten producing countries in 2002 (in thousands of tonnes)	
Brazil	20 004
USA	14 685
China	12 461
Mexico	6 165
Spain	5 783
India	4 580
Iran	3 732
Nigeria	3 250
Italy	2 789
Argentina	2 566
World	103 449

Steel: the top ten producing countries in 2002 (in thousands of tonnes)	
China	220 115
Japan	110 510
USA	91 360
Russia	61 325
South Korea	46 306
Germany	44 841
Ukraine	36 707
India	31 779
Brazil	31 105
Italy	26 740
World	945 140

Maize: the top ten producing countries in 2002 (in thousands of tonnes)	
USA	228 805
China	121 497
Brazil	35 500
Mexico	19 299
France	16 460
Argentina	15 000
India	11 110
Italy	10 824
South Africa	10 049
Indonesia	9 527
World	604 407

Seed cotton: the top ten producing countries in 2002 (in thousands of tonnes)	
China	14 748
USA	9 556
Pakistan	5 187
India	4 750
Uzbekistan	3 200
Turkey	2 240
Brazil	2 164
Greece	1 282
Australia	822
Egypt	820
World	53 143

Cars: the top ten producing countries in 2002 (in thousands of units)	
Japan	8 619
Germany	5 123
USA	5 016
France	3 284
South Korea	2 651
Spain	2 267
United Kingdom	1 628
Brazil	1 521
Canada	1 369
Italy	1 126
World	41 116

Coffee: the top ten producing countries in 2002 (in thousands of tonnes)	
Brazil	2 494
Colombia	697
Vietnam	689
Indonesia	623
India	317
Mexico	313
Ethiopia	220
Côte d'Ivoire	198
Uganda	198
Honduras	182
World	7 667

Yams: the top ten producing countries in 2002 (in thousands of tonnes)	
Nigeria	26 849
Ghana	3 900
Côte d'Ivoire	3 000
Benin	1 875
Togo	575
Central African Republic	350
Congo (Dem. Rep. of the)	320
Ethiopia	300
Cameroon	265
Colombia	237
World	39 685

Tourism revenue: the top ten countries in 2001 (in millions of US dollars)	
USA	72 295
Spain	32 873
France	29 979
Italy	25 787
China	17 792
Germany	17 225
United Kingdom	16 283
Canada	10 774
Austria	10 118
Turkey	8 932
World	457 890

THEMATIC MAPS

ORGANIZATIONS

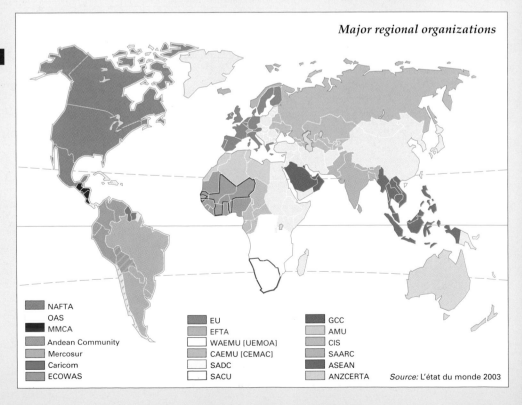

Major international organizations

| OECD |
| NATO |
| Commonwealth |
| OPEC |
| Arab League |
| APEC |

Council of Europe

OSCE
+Canada
+USA

Source:
L'état du monde 2003

Major regional organizations

NAFTA	EU	GCC
OAS	EFTA	AMU
MMCA	WAEMU [UEMOA]	CIS
Andean Community	CAEMU [CEMAC]	SAARC
Mercosur	SADC	ASEAN
Caricom	SACU	ANZCERTA
ECOWAS		

Source: L'état du monde 2003

LANGUAGES AND RELIGIONS

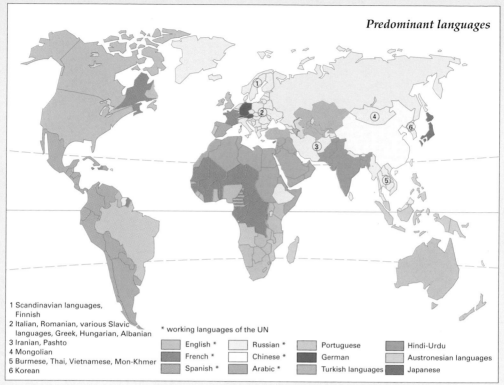

Predominant languages

1 Scandinavian languages, Finnish
2 Italian, Romanian, various Slavic languages, Greek, Hungarian, Albanian
3 Iranian, Pashto
4 Mongolian
5 Burmese, Thai, Vietnamese, Mon-Khmer
6 Korean

* working languages of the UN

English *	Russian *
French *	Chinese *
Spanish *	Arabic *

Portuguese	Hindi-Urdu
German	Austronesian languages
Turkish languages	Japanese

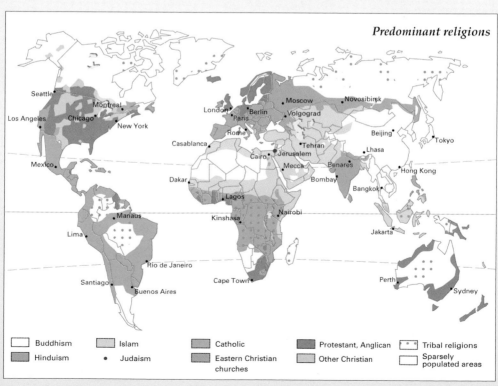

Predominant religions

Buddhism	Islam	Catholic	Protestant, Anglican	Tribal religions
Hinduism	• Judaism	Eastern Christian churches	Other Christian	Sparsely populated areas

POPULATION

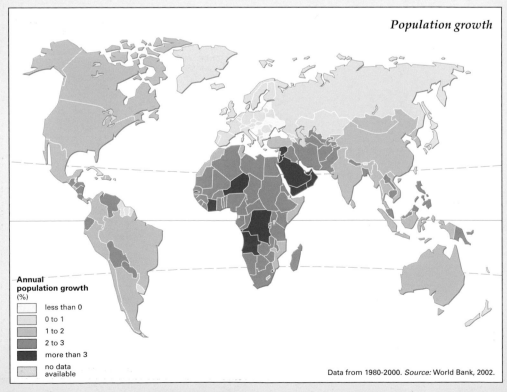

Population density

NORTHWEST
EUROPE

NORTHEAST
USA

MIDDLE
EAST

EASTERN ASIA

SOUTHERN ASIA

WEST AFRICAN
COAST

JAVA

SOUTHEAST
BRAZIL

Population density
(inhabitants/km²)

- less than 1
- 1 to 10
- 10 to 50
- 50 to 100
- more than 100

Population growth

**Annual
population growth**
(%)

- less than 0
- 0 to 1
- 1 to 2
- 2 to 3
- more than 3
- no data
  available

Data from 1980-2000. *Source:* World Bank, 2002.

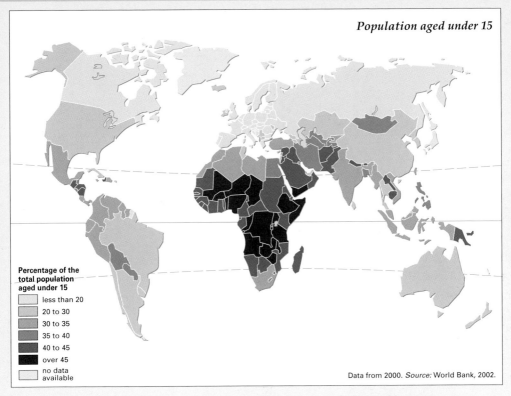

Population aged under 15

Percentage of the total population aged under 15

- less than 20
- 20 to 30
- 30 to 35
- 35 to 40
- 40 to 45
- over 45
- no data available

Data from 2000. *Source:* World Bank, 2002.

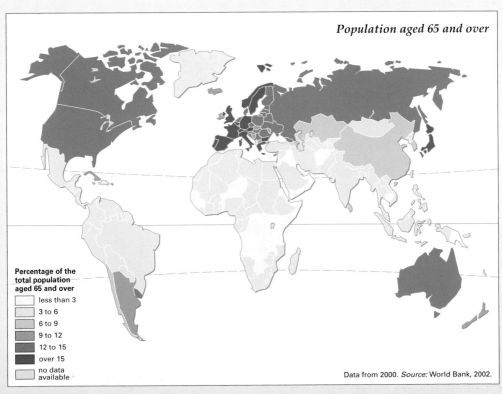

Population aged 65 and over

Percentage of the total population aged 65 and over

- less than 3
- 3 to 6
- 6 to 9
- 9 to 12
- 12 to 15
- over 15
- no data available

Data from 2000. *Source:* World Bank, 2002.

POPULATION

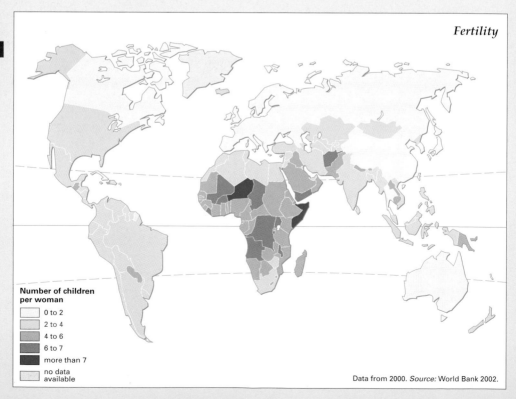

Life expectancy

Life expectancy at birth
(years)

- less than 40
- 40 to 50
- 50 to 60
- 60 to 70
- 70 to 75
- over 75
- no data available

Data from 2000. *Source:* World Bank, 2002.

Fertility

Number of children per woman

- 0 to 2
- 2 to 4
- 4 to 6
- 6 to 7
- more than 7
- no data available

Data from 2000. *Source:* World Bank 2002.

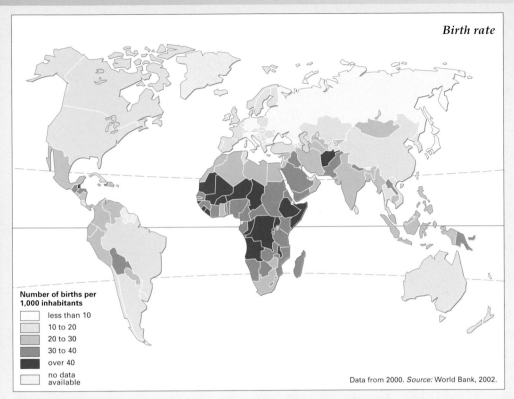

Birth rate

Number of births per 1,000 inhabitants

- less than 10
- 10 to 20
- 20 to 30
- 30 to 40
- over 40
- no data available

Data from 2000. *Source:* World Bank, 2002.

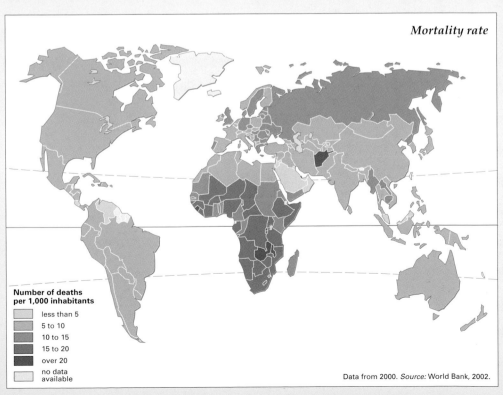

Mortality rate

Number of deaths per 1,000 inhabitants

- less than 5
- 5 to 10
- 10 to 15
- 15 to 20
- over 20
- no data available

Data from 2000. *Source:* World Bank, 2002.

ENVIRONMENT

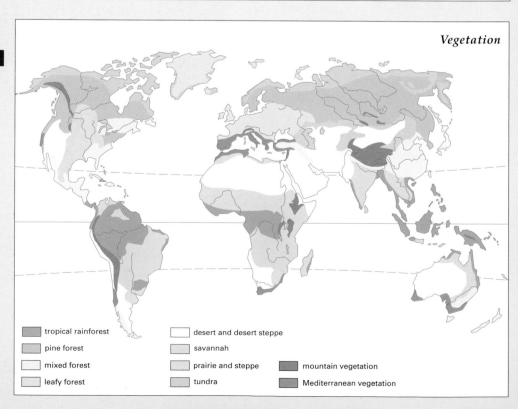

Climate

Tropical climate
- rainforest
- savannah

Arid climate
- semi-arid
- desert

Subtropical climate
- dry summers
- dry winters
- no dry season

Continental climate
- no dry season
- dry winters

Polar climate
- tundra climate
- snow and high mountains

Vegetation

- tropical rainforest
- pine forest
- mixed forest
- leafy forest
- desert and desert steppe
- savannah
- prairie and steppe
- tundra
- mountain vegetation
- Mediterranean vegetation

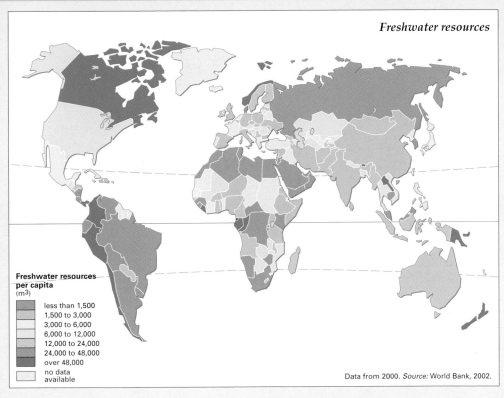

Freshwater resources

Freshwater resources per capita
(m³)

- less than 1,500
- 1,500 to 3,000
- 3,000 to 6,000
- 6,000 to 12,000
- 12,000 to 24,000
- 24,000 to 48,000
- over 48,000
- no data available

Data from 2000. *Source:* World Bank, 2002.

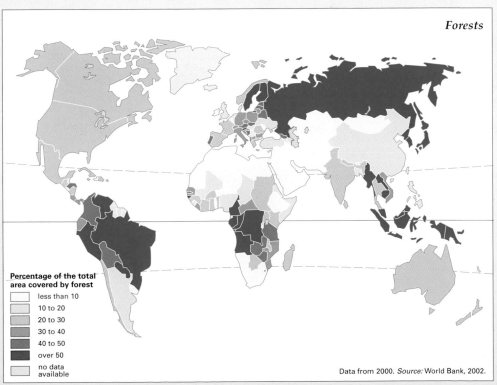

Forests

Percentage of the total area covered by forest

- less than 10
- 10 to 20
- 20 to 30
- 30 to 40
- 40 to 50
- over 50
- no data available

Data from 2000. *Source:* World Bank, 2002.

URBANIZATION

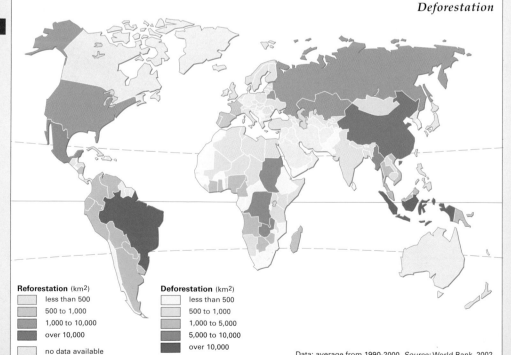

Urban population

Los Angeles
New York
Mexico
Tokyo
Beijing
Osaka-Kobe
Shanghai
Cairo
Karachi
Delhi
Dhaka
Bombay
Calcutta
Manilla
Lagos
Jakarta
Rio de Janeiro
São Paulo
Buenos Aires

Percentage of total population living in cities

- under 30
- 30 to 45
- 45 to 60
- 60 to 75
- over 75
- no data available

Large cities (million inhabitants)

10 to 15   15 to 20   over 20

Data from 2000. *Source:* World Bank, 2002.

Deforestation

Reforestation (km²)
- less than 500
- 500 to 1,000
- 1,000 to 10,000
- over 10,000
- no data available

Deforestation (km²)
- less than 500
- 500 to 1,000
- 1,000 to 5,000
- 5,000 to 10,000
- over 10,000

Data: average from 1990-2000. *Source:* World Bank, 2002.

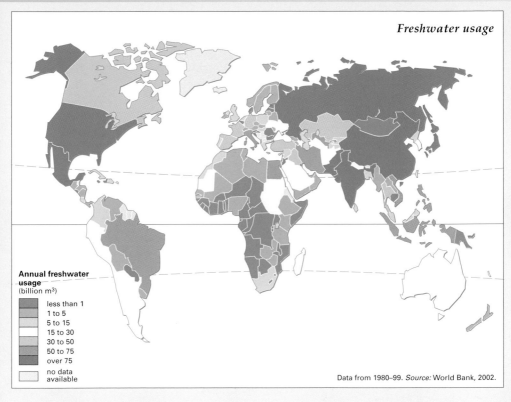

Freshwater usage

Annual freshwater usage
(billion m³)

- less than 1
- 1 to 5
- 5 to 15
- 15 to 30
- 30 to 50
- 50 to 75
- over 75
- no data available

Data from 1980–99. *Source:* World Bank, 2002.

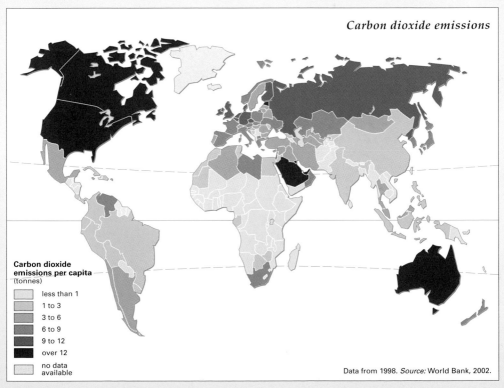

Carbon dioxide emissions

Carbon dioxide emissions per capita
(tonnes)

- less than 1
- 1 to 3
- 3 to 6
- 6 to 9
- 9 to 12
- over 12
- no data available

Data from 1998. *Source:* World Bank, 2002.

EDUCATION

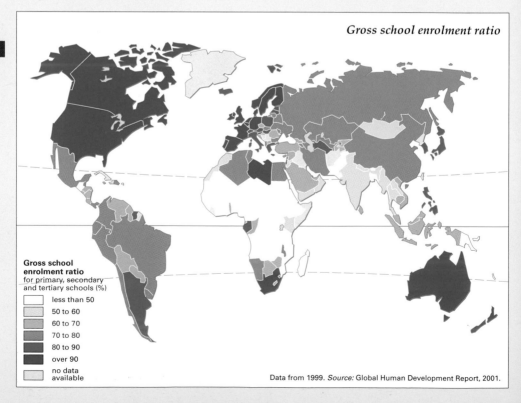

Adult illiteracy in developing countries

Percentage of people aged over 15 who are illiterate

- less than 10
- 10 to 20
- 20 to 30
- 30 to 40
- 40 to 50
- over 50
- no data available
- developed countries

Data from 1999. *Source:* Global Human Development Report, 2001.

Gross school enrolment ratio

Gross school enrolment ratio
for primary, secondary and tertiary schools (%)

- less than 50
- 50 to 60
- 60 to 70
- 70 to 80
- 80 to 90
- over 90
- no data available

Data from 1999. *Source:* Global Human Development Report, 2001.

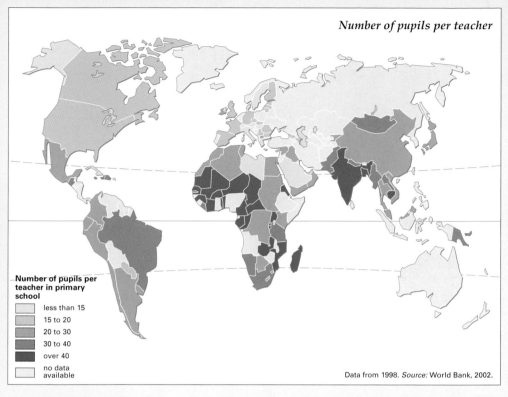

Number of pupils per teacher

Number of pupils per teacher in primary school

- less than 15
- 15 to 20
- 20 to 30
- 30 to 40
- over 40
- no data available

Data from 1998. *Source:* World Bank, 2002.

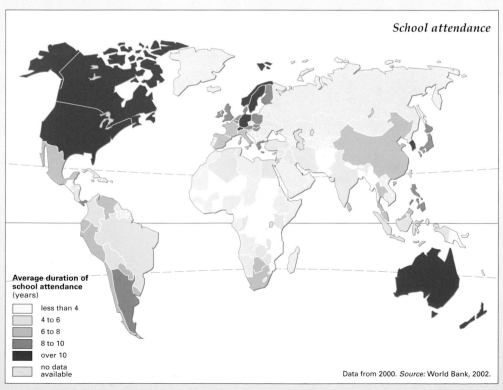

School attendance

Average duration of school attendance (years)

- less than 4
- 4 to 6
- 6 to 8
- 8 to 10
- over 10
- no data available

Data from 2000. *Source:* World Bank, 2002.

STANDARD OF LIVING

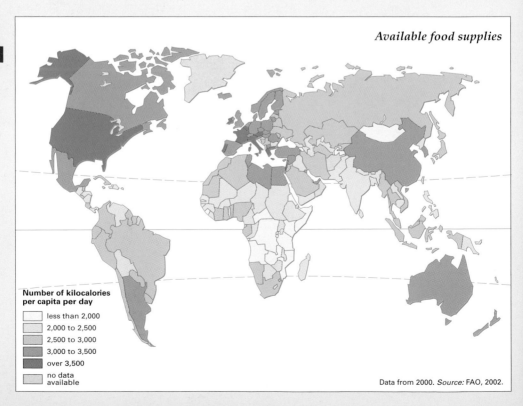

Human Development Index

Human Development Index

low
- less than 0.416
- 0.416 to 0.500

medium
- 0.500 to 0.662
- 0.662 to 0.800

high
- 0.800 to 0.904
- over 0.904

- no data available

Data from 1999. *Source:* Global Human Development Report, 2001.

Available food supplies

Number of kilocalories per capita per day
- less than 2,000
- 2,000 to 2,500
- 2,500 to 3,000
- 3,000 to 3,500
- over 3,500
- no data available

Data from 2000. *Source:* FAO, 2002.

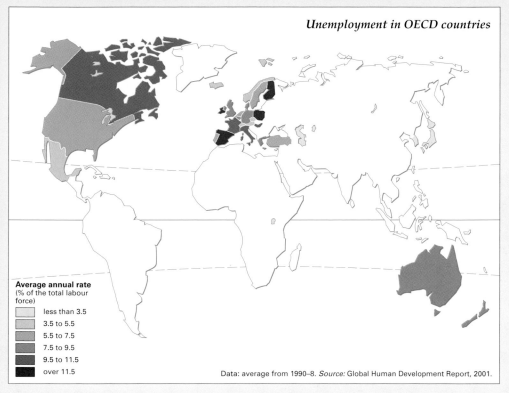

Unemployment in OECD countries

Average annual rate
(% of the total labour force)

- less than 3.5
- 3.5 to 5.5
- 5.5 to 7.5
- 7.5 to 9.5
- 9.5 to 11.5
- over 11.5

Data: average from 1990–8. *Source:* Global Human Development Report, 2001.

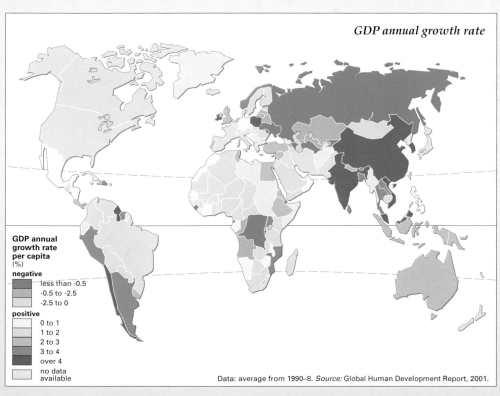

GDP annual growth rate

GDP annual growth rate per capita
(%)

negative
- less than -0.5
- -0.5 to -2.5
- -2.5 to 0

positive
- 0 to 1
- 1 to 2
- 2 to 3
- 3 to 4
- over 4
- no data available

Data: average from 1990–8. *Source:* Global Human Development Report, 2001.

HEALTH

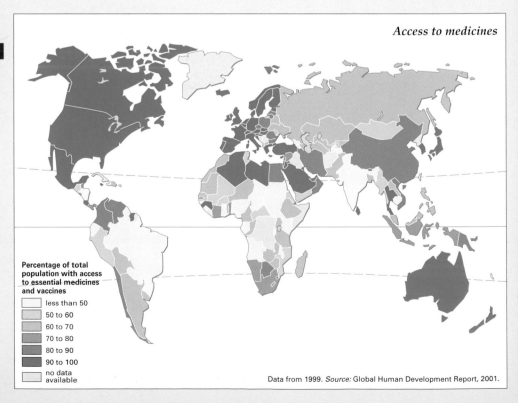

Healthcare spending

**Public and private
healthcare spending**
(% of GDP)
- less than 3
- 3 to 5
- 5 to 7
- 7 to 9
- over 9
- no data
  available

Data from 1995–9. *Source:* World Bank, 2002.

28

Access to medicines

**Percentage of total
population with access
to essential medicines
and vaccines**
- less than 50
- 50 to 60
- 60 to 70
- 70 to 80
- 80 to 90
- 90 to 100
- no data
  available

Data from 1999. *Source:* Global Human Development Report, 2001.

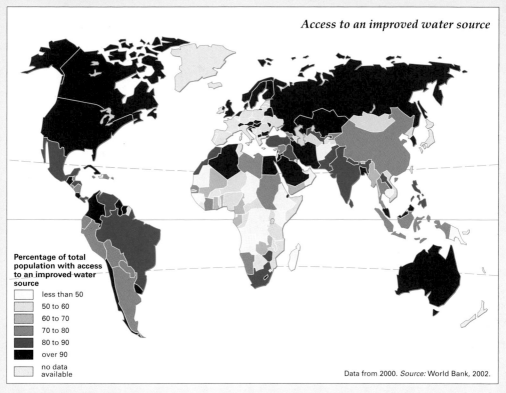

Access to an improved water source

Percentage of total population with access to an improved water source

- less than 50
- 50 to 60
- 60 to 70
- 70 to 80
- 80 to 90
- over 90
- no data available

Data from 2000. *Source:* World Bank, 2002.

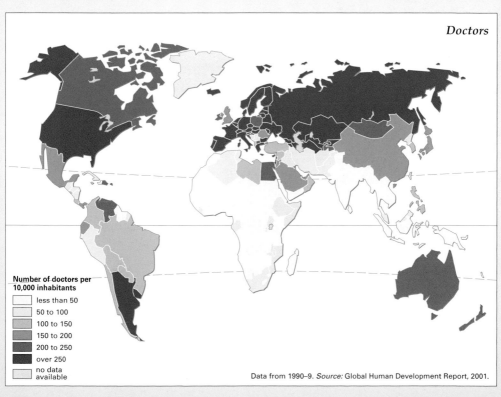

Doctors

Number of doctors per 10,000 inhabitants

- less than 50
- 50 to 100
- 100 to 150
- 150 to 200
- 200 to 250
- over 250
- no data available

Data from 1990–9. *Source:* Global Human Development Report, 2001.

ENERGY

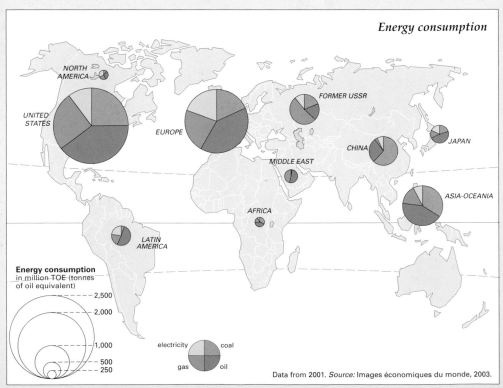

Energy production

NORTH AMERICA

EUROPE

FORMER USSR

AFRICA

MIDDLE EAST

ASIA-OCEANIA

LATIN AMERICA

Energy production
in million TOE (tonnes of oil equivalent)

2000

1000

500

electricity — coal

gas — oil

Data from 2001. *Source:* Images économiques du monde, 2003.

Energy consumption

NORTH AMERICA

UNITED STATES

EUROPE

FORMER USSR

CHINA

JAPAN

MIDDLE EAST

ASIA-OCEANIA

AFRICA

LATIN AMERICA

Energy consumption
in million TOE (tonnes of oil equivalent)

2,500

2,000

1,000

500
250

electricity — coal

gas — oil

Data from 2001. *Source:* Images économiques du monde, 2003.

NATIONS

OF THE

WORLD

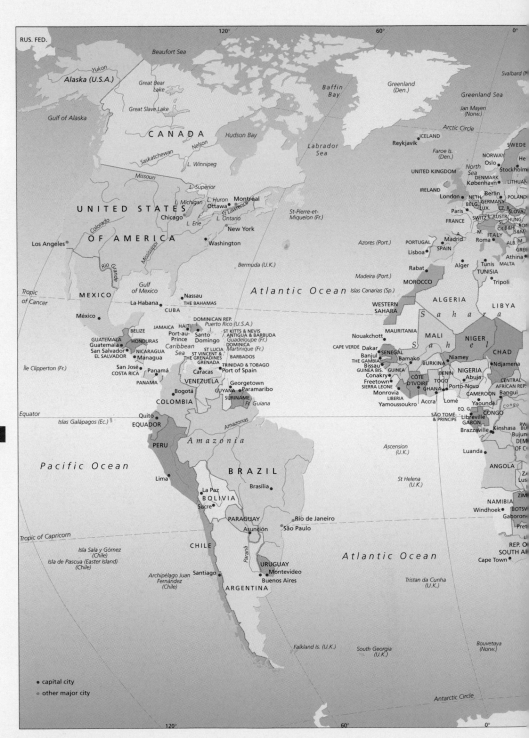

RUS. FED.

Beaufort Sea

Yukon

Alaska (U.S.A.)

Great Bear
Lake

Gulf of Alaska

Great Slave Lake

C A N A D A

Baffin
Bay

Greenland
(Den.)

Greenland Sea

Jan Mayen
(Norw.)

Svalbard (Nor.)

Arctic Circle

Reykjavík   ICELAND   SWEDE

Faroe Is.   NORWAY   He
(Den.)   Oslo

North   DENMARK   Stockholm
Sea   København   LITHUAN.

UNITED KINGDOM

IRELAND   London NETH. Berlin POLAND
                        BELG. GERMANY
Paris   LUX.   CZ. SLOVA.
FRANCE   SWITZ AUSTR. HUNG.
                 M. CR.B&H. S&M.
Madrid   ITALY   ALB.
PORTUGAL   Roma   GRE
Lisboa   SPAIN   Athina
                         MALTA
Rabat   Alger Tunis
MOROCCO   TUNISIA   Tripoli

Hudson Bay

Nelson

L. Winnipeg

Saskatchewan

Missouri

L. Superior

L. Michigan L. Huron Montreal
Chicago Ottawa St. Lawrence
         L. Erie L. Ontario
              New York

St-Pierre-et-
Miquelon (Fr.)

Labrador
Sea

Colorado

U N I T E D   S T A T E S

O F   A M E R I C A

Los Angeles

Rio Grande

Mississippi

Washington

Bermuda (U.K.)

Azores (Port.)

Atlantic Ocean

Madeira (Port.)

Islas Canarias (Sp.)

Tropic
of Cancer

MEXICO

Gulf
of Mexico

Nassau
THE BAHAMAS

México

La Habana   CUBA

DOMINICAN REP.
BELIZE   JAMAICA HAITI Puerto Rico (U.S.A.)
         Port-au- Santo ST KITTS & NEVIS
GUATEMALA HONDURAS Prince Domingo ANTIGUA & BARBUDA
Guatemala   Guadeloupe (Fr.)
San Salvador NICARAGUA   DOMINICA
EL SALVADOR Managua   ST LUCIA Martinique (Fr.)
                  ST VINCENT & BARBADOS
San José Caribbean THE GRENADINES
COSTA RICA Panamá Sea GRENADA TRINIDAD & TOBAGO
         Panamá   Caracas   Port of Spain

Île Clipperton (Fr.)

WESTERN
SAHARA

ALGERIA

LIBYA

Sahara

Nouakchott   MAURITANIA

MALI   NIGER

CAPE VERDE Dakar   *Sahel*

Banjul SENEGAL Bamako Niamey CHAD
THE GAMBIA Bissau BURKINA Ndjamena
GUINEA BIS. GUINEA   NIGERIA
Conakry   CÔTE BENIN Abuja
Freetown D'IVOIRE TOGO Porto-Novo CENTRAL
SIERRA LEONE   GHANA Lomé CAMEROON AFRICAN REP.
Monrovia Accra   Yaoundé Bangui
LIBERIA   EQ. G. CONGO
Yamoussoukro   SÃO TOMÉ Libreville
              & PRINCIPE GABON Kinshasa
                      Brazzaville   Bujun
                                    DEM
                                    OF C

VENEZUELA   Georgetown
            Paramaribo
Bogotá GUYANA SURINAME
COLOMBIA   Fr. Guiana

Equator

Islas Galápagos (Ec.)

Quito
EQUADOR

Amazonas

Ascension
(U.K.)

Luanda   ANGOLA

PERU

Amazonia

St Helena
(U.K.)

Pacific Ocean

Lima

B R A Z I L

La Paz Brasília
BOLIVIA
Sucre

PARAGUAY
Asunción

Río de Janeiro
São Paulo

Tropic of Capricorn

Isla Sala y Gómez
(Chile)
Isla de Pascua (Easter Island)
(Chile)

CHILE

Paraná

Atlantic Ocean

Cape Town

NAMIBIA
Windhoek   BOTSW
         Gaborone
                Pret
ZIM
Lu

REP. O
SOUTH AF

Archipélago Juan
Fernández
(Chile)

Santiago

URUGUAY
Montevideo
Buenos Aires

ARGENTINA

Tristan da Cunha
(U.K.)

Bouvetøya
(Norw.)

Falkland Is. (U.K.)

South Georgia
(U.K.)

● capital city
○ other major city

Antarctic Circle

32

120°   60°   0°

120°   60°   0°

TIME ZONES

| 23:00 | 24:00 | 01:00 | 02:00 | 03:00 | 04:00 | 05:00 | 06:00 | 07:00 | 08:00 | 09:00 | 10:00 |

International date line

ARCTIC

Ostrov Vrangelya
(Wrangel I.)

Ellesmere I.

Greenland
(Den.)

RUS.
FED.

Victoria I.

Baffin I.

Baffin
Bay

Rey

Arctic Circle

ALASKA
(U.S.A.)

Anchorage

CANADA

Aleutian Is. (U.S.A.)

Vancouver

Calgary

Winnipeg

Newfoundland
08:30

Hudson Bay

PACIFIC

Denver

Chicago

Ottawa

Montreal

ATLANTIC

Azo
(Por

UNITED STATES
OF AMERICA

Washington

New York

Los
Angeles

New Orleans

Bermuda (U.K.)

M
Po

Midway Is. (U.S.A.)

Tropic of Cancer

Miami

THE BAHAMAS

Wake I.
(U.S.A.)

Hawaiian Is. (U.S.A.)

La Habana

MÉXICO

CUBA

Antilles

DOMINICAN
REP.

CAPE VER

Johnston
(U.S.A.)

HAITI

(Fr.)

Guadeloupe

MARSHALL IS.

Kingman Reef
(U.S.A.)

BELIZE

GUATEMALA

JAMAICA

HONDURAS

Caribbean

Martinique (Fr.)

GUINEA-I

Wallis &
Futuna (Fr.)

Palmyra (U.S.A.)

EL SALVADOR

NICARAGUA

Sea

Trinidad

NAURU

Baker I. &
Howland I. (U.S.A.)

Île Clipperton
(Fr.)

COSTA RICA

PANAMÁ

Panamá

Caracas

VENEZUELA

GUYANA

SURINAME

French Guiana

KIRIBATI

Jarvis I. (U.S.A.)

Equator

Islas Galápagos
(Ecuador)

Bogotá

COLOMBIA

SOLOMON
Is.

TUVALU

Tokelau
(N.Z.)

Îles Marquises
(Fr.)

2:30

Quito

ECUADOR

PERU

Manaus

Recife

VANUATU

OCEAN

BRAZIL

Nouvelle-
Calédonie
(Fr.)

FIJI

Cook Is.
(N.Z.)

French
Polynesia
(Fr.)

Tahiti
(Fr.)

Tropic of Capricorn

Lima

La Paz

BOLIVIA

Brasilia

O

23:30
Norfolk I. (Aust.)

TONGA

SAMOA

Niue (N.Z.)

American Samoa
(U.S.A.)

3:30

Isla de Pascua
(Easter Island) (Ch.)

Sucre

PARAGUAY

Rio de Janeiro

São Paulo

22:30
Lord Howe I.(Aust.)

Kermadec Is.
(N.Z.)

Pitcairn I.
(U.K.)

Asunción

URUGUAY

NEW
ZEALAND

Auckland

Santiago

Buenos
Aires

Montevideo

Wellington

0:45

Chatham Is.
(N.Z.)

ARGENTINA

Campbell I.
(N.Z.)

Bounty Is.
(N.Z.)

Macquarie I.
(Austr.)

Falkland Is. (U.K.)

South Georgia
(U.K.)

STANDARD
TIME ZONES

NON-STANDARD TIME ZONES

Antarctic Circle

ANTARCTI

| +11 | +12 | -11 | -10 | -9 | -8 | -7 | -6 | -5 | -4 | -3 | -2 |

number of hours to subtract from zone 0 to obtain local time

NTERNATIONAL DATELINE

number of hours to add to zone 0 to obtain local time

• capital city

35

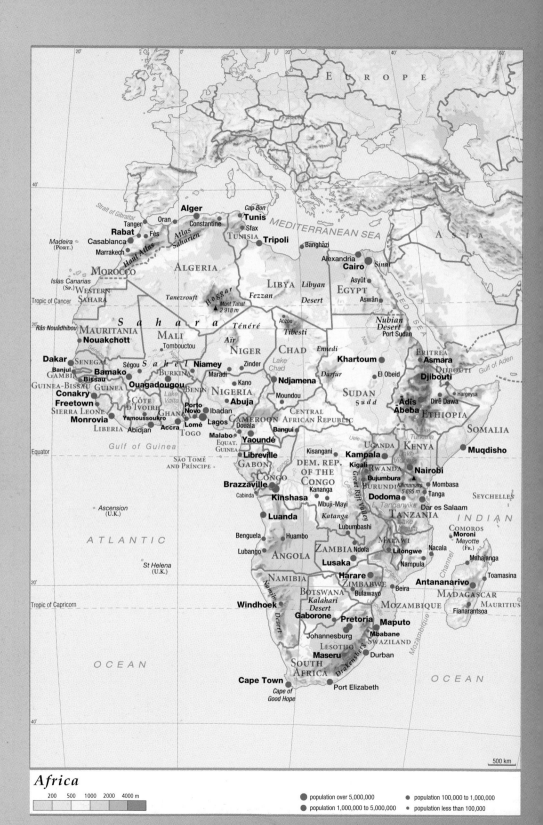

EUROPE

ASIA

MEDITERRANEAN SEA

Alger
Cap Bon
Tunis
Oran
Constantine
Tanger
Sfax
Rabat Fès
TUNISIA
Tripoli
Madeira
(PORT.)
Casablanca
Banghâzi
Marrakech
Atlas Saharien
Alexandria
Cairo
Asyût
Sinai
Islas Canarias
(SP.)
MOROCCO
Haut Atlas
ALGERIA
LIBYA
Libyan
EGYPT
WESTERN
Tropic of Cancer
SAHARA
Tanezrouft
Hoggar
Libyan Desert
Aswân
RED SEA
Fezzan
Mont Tahat
2 918 m
Nubian
Desert
Râs Nouâdhibou
S a h a r a
Ténéré
Aozou
Port Sudan
MAURITANIA
MALI
Air
Tibesti
Nouakchott
Tombouctou
Ennedi
NIGER
Khartoum
ERITREA
Asmara
Dakar
SENEGAL
Ségou
Sahel
Niamey
Zinder
CHAD
Darfur
El Obeid
DJIBOUTI
Banjul
Niger
BURKINA
Maradi
Lake
Chad
Djibouti
GAMBIA
Bamako
Ouagadougou
Kano
Ndjamena
Hargeysa
GUINEA-BISSAU
GUINEA
BENIN
NIGERIA
Moundou
SUDAN
Âdis
Âbeba
Dirê Dawa
Bissau
CÔTE
Conakry
D'IVOIRE
GHANA
Abuja
CAMEROON
CENTRAL
Sudd
ETHIOPIA
Freetown
Yamoussoukro
Porto
Novo
Ibadan
AFRICAN REPUBLIC
SOMALIA
SIERRA LEONE
Monrovia
Abidjan
Accra **Lomé**
Lagos
Douala
Bangui
Uele
Lake
Turkana
LIBERIA
TOGO
Malabo
Yaoundé
EQUAT.
UGANDA
KENYA
Gulf of Guinea
GUINEA
Libreville
Kisangani
Kampala
Muqdisho
Equator
SÃO TOMÉ
AND PRÍNCIPE
GABON
DEM. REP.
Kigali
Lake
Victoria
OF THE
RWANDA
Nairobi
Brazzaville
CONGO
Bujumbura
Kilimanjaro
5 895 m
Mombasa
Cabinda
Kinshasa
Kananga
BURUNDI
Dodoma
Tanga
SEYCHELLES
Mbuji-Mayi
Dar es Salaam
Ascension
(U.K.)
Luanda
Katanga
TANZANIA
INDIAN
Lake
Tanganyika
Moroni
COMOROS
Benguela
Huambo
Lubumbashi
MALAWI
Nacala
Mayotte
(FR.)
Mahajanga
Lubango
Ndola
Lilongwe
ATLANTIC
ANGOLA
ZAMBIA
Nampula
St Helena
(U.K.)
Lusaka
Harare
Beira
Antananarivo
Toamasina
Namib
NAMIBIA
ZIMBABWE
Bulawayo
MOZAMBIQUE
MADAGASCAR
MAURITIUS
BOTSWANA
Tropic of Capricorn
Windhoek
Kalahari
Desert
Fianarantsoa
Desert
Gaborone
Pretoria **Maputo**
Johannesburg
Mbabane
SWAZILAND
Mozambique Channel
Maseru
Durban
LESOTHO
Drakensberg
OCEAN
SOUTH
AFRICA
OCEAN
Cape Town
Cape of
Good Hope
Port Elizabeth

500 km

Africa

200 500 1000 2000 4000 m

● population over 5,000,000   ● population 100,000 to 1,000,000
● population 1,000,000 to 5,000,000   · population less than 100,000

AFRICA

ALGERIA		KENYA
ANGOLA	**AFRICA**	LESOTHO
BENIN	30,310,000 km^2	LIBERIA
BOTSWANA	population 842 million	LIBYA
BURKINA		MALAWI
BURUNDI		MALI
CAMEROON		MAURITANIA
CAPE VERDE		MOROCCO
CENTRAL AFRICAN REPUBLIC		MOZAMBIQUE
CHAD		NAMIBIA
CONGO		NIGER
CONGO (DEMOCRATIC REPUBLIC OF THE)		NIGERIA
CÔTE D'IVOIRE (IVORY COAST)	**THE AMERICAS** 42,000,000 km^2 population 880 million	RWANDA SÃO TOMÉ AND PRÍNCIPE
DJIBOUTI		SENEGAL
EGYPT		
EQUATORIAL GUINEA	**ASIA**	SIERRA LEONE
ERITREA	44,000,000 km^2	SOMALIA
ETHIOPIA	population 3,826 million	SOUTH AFRICA
GABON		SUDAN
THE GAMBIA		SWAZILAND
GHANA	**EUROPE**	
GUINEA	10,500,000 km^2	TANZANIA
GUINEA-BISSAU	population 731 million	TOGO
INDIAN OCEAN		TUNISIA
COMOROS	**OCEANIA**	UGANDA
MADAGASCAR	9,000,000 km^2	ZAMBIA
MAURITIUS	population 33 million	ZIMBABWE
SEYCHELLES		

The mountains in the north of the People's Democratic Republic of Algeria become narrower towards the east. The Saharan Atlas Ranges form a boundary between the coastal area, which has a Mediterranean climate, and the southern part of Algeria, which lies in the Sahara Desert. This vast, barren expanse of arid ground includes regions with varied reliefs: stony plateaux (regs), extensive dune areas (ergs) and massifs (such as the Hoggar) that rise abruptly from the desert.

Area: 2,381,741 km²
Population (2002): 31,403,000
Capital: Algiers 2,861,000 (2001 e) including the suburbs
Government type and political system: republic with a semi-presidential system
Head of state: (President of the Republic) Abdelaziz Bouteflika
Head of government: (Prime Minister) Ahmed Ouyahia
Administrative structure: 48 wilayas
Official languages: Arabic (official) and Tamazight (national)
Currency: Algerian dinar

DEMOGRAPHICS
Density: 13 inhab/km²
Percentage of population in urban areas (2001): 57.7%
Age structure of population (2000): 0–15 years: 34.8%, 15–65 years: 61.1%, over 65 years: 4.1%
Birth rate (2003): 22.8‰
Death rate (2003): 5.5‰
Infant mortality rate (2003): 43.9‰
Life expectancy at birth (2003): male: 68.1 years, female: 71.3 years

ECONOMY
GNP (2002): 54 billion US$
GNP per capita (2002): 1,720 US$
GNP per capita PPP (2002): 5,530 international dollars
HDI (2000): 0.697
GDP annual growth rate (2003): 6.7%
Annual inflation rate (1999): 2.65%
Labour force by occupation: n/a
GDP by sector (2000): agriculture: 8.6%, industry: 60.3%, services: 31.2%
Gross public debt: n/a
Unemployment rate (2000): 29.8%

Agriculture and fishing
Crops
citrus fruits (2002): 473,000t
almonds (2001): 26,000t
wheat (2002): 1,502,000t
dates (2001): 370,000t
olives (2002): 300,000t
oranges (2002): 330,000t
barley (2001): 500,000t
potatoes (2002): 1,000,000t
grapes (2002): 196,000t
Livestock farming and fishing
cattle (2002): 1,600,000 head
goats (2001): 3,500,000 head
camels (2001): 240,000 head
sheep (2002): 17,300,000 head
chickens (2002): 115,000,000 head
fish (1999): 106,000t

Energy generation and mining
total electricity (2001): 24,690 million kWh
hydroelectricity (2000): 100 million kWh
iron (2001): 760,000t
natural gas (2000): 89,300 million m³
oil (2001): 65,800,000t
phosphate (2001): 875,000t

Industrial production
milk (2001): 1,513,000t
meat (2001): 536,000t
olive oil (2001): 45,000t
steel (2003): 1,051,000t
cotton yarn (2001): 20t
wine (2002): 420,000hl

Tourism
Tourism revenue (1998): 24 million US$

Foreign trade
Exports (1997): 13,894 million US$
Imports (1997): 8,688 million US$

Defence
Armed forces (2001): 136,700 people
Defence budget (2001): 4.28% of GDP

Standard of living
Inhabitants per doctor (1993): 1,250
Average daily calorie intake (2000): 2,944 (FAO minimum: 2,400)
Cars per 1,000 inhabitants (1996): 25
Televisions per 1,000 inhabitants (2000): 110

HISTORY: KEY DATES

From ancient Algeria to the Regency of Algiers
Inhabited by the Berbers, Algeria was influenced by the Phoenician civilization (end of the 2nd millennium BC) and then the Carthaginian (7c BC–2c BC). The Berbers, Moors and Numidians set up powerful kingdoms in Numidia and Mauritania.
2c BC: Algeria prospered under Roman rule after Gaius Marius's victory over King Jugurtha of Numidia in 106 BC. Christianity was introduced.
AD 5c: Algeria was conquered and ravaged by the Vandals.
6c–7c: Algeria was ruled by Byzantium.
7c: Muslim Arabs arrived (Uqba ibn Nafi's raids, 681–2) and ousted the Byzantines. Algeria was converted to Islam and governed from Damascus by the Umayyad caliphs, then from Baghdad by the Abbasid caliphs.
10c–11c: the country was divided into many principalities (one of the most important was at Tlemcen), tribal confederations and free ports. In the early 10c, the suzerainty of the Fatimid dynasty began.
11c–13c: two Berber dynasties, the Almoravids and then the Almohads, dominated the Maghreb and part of Spain.
15c: Spain resisted the Muslim presence on its soil and captured the coastal cities of Algeria.
1518: the Turkish corsairs helped free Algeria from Spanish domination. One of them, Barbarossa, placed Algiers under Ottoman protection.
1587: Algeria formed the Regency of Algiers. It was governed by the deys from the 17c onwards, and the country's main source of revenue was protection payments from the privateering Barbary corsairs preying on Mediterranean shipping.

French colonization
1830: after a minor dispute, troops sent by Charles X of France captured Algiers.
1832–47: Berber leader Abd-el-Kader waged war on France, surrendering to General Bugeaud in 1847.
1852–70: the French successfully occupied Kabylia and the Saharan borders. Many colonists settled there.
1870–1940: an economic boom in Algeria was enjoyed by the colonists, but was of little benefit to the local population.
1954: an Algerian uprising marked the beginning of the war for Algerian independence.
1962: Algeria was declared independent.

Independent Algeria
1963: Ahmed Ben Bella, president of the new republic, established a one-party socialist government (FLN or Front de Libération Nationale).
1965: Houari Boumedienne, whose foreign policies were focused on non-alignment, deposed Ben Bella in a military coup.
1989: constitutional reforms took place and a multiparty system was established.
1991–2000: the country was plagued by violence linked to Islamic terrorism.
2000–3: issues such as poverty, unemployment and government corruption caused widespread civil unrest, which became worse in the aftermath of a catastrophic earthquake in 2003.

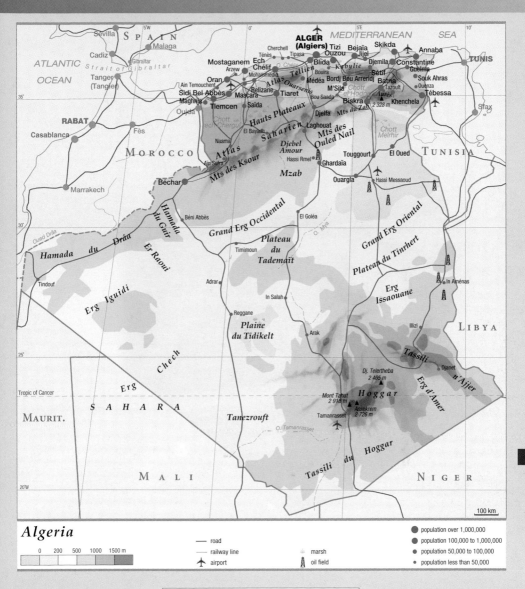

Algeria

| 0 | 200 | 500 | 1000 | 1500 m |

— road
✈ railway line
✈ airport

≈ marsh
🛢 oil field

● population over 1,000,000
● population 100,000 to 1,000,000
● population 50,000 to 100,000
· population less than 50,000

Maghreb and Mashreq

Algeria is part of the Maghreb. In Arabic, this name means 'land of the setting sun' or 'the west'. Morocco and Tunisia also belong to the Maghreb. The North African Arab countries also include Libya and Mauritania. In 1989, the countries in these five North African Arab States created an economic union, the Arab Maghreb Union (AMU). The name Mashreq ('the rising sun') is given to the Arab countries in Asia and in NE Africa (Egypt, Syria, Lebanon, etc).

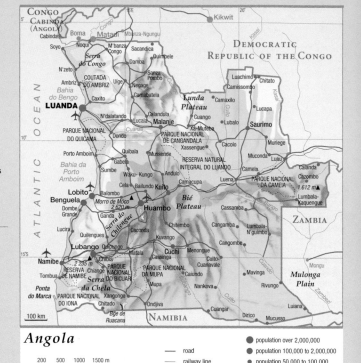

The Republic of Angola is a large country, more than five times the size of the UK. Its central area is the Bié Plateau, which receives ample rainfall and is covered in savannas. To the west, palm trees grow along the narrow, arid coastal plain.

Area: 1,246,700km²
Population (2002): 13,937,000
Capital: Luanda 2,819,000 (2001 e) including the suburbs
Government type and political system: republic with a semi-presidential system
Head of state: (President of the Republic) José Eduardo dos Santos
Head of government: (Prime Minister) Fernando da Piedade Dias dos Santos
Administrative structure: 18 provinces
Official language: Portuguese
Currency: kwanza

Angola

	road
—	railway line
✈	airport

200 500 1000 1500 m

● population over 2,000,000
● population 100,000 to 2,000,000
● population 50,000 to 100,000
• population less than 50,000

DEMOGRAPHICS
Density: 10 inhab/km²
Percentage of population in urban areas (2001): 34.8%
Age structure of population (2000): 0–15 years: 48.2%, 15–65 years: 49%, over 65 years: 2.8%
Birth rate (2003): 52.3‰
Death rate (2003): 23.6‰
Infant mortality rate (2003): 140.3‰
Life expectancy at birth (2003): male: 38.8 years, female: 41.5 years

ECONOMY
GNP (2002): 9.31 billion US$
GNP per capita (2002): 710 US$
GNP per capita PPP (2002): 1,840 international dollars
HDI (2000): 0.403
GDP annual growth rate (2003): 4.5%
Annual inflation rate (2000): 325.03%
Labour force by occupation: n/a
GDP by sector (2000): agriculture: 5.7%, industry: 76.1%, services: 18.2%
Gross public debt: n/a
Unemployment rate: n/a

Agriculture and fishing
Crops
bananas (2001): 300,000t
coffee (2002): 2,160t
sugar cane (2001): 360,000t
maize (2002): 430,000t
manioc (2001): 3,300,000t
millet (2001): 105,000t
sweet potatoes (2001): 185,000t
Livestock farming and fishing
cattle (2002): 4,150,000 head
goats (2001): 2,150,000 head
sheep (2002): 340,000 head
pigs (2002): 780,000 head
fish (1999): 177,000t

Energy generation and mining
diamonds (2001): 5,170,000 carats
total electricity (2001): 1,450 million kWh
hydroelectricity (2001): 921 million kWh
oil (2002): 44,600,000t

Industrial production
beer (2000): 1,000,000hl

Tourism
Tourism revenue (2000): 18 million US$

Foreign trade
Exports (2001): 6,534.3 million US$
Imports (2001): 3,179.2 million US$

Defence
Armed forces (2001): 100,000 people
Defence budget (2001): 0.76% of GDP

Standard of living
Inhabitants per doctor (1990): 14,290
Average daily calorie intake (2000): 1,903 (FAO minimum: 2,400)
Cars per 1,000 inhabitants (1996): 18
Televisions per 1,000 inhabitants (2000): 19

HISTORY: KEY DATES
1482: the Portuguese navigator Diogo Cão landed on the Angolan coast.
1580–1625: a Portuguese colony was established, and was active in the slave trade.
1902: the Bié Plateau was captured by Portuguese troops.
1961: the Luanda uprising began the war of independence, but the nationalist movement was divided.
1975: Angola declared its independence from Portugal.
1976–88: Cuban troops supported the MPLA government (Popular Movement for the Liberation of Angola) in its fight against the guerrillas (UNITA or National Union for the Total Independence of Angola).
1991: a multiparty system was introduced. A peace treaty between the MPLA and UNITA was signed.
1992: the government party won the first free elections. However, UNITA's refusal to concede defeat led to a resumption of the civil war, which continued despite another peace treaty in 1994.
2002: after the death of UNITA leader Jonas Savimbi in battle, a ceasefire was signed.

The Republic of Benin consists of a narrow strip of land that extends from north to south for almost 700km, from the Gulf of Guinea to the River Niger. The south has an equatorial climate and is dominated by plains, while the centre is drier and covered in savannas and plateaux. In the north, the Atakora Mountains rise to heights of up to 800m.

Area: 112,622km²
Population (2002): 6,629,000
Capital: Porto Novo 225,000 (2001 e)
Government type and political system: republic with a presidential system
Head of state and government: (President of the Republic) Mathieu Kérékou
Administrative structure: 12 departments
Official language: French
Currency: CFA franc

DEMOGRAPHICS

Density: 54 inhab/km²
Percentage of population in urban areas (2001): 43%
Age structure of population (2000): 0–15 years: 46.4%, 15–65 years: 50.9%, over 65 years: 2.7%
Birth rate (2003): 41.5‰
Death rate (2003): 14.3‰
Infant mortality rate (2003): 92.7‰
Life expectancy at birth (2003): male: 48.4 years, female: 53 years

ECONOMY

GNP (2002): 2.52 billion US$
GNP per capita (2002): 380 US$
GNP per capita PPP (2002): 1,060 international dollars

HDI (2000): 0.42
GDP annual growth rate (2003): 5.5%
Annual inflation rate (2000): 4.17%
Labour force by occupation: n/a
GDP by sector (2000): agriculture: 38%, industry: 14.4%, services: 47.6%
Gross public debt: n/a
Unemployment rate: n/a

Agriculture

Crops
groundnuts (2001): 81,000t
yams (2002): 1,875,000t
maize (2002): 622,000t
manioc (2001): 2,800,000t
cashew nuts (1998): 10,000t
sorghum (2002): 195,000t

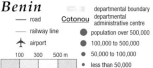

Benin

— road	**Cotonou** departmental administrative centre
— railway line	● population over 500,000
✈ airport	● 100,000 to 500,000
100 300 500 m	● 50,000 to 100,000
	● less than 50,000

— departmental boundary

Livestock farming
cattle (2002): 1,550,000 head
goats (2001): 1,183,000 head
sheep (2002): 670,000 head
pigs (2002): 550,000 head
chickens (2002): 10,000,000 head

Energy generation and mining
total electricity (2001): 274 million kWh
oil (2001): 50,000t

Industrial production
palm oil (2001): 15,000t
cotton yarn (2001): 141,000t
cement (2001): 250,000t

Tourism
Tourism revenue (1998): 33 million US$

Foreign trade
Exports (2001): 373.5 million US$
Imports (2001): 553 million US$

Defence
Armed forces (2001): 4,550 people
Defence budget (2001): 1.77% of GDP

Standard of living
Inhabitants per doctor (1994): 10,000
Average daily calorie intake (2000): 2,258 (FAO minimum: 2,400)
Cars per 1,000 inhabitants (1996): 7
Televisions per 1,000 inhabitants (2001): 44

HISTORY: KEY DATES

It is thought that around the 13c, the Aja people migrated from Tado (present-day Togo) and founded the Allada kingdom, which then broke up into the rival states of Great Ardra, Abomey and Porto Novo during the 17c.
Around 1720: Abomey became the kingdom of Dahomey. The king of Dahomey extended his authority, conquering the port of Ouidah, which gave access to Atlantic trade.
19c: the French influence grew, despite the efforts of King Béhanzin, who was ultimately defeated and exiled.
1895-1904: the colony of Dahomey was incorporated into French West Africa.
1946: Dahomey became a French overseas territory.
1958: it became an autonomous state within the French Community.
1960: Dahomey regained its independence.
1975: the country was renamed the People's Republic of Benin.

BOTSWANA

The majority of the Republic of Botswana is covered by the Kalahari Desert. In the northwest is the delta of the Okavango, a river that provides most of the country's natural resources.

Area: 581,730km²
Population (2002): 1,563,000
Capital: Gaborone 225,000 (2001 e)
Government type and political system: multiparty republic with a parliamentary system
Head of state and government: (President of the Republic) Festus Mogae
Administrative structure: 10 districts
Official language: English
Currency: pula

DEMOGRAPHICS

Density: 3 inhab/km²
Percentage of population in urban areas (2001): 49.4%
Age structure of population (2000): 0–15 years: 42.1%, 15–65 years: 55.1%, over 65 years: 2.8%
Birth rate (2003): 30.6‰
Death rate (2003): 21.4‰
Infant mortality rate (2003): 56.6‰
Life expectancy at birth (2003): male: 38.9 years, female: 40.5 years

ECONOMY

GNP (2002): 5.15 billion US$
GNP per capita (2002): 3,010 US$
GNP per capita PPP (2002): 7,740 international dollars
HDI (2000): 0.572
GDP annual growth rate (2003): 5.4%

Annual inflation rate (2000): 8.6%
Labour force by occupation: n/a
GDP by sector (2000): agriculture: 3.6%, industry: 44.4%, services: 52%
Gross public debt: n/a
Unemployment rate (1995): 21.5%

Agriculture

Crops
sorghum (2002): 15,000t
Livestock farming
cattle (2002): 1,700,000 head
goats (2001): 2,250,000 head

Energy generation and mining

copper (2001): 31,300t
diamonds (2001): 25,160,000 carats
total electricity (2001): 410 million kWh
coal (2001): 965,000t
nickel (2001): 26,200t

Industrial production

beer (2000): 390,000hl
meat (2001): 66,000t
milk (2001): 105,000t
timber (2000): 105,000m3

Tourism

Tourism revenue (1999): 234 million US$

Foreign trade

Exports (1999): 2,671 million US$
Imports (1999): 1,996.5 million US$

Defence

Armed forces (2001): 9,000 people
Defence budget (2001): 3.76% of GDP

Standard of living

Inhabitants per doctor (1993): 5,000
Average daily calorie intake (2000): 2,255 (FAO minimum: 2,400)
Cars per 1,000 inhabitants (1999): 29
Televisions per 1,000 inhabitants (2001): 30

HISTORY: KEY DATES

1885: Bechuanaland became a British protectorate.
1966: the country became independent and changed its name to Botswana.

Botswana

⟁	marsh
═══	motorway
——	road
------	railway line
✈	airport

● population over 100,000
● population 50,000 to 100,000
● population 10,000 to 50,000
• population less than 10,000

400   1000   1500   2000 m

150 km

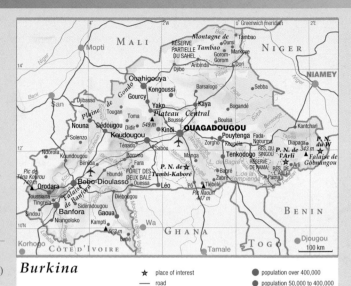

Burkina

200	300	500 m	

★	place of interest
—	road
—	railway line
✈	airport

●	population over 400,000
●	population 50,000 to 400,000
●	population 20,000 to 50,000
•	population less than 20,000

Burkina Faso (the country's official title) is a poor, landlocked country situated in the heart of the semi-arid Sahel region where the land merges into the Sahara Desert. Most of the country is arid and not very suitable for farming.

Area: 274,000km²
Population (2002): 12,210,000
Capital: Ouagadougou 862,000 (2001 e)
Government type and political system: republic with a semi-presidential system
Head of state: (President) Blaise Compaoré
Head of government: (Prime Minister) Paramanga Ernest Yonli
Administrative structure: 45 provinces
Official language: French
Currency: CFA franc

DEMOGRAPHICS

Density: 43 inhab/km²
Percentage of population in urban areas (2001): 16.9%
Age structure of population (2000): 0–15 years: 48.7%, 15–65 years: 48.1%, over 65 years: 3.2%
Birth rate (2003): 47.8‰
Death rate (2003): 17.4‰
Infant mortality rate (2003): 93.2‰
Life expectancy at birth (2003): male: 45.2 years, female: 46.2 years

ECONOMY

GNP (2002): 2.91 billion US$
GNP per capita (2002): 250 US$
GNP per capita PPP (2002): 1,090 international dollars
HDI (2000): 0.325
GDP annual growth rate (2003): 6.5%
Annual inflation rate (2000): −0.3%
Labour force by occupation: n/a
GDP by sector (2000): agriculture: 34.5%, industry: 17.2%, services: 48.3%
Gross public debt: n/a
Unemployment rate: n/a

Agriculture

Crops
groundnuts (2001): 169,000t
sugar cane (2002): 35,000t
cotton (2001): 395,000t
maize (2002): 653,000t
millet (2001): 957,000t
sorghum (2002): 1,373,000t
Livestock farming
cattle (2002): 4,800,000 head
goats (2001): 8,647,000 head
sheep (2002): 6,800,000 head

Energy generation and mining
total electricity (2001): 279 million kWh
gold (2001): 1,000kg

Industrial production
sugar (2001): 30,000t
cotton yarn (2001): 114,000t

Tourism
Tourism revenue (1998): 42 million US$

Foreign trade
Exports (1997): 190 million US$
Imports (1997): 506 million US$

Defence
Armed forces (2001): 10,200 people
Defence budget (2001): 1.56% of GDP

Standard of living
Inhabitants per doctor (1990): 33,330
Average daily calorie intake (2000): 2,293 (FAO minimum: 2,400)
Cars per 1,000 inhabitants (1996): 4

Televisions per 1,000 inhabitants (2001): 103

HISTORY: KEY DATES

The Bobo, Lobi and Gurunsi people inhabited part of present-day Burkina as early as 1100. The Mossi, who founded the kingdom of Ouagadougou in the late 15c, dominated the country for several hundred years.
18c: the Dioula people of the Kong kingdom (now the Côte d'Ivoire) unified the west of the country by creating the Gwiriko region, centred on the city of Bobo-Dioulasso.
1896–7: the French, through a mixture of negotiation and forceful occupation, gained control of the area.
1919: initially part of the Upper Senegal and Niger colony (1904), Upper Volta became a separate French colony.
1932: Upper Volta was dismantled and the territory divided up between Sudan, the Côte d'Ivoire and Niger.
1960: Upper Volta became fully independent.
1966–87: power changed hands frequently in a series of military coups.
1984: Upper Volta was renamed Burkina Faso, roughly translated as 'land of honest people'.
1991: a new constitution was approved, and a multiparty system established.

43

BURUNDI

The Republic of Burundi is a hilly country with high plateaux, situated close to the equator. Its high altitude (rarely below 1,000m) means that most of the country has a moderate, pleasant climate all year round.

Area: 27,834km²
Population (2002): 6,687,000
Capital: Bujumbura 346,000 (2001 e)
Government type and political system: republic
Head of state and government: (President of the Republic) Domitien Ndayizeye
Administrative structure: 15 provinces
Official languages: French and Kirundi
Currency: Burundi franc

DEMOGRAPHICS

Density: 239 inhab/km²
Percentage of population in urban areas (2001): 9.3%
Age structure of population (2000): 0–15 years: 47.6%, 15–65 years: 49.5%, over 65 years: 2.9%
Birth rate (2003): 44.2‰
Death rate (2003): 20.6‰
Infant mortality rate (2003): 107.4‰
Life expectancy at birth (2003): male: 40.4 years, female: 41.4 years

ECONOMY

GNP (2002): 0.704 billion US$
GNP per capita (2002): 100 US$
GNP per capita PPP (2002): 630 international dollars
HDI (2000): 0.313
GDP annual growth rate (2003): −0.5%
Annual inflation rate (2000): 24.32%
Labour force by occupation: n/a
GDP by sector (2000): agriculture: 50.7%, industry: 18.5%, services: 30.8%
Gross public debt: n/a
Unemployment rate: n/a

Agriculture and fishing

Crops
bananas (2001): 1,549,000t
sugar cane (2001): 200,000t
maize (2002): 127,000t
manioc (2001): 713,000t
sweet potatoes (2001): 781,000t
Livestock farming and fishing
cattle (2002): 324,000 head
goats (2001): 600,000 head
sheep (2002): 230,000 head
pigs (2002): 70,000 head
fish (1999): 9,250t

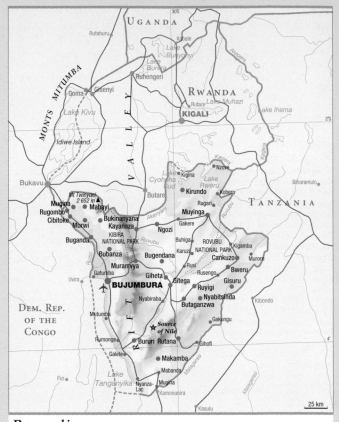

Burundi

— road
✈ airport
★ place of interest

| 500 | 1000 | 1500 m |

● population over 200,000
● population 20,000 to 200,000
● population less than 20,000

25 km

Energy generation and mining
total electricity (2001): 155 million kWh
gold (2001): 415kg

Industrial production
beer (2000): 1,170,000hl

Tourism
Tourism revenue (2000): 1 million US$

Foreign trade
Exports (2002): 31 million US$

Imports (2002): 104 million US$

Defence
Armed forces (2001): 45,500 people
Defence budget (2001): 4.92% of GDP

Standard of living
Inhabitants per doctor (1993): 17,240
Average daily calorie intake (2000): 1,605 (FAO minimum: 2,400)
Cars per 1,000 inhabitants: n/a
Televisions per 1,000 inhabitants (2000): 30

HISTORY: KEY DATES

Burundi's first known inhabitants were the Twa people, later outnumbered by the Hutus and Tutsis.
1890: Germany annexed Burundi and Rwanda, making them part of German East Africa.
1916–62: Belgian troops occupied the area and the League of Nations granted Belgium the mandate of Ruanda-Urundi, including present-day Rwanda and Burundi.
1962: Burundi became an independent kingdom.
1966: the Tutsi monarchy was abolished in a military coup, and Burundi became a republic. Political life was dominated by permanent intercommunity conflicts between the Hutu (85% of the population) and the Tutsi, a minority group who have traditionally dominated the Hutus.
1992: a new constitution established a multiparty system.
2001: a government of national union was introduced and a power-sharing agreement, the Arusha accords, was put in place, allowing for power to alternate between Tutsi and Hutu presidents.

The Republic of Cameroon has a varied terrain: there are narrow coastal plains in the south-west of the country, isolated volcanic peaks (Mount Cameroon), the Adamawa Massif in the centre, and hills and plateaux in the north and south. The climate is hot and dry, and temperatures are higher on the coast than on the inland plateaux. Rainfall is heavy in the highlands, decreasing towards the north.

Area: 475,442km²
Population (2002): 15,535,000
Capital: Yaoundé 1,481,000 (2001 e)
Government type and political system: republic with a semi-presidential system
Head of state: (President of the Republic) Paul Biya
Head of government: (Prime Minister) Peter Mafany Musonge
Administrative structure: 10 provinces
Official languages: English and French
Currency: CFA franc

DEMOGRAPHICS

Density: 32 inhab/km²
Percentage of population in urban areas (2001): 49.7%
Age structure of population (2000): 0–15 years: 43.1%, 15–65 years: 53.2%, over 65 years: 3.7%
Birth rate (2003): 35.4‰
Death rate (2003): 16.9‰
Infant mortality rate (2003): 88.1‰
Life expectancy at birth (2003): male: 45.1 years, female: 47.4 years

ECONOMY

GNP (2002): 8.75 billion US$
GNP per capita (2002): 550 US$
GNP per capita PPP (2001): 1,910 international dollars
HDI (2000): 0.512
GDP annual growth rate (2003): 4.2%
Annual inflation rate (2000): 1.24%
Labour force by occupation: n/a
GDP by sector (2000): agriculture: 43.8%, industry: 20.3%, services: 35.9%
Gross public debt: n/a
Unemployment rate: n/a

Agriculture and fishing

Crops
groundnuts (2001): 100,000t
bananas (2001): 850,000t
plantains (2001): 1,400,000t
cocoa (2001): 115,000t
sugar cane (2001): 1,350,000t
rubber (2001): 60,000t

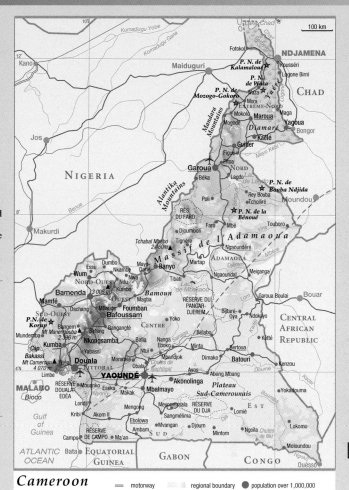

maize (2002): 825,000t
manioc (2001): 1,700,000t
millet (2001): 71,000t
oil palms (2001): 66,000t
sorghum (2002): 525,000t
Livestock farming and fishing
cattle (2002): 5,900,000 head
goats (2001): 4,400,000 head
sheep (2002): 3,800,000 head
pigs (2002): 1,350,000 head
chickens (2002): 31,000,000 head
fish (1999): 95,000t

Energy generation and mining
total electricity (2001): 3,613 million kWh
hydroelectricity (2001): 3,516 million kWh
gold (2001): 1,000kg
oil (2002): 3,700,000t

Industrial production
palm oil (2001): 130,000t
aluminium (2001): 81,000t
cotton yarn (2001): 97,000t
timber (2000): 1,894,000m3

Tourism
Tourism revenue (1998): 40 million US$

Foreign trade
Exports (1997): 1,814 million US$
Imports (1999): 15,616 million US$

Defence
Armed forces (2001): 23,100 people
Defence budget (2001): 1.3% of GDP

Standard of living
Inhabitants per doctor (1993): 12,000
Average daily calorie intake (2000): 2,255 (FAO minimum: 2,400)
Cars per 1,000 inhabitants (1996): 7
Televisions per 1,000 inhabitants (2000): 34

HISTORY: KEY DATES

Before colonization
Around the 13c, Bantu immigrants, including the Douala, arrived in the south. They were followed by the Fang. The Sao and Fulani peoples came from the Niger valley and settled in the north.

45

CAMEROON

In the south, the Bamiléké and the Bamoum founded chieftainships and kingdoms, while the Pygmies inhabited the forests.

The colonial period and independence
1472: the Portuguese reached the coast and eventually established a slave trade.
1850–60: British missionaries arrived and established trading posts.
1884: the country became a German colony.

HISTORY: KEY DATES

1911: the colony's borders were extended under a convention signed by Germany and France.
1916: the Allies drove out the Germans.
1919–22: Cameroon was divided into two zones, under British and French mandates.
1946: the two zones became UN trust territories.
1959: the part of Cameroon under the French trusteeship was granted independence as the Republic of Cameroon.

1961: after the unification of the southern sector of the former British Cameroon, the republic became a federation: the Federal Republic of Cameroon.
1972: the federation became a unitary state.
1994–2003: ongoing tensions between Cameroon and Nigeria over ownership of the oil-rich Bakassi peninsula led to hostilities, until a new border was established in late 2003.

A German colony

The German explorer Gustav Nachtigal signed treaties with several of Cameroon's local chiefs in 1884, creating the protectorate of Kamerun and marking the beginning of the German conquest of the country. During the First World War, the Belgians, French and British attacked Kamerun from their own possessions, eventually driving the Germans out in 1916. Despite its brevity, the German colonization helped to develop the country by setting up major infrastructures such as the railway system and various plantations (coffee, cocoa, banana, oil palm, rubber, etc).

CAPE VERDE

An island group in the Atlantic Ocean, 450km west of Senegal, the Republic of Cape Verde is made up of ten large islands and five smaller islets.

Area: 4,033km²
Population (2002): 446,000
Capital: Praia 82,000 (2001 e)
Government type and political system: republic with a semi-presidential system
Head of state: (President of the Republic) Pedro Pires
Head of government: (Prime Minister) José Maria Neves
Administrative structure: 2 districts
Official language: Portuguese
Currency: Cape Verde escudo

DEMOGRAPHICS

Density: 107 inhab/km²
Percentage of population in urban areas (2001): 63.3%

Age structure of population (2000): 0–15 years: 39.3%, 15–65 years: 56.1%, over 65 years: 4.6%
Birth rate (2003): 27.7‰
Death rate (2003): 5.4‰
Infant mortality rate (2003): 29.7‰
Life expectancy at birth (2003): male: 67 years, female: 72.8 years

ECONOMY

GNP (2002): 0.572 billion US$
GNP per capita (2002): 1,250 US$
GNP per capita PPP (2002): 4,920 international dollars
HDI (2000): 0.715
GDP annual growth rate (2003): 5%
Annual inflation rate (1998): 4.38%
Labour force by occupation: n/a
GDP by sector (2000): agriculture: 11.8%, industry: 17.6%, services: 70.6%
Gross public debt: n/a

Unemployment rate: n/a

Agriculture and fishing
Crops
sugar cane (2001): 14,000t
maize (2002): 5,070t
Livestock farming and fishing
goats (2001): 110,000 head
pigs (2002): 200,000 head
fish (1999): 10,400t

Industrial production
beer (2000): 5,520hl

Tourism
Tourism revenue (1999): 23 million US$

Foreign trade
Exports (2002): 41.76 million US$
Imports (2002): 278.02 million US$

Defence
Armed forces (2001): 1,200 people
Defence budget (2001): 1.83% of GDP

Standard of living
Inhabitants per doctor (1990): 5,130
Average daily calorie intake (2000): 3,278 (FAO minimum: 2,400)
Cars per 1,000 inhabitants (1996): 7
Televisions per 1,000 inhabitants (2001): 101

HISTORY: KEY DATES

1460: the Portuguese navigator Diogo Gomes visited the uninhabited archipelago.
1462: a Portuguese colony was established.
1975: Cape Verde became independent.
1991: the country's first free presidential elections were held.

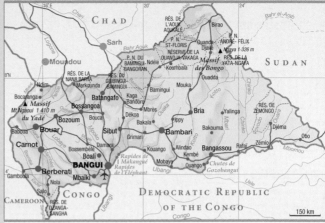

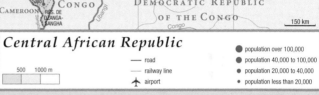

Central African Republic

— road
--- railway line
✈ airport

● population over 100,000
● population 40,000 to 100,000
● population 20,000 to 40,000
• population less than 20,000

500   1000 m

Although its total area is more than twice that of the UK, the Central African Republic is very sparsely populated. Rainfall is heavy in the south (near the equator) but the climate is drier in the north, where the land is covered by open forests and wooded savannas.

Area: 622,984km²
Population (2002): 3,844,000
Capital: Bangui 666,000 (2001 e)
Government type and political system: republic
Head of state: (President of the Republic) François Bozizé
Head of government: (Prime Minister) Celestin Gaombalet
Administrative structure: 14 prefectures, 2 economic prefectures and Bangui Federal District
Official language: French
Currency: CFA franc

DEMOGRAPHICS
Density: 6 inhab/km²
Percentage of population in urban areas (2001): 41.7%
Age structure of population (2000): 0–15 years: 43%, 15–65 years: 53%, over 65 years: 4%
Birth rate (2003): 37.7‰
Death rate (2003): 22.1‰
Infant mortality rate (2003): 100.4‰
Life expectancy at birth (2003): male: 38.5 years, female: 40.6 years

ECONOMY
GNP (2002): 0.969 billion US$
GNP per capita (2002): 250 US$
GNP per capita PPP (2002): 1,170 international dollars
HDI (2000): 0.375
GDP annual growth rate (2003): −5.8%
Annual inflation rate (1998): −1.89%
Labour force by occupation: n/a
GDP by sector (2000): agriculture: 54.6%, industry: 19.8%, services: 25.6%
Gross public debt: n/a
Unemployment rate: n/a

Agriculture
Crops
groundnuts (2001): 122,000t
bananas (2001): 118,000t
plantains (2001): 83,000t
coffee (2002): 13,000t
sugar cane (2001): 90,000t
cotton (2002): 20,000t
yams (2002): 350,000t
maize (2002): 113,000t
manioc (2001): 562,000t
Livestock farming
cattle (2002): 3,273,000 head
goats (2001): 2,600,000 head
pigs (2002): 738,000 head
Energy generation
total electricity (2001): 106 million kWh
hydroelectricity (2001): 85 million kWh
Industrial production
beer (2000): 110,000hl
diamonds (2001): 480,000 carats
timber (2000): 1,011,000m³
Tourism
Tourism revenue (1998): 6 million US$
Foreign trade
Exports (1997): 270 million US$
Imports (1997): 163 million US$
Defence
Armed forces (2001): 2,550 people
Defence budget (2001): 1.57% of GDP
Standard of living
Inhabitants per doctor (1990): 25,000
Average daily calorie intake (2000): 1,946 (FAO minimum: 2,400)

Cars per 1,000 inhabitants (1997): 0
Televisions per 1,000 inhabitants (2001): 6

HISTORY: KEY DATES
Pygmies and several Bantu tribes settled the country before other Bantu tribes (Baya, Banda) arrived in the 19c from Sudan, Congo and Chad to escape the slave trade.
1877: Henry Morton Stanley's descent of the Congo paved the way for other European explorers.
1889–1910: anxious to gain access to Chad and the Nile, France established an outpost at Bangui, then reinforced its presence with the Marchand mission (1896–8). In 1894 the area, then known as Ubangi-Shari, became a French territory, and in 1906 it was united administratively with Chad and incorporated into French Equatorial Africa.
1958–60: the Central African Republic was established as an autonomous republic within the French community, and later declared independent.
1965: following a military coup, Jean-Bédel Bokassa assumed power as president for life, and later as emperor.
1979: with the help of French commandos, Bokassa was removed from power and the republic was restored.
1979–2003: the leadership of the country changed hands repeatedly as a result of various elections and military coups.

47

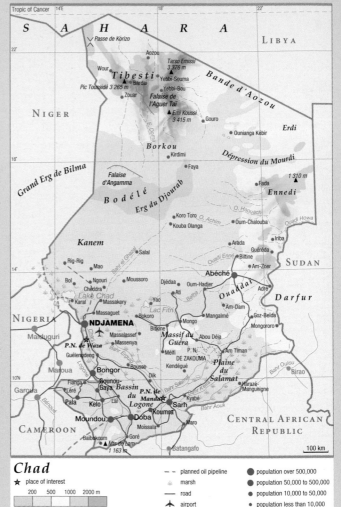

The northern part of the Republic of Chad lies in the southern Sahara Desert. It is partially mountainous and volcanic (Tibesti Massif).

Area: 1,284,000km²
Population (2002): 8,589,000
Capital: Ndjamena 735,000 (2001 e)
Government type and political system: republic with a semi-presidential system
Head of state: (President of the Republic) Idriss Déby
Head of government: (Prime Minister) Moussa Faki Mahamat
Administrative structure: 14 prefectures
Official languages: French and Arabic
Currency: CFA franc

DEMOGRAPHICS

Density: 6 inhab/km²
Percentage of population in urban areas (2001): 24.2%
Age structure of population (2000): 0–15 years: 46.5%, 15–65 years: 50.4%, over 65 years: 3.1%
Birth rate (2003): 48.4‰
Death rate (2003): 19.5‰
Infant mortality rate (2003): 115.3‰
Life expectancy at birth (2003): male: 43.7 years, female: 45.7 years

ECONOMY

GNP (2002): 1.78 billion US$
GNP per capita (2002): 210 US$
GNP per capita PPP (2002): 1010 international dollars
HDI (2000): 0.365
GDP annual growth rate (2003): 10%
Annual inflation rate (2000): 3.8%
Labour force by occupation: n/a
GDP by sector (2000): agriculture: 39.2%, industry: 13.8%, services: 47%
Gross public debt: n/a
Unemployment rate: n/a

Agriculture and fishing
Crops
groundnuts (2001): 333,000t
wheat (2001): 2,800t
sugar cane (2001): 355,000t
cotton (2002): 170,000t

yams (2002): 230,000t
manioc (2001): 342,000t
millet (2001): 321,000t
rice (2002): 135,000t
sorghum (2002): 481,000t
Livestock farming and fishing
cattle (2002): 5,900,000 head
goats (2001): 5,250,000 head
camels (2001): 725,000 head
sheep (2002): 2,450,000 head
chickens (2002): 5,000,000 head
fish (1999): 84,000t

Energy generation
total electricity (2001): 94 million kWh

Industrial production
beer (2000): 80,000hl

cotton yarn (2001): 70,000t

Tourism
Tourism revenue (1998): 10 million US$

Foreign trade
Exports (1997): 134 million US$
Imports (1997): 141 million US$

Defence
Armed forces (2001): 30,350 people
Defence budget (2001): 0.81% of GDP

Standard of living
Inhabitants per doctor (1993): 29,410
Average daily calorie intake (2000): 2,046 (FAO minimum: 2,400)
Cars per 1,000 inhabitants (1996): 3
Televisions per 1,000 inhabitants (1998): 1

Map legend

Chad
★ place of interest
200 500 1000 2000 m

-- planned oil pipeline
↟ marsh
— road
✈ airport

● population over 500,000
● population 50,000 to 500,000
● population 10,000 to 50,000
· population less than 10,000

HISTORY: KEY DATES

Chad's origins and the colonial period
Groups of hunters and livestock farmers, who left behind cave paintings and engravings, lived in this area until after 7000 BC, when the climate became too arid.
9c–19c: the Kanem kingdom, which rapidly adopted Islam, was founded in the 9c. After a period of strength in the 13c, the kingdom began to weaken. However, it grew powerful again in the 16c with Bornu as a centre. Other kingdoms were founded in the area (notably the kingdom of Bagirmi, which appeared in the 16c) and warred with Bornu, until the Sudanese Rabah el Zobaïr conquered the entire region.
19c: Lake Chad became a focal point for European explorers. The ambitions of Western countries clashed with those of the Arab slave traders. In the end, the Western countries were victorious.

Between 1884 and 1899, Chad's borders were artificially fixed under Franco-German and Franco-British agreements. Between 1895 and 1900, French missions led by Lamy, Foureau and Gentil eliminated the last armed resistance.
1920: Chad became a French colony.
1958: Chad became an autonomous member of the French community.

The independent state
1960: Chad became fully independent.
1966: guerrilla warfare erupted between the Muslim-controlled Chad National Liberation Front (Frolinat) and the government.
1973: Libyan forces invaded Chad, occupying the northern border area known as the Aozou Strip.
1979: a coalition government assumed power.
1981: Chad's president, Goukouni Oueddei, asked the Libyans to remove their troops. They withdrew from the

disputed Aozou Strip.
1982: Hissène Habré's troops occupied Ndjamena, which was evacuated by Libya. Habré became president.
1987: Habré's troops won several major victories over the Libyans.
1988: Chad and Libya restored diplomatic relations, but domestic peace remained fragile.
1990: Habré was overthrown by Idriss Déby.
1994: the International Court of Justice returned the Aozou Strip to Chad.
1996: multiparty elections were held for the first time.
2003: peace accords were signed between the rebels and the government, but internal conflict continued.
2004: refugees from the civil war in neighbouring Sudan sought shelter in Chad's desert border area. Fighting broke out between Chadian troops and Sudanese militias.

The Sahara

The Sahara is the largest desert in the world, covering over 8,000,000 km² and receiving less than 100mm of rain per year. Its boundaries are the Atlas Mountains of North Africa and the Mediterranean Sea to the north, the valley of the Niger River and the rest of Africa to the south, the Atlantic Ocean to the west and the Red Sea to the east. In the north, the Saharan Atlas Mountains mark the northernmost border of the desert, which reaches the sea in Libya and Egypt. In the south, no topographical relief allows a frontier to be fixed and it is generally considered that the Sahara ends in the zone where cram-cram, a low scattered grass typical of the Sahel, appears. The Sahara stretches across Morocco, Algeria, Tunisia, Libya, Egypt, Sudan, Chad, Niger, Mali and Mauritania.

Daytime temperatures in the Sahara can be as high as 55°C. The range of temperature between day and night is considerable (15–30°C). Apart from the two volcanic massifs of the Hoggar Mountains of southern Algeria (the highest point being Mount Tahat at 2,918m) and the Tibesti in the north of Chad (where the Emi Koussi volcano rises to 3,415m), the landscapes are often flat and stony (regs or flat gravel plains) or sandy (ergs or dune fields). Water is present at or just below the surface in temporary wadis. The only permanent rivers in the region are the Nile and the Niger.

Around 1.5 million people live in the Sahara. Nomadism, formerly a way of life for half the population, is gradually dying out. Crops are grown in oases, which produce large quantities of dates as well as cereals and vegetables. Mining resources are significant, including oil and natural gas in Algeria and Libya, phosphates in the western Sahara, uranium in Niger and iron in Mauritania. These natural resources play a role in the economic integration of Saharan countries.

49

**COMOROS
→ INDIAN OCEAN**

CÔTE D'IVOIRE (IVORY COAST)

In the north of the Republic of Côte d'Ivoire, uplands covered in savannas rise behind the coastal region, which is fringed by lagoons and partially occupied by dense forests.

Area: 322,463km²
Population (2002): 16,692,000
Capital: Yamoussoukro 155,803 (1998 census)
Government type and political system: republic with a presidential system
Head of state: (President of the Republic) Laurent Gbagbo
Head of government: (Prime Minister) Seydou Elimane Diarra
Administrative structure: 58 departments
Official language: French
Currency: CFA franc

DEMOGRAPHICS

Density: 46 inhab/km²
Percentage of population in urban areas (2001): 44%
Age structure of population (2000): 0–15 years: 42.1%, 15–65 years: 54.8%, over 65 years: 3.1%
Birth rate (2003): 35.5‰
Death rate (2003): 20‰
Infant mortality rate (2003): 101.3‰
Life expectancy at birth (2003): male: 40.8 years, female: 41.2 years

ECONOMY

GNP (2002): 10.2 billion US$
GNP per capita (2002): 620 US$
GNP per capita PPP (2002): 1,450 international dollars
HDI (2000): 0.428
GDP annual growth rate (2003): −3.8%
Annual inflation rate (2000): 2.46%
Labour force by occupation: n/a
GDP by sector (2000): agriculture: 29.2%, industry: 22.4%, services: 48.4%
Gross public debt: n/a
Unemployment rate: n/a

Agriculture and fishing

Crops
pineapples (2001): 226,000t
groundnuts (2001): 144,000t
cocoa (2001): 1,200,000t
coffee (2002): 198,000t
sugar cane (2001): 1,300,000t
rubber (2001): 108,000t
yams (2002): 3,000,000t
maize (2002): 625,000t
manioc (2001): 1,900,000t

cashew nuts (1998): 21,000t
oil palms (2001): 51,000t
rice (2002): 818,000t

Livestock farming and fishing
cattle (2002): 1,476,000 head
goats (2001): 1,134,000 head
sheep (2002): 1,522,000 head
chickens (2001): 29,400,000 head
fish (1999): 77,000t

Energy generation and mining

diamonds (2001): 320,000 carats
total electricity (2001): 4,605 million kWh
gold (2001): 3,100kg
oil (2002): 249,000t

Industrial production

copra (2001): 16,400t
palm oil (2001): 204,863t
cotton yarn (2001): 125,000t
timber (2000): 3,416,000m³

Tourism

Tourism revenue (1998): 108 million US$

Foreign trade

Exports (2002): 5,166.5 million US$
Imports (2002): 2,734.5 million US$

Defence

Armed forces (2001): 17,050 people
Defence budget (2001): 0.88% of GDP

Standard of living

Inhabitants per doctor (1990): 10,000
Average daily calorie intake (2000): 2,590 (FAO minimum: 2,400)

Cars per 1,000 inhabitants (1996): 18
Televisions per 1,000 inhabitants (2001): 60

Côte d'Ivoire

★ place of interest
200 300 400 500 m

═══ motorway
─── road
─── railway line
✈ airport

● population over 2,000,000
● population 100,000 to 2,000,000
● population 50,000 to 100,000
● population less than 50,000

HISTORY: KEY DATES

The earliest inhabitants of the Côte d'Ivoire were the Kru in the south-west and the Senufo in the north-east. Around the 15c, the Mandé, who founded the Kong kingdom, drove out the Kru. The Akan, who settled at the beginning of the 18c, founded chieftainships or kingdoms in the south-east.
1893: despite strong opposition from local people, France established a protectorate over the entire country, eventually incorporating it into French West Africa.
1958: the Côte d'Ivoire became an autonomous republic within the French Community.
1960: the Côte d'Ivoire became independent, with Félix Houphouët-Boigny as president.
1990: a multiparty system was adopted.
1993–2004: after the death of Houphouët-Boigny, the country's economic, social and political situation began to deteriorate. Multiple coups and uprisings led to the eventual division of the country into rebel-held territory (the north) and government-controlled territory (the south).

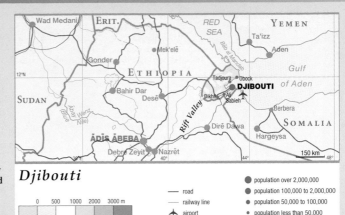

Djibouti

0	500	1000	2000	3000 m

— road
— railway line
✈ airport

● population over 2,000,000
● population 100,000 to 2,000,000
● population 50,000 to 100,000
· population less than 50,000

The Republic of Djibouti is a small country situated at the southernmost end of the Red Sea. It has a varied terrain and a hot, arid climate.

Area: 23,200km²
Population (2002): 651,000
Capital: Djibouti 542,000 (2001 e) including the suburbs
Government type and political system: republic with a presidential system
Head of state and government: (President of the Republic) Ismaïl Omar Guelleh
Prime minister: Dileïta Mohamed Dileïta
Administrative structure: 5 regions and 1 city
Official languages: Arabic and French
Currency: Djibouti franc

DEMOGRAPHICS
Density: 28 inhab/km²
Percentage of population in urban areas (2001): 84.2%
Age structure of population (2000): 0–15 years: 43.2%, 15–65 years: 53.6%, over 65 years: 3.2%
Birth rate (2003): 39.5‰
Death rate (2003): 17.7‰
Infant mortality rate (2003): 102.4‰
Life expectancy at birth (2003): male: 44.7 years, female: 46.8 years

ECONOMY
GNP (2002): 0.59 billion US$

GNP per capita (2002): 850 US$
GNP per capita PPP (2002): 2,040 international dollars
HDI (2000): 0.445
GDP annual growth rate (2003): 3.5%
Annual inflation rate (1992): 5.5%
Labour force by occupation: n/a
GDP by sector (2000): agriculture: 3.7%, industry: 14.2%, services: 82.1%
Gross public debt: n/a
Unemployment rate: n/a

Agriculture and fishing
Crops
tomatoes (2002): 1,100t
Livestock farming and fishing
cattle (2002): 297,000 head
goats (2001): 513,000 head
camels (2001): 70,000 head
sheep (2002): 466,000 head
fish (1999): 350t

Energy generation
total electricity (2001): 180 million kWh

Tourism
Tourism revenue (1998): 4 million US$

Foreign trade
Exports (1997): 144 million US$

Imports (1997): 383 million US$

Defence
Armed forces (2001): 9,850 people
Defence budget (2001): 3.92% of GDP

Standard of living
Inhabitants per doctor (1990): 4,180
Average daily calorie intake (2000): 2,050 (FAO minimum: 2,400)
Cars per 1,000 inhabitants (1996): 17
Televisions per 1,000 inhabitants (2000): 71

HISTORY: KEY DATES
1896: the country became a French colony, known as French Somaliland.
1977: the colony became independent and was renamed the Republic of Djibouti, with Hassan Gouled Aptidon as its president.
1991: the Afar population rebelled against the government.
1993: Djibouti held its first multiparty elections.
2003: the government expelled approximately 100,000 illegal imigrants from Djibouti.

53

ETHIOPIA

Ethiopia

★ place of interest

	marsh
—	road
—	railway line
✈	airport

0 500 1000 2000 3000 m

● population over 2,000,000
● population 100,000 to 2,000,000
● population 50,000 to 100,000
• population less than 50,000

150 km

Apart from the plains and plateaux in the east (Ogaden) and the Denakil depression farther north, Ethiopia is mainly a mountainous country (Ethiopian Massif). The climate varies greatly. Ethiopia's lowlands have a hot, dry climate, which produces semi-desert conditions. The rest of the country has a temperate climate.

Area: 1,104,300km²
Population (2002): 66,039,000
Capital: Addis Ababa 2,753,000 (2001 e)
Government type and political system: republic with a parliamentary system
Head of state: (President of the Republic) Girma Wolde-Giorgis
Head of government: (Prime Minister) Meles Zenawi
Administrative structure: 9 ethnically-based administrative states (*kililoch*) and 2 chartered cities
Official language: Amharic
Currency: birr

DEMOGRAPHICS

Density: 57 inhab/km²
Percentage of population in urban areas (2001): 15.9%
Age structure of population (2000): 0–15 years: 45.2%, 15–65 years: 51.8%, over 65 years: 3%
Birth rate (2003): 42.5‰
Death rate (2003): 17.7‰
Infant mortality rate (2003): 100.4‰
Life expectancy at birth (2003): male: 44.6 years, female: 46.3 years

ECONOMY

GNP (2002): 6.52 billion US$
GNP per capita (2002): 100 US$
GNP per capita PPP (2002): 780 international dollars
HDI (2000): 0.327
GDP annual growth rate (2003): –3.8%
Annual inflation rate (2003): 12.6%
Labour force by occupation: n/a
GDP by sector (2000): agriculture: 52.3%, industry: 11.2%, services: 36.5%
Gross public debt: n/a
Unemployment rate (1998): 29.49%

Agriculture and fishing

Crops
wheat (2002): 1,478,000t
coffee (2001): 228,000t
sugar cane (2001): 2,400,000t
yams (2001): 270,000t
maize (2002): 2,968,000t
honey (2001): 29,000t

millet (2001): 318,000t
barley (2002): 1,093,000t
potatoes (2002): 385,000t
sorghum (2002): 1,566,000t
Livestock farming and fishing
cattle (2002): 35,500,000 head
goats (2001): 17,000,000 head
camels (2001): 1,070,000 head
horses (2001): 2,750,000 head
sheep (2001): 11,438,000 head
chickens (2002): 38,000,000 head
fish (1999): 15,900t

Energy generation and mining
total electricity (2001): 1,713 million kWh
hydroelectricity (2001): 1,672 million kWh
gold (2001): 5,200kg

Industrial production
milk (2001): 1,197,000t
meat (2001): 654,000t

beer (2000): 3,999,000hl
cotton yarn (2001): 14,000t
cement (2001): 950,000t
timber (2000): 2,459,000m³
sisal (2001): 700t

Tourism
Tourism revenue (2000): 24 million US$

Foreign trade
Exports (2002): 480.2 million US$
Imports (2002): 1,455 million US$

Defence
Armed forces (2001): 252,500 people
Defence budget (2001): 9.76% of GDP

Standard of living
Inhabitants per doctor (1990): 33,330
Average daily calorie intake (2000): 2,022 (FAO minimum: 2,400)
Cars per 1,000 inhabitants (2000): 1
Televisions per 1,000 inhabitants (2000): 6

HISTORY: KEY DATES

AD 1c: the Axumite Kingdom extended its territories as far as the Blue Nile. Christianized by the Egyptian (Coptic) Church in the 4c, it reached its peak in the 6c.
16c: after the Axumite Kingdom collapsed, Ethiopia was conquered by the Somalis.
17c–18c: a number of separate, warring populations controlled various parts of the country.
19c: Menelik II defeated the Italians at Adwa (1896) and founded Addis Ababa.
1930: Ras Tafari Makonnen (later known as Haile Selassie I) became Emperor.
1935–6: Italy invaded Ethiopia, Eritrea and Somalia, making them part of Italian East Africa.

1941: British and Commonwealth troops liberated Ethiopia.
1962: Eritrea became an Ethiopian province. A rebellion began.
1974: a socialist state was proclaimed.
1977–8: supported by the USSR and Cuba, Ethiopia engaged in a border conflict against Somalia over the Ogaden region.
1987: Ethiopia became a popular, democratic, one-party republic.
1991: Eritrean rebels forced President Mengistu to resign and flee the country.
1993: Eritrea became independent.
1998–2000: border clashes between Ethiopia and Eritrea led to war.
2000–3: a ceasefire agreement was signed and UN mediation of the border dispute began.

58

The Gabonese Republic is a little larger than the UK and is located in the Ogooué River basin. It is a sparsely populated country with a hot, humid equatorial climate.

Area: 267,668km^2
Population (2002): 1,294,000
Capital: Libreville 573,000 (2001 e)
Government type and political system: republic with a semi-presidential system
Head of state: (President of the Republic) Omar Bongo
Head of government: (Prime Minister) Jean-François Ntoutoume-Emane
Administrative structure: 9 provinces
Official language: French
Currency: CFA franc

DEMOGRAPHICS

Density: 5 inhab/km^2
Percentage of population in urban areas (2001): 82.2%
Age structure of population (2000): 0–15 years: 40.2%, 15–65 years: 54%, over 65 years: 5.8%
Birth rate (2003): 31.6‰
Death rate (2003): 11.5‰
Infant mortality rate (2003): 56.8‰
Life expectancy at birth (2003): male: 55.8 years, female: 57.5 years

ECONOMY

GNP (2002): 4.03 billion US$
GNP per capita (2002): 3,060 US$
GNP per capita PPP (2002): 5,530 international dollars
HDI (2000): 0.637
GDP annual growth rate (2003): 2.8%
Annual inflation rate (1997): 4%
Labour force by occupation: n/a
GDP by sector (2000): agriculture: 6.4%, industry: 53.2%, services: 40.4%
Gross public debt: n/a
Unemployment rate: n/a

Agriculture and fishing

Crops
groundnuts (2001): 20,000t
cocoa (2001): 600t
sugar cane (2001): 235,000t
yams (2002): 155,000t
manioc (2001): 230,000t
Livestock farming and fishing
cattle (2002): 36,000 head
sheep (2002): 198,000 head
pigs (2002): 212,000 head
chickens (2002): 3,100,000 head

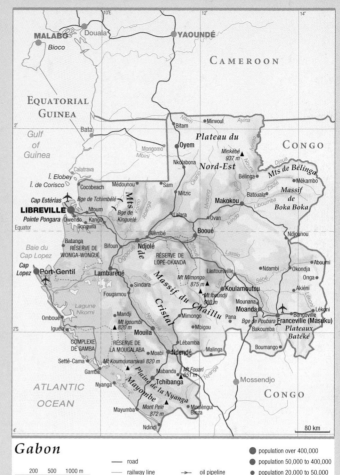

Gabon

— road
— railway line
✈ airport
→ oil pipeline
⌄ marsh

● population over 400,000
● population 50,000 to 400,000
● population 20,000 to 50,000
● population less than 20 000

200 500 1000 m

80 km

fish (1999): 53,000t

Energy generation and mining
total electricity (2001): 798 million kWh
hydroelectricity (2001): 523 million kWh
manganese (2001): 830,000t
oil (2002): 14,700,000t
uranium (1999): 294t

Industrial production
palm oil (2001): 6,400t
cement (2001): 210,000t
timber (2000): 2,584,000m^3

Tourism
Tourism revenue (2001): 7 million US$

Foreign trade
Exports (1999): 2,498.8 million US$
Imports (2000): 910.5 million US$

Defence
Armed forces (2001): 4,700 people
Defence budget (2001): 2.43% of GDP

Standard of living
Inhabitants per doctor (1993): 2,000
Average daily calorie intake (2000): 2,564 (FAO minimum: 2,400)
Cars per 1,000 inhabitants (1996): 17
Televisions per 1,000 inhabitants (2000): 326

HISTORY: KEY DATES

The earliest inhabitants were probably the Pygmies, who lived inland. Later, the Bantu-speaking Fang inhabited the north of the country.
c.1471: the Portuguese arrived on the coast of what is now Gabon.
17c–19c: the European settlers traded slaves as well as ivory and ebony.
1886: Gabon became a French colony. It was absorbed by French Congo (1888–1904) and then became part of French Equatorial Africa (1910).
1960: Gabon became an independent republic.
1990: a multiparty political system was introduced.
2003: constitutional reforms were passed, removing presidential term limitations.

The Gambia

50	100	200 m	

— road
— railway line
✈ airport

- ● population over 1,500,000
- ● population 100,000 to 1,500,000
- ● population 20,000 to 100,000
- ● population less than 20,000

The Republic of The Gambia consists of a narrow strip of land, 20–50km wide and 300km long, on either side of the River Gambia.

Area: 11,295km²
Population (2002): 1,371,000
Capital: Banjul 418,000 (2001 e) including the suburbs
Government type and political system: republic with a semi-presidential system
Head of state and government: (President of the Republic) Yahya Jammeh
Administrative structure: 5 divisions and 1 city
Official language: English
Currency: dalasi

DEMOGRAPHICS
Density: 116 inhab/km²
Percentage of population in urban areas (2001): 31.3%
Age structure of population (2000): 0–15 years: 40.3%, 15–65 years: 56.6%, over 65 years: 3.1%
Birth rate (2003): 35.8‰
Death rate (2003): 12.7‰
Infant mortality rate (2003): 80.5‰
Life expectancy at birth (2003): male: 52.7 years, female: 55.5 years

ECONOMY
GNP (2002): 0.375 billion US$
GNP per capita (2002): 270 US$
GNP per capita PPP (2002): 1,660 international dollars
HDI (2000): 0.405
GDP annual growth rate (2003): 8.7%
Annual inflation rate (2000): 0.84%

Labour force by occupation: n/a
GDP by sector (2000): agriculture: 37.9%, industry: 12.7%, services: 49.4%
Gross public debt: n/a
Unemployment rate: n/a

Agriculture and fishing
Crops
groundnuts (2001): 153,000t
millet (2001): 105,000t
Livestock farming and fishing
cattle (2002): 327,000 head
goats (2002): 146,000 head
sheep (2002): 146,000 head
chickens (2002): 591,000 head
fish (1999): 30,000t

Energy generation
total electricity (2001): 85 million kWh

Industrial production
palm oil (2001): 2,500t

Tourism
Tourism revenue (1998): 49 million US$

Foreign trade
Exports (2002): 583.4 million US$
Imports (2002): 1,041.6 million US$

Defence
Armed forces (2001): 800 people
Defence budget (2001): 0.71% of GDP

Standard of living
Inhabitants per doctor (1990): 11,690
Average daily calorie intake (2000): 2,473 (FAO minimum: 2,400)
Cars per 1,000 inhabitants (1996): 8
Televisions per 1,000 inhabitants (2000): 3

HISTORY: KEY DATES

13c–17c: once part of the empire of Mali, the country that is now known as The Gambia was settled by a group of Malinké people who became known as the Mandinka.
15c: European slave traders settled in The Gambia.
19c: The Gambia became a British Crown Colony.
1965: The Gambia achieved independence within the Commonwealth of Nations.
1970: The Gambia became a republic.
1982: Senegal and The Gambia signed a treaty of confederation, forming the Confederation of Senegambia.
1989: The Gambia withdrew from the Confederation of Senegambia and the alliance was dissolved.
2001: opposition parties were legalized prior to presidential elections.

Two Ghanas

The name Ghana was also given to a former kingdom in the western Sudan (5c–11c), which overlapped present-day Mauritania and Mali, in the Soninke country. Situated in the heart of the Sahel, this kingdom obtained its income from trading in salt and gold (the name Ghana originally referred to the ruler in control of the region's gold supply, and was later used to describe this empire, the 'Land of Gold'). The kingdom of Ghana was eventually sacked by the Almoravids, who conquered its capital in 1076.

The Republic of Ghana is a nation in West Africa with a tropical climate. Behind its coastal plains, which are lined with lagoons, lies a plateau region covered by dense rainforests. Savannas and open grasslands dominate in the north of the country.

Area: 238,533km²
Population (2002): 20,176,000
Capital: Accra 1,925,000 (2001 e) including the suburbs
Government type and political system: republic
Head of state and government: (President of the Republic) John Agyekum Kufuor
Administrative structure: 10 regions
Official language: English
Currency: cedi

DEMOGRAPHICS

Density: 84 inhab/km²
Percentage of population in urban areas (2001): 36.4%
Age structure of population (2000): 0–15 years: 40.9%, 15–65 years: 55.9%, over 65 years: 3.2%
Birth rate (2003): 31.9‰
Death rate (2003): 10‰
Infant mortality rate (2003): 57.8‰
Life expectancy at birth (2003): male: 56.5 years, female: 59.3 years

ECONOMY

GNP (2002): 5.51 billion US$
GNP per capita (2002): 270 US$
GNP per capita PPP (2002): 2,080 international dollars
HDI (2000): 0.548
GDP annual growth rate (2003): 4.7%
Annual inflation rate (2000): 25.19%
Labour force by occupation: n/a
GDP by sector (2000): agriculture: 35.3%, industry: 25.4%, services: 39.3%
Gross public debt: n/a
Unemployment rate: n/a

Agriculture
Crops
groundnuts (2001): 205,000t
plantains (2001): 1,932,000t
cocoa (2001): 410,000t
sugar cane (2001): 140,000t
yams (2001): 3,900,000t
maize (2002): 1,400,000t
manioc (2001): 8,512,000t
millet (2001): 169,000t
oranges (2002): 300,000t
oil palms (2001): 35,000t
rice (2002): 280,000t

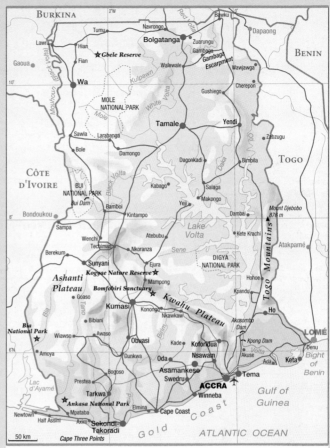

Ghana

⭐ place of interest
100   200   400 m

motorway
road
railway line
airport

● population over 1,000,000
● population 100,000 to 1,000,000
● population 20,000 to 100,000
• population less than 20,000

sorghum (2002): 316,000t
tomatoes (2002): 200,000t
Livestock farming
cattle (2002): 1,430,000 head
goats (2001): 3,077,000 head
sheep (2002): 2,970,000 head
pigs (2002): 350,000 head
chickens (2002): 22,000,000 head

Energy generation and mining
bauxite (2001): 715,000t
diamonds (2001): 870,000 carats
total electricity (2001): 8,801 million kWh
hydroelectricity (2001): 8,359 million kWh
manganese (2001): 260,000t
gold (2001): 68,700kg

Industrial production
palm oil (2001): 108,000t
aluminium (2001): 162,000t
cement (2001): 1,900,000t

Tourism
Tourism revenue (2001): 448 million US$

Foreign trade
Exports (2002): 2,015.2 million US$
Imports (2002): 2,705.1 million US$

Defence
Armed forces (2001): 7,000 people
Defence budget (2001): 0.66% of GDP

Standard of living
Inhabitants per doctor (1990): 25,000
Average daily calorie intake (2000): 2,699 (FAO minimum: 2,400)
Cars per 1,000 inhabitants (1996): 5
Televisions per 1,000 inhabitants (2000): 118

HISTORY: KEY DATES

1471: the Portuguese reached the coast of Ghana (then called the Gold Coast).
17c–18c: European traders competed for control of the coast.
19c: the Gold Coast gradually became a British protectorate.
1957: the Gold Coast became independent within the Commonwealth of Nations, and was renamed Ghana.
1992: Ghana's first multiparty elections were held.

Situated in the Indian Ocean north-west of Madagascar, the Union of the Comoros is made up of the islands of Njazidja (formerly named Grande Comore), Mwali (formerly Mohéli) and Nzwani (formerly Anjouan). In 1976, the fourth island in the archipelago, Mayotte, chose to remain under French administration.

Area: 2,235km²
Population (2002): 748,000
Capital: Moroni 49,000 (2001 e)
Government type and political system: republic
Head of state and government: (President of the Union) Azali Assoumani
Administrative structure: 3 governorates
Official languages: French and Arabic
Currency: Comoran franc

DEMOGRAPHICS

Density: 365 inhab/km²
Percentage of population in urban areas (2001): 33.8%
Age structure of population (2000): 0–15 years: 43%, 15–65 years: 54.4%, over 65 years: 2.6%
Birth rate (2003): 36.7‰
Death rate (2003): 8.4‰
Infant mortality rate (2003): 67‰
Life expectancy at birth (2003): male: 59.4 years, female: 62.2 years

ECONOMY

GNP (2002): 0.28 billion US$
GNP per capita (2002): 390 US$
GNP per capita PPP (2002): 1,690 international dollars
HDI (2000): 0.511
GDP annual growth rate (2003): 2.1%
Annual inflation rate: n/a
Labour force by occupation: n/a
GDP by sector (2000): agriculture: 40.9%, industry: 11.9%, services: 47.2%
Gross public debt: n/a
Unemployment rate: n/a

Agriculture and fishing

Crops
bananas (2001): 57,000t
manioc (2001): 45,000t
Livestock farming and fishing
cattle (2002): 52,000 head
goats (2001): 172,000 head
fish (1999): 12,200t

Energy generation

total electricity (2001): 21 million kWh

Tourism

Tourism revenue (1999): 19 million US$

Foreign trade

Exports (1997): 11 million US$

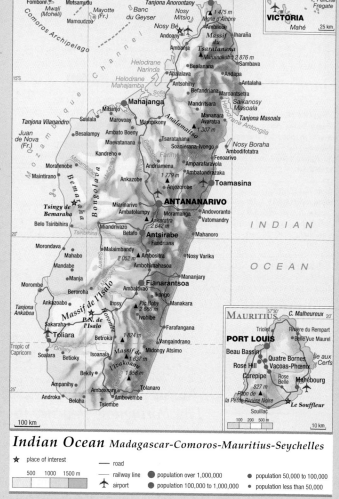

Indian Ocean Madagascar-Comoros-Mauritius-Seychelles

★ place of interest
── road
── railway line
✈ airport

| 500 | 1000 | 1500 m |

● population over 1,000,000
● population 100,000 to 1,000,000
● population 50,000 to 100,000
• population less than 50,000

Imports (1997): 157 million US$

Defence

Armed forces: n/a
Defence budget: n/a

Standard of living

Inhabitants per doctor: n/a
Average daily calorie intake (2000): 1,753 (FAO minimum: 2,400)
Cars per 1,000 inhabitants (1996): 13
Televisions per 1,000 inhabitants (1998): 4

HISTORY: KEY DATES

933: Shiragi Arabs came to the islands from Persia.
1841–1909: the islands were ceded to the French.
1975: three of the islands voted to become independent, while the fourth, Mayotte, remained a French dependency.
2001: a new constitution was established.

Beyond the rainforests and mangrove swamps of the Republic of Madagascar's narrow coastal plains, there are high plateaux from which volcanic peaks rise. The climate is tropical along the eastern coast, drier in the west, temperate inland due to the altitude and hot and very arid in the south, where the terrain is dominated by open forests, savannas and spiny thickets.

Area: 587,041km²
Population (2002): 16,913,000
Capital: Antananarivo 1,052,835 (1993 census), 1,689,000 (2001 e) including the suburbs
Government type and political system: republic with a semi-presidential system
Head of state: (President of the Republic) Marc Ravalomanana
Head of government: (Prime Minister) Jacques Sylla
Administrative structure: 6 provinces
Official languages: Malagasy and French
Currency: Ariary

DEMOGRAPHICS
Density: 27 inhab/km²
Percentage of population in urban areas (2001): 30.1%
Age structure of population (2000): 0–15 years: 44.7%, 15–65 years: 52.3%, over 65 years: 3%
Birth rate (2003): 41.6‰
Death rate (2003): 13.2‰
Infant mortality rate (2003): 91.5‰
Life expectancy at birth (2003): male: 52.5 years, female: 54.8 years

ECONOMY
GNP (2002): 3.84 billion US$
GNP per capita (2002): 230 US$
GNP per capita PPP (2002): 730 international dollars
HDI (2000): 0.469
GDP annual growth rate (2003): 9.6%
Annual inflation rate (2000): 12.03%
Labour force by occupation: n/a
GDP by sector (2000): agriculture: 34.9%, industry: 13.1%, services: 52%
Gross public debt: n/a
Unemployment rate: n/a

Agriculture and fishing
Crops
bananas (2001): 260,000t
coffee (2002): 65,000t
sugar cane (2001): 2,200,000t
maize (2002): 181,000t
manioc (2001): 2,228,000t
sweet potatoes (2001): 476,000t
potatoes (2002): 296,000t
rice (2002): 2,671,000t
Livestock farming and fishing
cattle (2002): 10,500,000 head
goats (2001): 1,350,000 head
sheep (2002): 650,000 head
pigs (2002): 1,600,000 head
chickens (2002): 24,000,000 head
fish (1999): 141,000t

Energy generation and mining
chromium (2001): 52,000t
total electricity (2001): 830 million kWh
hydroelectricity (2000): 520 million kWh

Industrial production
sugar (2002): 35,000t
beer (2000): 300,000hl
cement (2001): 54,000t
sisal (2001): 15,000t

Tourism
Tourism revenue (2000): 116 million US$

Foreign trade
Exports (2000): 824 million US$
Imports (2000): 997 million US$

Defence
Armed forces (2001): 13,500 people
Defence budget (2001): 1.03% of GDP

Standard of living
Inhabitants per doctor (1990): 10,000
Average daily calorie intake (2000): 2,007 (FAO minimum: 2,400)
Cars per 1,000 inhabitants (1996): 4
Televisions per 1,000 inhabitants (2000): 24

HISTORY: KEY DATES
14c–17c: Arab traders began to settle on the coasts of Madagascar, which was inhabited by Africans and Indonesians. The Europeans did not create any permanent settlements during this period.
18c: the Merina kingdom extended its rule over most of the island.
1817: the Merina ruler, King Radama I (1810–28), was designated king of Madagascar by Great Britain.
1885: the French protectorate of Madagascar was established.
1895–6: General Duchesne's expedition ended in the annexing of the island by France. The French abolished slavery.
1896–1905: Gallieni, the governor-general, worked towards establishing peace.
1947–8: a violent rebellion was harshly repressed by the French.
1960: the Malagasy Republic became fully independent.
1972: after serious civil unrest, President Tsiranana (in power since 1958) was forced to dissolve his government and resign.
1975–93: Didier Ratsiraka became president of Madagascar. After the failure of his socialist government, which lasted over ten years, the regime faced growing opposition from the Hery Veona or 'Active Forces'. Their leader, Albert Zafy, became president in 1993.
2002: After several years of political unrest, Marc Ravalomanana of the I Love Madagascar party became president.

65

The Republic of Mauritius consists of the large volcanic island of Mauritius, the island of Rodrigues and several smaller islands situated in the Indian Ocean to the east of Madagascar. Below an altitude of 400m Mauritius has a humid, subtropical climate, and at higher altitudes the climate is more temperate.

Area: 2,040km²
Population (2002): 1,180,000
Capital: Port Louis 176,000 (2001 e)
Government type and political system: republic with a parliamentary system

Head of state: (President of the Republic) Anerood Jugnauth
Head of government: (Prime Minister) Paul Berenger
Administrative structure: 5 municipalities, 9 districts and 3 dependencies
Official language: English
Currency: Mauritian rupee

DEMOGRAPHICS
Density: 568 inhab/km²
Percentage of population in urban areas (2001): 41.6%
Age structure of population (2000): 0–15 years: 25.6%, 15–65 years: 68.2%, over 65 years: 6.2%
Birth rate (2003): 16.2‰
Death rate (2003): 6.7‰
Infant mortality rate (2003): 16‰
Life expectancy at birth (2003): male: 68.4 years, female: 75.8 years

ECONOMY
GNP (2002): 4.68 billion US$
GNP per capita (2002): 3,860 $
GNP per capita PPP (2002): 10,820 international dollars

INDIAN OCEAN MAURITIUS

HDI (2000): 0.772
GDP annual growth rate (2003): 3.3%
Annual inflation rate (2000): 4.2%
Labour force by occupation: n/a
GDP by sector (2000): agriculture: 6%, industry: 32.1%, services: 61.9%
Gross public debt: n/a
Unemployment rate (2002): 9.7%

Agriculture and fishing
Crops
sugar cane (2001): 5,500,000t
Livestock farming and fishing
chickens (2002): 9,800,000 head
fish (1999): 12,100t

Energy generation
total electricity (2001): 1,311 million kWh
hydroelectricity (2001): 120 million kWh

Industrial production
sugar (2002): 521,000t
beer (2000): 390,000hl

Tourism
Tourism revenue (2001): 625 million US$
Foreign trade
Exports (2002): 1,830.2 million US$
Imports (2002): 2,018.3 million US$
Defence
Armed forces (2001): 2,000 people
Defence budget (2001): 0.19% of GDP

Standard of living
Inhabitants per doctor (1995): 1,111
Average daily calorie intake (2000): 2,985 (FAO minimum: 2,400)
Cars per 1,000 inhabitants (1999): 73
Televisions per 1,000 inhabitants (2001): 301

HISTORY: KEY DATES

1598: the Dutch claimed the uninhabited island, naming it after Prince Maurice of Nassau.
1638–1710: a Dutch settlement was founded on the island. Convicts from Indonesia and natives of Madagascar were used as slave labour. The dodo was hunted to extinction.
1715: the French took control of the island and renamed it Île de France.
1814: under the Treaty of Paris, the island was ceded to the British and renamed Mauritius.
1834: the British abolished slavery. The freeing of the slaves led to a significant influx of Indian workers.
1968: the island became an independent state within the Commonwealth of Nations.
1992: Mauritius became a republic.
2003: Paul Berenger became the first non-Hindu prime minister of Mauritius.

INDIAN OCEAN SEYCHELLES

The Republic of Seychelles is an archipelago in the Indian Ocean made up of 115 granitic and coralline islands. The principal island is Mahé. The Seychelles' climate is tropical and oceanic, tempered by marine influences. Rainfall varies from island to island, and from one season to another.

Area: 455km²
Population (2002): 76,000
Capital: Victoria 30,000 (2001 e) including the suburbs
Government type and political system: republic with a semi-presidential system
Head of state and government: (President of the Republic) James Michel
Administrative structure: 23 districts
Official languages: English, French and Creole
Currency: Seychelles rupee

DEMOGRAPHICS
Density: 189 inhab/km²
Percentage of population in urban areas (2001): 64.5%
Age structure of population (1993): 0–15 years: 35%, 15–65 years: 59%, over 65 years: 6%

Birth rate (1999): 18.23‰
Death rate (1999): 7.05‰
Infant mortality rate (1998): 14.5‰
Life expectancy at birth: n/a

ECONOMY
GNP (2000): 0.569 billion US$
GNP per capita (2000): 6,780 US$
GNP per capita PPP (1999): 10,381 international dollars
HDI (2000): 0.811
GDP annual growth rate (2003): −5.1%
Annual inflation rate (2000): 6.29%
Labour force by occupation: n/a
GDP by sector (2000): agriculture: 3%, industry: 21.6%, services: 75.4%
Gross public debt: n/a
Unemployment rate: n/a

Agriculture and fishing
Crops
bananas (2001): 1,970t
tea (2001): 230 t
Fishing
fish (1999): 38,000t
Energy generation
total electricity (2001): 160 million kWh
Tourism
Tourism revenue (2001): 113 million US$

Foreign trade
Exports (2002): 236.7 million US$
Imports (2002): 376.26 million US$
Defence
Armed forces (2001): 450 people
Defence budget (2001): 1.83% of GDP
Standard of living
Inhabitants per doctor (1991): 172
Average daily calorie intake (2000): 2,432 (FAO minimum: 2,400)
Cars per 1,000 inhabitants (1996): 89
Televisions per 1,000 inhabitants (2001): 202

HISTORY: KEY DATES
16c: the Portuguese navigator Vasco da Gama claimed discovery of the islands, which had probably been used as a provisioning stop by earlier seafaring peoples.
18c: the archipelago was taken over by France.
1814: under the Treaty of Paris, the Seychelles passed from French to British rule.
1976: the Seychelles became an independent republic within the Commonwealth of Nations.

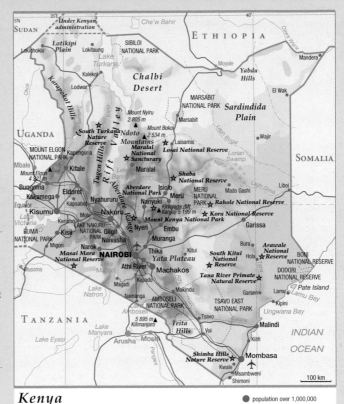

The high volcanic massifs in the south-west of the Republic of Kenya are densely populated, because the altitude moderates the temperatures in this equatorial zone. The steppe-like low plateaux and plains in the north and north-east are almost empty.

Area: 580,367 km²
Population (2002): 31,905,000
Capital: Nairobi 2,343,000 (2001 e)
Government type and political system: republic
Head of state and government: (President of the Republic) Mwai Kibaki
Administrative structure: 7 provinces and 1 area
Official languages: English (official) and Swahili (native)
Currency: Kenyan shilling

DEMOGRAPHICS

Density: 52 inhab/km²
Percentage of population in urban areas (2001): 34.3%
Age structure of population (2000): 0–15 years: 43.5%, 15–65 years: 53.7%, over 65 years: 2.8%
Birth rate (2003): 32.5‰
Death rate (2003): 16.7‰
Infant mortality rate (2003): 69.3‰
Life expectancy at birth (2003): male: 43.5 years, female: 45.6 years

ECONOMY

GNP (2002): 11.2 billion US$
GNP per capita (2002): 360 US$
GNP per capital PPP (2002): 1,010 international dollars
HDI (2000): 0.513
GDP annual growth rate (2003): 1.5%
Annual inflation rate (2000): 5.86%
Labour force by occupation: n/a
GDP by sector (2000): agriculture: 19.9%, industry: 18.7%, services: 61.4%
Gross public debt: n/a
Unemployment rate: n/a

Agriculture and fishing

Crops
pineapples (2001): 280,000t
bananas (2001): 210,000t
plantains (2001): 370,000t
wheat (2002): 234,000t
coffee (2002): 48,000t
sugar cane (2001): 5,150,000t
maize (2002): 2,340,000t
manioc (2001): 950,000t
honey (2001): 24,940t

cashew nuts (1998): 9,000t
sweet potatoes (2001): 535,000t
sorghum (2002): 72,000t
tea (2001): 240,000t

Livestock farming and fishing
cattle (2002): 11,500,000 head
goats (2001): 9,000,000 head
camels (2001): 830,000 head
sheep (2002): 7,700,000 head
chickens (2002): 27,900,000 head
fish (1999): 206,000t

Energy generation

total electricity (2001): 4,033 million kWh
hydroelectricity (2001): 714 million kWh

Industrial production

beer (2000): 2,600,000hl
sugar (2002): 494,000t

timber (2000): 1,977,000m³
sisal (2001): 25,000t

Tourism

Tourism revenue (2001): 308 million US$

Foreign trade

Exports (2001): 1,894 million US$
Imports (2001): 3,176.1 million US$

Defence

Armed forces (2001): 24,400 people
Defence budget (2001): 2.39% of GDP

Standard of living

Inhabitants per doctor (1990): 20,000
Average daily calorie intake (2000): 1,965 (FAO minimum: 2,400)
Cars per 1,000 inhabitants (1996): 11
Televisions per 1,000 inhabitants (2001): 26

HISTORY: KEY DATES

Some of the earliest known fossil hominid remains have been found in Kenya.
1888: Great Britain was granted concessionary rights to the Kenya coast by the Sultan of Zanzibar.
1920: Kenya became a British Crown Colony.
1925: Jomo Kenyatta became the leader of the nationalist movement, which demanded the return of land to the Kikuyu people.
1952–6: the Mau Mau rebellion against British rule was severely repressed.
1963: Kenya became independent within the Commonwealth of Nations.
1998: thousands were injured in a bomb attack on the US Embassy in Nairobi.
2004: a new constitution was drafted.

LESOTHO

Lesotho

★ place of interest

| 500 | 1000 | 1500 | 2000 m |

═══ motorway	● population over 1,000,000
— road	● population 500,000 to 1,000,000
--- railway line	● population 100,000 to 500,000
✈ airport	• population less than 100,000

The Kingdom of Lesotho is a landlocked, mountainous country, totally enclosed within South Africa.

Area: 30,355km²
Population (2002): 2,076,000
Capital: Maseru 271,000 (2001 e) including the suburbs
Government type and political system: monarchy
Head of state: (King) Letsie III
Head of government: (Prime Minister) Bethuel Pakalitha Mosisili
Administrative structure: 10 districts
Official languages: Sesotho and English
Currency: loti

DEMOGRAPHICS
Density: 71 inhab/km²
Percentage of population in urban areas (2001): 28.7%
Age structure of population (2000): 0–15 years: 39.3%, 15–65 years: 56.5%, over 65 years: 4.2%
Birth rate (2003): 31.1‰
Death rate (2003): 25.7‰
Infant mortality rate (2003): 92.1‰
Life expectancy at birth (2003): male: 32.3 years, female: 37.7 years

ECONOMY
GNP (2002): 0.973 billion US$
GNP per capita (2002): 550 US$
GNP per capita PPP (2002): 2,970 international dollars
HDI (2000): 0.535
GDP annual growth rate (2003): 3.9%
Annual inflation rate (2000): 6.13%
Labour force by occupation: n/a
GDP by sector (2000): agriculture: 16.9%, industry: 43.8%, services: 39.3%
Gross public debt: n/a

Unemployment rate: n/a
Agriculture
Crops
maize (2002): 150,000t
Livestock farming
cattle (2002): 540,000 head
goats (2001): 570,000 head
sheep (2002): 850,000 head
Industrial production
milk (2001): 23,800t
Tourism
Tourism revenue (1999): 19 million US$
Foreign trade
Exports (2002): 354.8 million US$
Imports (2002): 736 million US$
Defence
Armed forces (2001): 2,000 people

Defence budget (2001): 3.09% of GDP
Standard of living
Inhabitants per doctor (1990): 18,610
Average daily calorie intake (2000): 2,300 (FAO minimum: 2,400)
Cars per 1,000 inhabitants (1996): 6
Televisions per 1,000 inhabitants (2000): 16

HISTORY: KEY DATES
1868: the kingdom of Lesotho, created in the 19c, became a British protectorate with the name Basutoland.
1966: the country became independent and was renamed Lesotho.

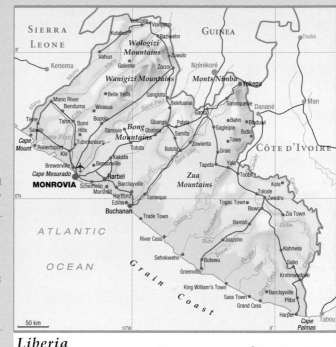

Liberia

200	500	1000 m	

— road   ● population over 500,000

— railway line   ● population 20,000 to 100,000

✈ airport   ● population less than 20,000

Beyond the Republic of Liberia's narrow coastal plain, the land rises gradually towards the Nimba Mountains. The hot and humid climate favours dense inland forests, which cover one-third of the country.

Area: 111,369km²
Population (2002): 3,298,000
Capital: Monrovia 491,000 (2001 e)
Government type and political system: republic
Head of state and government: (President of the Republic) Gyude Bryant
Administrative structure: 13 counties
Official language: English
Currency: Liberian dollar

DEMOGRAPHICS
Density: 29 inhab/km²
Percentage of population in urban areas (2001): 45.5%
Age structure of population (2000): 0–15 years: 42.7%, 15–65 years: 54.4%, over 65 years: 2.9%
Birth rate (2003): 50‰
Death rate (2003): 21.5‰
Infant mortality rate (2003): 147.4‰
Life expectancy at birth (2003): male: 40.7 years, female: 42.2 years

ECONOMY
GNP (2002): 0.476 billion US$
GNP per capita (2002): 460 US$
GNP per capita PPP: n/a
HDI: n/a
GDP annual growth rate (2001): 5.3%
Annual inflation rate (1992): 75%
Labour force by occupation: n/a
GDP by sector (1991): agriculture: 41%, industry: 20%, services: 39%
Gross public debt: n/a
Unemployment rate: n/a

Agriculture and fishing
Crops
sugar cane (2001): 250,000t
rubber (2001): 135,000t
manioc (2001): 441,000t
rice (2002): 190,000t

Livestock farming and fishing
goats (2001): 220,000 head
sheep (2002): 210,000 head
pigs (2002): 130,000 head
chickens (2002): 5,000,000 head
fish (1999): 15,500t

Energy generation and mining
diamonds (2001): 170,000 carats
total electricity (2001): 469 million kWh
gold (2001): 1,000kg

Industrial production
palm oil (2001): 42,000t

Tourism
Tourism revenue: n/a

Foreign trade
Exports (1997): 949 million US$
Imports (1997): 3,875 million US$

Defence
Armed forces (2001): 11,000 people
Defence budget (2001): 3.33% of GDP

Standard of living
Inhabitants per doctor (1990): 9,340
Average daily calorie intake (2000): 2,076 (FAO minimum: 2,400)
Cars per 1,000 inhabitants (1996): 3
Televisions per 1,000 inhabitants (2000): 25

HISTORY: KEY DATES
15c–18c: Mande and Kru-speaking populations occupied the region.
1822: the American Colonization Society, founded in 1816, began to land freed slaves from the Americas at a settlement on the coast, which they named Monrovia after the American President James Monroe.
1847: Liberia became a fully independent republic, with Monrovia as its capital.
1926: the state began to lease large areas of land to American companies as a means of raising revenue.
1980: Master Sergeant Samuel Doe became president in a military coup.
1990–6: a rebellion led by Charles Taylor resulted in civil war.
1997–2003: Taylor presided over a corrupt regime until forced into exile in 2003. A transitional government then began peace talks with rebel forces.

LIBYA

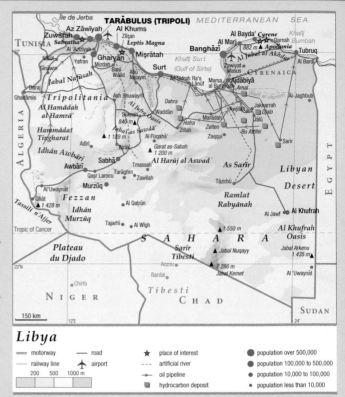

Libya

motorway	road	★ place of interest	● population over 500,000
railway line	✈ airport	--- artificial river	● population 100,000 to 500,000
200 500 1000 m		→ oil pipeline	● population 10,000 to 100,000
		⬛ hydrocarbon deposit	• population less than 10,000

The Great Socialist People's Libyan Arab Jamahiriya, as Libya is officially called, is a flat, barren country in Northern Africa bordering on the Mediterranean Sea. The Sahara Desert occupies around 95% of Libya, and this part of the country is virtually uninhabited except around scattered oases. The less arid coastal regions of Tripolitania in the west and Cyrenaica in the east, separated by 500km of arid coastline (the Gulf of Sirte), are where most of the population is concentrated.

Area: 1,759,540km²
Population (2002): 5,529,000
Capital: Tripoli 1,776,000 (2001 e)
Government type and political system: republic
Head of state and government: (revolutionary leader) Muammar Al-Gaddafi (or Qaddafi)
Administrative structure: 13 regions
Official language: Arabic
Currency: Libyan dinar

DEMOGRAPHICS

Density: 3 inhab/km²
Percentage of population in urban areas (2001): 87.9%
Age structure of population (2000): 0–15 years: 33.9%, 15–65 years: 62.7%, over 65 years: 3.4%
Birth rate (2003): 23.2‰
Death rate (2003): 4.2‰
Infant mortality rate (2003): 20.7‰
Life expectancy at birth (2003): male: 70.8 years, female: 75.4 years

ECONOMY

GNP (1985): 27.29 billion US$
GNP per capita (1985): 6,520 $
GNP per capita PPP: n/a
HDI (2000): 0.773
GDP annual growth rate (2003): 4.7%
Annual inflation rate (1992): 7%
Labour force by occupation: n/a
GDP by sector (1991): agriculture: 8%, industry: 48%, services: 44%
Gross public debt: n/a
Unemployment rate: n/a

Agriculture and fishing

Crops
citrus fruits (2002): 66,000t
almonds (2001): 31,000t
wheat (2002): 125,000t
dates (2001): 133,000t
olives (2002): 150,000t

barley (2002): 80,000t
potatoes (2002): 195,000t
tomatoes (2002): 160,000t
Livestock farming and fishing
cattle (2002): 130,000 head
goats (2001): 1,950,000 head
camels (2001): 72,000 head
sheep (2001): 4,130,000 head
fish (1999): 32,600t

Energy generation and mining
total electricity (2001): 20,180 million kWh
natural gas (2000): 5,500 million m³
oil (2002): 64,700,000t

Industrial production
olive oil (2001): 6,000t

steel (2003): 989,000t
wool (2001): 8,625t

Tourism
Tourism revenue (1999): 28 million US$

Foreign trade
Exports (1999): 6,758 million US$
Imports (1999): 3,996 million US$

Defence
Armed forces (2001): 76,000 people
Defence budget (2001): 8.88% of GDP

Standard of living
Inhabitants per doctor (1990): 909
Average daily calorie intake (2000): 3,305 (FAO minimum: 2,400)
Cars per 1,000 inhabitants (1996): 145
Televisions per 1,000 inhabitants (2000): 137

HISTORY: KEY DATES

7c BC: the western part of present-day Libya was settled by Phoenician peoples.
4c BC: Greek colonists in Cyrenaica named the country Libya.
1c BC: Libya was conquered by Rome.
642–3: the Arab conquest introduced Islam.
1517: the Ottomans conquered Cyrenaica and then Tripolitania (1551).
1934: the Italian colony of Libya was created.
1940–3: the Allies ousted Italy from Libya, which was then divided between the French (who administered Fezzan) and the British (who administered Tripolitania and Cyrenaica).
1951: Libya became an independent kingdom under King Idris I.
1969: the monarchy was abolished in a military coup led by Colonel Muammar Al-Gaddafi, who became the leader of the country. He nationalized Libya's oil companies (1971) and launched the Islamic Cultural Revolution (1973).
1973–2002: Libyan military activity led to conflict in neighbouring Chad and with the West.
2003: UN sanctions against Libya were lifted after the country's relations with the West improved.

MADAGASCAR
➡ INDIAN OCEAN

The Republic of Malawi is a landlocked country in southern Africa. High plateaux cover the north and centre of the country, while in the south the terrain is more uneven and the land only rises to around 90m above sea level. In total, Malawi is 900km in length, and most of the country borders on the western bank of Lake Malawi. The climate is generally subtropical, with a dry season that lasts from May to October.

Area: 118,484km²
Population (2002): 11,828,000
Capital: Lilongwe 440,000 (1998 census), 523,000 (2001 e) including the suburbs
Government type and political system: republic with a presidential system
Head of state and government: (President of the Republic) Bingu wa Mutharika
Administrative structure: 27 districts
Official languages: English (official) and Chichewa (national)
Currency: Malawian kwacha

DEMOGRAPHICS

Density: 93 inhab/km²
Percentage of population in urban areas (2001): 15.1%
Age structure of population (2000): 0–15 years: 46.3%, 15–65 years: 50.8%, over 65 years: 2.9%
Birth rate (2003): 44.6‰
Death rate (2003): 24.1‰
Infant mortality rate (2003): 115.4‰
Life expectancy at birth (2003): male: 37.3 years, female: 37.7 years

ECONOMY

GNP (2002): 1.7 billion US$
GNP per capita (2002): 160 US$

Malawi

- ● population over 200,000
- ✈ airport ● population 40,000 to 200,000
- — road ● population 10,000 to 40,000
- — railway line • population less than 10,000

| 800 | 1000 | 1500 m |

★ place of interest

GNP per capita PPP (2002): 570 international dollars
HDI (2000): 0.4
GDP annual growth rate (2003): 4.4%
Annual inflation rate (2000): 29.49%
Labour force by occupation: n/a
GDP by sector (2000): agriculture: 41.5%, industry: 19.1%, services: 39.4%
Gross public debt: n/a
Unemployment rate: n/a

Agriculture and fishing

Crops
plantains (2001): 200,000t
sugar cane (2001): 1,900,000t
maize (2002): 1,557,000t
manioc (2001): 900,000t
potatoes (2002): 1,061,000t
tobacco (2001): 83,000t

Livestock farming and fishing

cattle (2002): 750,000 head
goats (2001): 1,450,000 head
sheep (2002): 115,000 head
pigs (2002): 456,000 head
fish (1999): 46,000t

Energy generation and mining

total electricity (2001): 769 million kWh
coal (1999): 54,000t

Industrial production

sugar (2002): 217,000t
beer (2000): 117,000hl
timber (2000): 520,000m3

Tourism

Tourism revenue (2000): 27 million US$

Foreign trade

Exports (2002): 422.4 million US$
Imports (2002): 573.2 million US$

Defence

Armed forces (2001): 5,300 people
Defence budget (2001): 0.33% of GDP

Standard of living

Inhabitants per doctor (1993): 50,360
Average daily calorie intake (2000): 2,180 (FAO minimum: 2,400)
Cars per 1,000 inhabitants (1996): 2
Televisions per 1,000 inhabitants (2001): 3

HISTORY: KEY DATES

1840: slave traders from Zanzibar began subjecting Malawi's Bantu population to frequent raids.
1859: the Scottish missionary David Livingstone visited Lake Nyasa.
1889: a British protectorate was established in the region.
1907: the country was renamed Nyasaland.
1953: Great Britain formed the Federation of Rhodesia and Nyasaland. The Nyasaland African Congress, a party led by Dr Hastings Kamuzu Banda, demanded independence.
1964: Nyasaland became independent, and was renamed Malawi.
1966: Malawi became a republic with Banda as president, and the new constitution established a one-party political system. Opposition parties were suppressed.
1993: voters rejected the one-party political system in a referendum, and a multiparty system was re-established.
1994: Malawi's first multiparty presidential and municipal elections were held. President Banda was defeated, and retired from politics.
2002: a serious drought in southern Africa caused grain shortages in Malawi.

MOROCCO

The Kingdom of Morocco has a varied terrain. Beyond its coastal plains, the land rises up to a broad plateau and then to the Atlas Mountains, which separate the Mediterranean coast from eastern Morocco. The Moulouya River valley lies between the High and Middle Atlas ranges. An area of highlands called Er Rif (or the Rif Atlas) runs parallel to the Mediterranean Sea in the north of the country. In the south, the plains and valleys merge with the Sahara Desert. A relatively humid climate predominates in the area of Morocco bordering on the Atlantic Ocean, while the eastern and southern parts of the country are more arid.

Area: 710,000km² (including the annexed Western Sahara, formerly the Spanish Sahara)
Population (2002): 30,988,000
Capital: Rabat 1,668,000 (2001 e) including the suburbs
Government type and political system: constitutional monarchy with a parliamentary system
Head of state: (King) Mohammed VI
Head of government: (Prime Minister) Driss Jettou
Administrative structure: 16 regions
Official language: Arabic
Currency: Moroccan dirham

DEMOGRAPHICS
Density: 40 inhab/km²
Percentage of population in urban areas (2001): 56.1%
Age structure of population (2000): 0–15 years: 34.7%, 15–65 years: 61.2%, over 65 years: 4.1%
Birth rate (2003): 23.2‰
Death rate (2003): 6‰
Infant mortality rate (2003): 42.1‰
Life expectancy at birth (2003): male: 66.8 years, female: 70.5 years

ECONOMY
GNP (2002): 34.7 billion US$

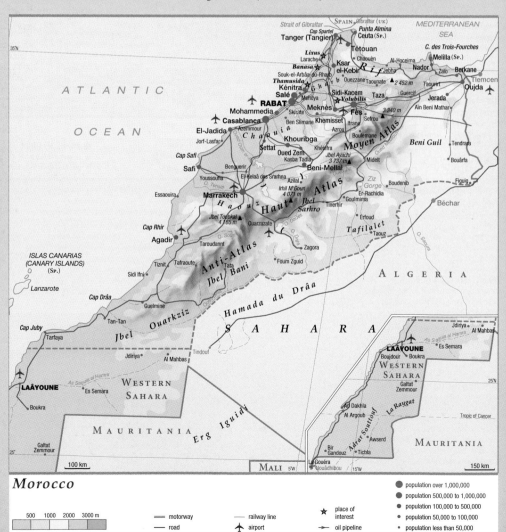

Morocco

500 1000 2000 3000 m

— motorway
— road
— railway line
✈ airport
★ place of interest
→ oil pipeline

● population over 1,000,000
● population 500,000 to 1,000,000
● population 100,000 to 500,000
● population 50,000 to 100,000
• population less than 50,000

GNP per capita (2002): 1,170 US$
GNP per capita PPP (2002): 3,730 international dollars
HDI (2000): 0.602
GDP annual growth rate (2003): 5.5%
Annual inflation rate (2000): 1.89%
Labour force by occupation: n/a
GDP by sector (2000): agriculture: 13.5%, industry: 32.2%, services: 54.3%
Gross public debt: n/a
Unemployment rate (2002): 11.6%

Agriculture and fishing
Crops
citrus fruits (2002): 1,152,000t
almonds (2001): 65,000t
wheat (2002): 3,359,000t
sugar cane (2001): 1,321,000t
dates (2001): 32,400t
mandarin oranges (1998): 462,000t
walnuts (2001): 8,000t
olives (2002): 470,000t
oranges (2002): 723,000t
barley (2002): 1,671,000t
potatoes (2002): 1,334,000t
grapes (2002): 331,000t
tomatoes (2001): 991,000t
Livestock farming and fishing
cattle (2002): 2,670,000 head
goats (2001): 5,372,000 head
sheep (2002): 16,336,000 head
fish (1999): 748,000t

Energy generation and mining
silver (2001): 240t
hydroelectricity (2000): 1,243 million kWh
total electricity (2001): 14,243 million kWh
coal (1999): 130,000t
phosphate (2001): 21,766,000t
lead (2001): 83,000t
zinc (2001): 123,000t

Industrial production
olive oil (2001): 35,000t
lead (2001): 70,000t
cars (2002): 17,000 units
commercial vehicles: n/a
cotton yarn (2001): 300t
wool (2001): 40,000t
sisal (2001): 2,200t
cement (2001): 8,450,000t

Tourism
Tourism revenue (2001): 2,460 million US$

Foreign trade
Exports (2002): 7,839 million US$
900654 million US$

Defence
Armed forces (1998): 196,300 people

Defence budget (2001): 4.18% of GDP

Standard of living
Inhabitants per doctor (1994): 2,500
Average daily calorie intake (2000): 2,964 (FAO minimum: 2,400)
Cars per 1,000 inhabitants (1999): 41
Televisions per 1,000 inhabitants (2001): 159

HISTORY: KEY DATES

Ancient Morocco
9c bc–8c bc: the Phoenicians created trading posts on the coast.
6c bc: the trading posts fell under the control of Carthage.
5c bc: the kingdom of Mauritania was created.
AD 40: Mauritania was annexed by Rome.
AD 425–AD 442: the Vandals invaded the country.

Islamic Morocco
700–10: the Arabs conquered the country and imposed Islam on the Berber, Christian, Jewish and animist tribes.
789–985: the Idrisside dynasty governed the country.
1061–1147: the Maghreb and Andalusia were both made part of the Almoravids' vast empire.
1147–1269: under the Almohad dynasty, a brilliant Arab-Andalusian civilization flourished.
1269–1465: Morocco was in the hands of the Merinids.
1415: the Portuguese conquered Ceuta.
1472–1554: under the Wattasids, urban life declined. Nomadism and tribal customs became widespread.
1554–1659: under the Saadians, the Portuguese were defeated at Alcazarquivir (1578) by Al-Mansur.
1666: Mulay Al-Rachid founded the Alawite dynasty, which has ruled over Morocco ever since.
17c–18c: disputes over succession took place, and Morocco underwent a serious economic decline.

19c: Great Britain, Spain and France forced the sultans to open up the country to their goods; their rivalry allowed Morocco to retain its independence.

From the French and Spanish protectorates to the present day
1906–12: after the Algeciras Conference, France occupied most of the country.
1912: the Treaty of Fez established a French protectorate. Spain maintained its coastal protectorate in the northern zone (Rif) and the southern zone (Ifni).
1912–25: Lyautey, the French resident-general, administered the protectorate.
1921–6: Abd el-Krim led the Rif Rebellion against the Spanish.
1933–4: the High Atlas Berber resistance came to an end; France controlled the whole country. Sultan Muhammad V retained purely religious powers.
1944: the Istiqlal Party, supported by Muhammad V, demanded independence.
1953–5: Sultan Muhammad V was deposed and forced into exile by the French authorities.
1956–7: independence was declared and Morocco was made a kingdom.
1961: Hassan II came to the throne.
1975–9: Morocco recovered the former Spanish Sahara.
1999: King Hassan II died and was succeeded by his eldest son, who became King Muhammad VI.
2002–4: a dispute arose between Morocco and Spain over possession of the island of Perejil.

75

The Republic of Mozambique has a humid subtropical to tropical climate and is mainly covered by forests. Behind the coastal plains rise plateaux and hills.

Area: 801,590km^2
Population (2002): 18,987,000
Capital: Maputo 966,837 (1997 census)
Government type and political system: republic with a semi-presidential system
Head of state and government: (President of the Republic) Joaquim Alberto Chissano
Prime Minister: Luisa Diogo
Administrative structure: 10 provinces and 1 city
Official language: Portuguese
Currency: metical

DEMOGRAPHICS

Density: 25 inhab/km^2
Percentage of population in urban areas (2001): 33.2%
Age structure of population (2000): 0–15 years: 43.9%, 15–65 years: 52.9%, over 65 years: 3.2%
Birth rate (2003): 41.2‰
Death rate (2003): 23.5‰
Infant mortality rate (2003): 122‰
Life expectancy at birth (2003): male: 36.6 years, female: 39.6 years

ECONOMY

GNP (2002): 3.65 billion US$
GNP per capita (2002): 200 US$
GNP per capita PPP (2002): 990 international dollars
HDI (2000): 0.322
GDP annual growth rate (2003): 7%
Annual inflation rate (1999): 2.03%
Labour force by occupation: n/a
GDP by sector (2000): agriculture: 24.4%, industry: 25.1%, services: 50.5%
Gross public debt: n/a
Unemployment rate: n/a

Agriculture and fishing

Crops
groundnuts (2001): 109,000t
sugar cane (2001): 397,000t
jute (1997): 5,000t
maize (2002): 1,236,000t
manioc (2001): 5,362,000t
cashew nuts (1998): 51,716t
rice (2002): 167,000t
sisal (2001): 600t
sorghum (2002): 314,000t
Livestock farming and fishing
cattle (2002): 1,320,000 head

Mozambique

200	500	1000 m

— road
— railway line
✈ airport

● population over 1,000,000
● population 100,000 to 1,000,000
● population 50,000 to 100,000
• population less than 50 000

chickens (2002): 28,000,000 head
fish (1999): 35,600t

Energy generation and mining
bauxite (2001): 8,000t
total electricity (2001): 7,193 million kWh
coal (2001): 19,000t

Industrial production
beer (2000): 480,000hl
sugar (2002): 35,000t
copra (2001): 19,100t
aluminium (2001): 266,000t
cement (2001): 380,000t
timber (2000): 1,319,000m^3

Tourism
Tourism revenue: n/a

Foreign trade
Exports (2001): 726 million US$
Imports (2001): 997.3 million US$

Defence
Armed forces (2001): 10,000 people

Defence budget (2001): 1.86% of GDP

Standard of living
Inhabitants per doctor (1990): 50,000
Average daily calorie intake (2000): 1,927 (FAO minimum: 2,400)
Cars per 1,000 inhabitants (1996): 0
Televisions per 1,000 inhabitants (2000): 5

HISTORY: KEY DATES

10c–15c: the country was inhabited by Bantu-speaking peoples before the Portuguese settled on the coast.
1951: Mozambique became an overseas province of Portugal.
1975: Mozambique became independent.
1977–92: civil war left nearly a million Mozambicans dead.
2000–2: floods and drought caused severe damage throughout the country.

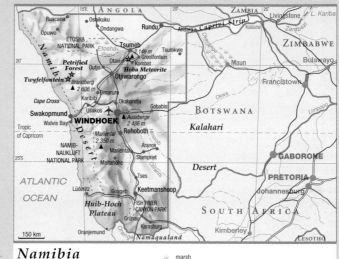

Beyond the coastal Namib Desert (150–300km in width), the land rises abruptly to the central plateau of eastern Namibia (over 1,350m). This plateau takes up almost four-fifths of the Republic of Namibia, sloping gently down eastwards towards the Kalahari Desert and northwards towards the Etosha Pan, a large salt marsh.

Namibia

★ place of interest
400 1000 1500 2000 m

⟂ marsh
═══ motorway
── road
── railway line
✈ airport

● population over 100,000
● population 50,000 to 100,000
● population 10,000 to 50,000
• population less than 10,000

Area: 824,292km^2
Population (2002): 1,819,000
Capital: Windhoek 216,000 (2001 e) including the suburbs
Government type and political system: republic with a semi-presidential system
Head of state and government: (President of the Republic) Samuel (Sam) Nujoma
Prime Minister: Theo-Ben Gurirab
Administrative structure: 13 districts
Official language: English
Currency: Namibian dollar

DEMOGRAPHICS

Density: 2 inhab/km^2
Percentage of population in urban areas (2001): 31.4%
Age structure of population (2000): 0–15 years: 43.7%, 15–65 years: 52.5%, over 65 years: 3.8%
Birth rate (2003): 33.4‰
Death rate (2003): 17.9‰
Infant mortality rate (2003): 59.8‰
Life expectancy at birth (2003): male: 42.9 years, female: 45.6 years

ECONOMY

GNP (2002): 3.55 billion US$
GNP per capita (2002): 1,790 U$
GNP per capita PPP (2002): 6,700 international dollars
HDI (2000): 0.61
GDP annual growth rate (2003): 3.7%
Annual inflation rate (1999): 8.6%
Labour force by occupation: n/a
GDP by sector (2000): agriculture: 11%, industry: 28%, services: 61%
Gross public debt: n/a
Unemployment rate: n/a

Agriculture and fishing

Crops
maize (2002): 29,000t
millet (2001): 65,000t
Livestock farming and fishing
cattle (2002): 2,509,000 head
goats (2001): 1,700,000 head
sheep (2002): 2,370,000 head
chickens (2002): 2,600,000 head
fish (1999): 299,000t

Energy generation and mining
copper (2001): 12,400t
diamonds (2001): 1,490,000 carats
total electricity (2001): 27 million kWh
gold (2001): 2,851kg
lead (2001): 12,000t
uranium (2001): 2,239t
zinc (2001): 42,000t

Industrial production
copper (2001): 12,400t

Tourism
Tourism revenue (1998): 288 million US$

Foreign trade
Exports (1998): 1,278.3 million US$
Imports (1998): 1,450.9 million US$

Defence
Armed forces (2001): 9,000 people
Defence budget (2001): 3.08% of GDP

Standard of living
Inhabitants per doctor (1993): 4,320
Average daily calorie intake (2000): 2,649 (FAO minimum: 2,400)
Cars per 1,000 inhabitants (1996): 46
Televisions per 1,000 inhabitants (2000): 38

HISTORY: KEY DATES

15c–18c: Portuguese and Dutch explorers reached present-day Namibia. The interior was occupied by Bantu-speaking peoples (Herero and Nama), who drove out the Bushmen.
1892: Germany dominated the region (then known as South-West Africa) apart from one enclave, Walvis Bay, which became a British colony in 1878.
1903–8: Germany suppressed uprisings by the Herero and the Nama people.
1914: South African forces occupied the region.
1920: the League of Nations granted South Africa a mandate to govern the territory.
1922: the British enclave was attached to South-West Africa.
1968: the UN changed the region's name from South-West Africa to Namibia. At around the same time, a Marxist pro-independence party, the SWAPO (South-West Africa People's Organization), began guerrilla oper-ations against the Union of South Africa.
1988: agreements between South Africa, Angola and Cuba led to a ceasefire in the north of Namibia and paved the way for the country's independence.
1990: Namibia became independent.
2002–3: the government encouraged land reform to redistribute land away from Namibia's white minority.

77

RWANDA

The Republic of Rwanda is a small, landlocked country made up of high plateaux, where the altitude moderates the equatorial temperatures.

Area: 26,338km²
Population (2002): 8,148,000
Capital: Kigali 412,000 (2001 e)
Government type and political system: republic
Head of state: (President of the Republic) Paul Kagame
Head of government: (Prime Minister) Bernard Makuza
Administrative structure: 12 prefectures
Official languages: English, French and Kinyarwanda
Currency: Rwandan franc

DEMOGRAPHICS
Density: 294 inhab/km²
Percentage of population in urban areas (2001): 6.3%
Age structure of population (2000): 0–15 years: 44.3%, 15–65 years: 53.1%, over 65 years: 2.6%
Birth rate (2003): 44‰
Death rate (2003): 21.8‰
Infant mortality rate (2003): 111.5‰
Life expectancy at birth (2003): male: 38.8 years, female: 39.7 years

ECONOMY
GNP (2002): 1.85 billion US$
GNP per capita (2002): 230 US$
GNP per capita PPP (2002): 1,260 international dollars
HDI (2000): 0.403
GDP annual growth rate (2003): 0.9%
Annual inflation rate (2000): 3.9%
Labour force by occupation: n/a
GDP by sector (2000): agriculture: 43.7%, industry: 21.2%, services: 35.1%
Gross public debt: n/a
Unemployment rate: n/a
Agriculture and fishing
Crops
plantains (2001): 1,573,000t
manioc (2001): 688,000t
sweet potatoes (2001): 1,137,000t
sorghum (2002): 194,000t

Rwanda
500   1000   1500 m

▲ volcano
— road
✈ airport
★ place of interest

● population over 200,000
● population 20,000 to 200,000
• population less than 20,000

25 km

Livestock farming and fishing
cattle (2002): 815,000 head
goat (2001): 700,000 head
sheep (2002): 260,000 head
fish (1999): 6,730t
Energy generation and mining
total electricity (2001): 97 million kWh
tin (2001): 260t
gold (2001): 10kg
Industrial production
beer (2000): 400,000hl
cement (2001): 75,000t
Tourism
Tourism revenue (1999): 17 million US$

Foreign trade
Exports (2002): 67.2 million US$
Imports (2002): 233.3 million US$
Defence
Armed forces (2001): 60,000 people
Defence budget (2001): 2.88% of GDP
Standard of living
Inhabitants per doctor (1990): 50,000
Average daily calorie intake (2000): 2,077 (FAO minimum: 2,400)
Cars per 1,000 inhabitants (1996): 1
Televisions per 1,000 inhabitants (1998): 0

HISTORY: KEY DATES

Rwanda's first known inhabitants were the Twa people, later displaced by the Hutus and the Tutsis.
1890: Germany annexed Rwanda and Burundi, making them part of German East Africa.
1916–62: Belgian troops occupied the area and the League of Nations granted Belgium the mandate of Ruanda-Urundi, including present-day Rwanda and Burundi.
1962: Rwanda became independent. There were serious conflicts between the Hutus and the Tutsis, who emigrated or were forced to leave the country.

1973: a military coup, led by the Hutu General Juvénal Habyarimana, ousted president Grégoire Kayibanda.
1991: a new constitution established a multiparty political system.
1994: the death of the Rwandan and Burundian presidents opened an extremely bloody episode in the country's history. Rwanda was ravaged by war, and an estimated 800,000 Tutsi and Hutu moderates were killed by Hutu extremists during this genocide.
1996: Rwandan troops invaded Zaire.
2003: a new constitution, designed to prevent another genocide, was approved.

The Democratic Republic of São Tomé and Príncipe lies in the Gulf of Guinea, about 300km off the coast of Gabon in West Africa. It consists of two main islands of volcanic origin, and a number of smaller islets. Over 95% of the population live on the island of São Tomé. The terrain is mountainous, with summits over 2,000m, and the climate is hot and humid.

Area: 964km²
Population (2002): 127,000
Capital: São Tomé 67,000 (2001 e)
Government type and political system: republic with a semi-presidential system
Head of state: (President of the Republic) Fradique de Menezes
Head of government: (Prime Minister) Damaio Vaz d'Almeida
Administrative structure: 2 provinces
Official language: Portuguese
Currency: dobra

DEMOGRAPHICS
Density: 152 inhab/km²
Percentage of population in urban areas (2001): 47.6%
Age structure of population (1993): 0–15 years: 42%, 15–65 years: 53%, over 65 years: 5%
Birth rate (2003): 33.2‰
Death rate (2003): 5.8‰

São Tomé and Príncipe

- oil pipeline
- population 20,000 to 50,000
- population less than 20 000
- marsh
- road
- railway line
- airport

200 500 1000 m

80 km

Infant mortality rate (2003): 31.6‰
Life expectancy at birth (2003): male: 67 years, female: 72.8 years

ECONOMY
GNP (2002): 0.046 billion US$
GNP per capita (2002): 300 US$
GNP per capita PPP (1999): 1,335 international dollars
HDI (2000): 0.632

GDP annual growth rate (2003): 4.5%
Annual inflation rate (1992): 27.4%
Labour force by occupation: n/a
GDP by sector (2000): agriculture: 20.5%, industry: 17%, services: 62.5%
Gross public debt: n/a
Unemployment rate: n/a

Agriculture and fishing
Crops
bananas (2001): 20,000t
coffee (2002): 20t
copra (2001): 10t
maize (2002): 2,500t
Fishing
fish (1999): 3,760t

Energy generation
total electricity (2001): 17 million kWh

Industrial production
palm oil (2001): 2,025t

Tourism
Tourism revenue (1998): 2 million US$

Foreign trade
Exports (1997): 8 million US$
Imports (2002): 28 million US$

Defence
Armed forces: n/a
Defence budget: n/a

Standard of living
Inhabitants per doctor (1990): 2,000
Average daily calorie intake (2000): 2,390 (FAO minimum: 2,400)
Cars per 1,000 inhabitants (1996): 29
Televisions per 1,000 inhabitants (2000): 228

HISTORY: KEY DATES
1471: the two main islands were reached by Portuguese explorers.
1483: the Portuguese founded the settlement of São Tomé.
1975: São Tomé and Príncipe became independent.
1991: the country's first multiparty elections took place.
1995: Príncipe assumed local authority.

81

SWAZILAND

The Kingdom of Swaziland is a small, green and mountainous landlocked country, which is mainly surrounded by South Africa. The north-eastern part of the country borders on Mozambique.

Area: 17,364km²
Population (2002): 947,000
Capital: Mbabane (administrative) 80,000 (2001 e)
Capital: Lobamba (legislative)
Government type and political system: monarchy
Head of state: (King) Mswati III
Head of government: (Prime Minister) Absalom Themba Dlamini
Administrative structure: 4 districts
Official languages: English and SiSwati
Currency: lilangeni

DEMOGRAPHICS

Density: 58 inhab/km²
Percentage of population in urban areas (2001): 26.7%
Age structure of population (2000): 0–15 years: 41.6%, 15–65 years: 54.9%, over 65 years: 3.5%
Birth rate (2003): 34.5‰
Death rate (2003): 25.4‰
Infant mortality rate (2003): 78.3‰
Life expectancy at birth (2003): male: 33.3 years, female: 35.4 years

ECONOMY

GNP (2002): 1.35 billion US$
GNP per capita (2002): 1,240 US$
GNP per capita PPP (2002): 4,730

Swaziland

— road	● population over 1,000,000
— railway line	● population 100,000 to 1,000,000
✈ airport	● population 50,000 to 100,000
	• population less than 50 000

200 500 1000 m

international dollars
HDI (2000): 0.577
GDP annual growth rate (2003): 2.2%
Annual inflation rate (2000): 12.21%
Labour force by occupation: n/a
GDP by sector (2000): agriculture: 16.8%, industry: 44.3%, services: 38.9%
Gross public debt: n/a
Unemployment rate: n/a

Agriculture
Crops
citrus fruits (2002): 74,000t
maize (2002): 85,000t
oranges (2002): 36,000t
timber (2000): 330,000m³
Livestock farming
cattle (2002): 615,000 head
goats (2001): 445,000 head

Energy generation
total electricity (2001): 348 million kWh

Industrial production
sugar (2002): 520,000t

Tourism
Tourism revenue (1999): 35 million US$

Foreign trade
Exports (2002): 955.2 million US$
Imports (2002): 1,034.6 million US$

Defence
Armed forces: n/a
Defence budget: n/a

Standard of living
Inhabitants per doctor (1990): 18,820
Average daily calorie intake (2000): 2,620 (FAO minimum: 2,400)
Cars per 1,000 inhabitants (1998): 34
Televisions per 1,000 inhabitants (2001): 128

HISTORY: KEY DATES

1815: the independent Bantu kingdom of Swaziland was founded.
1903: Swaziland became a British protectorate.
1968: Swaziland regained independence.
2004: drought, poverty and the AIDS epidemic led to a humanitarian crisis.

As well as three islands, the United Republic of Tanzania consists of a narrow coastal plain that borders on a vast plateau, broken by arms of the Great African Rift Valley. High volcanic massifs, including the extinct volcano Kilimanjaro (Africa's highest point), rise above the plains.

Area: 883,749km²
Population (2002): 36,820,000
Capital: Dodoma 168,500 (2004 e)
Government type and political system: republic
Head of state and government: (President of the Republic) Benjamin William Mkapa
Administrative structure: 25 regions
Official languages: Kiswahili and English
Currency: Tanzanian shilling

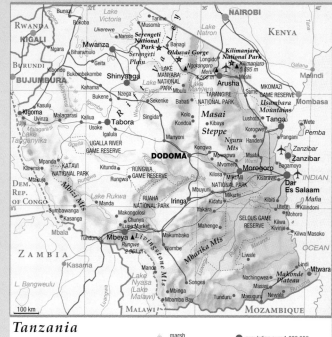

Tanzania

☆	place of interest
	500 1000 2000 3000 m
🔆	marsh
✈	airport
—	road
—	railway line
●	population over 1,000,000
●	population 100,000 to 1,000,000
●	population 50,000 to 100,000
●	population less than 50,000

DEMOGRAPHICS

Density: 36 inhab/km²
Percentage of population in urban areas (2001): 33.2%
Age structure of population (2000): 0–15 years: 45%, 15–65 years: 52.6%, over 65 years: 2.4%
Birth rate (2003): 39.3‰
Death rate (2003): 18.1‰
Infant mortality rate (2003): 99.8‰
Life expectancy at birth (2003): male: 42.5 years, female: 44.1 years

ECONOMY

GNP (2002): 9.67 billion US$
GNP per capita (2002): 290 US$
GNP per capita PPP (2002): 580 international dollars
HDI (2000): 0.44
GDP annual growth rate (2003): 5.5%
Annual inflation rate (2000): 5.92%
Labour force by occupation: n/a
GDP by sector (2000): agriculture: 45.1%, industry: 15.8%, services: 39.1%
Gross public debt: n/a
Unemployment rate: n/a

Agriculture and fishing

Crops
bananas (2001): 800,000t
plantains (2001): 652,000t
coffee (2002): 58,000t
sugar cane (2001): 1,500,000t
maize (2002): 2,701,000t
manioc (2001): 5,650,000t
honey (2001): 26,000t
cashew nuts (1998): 70,000t
sweet potatoes (2001): 453,000t

timber (2000): 2,314,000m³
rice (2002): 514,000t
sorghum (2002): 700,000t
tobacco (2001): 24,300t
tea (2001): 25,500t

Livestock farming and fishing

cattle (2002): 17,700,000 head
goats (2001): 10,000,000 head
sheep (2002): 3,550,000 head
chickens (2002): 29,000,000 head
fish (1999): 310,000t

Energy generation and mining

diamonds (2001): 355,000 carats
total electricity (2001): 2,906 million kWh
lignite (2000): 35,000t
gold (2001): 32,300kg

Industrial production

milk (2001): 781,000t
meat (2001): 331,000t
sugar (2002): 165,000t
beer (2000): 1,800,000hl
copra (2001): 20,400t
cotton yarn (2001): 81,000t
cement (2001): 875,000t
sisal (2001): 20,500t

Tourism

Tourism revenue (2001): 725 million US$

Foreign trade

Exports (2002): 902.5 million US$
Imports (2002): 1,511.3 million US$

Defence

Armed forces (2001): 27,000 people
Defence budget (2001): 1.58% of GDP

Standard of living

Inhabitants per doctor (1990): 33,330

Average daily calorie intake (2000): 1,906 (FAO minimum: 2,400)
Cars per 1,000 inhabitants (1996): 1
Televisions per 1,000 inhabitants (2001): 42

HISTORY: KEY DATES

12c: the country was inhabited by Bantu-speaking tribes, and ports such as Kilwa and Zanzibar flourished.
1498: the Portuguese explorer Vasco da Gama reached the country.
17c: Arab settlers drove out the Portuguese.
19c: the Sultan of Oman claimed Zanzibar and the coast; the Arabs controlled the inland trade routes along which British explorers travelled.
1880–1920: Germany took control of the country, making it a protectorate.
1920–46: the area, renamed Tanganyika, was made a British mandate by the League of Nations.
1961: independence was declared (excluding the Sultanate of Zanzibar, which remained a British protectorate until 1963).
1964: the United Republic of Tanzania was formed by the union of Zanzibar and Tanganyika.
1992: the constitution was amended to legalize opposition parties.
1990s: large numbers of refugees from Rwanda and Burundi arrived in Tanzania.

89

TUNISIA

HISTORY: KEY DATES

Ancient Tunisia
c.814 BC: the Phoenicians founded the colonies of Utica and Carthage.
146 BC: Carthage was destroyed and the Roman Province of Africa was created.
AD 3c–AD 4c: Christianity flourished.
AD 429–AD 533: the Vandals occupied the country.
AD 533: the Byzantines took control of Carthage.

Muslim Tunisia
660–705: the Arabs founded Kairouan (670), where the Umayyad governors of Ifriqiya resided.
800–909: the Aghlabids governed the country.
909: the Aghlabids were ousted by the Fatimids.
969: the Fatimids conquered Egypt and left Ifriqiya to their Zirid vassals.
11c: the invasions of the Banu Hilal tribe destroyed the country.

1160–1229: the Almohads ruled over Tunisia.
1229–1574: under the Hafsids, the capital, Tunis, developed as a result of trade.
1574: Tunisia became part of the Turkish Ottoman Empire.
1869: political unrest led to debt and eventually bankruptcy. France, Great Britain and Italy intervened and took control of the economy.

Independent Tunisia
1881: the Treaty of Bardo established a French protectorate over Tunisia.
1920: the Destour Party (Tunisian Liberal Constitutional Party) was founded.
1934: Habib Bourguiba's more radical Neo-Destour (New Constitution) Party was founded.
1942–3: Tunisia was occupied by

Germany.
1956: Tunisia became independent.
1963: Tunisia demanded that the French forces leave their base in Bizerte.
1964: the Neo-Destour Party was renamed the Socialist Destour Party. The colonists' lands were nationalized.
1970–8: trade union and student opposition to the one-party regime of Bourguiba (who was elected president for life in 1975) grew; strikes and riots broke out.
1983: a multiparty political system was officially established.
1987: Bourguiba was removed from office on grounds of senility.
1987–2004: Zine Al-Abidine Bin Ali was repeatedly elected president, changing the constitution in 2002 to remove term limitations on his presidency.

Carthage

Phoenician colonists from the city of Tyre established the colony of Carthage (the name meant 'new city') on a site near present-day Tunis. According to legend, Queen Dido founded the city in 814 BC. Carthage became the capital of a very powerful maritime republic, dominating the western Mediterranean almost completely. It built up a wide network of trade, established colonies in Sicily and Spain and sent sailors to the North Atlantic and the western coasts of Africa. It waged long battles known as the Punic Wars (264 BC–146 BC) against its rival, Rome. The Romans were so obsessed by Carthage that the Consul Cato the Elder (234 BC–149 BC) ended all his speeches with a phrase he became famous for: '*Carthago delenda est*' ('Carthage must be destroyed'). Conquered, despite the efforts of the Carthaginian general Hannibal, by Scipio Africanus (201 BC), Carthage was then destroyed by Scipio Aemilianus (146 BC). Re-established as a Roman colony (1 BC), Carthage became the capital of Roman and Christian Africa. The city was taken in AD 439 by the Vandals, and was virtually annihilated by the Arabs in around 698.

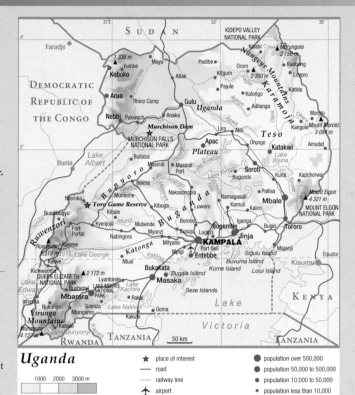

The Republic of Uganda lies on the equator. It is a landlocked country that consists mainly of a high plateau, above which rise lofty peaks such as the Ruwenzori Mountains and Mount Elgon. Apart from the steppes in the semi-arid north, the rainforests in the south and the wood-covered massifs, most of the country is covered in savannas.

Area: 241,038km²
Population (2002): 24,780,000
Capital: Kampala 774,241 (1991 census), 1,274,000 (2001 e) including the suburbs
Government type and political system: republic with a semi-presidential system
Head of state and government: (President of the Republic) Yoweri Kaguta Museveni
Prime Minister: Apollo Nsibambi
Administrative structure: 56 districts
Official language: English
Currency: Ugandan shilling

DEMOGRAPHICS
Density: 92 inhab/km²
Percentage of population in urban areas (2001): 14.5%
Age structure of population (2000): 0–15 years: 49.2%, 15–65 years: 48.3%, over 65 years: 2.5%
Birth rate (2003): 50.7‰
Death rate (2003): 16.7‰
Infant mortality rate (2003): 86.1‰
Life expectancy at birth (2003): male: 45.4 years, female: 46.9 years

ECONOMY
GNP (2002): 5.93 billion US$
GNP per capita (2002): 240 US$
GNP per capita PPP (2002): 1,360 international dollars
HDI (2000): 0.444
GDP annual growth rate (2003): 4.9%
Annual inflation rate (2000): 2.83%
Labour force by occupation: n/a
GDP by sector (2000): agriculture: 42.5%, industry: 19.1%, services: 38.4%
Gross public debt: n/a
Unemployment rate: n/a

Agriculture and fishing
Crops
groundnuts (2001): 146,000t
plantains (2001): 9,533,000t
coffee (2002): 198,000t
sugar cane (2001): 1,500,000t
maize (2002): 1,200,000t
manioc (2001): 5,265,000t
millet (2001): 584,000t
sweet potatoes (2001): 2,515,000t
potatoes (2001): 510,000t
sorghum (2002): 430,000t
tobacco (2001): 22,600t
tea (2001): 32,900t

Livestock farming and fishing
cattle (2002): 5,900,000 head
goats (2001): 6,200,000 head
sheep (2002): 1,200,000 head
pigs (2002): 1,550,000 head
chickens (2002): 25,500,000 head
fish (1999): 226,000t

Energy generation
total electricity (2001): 1,928 million kWh

Industrial production
sugar (2001): 180,000t
beer (2000): 850,000hl
cotton yarn (2001): 12,800t

Tourism
Tourism revenue (1999): 149 million US$

Foreign trade
Exports (2001): 451.6 million US$
Imports (2001): 1,026.6 million US$

Defence
Armed forces (2001): 50,000 people
Defence budget (2001): 2.24% of GDP

Standard of living
Inhabitants per doctor (1990): 25,000
Average daily calorie intake (2000): 2,359 (FAO minimum: 2,400)
Cars per 1,000 inhabitants (1999): 2
Televisions per 1,000 inhabitants (2000): 27

93

HISTORY: KEY DATES
The present-day population of Uganda is descended from the Bantu and Nilotic-speaking tribes who were among the country's earliest inhabitants.
16c–19c: these populations formed small, loosely structured states. In the 17c, the kingdom of Buganda began to expand and take over the other states.
1894: Uganda became a British protectorate.
1962: Uganda became an independent federal state.
1963: Uganda became a republic.
1971–9: Idi Amin Dada led a tyrannical regime until he was ousted by the Uganda National Liberation Front.
1979–86: after several years of anarchy, tribal rebellions, repression and military coups, Yoweri Museveni became president.
1986–2003: Museveni introduced democratic and economic reforms.

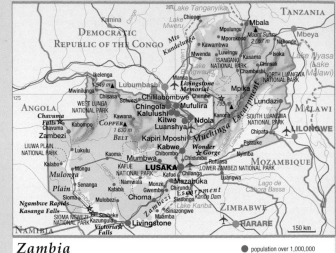

Zambia

500	1000	1500 m

— road
— railway line

✷ marsh
★ place of interest
✈ airport

● population over 1,000,000
● population 100,000 to 1,000,000
● population 50,000 to 100,000
• population less than 50,000

The Republic of Zambia is a landlocked country in Southern Africa with a tropical climate, moderated by altitude. Zambia is mainly made up of hills and plateaux, drained by the Zambezi River and its tributaries. Only the far north-east of the country belongs to the Congo basin. The natural vegetation is open forest, which has degraded in many places and become savanna.

Area: 752,618km²
Population (2002): 10,872,000
Capital: Lusaka 1,718,000 (2001 e)
Government type and political system: republic with a semi-presidential system
Head of state and government: (President of the Republic) Levy Mwanawasa
Administrative structure: 9 provinces
Official language: English
Currency: kwacha

DEMOGRAPHICS
Density: 12 inhab/km²
Percentage of population in urban areas (2001): 39.8%
Age structure of population (2000): 0–15 years: 46.5%, 15–65 years: 50.6%, over 65 years: 2.9%
Birth rate (2003): 42.2‰
Mortality rate (2000): 28‰
Infant mortality rate (2003): 104.8‰
Life expectancy at birth (2003): male: 32.7 years, female: 32.1 years

ECONOMY
GNP (2002): 3.46 billion US$
GNP per capita (2002): 340 US$
GNP per capita PPP (2002): 800 international dollars
HDI (2000): 0.433
GDP annual growth rate (2003): 4.2%
Annual inflation rate (1997): 24.8%
Labour force by occupation: n/a
GDP by sector (2000): agriculture: 27.3%, industry: 24.1%, services: 48.6%

Gross public debt: n/a
Unemployment rate: n/a

Agriculture and fishing
Crops
sugar cane (2001): 1,800,000t
maize (2002): 602,000t
manioc (2001): 950,000t
Livestock farming and fishing
cattle (2002): 2,600,000 head
goats (2001): 1,270,000 head
chickens (2002): 30,000,000 head
fish (1999): 72,000t

Energy generation and mining
silver (2001): 5t
copper (2001): 299,000t
total electricity (2001): 7,751 million kWh
gold (2001): 130kg

Industrial production
sugar (2001): 222,000t
copper (2000): 225,000t

Tourism
Tourism revenue (2000): 91 million US$

Foreign trade
Exports (1997): 1,178 million US$
Imports (1997): 1,070 million US$

Defence
Armed forces (2001): 21,600 people
Defence budget (2001): 0.68% of GDP

Standard of living
Inhabitants per doctor (1993): 11,430
Average daily calorie intake (2000): 1,912

(FAO minimum: 2,400)
Cars per 1,000 inhabitants (1996): 15
Televisions per 1,000 inhabitants (2001): 145

HISTORY: KEY DATES
Present-day Zambia, which is thought to have been first inhabited by Pygmies and then Bantu-speaking tribes, was divided into chieftainships prior to the arrival of European colonists.
1851–73: the Scottish missionary David Livingstone explored the region.
1899: the country was occupied by Britain.
1911: the British occupied zone was divided into two regions, Northern Rhodesia (now Zambia) and Southern Rhodesia (now Zimbabwe).
1924: Northern Rhodesia became a British Crown Colony.
1953–63: the Central African Federation united Northern Rhodesia, Southern Rhodesia and Nyasaland (now Malawi).
1964: Northern Rhodesia was renamed Zambia, and became independent within the Commonwealth of Nations.
1991: a multiparty system of democracy was established.
2001: an appeal for aid was launched to combat severe food shortages.

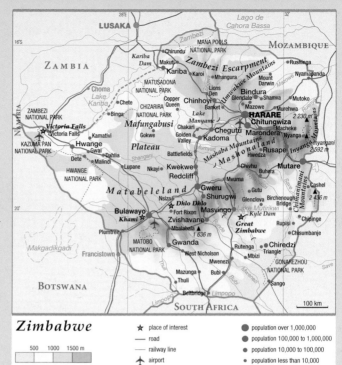

The Republic of Zimbabwe is a landlocked country in southern Africa. Most of the country lies on a high plateau and is covered in dry, deciduous woodlands and savannas.

Area: 390,757km²
Population (2002): 13,076,000
Capital: Harare 1,868,000 (2001 e)
Government type and political system: multiparty republic with a parliamentary system
Head of state and government: (President of the Republic) Robert Gabriel Mugabe
Administrative structure: 8 provinces and 2 cities
Official language: English
Currency: Zimbabwe dollar

Zimbabwe

★ place of interest
— road
— railway line
✈ airport

● population over 1,000,000
● population 100,000 to 1,000,000
● population 10,000 to 100,000
• population less than 10,000

DEMOGRAPHICS
Density: 30 inhab/km²
Percentage of population in urban areas (2001): 36%
Age structure of population (2000): 0–15 years: 45.2%, 15–65 years: 51.6%, over 65 years: 3.2%
Birth rate (2003): 32.1‰
Death rate (2003): 27‰
Infant mortality rate (2003): 58.4‰
Life expectancy at birth (2003): male: 33.7 years, female: 32.6 years

ECONOMY
GNP (2002): 6.16 billion US$
GNP per capita (2002): 480 US$
GNP per capita PPP (2002): 2,180 international dollars
HDI (2000): 0.551
GDP annual growth rate (2003): −13.2%
Annual inflation rate (1998): 31.82%
Labour force by occupation: n/a
GDP by sector (2000): agriculture: 18.5%, industry: 25%, services: 56.5%
Gross public debt: n/a
Unemployment rate: n/a

Agriculture
Crops
groundnuts (2001): 180,000t
wheat (2002): 150,000t
sugar cane (2001): 4,100,000t
cotton (2001): 200,000t
maize (2002): 1,000,000t
manioc (2001): 175,000t
tobacco (2001): 196,000t

Livestock farming
cattle (2002): 5,753,000 head
goats (2001): 2,800,000 head
sheep (2002): 600,000 head
pigs (2002): 605,000 head
chickens (2002): 22,000,000 head

Energy generation and mining
silver (2000): 3t
chromium (2001): 780,000t
diamonds (2001): 15,000 carats
total electricity (2001): 6,735 million kWh
iron (2001): 184,000t
coal (2001): 4,499,000t
nickel (2001): 8,100t
gold (2001): 18,050kg

Industrial production
sugar (2002): 554,000t
cotton yarn (2001): 128,000t
steel (2003): 137,000t
copper (2001): 2,060t
cement (2001): 1,000,000t

Tourism
Tourism revenue (1999): 202 million US$

Foreign trade
Exports (1997): 2,119 million US$
Imports (1997): 3,090 million US$

Defence
Armed forces (2001): 36,000 people
Defence budget (2001): 2.92% of GDP

Standard of living
Inhabitants per doctor (1990): 10,000
Average daily calorie intake (2000): 2,117 (FAO minimum: 2,400)

Cars per 1,000 inhabitants (1996): 28
Televisions per 1,000 inhabitants (2000): 30

95

HISTORY: KEY DATES
Among the early inhabitants of present-day Zimbabwe were the Bushmen and the Bantus.
19c: Ndebele settlers migrated from South Africa to present-day Zimbabwe. European explorers colonized the country.
1923: the country (then Southern Rhodesia) became a self-governing British Crown Colony.
1953–63: Nyasaland (present-day Malawi), Northern and Southern Rhodesia were joined in the Central African Federation.
1970: Rhodesia was declared a republic. The international community condemned the new state's repressive racial policies.
1979: the first multiracial elections were held and a multiracial government was formed.
1980: Zimbabwe's independence was recognized, and the Republic of Zimbabwe came into being.
1980–2004: under Robert Mugabe's regime, opposition parties were repressed and Zimbabwe's economy suffered. Controversial land reform measures led to widespread violence and food shortages.

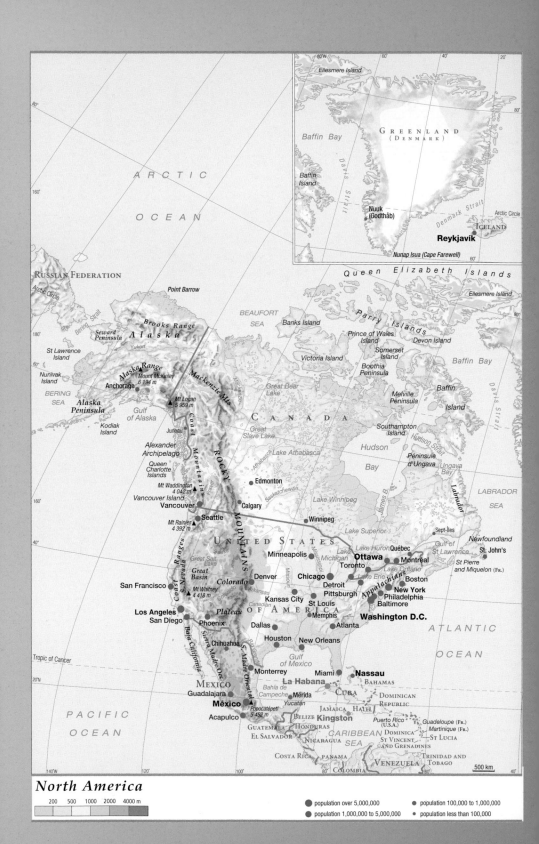

North America

80°W 60° 40° 20°

Ellesmere Island

G R E E N L A N D
(D E N M A R K)

Baffin Bay

Baffin
Island

Davis Strait

80°

Denmark Strait

ICELAND

Nuuk
(Godthåb)

Arctic Circle

Reykjavík

Nunap Isua (Cape Farewell)

60°

A R C T I C

O C E A N

Queen Elizabeth Islands

Ellesmere Island

80°

RUSSIAN FEDERATION

Arctic Circle

Point Barrow

BEAUFORT
SEA

Banks Island

Parry Islands

Baffin Bay

160°

Bering Strait

Brooks Range

Alaska

Prince of Wales
Island

Devon Island

180°

Seward
Peninsula

Yukon

Somerset
Island

St Lawrence
Island

Alaska Range

Mount McKinley
6 194 m

Mackenzie Mts

Victoria Island

Boothia
Peninsula

Melville
Peninsula

Baffin

60°

Nunivak
Island

Anchorage

Mt Logan
5 959 m

Great Bear
Lake

Southampton
Island

Island

BERING
SEA

Alaska
Peninsula

Gulf
of Alaska

C A N A D A

Hudson
Bay

Péninsule
d'Ungava

Ungava
Bay

Davis Strait

Kodiak
Island

Juneau

Great
Slave Lake

LABRADOR
SEA

Alexander
Archipelago

Coast Mountains

Lake Athabasca

Fraser

Athabasca

Queen
Charlotte
Islands

R O C K Y

Edmonton

Saskatchewan

Lake Winnipeg

James B.

Labrador

160°

Mt Waddington
4 042 m

Vancouver Island

Vancouver

Calgary

Winnipeg

Sept-Îles

Seattle

Mt Rainier
4 392 m

M O U N T A I N S

Lake Superior

Lake Huron

Québec

Gulf of
St Lawrence

Newfoundland

40°

San Francisco

Coast Ranges

S. Nevada

U N I T E D   S T A T E S

Minneapolis

Lake
Michigan

Missouri

Ottawa

Toronto

Lake Ontario
Lake Erie

Montréal

Boston

St Pierre
and Miquelon (Fr.)

St John's

Great Salt
Lake

Great
Basin

Mt Whitney
4 418 m

Colorado

Denver

Colorado

Chicago

Detroit

Pittsburgh

New York

Appalachians

Philadelphia

Los Angeles
San Diego

Plateau

Kansas City

Arkansas

Canadian

St Louis

O F   A M E R I C A

Memphis

Baltimore

Washington D.C.

Phoenix

Sierra Madre Occ.

Dallas

Atlanta

ATLANTIC

Baja California

Houston

New Orleans

OCEAN

Tropic of Cancer

S. Madre Oriental

Gulf
of Mexico

20°N

MÉXICO

Monterrey

Miami

Nassau

BAHAMAS

Guadalajara

Bahía de
Campeche

Mérida

La Habana

CUBA

DOMINICAN
REPUBLIC

México

Yucatán

JAMAICA

HAITI

PACIFIC

OCEAN

Popocatépetl
5 452 m

Acapulco

GUATEMALA

BELIZE

HONDURAS

Kingston

Puerto Rico
(U.S.A.)

Guadeloupe (Fr.)
Martinique (Fr.)

CARIBBEAN

DOMINICA

St LUCIA

EL SALVADOR

NICARAGUA

SEA

St VINCENT
AND GRENADINES

COSTA RICA

PANAMA

VENEZUELA

TRINIDAD AND
TOBAGO

COLOMBIA

500 km

140°W   120°   100°   80°   60°   40°

North America

200 500 1000 2000 4000 m

● population over 5,000,000

● population 1,000,000 to 5,000,000

● population 100,000 to 1,000,000

• population less than 100,000

THE AMERICAS

ARGENTINA

THE BAHAMAS

BELIZE

BOLIVIA

BRAZIL

CANADA

CHILE

COLOMBIA

COSTA RICA

CUBA

DOMINICAN
REPUBLIC

ECUADOR

EL SALVADOR

FRENCH GUIANA

GUATEMALA

GUYANA

HAITI

HONDURAS

JAMAICA

LESSER ANTILLES
ANTIGUA AND BARBUDA
BARBADOS
DOMINICA
GRENADA
ST KITTS AND NEVIS
ST LUCIA
ST VINCENT AND THE
GRENADINES
TRINIDAD AND TOBAGO

MEXICO

NICARAGUA

PANAMA

PARAGUAY

PERU

SURINAME

UNITED STATES
OF AMERICA

URUGUAY

VENEZUELA

THE AMERICAS
42,000,000km^2
880 million inhabitants

AFRICA
30,310,000km^2
842 million inhabitants

ASIA
44,000,000km^2
3,826 million inhabitants

EUROPE
10,500,000km^2
731 million inhabitants

OCEANIA
9,000,000km^2
33 million inhabitants

Central and South America

200 500 1000 2000 4000 m

● population over 5,000,000
● population 1,000,000 to 5,000,000
● population 100,000 to 1,000,000
• population less than 100,000

500 km

Tropic of Cancer

20°N

La Habana

CUBA

MEXICO

GUAT. BELIZE

Belmopan

DOMINICAN REPUBLIC

HAITI

Puerto Rico (U.S.A.)

Port-au-Prince

Kingston **St-Dominique**

JAMAICA

San Juan

Guadeloupe (Fr.)

DOMINICA

Lesser Antilles

ATLANTIC

Guatemala HONDURAS

Tegucigalpa

EL SALVADOR

San Salvador

HONDURAS

Managua

NICARAGUA

CARIBBEAN SEA

ST LUCIA

Martinique (Fr.)

ST VINCENT AND THE GRENADINES

BARBADOS

GRENADA

OCEAN

10°

San José

COSTA RICA

Panamá

PANAMA

Barranquilla

Maracaibo

Caracas

Valencia

Ciudad Bolívar

TRINIDAD AND TOBAGO

Port of Spain

Medellín

Llanos

VENEZUELA

Georgetown

GUYANA

Paramaribo

Cayenne

Cali

Bogotá

SURINAME

French Guiana

COLOMBIA

Equator

Islas Galápagos (Ec.)

Quito

Chimborazo 6 310 m

Cotopaxi 5 897 m

Mouths of the Amazon

Belém

ECUADOR

Guayaquil

Iquitos

Putumayo

Japurá

A m a z o n

Manaus

(Amazon)

B a s i n

BRAZIL

Fortaleza

Ponta do Calcanhar

Trujillo

Marañón

Huascarán 6 768 m

La Montaña

Juruá

Purus

Madeira

Tapajós

Xingu

Caatinga

Recife

10°

Lima

Cusco (Cuzco)

Ancohuma 6 550 m

PERU

ANDES

Tocantins

Salvador

Arequipa

La Paz

Cochabamba

BOLIVIA

Santa Cruz

Sucre

Sajama 6 542 m

Altiplano

Planalto do Mato Grosso

Brasília

Belo Horizonte

20°

Desierto de Atacama

Gran Chaco

Paraná

PARAGUAY

Campinas

Rio de Janeiro

Tropic of Capricorn

PACIFIC

I. San Ambrosio (CHILE)

I. San Félix (CHILE)

Volcán Llullaillaco 6 723 m

Ojos del Salado 6 880 m

Pissis 6 779 m

Asunción

San Miguel de Tucumán

Ciudad del Este

Curitiba

São Paulo

Porto Alegre

OCEAN

Bonete 6 872 m

Aconcagua 6 959 m

Salado

Córdoba

Salto

Paraná

Uruguay

URUGUAY

30°

Islas Juan Fernández (CHILE)

Viña del Mar

Mendoza

Rosario

Buenos Aires

Montevideo

I. Alejandro Selkirk

I. Robinson Crusoe

Valparaíso

Santiago

Tupungato 6 800 m

La Plata

Río de la Plata

Concepción

ARGENTINA

Pampas

CHILE

ANDES

Colorado

Bahía Blanca

ATLANTIC

100°

40°

Golfo San Matías

Patagonia

OCEAN

Arch. de los Chonos

Golfo de San Jorge

Archipiélago de la Reina Adelaida

Bahía Grande

Falkland Islands (U.K.)

Estrecho de Magallanes

50°S

Punta Arenas

Isla Grande de Tierra del Fuego

Estrecho de Magallanes

Cabo de Hornos (Cape Horn)

90°W   80°   70°   60°   50°   40°

Apart from its western boundary, which lies in the Andes Mountains, the Argentine Republic – eleven times larger than the United Kingdom – is made up of rolling plateaux in the south (Patagonia) and fertile plains in the east and north (the Pampas, Chaco). The climate is subtropical in the north, temperate around the Río de la Plata area, and arid and sub-Antarctic in Patagonia and Tierra del Fuego.

Area: 2,780,400km²
Population (2002): 37,944,000
Capital: Buenos Aires 2,768,772 (2001 e), 12,106,000 (2001 e) including the suburbs
Government type and political system: republic with a semi-presidential system
Head of state and government: (President of the Republic) Néstor Kirchner
Administrative structure: 23 provinces and 1 federal district
Official language: Spanish
Currency: Argentine peso

DEMOGRAPHICS

Density: 13 inhab/km²
Percentage of population in urban areas (2001): 88.3%
Age structure of population (2000): 0–15 years: 27.7%, 15–65 years: 62.6%, over 65 years: 9.7%
Birth rate (2003): 19‰
Death rate (2003): 7.6‰
Infant mortality rate (2003): 20‰
Life expectancy at birth (2003): male: 70.6 years, female: 77.7 years

ECONOMY

GNP (2002): 154 billion US$
GNP per capita (2002): 4,220 US$
GNP per capita PPP (2002): 10,190 international dollars
HDI (2000): 0.844
GDP annual growth rate (2003): 8.7%
Annual inflation rate (2000): −0.94%
Labour force by occupation: n/a
GDP by sector (2000): agriculture: 4.8%, industry: 27.5%, services: 67.7%
Gross public debt: n/a
Unemployment rate (2002): 19.6%

Agriculture and fishing

Crops
citrus fruits (2002): 2,566,000t

Argentina

provincial boundary	═══ motorway	─── railway line	● population over 1,000,000
S. Luis provincial capital	─── road	✈ airport	● population 500,000 to 1,000,000
400 1000 2000 4000 m		★ place of interest	● population 100,000 to 500,000
			● population less than 100,000

groundnuts (2001): 563,000t
sunflowers (2002): 3,844,000t
wheat (2002): 12,300,000t
lemons (2002): 1,200,000t
cotton (2002): 190,000t
maize (2002): 15,000,000t

mandarin oranges (1998): 410,000t
honey (2001): 90,000t
olives (2002): 93,000t
oranges (2002): 780,000t
grapefruits (2001): 191,000t
peaches (2002): 213,000t

99

ARGENTINA

apples (2001): 1,428,000t
potatoes (2002): 2,133,000t
grapes (2002): 2,460,000t
soya beans (2002): 30,000,000t
sorghum (2002): 2,847,000t
tobacco (2001): 101,000t
tea (2001): 50,000t

Livestock farming and fishing
cattle (2002): 48,100,000 head
horses (2001): 3,600,000 head
sheep (2002): 12,400,000 head
chickens (2002): 111,000,000 head
fish (1999): 1,026,000t

Energy generation and mining
silver (2001): 153t
total electricity (2001): 97,167 million kWh
natural gas (2002): 36,100 million m³

gold (2001): 30,630kg
oil (2002): 39,400,000t
lead (2001): 14,000t
uranium (1999): 28t
zinc (2001): 34,500t

Industrial production
milk (2001): 9,600,000t
cheese (2001): 420,000t
meat (2001): 3,995,000t
olive oil (2001): 8,000t
beer (2000): 12,090,000hl
wine (2002): 12,150,000hl
cars (2002): 111,000 units
copper (2001): 192,000t
lead (2001): 28,500t
zinc (2001): 43,000t
wool (2001): 58,000t
synthetic rubber (2001): 48,000t

cement (2001): 7,000,000t

Tourism
Tourism revenue (2001): 2,534 million US$

Foreign trade
Exports (2002): 25,709 million US$
Imports (2002): 8,470 million US$

Defence
Armed forces (2001): 69,900 people
Defence budget (2001): 1.23% of GDP

Standard of living
Inhabitants per doctor (1990): 370
Average daily calorie intake (2000): 3,181 (FAO minimum: 2,400)
Cars per 1,000 inhabitants (1998): 140
Televisions per 1,000 inhabitants (2001): 326

HISTORY: KEY DATES

The Spanish colonial era and independence
1516: the Spanish navigator Juan Díaz de Solís visited the Río de la Plata.
1536–80: Buenos Aires was founded, abandoned and then re-established as a settlement.
18c: the area underwent a considerable economic boom, and Buenos Aires flourished. In 1776, the Spanish government made Buenos Aires a free port and capital of the Viceroyalty of Río de la Plata.
1806–7: the Argentine militia fought off two attacks on Buenos Aires by British forces.
1810: the viceroy was deposed by a revolutionary junta, and Buenos Aires declared itself independent.
1816: the Tucumán Congress proclaimed Argentina's independence, naming it the United Provinces of the Río de la Plata.

Political conflict and economic and demographic expansion
1820–35: the mazorqueros (federalists), led by provincial leaders, and the unitarios (centralists) in Buenos Aires engaged in fierce conflict.
1835–52: federalist leader Juan Manuel de Rosas established a dictatorship.
1853: after Rosas was overthrown,

Argentina established a federal and liberal constitution.
1862–80: liberal politician Bartolomé Mitre became president and the country was finally unified. Argentina, Brazil and Uruguay fought the War of the Triple Alliance against Paraguay. Plans for economic growth were drawn up, based on the expansion of cattle and sheep farming and the construction of a railway network. Indigenous peoples were either subjugated or wiped out by General Julio A Roca, who eventually became president of Argentina.
1880–1930: in parallel with an influx of European immigrants, the economy underwent a boom, but was extremely dependent on foreign capital and markets (particularly the British). The middle and working classes, or Radicals, asserted their opposition to the dominance of the liberal oligarchy made up of wealthy landowners and merchants. President Hipólito Yrigoyen (1916–22 and 1928–30), a Radical, imposed social legislation without agrarian reform.

Military regimes and the return to democracy
1929: the global economic crisis that followed the 1929 Wall Street Crash

created favourable conditions for the establishment of conservative military regimes.
1943–55: a junta of nationalist military officers, including Juan Domingo Perón, deposed President Ramón Castillo. When Perón became president (1946–55), he applied a populist, so-called 'justicialist' doctrine aimed at giving a political voice to the working class.
1955: Perón was ousted by a military coup.
1973: Perón became president again. When he died in 1974, his third wife, Isabel, succeeded him.
1976: a military junta led by General Jorge Videla deposed Isabel Perón and imposed an emergency regime during the so-called Dirty War. Thousands of opponents of the regime 'disappeared'.
1982: Argentina invaded the Falkland Islands, but was defeated. Civilian rule was re-established in Argentina.
1982–2003: despite constitutional reform and privatization programmes, the Argentine economy went into recession in 1999. Austerity measures and aid from the International Monetary Fund (IMF) led to slight improvements in 2003, when Néstor Kirchner was elected president.

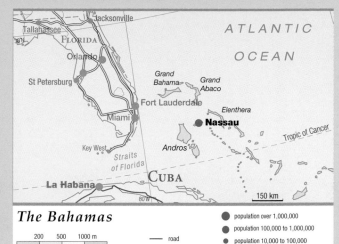

The Bahamas

200 500 1000 m

— road
✈ airport

● population over 1,000,000
● population 100,000 to 1,000,000
● population 10,000 to 100,000
• population less than 10,000

150 km

The Commonwealth of The Bahamas is an archipelago of around 700 islands and 2,000 cays. The majority of the population lives on two of the islands: New Providence (which contains the capital city, Nassau) and Grand Bahama.

Area: 13,878km²
Population (2002): 312,000
Capital: Nassau 220,000 (2001 e) including the suburbs
Government type and political system: constitutional monarchy with a parliamentary system
Head of state: (Queen) Elizabeth II, represented by the Governor-General Dame Ivy Dumont
Head of government: (Prime Minister) Perry Christie
Administrative structure: 21 districts
Official language: English
Currency: Bahamian dollar

DEMOGRAPHICS

Density: 22 inhab/km²
Percentage of population in urban areas (2001): 88.8%
Age structure of population (2000): 0–15 years: 29.6%, 15–65 years: 65%, over 65 years: 5.4%
Birth rate (2003): 19.4‰
Death rate (2003): 8.2‰
Infant mortality rate (2003): 17.7‰
Life expectancy at birth (2003): male: 63.9 years, female: 70.3 years

ECONOMY

GNP (2002): 4.53 billion US$
GNP per capita (2002): 14,860 US$

GNP per capita PPP (2002): 16,080 international dollars
HDI (2000): 0.826
GDP annual growth rate (2003): 0.9%
Annual inflation rate (2001): 2%
Labour force by occupation (1998): industry: 7%, services: 90%
GDP by sector (1991): agriculture: 3%, industry: 15.3%, services: 81.2%
Gross public debt: n/a
Unemployment rate (1998): 7.7%

Agriculture

Crops
citrus fruits (2002): 21,000t
bananas (2001): 3,300t
sugar cane (2001): 45,000t
maize (2002): 380t
Livestock farming
goats (2001): 13,582 head
chickens (2002): 3,550,000 head

Energy generation

total electricity (2001): 1,560 million kWh

Tourism

Tourism revenue (1999): 1,503 million US$

Foreign trade

Exports (2001): 614.1 million US$

Imports (2001): 1,764.7 million US$

Defence

Armed forces (2001): 860 people
Defence budget (2001): 0.64% of GDP

Standard of living

Inhabitants per doctor (1993): 714
Average daily calorie intake (2000): 2,443 (FAO minimum: 2,400)
Cars per 1,000 inhabitants (1996): 159
Televisions per 1,000 inhabitants (2000): 247

HISTORY: KEY DATES

18c: America, Britain and Spain fought over The Bahamas. In 1783, the islands were ceded to Britain under the Treaty of Paris.
1973: The Bahamas gained independence within the Commonwealth of Nations.

BARBADOS ➡ LESSER ANTILLES

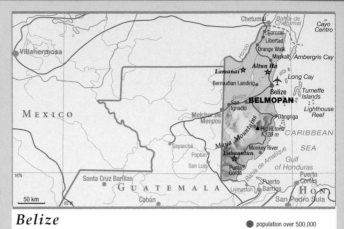

Belize

★ place of interest

| 200 | 500 | 1500 | 3000 m |

— road
--- railway line
✈ airport

● population over 500,000
● population 100,000 to 500,000
● population 10,000 to 100,000
• population less than 10,000

Belize has a subtropical climate, and 40% of its land is covered with forests. Beyond a swampy coastal plain in the north, the land rises to the Maya Mountains in the south.

Area: 22,696km²
Population (2002): 235,000
Capital: Belmopan 9,000 (2001 e)
Government type and political system: constitutional monarchy with a parliamentary regime
Head of state: (Queen) Elizabeth II, represented by the Governor-General Sir Colville Young
Head of government: (Prime Minister) Said Musa
Administrative structure: 6 districts
Official language: English
Currency: Belizean dollar

DEMOGRAPHICS

Density: 10 inhab/km²
Percentage of population in urban areas (2001): 48.1%
Age structure of population (2000): 0–15 years: 38.4%, 15–65 years: 57.4%, over 65 years: 4.2%
Birth rate (2003): 27‰
Death rate (2003): 5.3‰
Infant mortality rate (2003): 31.1‰
Life expectancy at birth (2003): male: 69.9 years, female: 73 years

ECONOMY

GNP (2002): 0.75 billion US$
GNP per capita (2002): 2,970 US$
GNP per capita PPP (2002): 5,490 international dollars

HDI (2000): 0.784
GDP annual growth rate (2003): 2.1%
Annual inflation rate (2000): 0.61%
Labour force by occupation: n/a
GDP by sector (2000): agriculture: 21.4%, industry: 27%, services: 51.6%
Gross public debt: n/a
Unemployment rate (1996): 13.8%

Agriculture and fishing

Crops
bananas (2001): 85,000t
sugar cane (2001): 1,150,000t
maize (2002): 33,500t
oranges (2002): 169,000t
Livestock farming and fishing
cattle (2002): 57,000 head
pigs (2002): 22,900 head
chickens (2002): 1,400,000 head
fish (1999): 43,100t

Energy generation
total electricity (2001): 199 million kWh

Industrial production
sugar (2002): 111,000t
beer (2000): 32,500hl

Tourism
Tourism revenue (2001): 121 million US$

Foreign trade
Exports (2002): 310.4 million US$
Imports (2002): 500.3 million US$

Defence
Armed forces (2001): 1,050 people
Defence budget (2001): 2.4% of GDP

Standard of living
Inhabitants per doctor (1995): 2,027
Average daily calorie intake (2000): 2,888 (FAO minimum: 2,400)
Cars per 1,000 inhabitants (1998): 44
Televisions per 1,000 inhabitants (2000): 183

HISTORY: KEY DATES

c.900 BC: Maya settlements were established in the area that later became Belize.
17c–18c: British buccaneers and logwood cutters settled in the region. Spain fought with Britain to control it.
1862: the area became a British Crown Colony, named British Honduras.
1964: it was granted full internal self-government.
1972: the official name of the territory was changed to Belize.
1981: Belize gained independence within the Commonwealth of Nations.
1991: Guatemala recognized Belize as a sovereign and independent state.

The eastern part of the Republic of Bolivia is lowland, covered by Amazonian rainforests. To the west are the Andes Mountains. In the centre of the country is the altiplano, a region of high plateaux where the population and the main cities are concentrated.

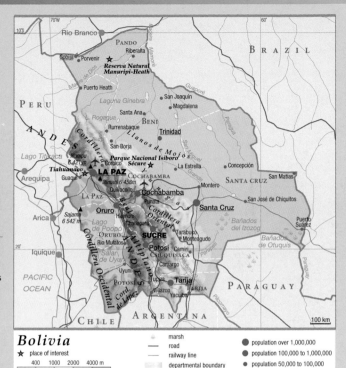

Bolivia

⛯ marsh
★ place of interest
— road
railway line
400 1000 2000 4000 m
departmental boundary
Tarija departmental capital

● population over 1,000,000
● population 100,000 to 1,000,000
● population 50,000 to 100,000
• population less than 50,000

100 km

Area: 1,098,581km²
Population (2002): 8,706,000
Capital: La Paz (administrative)
1,499,000 (2001 e) including the suburbs
Capital: Sucre (official and legislative)
Government type and political system:
republic with a presidential system
Head of state and government: (President
of the Republic) Carlos Mesa
Administrative structure: 9 departments
Official languages: Spanish, Aymara and
Quechua
Currency: boliviano

DEMOGRAPHICS

Density: 8 inhab/km²
Percentage of population in urban areas
(2001): 62.9%
Age structure of population (2000): 0–15
years: 39.6%, 15–65 years: 56.4%, over
65 years: 4%
Birth rate (2003): 29.3‰
Death rate (2003): 8.1‰
Infant mortality rate (2003): 55.6‰
Life expectancy at birth (2003): male: 61.8
years, female: 66 years

ECONOMY

GNP (2002): 7.95 billion US$
GNP per capita (2002): 900 US$
GNP per capita PPP (2002): 2,390
international dollars
HDI (2000): 0.653
GDP annual growth rate (2003): 2.6%
Annual inflation rate (2000): 4.6%
Labour force by occupation: n/a
GDP by sector (2000): agriculture: 22%,
industry: 15.3%, services: 62.7%
Gross public debt: n/a
Unemployment rate (2000): 7.4%

Agriculture and fishing

Crops
bananas (2001): 688,000t
sugar cane (2001): 3,859,000t
maize (2002): 725,000t
potatoes (2002): 944,000t
soya beans (2002): 1,167,000t
Livestock farming and fishing
cattle (2002): 6,576,000 head
horses (2001): 322,000 head
sheep (2002): 8,902,000 head

pigs (2002): 2,851,000 head
chickens (2002): 75,000,000 head
fish (1999): 6,450t

Energy generation and mining

silver (2001): 408t
copper (2000): 110,000t
total electricity (2001): 3,901 million kWh
tin (2001): 12,500t
natural gas (2002): 5,400 million m³
gold (2001): 12,395kg
oil (2002): 1,544,000t
lead (2001): 9,600t
zinc (2001): 150,000t

Industrial production

meat (2001): 409,000t
sugar (2002): 405,000t
beer (2000): 2,195,000hl

cement (2001): 1,100,000t
timber (2000): 468,000m³

Tourism

Tourism revenue (2001): 156 million US$

Foreign trade

Exports (2002): 1,298.7 million US$
Imports (2002): 1,532.1 million US$

Defence

Armed forces (2001): 31,500 people
Defence budget (2001): 1.76% of GDP

Standard of living

Inhabitants per doctor (1993): 2,500
Average daily calorie intake (2000): 2,218
(FAO minimum: 2,400)
Cars per 1,000 inhabitants (2000): 22
Televisions per 1,000 inhabitants (2000): 119

103

HISTORY: KEY DATES

1532–8: Spanish conquerors defeated indigenous peoples and settled in the Alto Peru region.
1545: the discovery of silver mines in Potosi made the region the richest area in the Spanish empire.
1559: the region became a dependency of the Viceroyalty of Peru.
1824–5: after the Battle of Ayacucho, Bolivia became independent.
1836: Peru established a confederation with Bolivia that would last until 1839.
1879–84: during the War of the Pacific, Bolivia lost its coastal territory in the Atacama to Chile and became landlocked.
1932–5: after losing the Chaco War, Bolivia surrendered its territory in the

Gran Chaco region to Paraguay.
1943: the Nationalist Revolutionary Movement (MNR, or Movimiento Nacionalista Revolucionario) seized power. It introduced far-reaching reforms before being overthrown by the military in 1964.
1982: following a number of coups and emergency regimes, civilian government was restored.
1982–2003: governmental efforts to replace the widespread cultivation of coca with alternative crops were met with resistance by indigenous farmers. An economic recession and increasing poverty gave rise to continuing social unrest.

As well as the immense Amazon Basin, the Federative Republic of Brazil contains a number of plateaux that rise up to mountain ranges. From these the land drops directly to the Atlantic Ocean, or to narrow coastal flood plains. The climate is equatorial in the Amazon, constantly hot and humid and covered by dense permanent rainforests. In the south, however, the climate is drier and more temperate. In northern Brazil, campos (grasslands) and other types of savanna such as caatinga (thorn forest) predominate. There are also steppes, especially in the north-east.

Area: 8,547,403km²
Population (2002): 174,706,000
Capital: Brasília 2,043,169 (2000 census)
Government type and political system: republic with a presidential system
Head of state and government: (President of the Republic) Luiz Inácio Lula da Silva
Administrative structure: 26 states and 1 federal district
Official language: Portuguese
Currency: Brazilian real

DEMOGRAPHICS

Density: 20 inhab/km²
Percentage of population in urban areas (2001): 81.7%
Age structure of population (2000): 0–15 years: 28.8%, 15–65 years: 66.1%, over 65 years: 5.1%
Birth rate (2003): 19.7‰
Death rate (2003): 7.1‰
Infant mortality rate (2003): 38.4‰
Life expectancy at birth (2003): male: 64 years, female: 72.6 years

ECONOMY

GNP (2002): 495 billion US$
GNP per capita (2002): 2,830 US$
GNP per capita PPP (2002): 7,450 international dollars
HDI (2000): 0.757
GDP annual growth rate (2003): –0.2%
Annual inflation rate (2000): 7.04%
Labour force by occupation (1999): agriculture: 24.2%, industry: 19.3%, services: 56.5%
GDP by sector (2000): agriculture: 7.4%, industry: 28.6%, services: 64%

Gross public debt: n/a
Unemployment rate (1999): 9.6%

Agriculture and fishing
Crops
citrus fruits (2002): 20,004,000t
pineapples (2001): 1,442,000t
groundnuts (2001): 198,000t
bananas (2001): 5,744,000t
cocoa (2001): 187,000t
coffee (2002): 2,494,000t
sugar cane (2001): 339,136,000t
lemons (2002): 580,000t
yams (2002): 230,000t
maize (2002): 35,500,000t
mandarin oranges (1998): 749,000t
manioc (2001): 24,088,000t
cashew nuts (1998): 45,478t
oranges (2002): 18,447,000t
grapefruits (2001) : 66,000t
sweet potatoes (2001): 485,000t
peaches (2002): 184,000t
apples (2001): 706,000t
rice (2002): 10,472,000t
soya beans (2002): 42,027,000t
sorghum (2002): 773,000t
tobacco (2001): 565,000t
tomatoes (2002): 3,608,000t
Livestock farming and fishing
cattle (2002): 176,000,000 head
buffaloes (2001): 1,150,000 head
goats (2001): 8,700,000 head
horses (2001): 5,850,000 head
sheep (2002): 15,500,000 head
pigs (2002): 30,000,000 head
chickens (2002): 1,050,000,000 head
fish (1999): 775,000t

Energy generation and mining
bauxite (2001): 13,900,000t
chromium (2001): 420,000t
diamonds (2001): 1,000,000 carats
total electricity (2001): 321,165 million kWh
hydroelectricity (2001): 265,459 million kWh
tin (2001): 14,000t
iron (2001): 137,742,000t
coal (2001): 4,108,000t
manganese (2001): 1,430,000t
nickel (2001): 45,400t
gold (2001): 52,400kg
phosphate (2001): 4,700,000t

Industrial production
milk (2001): 22,718,000t
meat (2001): 15,161,000t
sugar (2002): 23,810,000t
palm oil (2001): 108,000t
oil palms (2001): 130,000t
cars (2002): 1,521,000 units
commercial vehicles (1998): 329,000 units

HISTORY: KEY DATES

The colonial period
1500: the Portuguese explorer Pedro Álvares Cabral led an expedition that claimed Brazil for Portugal.
1555–67: French attempts to settle in Brazil were thwarted by the Portuguese.
1624–54: attracted by the money that could be made from sugar production, the Dutch occupied the coasts of Brazil.
1720–70: the search for gold led to the development of inland Brazil. Large cotton, cocoa and tobacco plantations ensured the country's economic revival.
1808–21: the Portuguese royal family, fleeing from Napoleon's armies, settled in Rio de Janeiro, making it the capital of the Portuguese empire.
1815: the Portuguese king, Dom João VI, elevated Brazil to the status of a kingdom (equal with Portugal).

The empire of Brazil
1822–89: under Dom Pedro I (1822–31) and Dom Pedro II (1831–89), Brazil, now an independent empire, experienced an influx of immigrants and an economic boom. Its borders were adjusted after the war against Paraguay. The abolition of slavery in 1888 angered the aristocratic landowners.

The federalist republic and the Vargas era
1889: Dom Pedro II was overthrown in a bloodless coup, and a federalist republic was established. Coffee growing continued to predominate, ensuring economic prosperity; the production of

wheat and rubber also developed.
1917: Brazil declared war on Germany.
1930: economic crisis led to the fall of the regime, and Getúlio Vargas came to power through a coup. He was elected president in 1934, and established a dictatorship in 1937.
1942: Brazil's participation in World War II alongside the Allies stimulated the country's economy.
1945: Vargas was ousted by another military coup.
1950–4: Vargas was re-elected president, but committed suicide in 1954.

Contemporary Brazil
1956–64: a series of reformist governments struggled against the power of multinational companies.
1960: Brasília became the capital of Brazil.
1964–85: after a military coup, a series of generals came to power. The national economy was mainly subordinated to North America.
1985: a civilian government was restored, but inflation continued to increase.
1988: a new constitution came into force.
1990–2002: economic reforms were implemented in response to fiscal crises in several Brazilian states. Lula da Silva's election as president in 2002 marked the first transfer of power between elected Brazilian presidents for over forty years.

steel *(2003):* 31,105,000t
aluminium *(2001):* 1,131,000t
cast iron *(1998):* 25,132,000t
copper *(2001):* 32,000t
lead *(2001):* 47,000t
zinc *(2001):* 199,000t
tin *(2001):* 14,000t
nickel *(2001):* 45,400t
cotton yarn *(2001):* 868,000t
jute *(2001):* 235,000t
sisal *(2001):* 183,000t

silk *(2001):* 1,400t
artificial textiles *(1999):* 48,400t
cement *(2001):* 39,500,000t
paper *(2000):* 6,473,000t
timber *(2000):* 102,994,000m³

Tourism
Tourism revenue (2001): 3,701 million US$

Foreign trade
Exports (2002): 60,362 million US$
Imports (2002): 47,219 million US$

Defence
Armed forces (2001): 287,600 people
Defence budget (2001): 1.7% of GDP

Standard of living
Inhabitants per doctor (1995): 714
Average daily calorie intake (2000): 2,985
(FAO minimum: 2,400)
Cars per 1,000 inhabitants (2000): 137
Televisions per 1,000 inhabitants (2001): 349

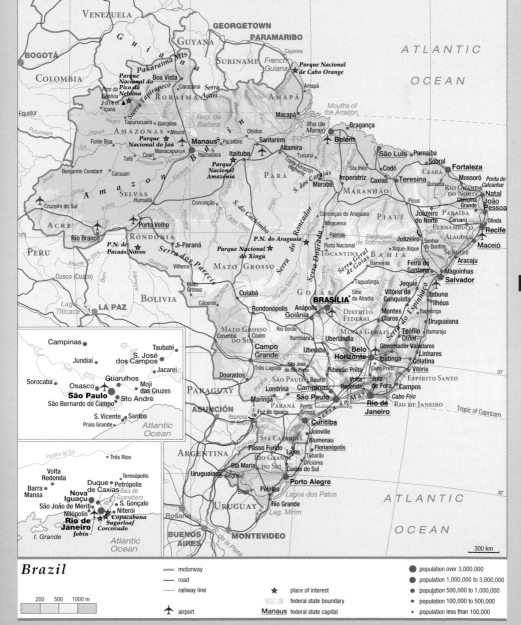

Brazil

═══	motorway
───	road
───	railway line

★ place of interest
▨ federal state boundary
✈ airport
Manaus federal state capital

● population over 3,000,000
● population 1,000,000 to 3,000,000
● population 500,000 to 1,000,000
• population 100,000 to 500,000
· population less than 100,000

200 500 1000 m

300 km

ATLANTIC OCEAN

ICELAND
REYKJAVÍK

Denmark Strait

Greenland (Denmark)

Nunap Isua (Cape Farewell)

Qeqertarsuaq (Disko)

LABRADOR SEA

Davis Strait

Baffin Bay

Cape Chidley

Cumberland Peninsula

ELLESMERE ISLAND NATIONAL PARK
Ellesmere Island
Queen Elizabeth Islands
Sverdrup Islands
Axel Heiberg Island
Eureka
Magnetic North Pole
Devon Island
Cornwallis Island
Resolute
Bathurst Island
Prince of Wales Island
King William Island
Boothia Peninsula
Borden Island
Prince Patrick Island
Melville Island
Banks Island
Sachs Harbour
Victoria Island
Wollaston Peninsula
Cambridge Bay
Kugluktuk

NEWFOUNDLAND AND LABRADOR

Labrador

Nain
Hopedale
Happy Valley-Goose Bay
Churchill Falls
Labrador City
Smallwood Reservoir

Cape St. Charles
Blanc-Sablon
Corner Brook
Gander St. John's
Newfoundland
Cape Race

St-Pierre and Miquelon (Fr.)
Cape Breton Island
Sydney
Louisbourg
Cape Sable

PRINCE EDWARD ISLAND
Charlottetown
NOVA SCOTIA
Moncton
Dartmouth
Halifax
Bridgewater
NEW BRUNSWICK
Fredericton
Saint John
Bay of Fundy

QUÉBEC
Kuujjuaq
Péninsule d'Ungava
Ungava Bay
Inukjuak
Puvirnituq
Chisasibi
Akimiski Island

Sept-Îles
Port-Cartier
Baie-Comeau
Rimouski
Chicoutimi
Shawinigan
Trois-Rivières
Québec
Sherbrooke
Montréal
OTTAWA

HUDSON BAY

NUNAVUT

Hall Beach
Igloolik
Repulse Bay
Chesterfield Inlet
Rankin Inlet
Arviat
Baker Lake
Coral Harbour
Southampton Island
Coats Island
Mansel Island
Belcher Islands

Churchill

Iqaluit
Frobisher Bay
Baffin Island
Foxe Basin
Hudson Strait

ONTARIO
North Bay
Sudbury
Sault Ste Marie
Thunder Bay
Toronto
Hamilton
London
Mississauga
Oshawa
St. Catharines
Niagara Falls
Kingston
Windsor
Manitoulin Island
Lake Huron
Lake Erie
Lake Ontario

New York
Boston
Philadelphia
Detroit
Chicago

MANITOBA
Winnipeg
Brandon
The Pas
Lynn Lake
Thompson
Lake Winnipeg

SASKATCHEWAN
Regina
Saskatoon
Prince Albert
Moose Jaw
Weyburn
La Ronge
North Battleford
Yorkton

ALBERTA
Edmonton
Calgary
Red Deer
Lethbridge
Medicine Hat
Fort McMurray
Grande Prairie
Peace River

NORTHWEST TERRITORIES
Yellowknife
Hay River
Fort Smith
Fort Simpson
Fort Providence
Rae-Edzo
Fort Liard
Fort Nelson
Great Slave Lake
Great Bear Lake
Franklin Mountains
Mackenzie Mountains
Wood Buffalo National Park

YUKON TERRITORY
Whitehorse
Dawson
Mayo
Watson Lake
Old Crow
Ivvavik National Park
Inuvik
Aklavik
Fort McPherson
Fort Good Hope
Norman Wells
Ogilvie Mts
Selwyn Mts
Kluane National Park

BRITISH COLUMBIA
Vancouver
Victoria
Prince George
Prince Rupert
Kamloops
Kelowna
Nanaimo
Port McNeill
Queen Charlotte Islands
Vancouver Island
Coast Mountains
Rocky Mountains
Selkirk Mts
Mt Columbia 3 747 m
Mt Waddington 4 042 m
Jasper National Park
Banff National Park

ARCTIC OCEAN
BEAUFORT SEA
Cape Bathurst
Prudhoe Bay
Point Barrow
Barrow

ALASKA (U.S.A.)
Mt McKinley 6 194 m
Anchorage
Fairbanks
Brooks Range
Alaska Range
Gulf of Alaska
Kodiak Island
St Lawrence Island
Alaska Peninsula

Mt St Elias 5 489 m
Mt Logan 5 959 m
St Elias Mts

RUSSIAN FEDERATION

PACIFIC OCEAN

UNITED STATES OF AMERICA
Seattle
Portland
Minneapolis
St. Paul
Columbia
Missouri
Snake

Juan de Fuca Strait

300 km

airport
place of interest

population over 1,000,000
population 100,000 to 1,000,000
population 50,000 to 100,000
population less than 50,000

provincial or territorial boundary
Victoria provincial or territorial capital

motorway
road
railway line

glacier
200 500 1000 2000 m

106

Canada is the world's second-largest country (after Russia), with a population just over half that of the United Kingdom. Plateaux predominate in the east and centre. In the west, the Rocky Mountains form a barrier to the rainy and moderating influence of the Pacific. The deciduous trees of the lowlands in the south, around the fertile St Lawrence Valley, give way to conifers; these are followed by tundra and, in the Arctic, ice. There are very harsh winters in the north of the country.

Area: 9,970,610km²
Population (2002): 31,268,000
Capital: Ottawa 323,340 (1996 census), 1,094,000 (2001 e) including the suburbs
Government type and political system: constitutional monarchy with a parliamentary system
Head of state: (Queen) Elizabeth II, represented by the Governor-General Adrienne Clarkson
Head of government: (Prime Minister) Paul Martin
Administrative structure: 10 provinces and 3 territories
Official languages: English and French
Currency: Canadian dollar

DEMOGRAPHICS
Density: 3 inhab/km²
Percentage of population in urban areas (2001): 78.9%
Age structure of population (2000): 0–15 years: 19.1%, 15–65 years: 68.3%, over 65 years: 12.6%
Birth rate (2003): 10.3‰
Death rate (2003): 7.5‰
Infant mortality rate (2003): 5.3‰
Life expectancy at birth (2003): male: 76.7 years, female: 81.9 years

ECONOMY
GNP (2002): 702 billion US$
GNP per capita (2002): 22,390 US$
GNP per capita PPP (2002): 28,930 international dollars
HDI (2000): 0.94
GDP annual growth rate (2003): 1.7%
Annual inflation rate (2000): 2.75%
Labour force by occupation (2000): agriculture: 3.3%, industry: 22.6%, services: 74.1%
GDP by sector (1998): agriculture: 2.6%, industry: 33.2%, services: 64.2%
Gross public debt (1998): 89.8% of GDP
Unemployment rate (2002): 7.7%

Agriculture and fishing
Crops
oats (2001): 2,769,000t
wheat (2002): 16,198,000t
rape (2001): 5,062,000t
maize (2002): 8,995,000t
honey (2001): 31,733t
barley (2002): 7,489,000t
potatoes (2002): 4,697,000t
rye (2001): 194,000t
soya beans (2002): 2,335,000t
tobacco (2001): 58,000t
Livestock farming and fishing
cattle (2002): 13,762,000 head
pigs (2002): 14,367,000 head
fish (1999): 1,136,000t

Energy generation and mining
silver (2001): 1,271t
copper (2001): 632,000t
diamonds (2001): 2,600,000 carats
total electricity (2001): 566,310 million kWh
nuclear electricity (2001): 72,858 million kWh
hydroelectricity (2000): 352,750 million kWh
iron (2001): 17,186,000t
natural gas (2000): 180,338 million m³
molybdenum (2001): 7,000t
nickel (2001): 193,000t
gold (2001): 159,714kg
oil (2002): 123,347,000t
lead (2001): 149,400t
uranium (2001): 12,520t
zinc (2001): 1,009,000t

Industrial production
milk (2001): 8,170,000t
cheese (2001): 359,720t
meat (2001): 4,121,000t
steel (2003): 15,399,000t
aluminium (2001): 2,583,000t
cast iron (1998): 8,937,000t
copper (2001): 632,000t
nickel (2001): 193,000t
lead (2001): 149,400t
zinc (2001): 1,009,000t
cars (2002): 1,369,000 units
commercial vehicles (1998): 1,079,000 units
synthetic rubber (2001): 145,000t
paper (2000): 20,921,000t
timber (2000): 176,572,000m³

Tourism
Tourism revenue (2001): 10,774 million US$

Foreign trade
Exports (2002): 264,078 million US$
Imports (2002): 227,240 million US$

Defence
Armed forces (2001): 52,300 people
Defence budget (2001): 1.05% of GDP

Standard of living
Inhabitants per doctor (1996): 476
Average daily calorie intake (2000): 3,174 (FAO minimum: 2,400)
Cars per 1,000 inhabitants (1997): 445
Televisions per 1,000 inhabitants (2001): 715

HISTORY: KEY DATES

French-British rivalry
The earliest inhabitants of Canada were prehistoric peoples who arrived from Asia via the Bering Strait.
1497: English explorer John Cabot reached Canada's east coast.
1534–6: Frenchman Jacques Cartier claimed discovery of Canada and explored the St Lawrence River.
1604–8: French explorer Samuel de Champlain founded the country's first permanent European settlement, Port Royal in Acadia, and later established a trading post at Quebec.
1627: France created the Company of One Hundred Associates (aka the Company of New France) with a view to establishing French colonies and trading in furs. However, few French immigrants arrived. The French and their allies, the Huron, were unsuccessful in their warfare against the Iroquois.
1663–70: France made Canada a royal province and granted it a new administration. New France flourished, and the St Lawrence River region began to be colonized.
1670–89: British settlers on the Atlantic coast to the south challenged France's control of the territory and the local fur trade. Their struggle for domination of the eastern part of the continent grew into the French and Indian Wars.
1713: under the Treaty of Utrecht, the French lost Hudson Bay, Acadia and most of Newfoundland.
1756–63: in the Seven Years' War, Britain took control of Quebec in 1759 and of Montreal in 1760. The Treaty of Paris in 1763 gave Britain control of all French territories east of the Mississippi.

British Canada
1783: the second Treaty of Paris, recognizing the independence of the USA, led to the arrival of large numbers of American loyalists. Exploration continued, leading to expansion of Canada's territory.
1791: the Constitutional Act divided the country into two colonies, the predominantly British Upper Canada and the predominantly French Lower Canada.
1812–14: American attempts to invade Canada were driven back by British and Canadian forces.
1815: large numbers of Scottish and Irish immigrants began to arrive in Canada.
1820–37: campaigns for political reform by William Lyon Mackenzie in Upper

CANADA

⇒

HISTORY: KEY DATES

Canada and Louis Joseph Papineau in Lower Canada were met with refusal from London, leading to rebellion in both parts of Canada.

1840: the Act of Union made Upper Canada and Lower Canada into a single province, controlled by the same parliament, with English as the only official language.

1848: French was restored to the status of an official Canadian language.

Modern Canada

1867: the British North America Act created the Dominion of Canada, which confederated Ontario (formerly Upper Canada/Canada West), Quebec (formerly Lower Canada/Canada East), Nova Scotia and New Brunswick.

1870: the rebellion of the Métis ethnic group, led by Louis Riel, was unsuccessful in securing protection for their rights to their Red River settlement, which eventually became the Canadian province of Manitoba.

1870–1905: the provinces of British Columbia, Prince Edward Island, Saskatchewan and Alberta were instituted.

1896–1911: commercial ties with Great Britain were tightened whilst the autonomy of the Dominion was reinforced. Large numbers of immigrants continued to arrive in Canada, attracted by its growing economy.

1914–18: Canada participated in World War I alongside the Allies.

1921–48: William Lyon Mackenzie King, leader of the Liberal Party, served as Canadian prime minister (except for three months in 1926 and the period 1930–5).

1926: the Imperial Conference recognized Canada's independence within the Commonwealth of Nations, sanctioned by the Westminster Statute (1931).

1940–45: Canada developed a powerful war industry during World War II.

1949: the island of Newfoundland became a Canadian province, and Canada joined the North Atlantic Treaty Organization (NATO).

1948–84: Canada pursued a policy of increasingly close rapprochement with the USA. The demands of separatists in the French-speaking province of Quebec culminated in a referendum on Quebec's independence, in which the pro-independence movement was defeated.

1982: the Canada Act made Canada a fully sovereign state with the right to amend its own constitution. The inhabitants of Quebec were not satisfied that their demands had been properly addressed, and Quebec refused to accept the Act.

1984: the Progressive Conservative politician Brian Mulroney came to power.

1990: Canada joined the Organization of American States (OAS). The constitutional reform project known as the Meech Lake Accord (aimed at satisfying Quebec's demands) collapsed under the weight of objection from Canada's English-speaking population to the limitations on the use of English that the Quebecois sought to put in place. This created an unprecedented constitutional crisis, exacerbated by the concurrent territorial claims made by Native American peoples.

1992: a new constitutional reform project known as the Charlottetown Accord was rejected in a referendum.

1993: the Conservative politician Kim Campbell became Canada's first woman prime minister.

1994: the North American Free Trade Agreement (NAFTA), negotiated in 1992 with the USA and Mexico, came into force.

1995: a further referendum on Quebec's sovereignty was defeated by an extremely narrow margin.

1998–9: the federal government issued an apology to Canada's indigenous people for past mistreatment and injustice. A fund for reparations was established, and the largest native-claim settlement in Canada's history was completed when the eastern part of the Northwest Territories, with an Inuit-dominated population, became the Territory of Nunavut.

2003–4: Quebec's pro-independence party was defeated in provincial elections. Following the resignation of prime minister Jean Chrétien, his fellow Liberal Paul Martin succeeded him in office.

The Provinces

provinces or territories	area (in km²)	number of inhabitants**	capital
Alberta	661 000	2 974 807	Edmonton
British Columbia	950 000	3 907 738	Victoria
Prince Edward Island	5 657	135 294	Charlottetown
Manitoba	600 000	1 119 583	Winnipeg
New Brunswick	73 437	729 498	Fredericton
Nova Scotia	55 490	908 007	Halifax
Nunavut *	1 900 000	26 745	Iqaluit
Ontario	1 068 582	11 410 046	Toronto
Quebec	1 540 680	7 237 479	Quebec
Saskatchewan	652 000	978 933	Regina
Newfoundland	406 000	512 930	Saint John's
Northwest Territories *	1 480 000	37 360	Yellowknife
Yukon *	482 515	28 674	Whitehorse

* denotes territory   ** 2001 census

The Republic of Chile stretches about 4,000km from north to south, and is on average only 100–200km wide. It is made up of a discontinuous central valley that lies between the Andes Mountains to the east and a coastal range to the west. Chile has several different climatic and vegetation zones: the Atacama Desert in the north, a Mediterranean climate in the Santiago region, an oceanic climate around Osorno and a cold and wet alpine climate in the south, where the forests gradually give way to glaciers, fjords and lakes.

Area: 756,626km²
Population (2002): 15,589,000
Capital: Santiago 4,311,133 (1992 census), 5,551,000 (2001 e) including the suburbs
Government type and political system: republic with a presidential system
Head of state and government: (President of the Republic) Ricardo Lagos Escobar
Administrative structure: 13 regions
Official language: Spanish
Currency: Chilean peso

DEMOGRAPHICS

Density: 20 inhab/km²
Percentage of population in urban areas (2001): 86%
Age structure of population (2000): 0–15 years: 28.5%, 15–65 years: 64.3%, over 65 years: 7.2%
Birth rate (2003): 18.2‰
Death rate (2003): 5.6‰
Infant mortality rate (2003): 11.6‰
Life expectancy at birth (2003): male: 73 years, female: 79 years

ECONOMY

GNP (2002): 66 billion US$
GNP per capita (2002): 4,250 US$
GNP per capita PPP (2002): 9,420 international dollars
HDI (2000): 0.831
GDP annual growth rate (2003): 3.3%
Annual inflation rate (2000): 3.84%
Labour force by occupation (2003): agriculture: 13.6%, industry: 23.4%, services: 63%
GDP by sector (2000): agriculture: 10.5%, industry: 33.5%, services: 56%
Gross public debt: n/a

Chile

- ● population over 1,000,000
- ● population 100,000 to 1,000,000
- ● population 50,000 to 100 000
- • population less than 50,000

—— motorway
—— road
—— railway line
▨ regional boundary
Talca regional capital
glacier

✈ airport
★ place of interest

400 1000 2000 4000 m
200 km

Unemployment rate (2002): 7.8%

Agriculture and fishing

Crops
tomatoes (2002): 1,287,000t
sugar beets (2002): 3,540,000t
wheat (2002): 1,820,000t
lemons (2002): 140,000t
maize (2002): 924,000t
walnuts (2001): 12,500t
peaches (2002): 274,000t
apples (2001): 1,075,000t
potatoes (2002): 1,303,000t
grapes (2002): 1,720,000t

Livestock farming and fishing
cattle (2002): 3,566,000 head
horses (2001): 650,000 head
sheep (2002): 3,890,000 head
pigs (2002): 3,100,000 head
chickens (2002): 75,000,000 head
fish (1999): 5,325,000t

Energy generation and mining

silver (2001): 1,240t
copper (2001): 4,739,000t
total electricity (2001): 41,663 million kWh
iron (2001): 5,900,000t
natural gas (2000): 2,702 million m³
molybdenum (2001): 33,000t
gold (2001): 42,673kg
oil (2002): 349,000t
zinc (2001): 31,500t

Industrial production

milk (2001): 2,210,000t
sugar (2002): 576,000t
meat (2001): 956,000t
wine (2002): 5,752,000hl
beer (2000): 3,025,000hl
steel (2003): 1,344,000t
copper (2001): 4,739,300t
cement (2001): 3,500,000t

Tourism

Tourism revenue (2001): 788 million US$

Foreign trade

Exports (2002): 18,340 million US$
Imports (2002): 15,827 million US$

Defence

Armed forces (2001): 80,500 people
Defence budget (2001): 1.78% of GDP

Standard of living

Inhabitants per doctor (1993): 2,150
Average daily calorie intake (2000): 2,881 (FAO minimum: 2,400)
Cars per 1,000 inhabitants (2000): 87
Televisions per 1,000 inhabitants (2001): 286

HISTORY: KEY DATES

The colonial period
Chile was originally inhabited by the Araucanian people, who were dominated by the Incas in the north.
1541: following initial failure by Spanish explorers to establish a presence in Chile, Spanish conquistador Pedro de Valdivia founded Santiago. He went on to establish several other settlements, despite strong resistance from the indigenous people.
⇨

CHILE

HISTORY: KEY DATES

1553: de Valdivia was killed during a massacre of Spanish forces by indigenous people. Spanish colonists were not driven out, and eventually succeeded in defeating the Araucanians.
1778: after a long period of dependency on the Viceroyalty of Peru, Chile became a separate entity within the Spanish empire.

Chilean independence
1810: the movement towards independence began with the formation of a patriotic junta in Santiago.
1814: Chilean insurgents including Bernardo O'Higgins and José Miguel Carrera were defeated by the Spanish at Rancagua.
1817–18: José de San Martín brought an army from Argentina to fight the Spanish; his victory at Maipú liberated the country. O'Higgins became the Supreme Leader of Chile, and an independent republic was proclaimed.
1823–31: O'Higgins' policies were met with strong opposition, forcing his resignation. A period of anarchy followed.
1831–71: under a conservative regime, a constitution was put into place, leading to increased stability.

1871–91: a coalition of liberals and radicals led the country during the War of the Pacific against Peru and Bolivia (1879–84). Chile was victorious, and took possession of all of Bolivia's maritime territory as well as the provinces of Tarapacá, Tacna and Arica, which had belonged to Peru. Disputes over ownership of these provinces, as well as border disputes with Argentina, continued into the twentieth century.

The 20c
1891–1925: the 1891 Chilean Civil War ended in victory for the parliamentary regime over the presidential regime. During World War I, Chile benefited from the exploitation of its natural resources, including copper and nitrates.
1925: the army re-established a presidential regime.
1938–52: government by the Popular Front, a democratic leftist coalition elected in 1938, was succeeded by other centre-left governments which worked to stabilize the economy and improve labour conditions.
1958–70: the conservative government of Jorge Alessandri (1958–64) was followed by the Christian Democrat government of Eduardo Frei Montalva.

1970: the Marxist Salvador Allende, a member of Chile's Socialist Party, was elected president. He set about nationalizing the private industries, the mines and the banks.
1973–4: armed forces bombarded the presidential palace in a military coup, killing Allende. General Augusto Pinochet Ugarte declared a state of emergency and was proclaimed the Supreme Leader of Chile.
1980: a new constitution confirmed the authoritarian character of the regime. However, Pinochet's brutal dictatorship was being met with growing resistance.
1988: Pinochet organized a plebiscite, aimed at ensuring the continuation of his regime. Pinochet lost the plebiscite on whether he should stay in power, but decided to remain head of state until 1990, legally the end of his mandate.
1998–2000: Pinochet was arrested and detained in London, reopening debate over the events of 1970–80. His failing health led to his eventual release and return to Chilean custody. Elections in 2000 made Ricardo Lagos Escobar the first Socialist president of Chile since Allende.

Tierra del Fuego

This mountainous archipelago is located at the end of the Andes Mountains, at the southernmost tip of South America. It is separated from the continent by the Strait of Magellan. Magellan himself, who explored the archipelago in 1520, chose the name Tierra del Fuego (which literally means 'Land of Fire'), inspired by the columns of smoke he saw rising from the Native Americans' fires. Colonized since the 19c, it is divided between Argentina and Chile; the capital of the Argentinian sector of Tierra del Fuego is Ushuaia, the world's most southerly city. The region is mainly covered with forests and is very sparsely populated. It is cold, wet and misty. Whilst its terrestrial fauna is somewhat limited, there is a wealth of marine fauna including whales, dolphins, walruses and seals.

Colombia

★ place of interest

| 400 | 1000 | 2000 | 3000 m |

— road
— railway line
✈ airport

● population over 1,000,000
● population 250,000 to 1,000,000
● population 100,000 to 250,000
• population less than 100,000

The Republic of Colombia is situated in north-western South America on the borders of Central America, and has coastlines on both the Caribbean Sea and the Pacific Ocean. Over half of the country is covered in Amazonian rainforest. The west of the country is dominated by the Andes Mountains, and the east by the llanos (grasslands, seasonally-flooded plains and forests).

Area: 1,138,914km²
Population (2002): 43,495,000
Capital: Bogotá 4,945,448 (1993 census), 6,957,000 (2001 e) including the suburbs
Government type and political system: republic with a presidential system
Head of state and government: (President of the Republic) Álvaro Uribe Vélez
Administrative structure: 32 departments and 1 capital district (Bogotá DC)
Official language: Spanish
Currency: Colombian peso

DEMOGRAPHICS
Density: 37 inhab/km²
Percentage of population in urban areas (2001): 75.5%
Age structure of population (2000): 0–15 years: 32.8%, 15–65 years: 62.5%, over 65 years: 4.7%
Birth rate (2003): 22.2‰
Death rate (2003): 5.4‰
Infant mortality rate (2003): 25.6‰
Life expectancy at birth (2003): male: 69.2 years, female: 75.3 years

ECONOMY
GNP (2002): 80 billion US$
GNP per capita (2002): 1,820 US$
GNP per capita PPP (2002): 6,150 international dollars
HDI (2000): 0.772
GDP annual growth rate (2003): 3.6%
Annual inflation rate (2000): 9.49%
Labour force by occupation (1998): agriculture: 1%, industry: 26.5%, services: 72.5%
GDP by sector (2000): agriculture: 13.8%, industry: 30.5%, services: 55.7%
Gross public debt: n/a
Unemployment rate (2002): 15.7%

Agriculture and fishing
Crops
pineapples (2001): 360,000t
bananas (2001): 1,380,000t
plantains (2001): 2,827,000t
cocoa (2001): 45,200t
coffee (2002): 697,000t
sugar cane (2001): 33,400,000t
yams (2002): 237,000t
manioc (2001): 1,982,000t
oranges (2002): 298,000t
potatoes (2002): 2,841,000t
Livestock farming and fishing
cattle (2002): 24,765,000 head
horses (2001): 2,600,000 head
sheep (2002): 2,045,000 head
pigs (2002): 2,234,000 head
chickens (2002): 115,000,000 head
fish (1999): 171,000t

Energy generation and mining
silver (2001): 7,242t
total electricity (2001): 42,992 million kWh
coal (2001): 43,432,000t
nickel (2001): 53,000t
gold (2001): 21,813kg
oil (2002): 29,700,000t

Industrial production
milk (2001): 5,980,000t
meat (2001): 1,381,000t
sugar (2002): 2,523,000t
palm oil (2001): 560,000t
oil palms (2001): 113,000t
steel (2003): 665,000t
nickel (2001): 53,000t
cotton yarn (2001): 42,000t
cement (2001): 9,800,000t

Tourism
Tourism revenue (2001): 1,209 million US$

Foreign trade
Exports (2002): 12,303 million US$
Imports (2002): 12,077 million US$

Defence
Armed forces (2001): 158,000 people
Defence budget (2001): 1.94% of GDP

Standard of living
Inhabitants per doctor (1993): 1,111
Average daily calorie intake (2000): 2,597 (FAO minimum: 2,400)
Cars per 1,000 inhabitants (1999): 43
Televisions per 1,000 inhabitants (2001): 286

COLOMBIA

HISTORY: KEY DATES

Colonization
During its precolonial period, Colombia was inhabited by Chibcha, sub-Andean and Caribbean peoples.
1500–25: the Spanish conquest of the country began.
1538: Gonzalo Jiménez de Quesada founded Bogotá, and named the area New Granada.
18c: the Viceroyalty of New Granada was created. The colony prospered, exporting precious metals and minerals.

Independence
1810–15: the Spanish government repressed a movement towards independence.
1817–19: revolutionary leader Simón Bolívar continued to fight, and defeated the Spanish at the Battle of Boyacá (1819). At the Congress of Angostura later that year, he proclaimed the Republic of Gran Colombia, comprising New Granada, Venezuela and Panama. He also annexed Ecuador in 1822.
1820: upon Bolívar's death, Venezuela and Ecuador seceded.

Liberals and Conservatives in power
1833–49: after the authoritarian presidency of Francisco de Paula Santander (1833–37), a centralist Conservative government came to power.
1849–52: reforms were carried out under a Liberal government.
1861–64: under the presidency of T C Mosquera, church goods were confiscated, the church was separated from the state and a federal constitution was adopted.
1880–8: the president, Rafael Núñez, re-established ties with the church and granted the country a common constitution.
1899–1903: the 'War of a Thousand Days' between the Liberals and Conservatives devastated the country, and ended in Conservative victory.

The 20c
1903: under pressure from the USA, Colombia accepted the declaration of Panama's independence. Panama became an independent state.
1904–30: political stability was accompanied by economic growth, supported by the trade in coffee and oil.
1930–48: the Liberals returned to power, and attempted to pursue reformist policies.
1948–58: the assassination of the Liberal leader Jorge Gaitán led to a difficult period of violence, martial law and civil war.
1958–70: Liberals and Conservatives agreed to form a National Front coalition and took turns at being in power, fighting to stabilize the country's economy.
1970: over the next three decades, drug cartels and leftist guerrilla groups grew in power and influence. Despite granting amnesty to the guerrillas, the authorities were faced with an increase in violence linked to political tensions and drug trafficking.
1999–2004: economic recession and a devastating earthquake in 1999 further undermined the government's struggle to control Colombia's ongoing internal problems. Some economic recovery and governmental reform followed, but tensions between the government and rebels continued.

The Andes

The Andes Mountains extend over seven countries (Argentina, Bolivia, Chile, Colombia, Ecuador, Peru and Venezuela). Their highest peak is Aconcagua (6,959m). From Venezuela to Tierra del Fuego, the Andes stretch for around 8,000km on the edge of the Pacific, constituting the largest geographical relief in the world, with summits of almost 7,000m and accompanying oceanic trenches of a similar depth.

Once the most densely inhabited part of South America, with populations and agriculture adapted to the high altitudes, the Andes have been partially depopulated since people have moved closer to the coasts. However, several large cities such as Bogotá, Quito and La Paz remain, as well as mines (mainly iron and copper) and oil wells near the coasts.

COSTA RICA

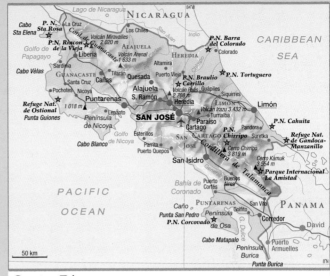

Costa Rica

★ place of interest
200 500 1500 3000 m

— road
— railway line
  provincial boundary
Limón provincial capital

▲ volcano
✈ airport

● population over 100,000
● population 30,000 to 100,000
● population 10,000 to 30,000
• population less than 10,000

The Republic of Costa Rica is bounded to the east by the Caribbean Sea and to the west by the Pacific Ocean. Its terrain is varied, with mountain ranges and plateaux as well as many volcanoes, and one-third of the total land area is covered by forest. The Meseta Central (a high plateau) is the most densely populated part of the country. The coastal areas and the north of Costa Rica are made up of low-lying plains and pasture lands.

Area: 51,100km²
Population (2002): 4,200,000
Capital: San José 983,000 (2001 e) including the suburbs
Government type and political system: republic with a presidential regime
Head of state and government: (President of the Republic) Abel Pacheco de la Espriella
Administrative structure: 7 provinces
Official language: Spanish
Currency: Costa Rican colón

DEMOGRAPHICS

Density: 79 inhab/km²
Percentage of population in urban areas (2001): 59.5%
Age structure of population (2000): 0–15 years: 32.4%, 15–65 years: 62.5%, over 65 years: 5.1%
Birth rate (2003): 19.1‰
Death rate (2003): 3.9‰
Infant mortality rate (2003): 10.5‰
Life expectancy at birth (2003): male: 75.8 years, female: 80.6 years

ECONOMY

GNP (2002): 16.1 billion US$
GNP per capita (2002): 4,070 US$
GNP per capita PPP (2002): 8,560 international dollars
HDI (2000): 0.82
GDP annual growth rate (2003): 5.6%
Annual inflation rate (2000): 10.99%
Labour force by occupation (2001): agriculture: 15.6%, industry: 23.3%, services: 61.1%

GDP by sector (2000): agriculture: 9.4%, industry: 31.2%, services: 59.4%
Gross public debt: n/a
Unemployment rate (2002): 6.1%

Agriculture and fishing
Crops
pineapples (2001): 475,000t
bananas (2001): 2,270,000t
coffee (2002): 141,000t
sugar cane (2001): 3,750,000t
rice (2002): 252,000t
Livestock farming and fishing
cattle (2002): 1,220,000 head
pigs (2002): 535,000 head
fish (1999): 35,000t

Energy generation
total electricity (2001): 6,839 million kWh

Industrial production
milk (2001): 730,000t
meat (2001): 190,000t
palm oil (2001): 130,000t
cement (2001): 1,100,000t

Tourism
Tourism revenue (2001): 1,278 million US$

Foreign trade
Exports (2002): 5,259.3 million US$
Imports (2002): 6,522.7 million US$

Defence
Armed forces (2001): 8,400 people
Defence budget (2001): 0.64% of GDP

Standard of living
Inhabitants per doctor (1993): 1,111

Average daily calorie intake (2000): 2,783 (FAO minimum: 2,400)
Cars per 1,000 inhabitants (1999): 88
Televisions per 1,000 inhabitants (2000): 231

HISTORY: KEY DATES

1563: the Spanish settlement of Cartago was founded, and the indigenous peoples were largely wiped out.
1569: Costa Rica became part of the Captaincy General of Guatemala.
1821–3: the country became independent from Spain, and for a short time was part of the Mexican empire.
1824–39: Costa Rica became one of the five republics of the Central American Federation before becoming a sovereign state in 1839.
19c: the cultivation of coffee and bananas brought economic prosperity, eventually leading to the establishment of democracy. The United Fruit Company was founded, and Costa Rica became economically dependent on the USA.
1949–74: José Figueres Ferrer, co-founder of the National Liberation Party (PLN), was elected president in 1949 and dominated political life for the next twenty-five years.
1987–9: Costa Rica, Guatemala, Honduras, Nicaragua and El Salvador signed agreements aimed at re-establishing peace in Central America.

CUBA

Situated less than 250km south of Florida, the Republic of Cuba comprises an archipelago which includes the largest island in the Caribbean Sea. Cuba contains many plains and limestone plateaux, with more rugged hills and mountains in the south-east. Due to the country's latitude, the climate is tropical with a constant temperature (around 25°C), and relatively heavy rainfall (1,200mm) which mainly falls in the wet season between June and December.

Area: 110,861km²
Population (2002): 11,272,000
Capital: Havana 2,268,000 (2001 census)
Government type and political system: republic with a socialist regime
Head of state and government: (President) Fidel Castro
Administrative structure: 14 provinces and 1 municipality
Official language: Spanish
Currency: Cuban peso

DEMOGRAPHICS

Density: 101 inhab/km²
Percentage of population in urban areas (2001): 75.5%
Age structure of population (2000): 0–15 years: 21.2%, 15–65 years: 69.2%, over 65 years: 9.6%
Birth rate (2003): 11.6‰
Death rate (2003): 7.2‰
Infant mortality rate (2003): 7.3‰
Life expectancy at birth (2003): male: 74.8 years, female: 78.7 years

ECONOMY

GNP: n/a
GNP per capita: n/a
GNP per capita PPP: n/a
HDI (2000): 0.795
GDP annual growth rate (2000): 5.6%
Annual inflation rate: n/a
Labour force by occupation: n/a
GDP by sector (2000): agriculture: 6.7%, industry: 46.4%, services: 46.9%
Gross public debt: n/a
Unemployment rate: n/a

Agriculture and fishing

Crops
citrus fruits (2001): 546,000t
pineapples (2001): 19,000t
bananas (2001): 180,000t
plantains (2001): 380,000t
coffee (2002): 15,000t
sugar cane (2001): 35,000,000t
maize (2002): 309,000t
manioc (2001): 300,000t
oranges (2002): 297,000t
grapefruits (2001): 170,000t
potatoes (2002): 345,000t
rice (2002): 692,000t
tobacco (2001): 35,000t

Livestock farming and fishing

cattle (2002): 3,972,000 head
horses (2001): 400,000 head
goats (2001): 240,000 head
sheep (2002): 310,000 head
pigs (2002): 1,554,000 head
chickens (2002): 24,200,000 head
fish (1999): 122,000t

Energy generation and mining

chromium (2001): 50,000t
total electricity (2001): 14,385 million kWh
hydroelectricity (2001): 93 million kWh
nickel (2001): 71,000t
oil (2002): 1,992,000t

Industrial production

milk (2001): 614,000t
meat (2001): 252,000t
sugar (2002): 3,775,000t
steel (2003): 211,000t
nickel (2001): 71,000t
cotton yarn (1998): 5,000t
cement (2001): 1,700,000t

Tourism

Tourism revenue (2001): 1,692 million US$

Foreign trade

Exports (1997): 1,755 million US$
Imports (1997): 2,642 million US$

Defence

Armed forces (2001): 46,000 people
Defence budget (2001): 3.82% of GDP

Standard of living

Inhabitants per doctor (1990): 278
Average daily calorie intake (2000): 2,564 (FAO minimum: 2,400)
Cars per 1,000 inhabitants (1997): 16
Televisions per 1,000 inhabitants (2001): 251

114

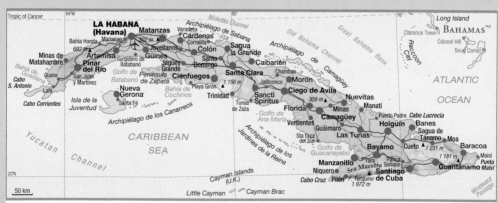

Cuba

200 500 1000 m

—— road
—— railway line
✈ airport

● population over 1,000,000
● population 100,000 to 1,000,000
● population 10,000 to 100,000
· population less than 10,000

50 km

DOMINICA ➜ LESSER ANTILLES

HISTORY: KEY DATES

The colonial period

The island's earliest inhabitants were the Ciboney and Arawak people.

1492: Christopher Columbus visited Cuba.

1511: Diego Velázquez de Cuéllar began the conquest of Cuba. The indigenous peoples were largely wiped out by early colonists, and African slaves took their place as labourers.

1762: the city of Havana was captured by British forces, but was returned to Spain under the Treaty of Paris the following year.

1818: Spain allowed Cuba to trade with the rest of the world. The slave trade was at its height, and Spain struggled to repress slave rebellions.

1868–78: abuse by the colonial administration led to a general uprising known as the Ten Years' War. Cuba obtained a limited amount of autonomy.

1886: slavery was abolished.

1895: the second war of independence broke out, led by the poet and revolutionary José Martí.

1898–1902: after the battleship USS Maine exploded while lying at anchor in Havana harbour, the USA went to war against Spain. Spain was then forced to relinquish all claims to Cuba, which was established as an independent republic.

Independence

1902: the Republic of Cuba was granted a constitution, but remained under official US protection. The USA retained the right to intervene in the island's affairs, and strengthened its economic domination. An economic boom during World War I was followed by collapse, and corrupt political regimes did little to improve the situation.

1925–33: the dictatorial president Gerardo Machado failed to follow through on planned economic and social improvements, and was eventually overthrown by the army.

1933–44: General Fulgencio Batista, protected by the USA, seized power in 1933 and ruled as a dictator until 1940, when he was elected president.

1952: Batista again seized power in a bloodless coup and suspended the constitution.

1953: after leading an unsuccessful revolt against the Batista regime, Fidel Castro was imprisoned and went into exile in Mexico.

1956: Castro returned to eastern Cuba and took to the maquis in the Sierra Maestra, where he assembled a guerrilla army.

1959: Castro's army forced Batista to flee the country.

Fidel Castro's regime

When he became leader, Castro pursued nationalization policies that led to a US embargo on Cuban trade. The USSR was supportive of the new Cuban regime.

1961: an attempted invasion by anti-Castro Cuban exiles at the Bay of Pigs, supported by the USA, failed.

1962: the installation of Soviet nuclear missile bases in Cuba led to the international incidents that became known as the Cuban Missile Crisis.

1965–79: the hardening of the regime (nationalization of private companies; military training in schools) was accompanied by massive emigration, particularly to the US city of Miami, Florida. Cuba received economic and military aid from the USSR, and in return lent its support to Soviet foreign

policy. Cuba sent troops to Africa to help Angola's left-wing MPLA in 1975, and to help Ethiopia defeat the Eritreans and Somalis in 1977.

1976: Castro became president of the Republic of Cuba.

1979: Cuba became president of the movement of non-aligned countries.

1980: the emigration of Cubans to Florida continued until it was halted by the Cuban government.

1989–90: Cuba withdrew its troops from Africa.

1993: the US dollar became legal tender in Cuba, eventually leading to a severe economic divide.

1994: a new wave of Cuban emigrants tried to enter Florida, leading to tensions with the USA. Weakened by the collapse of the Eastern Bloc countries and the disintegration of the USSR, the regime continued to follow a Marxist orthodoxy, despite some concessions to a market economy.

1996: the US economic embargo was made permanent during a time of increased political tension between the USA and Cuba.

1998: the visit of Pope John Paul II to the island marked Cuba's return to the international scene, and US restrictions were relaxed very slightly. Investment from Canada, Europe and Latin America had a positive impact on the Cuban economy.

2002: former US president Jimmy Carter visited Cuba and criticized its treatment at the hands of the USA.

2004: US President George W Bush strengthened some aspects of the embargo.

The Cuban Missile Crisis

This is the name given to the crisis that occurred between the USA and the USSR in 1962, centring around the installation of Soviet nuclear missile bases in Cuba. In September 1962, acting on evidence that bases for offensive weapons were being constructed, President John F Kennedy decided to impose a naval blockade on Cuba. This prevented arms being sent to Cuba in Soviet freighters. The USSR protested vehemently, and for a time the two countries appeared to be on the brink of a nuclear war. Soviet premier Nikita Khrushchev finally proposed a solution to the crisis. He agreed that the USSR would withdraw its missiles under UN control, if Cuba promised not to receive any arms in the future and the USA pledged not to invade Cuba. On 28th October 1962 the crisis was resolved along these lines, and work to dismantle the missile sites began on 12th November. The blockade was then lifted on 20th November. All missiles and bombers were removed from Cuba by the end of the year.

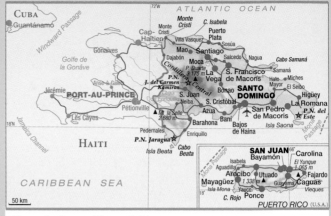

The Dominican Republic comprises the eastern two-thirds of the island of Hispaniola, with Haiti occupying the western part. It has a moderate subtropical climate with fertile soil and ample rainfall. In the centre and the west are several mountain ranges; in the east are rolling hills and plains.

Dominican Republic

200	500	1000	2000 m

★ place of interest
— road
✈ airport

● population over 1,000,000
● population 100,000 to 1,000,000
● population 30,000 to 100,000
• population less than 30,000

Area: 48,511km²
Population (2002): 8,640,000
Capital: Santo Domingo 2,629,000 (2001 e) including the suburbs
Government type and political system: republic with a presidential system
Head of state and government: (President of the Republic) Leonel Fernandez
Administrative structure: 29 provinces and 1 district
Official language: Spanish
Currency: Dominican peso

DEMOGRAPHICS

Density: 176 inhab/km²
Percentage of population in urban areas (2001): 66%
Age structure of population (2000): 0–15 years: 33.5%, 15–65 years: 62.2%, over 65 years: 4.3%
Birth rate (2003): 23.3‰
Death rate (2003): 7‰
Infant mortality rate (2003): 35.7‰
Life expectancy at birth (2003): male: 64.4 years, female: 69.2 years

ECONOMY

GNP (2002): 17.9 billion US$
GNP per capita (2002): 2,140 US$
GNP per capita PPP (2002): 6,270 international dollars
HDI (2000): 0.727
GDP annual growth rate (2003): –1.3%
Annual inflation rate (2001): 8.9%
Labour force by occupation (1997): agriculture: 19.9%, industry: 25.1%, services: 55%
GDP by sector (2000): agriculture: 11.1%, industry: 34.1%, services: 54.8%
Gross public debt: n/a
Unemployment rate (1997): 15.9%

Agriculture and fishing

Crops
bananas (2001): 445,000t
plantains (2001): 343,000t
cocoa (2001): 44,900t
coffee (2002): 49,000t

sugar cane (2001): 4,645,000t
manioc (2001): 124,000t
oranges (2002): 86,000t
rice (2002): 731,000t
tobacco (2001): 17,500t
tomatoes (2002): 155,000t

Livestock farming and fishing
cattle (2002): 2,160,000 head
horses (2001): 330,000 head
pigs (2002): 577,000 head
chickens (2002): 46,000,000 head
fish (1999): 9,270t

Energy generation and mining

silver (1999): 3.14t
total electricity (2001): 9,186 million kWh
nickel (2001): 31,000t
gold (2000): 650kg

Industrial production

milk (2001): 410,000t

meat (2001): 338,000t
sugar (2002): 494,000t
beer (2000): 3,500,000hl
cement (2001): 2,000,000t

Tourism

Tourism revenue (2001): 2,689 million US$

Foreign trade

Exports (2002): 5,183.4 million US$
Imports (2002): 8,882.5 million US$

Defence

Armed forces (2001): 24,500 people
Defence budget (2001): 0.69% of GDP

Standard of living

Inhabitants per doctor (1993): 909
Average daily calorie intake (2000): 2,325 (FAO minimum: 2,400)
Cars per 1,000 inhabitants (1996): 27
Televisions per 1,000 inhabitants (1998): 96

HISTORY: KEY DATES

1492: Christopher Columbus reached the island, which he named Hispaniola ('Little Spain').
16c–18c: Spanish colonization led to the disappearance of the island's original inhabitants, the Tainos.
1697: the Treaty of Ryswick gave Haiti to France and the Dominican Republic to Spain.
1795: Spain ceded its part of Hispaniola to France.
1822–44: the whole of the island was ruled by Haiti.
1844: the Dominican Republic became independent.
1861: in order to ward off Haitian aggression, the Dominican Republic voluntarily returned to the Spanish empire.
1865–1905: independence was restored. A period of chaos and revolution followed, with numerous leadership changes, until the country became bankrupt.
1905–24: the US government arranged a customs receivership in the country, gaining fiscal control and political domination. In 1916, US marines occupied the country and established a military government, favouring the arrival of General Rafael Leónidas Trujillo Molina.
1930–61: Trujillo established a dictatorship that lasted until his assassination in 1961.
1962–3: Juan Bosch was elected president in 1962, but was ousted in a right-wing military coup in 1963.
1965: military intervention by the USA led to a planned election in which Bosch lost the presidency.
1996–2003: some economic growth took place under successive democratic leaders, but a severe fiscal crisis in 2003 led to nationwide strikes.

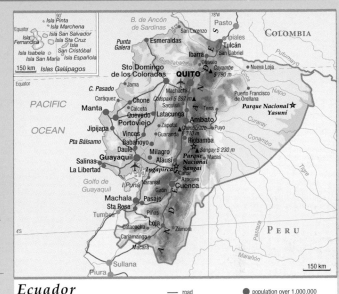

In the Republic of Ecuador the Andes Mountains form high plateaux dominated by volcanoes, and separate the coastal plain – broader and wetter in the north – from the eastern, Amazonian region, which is covered in dense rainforests. Ecuador also includes the Galápagos Islands.

Area: 283,561km²
Population (2002): 13,112,000
Capital: Quito 1,660,000 (2001 e)
Government type and political system: republic with a presidential system
Head of state and government: (President of the Republic) Lucio Gutiérrez
Administrative structure: 21 provinces
Official language: Spanish
Currency: US dollar

DEMOGRAPHICS

Density: 47 inhab/km²
Percentage of population in urban areas (2001): 63.4%
Age structure of population (2000): 0–15 years: 33.8%, 15–65 years: 61.5%, over 65 years: 4.7%
Birth rate (2003): 23‰
Death rate (2003): 5.8‰
Infant mortality rate (2003): 41.5‰
Life expectancy at birth (2003): male: 68.3 years, female: 73.5 years

ECONOMY

GNP (2002): 19.1 billion US$
GNP per capita (2002): 1,490 US$
GNP per capita PPP (2002): 3,340 international dollars
HDI (2000): 0.732
GDP annual growth rate (2003): 2.6%
Annual inflation rate (2001): 37.7%
Labour force by occupation (1998): agriculture: 7.3%, industry: 21.4%, services: 71.3%
GDP by sector (2000): agriculture: 10%, industry: 40.2%, services: 49.8%
Gross public debt: n/a
Unemployment rate (2002): 9.3%

Agriculture and fishing

Crops
bananas (2001): 7,561,000t
plantains (2001): 476,000t
cocoa (2001): 107,000t
coffee (2002): 179,000t
sugar cane (2001): 5,962,000t
maize (2002): 602,000t

oil palms (2001): 46,300t
potatoes (2002): 485,000t
rice (2002): 1,285,000t
Livestock farming and fishing
cattle (2002): 5,578,000 head
horses (2001): 525,000 head
sheep (2002): 2,381,000 head
pigs (2002): 2,806,000 head
chickens (2002): 140,000,000 head
fish (1999): 625,000t

Energy generation and mining

total electricity (2001): 10,741 million kWh
natural gas (1996): 1,057 million m³
gold (2001): 2,297kg
oil (2002): 20,800,000t

Industrial production

palm oil (2001): 280,308t

cement (2001): 2,800,000t

Tourism

Tourism revenue (2001): 430 million US$

Foreign trade

Exports (2002): 5,192 million US$
Imports (2002): 6,196 million US$

Defence

Armed forces (2001): 59,500 people
Defence budget (2001): 1.92% of GDP

Standard of living

Inhabitants per doctor (1993): 960
Average daily calorie intake (2000): 2,693 (FAO minimum: 2,400)
Cars per 1,000 inhabitants (1999): 43
Televisions per 1,000 inhabitants (2001): 225

HISTORY: KEY DATES

1534: Sebastián de Benalcázar passed through the area without establishing a significant Spanish presence there.
1563: the Spanish created the audiencia (administrative district) of Quito, which was attached to the Viceroyalty of Peru, then to that of New Grenada (1739).
1822: the country was liberated from the Spanish and became part of Gran Colombia (with present-day Colombia and Venezuela).
1830: the fully independent Republic of Ecuador was created.
1845–95: a struggle for power between Liberal and Conservative politicians with strongly opposed ideologies dominated political life.
1895–1930: a Liberal government secularized the state.
1934: José María Velasco Ibarra was elected president for the first of six terms.
1941–2: Ecuador lost its Amazonian territory in a war with Peru.
1972: Velasco was overthrown in a military coup.
1979: after constitutional reform, there was a return to democracy with a civilian government.
1990–2: indigenous peoples were given title to a significant area of rainforest land.
1992–2004: a series of changes of government through elections and coups was accompanied by environmental crises and economic recession. In 2001, the US dollar was adopted as the national currency in an attempt to stabilize the economy.

EL SALVADOR

agriculture: 22.1%, industry: 25%, services: 52.9%
GDP by sector (2000): agriculture: 10.2%, industry: 30.2%, services: 59.6%
Gross public debt: n/a
Unemployment rate (2002): 10.2%

Agriculture
Crops
coffee (2002): 92,000t
sugar cane (2001): 4,589,000t
jute (1997): 7,000t
maize (2002): 644,000t
sorghum (2002): 141,000t
Livestock farming
cattle (2002): 1,100,000 head
horses (2001): 96,000 head
pigs (2002): 153,000 head

Energy generation
total electricity (2001): 3,729 million kWh

Industrial production
sugar (2002): 476,000t
cement (2001): 2,500,000t

Tourism
Tourism revenue (2001): 235 million US$

Foreign trade
Exports (2002): 3,016.8 million US$
Imports (2002): 4,922.3 million US$

Defence
Armed forces (2001): 16,800 people
Defence budget (2001): 0.82% of GDP

Standard of living
Inhabitants per doctor (1993): 1,429
Average daily calorie intake (2000): 2,503 (FAO minimum: 2,400)
Cars per 1,000 inhabitants (1997): 30
Televisions per 1,000 inhabitants (2000): 201

The Republic of El Salvador is a mountainous and volcanic country that borders the Pacific Ocean. It is the smallest state in Central America, but also the most densely populated. The coastal climate is tropical (hot and humid), while the inland climate is moderated by altitude.

Area: 21,041km²
Population (2002): 6,520,000
Capital: San Salvador 1,381,000 (2001 e) including the suburbs
Government type and political system: republic with a presidential system
Head of state and government: (President of the Republic) Elias Antonio Saca
Administrative structure: 14 departments
Official language: Spanish
Currencies: Salvadoran colon and the US dollar

DEMOGRAPHICS
Density: 299 inhab/km²
Percentage of population in urban areas (2001): 61.3%

Age structure of population (2000): 0–15 years: 35.6%, 15–65 years: 59.4%, over 65 years: 5%
Birth rate (2003): 25.1‰
Death rate (2003): 5.9‰
Infant mortality rate (2003): 26.4‰
Life expectancy at birth (2003): male: 67.7 years, female: 73.7 years

ECONOMY
GNP (2002): 13.6 billion US$
GNP per capita (2002): 2,110 US$
GNP per capita PPP (2002): 4,790 international dollars
HDI (2000): 0.706
GDP annual growth rate (2003): 2.2%
Annual inflation rate (2001): 0.1%
Labour force by occupation (1999):

HISTORY: KEY DATES
1524: the Spanish conquered the region.
1821–2: after achieving independence from Spain, El Salvador became part of the Mexican empire until its collapse.
1823–39: El Salvador became part of the Central American Federation.
1841: El Salvador became a fully independent republic.
LATE 19c–EARLY 20c: bitter ideological conflict between Liberals and Conservatives led to ongoing political unrest.
1969: El Salvador fought Honduras in what became known as the Football War.
1972: José Napoléon Duarte was elected president but was subsequently exiled by the army. For several years, guerrilla warfare and terrorism held sway; civil war broke out in 1980.
1987–9: agreements were signed with neighbouring countries with the aim of restoring peace in Central America.
1992: the Chapultepec Peace Accords between the government and the guerrillas were signed in Mexico, ending the civil war. Economic and land reforms began to take effect.
1998–2001: the country was devastated by natural disasters, including a hurricane and two major earthquakes.

The Football War

To ease the problem of overpopulation, El Salvador has for many years sent workers to Honduras. Agrarian reform undertaken by Honduras to the detriment of the Salvadoran immigrants led to an outbreak of disturbances in June 1969, when passion for football was used as a pretext for letting off political and nationalistic steam. El Salvador and Honduras were competing for the chance to take part in the finals of the 1970 football World Cup. On 8th June, the Honduran team defeated the Salvadoran team. The return match on 15th June ended in a victory for El Salvador: the violent reaction of the Honduran population led to the exodus of thousands of Salvadorans. Another match took place in Mexico at the end of June; El Salvador won, and again the result was violence against Salvadoran nationals. On 14th July 1969, Salvadoran troops entered Honduras, but the conflict lasted for only four days; the Organization of American States ordered an immediate ceasefire and the withdrawal of the Salvadoran troops from Honduras.

French Guiana

- road
— railway line
✈ airport
200 500 1000 m

- ● population over 50,000
- ● population 20,000 to 50,000
- ● population 10,000 to 20,000
- ● population 5,000 to 10,000
- · population less than 5,000

The Department of Guiana is an overseas department of France situated on mainland South America. Its coastal plains give way to a low inland plateau, with hills and small mountains in the south. The climate is equatorial, with heavy rainfall throughout the year.

Area: 91,000km²
Population (2004 e): 191,309
Capital: Cayenne
Government type and political system: overseas department of France
Head of state: (President of the Republic) Jacques Chirac
Head of government: (Prime Minister) Jean-Pierre Raffarin
Administrative structure: 2 regions
Official language: French
Currency: euro

DEMOGRAPHICS

Density: n/a

Percentage of population in urban areas: n/a
Age structure of the population (2004 e):
0–14 years: 29.6%, 15–64 years: 64.5%, over 65 years: 5.9%
Birth rate (2004 e): 21‰
Death rate (2004 e): 4.8‰
Infant mortality rate (2004 e): 12.5‰
Life expectancy at birth (2004 e): male: 73.6 years, female: 80.4 years

ECONOMY

GNP: n/a

GNP per capita: n/a
GNP per capita PPP: n/a
HDI: n/a
GDP annual growth rate: n/a
Annual inflation rate (2002 e): 1.5%
Labour force by occupation (1980):
agriculture: 18.2%, industry: 21.2%, services: 60.6%
GDP by sector: n/a
Gross public debt: n/a
Unemployment rate (2002): 22%

Energy generation
total electricity (2001): 455 million kWh

Foreign trade
Exports (2002 e): 155 million US$
Imports (2002 e): 625 million US$

Defence
Armed forces (2004): 0 (defence is the responsibility of France)
Defence budget (2004): 0 (defence is the responsibility of France)

Standard of living
Inhabitants per doctor: n/a
Average daily calorie intake: n/a (FAO minimum: 2,400)
Cars per 1,000 inhabitants: n/a
Televisions per 1,000 inhabitants: n/a

HISTORY: KEY DATES

1500: European explorers reached the coast of present-day French Guiana.
1604: the French settled the territory.
18c: France began to use French Guiana as a penal settlement, establishing notoriously harsh penal colonies that remained in place until the end of World War II, when the territory became an overseas department of France.

The southern part of the Republic of Guatemala is covered in mountains, some of which are volcanic. There are low plateaux in the north of the country.

Area: 108,889km²
Population (2002): 11,995,000
Capital: Guatemala City 3,366,000 (2001 e)
Government type and political system: republic with a presidential system
Head of state and government: (President of the Republic) Óscar Berger
Administrative structure: 22 departments
Official currency: Spanish
Currency: quetzal

Guatemala

★ place of interest
  200 500 1500 3000 m

— road
— railway line
✈ airport

● population over 500,000
● population 100,000 to 500,000
● population 10,000 to 100,000
• population less than 10,000

DEMOGRAPHICS

Density: 104 inhab/km²
Percentage of population in urban areas (2001): 40%
Age structure of population (2000): 0–15 years: 43.6%, 15–65 years: 52.9%, over 65 years: 3.5%
Birth rate (2003): 34.2‰
Death rate (2003): 6.7‰
Infant mortality rate (2003): 41.2‰
Life expectancy at birth (2003): male: 63 years, female: 68.9 years

ECONOMY

GNP (2002): 21 billion US$
GNP per capita (2002): 1,760 US$
GNP per capita PPP (2002): 4,030 international dollars
HDI (2000): 0.631
GDP annual growth rate (2003): 2.1%
Annual inflation rate (2000): 5.98%
Labour force by occupation: n/a
GDP by sector (2000): agriculture: 22.8%, industry: 19.9%, services: 57.3%
Gross public debt: n/a
Unemployment rate (2002): 1.8%

Agriculture and fishing

Crops
coffee (2002): 180,000t
sugar cane (2001): 16,935,000t
rubber (2001): 47,500t
lemons (2002): 143,000t
Livestock farming and fishing
cattle (2002): 2,400,000 head
horses (2001): 120,000 head
sheep (2002): 250,000 head

pigs (2002): 800,000 head
chickens (2002): 26,000,000 head
fish (1999): 15,900t

Energy generation and mining
total electricity (2001): 6,237 million kWh
oil (2002): 1,170,000t

Industrial production
sugar (2002): 1,912,000t
cement (2001): 1,600,000t

Tourism
Tourism revenue (2001): 493 million US$

Foreign trade
Exports (2002): 2,628.4 million US$
Imports (2002): 5,578.4 million US$

Defence
Armed forces (2001): 31,400 people
Defence budget (2001): 0.52% of GDP

Standard of living
Inhabitants per doctor (1993): 3,333
Average daily calorie intake (2000): 2,171 (FAO minimum: 2,400)
Cars per 1,000 inhabitants (1999): 52
Televisions per 1,000 inhabitants (2000): 61

HISTORY: KEY DATES

During the first millennium, Guatemala was one of the centres of the flourishing Mayan civilization.
1524: the Spanish, led by Pedro de Alvarado, conquered Guatemala.
1821–3: Guatemala joined the Mexican empire.
1824–39: Guatemala became part of the Central American Federation.
1839: the country regained its independence under the Conservative dictator Rafael Carrera.
1873–85: the Liberal president Justo Rufino Barrios modernized the country.
1898–1920: his successor, Manuel José Estrada Cabrera, continued the work of modernization.
1931–44: Jorge Ubico became president and ruled as a dictator. Guatemala

declared war on the Axis powers in 1941.
1951–4: the reformist president Jacobo Arbenz Guzmán was overthrown in a military coup backed by the USA. A guerrilla movement was formed, and civil war broke out.
1970–82: a state of siege was declared in an unsuccessful bid to curtail guerrilla violence; the kidnapping and murder of labour and political leaders was common. Fraudulent elections only exacerbated the crisis of leadership.
1987–9: agreements were signed with neighbouring countries with the aim of restoring peace in Central America.
1996: a peace agreement was signed between the government of president Álvaro Arzú Irigoyen and the guerrillas, ending the 36-year civil war.

Guyana

★	place of interest
—	road
✈	airport
●	population over 200,000
●	population 10,000 to 200,000
•	population less than 10,000

100   200   500   1000 m

The Co-operative Republic of Guyana has a tropical, hot and humid climate. Forests, divided by strongly flowing rivers that serve as transport links, cover three-quarters of the country. The altitude rises in the south, where there is a drier climate, and in the west.

Area: 214,969km²
Population (2002): 766,000
Capital: Georgetown 280,000 (2001 e) including the suburbs
Government type and political system: republic with a parliamentary system
Head of state: (President of the Republic) Bharrat Jagdeo
Head of government: (Prime Minister) Samuel Hinds
Administrative structure: 10 regions
Official language: English
Currency: Guyanese dollar

DEMOGRAPHICS

Density: 4 inhab/km²
Percentage of population in urban areas (2001): 36.7%
Age structure of population (2000): 0–15 years: 30.6%, 15–65 years: 64.4%, over 65 years: 5%
Birth rate (2003): 21.9‰
Death rate (2003): 9‰
Infant mortality rate (2003): 51.2‰
Life expectancy at birth (2003): male: 60.1 years, female: 66.3 years

ECONOMY

GNP (2002): 0.656 billion US$
GNP per capita (2002): 860 US$
GNP per capita PPP (2002): 3,940 international dollars
HDI (2000): 0.708
GDP annual growth rate (2003): –0.2%
Annual inflation rate (2001): 2.7%
Labour force by occupation: n/a
GDP structure (1999): agriculture: 35.1%, industry: 28.5%, services: 36.4%

Gross public debt: n/a
Unemployment rate: n/a

Agriculture and fishing

Crops
sugar cane (2001): 3,000,000t
rice (2002): 444,000t
Livestock farming and fishing
cattle (2002): 100,000 head
chickens (2002): 12,500,000 head
fish (1999): 54,000t

Energy generation and mining

bauxite (2001): 1,985,000t
total electricity (2001): 852 million kWh
gold (2001): 14,183kg

Industrial production

beer (2000): 118,000hl
sugar (2002): 331,000t

Tourism

Tourism revenue (1999): 59 million US$

Foreign trade

Exports (2002): 494.9 million US$
Imports (2002): 536.1 million US$

Defence

Armed forces (2001): 1,600 people
Defence budget (2001): 0.74% of GDP

Standard of living

Inhabitants per doctor (1995): 8,947
Average daily calorie intake (2000): 2,582 (FAO minimum: 2,400)
Cars per 1,000 inhabitants: n/a
Televisions per 1,000 inhabitants (2000): 81

121

HISTORY: KEY DATES

1621–1791: Dutch colonists developed sugar cane and cotton plantations in Guyana.
1814: the British, having occupied Guyana since 1796, took control of the western part of the country (British Guiana).
1834: slavery was abolished.
1966–70: the country achieved full independence and became a republic within the Commonwealth of Nations.
1980s–2004: many state-owned industries were privatized under successive governments. Ongoing ethnic conflict meant that the standard of living for most of the population remained low.

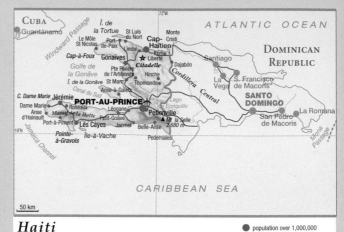

Haiti

| place of interest |
| road |
| airport |

- ● population over 1,000,000
- ● population 100,000 to 1,000,000
- ● population 30,000 to 100,000
- ● population less than 30,000

200   500   1000   2000 m

The Republic of Haiti occupies the western third of the island of Hispaniola. It has a tropical climate, and the east of the country receives more rain than the west, which is often devastated by cyclones. A series of mountain ranges and valleys filled with alluvia runs across the country from north to south.

Area: 27,750km²
Population (2002): 8,400,000
Capital: Port-au-Prince 1,838,000 (2001 e) including the suburbs
Government type and political system: republic with a semi-presidential system
Head of state: (Interim President of the Republic) Boniface Alexandre
Head of government: (Interim Prime Minister) Gérard Latortue
Administrative structure: 9 departments
Official languages: Creole and French
Currency: gourde

DEMOGRAPHICS

Density: 296 inhab/km²
Percentage of population in urban areas (2001): 36.3%
Age structure of population (2000): 0–15 years: 40.6%, 15–65 years: 55.7%, over 65 years: 3.7%
Birth rate (2003): 30.3‰
Death rate (2003): 14.6‰
Infant mortality rate (2003): 63.2‰
Life expectancy at birth (2003): male: 49 years, female: 50 years

ECONOMY

GNP (2002): 3.61 billion US$
GNP per capita (2002): 440 US$
GNP per capita PPP (2002): 1,610 international dollars
HDI (2000): 0.471
GDP annual growth rate (2003): −1.1%
Annual inflation rate (2001): 16.7%
Labour force by population: n/a
GDP by sector (2000): agriculture: 28.4%, industry: 20.2%, services: 51.4%
Gross public debt: n/a
Unemployment rate: n/a

Agriculture

Crops
bananas (2001): 290,000t
coffee (2002): 30,000t
sugar cane (2001): 1,008,000t
yams (2002): 198,000t
maize (2002): 185,000t
sweet potatoes (2001): 174,000t
sisal (2001): 5,660t
Livestock farming
cattle (2002): 1,450,000 head
goats (2001): 1,942,000 head
horses (2001): 501,000 head
pigs (2002): 1,001,000 head

Energy generation
total electricity (2001): 580 million kWh

Tourism
Tourism revenue (1999): 55 million US$

Foreign trade
Exports (1998): 299.3 million US$
Imports (1998): 640.7 million US$

Defence
Armed forces (2001): n/a
Defence budget (2001): 1.17% of GDP

Standard of living
Inhabitants per doctor (1995): 10,855
Average daily calorie intake (2000): 2,056 (FAO minimum: 2,400)
Cars per 1,000 inhabitants (1996): 4
Televisions per 1,000 inhabitants (2001): 6

HISTORY: KEY DATES

1492: Christopher Columbus visited the island (which was originally inhabited by Arawak-speaking peoples) and named it Hispaniola (Little Spain).
1697: the Treaty of Ryswick gave Haiti to France.
18c: Haiti became the most prosperous of all the French colonies. Around 90% of the population were black slaves, emancipated slaves and mulattoes.
1791: a former slave, Toussaint Louverture, led a rebellion that would last until independence was achieved.
1804: with help from the USA, the French were driven out, and Haiti declared its independence.
1806–18: secession divided Haiti into a northern kingdom and a southern republic.
1822: Hispaniola was reunified under Haitian control.
1844: the eastern part of the island became independent again as the Dominican Republic.
1859: Haiti became a republic after the death of its last emperor.
1915–34: US troops occupied Haiti.
1957–71: François Duvalier ('Papa Doc') was elected president, and eventually established a dictatorship.
1971–86: following Duvalier's death, his son Jean-Claude Duvalier ('Baby Doc') succeeded him and also declared himself president for life. In 1986, Baby Doc was forced to flee Haiti in the wake of a serious political crisis.
1990: Jean-Bertrand Aristide became the country's first democratically-elected president, but was overthrown shortly afterwards in a military coup.
1994–2004: Aristide was returned to power, but ongoing violent opposition to his government led to his exile in 2004, the 200th anniversary of Haitian independence.

Honduras

	road	★ place of interest	● population over 500,000
200 500 1500 m	--- railway line	✈ airport	● population 100,000 to 500,000
			● population 50,000 to 100,000
			● population less than 50,000

The Republic of Honduras is a mountainous, forested country with a relatively humid and temperate climate. It has an outlet to the Pacific Ocean via the Golfo de Fonseca, and a much longer coastline facing the Caribbean Sea. Offshore, in the Caribbean, lie the Islas de la Bahia (Bay Islands).

Area: 112,088km²
Population (2002): 6,732,000
Capital: Tegucigalpa 980,000 (2001 e)
Government type and political system: republic with a presidential system
Head of state and government: (President of the Republic) Ricardo Maduro Joest
Administrative structure: 18 departments
Official language: Spanish
Currency: Honduran lempira

DEMOGRAPHICS

Density: 58 inhab/km²
Percentage of population in urban areas (2001): 53.6%
Age structure of population (2000): 0–15 years: 41.8%, 15–65 years: 54.8%, over 65 years: 3.4%
Birth rate (2003): 30‰
Death rate (2003): 5.7‰
Infant mortality rate (2003): 32.1‰
Life expectancy at birth (2003): male: 66.5 years, female: 71.4 years

ECONOMY

GNP (2002): 6.32 billion US$
GNP per capita (2002): 930 US$
GNP per capita PPP (2002): 2,540 international dollars
HDI (2000): 0.638
GDP annual growth rate (2003): 3%
Annual inflation rate (2001): 9.7%
Labour force by occupation (1998) : agriculture: 34.6%, industry: 23%, services: 42.4%
GDP by sector (2000): agriculture: 17.7%, industry: 31.6%, services: 50.7%
Gross public debt: n/a

Unemployment rate (2002): 4.2%

Agriculture

Crops
bananas (2001): 457,000t
plantains (2001): 240,000t
coffee (2002): 182,000t
sugar cane (2001): 4,117,000t
maize (2002): 392,000t
oil palms (2001): 22,300t
Livestock farming
cattle (2002): 1,860,000 head
horses (2001): 180,000 head
pigs (2002): 538,000 head

Energy generation and mining

silver (2001): 35t
total electricity (2001): 3,778 million kWh
lead (2001): 6,800t
zinc (2001): 32,600t

Industrial production

palm oil (2001): 94,000t
sugar (2002): 337,000t
beer (2000): 870,000hl
cement (2001): 1,100,000t

Tourism

Tourism revenue (2000): 240 million US$

Foreign trade

Exports (2002): 1,930.4 million US$
Imports (2002): 2,804.4 million US$

Defence

Armed forces (2001): 8,300 people
Defence budget (2001): 0.72% of GDP

Standard of living

Inhabitants per doctor (1993): 2,330
Average daily calorie intake (2000): 2,395 (FAO minimum: 2,400)
Cars per 1,000 inhabitants (1999): 52
Televisions per 1,000 inhabitants (2000): 96

HISTORY: KEY DATES

4C AD: the Mayan culture was present in the area.
1502: Christopher Columbus sighted the country and gave it the name Honduras.
1524: Spanish explorer Pedro de Alvarado established coastal settlements.
1544: the country was attached to the Captaincy General of Guatemala.
1821: Honduras became part of the Mexican empire.
1824–38: the country was part of the Central American Federation.
1838: Honduras became an independent sovereign state.
1859: Britain ceded the Bay Islands to Honduras.
LATE 19C–EARLY 20C: Honduras was divided between rival local oligarchies. It was under the sway of the United Fruit Company, which controlled most of the country's banana exports.
1933–48: the dictatorship of Tiburcio Carías Andino was followed by a presidential election.
1969: Honduras fought El Salvador in what became known as the Football War.
1987–92: in 1987 and 1989, Honduras signed agreements with Costa Rica, Guatemala, Nicaragua and El Salvador, aimed at re-establishing peace in the region. A further agreement with El Salvador in 1992 settled the long-running border conflict between the two countries.
1998: the destruction caused by Hurricane Mitch had a lasting impact on the country's economic and social development.

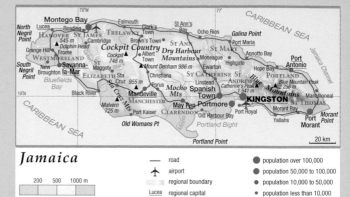

Jamaica

— road
✈ airport
— regional boundary
Lucea regional capital

● population over 100,000
● population 50,000 to 100,000
● population 10,000 to 50,000
• population less than 10,000

200 500 1000 m

The island of Jamaica has a tropical maritime climate, with rainfall heaviest in the northern and eastern regions; it is sometimes affected by cyclones. Mountains extend across the island (the highest is Blue Mountain, at 2,256m), limestone plateaus dominate the centre and west and there are many alluvial plains, particularly on the coasts.

Area: 10,990km²
Population (2002): 2,621,000
Capital: Kingston 672,000 (2001 e)
Government type and political system: constitutional monarchy with a parliamentary system
Head of state: (Queen) Elizabeth II, represented by the Governor-General Sir Howard Felix Cooke
Head of government: (Prime Minister) Percival James Patterson
Administrative structure: 14 parishes
Official language: English
Currency: Jamaican dollar

DEMOGRAPHICS
Density: 226 inhab/km²
Percentage of population in urban areas (2001): 56.6%
Age structure of population (2000): 0–15 years: 31.5%, 15–65 years: 61.3%, over 65 years: 7.2%
Birth rate (2003): 20.5‰
Death rate (2003): 5.7‰
Infant mortality rate (2003): 19.9‰
Life expectancy at birth (2003): male: 73.7 years, female: 77.8 years

ECONOMY
GNP (2002): 7.05 billion US$
GNP per capita (2002): 2,690 US$
GNP per capita PPP (2002): 3,680 international dollars
HDI (2000): 0.742

GNP annual growth rate (2003): 2.2%
Annual inflation rate (2001): 5%
Labour force by occupation (1998): agriculture: 21%, industry: 18.2%, services: 60.8%
GNP by sector (2000): agriculture: 6.5%, industry: 31.3%, services: 62.2%
Gross public debt: n/a
Unemployment rate (1996): 16%

Agriculture
Crops
bananas (2001): 130,000t
coffee (2002): 2,700t
sugar cane (2001): 2,400,000t
yams (2002): 148,000t
Livestock farming
cattle (2002): 400,000 head
goats (2001): 440,000 head
pigs (2002): 180,000 head

Energy generation and mining
bauxite (2001): 12,370,000t
total electricity (2001): 6,272 million kWh

Industrial production
sugar (2002): 197,000t
beer (2000): 699,000hl
aluminium (1996): 3,302,000t
cement (2001): 500,000t

Tourism
Tourism revenue (2001): 1,233 million US$

Foreign trade
Exports (2002): 1,309.1 million US$
Imports (2002): 3,179.6 million US$

Defence
Armed forces (2001): 2,830 people
Defence budget (2001): 0.5% of GDP

Standard of living
Inhabitants per doctor (1995): 6,419

Average daily calorie intake (2000): 2,693 (FAO minimum: 2,400)
Cars per 1,000 inhabitants (1996): 39
Televisions per 1,000 inhabitants (2000): 194

HISTORY: KEY DATES
1494: Christopher Columbus sighted the island of Jamaica.
1509: Spanish settlers arrived and destroyed the local Arawak population.
1655–70: the British seized the island and eventually took formal control of it, cultivating sugarcane and developing the slave trade.
18c: Jamaica became the centre of South America's slave trade.
1830s–40s: the abolition of slavery and customs privileges led to the ruin of the island's large plantations.
1866–84: Jamaica was a British Crown Colony.
1938–40: labour reforms failed to improve conditions for the black population, and the independence movement grew.
1942: rich deposits of bauxite were discovered in Jamaica.
1944: constitutional reforms introduced self-government and universal adult suffrage.
1962: Jamaica became independent within the Commonwealth of Nations.
1980–8: two devastating hurricanes presented setbacks to Jamaica's economic development.
1992–2004: inflation and national debt were gradually brought under control, but continuing social inequality caused frequent outbreaks of violent unrest.

Antigua and Barbuda is an island nation with a tropical climate, situated to the north of Guadeloupe in the Leeward group of the Lesser Antilles. The archipelago is made up of the islands of Antigua, Barbuda and Redonda.

Area: 442 km²
Population (2002): 77,000
Capital: Saint John's 24,000 (2001 e)
Government type and political system: constitutional monarchy with a parliamentary system
Head of state: (Queen) Elizabeth II, represented by the Governor-General Sir James Carlisle
Head of government: (Prime Minister) Baldwin Spencer
Administrative structure: 6 parishes and 2 dependencies
Official language: English
Currency: East Caribbean dollar

DEMOGRAPHICS

Density: 153 inhab/km²
Percentage of population in urban areas (2001): 37.1%
Age structure of population (1993): 0–15 years: 27%, 15–65 years: 67%, over 65 years: 6%
Birth rate (1999): 20.38‰
Death rate (1999): 4.98‰
Infant mortality rate (1998): 16.7‰
Life expectancy at birth: n/a

ECONOMY

GNP (2002): 0.671 billion US$
GNP per capita (2002): 9,720 US$
GNP per capita PPP (2002): 10,390 international dollars
HDI (2000): 0.8
GDP annual growth rate (2003): 2.5%
Annual inflation rate (1992): 4.5%
Labour force by occupation: n/a
GDP by sector (2000): agriculture: 3.9%, industry: 19.1%, services: 77%
Gross public debt: n/a
Unemployment rate: n/a

Agriculture and fishing
Livestock farming and fishing
cattle (2002): 13,800 head
goats (2001): 11,800 head
sheep (2002): 18,500 head
pigs (2002): 5,300 head
chickens (2002): 98,000 head
fish (1999): 3,190t

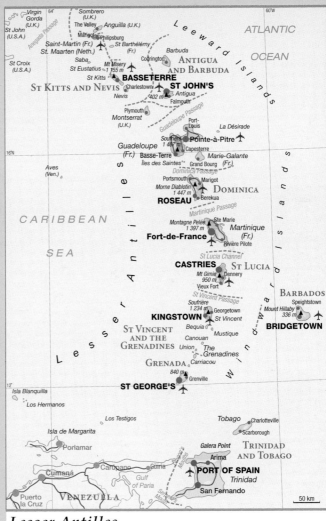

Lesser Antilles

- population over 100,000
- population 30,000 to 100,000
- population 10,000 to 30,000
- population less than 10,000

— road
✈ airport

Energy generation
total electricity (2001): 105 million kWh
Tourism
Tourism revenue (1999): 291 million US$
Foreign trade
Exports (2001): 38.62 million US$
Imports (2001): 321.17 million US$
Defence
Armed forces (2001): 170 people

Defence budget (2001): 0.67% of GDP
Standard of living
Inhabitants per doctor (1993): 333
Average daily calorie intake (2000): 2,396 (FAO minimum: 2,400)
Cars per 1,000 inhabitants: n/a
Televisions per 1,000 inhabitants (2000): 443

HISTORY: KEY DATES

17c: the British colonized Antigua and Barbuda.
1834: slavery was abolished, to the detriment of the islands' sugar industry.
1966: the islands became self-governing.
1967: Antigua, Barbuda and Redonda formed an associated state of the Commonwealth of Nations.
1981: Antigua and Barbuda achieved full independence within the Commonwealth.
1995: Hurricane Luis caused extensive damage to the islands.

LESSER ANTILLES **BARBADOS**

Barbados is the most easterly of the Caribbean islands. Of volcanic origin, the island has a fertile soil and rainy tropical climate.

Area: 430km²
Population (2002): 270,000
Capital: Bridgetown 136,000 (2001 e) including the suburbs
Government type and political system: constitutional monarchy with a parliamentary system
Head of state: (Queen) Elizabeth II, represented by the Governor-General Sir Clifford Husbands
Head of government: (Prime Minister) Owen Arthur
Administrative structure: 11 parishes
Official language: English
Currency: Barbados dollar

DEMOGRAPHICS

Density: 627 inhab/km²
Percentage of population in urban areas (2001): 50.5%
Age structure of population (2000): 0–15 years: 20.7%, 15–65 years: 68.9%, over 65 years: 10.4%
Birth rate (2003): 12.2‰
Death rate (2003): 7.8‰
Infant mortality rate (2003): 10.9‰

Life expectancy at birth (2003): male: 74.5 years, female: 79.5 years

ECONOMY

GNP (2002): 237 billion US$
GNP per capita (2002): 8,790 US$
GNP per capita PPP (2002): 14,660 international dollars
HDI (2000): 0.871
GDP annual growth rate (2003): 1.6%
Annual inflation rate (2000): 2.44%
Labour force by occupation: n/a
GDP by sector (2000): agriculture: 6.3%, industry: 21%, services: 72.7%
Gross public debt: n/a
Unemployment rate (2002): 9.9%

Agriculture and fishing
Crops
bananas (2001): 500t
sugar cane (2001): 520,000t
maize (2002): 2,200t
sweet potatoes (2001): 5,100t
Livestock farming and fishing
cattle (2002): 21,000 head
sheep (2002): 41,400 head
pigs (2002): 35,000 head
chickens (2002): 3,430,000 head
fish (1999): 3,210t

Energy generation and mining
total electricity (2001): 780 million kWh
natural gas (2000): 38 million m³

oil (2000): 78,000t
Industrial production
sugar (2002): 45,000t
beer (2000): 69,000hl

Tourism
Tourism revenue (2000): 745 million US$

Foreign trade
Exports (2001): 271.2 million US$
Imports (2001): 952.3 million US$

Defence
Armed forces (2001): 610 people
Defence budget (2001): 0.49% of GDP

Standard of living
Inhabitants per doctor (1990): 1,120
Average daily calorie intake (2000): 3,022 (FAO minimum: 2,400)
Cars per 1,000 inhabitants (1999): 229
Televisions per 1,000 inhabitants (2001): 325

HISTORY: KEY DATES
It is thought that Arawaks may have been the original inhabitants of Barbados.
17c: the island was occupied by the British.
19c: it was the administrative centre of the Windward Islands before becoming a separate colony in 1885.
1966: Barbados became independent within the Commonwealth of Nations.

LESSER ANTILLES **DOMINICA**

An island of volcanic origin with a tropical climate and heavy summer rain, the Commonwealth of Dominica is one of the Windward Islands of the Lesser Antilles.

Population (2002): 71,000
Capital: Roseau 26,000 (2001 e)
Government type and political system: republic with a parliamentary system
Head of state: (President of the Republic) Nicholas Liverpool
Head of government: (Prime Minister) Roosevelt Skerrit
Administrative structure: 10 parishes
Official language: English
Currency: East Caribbean dollar

DEMOGRAPHICS

Density: 94 inhab/km²
Percentage of population in urban areas (2001): 71.3%
Age structure of population (1993): 0–15 years: 31%, 15–65 years: 62%, over 65 years: 7%
Birth rate (1999): 20.18‰
Death rate (1999): 5.96‰
Infant mortality rate (1998): 15‰
Life expectancy at birth: n/a

ECONOMY

GNP (2002): 0.216 billion US$
GNP per capita (2002): 3,000 US$
GNP per capita PPP (2002): 4,960 international dollars
HDI (2000): 0.779
GDP annual growth rate (2002): –3.6%
Annual inflation rate (2000): 0.85%
Labour force by occupation: n/a
GDP by sector (2000): agriculture: 17.4%, industry: 23.5%, services: 59.1%
Gross public debt: n/a
Unemployment rate: n/a

Agriculture and fishing
Crops
bananas (2001): 31,000t
plantains (2001): 7,900t
sugar cane (2001): 4,400t
oranges (2002): 7,200t
Livestock farming and fishing
cattle (2002): 13,400 head
goats (2001): 9,700 head
sheep (2002): 7,600 head
pigs (2002): 5,000 head
fish (1999): 1,210t

Energy generation
total electricity (2001): 72 million kWh

Industrial production
copra (2001): 1,200t

Tourism
Tourism revenue (1999): 49 million US$

Foreign trade
Exports (2001): 44.4 million US$
Imports (2001): 115.29 million US$

Defence
Armed forces: n/a
Defence budget: n/a

Standard of living
Inhabitants per doctor (1991): 2,000
Average daily calorie intake (2000): 2,994 (FAO minimum: 2,400)
Cars per 1,000 inhabitants: n/a
Televisions per 1,000 inhabitants (2000): 220

HISTORY: KEY DATES
1493: Christopher Columbus reached Dominica.
1805: after nearly 300 years of European attempts to settle in Dominica, the island became a British colony.
1978: Dominica became independent within the Commonwealth of Nations.

Grenada is an island nation consisting of the mountainous, volcanic island of Grenada and the southern Grenadine islands (including Carriacou and Petite Martinique).

Area: 344km²
Population (2002): 103,000
Capital: Saint George's 36,000 (2001 e) including the suburbs
Government type and political system: constitutional monarchy with a parliamentary system
Head of state: (Queen) Elizabeth II, represented by the Governor-General Daniel Williams
Head of government: (Prime Minister) Keith Mitchell
Administrative structure: 6 parishes and 1 dependency
Official language: English
Currency: East Caribbean dollar

DEMOGRAPHICS

Density: 272 inhab/km²
Percentage of population in urban areas (2001): 38.4%
Age structure of population (1993): 0–15 years: 42%, 15–65 years: 53%, over 65 years: 5%
Birth rate (1999): 25.26‰
Death rate (1999): 7.12‰
Infant mortality rate (1998): 13.6‰

Life expectancy at birth: n/a

ECONOMY

GNP (2002): 0.361 billion US$
GNP per capita (2002): 3,530 US$
GNP per capita PPP (2002): 6,600 international dollars
HDI (2000): 0.747
GDP annual growth rate (2003): 2.5%
Annual inflation rate (1999): 0.24%
Labour force by occupation: n/a
GDP by sector (2000): agriculture: 7.7%, industry: 23.9%, services: 68.3%
Gross public debt: n/a
Unemployment rate: n/a

Agriculture and fishing

Crops
bananas (2001): 5,000t
sugar cane (2001): 6,750t
oranges (2002): 900t
grapefruits (2001): 2,000t
Livestock farming and fishing
cattle (2002): 4,400 head
goats (2001): 7,100 head
sheep (2002): 13,100 head
pigs (2002): 5,850 head
fish (1999): 1,630t

Energy generation
total electricity (2001): 138 million kWh

Industrial production
beer (2000): 20,000hl

Tourism
Tourism revenue (2001): 63 million US$
Foreign trade
Exports (2001): 63.6 million US$
Imports (2001): 196.83 million US$
Defence
Armed forces: n/a
Defence budget: n/a
Standard of living
Inhabitants per doctor (1993): 1,667
Average daily calorie intake (2000): 2,764 (FAO minimum: 2,400)
Cars per 1,000 inhabitants: n/a
Televisions per 1,000 inhabitants (1998): 368

HISTORY: KEY DATES

15c–18c: sighted by Christopher Columbus in 1498, Grenada later became a French and then a British colony.
1974: Grenada became independent within the Commonwealth of Nations.
1979: a bloodless coup led to the establishment of the People's Revolutionary Government, with Maurice Bishop as prime minister.
1983: Bishop's assassination by radical members of his own party led to military intervention by the USA, which occupied Grenada.
1984: democratic government was re-established.

The Federation of St Kitts (also known as St Christopher) and Nevis consists of the islands of St Kitts, Nevis and Sombrero.

Area: 261km²
Population (2002): 46,000
Capital: Basseterre 12,000 (2001 e)
Government type and political system: constitutional monarchy with a parliamentary system
Head of state: (Queen) Elizabeth II, represented by the Governor-General Sir Cuthbert Montroville Sebastian
Head of government: (Prime Minister) Denzil Douglas
Administrative structure: 2 states
Official language: English
Currency: East Caribbean dollar

DEMOGRAPHICS

Density: 147 inhab/km²
Percentage of population in urban areas (2001): 34.3%
Age structure of population (1993): 0–15 years: 32%, 15–65 years: 59%, over 65 years: 9%
Birth rate (1999): 19.22‰

Death rate (1999): 11.7‰
Infant mortality rate (1998): 21‰
Life expectancy at birth (2003): male: 68.2 years, female: 71.6 years

ECONOMY

GNP (2002): 0.301 billion US$
GNP per capita (2002): 6,540 US$
GNP per capita PPP (2002): 10,750 international dollars
HDI (2000): 0.814
GDP annual growth rate (2003): 2.1%
Annual inflation rate (1999): 3.91%
Labour force by occupation: n/a
GDP by sector (2000): agriculture: 3.6%, industry: 26%, services: 70.4%
Gross public debt: n/a
Unemployment rate: n/a

Agriculture and fishing
Crops
sugar cane (2001): 188,000t
Fishing
fish (1999): 350t

Energy generation
total electricity (2001): 100 million kWh

Industrial production
sugar (2002): 19,000t

Tourism
Tourism revenue (1999): 70 million US$
Foreign trade
Exports (2001): 55 million US$
Imports (2001): 166 million US$
Defence
Armed forces: n/a
Defence budget: n/a
Standard of living
Inhabitants per doctor (1990): 1,111
Average daily calorie intake (2000): 2,685 (FAO minimum: 2,400)
Cars per 1,000 inhabitants: n/a
Televisions per 1,000 inhabitants (2000): 260

HISTORY: KEY DATES

17c–18c: French and British colonists settled on St Kitts, which was then ceded to Britain under the Treaty of Paris in 1793.
1967: St Kitts, along with Nevis and Anguilla, formed a self-governing state within the Commonwealth of Nations.
1983: St Kitts and Nevis gained full independence as part of the Commonwealth of Nations.

Saint Lucia is a mountainous island of extinct volcanoes situated in the Windward Islands of the Lesser Antilles.

Area: 622km²
Population (2002): 151,000
Capital: Castries 57,000 (2001 e) including the suburbs
Government type and political system: constitutional monarchy with a parliamentary system
Head of state: (Queen) Elizabeth II, represented by the Governor-General Dame Pearlette Louisy
Head of government: (Prime Minister) Kenny Anthony
Administrative structure: 11 quarters
Official language: English
Currency: East Caribbean dollar

DEMOGRAPHICS

Density: 251 inhab/km²
Percentage of population in urban areas (2001): 38%
Age structure of population (2000): 0–15 years: 32.1%, 15–65 years: 62.2%, over 65 years: 5.7%

Birth rate (2003): 20.4‰
Death rate (2003): 5.9‰
Infant mortality rate (2003): 14.8‰
Life expectancy at birth (2003): male: 70.8 years, female: 74.1 years

ECONOMY

GNP (2002): 0.6 billion US$
GNP per capita (2002): 3,750 US$
GNP per capita PPP (2002): 4,950 international dollars
HDI (2000): 0.772
GDP annual growth rate (2003): 2.3%
Annual inflation rate (1999): 5.35%
Labour force by occupation: n/a
GDP by sector (2000): agriculture: 7.9%, industry: 19.6%, services: 72.5%
Gross public debt: n/a
Unemployment rate (1996): 16.3%

Agriculture and fishing

Crops
bananas (2001): 80,000t
Fishing
fish (1999): 1,720t

Energy generation
total electricity (2001): 120 million kWh

Industrial production
copra (2001): 1,200t

Tourism
Tourism revenue (2001): 232 million US$

Foreign trade
Exports (2001): 51.81 million US$
Imports (2001): 258.74 million US$

Defence
Armed forces: n/a
Defence budget: n/a

Standard of living
Inhabitants per doctor (1995): 1,875
Average daily calorie intake (2000): 2,838 (FAO minimum: 2,400)
Cars per 1,000 inhabitants (1996): 728
Televisions per 1,000 inhabitants (2000): 365

HISTORY: KEY DATES

1814: St Lucia became a British Crown Colony.
1979: St Lucia became independent within the Commonwealth of Nations.

LESSER ANTILLES
ST VINCENT AND THE GRENADINES

Saint Vincent and the Grenadines is an island nation situated in the eastern Caribbean Sea. It consists of the main island of St Vincent – which is mountainous with areas of rainforest and an active volcano – and some of the smaller Grenadine islands.

Area: 388km²
Population (2002): 112,000
Capital: Kingstown 28,000 (2001 e) including the suburbs
Government type and political system: constitutional monarchy with a parliamentary system
Head of state: (Queen) Elizabeth II, represented by the Governor-General Dr Sir Frederick Ballantyne
Head of government: (Prime Minister) Ralph Gonsalves
Administrative structure: 6 parishes
Official language: English
Currency: East Caribbean dollar

DEMOGRAPHICS

Density: 294 inhab/km²
Percentage of population in urban areas (2001): 55.9%
Age structure of population (2000): 0–15 years: 32.9%, 15–65 years: 60.5%, over 65 years: 6.6%
Birth rate (2003): 20‰
Death rate (2003): 5.8‰
Infant mortality rate (2003): 15.7‰
Life expectancy at birth (2003): male: 72.6 years, female: 75.6 years

ECONOMY

GNP (2002): 0.33 billion US$
GNP per capita (2002): 2,820 US$
GNP per capita PPP (2002): 5,190 international dollars
HDI (2000): 0.733
GDP annual growth rate (2003): 2.2%
Annual inflation rate (2000): 0.2%
Labour force by occupation: n/a
GDP by sector (2000): agriculture: 9.8%, industry: 25.5%, services: 64.7%
Gross public debt: n/a
Unemployment rate: n/a

Agriculture and fishing

Crops
bananas (2001): 43,300t
sugar cane (2001): 20,000t
coffee (2002): 170t
cocoa (2001): 175t
Fishing
fish (1999): 15,600t

Energy generation
total electricity (2001): 92 million kWh

Tourism
Tourism revenue (1999): 77 million US$

Foreign trade
Exports (2001): 45.7 million US$
Imports (2001): 151.96 million US$

Defence
Armed forces: n/a
Defence budget: n/a

Standard of living
Inhabitants per doctor (1995): 2,610
Average daily calorie intake (2000): 2,579 (FAO minimum: 2,400)
Cars per 1,000 inhabitants: n/a
Televisions per 1,000 inhabitants (2000): 234

HISTORY: KEY DATES

18c: a British settlement was founded on the island of St Vincent, and the colonists deported most of the indigenous Caribs.
1969: self-government was introduced.
1979: St Vincent and the Grenadines became independent within the Commonwealth of Nations.

The Republic of Trinidad and Tobago is made up of two islands: Trinidad (4,828km²), where 96% of the total population is concentrated, and Tobago (300km²). It has a humid, tropical climate, with heavier rainfall in the east than in the west. Trinidad is mainly flat apart from the rugged Northern Range.

Area: 5,128km²
Population (2002): 1,306,000
Capital: Port of Spain 54,000 (2001 e) including the suburbs
Government type and political system: republic with a presidential system
Head of state: (President of the Republic) George Maxwell Richards
Head of government: (Prime Minister) Patrick Manning
Administrative structure: 11 regions and 5 municipalities
Official language: English

Currency: Trinidad and Tobago dollar

DEMOGRAPHICS

Density: 253 inhab/km²
Percentage of population in urban areas (2001): 74.5%
Age structure of population (2000): 0–15 years: 25%, 15–65 years: 68.3%, over 65 years: 6.7%
Birth rate (2003): 13.7‰
Death rate (2003): 7.3‰
Infant mortality rate (2003): 14.1‰
Life expectancy at birth (2003): male: 68.4 years, female: 74.4 years

ECONOMY

GNP (2002): 8.8 billion US$
GNP per capita (2002): 6,750 US$
GNP per capita PPP (2002): 9,000 international dollars
HDI (2000): 0.805
GDP annual growth rate (2003): 3.8%
Annual inflation rate (2001): 2.5%
Labour force by occupation (2001): agriculture: 7.8%, industry: 28.8%, services: 63.4%
GDP by sector (2000): agriculture: 1.6%, industry: 43.2%, services: 55.2%
Gross public debt: n/a
Unemployment rate (2001): 10.8%

Agriculture
Crops
sugar cane (2001): 1,500,000t
Livestock farming
cattle (2002): 31,600 head
goats (2001): 59,000 head
pigs (2002): 64,000 head

Energy generation and mining
total electricity (2001): 5,315 million kWh
natural gas (2002): 16,800 million m³
oil (2002): 7,500,000t

Tourism
Tourism revenue (1999): 210 million US$

Foreign trade
Exports (2001): 4,304.2 million US$
Imports (2001): 3,586.1 million US$

Defence
Armed forces (2001): 2,700 people
Defence budget (2001): 0.81% of GDP

Standard of living
Inhabitants per doctor (1995): 1,520
Average daily calorie intake (2000): 2,777 (FAO minimum: 2,400)
Cars per 1,000 inhabitants (1996): 90
Televisions per 1,000 inhabitants (2000): 340

HISTORY: KEY DATES

1498: Christopher Columbus visited Trinidad, which was occupied in turn by Dutch, Spanish, French and British colonists.
1802: France, Spain and Great Britain fought for possession of the islands; Spain ceded Trinidad to Britain in 1802, and France ceded Tobago to Britain shortly afterwards.
1962: Trinidad and Tobago left the West Indies Federation to become an independent state and a member of the Commonwealth of Nations.
1976: Trinidad and Tobago became a republic.

MEXICO

The Tropic of Cancer runs through the United Mexican States. Mountain ranges and plateaux cover about two-thirds of the country, and the altitude moderates the temperature in these areas. Most of the population is concentrated on the central plateaux. The north is an arid semi-desert, while the south has a humid tropical climate and is partially covered by forests. Earthquakes are frequent, and there are also volcanoes, particularly in the south.

Area: 1,970,577km²
Population (2002): 101,843,000
Capital: Mexico City 18,268,000 (2001 e) including the suburbs
Government type and political system: republic with a presidential system
Head of state and government: (President of the Republic) Vicente Fox Quesada

Administrative structure: 31 states and one federal district
Official language: Spanish
Currency: Mexican peso

DEMOGRAPHICS
Density: 50 inhab/km²
Percentage of population in urban areas (2001): 74.6%
Age structure of population (2000): 0–15 years: 33.1%, 15–65 years: 62.2%, over 65 years: 4.7%
Birth rate (2003): 22.4‰
Death rate (2003): 5‰
Infant mortality rate (2003): 28.2‰
Life expectancy at birth (2003): male: 70.4 years, female: 76.4 years

ECONOMY
GNP (2002): 597 billion US$
GNP per capita (2002): 5,920 US$
GNP per capita PPP (2002): 8,800 international dollars
HDI (2000): 0.796
GDP annual growth rate (2003): 1.3%
Annual inflation rate (2001): 6.4%
Labour force by occupation (2001): agriculture: 18.1%, industry: 25.9%, services: 56%
GDP by sector (2000): agriculture: 4.4%, industry: 28.4%, services: 67.2%
Gross public debt: n/a
Unemployment rate (2002): 2.7%

Agriculture and fishing
Crops
citrus fruits (2002): 6,165,000t
pineapples (2001): 535,000t
bananas (2001): 1,977,000t
cocoa (2001): 44,700t
coffee (2002): 313,000t
sugar cane (2001): 49,500,000t
lemons (2002): 1,680,000t
cotton (2002): 123,000t
maize (2002): 19,299,000t
mandarin oranges (1998): 190,000t
honey (2001): 55,783t
walnuts (2001): 18,500t
oranges (2002): 3,844,000t
barley (2002): 737,000t
grapefruits (2001): 212,000t
peaches (2002): 198,000t
timber (2000): 8,105,000m³
grapes (2002): 363,000t
rice (2002): 227,000t
sisal (2001): 46,500t
sorghum (2002): 5,206,000t
tobacco (2001): 40,600t
tomatoes (2002): 1,990,000t
Livestock farming and fishing
cattle (2002): 30,700,000 head
goats (2001): 9,100,000 head
horses (2001): 6,255,000 head
sheep (2002): 6,260,000 head
pigs (2002): 18,000,000 head
chickens (2002): 521,000,000 head
fish (1999): 1,251,000t

Mexico

500 1000 2000 m

200 km

▲ volcano
★ place of interest

═══ motorway
─── road
─── railway line

● population over 1,000,000
● population 500,000 to 1,000,000
● population 100,000 to 500,000
• population less than 100,000

Energy generation and mining

silver (2001): 2,760t
copper (2001): 367,000t
total electricity (2001): 198,561 million kWh
iron (2000): 6,795,000t
natural gas (2002): 38,770 million m³
manganese (2001): 100,000t
molybdenum (2001): 7,000t
gold (2001): 26,300kg
oil (2002): 177,999,000t
lead (2001): 135,000t
zinc (2001): 400,000t

Industrial production

eggs (2001): 1,881,645t
meat (2001): 4,636,000t

copra (2001): 83,000t
sugar (2002): 4,872,000t
beer (2000): 52,500,000hl
steel (2003): 15,237,000t
aluminium (2001): 65,000t
copper (2001): 367,600t
lead (2001): 150,000t
zinc (2001): 250,000t
cars (2002): 961,000 units
commercial vehicles (1998): 475,000 units
synthetic textiles (1999): 588,000t
cement (2001): 29,966,000t
cotton yarn (2001): 98,000t
synthetic rubber (2001): 173,000t

Tourism

Tourism revenue (2001): 8,401 million US$

Foreign trade

Exports (2002): 160,763 million US$
Imports (2002): 168,769 million US$

Defence

Armed forces (2001): 192,770 people
Defence budget (2001): 0.53% of GDP

Standard of living

Inhabitants per doctor (1996): 666
Average daily calorie intake (2000): 3,165 (FAO minimum: 2,400)
Cars per 1,000 inhabitants (2000): 107
Televisions per 1,000 inhabitants (2000): 283

HISTORY: KEY DATES

Pre-Columbian Mexico to the colonial period

c.8000 BC: hunter-gatherers inhabited Mexico.
5200 BC–3400 BC: the earliest known use of maize was in the Tehuacán area at this time.
1200 BC–600 BC: the elaborate Olmec civilization flourished on the Gulf Coast.
AD 250–AD 950: the classic period of Mesoamerica; the Mayan civilization flourished and the Toltec warrior culture developed.
950–1170: the Toltec people controlled most of central Mexico during this period. Their capital, Tula (about 80km from present-day Mexico City), was eventually destroyed by the Chichimecs, ancestors of the Aztecs.
13c: the Mixtec people were dominant during this period, which also saw the development of the Totonac, Cempoala and Huaxtec civilizations. The last wave of Chichimec invaders eventually overwhelmed resistance from the Mixtec and Zapotec peoples. The Aztecs founded Tenochtitlán (now Mexico City) in the 14c.
1519–35: Spanish conquistador Hernán Cortés led the destruction of the Aztec empire, and became governor of New Spain. The colony became a viceroyalty in 1535. Epidemics and forced labour wiped out most of the indigenous population. Spanish colonization led to large-scale conversion of native people to the Catholic faith.
17c–18c: Mexico became wealthier through the exploitation of silver mines. Agriculture and farming developed.

Independence to the present day

1810–15: a movement towards independence began with the issuing of a revolutionary tract known as the 'grito de Dolores'; rebel armies of the poorer classes rose up against the Spanish and the Creoles.
1821–2: Mexico gained independence from Spain. Agustín de Iturbide proclaimed himself emperor in 1822.
1823: after the abdication of Iturbide, General Antonio López de Santa Anna established the Republic of Mexico.
1836: Texas seceded and became an independent republic.
1846–8: Mexico lost a large area of territory, including California, Nevada and Arizona, in its war with the USA.
1862–4: France intervened in Mexico and created a Catholic empire. With the military support of France, Maximilian of Habsburg, brother of the emperor of Austria, was proclaimed emperor.
1867–1911: the republic was restored. Porfirio Díaz became president of an authoritarian government that continued, with only a brief hiatus (1880–4), until 1911.
1910–17: the Mexican Revolution began a long period of conflict. The demands of agrarian workers and nationalists were sometimes overlooked in the struggle for power by the leaders of different factions, several of whom were supported by the USA: Pancho Villa, Emiliano Zapata, Venustiano Carranza and Álvaro Obregón.
1934–40: under the presidency of Lázaro Cárdenas, a political system centred on the National Revolutionary Party (PRN) was established. The party was re-named the Institutional Revolutionary Party, or PRI, in 1946, and maintained its hegemony until 2000.
1980s: economic downturn brought a crisis of unemployment and inflation; relations with the USA were strained by problems of drug smuggling and illegal immigration at the border between the two countries.
1992–4: the North American Free Trade Agreement (NAFTA) was negotiated with the USA and Canada.
1998: Mexico joined with the Organization of Petroleum Exporting Countries (OPEC) to control oil prices and stabilize the economy.
2000: Vicente Fox Quesada of the Alliance for Change became the first non-PRI candidate to be elected president of Mexico.

The interior of the Republic of Nicaragua is mountainous, especially in the west. Fertile valleys contain two large lakes, Nicaragua and Managua. A narrow but fertile plain borders the Pacific Ocean, while a wider, heavily forested plain borders the Caribbean Sea.

Area: 130,000km²
Population (2002): 5,347,000
Capital: Managua 1,039,000 (2001 e)
Government type and political system: republic with a presidential system
Head of state and government: (President of the Republic) Enrique Bolaños
Administrative structure: 15 departments and 2 autonomous regions
Official language: Spanish
Currency: córdoba oro

DEMOGRAPHICS

Density: 34 inhab/km²
Percentage of population in urban areas (2001): 56.5%
Age structure of population (2000): 0–15 years: 42.6%, 15–65 years: 54.4%, over 65 years: 3%
Birth rate (2003): 31.6‰
Death rate (2003): 5.1‰
Infant mortality rate (2003): 35.7‰
Life expectancy at birth (2003): male: 67.2 years, female: 71.9 years

ECONOMY

GNP (2002): 3.82 billion US$
GNP per capita (2002): 710 US$
GNP per capita PPP (2002): 2,350 international dollars
HDI (2000): 0.635
GDP annual growth rate (2003): 2.3%
Annual inflation rate (2001): 7.4%
Labour force by occupation (2001): agriculture: 43.4%, industry: 14.7%, services: 41.9%
GDP by sector (2000): agriculture: 32.3%, industry: 22.6%, services: 45.1%
Gross public debt: n/a
Unemployment rate (2002): 12.2%

Agriculture and fishing

Crops
coffee (2002): 60,000t
sugar cane (2001): 3,992,000t
maize (2002): 495,000t
rice (2002): 284,000t

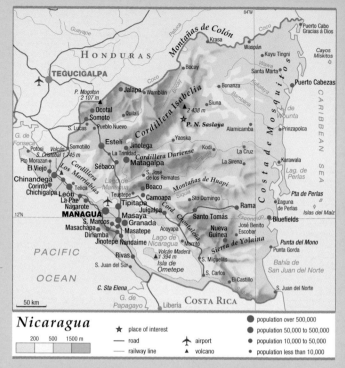

Nicaragua

200 500 1500 m

★ place of interest
— road
— railway line
✈ airport
▲ volcano

● population over 500,000
● population 50,000 to 500,000
● population 10,000 to 50,000
• population less than 10,000

Livestock farming and fishing
cattle (2002): 3,350,000 head
horses (2001): 248,000 head
pigs (2002): 430,000 head
fish (1999): 24,800t

Energy generation and mining
silver (2001): 2t
total electricity (2001): 2,549 million kWh
gold (2001): 3,650kg

Industrial production
sugar (2002): 334,000t

Tourism
Tourism revenue (2001): 109 million US$

Foreign trade
Exports (2002): 605.1 million US$
Imports (2002): 1,636.4 million US$

Defence
Armed forces (2001): 14,000 people
Defence budget (2001): 1.11% of GDP

Standard of living
Inhabitants per doctor (1993): 1,490
Average daily calorie intake (2000): 2,227 (FAO minimum: 2,400)
Cars per 1,000 inhabitants (2000): 12
Televisions per 1,000 inhabitants (2000): 69

HISTORY: KEY DATES

16c: under Spanish rule, Nicaragua became part of the Captaincy General of Guatemala.
1821–38: Nicaragua gained independence from Spain, and was part of the Central American Federation from 1825–38.
1912–33: US troops occupied Nicaragua, to provide support for particular political regimes and to safeguard US interests in a proposed Nicaraguan canal.
1937: Anastasio Somoza established a dictatorship that continued until he was assassinated in 1956.
1956–79: despite growing opposition, the Somoza family maintained its domination of Nicaraguan politics.
1979: the opposition Sandinista National Liberation Front (FSLN) brought down the dictatorship and established a socialist political regime, backed by Cuba and the USSR. The USA was not supportive of the new regime.
1983: the USA gave open, and later covert, support to counter-revolutionary military forces known as contras.
1984: Daniel Ortega Saavedra, a Sandinista, was elected president.
1987–9: Nicaragua signed agreements with neighbouring states aimed at restoring peace in the region.
1990: Violeta Barrios de Chamorro was elected president, becoming the first woman to govern a Central American country. Relations between Nicaragua and the USA improved.
2001: Enrique Bolaños Geyer became president.

Panama

200	500	1500 m		

— road   — — railway line
▲ volcano   ✈ airport

● population over 500,000
● population 250,000 to 500,000
● population 50,000 to 250,000
• population less than 50,000

The Republic of Panama has a tropical climate with plenty of rainfall; it contains mountainous and forested areas and has fertile coastal plains. The Panama Canal Zone, which links the Pacific and Atlantic oceans, is of primary importance to the country.

Area: 75,517km²
Population (2002): 2,942,000
Capital: Panama City 1,202,000 (2001 e) including the suburbs
Government type and political system: republic with a presidential system
Head of state and government: (President of the Republic) Martin Torrijos
Administrative structure: 9 provinces and 3 autonomous territories for indigenous people
Official language: Spanish
Currency: balboa

DEMOGRAPHICS

Density: 37 inhab/km²
Percentage of population in urban areas (2001): 56.6%
Age structure of population (2000): 0–15 years: 31.3%, 15–65 years: 63.2%, over 65 years: 5.5%
Birth rate (2003): 22.7‰
Death rate (2003): 5‰
Infant mortality rate (2003): 20.6‰
Life expectancy at birth (2003): male: 72.3 years, female: 77.4 years

ECONOMY

GNP (2002): 11.8 billion US$
GNP per capita (2002): 4,020 US$
GNP per capita PPP (2002): 6,060 international dollars
HDI (2000): 0.787
GDP annual growth rate (2003): 4.1%
Annual inflation rate (2000): 0.7%
Labour force by occupation (1998): agriculture: 19.3%, industry: 18.5%, services: 62.2%
GDP by sector (2000): agriculture: 6.7%, industry: 17%, services: 76.3%

Gross public debt: n/a
Unemployment rate (2002): 14.1%

Agriculture

Crops
bananas (2001): 489,000t
sugar cane (2001): 1,789,000t
rice (2002): 245,000t
Livestock farming
cattle (2002): 1,533,000 head
horses (2001): 166,000 head
pigs (2002): 303,000 head

Energy generation

total electricity (2001): 4,039 million kWh

Industrial production

sugar (2002): 152,000t

Tourism

Tourism revenue (2001): 626 million US$

Foreign trade

Exports (2002): 5,283.8 million US$
Imports (2002): 6,460.2 million US$

Defence

Armed forces (2001): 11,800 people
Defence budget (2001): 1.3% of GDP

Standard of living

Inhabitants per doctor (1993): 556
Average daily calorie intake (2000): 2,488 (FAO minimum: 2,400)
Cars per 1,000 inhabitants (1998): 83
Televisions per 1,000 inhabitants (2000): 194

HISTORY: KEY DATES

1501: Spanish explorers first sighted Panama. The country was subsequently colonized by Spain, and became strategically important for the Spanish colonization of Peru.
16c–18c: initially part of the Viceroyalty of Peru, Panama was later transferred to the Viceroyalty of New Grenada.
1821: Panama joined the union known as Gran Colombia.
1881–9: a French company attempted the building of a canal across the isthmus of Panama, linking the Atlantic and Pacific oceans. Financial difficulties and illness forced the suspension of the project.
1903–14: Panama split from Colombia, and was established as an independent republic after a rebellion encouraged by the USA. The USA established its authority over the Panama Canal Zone, and undertook to complete the building of the canal.
1908–66: resistance to US control of the

Canal Zone gave rise to increased nationalism, political unrest and frequent changes of administration in Panama.
1968–81: after a military coup, General Omar Torrijos Herrera became president. In 1977 he signed a treaty with the USA stating that the Canal Zone would be returned to Panamanian jurisdiction at the end of 1999.
1983: Colonel Manuel Noriega became head of the National Guard, which expanded and renamed the Panamanian Defence Force. Drug trafficking and corruption permeated Panamanian politics.
1989: Noriega became Panama's president, but was removed from power during an invasion by US forces.
1999: Panama's authority over the Canal Zone was re-established.
2004: Martin Torrijos, the son of former president Omar Torrijos, was elected president.

PARAGUAY

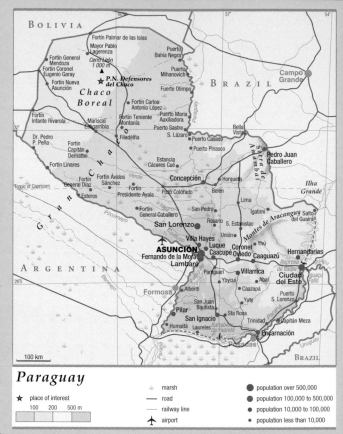

Paraguay

★ place of interest
100 200 500 m

⚓ marsh
— road
— railway line
✈ airport

● population over 500,000
● population 100,000 to 500,000
● population 10,000 to 100,000
• population less than 10,000

The Republic of Paraguay is a landlocked country in South America. The Chaco region, a vast, sparsely populated, semi-arid plain, lies west of the River Paraguay. The rest of the country, between the rivers Paraguay and Paraná, is wetter (over 1,200mm rainfall per year) and made up of plateaux and plains.

Area: 406,752km²
Population (2002): 5,779,000
Capital: Asunción 1,302,000 (2001 e) including the suburbs
Government type and political system: republic with a semi-presidential system
Head of state and government: (President of the Republic) Nicanor Duarte Frutos
Administrative structure: 17 departments and 1 capital city
Official languages: Spanish and Guaraní
Currency: guaraní

134

DEMOGRAPHICS
Density: 14 inhab/km²
Percentage of population in urban areas (2001): 56.6%
Age structure of population (2000): 0–15 years: 39.5%, 15–65 years: 57%, over 65 years: 3.5%
Birth rate (2003): 6.43‰
Death rate (2003): 5.1‰
Infant mortality rate (2003): 37‰
Life expectancy at birth (2003): male: 68.6 years, female: 73.1 years

ECONOMY
GNP (2002): 6.43 billion US$
GNP per capita (2002): 1,170 US$
GNP per capita PPP (2002): 4,590 international dollars
HDI (2000): 0.74
GDP annual growth rate (2003): 2.3%
Annual inflation rate (2001): 7.7%
Labour force by occupation: n/a
GDP by sector (2000): agriculture: 20.6%, industry: 27.4%, services: 52%
Gross public debt: n/a
Unemployment rate (1996): 8.2%

Agriculture
Crops
wheat (2002): 359,000t
sugar cane (2001): 3,854,000t
maize (2002): 867,000t

manioc (2001): 3,854,000t
oranges (2002): 207,000t
grapefruits (2001): 47,900t
soya beans (2002): 3,300,000t
Livestock farming
cattle (2002): 9,378,000 head
horses (2001): 400,000 head
sheep (2002): 410,000 head
pigs (2002): 1,822,000 head

Energy generation
total electricity (2001): 44,894 million kWh
hydroelectricity (2000): 44,857 million kWh

Industrial production
beer (2000): 2,200,000hl
sugar (2002): 165,000t
cement (2001): 700,000t
cotton yarn (2001): 98,000t

Tourism
Tourism revenue (2000): 66 million US$

Foreign trade
Exports (2002): 2,319.3 million US$
Imports (2002): 2,390.9 million US$

Defence
Armed forces (2001): 18,600 people
Defence budget (2001): 0.9% of GDP

Standard of living
Inhabitants per doctor (1994): 3,333
Average daily calorie intake (2000): 2,533 (FAO minimum: 2,400)

Cars per 1,000 inhabitants (1996): 14
Televisions per 1,000 inhabitants (2000): 218

HISTORY: KEY DATES
16c: originally inhabited by the Guaraní people, the Paraguay basin was explored and settled by the Spanish after 1537.
1604: the region was placed under the sole rule of Spanish Jesuit missionaries. The indigenous population was resettled in communities administered by religious and colonial authorities.
1767: the Spanish king Charles III expelled the Jesuits; the settlements were destroyed and the indigenous people dispersed.
1813: Paraguay's independence was proclaimed. The country was then ruled by a series of dictators.
1865–70: war against Argentina, Uruguay and Brazil over sea access ruined Paraguay, which lost half of its population and large tracts of land.
1932–89: the 1932–5 Chaco War against Bolivia, which Paraguay won, was followed by a series of military dictatorships.
1990–2004: Paraguay moved closer to democratic government, but economic difficulties and widespread political corruption hampered its development.

The Republic of Peru can be divided into three geographical regions: the narrow, arid coastal plain; the central Andes Mountains (with altitudes of over 4,000m), which contain high basins and a high plateau (altiplano); and the Amazonian plain, covered with rainforests, which is drained by the Upper Amazon and its tributaries and extends over more than half of the country.

Area: 1,285,216km²
Population (2002): 26,523,000
Capital: Lima 7,594,000 (2001 e) including the suburbs
Government type and political system: republic with a semi-presidential system
Head of state: (President of the Republic) Alejandro Toledo Manrique
Head of government: (Prime Minister) Carlos Ferrero Costa
Administrative structure: 24 departments and 1 constitutional province (Callao)
Official languages: Spanish, Aymara and Quechua
Currency: nuevo sol

Peru

★ place of interest
⌖ oil field

| 200 | 400 | 1000 | 2000 | 3000 m |

motorway
road
railway line
✈ airport

● population over 1,000,000
● population 250,000 to 1,000,000
● population 100,000 to 250,000
• population less than 100,000

DEMOGRAPHICS

Density: 20 inhab/km²
Percentage of population in urban areas (2001): 73.1%
Age structure of population (2000): 0–15 years: 33.4%, 15–65 years: 61.8%, over 65 years: 4.8%
Birth rate (2003): 23.3‰
Death rate (2003): 6.1‰
Infant mortality rate (2003): 33.4‰
Life expectancy at birth (2003): male: 67.3 years, female: 72.4 years

ECONOMY

GNP (2002): 54 billion US$
GNP per capita (2002): 2,020 US$
GNP per capita PPP (2002): 4,880 international dollars
HDI (2000): 0.747
GDP annual growth rate (2003): 4%
Annual inflation rate (2001): 2%
Labour force by occupation (1998): agriculture: 5.3%, industry: 20.3%, services: 74.4%
GDP by sector (2000): agriculture: 7.9%, industry: 27.2%, services: 64.9%

Gross public debt: n/a
Unemployment rate (2002): 7.9%

Agriculture and fishing

Crops
plantains (2001): 1,450,000t
wheat (2002): 187,000t
cocoa (2001): 22,000t
coffee (2002): 170,000t
sugar cane (2001): 7,950,000t
lemons (2002): 254,000t
maize (2002): 1,293,000t
mandarin oranges (1998): 89,000t
oranges (2002): 293,000t
barley (2002): 200,000t
sweet potatoes (2001): 273,000t
apples (2001): 158,000t
potatoes (2002): 3,299,000t
rice (2002): 2,119,000t
tomatoes (2002): 130,000t
Livestock farming and fishing
cattle (2002): 4,973,000 head
goats (2001): 2,000,000 head
horses (2001): 700,000 head
sheep (2002): 14,047,000 head

pigs (2002): 2,858,000 head
chickens (2002): 90,000,000 head
fish (1999): 8,438,000t

Energy generation and mining

silver (2001): 2,353t
copper (2001): 722,000t
total electricity (2001): 20,590 million kWh
hydroelectricity (2001): 17,439 million kWh
tin (2001): 38,182t
iron (2002): 3,087,000t
molybdenum (2001): 7,500t
gold (2001): 138,022kg
oil (2002): 4,800,000t
lead (2001): 271,000t
zinc (2001): 1,056,000t

Industrial production

beer (2000): 8,310,000hl
steel (2003): 676,000t
copper (2001): 722,726t
lead (2001): 116,000t
zinc (2001): 201,498t

PERU

cement (2001): 3,589,000t
cotton yarn (2001): 48,000t
synthetic textiles (1998): 41,000t

Tourism
Tourism revenue (2001): 865 million US$
Foreign trade
Exports (2002): 7,647 million US$
Imports (2002): 7,440 million US$
Defence
Armed forces (2001): 110,000 people
Defence budget (2001): 1.58% of GDP
Standard of living
Inhabitants per doctor (1993): 940
Average daily calorie intake (2000): 2,624
(FAO minimum: 2,400)
Cars per 1,000 inhabitants (1999): 27
Televisions per 1,000 inhabitants (2000): 148

ST KITTS AND NEVIS ➡ LESSER ANTILLES

ST LUCIA ➡ LESSER ANTILLES

ST VINCENT AND THE GRENADINES ➡ LESSER ANTILLES

HISTORY: KEY DATES

Peru was the centre of many Amerindian civilizations including the Chavín, Moche, Chimú, Nazca and Paracas.
12c–16c: the Incas extended their rule over the Andean plateaux, encompassing most of present-day Peru within their empire.
1532–3: the Spanish explorer Francisco Pizzaro captured the Incan capital Cuzco and had the Inca king Atahualpa killed; over the next few years, the Incas disappeared.
1544: the discovery of silver deposits at Potosí (in present-day Bolivia) enabled the colonial society to become wealthy very quickly.
1569–81: the viceroy Francisco Toledo developed the colonial administration and began to arrange resettlement of the local people into communities administered by religious and colonial authorities.
1780–2: a rebellion against the colonists, led by José Gabriel Condorcanqui (Túpac Amaru), shook the country.
1821: South American revolutionary leader José de San Martín captured Lima from the Spanish and proclaimed Peru independent. The country's independent status was reinforced by General Antonio José de Sucre's victory against the Spanish troops at Ayacucho (1824). A series of military coups followed.
1836–9: Peru and Bolivia were joined in a confederation that ended after military intervention from Chile.
1879–84: the War of the Pacific against Chile ended in defeat for Peru, which then ceded various territories to Chile. This eventually led to the Tacna-Arica controversy, a long period of wrestling over ownership of two disputed provinces.
1980–92: a new constitution was established, but an economic downturn led to civil unrest and armed conflict. The most active insurgent groups were the Maoist guerrillas known as the Shining Path, and the Túpac Amaru Revolutionary Movement (MRTA). In 1992 the constitution was suspended in order to allow the government more power to act against the guerillas.
1993: another new constitution came into effect.
1998: an agreement resolved the long-running border disputes between Peru and Ecuador.

Machu Picchu

Not far from the city of Cuzco is the ancient Inca city of Machu Picchu, located approximately 2,000m above the valley of the River Urubamba. Spanish conquerors never found Machu Picchu, and its remarkably well-preserved ruins were eventually rediscovered in 1911 by the US archaeologist Hiram Bingham. The exact function of the site – religious sanctuary, fortress or last capital – remains uncertain. It appears to have been built after 1450 and was planned as a single unit containing agricultural terraces, living quarters, palaces and temples, as well as a complex system of pools fed by natural springs. Temples and palaces in dressed stone are the most notable buildings. The houses were also built of stone, and were probably covered in a clay coating.

The Republic of Suriname is situated in north-eastern South America towards the east of the Guyana Plateau. The climate is equatorial, and rainforests cover 95% of the country.

Area: 163,265km²
Population (2002): 421,000
Capital: Paramaribo 240,000 (2001 e)
Government type and political system: republic with a parliamentary system
Head of state and government: (President of the Republic) Ronald Venetiaan
Administrative structure: 10 districts
Official language: Dutch
Currency: Suriname dollar

DEMOGRAPHICS

Density: 3 inhab/km²
Percentage of population in urban areas (2001): 74.7%
Age structure of population (2000): 0–15 years: 30.5%, 15–65 years: 63.9%, over 65 years: 5.6%
Birth rate (2003): 21.7‰
Death rate (2003): 5.9‰
Infant mortality rate (2003): 25.7‰
Life expectancy at birth (2003): male: 68.5 years, female: 73.7 years

ECONOMY

GNP (2002): 0.841 billion US$
GNP per capita (2002): 1,940 US$
GNP per capita PPP (2002): 3,310 international dollars
HDI (2000): 0.756
GDP annual growth rate (2003): 5.8%
Annual inflation rate (2001): 42.3%
Labour force by occupation: n/a
GDP by sector (2000): agriculture: 9.7%, industry: 20.4%, services: 69.9%

Gross public debt: n/a
Unemployment rate (1999): 14%

Agriculture

Crops
bananas (2001): 50,000t
rice (2002): 57,000t
Livestock farming
cattle (2002): 136,000 head
chickens (2002): 3,700,000 head

Energy generation and mining
bauxite (2001): 4,512,000t
total electricity (2001): 1,959 million kWh
oil (1999): 588,000t

Industrial production
palm oil (2001): 220t
aluminium (1999): 10,000t

Tourism
Tourism revenue (1999): 53 million US$

Foreign trade
Exports (2002): 369.3 million US$
Imports (2002): 321.9 million US$

Defence
Armed forces (2001): 1,840 people
Defence budget (2001): 5.26% of GDP

Standard of living
Inhabitants per doctor (1995): 1,273

Average daily calorie intake (2000): 2,652 (FAO minimum: 2,400)
Cars per 1,000 inhabitants (1996): 122
Televisions per 1,000 inhabitants (2001): 261

HISTORY: KEY DATES

1667: Britain ceded its part of Suriname (then known as Dutch Guiana) to the Netherlands in exchange for the city of New Amsterdam (present-day New York).
18c: successful sugar cane plantations were established in the country.
1863–6: slavery was abolished, and the Netherlands granted Dutch Guiana a parliament.
1975: the country, by this time known as Suriname, became an independent republic.
1982–92: guerrilla warfare did serious damage to Suriname, particularly under the regime of army chief Désiré Bouterse.
1992: a peace treaty was signed between the government and the guerrillas.
1999–2000: Bouterse and his political allies were discredited. Former president Ronald Venetiaan was restored to office.

137

Suriname

★	place of interest	●	population over 200,000
—	road	●	population 10,000 to 200,000
✈	airport	•	population less than 10,000

100 200 500 1000 m

The Dutch colonial empire

During the 17c, the Dutch East and West India Companies enabled the Dutch to settle and establish trading posts across present-day Indonesia and the Far East. The Dutch empire in the Americas reached its peak around the middle of the 17c. It comprised part of Brazil (taken from the Portuguese), former Spanish possessions in the Caribbean and, in the north, a series of settlements that formed the New Netherlands (including New Amsterdam, which the British later renamed New York). The Dutch lost their North American colonies to the British, but under the Treaty of Breda, which ended the second Anglo-Dutch War in 1667, they kept Dutch Guiana (present-day Suriname) and their Caribbean possessions.

During the 17c, the Dutch state expanded its hegemony in Indonesia. In 1814, Great Britain returned Dutch colonies to the Netherlands, except the Cape Colony, part of Guyana, Tobago and Ceylon.

There is an extremely wide variety of landscapes in the United States of America: the country is almost as large as the whole of Europe, from the Atlantic Ocean to the Urals. In the west, the Rocky Mountains, made up of a series of ranges running north to south, tower above high plateaus and river basins. They form a climatic barrier, in particular reducing precipitation in the east, on the Great Plains. The latter, which are roughly situated in the Mississippi–Missouri Basin, constitute a huge area that stretches from the Great Lakes to the Gulf of Mexico and reaches the Appalachian Mountains in the east. The Midwest has a continental climate with cold winters and occasionally very hot summers, with precipitation levels increasing towards the east. Heavy rainfall, sometimes linked to cyclones and associated with high temperatures, characterizes the subtropical south-east (particularly Florida).

Area: 9,151,670km²
Population (2002): 288,530,000
Capital: Washington, DC 572,059 (2000 census), 3,997,000 (2001 e) including the suburbs
Government type and political system: republic with a presidential system
Head of state and government: (President of the Republic) George W Bush
Administrative structure: 50 states, 1 federal district, 14 dependencies and associated states
Official language: English
Currency: United States dollar

DEMOGRAPHICS

Density: 30 inhab/km²
Percentage of population in urban areas (2001): 77.4%
Age structure of population (2000): 0–15 years: 21.7%, 15–65 years: 66%, over 65 years: 12.3%
Birth rate (2003): 14.5‰
Death rate (2003): 8.3‰
Infant mortality rate (2003): 6.7‰
Life expectancy at birth (2003): male: 74.3 years, female: 79.9 years

ECONOMY

GNP (2002): 10,207 billion US$
GNP per capita (2002): 35,400 US$
GNP per capita PPP (2002): 36,110 international dollars
HDI (2000): 0.939
GDP annual growth rate (2002): 2.4%

HAWAIIAN ISLANDS

Kauai Hanalei
Lehua Kapaa
Niihau Lihue
Kaula Waialua Oahu
Wahiawa Kaneohe
Pearl Hooleihua Molokai
Harbor Honolulu Halawa Maui
Lanai Wailuku
Kahoolawe Upolu Hawi
Point Honokaa
Kiholo Waimea
Kealakekua Mauna Kea Hilo
Bay 4 205 m
Captain Kilauea Crater
Cook Pahala
Ka Lae

PACIFIC OCEAN

100 km

ATLANTIC OCEAN

139

GULF OF MEXICO

CARIBBEAN SEA

Legend

150 km

● population over 5,000,000
● population 1,000,000 to 5,000,000
● population 100,000 to 1,000,000
• population less than 100,000

— road
— railway line
✈ airport
★ place of interest

international boundary
state boundary
Denver state capital

0   200   500   1000   2000 m

UNITED STATES OF AMERICA

Inflation rate (2001): 2.3%
Labour force by occupation (2000):
agriculture: 2.6%, industry: 22.9%,
services: 74.5%
GDP by sector (1999): agriculture: 1.6%,
industry: 24.7%, services: 73.7%
Gross public debt (2002): 61% of GDP
Unemployment rate (2002): 5.8%

Agriculture and fishing

Crops
citrus fruits (2002): 14,685,000t
almonds (2001): 386,000t
pineapples (2001): 44,300t
groundnuts (2001): 1,923,000t
oats (2001): 1,696,000t
sugar beets (2002): 25,145,000t
butter (2001): 578,350t
wheat (2002): 44,062,000t
sugar cane (2001): 31,891,000t
lemons (2002): 727,000t
rape (2001): 908,000t
cotton (2002): 9,556,000t
dates (2001): 15,900t
maize (2002): 228,805,000t
mandarin oranges (1998): 534,000t

honey (2001): 100,293t
hazelnuts (2001): 43,540t
walnuts (2001): 254,010t
olives (2002): 82,000t
oranges (2002): 11,251,000t
barley (2002): 4,933,000t
grapefruits (2001): 2,240,000t
sweet potatoes (2001): 653,000t
peaches (2002): 1,439,000t
pistachios (2001): 90,720,000t
apples (2001): 4,337,000t
potatoes (2002): 20,856,000t
timber (2000): 427,654,000m³
grapes (2002): 6,681,000t
rice (2002): 9,569,000t
rye (2001): 177,000t
soya beans (2002): 74,825,000t
sorghum (2002): 9,392,000t
tobacco (2001): 450,000t
tomatoes (2002): 12,267,000t
sunflowers (2002): 1,133,000t
Livestock farming and fishing
cattle (2002): 97,102,000 head
horses (2001): 5,326,000 head
sheep (2002): 6,685,000 head

pigs (2002): 59,922,000 head
chickens (2002): 1,940,000,000 head
fish (1999): 5,233,000t

Energy generation and mining
silver (2001): 1,740t
copper (2001): 1,340,000t
nuclear electricity (2001): 768,826
million kWh
hydroelectricity (2001): 208,726 million
kWh
total electricity (2001): 3,719,485
million kWh
iron (2001): 27,480,000t
natural gas (2002): 547,700 million m³
coal (2001): 937,435,000t
molybdenum (2001): 37,600t
gold (2001): 335,000kg
oil (2002): 346,816,000t
phosphate (2001): 31,900,000t
lead (2001): 466,000t
uranium (2001): 1,000t
zinc (2001): 842,000t

Industrial production
cheese (2001): 4,073,000t

The United States of America

state	area (in km²)	number of inhabitants*	capital	state	area (in km²)	number of inhabitants*	capital
Alabama	131 427	4 447 100	Montgomery	Mississippi	121 489	2 844 658	Jackson
Alaska	1 481 354	626 932	Juneau	Missouri	178 415	5 595 211	Jefferson
Arizona	294 314	5 130 632	Phoenix	Montana	376 981	902 195	Helena
Arkansas	134 857	2 673 400	Little Rock	Nebraska	199 100	1 711 263	Lincoln
California	403 935	33 871 648	Sacramento	Nevada	284 449	1 998 257	Carson
North Carolina	126 161	8 049 313	Raleigh	New Hampshire	23 227	1 235 786	Concord
South Carolina	77 984	4 012 012	Columbia	New Jersey	19 211	8 414 350	Trenton
Colorado	268 628	4 301 261	Denver	New York	122 284	18 976 457	Albany
Connecticut	12 548	3 405 565	Hartford	New Mexico	314 311	1 819 046	Santa Fe
North Dakota	178 648	642 200	Bismarck	Ohio	106 056	11 353 140	Columbus
South Dakota	196 541	754 844	Pierre	Oklahoma	177 848	3 450 654	Oklahoma C.
Delaware	5 060	783 600	Dover	Oregon	248 632	3 421 399	Salem
Florida	139 670	15 982 378	Tallahassee	Pennsylvania	116 075	12 281 054	Harrisburg
Georgia	149 977	8 186 453	Atlanta	Rhode Island	2 706	1 048 319	Providence
Hawaii	16 635	1 211 537	Honolulu	Tennessee	106 752	5 689 283	Nashville
Idaho	214 315	1 293 953	Boise	Texas	678 055	20 851 820	Austin
Illinois	143 961	12 419 293	Springfield	Utah	212 752	2 233 169	Salt Lake City
Indiana	92 895	6 080 485	Indianapolis	Vermont	23 956	608 827	Montpelier
Iowa	144 772	2 926 324	Des Moines	Virginia	102 549	7 078 515	Richmond
Kansas	211 901	2 688 418	Topeka	West Virginia	62 361	1 808 344	Charleston
Kentucky	102 896	4 041 769	Frankfort	Washington	172 349	5 894 121	Olympia
Louisiana	112 825	4 468 976	Baton Rouge	Wisconsin	140 663	5 363 675	Madison
Maine	79 931	1 274 923	Augusta	Wyoming	251 490	493 782	Cheyenne
Maryland	25 314	5 296 486	Annapolis	**Federal District**			
Massachusetts	20 306	6 349 097	Boston	District of Columbia	159	572 059	Washington
Michigan	147 122	9 938 444	Lansing				
Minnesota	206 190	4 919 479	Saint Paul				

* 2000 census.

milk *(2001)*: 75,404,000t
eggs *(2001)*: 5,096,040t
meat *(2001)*: 37,898,000t
sugar *(2002)*: 7,624,000t
wine *(2002)*: 25,400,000hl
steel *(2003)*: 91,360,000t
cast iron *(1998)*: 48,238,000t
aluminium *(2001)*: 2,637,000t
copper *(2001)*: 1,340,000t
tin *(2001)*: 13,900t
lead *(2001)*: 1,390,000t
zinc *(2001)*: 311,000t

cars *(2002)*: 5,016,000 units
commercial vehicles *(1998)*: 6,488,000 units
shipbuilding *(2001)*: 88,000dwt
timber *(2000)*: 427,654,000m³
artificial textiles *(1999)*: 134,200t
synthetic textiles *(1999)*: 3,913,500t

Tourism
Tourism revenue **(2001)**: 72,295 million US$

Foreign trade
Exports **(2002)**: 685,380 million US$

Imports **(2002)**: 1,164,760 million US$

Defence
Armed forces **(2001)**: 1,414,000 people
Defence budget **(2001)**: 3.84% of GDP

Standard of living
Inhabitants per doctor **(1996)**: 384
Average daily calorie intake **(2000)**: 3,772
(FAO minimum: 2,400)
Cars per 1,000 inhabitants **(1999)**: 475
Televisions per 1,000 inhabitants **(2000)**: 854

HISTORY: KEY DATES

The colonial period and independence

16c: already occupied by a number of indigenous Native American groups, the territory that is now the USA was explored by the French, Spanish and English.

17c: English settlers arrived in large numbers, fleeing political and religious upheavals in Britain. They settled on the east coast, whilst the French spread out along the Mississippi River, establishing the colony of Louisiana. Through successive foundations and by annexing Dutch territories, thirteen British colonies were created.

1754–60: colonial and British forces joined together in the French and Indian War.

1763: under the Treaty of Paris, France ceded its North American territories to Britain, opening the west to British colonists.

1763–73: dissatisfaction with Britain's administration led to rebellion amongst the colonists.

1775–83: ongoing tension between Britain and the colonists led to the American Revolution (or War of Independence), which resulted in the independence of the thirteen American colonies.

1776: the Declaration of Independence was signed on 4th July.

1781: the Articles of Confederation, establishing the terms of the union of states, were signed.

1783: the second Treaty of Paris was signed, fully recognizing the independence of the USA.

Independence to the Civil War

1787: a constitution for the USA was drawn up.

1789: George Washington became the country's first president.

1803: the USA purchased Louisiana from France.

1812–14: the War of 1812, provoked in part by Britain's failure to observe American neutral and maritime rights, was eventually won by the USA.

1819: the USA purchased Florida from Spain.

1846–8: after the Mexican War, the USA annexed a large area of Mexican territory including Texas, New Mexico and California.

1853–61: antagonism between the free-trade ethos of the agricultural South and the protectionist and increasingly industrialized North was made worse by the conflict over slavery.

1860: Abraham Lincoln, a Republican from the North, was elected president. Eleven Southern states then seceded from the Union in protest and formed the Confederate States of America.

1865: the American Civil War (1861–5) was won by the Union, or Northern states, leading to the complete abolition of slavery. President Lincoln was assassinated shortly afterwards.

Reconstruction to World War II

1867: the USA purchased Alaska from Russia.

1877: the post-Civil War period known as Reconstruction, during which the Southern states were gradually reintegrated with the Union, came to a close.

1890: a massacre of Sioux men, women and children by the US army at Wounded Knee, South Dakota, marked the end of the 'Sioux Wars', during which the Sioux people had resisted the systematic conquest of their territory.

1898: the USA assisted Cuba's struggle for independence and annexed Guam, Puerto Rico and the Philippines.

1901–9: Panama was established as a republic after a rebellion encouraged by the USA. The USA established authority over the Panama Canal Zone, and undertook to complete the building of the canal.

1917: the USA intervened in World War I, declaring war on Germany.

1929: a Wall Street stock market crash on Thursday 24th October ('Black Thursday') marked the start of the unprecedented economic and social crisis known as the Great Depression.

1933–45: President Franklin D Roosevelt's 'New Deal' recovery programme introduced significant social and economic reform.

1941: the USA entered World War II after the bombing of Pearl Harbor by Japanese forces.

1945: the USA used the recently developed atomic bomb against the Japanese cities of Hiroshima and Nagasaki.

America since 1945

1945–53: the USA affirmed its opposition to Soviet expansion, leading to the Cold War.

1948: the Marshall Plan, an economic aid plan to help post-war Europe, was adopted.

1949: the establishment of the North Atlantic Treaty Organization (NATO) reinforced the alliance between Western powers.

1950: the USA joined the Korean War.

1962: the USA demanded that Soviet nuclear missile bases in Cuba be dismantled. The resulting tensions between the USA and the USSR became known as the Cuban Missile Crisis.

1963: President John F Kennedy was assassinated in Dallas.

1964: the USA intervened directly in the Vietnam War.

1969–74: President Richard Nixon paid a visit to China, and worked to improve relations with the USSR.

1973: US troops withdrew from Vietnam. Nixon was forced to resign in the wake of the Watergate scandal.

1983: the USA occupied Grenada.

1989: a US military invasion of Panama ousted the Panamanian president, Manuel Noriega.

1991: the USA and its allies won a decisive victory over Iraq in the first Gulf War.

1994: the North American Free Trade Agreement (NAFTA) between the USA, Canada and Mexico took effect.

2001: terrorist attacks destroyed the twin towers of the World Trade Center in New York City and struck the Pentagon in Washington, DC. The attacks were attributed to the Saudi-born terrorist leader Osama Bin Laden and the Islamic militant group Al-Qaeda. US forces responded to the attack with military intervention in Afghanistan, where Bin Laden was thought to have taken refuge.

2003: the USA, with the support of the UK, launched a military offensive against Iraq.

Uruguay

— road
— railway line
✈ airport

200 m

● population over 1,000,000
● population 50,000 to 1,000,000
● population 10,000 to 50,000
• population less than 10,000

50 km

The Oriental Republic of Uruguay's terrain consists mainly of hills and low-lying plains. The country, which borders Brazil to the north, the Atlantic Ocean to the south-east and the Río de la Plata – one of the longest estuaries in the world – to the south-west, is a transition zone between the Brazilian Plateau and the Argentinian Pampas. The climate is temperate, and rainfall is heavier in the north than in the south.

Area: 175,016km²
Population (2002): 3,385,000
Capital: Montevideo 1,329,000 (2001 e)
Government type and political system: republic with a semi-presidential system
Head of state and government: (President of the Republic) Tabare Vazquez
Administrative structure: 19 departments
Official language: Spanish
Currency: Uruguayan peso

142

DEMOGRAPHICS
Density: 19 inhab/km²
Percentage of population in urban areas (2001): 92.1%
Age structure of population (2000): 0–15 years: 24.8%, 15–65 years: 62.3%, over 65 years: 12.9%
Birth rate (2003): 16.8‰
Death rate (2003): 9.1‰
Infant mortality rate (2003): 13.1‰
Life expectancy at birth (2003): male: 71.6 years, female: 78.9 years

ECONOMY
GNP (2002): 14.6 billion US$
GNP per capita (2002): 4,340 US$
GNP per capita PPP (2002): 7,710 international dollars
HDI (2000): 0.831
GDP annual growth rate (2003): 2.5%
Annual inflation rate (2001): 4.4%
Labour force by occupation: n/a
GDP by sector (2000): agriculture: 6%, industry: 27.3%, services: 66.7%
Gross public debt: n/a
Unemployment rate (2002): 15.3%

Agriculture and fishing
Crops
wheat (2002): 206,000t

sugar cane (2001): 160,000t
maize (2002): 163,000t
potatoes (2002): 147,000t
rice (2002): 939,000t
Livestock farming and fishing
cattle (2002): 11,115,000 head
sheep (2002): 10,986,000 head
chickens (2002): 13,500,000 head
fish (1999): 103,000t

Energy generation
total electricity (2001): 7,963 million kWh

Industrial production
milk (2001): 1,422,000t
wool (2001): 54,425t

wine (2002): 714,000hl

Tourism
Tourism revenue (2001): 561 million US$

Foreign trade
Exports (2002): 1,933.1 million US$
Imports (2002): 1,872.9 million US$

Defence
Armed forces (2001): 23,900 people
Defence budget (2001): 1.97% of GDP

Standard of living
Inhabitants per doctor (1990): 350
Average daily calorie intake (2000): 2,878 (FAO minimum: 2,400)
Cars per 1,000 inhabitants (1997): 158
Televisions per 1,000 inhabitants (2000): 530

HISTORY: KEY DATES

16c–17c: the Spanish explored the coast of Uruguay, and later established a settlement in the south-west; a Portuguese settlement was also founded.
18c: Spanish colonists founded the military stronghold of Montevideo, and drove the Portuguese settlers out of the area.
1825–8: Uruguay became independent, forming a buffer state between its two powerful neighbours, Argentina and Brazil.
1838–65: political life was marked by a struggle between the Colorados, or 'Redshirts' – the future Liberals – and the Blancos, or 'Whites' – the future Conservative Party.
1930: the first football World Cup was staged in Uruguay.

1931–8: Gabriel Terra became president in a coup and suspended the constitution, but continued development of the country by socialist principles.
1960s: the Tupamaros, a Marxist terrorist guerrilla group, emerged during a period of ongoing social unrest.
1976: a military coup led to a period of harsh government by a regime with little concern for human rights; many people were killed.
1985: civilian rule was restored.
2002: economic crises in neighbouring countries had a negative impact on the economy of Uruguay.
2003: the government announced plans to compensate families of those killed during the country's years of guerrilla warfare and military dictatorship.

VENEXUELA

The Andes Mountains contain the highest elevation in the Bolivarian Republic of Venezuela, Pico Bolívar (5,007m), and surround the Gulf of Venezuela. The centre of the country is made up of the llanos, a lowland area of plains drained by tributaries of the River Orinoco. This area is surrounded by mountain ranges that run along the coast of the Caribbean Sea. Venezuela's climate is tropical, with heavier rainfall in the south where Amazonian rainforests predominate.

Venezuela

Area: 912,050km²
Population (2002): 25,093,000
Capital: Caracas 3,177,000 (2001 e) including the suburbs
Government type and political system: republic with a presidential system
Head of state and government: (President of the Republic) Hugo Chávez Frías
Administrative structure: 23 states, 1 federal district and 1 federal dependency (made up of 72 islands)
Official language: Spanish
Currency: bolívar

DEMOGRAPHICS
Density: 27 inhab/km²
Percentage of population in urban areas (2001): 87.2%
Age structure of population (2000): 0–15 years: 34%, 15–65 years: 61.6%, over 65 years: 4.4%
Birth rate (2003): 22‰
Death rate (2003): 4‰
Infant mortality rate (2003): 18.9‰
Life expectancy at birth (2003): male: 70.9 years, female: 76.7 years

ECONOMY
GNP (2002): 102 billion US$
GNP per capita (2002): 4,080 US$
GNP per capita PPP (2002): 5,220 international dollars
HDI (2000): 0.77
GDP annual growth rate (2003): –9.2%
Annual inflation rate (2001): 12.5%
Labour force by occupation: n/a
GDP by sector (2000): agriculture: 5%, industry: 36.4%, services: 58.6%
Gross public debt: n/a
Unemployment rate (2002): 15.8%

Agriculture
Crops
pineapples (2001): 300,000t

bananas (2001): 1,050,000t
plantains (2001): 700,000t
cocoa (2001): 18,000t
sugar cane (2001): 8,857,000t
maize (2002): 1,546,000t
manioc (2001): 571,000t
oranges (2002): 383,000t
rice (2002): 661,000t
sisal (2001): 10,500t
Livestock farming
cattle (2002): 16,000,000 head
goats (2001): 4,000,000 head
horses (2001): 500,000 head
pigs (2002): 5,655,000 head
chickens (2002): 150,000,000 head

Energy generation and mining
bauxite (2001): 4,400,000t
diamonds (2001): 125,000 carats
total electricity (2001): 87,598 million kWh
hydroelectricity (2001): 59,849 million kWh
iron (2001): 12,160,000t

coal (2001): 7,584,000t
gold (2001): 9,076kg
oil (2002): 151,400,000t
Industrial production
sugar (2002): 590,000t
steel (2003): 3,664,000t
aluminium (2001): 570,000t
cement (2001): 8,700,000t
Tourism
Tourism revenue (1999): 656 million US$
Foreign trade
Exports (2002): 26,656 million US$
Imports (2002): 13,732 million US$
Defence
Armed forces (2001): 82,300 people
Defence budget (2001): 1.49% of GDP
Standard of living
Inhabitants per doctor (1993): 640
Average daily calorie intake (2000): 2,256 (FAO minimum: 2,400)
Cars per 1,000 inhabitants (1996): 69
Televisions per 1,000 inhabitants (2000): 185

143

HISTORY: KEY DATES
1498–1520: Spanish navigators explored the coast and eventually established settlements.
1821–30: Simón Bolívar liberated Venezuela from Spain; Venezuela joined Gran Colombia.
1830–48: Venezuela seceded from Gran Colombia. José Antonio Páez ruled the country as a military dictator.
1858–70: civil war developed.
1870–1935: Venezuela was ruled by successive dictatorships.
1935–47: a process of democratization began.
1948–58: the army imposed General Marcos Pérez Jiménez as president.
1959–64: a democratic government was again established.
2000–4: political and economic problems continued to plague the country during the presidency of Hugo Chávez Frías.

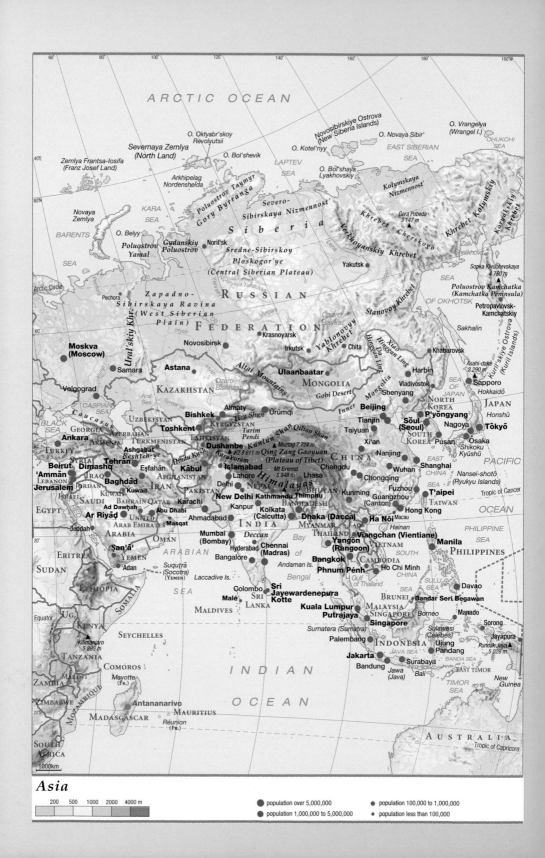

Asia

| | 200 | 500 | 1000 | 2000 | 4000 m |

● population over 5,000,000
● population 1,000,000 to 5,000,000
● population 100,000 to 1,000,000
· population less than 100,000

ASIA

AFGHANISTAN	JORDAN
ARABIAN PENINSULA	KAZAKHSTAN
BAHRAIN	KOREA, NORTH
OMAN	KOREA, SOUTH
QATAR	KUWAIT
SAUDI ARABIA	KYRGYZSTAN
UAE	LAOS
YEMEN	LEBANON
ARMENIA	MALAYSIA
AZERBAIJAN	MONGOLIA
BANGLADESH	MYANMAR
BHUTAN	(BURMA)
BRUNEI	NEPAL
CAMBODIA	PAKISTAN
CHINA	PHILIPPINES
CYPRUS	SINGAPORE
EAST TIMOR	SRI LANKA
GEORGIA	SYRIA
INDIA	TAIWAN
INDIAN OCEAN	TAJIKISTAN
MALDIVES	THAILAND
INDONESIA	TURKEY
IRAN	TURKMENISTAN
IRAQ	UZBEKISTAN
ISRAEL	VIETNAM
JAPAN	

ASIA
44,000,000 km^2
population 3,826 million

AFRICA
30,310,000 km^2
population 842 million

THE AMERICAS
42,000,000 km^2
population 880 million

EUROPE
10,500,000 km^2
population 731 million

OCEANIA
9,000,000 km^2
population 33 million

AFGHANISTAN

The Islamic State of Afghanistan is a landlocked, mainly mountainous country, dominated by the Hindu Kush system. Its climate is arid, often with less than 250mm rainfall per year. Major river valleys include Amu-Daria in the north and Helmand in the south. At the foot of the mountains, which receive more rainfall than the average, lie the principal cities of Kabul, Kandahar, and Harat.

Area: 652,090km²
Population (2002): 23,294,000
Capital: Kabul 2,734,000 (2001 e)
Head of state and government:
(President) Hamid Karzai
Administrative structure: 34 provinces
Official languages: Persian Dari and Afghan Pashto
Currency: afghani

DEMOGRAPHICS

Density: 35 inhab/km²
Percentage of population in urban areas (2001): 22.3%
Age structure of population (2000): 0–15 years: 43.5%, 15–65 years: 53.7%, over 65 years: 2.8%
Birth rate (2003): 47.4‰
Death rate (2003): 21.5‰
Infant mortality rate (2003): 161.7‰
Life expectancy at birth (2003): male: 43 years, female: 43.3 years

ECONOMY

GNP: n/a
GNP per capita: n/a
GNP per capita PPP: n/a
HDI: n/a
GDP annual growth rate: n/a
Inflation rate (1990): 41%
Labour force by occupation: n/a
GDP by sector: n/a
Gross public debt: n/a
Unemployment rate: n/a

Agriculture

Crops
wheat (2002): 2,686,000t
sugar cane (2000): 38,000t
maize (2002): 298,000t
barley (2002): 345,000t
pistachios (1998): 2,000t
grapes (2002): 365,000t
rice (2002): 388,000t
Livestock farming:
cattle (2002): 3,500,000 head
goats (2000): 2,200,000 head

Afghanistan

1000 2000 4000 m

— road
--- railway line
✈ airport

● population over 1,000,000
● population 100,000 to 1,000,000
● population 25,000 to 100,000
· population less than 25,000

150 km

camels (1998): 265,000 head
horses (1998): 300,000 head
sheep (2002): 11,000,000 head

Energy generation and mining
total electricity (2001): 335 million kWh
natural gas (2000): 3,000 million m³
coal (2001): 1,000t

Tourism
Tourism revenue (1998): 1 million US$

Foreign trade
Exports (1997): 148 million US$

Imports (1997): 566 million US$

Defence
Armed forces (2001): 50,000 people
Defence budget: n/a

Standard of living
Inhabitants per doctor (1993): 7,000
Average daily calorie intake: n/a
Cars per 1,000 inhabitants (1996): 1
Televisions per 1,000 inhabitants (2001): 14

HISTORY: KEY DATES

Ancient and medieval Afghanistan
A province of the Iranian Achaemenid empire (6c BC–4c BC), the territory of present-day Afghanistan was 'Hellenized' after the arrival of Alexander the Great (329 BC). Bactria (present-day Balkh), a region which was part of the Kushana empire (1c BC–AD 5c), was influenced by Buddhism, and Afghanistan was later incorporated into the Muslim world. This began when Harat was conquered by the Arabs (651). The Islamization of Afghanistan continued under the Ghaznavids (10c–11c). In 1221–2, Mongols under Genghis Khan conquered the region.

The modern and contemporary period
16c–17c: India and Iran divided the territory of Afghanistan between them.
1747: the first national Afghan dynasty was founded under Ahmad Shah Durrani.
1839–1919: the first, second and third Anglo–Afghan wars took place.
1919: Afghanistan regained its independence.
1973–9: a series of coups took place, beginning when the king was deposed and the Republic of Afghanistan proclaimed. Three further coups followed before the end of the decade.
1979–89: Soviet military forces intervened to support the Afghan government in its struggle against the Mujahidin (Muslim guerrillas).
1992: the Mujahidin proclaimed the Islamic State of Afghanistan.
1996: the Taliban, a fundamentalist group supported by Pakistan, seized power and imposed a radical Islamic regime.
2001: following terrorist attacks against the USA on 11th September, US troops intervened in Afghanistan. Following US bombings and assaults by the North Atlantic Alliance, the Taliban regime collapsed. A multiethnic transitional government was established.
2003: NATO assumed control of security in Kabul.
2004: a new constitution was adopted.

The Kingdom of Bahrain is an archipelago of 35 mainly flat, sandy islands. A 25km causeway connects Bahrain to Saudi Arabia.

Area: 694km²
Population (2002): 664,000
Capital: Manama 150,000 (2001 e) including the suburbs
Government type and political system: constitutional monarchy
Head of state: (King) Sheikh Hamad ibn Isa al-Khalifa
Head of government: (Prime Minister) Sheikh Khalifa ibn Salman al-Khalifa
Administrative structure: 12 municipalities
Official language: Arabic
Currency: Bahraini dinar

DEMOGRAPHICS
Density: 935 inhab/km²
Percentage of population in urban areas
(2001): 92.5%
Age structure of population (2000): 0–15 years: 28.2%, 15–65 years: 68.9%, over 65 years: 2.9%
Birth rate (2003): 19.9‰
Death rate (2003): 3.1‰
Infant mortality rate (2003): 14.2‰
Life expectancy at birth (2003): male: 72.5 years, female: 75.9 years

ECONOMY
GNP (2002): 7.33 billion US$
GNP per capita (2002): 10,500 US$
GNP per capita PPP (2002): 16,190 international dollars
HDI (2000): 0.831
GDP annual growth rate (2003): 5%
Annual inflation rate (1998): −0.37%
Labour force by occupation: n/a
GDP by sector (1995): agriculture: 0.93%, industry: 43.32%, services: 55.75%
Gross public debt: n/a
Unemployment rate: n/a

Agriculture
Crops
dates (2001): 16,500t
tomatoes (2002): 3,400t
Livestock farming
cattle (2002): 13,000 head
goats (2001): 16,300 head
camels (2001): 920 head
sheep (2002): 17,500 head

Energy generation and mining
total electricity (2001): 6,257 million kWh
natural gas (2002): 9,200 million m³
oil (2002): 8,664,000t

Industrial production
milk (2001): 14,400t
aluminium (2001): 510,000t
cement (2001): 89,000t

Tourism
Tourism revenue (1999): 408 million US$

Foreign trade
Exports (2002): 5,785.6 million US$
Imports (2000): 4,672.9 million US$

Defence
Armed forces (2001): 10,700 people
Defence budget (2001): 4.82% of GDP

Standard of living
Inhabitants per doctor (1991): 769
Average daily calorie intake: n/a
Cars per 1,000 inhabitants (2000): 266
Televisions per 1,000 inhabitants (2000): 402

HISTORY: KEY DATES
1861: Bahrain became a British protectorate.
1971: Bahrain gained full independence.
2002: the country became a constitutional monarchy.

147

Arabian Peninsula – Bahrain – Oman – Qatar – Saudi Arabia – UAE – Yemen

| 200 500 1000 2000 3000 m | road | oil field | population over 1,000,000 | population 50,000 to 100,000 |
| | railway line | airport | oil and gas pipeline | population 100,000 to 1,000,000 | population less than 50,000 |

ARABIAN PENINSULA OMAN

A vast desert plain covers most of the interior of the Sultanate of Oman, and there are mountain ranges along the north and south-east coasts.

Area: 212,457km²
Population (2002): 2,709,000
Capital: Muscat 540,000 (2001 e)
Government type and political system: monarchy
Head of state and government: (Sultan) Qaboos Bin Said
Administrative structure: 6 regions and 2 governorates
Official language: Arabic
Currency: rial

DEMOGRAPHICS

Density: 12 inhab/km²
Percentage of population in urban areas (2001): 76.5%
Age structure of population (2000): 0–15 years: 44.1%, 15–65 years: 53.4%, over 65 years: 2.5%
Birth rate (2003): 31.8‰
Death rate (2003): 3.3‰
Infant mortality rate (2003): 19.7‰
Life expectancy at birth (2003): male: 71 years, female: 74.4 years

ECONOMY

GNP (2002): 19.9 billion US$
GNP per capita (2002): 7,830 US$
GNP per capita PPP (2002): 13,000 international dollars
HDI (2000): 0.751
GDP annual growth rate (2003): 2.2%
Annual inflation rate (2000): −1.11%
Labour force by occupation: n/a
GDP by sector (1994): agriculture: 3%, industry: 53%, services: 44%
Gross public debt: n/a
Unemployment rate: n/a

Agriculture and fishing

Crops
bananas (2001): 30,500t
dates (2001): 260,000t
potatoes (2002): 15,500t
tobacco (2001): 1,270t
Livestock farming and fishing
cattle (2002): 314,000 head
goats (2001): 980,000 head
camels (2001): 98,000 head
sheep (2002): 354,000 head
chickens (2002): 3,400,000 head
fish (1999): 109,000t

Energy generation and mining
silver (2000): 1t
copper (2001): 24,281t
total electricity (2001): 9,274 million kWh
natural gas (2002): 14,800 million m³
gold (2001): 610kg
oil (2002): 44,600,000t

Tourism
Tourism revenue (2001): 118 million US$

Foreign trade
Exports (2001): 11,074 million US$
Imports (2001): 5,311 million US$

Defence
Armed forces (2001): 41,700 people
Defence budget (2001): 12.02% of GDP

Standard of living
Inhabitants per doctor (1993): 1,111
Average daily calorie intake: n/a
Cars per 1,000 inhabitants (1996): 103
Televisions per 1,000 inhabitants (2000): 563

HISTORY: KEY DATES

17c–19c: the Sultans of Oman took possession of a maritime empire centred on Zanzibar, which had previously been controlled by Portugal.
1970–2004: after seizing power from his father in a bloodless coup, Sultan Qaboos Bin Said attempted to modernize the country by using oil revenues to develop its infrastructure.

ARABIAN PENINSULA QATAR

The State of Qatar occupies a small, low-lying, barren peninsula covered with sand, which projects from the Arabian Peninsula into the Persian Gulf. It has a number of islands and is rich in oil and gas.

Area: 11,000km²
Population (2002): 584,000
Capital: Doha 285,000 (2001 e) including the suburbs
Government type and political system: monarchy
Head of state and government: (Emir) Sheikh Hamad bin Khalifa al-Thani
Prime minister: Sheikh Abdullah bin Khalifa al-Thani
Administrative structure: 9 municipalities
Official language: Arabic
Currency: Qatari riyal

DEMOGRAPHICS

Density: 53 inhab/km²
Percentage of population in urban areas (2001): 92.9%
Age structure of population (2000): 0–15 years: 26.7%, 15–65 years: 71.8%, over 65 years: 1.5%
Birth rate (2003): 17.4‰
Death rate (2003): 3.7‰
Infant mortality rate (2003): 12.3‰
Life expectancy at birth (2003): male: 70.5 years, female: 75.4 years

ECONOMY

GNP (1997): 9.51 billion US$
GNP per capita (1995): 15,570 US$
GNP per capita PPP (1996): 16,330 international dollars
HDI (2000): 0.803
GDP annual growth rate (2003): 4%
Annual inflation rate (2000): −1.02%
Labour force by occupation: n/a
GDP by sector (1991): agriculture: 1%, industry: 45%, services: 54%
Gross public debt: n/a
Unemployment rate: n/a

Agriculture and fishing

Crops
dates (2001): 16,500t
Livestock farming and fishing
cattle (2002): 15,000 head
goats (2001): 179,000 head
camels (2001): 50,000 head
horses (2001): 3,780 head
sheep (2002): 200,000 head
chickens (2002): 4,000,000 head
fish (1999): 4,210t

Energy generation and mining
total electricity (2001): 9,264 million kWh
natural gas (2002): 29,300 million m³
oil (2002): 34,700,000t

Industrial production
steel (2003): 1,054,000t

Tourism
Tourism revenue: n/a

Foreign trade
Exports (1997): 5,560 million US$
Imports (1997): 4,489 million US$

Defence
Armed forces (2001): 12,400 people
Defence budget (2001): 7.07% of GDP

Standard of living
Inhabitants per doctor (1990): 667
Average daily calorie intake: n/a
Cars per 1,000 inhabitants (1996): 217
Televisions per 1,000 inhabitants (2001): 869

HISTORY: KEY DATES

1971: Qatar, formerly a British protectorate, became independent.
1999–2003: municipal elections and a new constitution were introduced.

The Kingdom of Saudi Arabia is a huge country that takes up about four-fifths of the Arabian Peninsula, and owes its economic and political importance to its vast oil reserves (the Al Hasa plain on the Arabian Gulf is rich in oil). Its climate is hot and dry, with higher humidity on the Red Sea coast. An influential member of OPEC (Organization of Petroleum Exporting Countries), Saudi Arabia is the world's leading oil producer and exporter.

Area: 2,149,690km²
Population (2002): 21,700,000
Capital: Riyadh 4,761,000 (2001 e)
Government type and political system: monarchy
Head of state and government: (King) Fahd bin Abdulaziz al-Saud
Administrative structure: 13 provinces
Official language: Arabic
Currency: Saudi riyal

DEMOGRAPHICS

Density: 10 inhab/km²
Percentage of population in urban areas (2001): 86.6%
Age structure of population (2000): 0–15 years: 42.9%, 15–65 years: 54.1%, over 65 years: 3%
Birth rate (2003): 31.5‰
Death rate (2003): 3.7‰
Infant mortality rate (2003): 20.6‰
Life expectancy at birth (2003): male: 71.1 years, female: 73.7 years

ECONOMY

GNP (2002): 187 billion US$
GNP per capita (2002): 8,530 US$
GNP per capita PPP (2002): 12,660 international dollars
HDI (2000): 0.759
GDP annual growth rate (2003): 6.4%
Annual inflation rate (2000): −0.85%
Labour force by occupation: n/a
GDP by sector (1998): agriculture: 7%, industry: 47.6%, services: 45.4%
Gross public debt: n/a
Unemployment rate (2001): 4.6%

Agriculture
Crops
wheat (2002): 2,431,000t
dates (2001): 712,000t
sorghum (2002): 239,000t
Livestock farming
cattle (2001): 330,000 head
goats (2001): 4,305,000 head
camels (2001): 400,000 head
horses (2001): 3,000 head
sheep (2002): 8,170,000 head

Energy generation and mining
total electricity (2001): 122,401 million kWh
natural gas (2002): 56,400 million m³
gold (2001): 5,000kg
oil (2002): 418,100,000t

Industrial production
steel (2003): 3,944,000t
cement (2001): 20,608,000t

Tourism
Tourism revenue (1998): 1,462 million US$

Foreign trade
Exports (2002): 71,679 million US$
Imports (2002): 29,642 million US$

Defence
Armed forces (2001): 124,500 people
Defence budget (2001): 11.68% of GDP

Standard of living
Inhabitants per doctor (1993): 769
Average daily calorie intake (2000): 2,875 (FAO minimum: 2,400)
Cars per 1,000 inhabitants (1996): 98
Televisions per 1,000 inhabitants (2000): 264

HISTORY: KEY DATES

1930: Oil was discovered in Saudi Arabia.
1932: the kingdom of Saudi Arabia was created by the unification of areas conquered by Abdulaziz bin Abdur-Rahman (known as Ibn Saud) since 1902. Ibn Saud was proclaimed king, and used oil revenues to modernize the country during his reign.
1953–64: Ibn Saud was succeeded by his son, Saud Bin Abdulaziz al-Saud. In 1958 Saud ceded power to his brother, Faisal bin Abdulaziz al-Saud, who deposed him in 1964.
1960: Saudi Arabia became one of the founding members of the Organization of Petroleum Exporting Countries (OPEC).
1972–3: Saudi Arabia attempted to limit US control of its oil reserves. It led an oil boycott against various Western countries in 1973, causing the price of oil to escalate sharply.
1975: Faisal was assassinated by his nephew and then succeeded by his brother Khalid.
1982: Khalid's brother Fahd succeeded him.
1991: a multinational force deployed on Saudi Arabian territory intervened against Iraq during the Gulf War.
2003: following an unprecedented level of protest against the existing regime, plans for significant political reforms were announced.

The United Arab Emirates is a federation in the eastern central Arabian Peninsula. It comprises seven emirates: Abu Dhabi, Ajman, Dubai, Fujairah, Ras al-Khaimah, Sharjah and Umm al-Qaiwain. The climate is hot, and sandstorms are frequent.

Area: 83,600km²
Population (2002): 2,701,000
Capital: Abu Dhabi 398,695 (1995 census), 471,000 (2001 e) including the suburbs
Government type and political system: monarchy
Head of state: (President of the Supreme Council and ruler of Abu Dhabi) Sheikh Khalifa Bin Zayed
Head of government: (Prime Minister) Sheikh Maktoum Bin Rashid al-Maktoum
Administrative structure: 7 emirates
Official language: Arabic
Currency: UAE dirham

DEMOGRAPHICS

Density: 31 inhab/km²
Percentage of population in urban areas (2001): 87.1%
Age structure of population (2000): 0–15 years: 26%, 15–65 years: 71.3%, over 65 years: 2.7%
Birth rate (2003): 16.7‰
Death rate (2003): 2.4‰
Infant mortality rate (2003): 13.6‰
Life expectancy at birth (2003): male: 73.3 years, female: 77.4 years

ECONOMY

GNP (1998): 49.2 billion US$
GNP per capita (1998): 18,060 US$
GNP per capita PPP (2002): 24,030 international dollars
HDI (2000): 0.812
GDP annual growth rate (2003): 7%
Annual inflation rate: n/a
Labour force by occupation: n/a
GDP by sector (1993): agriculture: 2%, industry: 57%, services: 41%
Gross public debt: n/a

Unemployment rate (2000): 2.3%

Agriculture and fishing
Crops
dates (2001): 318,000t
tomatoes (2002): 400,000t
Livestock farming and fishing:
cattle (2002): 106,000 head
goats (2001): 1,200,000 head
camels (2001): 200,000 head
sheep (2002): 550,000 head
fish (1999): 118,000t

Energy generation and mining
chromium (2001): 10,000t
total electricity (2001): 37,745 million kWh
natural gas (2002): 46,000 million m³
oil (2002): 105,600,000t

Industrial production
aluminium (2001): 500,000t
cement (2001): 6,100,000t

Tourism
Tourism revenue (1999): 607 million US$

Foreign trade
Exports (1997): 30,423 million US$
Imports (1997): 31,050 million US$

Defence
Armed forces (2001): 41,500 people
Defence budget (2001): 2.41% of GDP

Standard of living
Inhabitants per doctor (1993): 1,100
Average daily calorie intake (2000): 3,192
(FAO minimum: 2,400)
Cars per 1,000 inhabitants (1996): 11

Televisions per 1,000 inhabitants (2001): 252

HISTORY: KEY DATES
19c: the Trucial States (so-called because their rulers were bound by truces) signed a perpetual maritime peace treaty with Great Britain and became a British protectorate.
1962: oil exports from Abu Dhabi began.
1971–2: following independence from Britain, the seven emirates constituting these states formed a federation.
1973: a rise in global oil prices dramatically boosted the UAE's economic power.

ARABIAN PENINSULA YEMEN

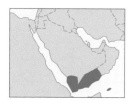

Most of the Republic of Yemen is an arid desert. A high plateau that reaches altitudes of up to 3,760m occupies the western part of the country. These highlands are home to most of the country's population, and Yemen's capital, Sana'a, is also situated on this high plateau. Aden, the country's main port and economic capital, is located on the southern coast.

Area: 537,968km²
Population (2002): 19,911,000
Capital: Sana'a 1,410,000 (2001 e)
Government type and political system: republic with a semi-presidential system
Head of state: (President of the Republic) Ali Abdullah Saleh
Head of government: (Prime Minister) Abdul Qadir Abd al-Rahman Bajammal
Administrative structure: 17 governorates
Official language: Arabic
Currency: Yemeni riyal

DEMOGRAPHICS
Density: 37 inhab/km²
Percentage of population in urban areas (2001): 25%
Age structure of population (2000): 0–15 years: 50.1%, 15–65 years: 47.6%, over 65 years: 2.3%

Birth rate (2003): 45‰
Death rate (2003): 9.2‰
Infant mortality rate (2003): 70.6‰
Life expectancy at birth (2003): male: 58.9 years, female: 61.1 years

ECONOMY
GNP (2002): 9.15 billion US$
GNP per capita (2002): 490 US$
GNP per capita PPP (2002): 800 international dollars
HDI (2000): 0.479
GDP annual growth rate (2003): 3.8%
Annual inflation rate (1998): 7.92%
Labour force by occupation (1999): agriculture: 54.1%, industry: 11.1%, services: 34.8%
GDP by sector (2000): agriculture: 15.4%, industry: 46.2%, services: 38.4%
Gross public debt: n/a
Unemployment rate: n/a

Agriculture
Crops
bananas (2001): 90,000t
wheat (2002): 150,000t
dates (2001): 29,800t
potatoes (2002): 211,000t
grapes (2002): 165,000t
sorghum (2002): 289,000t
tomatoes (2002): 267,000t
Livestock farming
cattle (2002): 1,342,000 head
goats (2001): 4,252,000 head
sheep (2002): 6,483,000 head

Energy generation and mining
total electricity (2001): 3,010 million kWh
oil (2002): 22,400,000t

Tourism
Tourism revenue (2001): 38 million US$

Foreign trade
Exports (2002): 3,620.7 million US$

Imports (2002): 2,932 million US$

Defence
Armed forces (2001): 66,500 people
Defence budget (2001): 7.64% of GDP

Standard of living
Inhabitants per doctor (1990): 10,000
Average daily calorie intake (2000): 2,038
(FAO minimum: 2,400)
Cars per 1,000 inhabitants (1996): 14
Televisions per 1,000 inhabitants (2000): 283

HISTORY: KEY DATES
AD 6c: present-day Yemen was occupied by the Ethiopians and the Sassanid Persians.
628: the Muslim caliphate took control of the region.
1570: Yemen became part of the Ottoman Empire.
1839: the British conquered Aden and established a protectorate in the south of Yemen.
1918: the Ottoman Empire dissolved.
1920: the independence of northern Yemen was officially recognized.
1967: Southern Yemen was established as an independent country.
1970: Southern Yemen became the Marxist-Leninist People's Democratic Republic of Yemen (PDRY).
1990: the two republics were formally unified as the Republic of Yemen.
1994: the southern part of the country attempted to secede after relations between the two areas broke down.
2002: a number of foreign Islamic scholars were expelled from Yemen in an attempt to rid the country of terrorism.

The Republic of Armenia is a landlocked country, situated in southern Transcaucasia, bordering on Turkey to the west. Armenia is mountainous (90% of the territory is over 1,000m), cut through by depressions such as the Araz valley, or basins such as the one in which Lake Sevan is situated.

Area: 29,800km²
Population (2002): 3,790,000
Capital: Yerevan 1 420 000 (2001 e) including the suburbs
Government type and political system: republic with a semi-presidential system
Head of state: (President of the Republic) Robert Kocharyan
Head of government: (Prime Minister) Andranik Markaryan
Administrative structure: 10 provinces and a capital district
Official language: Armenian
Currency: Armenian dram

DEMOGRAPHICS

Density: 118 inhab/km²
Percentage of population in urban areas (2001): 67.3%
Age structure of population (2000): 0–15 years: 23.7%, 15–65 years: 67.7%, over 65 years: 8.6%
Birth rate (2003): 9.7‰
Death rate (2003): 7.7‰
Infant mortality rate (2003): 17.3‰
Life expectancy at birth (2003): male: 69 years, female: 75.6 years

ECONOMY

GNP (2002): 2.43 billion US$
GNP per capita (2002): 790 US$
GNP per capita PPP (2002): 3,230 international dollars
HDI (2000): 0.754
GDP annual growth rate (2003): 12%
Annual inflation rate (2000): −0.81%
Labour force by occupation: n/a
GDP by sector (2000): agriculture: 25.4%, industry: 35.6%, services: 39%
Gross public debt: n/a
Unemployment rate (2002): 9.4%

Agriculture

Crops
wheat (2002): 285,000t
barley (2002): 109,000t

Armenia

| 500 | 1000 | 1500 | 2000 m |

— road
— railway line
★ place of interest

● population over 1,000,000
● population 100,000 to 1,000,000
● population 30,000 to 100,000
• population less than 30,000

apples (2001): 22,200t
potatoes (2002): 374,000t
grapes (2002): 104,000t
tomatoes (2002): 170,000t
Livestock farming
cattle (2002): 497,000 head
sheep (2002): 546,000 head
pigs (2002): 98,000 head

Energy generation and mining
copper (2001): 9,700t
nuclear electricity (2001): 1,987 million kWh
total electricity (2001): 6,479 million kWh
molybdenum (2001): 3,300t

Industrial production
wine (2002): 72,000hl
wool (2001): 1,356t

cement (2001): 300,000t

Tourism
Tourism revenue (2000): 45 million US$

Foreign trade
Exports (2002): 513.78 million US$
Imports (2002): 882.54 million US$

Defence
Armed forces (2001): 44,610 people
Defence budget (2001): 3.1% of GDP

Standard of living
Inhabitants per doctor (1995): 323
Average daily calorie intake (2000): 1,943 (FAO minimum: 2,400)
Cars per 1,000 inhabitants: n/a
Televisions per 1,000 inhabitants (2001): 230

HISTORY: KEY DATES

640: the Arabs invaded Armenia.
11c–15c: Great Armenia was invaded by the Turks and Mongols. Lesser Armenia, created in Cilicia by King Ruben I, supported the Crusades in the fight against Islam and then fell to the Mamluks in 1375. The Ottomans ruled the whole of Armenia.
1813–28: the Russians conquered eastern Armenia.
1915–17: between 600,000 and 1.75 million Armenians were victims of enforced deportation and genocide carried out by the Turkish government.
1918: the Republic of Armenia was proclaimed.

1920: Turkish Kemalist and Russian Bolshevik troops invaded and occupied the country.
1922: Armenia became part of the USSR.
1988: Armenia claimed unification with the Azerbaijani region of Nagorno-Karabakh, despite opposition from the Soviet and Azerbaijani governments.
1991: Armenia became independent.
1992: the conflict over Nagorno-Karabakh became a war between Armenia and Azerbaijan.
1994: a ceasefire was signed, and Karabakh became an independent republic.

AZERBAIJAN

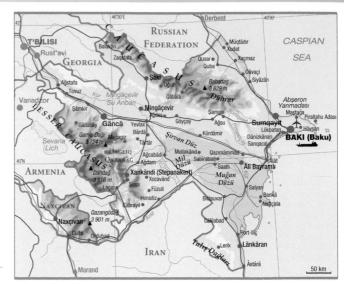

Azerbaijan

oil-exporting port

0   500   1000   2000 m

——	road
——	railway line
✈	airport
✈	oil pipeline

- ● population over 1,000,000
- ● population 100,000 to 1,000,000
- ● population 30,000 to 100,000
- • population less than 30,000

Azerbaijan is a republic in eastern Transcaucasia, bounded to the east by the Caspian Sea. It consists of the vast delta of the rivers Kura and Araz, and its mountainous perimeter. The climate is continental, hot in the summer and cold in winter.

Area: 86,600km²
Population (2002): 8,147,000
Capital: Baku 1,964,000 (2001 e) including the suburbs
Government type and political system: republic with a presidential system
Head of state: (President of the Republic) Ilham Aliyev
Head of government: (Prime Minister) Artur Rasizada
Administrative structure: 65 regions, 13 municipalities and one autonomous republic
Official language: Azeri
Currency: Azerbaijani manat

DEMOGRAPHICS

Density: 89 inhab/km²
Percentage of population in urban areas (2001): 51.9%
Age structure of population (2000): 0–15 years: 29%, 15–65 years: 64.2%, over 65 years: 6.8%
Birth rate (2003): 17.8‰
Death rate (2003): 5.6‰
Infant mortality rate (2003): 29.3‰
Life expectancy at birth (2003): male: 68.7 years, female: 75.5 years

ECONOMY

GNP (2002): 5.8 billion US$
GNP per capita (2002): 710 US$
GNP per capita PPP (2002): 3,010 international dollars
HDI (2000): 0.741
GDP annual growth rate (2003): 11.2%
Annual inflation rate (2000): 1.77%
Labour force by occupation (1998): agriculture: 29.3%, industry: 14%, services: 56.7%
GDP by sector (2000): agriculture: 18.9%, industry: 37.9%, services: 43.2%
Gross public debt: n/a
Unemployment rate (2002): 1.3%

Agriculture

Crops
wheat (2002): 1,693,000t

barley (2002): 295,000t
apples (2001): 291,000t
potatoes (2002): 695,000t
grapes (2002): 62,000t
tomatoes (2002): 404,000t
Livestock farming
cattle (2002): 2,098,000 head
buffaloes (2001): 302,000 head
goats (2001): 416,000 head
horses (2001): 64,000 head
sheep (2002): 6,003,000 head
pigs (2002): 16,900 head

Energy generation and mining
total electricity (2001): 18,225 million kWh
natural gas (2002): 4,800 million m³
oil (2002): 15,300,000t

Industrial production
milk (2001): 1,018,000t
meat (2001): 114,000t
wine (2002): 529,000hl
steel (2000): 25,000t

Tourism
Tourism revenue (1999): 81 million US$

Foreign trade
Exports (2002): 2,304.9 million US$
Imports (2002): 1,823.3 million US$

Defence
Armed forces (2001): 72,100 people
Defence budget (2001): 2.07% of GDP

Standard of living
Inhabitants per doctor (1996): 263
Average daily calorie intake (2000): 2,468 (FAO minimum: 2,400)
Cars per 1,000 inhabitants (2000): 41
Televisions per 1,000 inhabitants (2001): 321

HISTORY: KEY DATES

11c: Azerbaijan, formerly a province of Iran, was invaded by the Seljuk Turks.
1828: northern Azerbaijan was ceded to Russia, while southern Azerbaijan remained part of Persia.
1918: Azerbaijan was proclaimed an independent republic.
1920: Azerbaijan was occupied by the Red Army and became a Soviet republic.
1922: Azerbaijan became one of the founder members of the USSR.
1923–4: the Autonomous Republic of Nakitchevan and the Autonomous Region of Nagorno-Karabakh were instituted and united with Azerbaijan.
1936: Azerbaijan became a federated republic.
1988: Azerbaijani opposition to Armenian claims on Nagorno-Karabakh led to the development of nationalism and anti-Armenian pogroms.
1990: the Communist Party won the country's first multiparty elections.
1991: Azerbaijan gained full independence and became part of the Commonwealth of Independent States (CIS).
1992–4: the conflict over Nagorno-Karabakh escalated into a war between Armenia and Azerbaijan. After a ceasefire was signed, Karabakh began to act as an independent republic.
1994–2004: Azerbaijan's offshore oil resources were developed and exploited.

BAHRAIN
➡ ARABIAN PENINSULA

152

Lying to the north of the Bay of Bengal, the People's Republic of Bangladesh extends over the majority of the delta of the Ganges, Meghna and Brahmaputra rivers. It has an extremely hot and humid climate and is frequently flooded, especially during the summer monsoon season.

Area: 143,998km²
Population (2002): 143,364,000
Capital: Dhaka 3,690,066 (1991 census), 13,181,000 (2001 e) including the suburbs
Government type and political system: republic with a parliamentary system
Head of state: (President of the Republic) Iajuddin Ahmed
Head of government: (Prime Minister) Khaleda Zia
Administrative structure: 6 administrative divisions
Official language: Bengali
Currency: taka

DEMOGRAPHICS

Density: 903 inhab/km²
Percentage of population in urban areas (2001): 25.6%
Age structure of population (2000): 0–15 years: 38.7%, 15–65 years: 58.2%, over 65 years: 3.1%
Birth rate (2003): 28.9‰
Death rate (2003): 8.3‰
Infant mortality rate (2003): 64‰
Life expectancy at birth (2003): male: 61 years, female: 61.8 years

ECONOMY

GNP (2002): 51 billion US$
GNP per capita (2002): 380 US$
GNP per capita PPP (2002): 1,770 international dollars
HDI (2000): 0.478
GDP annual growth rate (2003): 5.4%
Annual inflation rate (2000): 2.38%
Labour force by occupation: n/a
GDP by sector (2000): agriculture: 24.6%, industry: 24.4%, services: 51%
Gross public debt: n/a
Unemployment rate (1996): 2.5%

Agriculture and fishing

Crops
groundnuts (2001): 40,000t
wheat (2002): 1,606,000t

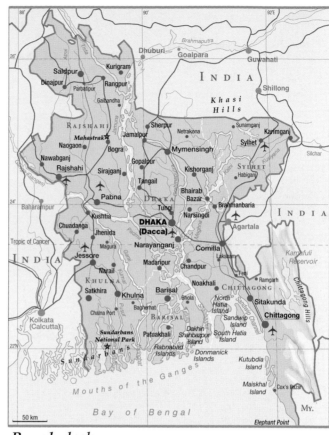

Bangladesh

★	place of interest
▨	divisional boundary
Sylhet	divisional capital

—	road
—	railway line
✈	airport

●	population over 1,000,000
●	population 100,000 to 1,000,000
●	population 30,000 to 100,000
•	population less than 30,000

sugar cane (2001): 6,742,000t
rape (2001): 260,000t
potatoes (2002): 2,994,000t
rice (2002): 37,851,000t
tea (2001): 52,000t

Livestock farming and fishing
cattle (2002): 24,000,000 head
buffaloes (2001): 830,000 head
goats (2001): 34,100,000 head
sheep (2002): 1,154,000 head
chickens (2002): 140,000,000 head
fish (1999): 1,544,000t

Energy generation and mining
total electricity (2001): 15,325 million kWh
natural gas (2002): 11,200 million m³

Industrial production
milk (2001): 2,112,000t
sugar (2002): 222,000t
meat (2001): 428,000t
tea (2001): 52,000t
tobacco (2001): 37,000t
cotton yarn (2001): 18,000t
jute (1997): 883,000t
synthetic textiles: n/a
cement (2001): 5,005,000t

paper (2000): 46,000t

Tourism
Tourism revenue (2001): 48 million US$

Foreign trade
Exports (2002): 6,078.4 million US$
Imports (2002): 7,714 million US$

Defence
Armed forces (2001): 120,000 people
Defence budget (2001): 1.41% of GDP

Standard of living
Inhabitants per doctor (1995): 5,000
Average daily calorie intake (2000): 2,103 (FAO minimum: 2,400)
Cars per 1,000 inhabitants (1999): 0
Televisions per 1,000 inhabitants (2001): 17

HISTORY: KEY DATES

1947: British rule over India ended; East and West Pakistan were established.
1971: East Pakistan obtained its independence and became Bangladesh.

153

The Kingdom of Bhutan is situated in the eastern Himalayas, bordered to the north by China and to the south by India. It is a small country, with high mountains separated by valleys running from north to south. The majority of Bhutan is covered with forest, and the climate is temperate or very humid depending on the altitude.

Area: 47,000km²
Population (2002): 2,198,000
Capital: Thimphu 32,000 (2001 e)
Government type and political system: monarchy
Head of state: (King) Jigme Singye Wangchuk
Head of government: (Prime Minister) Lyonpo Jigme Yozer Thinley
Administrative structure: 20 administrative districts
Official language: Dzongkha
Currencies: ngultrum and Indian rupee

DEMOGRAPHICS

Density: 45 inhab/km²
Percentage of population in urban areas (2001): 7.4%
Age structure of population (2000): 0–15 years: 42.7%, 15–65 years: 53.1%, over 65 years: 4.2%
Birth rate (2003): 34.5‰
Death rate (2003): 8.6‰
Infant mortality rate (2003): 53.6‰
Life expectancy at birth (2003): male: 62 years, female: 64.5 years

ECONOMY

GNP (2002): 0.5112 billion US$
GNP per capita (2002): 600 US$
GNP per capita PPP (2001): 1,530 international dollars
HDI (2000): 0.494
GDP annual growth rate (2003): 7.3%
Annual inflation rate (1997): 6.5%
Labour force by occupation: n/a
GDP by sector (2000): agriculture: 33.2%, industry: 37.3%, services: 29.5%
Gross public debt: n/a
Unemployment rate: n/a

Agriculture

Crops
maize (2002): 48,500t
oranges (2002): 30,000t
potatoes (2002): 22,000t
rice (2002): 44,300t
Livestock farming
cattle (2002): 355,000 head
goats (2001): 42,100 head
sheep (2002): 22,900 head
pigs (2002): 41,400 head

Energy generation and mining
total electricity (2001): 1,896 million kWh
hydroelectricity (2001): 1,895 million kWh
coal (2001): 50,000t

Industrial production
milk (2001): 32,000t
meat (2001): 7,760t
cement (2001): 160,000t
timber (2000): 134,000m³

Tourism
Tourism revenue (2000): 9 million US$

Foreign trade
Exports (1995): 3,349 million US$
Imports (1995): 3,802 million US$

Defence
Armed forces (1999): 6,000 people
Defence budget: n/a

Standard of living
Inhabitants per doctor (1994): 5,000
Average daily calorie intake (1995): 2,058 (FAO minimum: 2,400)
Cars per 1,000 inhabitants: n/a
Televisions per 1,000 inhabitants (2001): 26

HISTORY: KEY DATES

1865: southern Bhutan was annexed by Britain.
1907: Bhutan's first hereditary monarchy was established.
1910–49: Britain controlled Bhutan's foreign affairs until 1949, when that role was assumed by India.
1971: Bhutan became a member of the UN.
2002: a new constitution was drafted.

Map

Bhutan
● population over 500,000
● population 100,000 to 500,000
● population 30,000 to 100,000
● population less than 30,000
— road
— railway line
★ place of interest
✈ airport

CHINA
Lhasa
Yarlung Zangbo (Brahmaputra)
Yamzho Yumco
Puma Yumco
Kula Kangri 7,554 m
HIMALAYAS
Chomo Lhari 7,314 m
Lingzhi
Gasa
Thunkar
THIMPHU
Punakha
Wandue-Phodrang
Trongsa
Shongar
Trashigang
Ha
Chengmari
Samchi
Chhukha
Sarbhang
Gelephu
Dewangiri
Mongar
Samdrup Jongkhar
BANGLADESH
INDIA
Brahmaputra

Brunei

— road

✈ airport

● population 100,000 to 1,000,000

● population 50,000 to 100,000

● population less than 50,000

The State of Brunei Darussalam is a low-lying, humid region, made up of two enclaves on the north-west coast of the island of Borneo. Although very small, the country possesses large deposits of oil and gas.

Area: 5,765km²
Population (2002): 341,000
Capital: Bandar Seri Begawan 46,000 (2001 e)
Government type and political system: monarchy
Head of state and government: (Sultan) Muda Hassanal Bolkiah Mu'izzadin Waddaulah
Administrative structure: 4 districts
Official language: Malaysian
Currency: Bruneian dollar

DEMOGRAPHICS

Density: 57 inhab/km²
Percentage of population in urban areas (2001): 72.7%
Age structure of population (2000): 0–15 years: 31.9%, 15–65 years: 64.9%, over 65 years: 3.2%
Birth rate (2003): 23.5‰
Death rate (2003): 2.8‰
Infant mortality rate (2003): 6.1‰
Life expectancy at birth (2003): male: 74.2 years, female: 78.9 years

ECONOMY

GNP (1998): 7.75 billion US$
GNP per capita (1998): 24,100 US$
GNP per capita PPP (1998): 24,910 international dollars
HDI (2000): 0.856
GDP annual growth rate (2003): 3.6%
Annual inflation rate (1992): 2%
Labour force by occupation: n/a
GDP by sector (1998): agriculture: 2.8%, industry: 44.4%, services: 52.7%
Gross public debt: n/a
Unemployment rate: n/a

Agriculture and fishing

Crops
pineapples (2001): 750t
bananas (2001): 600t
rubber (2001): 210t
manioc (2001): 1,600t
coconuts (2001): 170t
rice (2002): 400t
Livestock farming and fishing
cattle (2002): 2,000 head
buffaloes (2001): 6,000 head
goats (2001): 3,500 head
chickens (2002): 12,500,000 head
fish (1999): 3,310t

Energy generation and mining

total electricity (2001): 2,497 million kWh
natural gas (2002): 11,500 million m³
oil (2002): 10,200,000t

Industrial production

milk (2001): 110t
meat (2001): 18,190t
timber (2000): 217,000m³

Tourism

Tourism revenue (1998): 37 million US$

Foreign trade

Exports (1997): 2,330 million US$
Imports (1997): 3,919 million US$

Defence

Armed forces (2001): 7,000 people
Defence budget (2001): 5.5% of GDP

Standard of living

Inhabitants per doctor (1991): 1,429
Average daily calorie intake (2000): 2,832 (FAO minimum: 2,400)
Cars per 1,000 inhabitants (1999): 225
Televisions per 1,000 inhabitants (2001): 642

HISTORY: KEY DATES

1888: Brunei became a British protectorate.
1984: Brunei became independent within the Commonwealth of Nations.

CAMBODIA

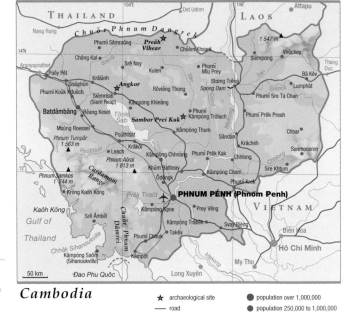

The Kingdom of Cambodia is made up of plains and plateaux covered with forests and savannas, which surround a central depression drained by the Mekong River. Most of the population is concentrated in this central region.

Area: 181,035km²
Population (2002): 13,776,000
Capital: Phnom Penh 1,109,000 (2001 e)
Government type and political system: constitutional monarchy with a parliamentary system
Head of state: (King) Norodom Sihamoni
Head of government: (Prime Minister) Hun Sen
Administrative structure: 20 provinces and 4 autonomous municipalities
Official language: Khmer
Currency: riel

DEMOGRAPHICS
Density: 62 inhab/km²
Percentage of population in urban areas (2001): 17.4%
Age structure of population (2000): 0–15 years: 43.9%, 15–65 years: 53.3%, over 65 years: 2.8%
Birth rate (2003): 33.9‰
Death rate (2003): 10‰
Infant mortality rate (2003): 73.2‰
Life expectancy at birth (2003): male: 55.2 years, female: 59.5 years

ECONOMY
GNP (2002): 3.77 billion US$
GNP per capita (2002): 300 US$
GNP per capita PPP (2002): 1,970 international dollars
HDI (2000): 0.543
GDP annual growth rate (2003): 4.8%
Annual inflation rate (2000): −0.79%
Labour force by occupation: n/a
GDP by sector (2000): agriculture: 37.1%, industry: 20.5%, services: 42.4%
Gross public debt: n/a
Unemployment rate (2001): 1.8%

Agriculture and fishing
Crops
bananas (2001): 146,000t
sugar cane (2001): 167,000t
rubber (2001): 35,900t
rice (2002): 3,823,000t
soya beans (2002): 38,800t
tobacco (2001): 7,750t
Livestock farming and fishing
cattle (2002): 2,924,000 head
buffaloes (2001): 626,000 head
pigs (2002): 2,105,000 head
fish (1999): 284,000t

Energy generation
total electricity (2001): 119 million kWh

Industrial production
sugar (2002): 9,400t
meat (2001): 204,000t
timber (2000): 179,000m³

Tourism
Tourism revenue (2000): 228 million US$

Foreign trade
Exports (2002): 1,750.1 million US$
Imports (2002): 2,315.5 million US$

Defence
Armed forces (2001): 125,000 people
Defence budget (2001): 1.19% of GDP

Standard of living
Inhabitants per doctor (1994): 10,000
Average daily calorie intake (2000): 2,070 (FAO minimum: 2,400)
Cars per 1,000 inhabitants (2000): 26
Televisions per 1,000 inhabitants (2001): 8

HISTORY: KEY DATES

6c: previously part of the kingdom of Fou-nan, Cambodia was conquered by the Khmers.
1432: Cambodia's capital, Angkor, was abandoned, and Phnom Penh became the new capital.
16c: Cambodia became a vassal of the kingdom of Siam. Cambodia was then used as a battleground by the Siamese and the Vietnamese, who colonized the Mekong Delta in the 18c.
1863: the country became a French protectorate.
1953: King Norodom Sihanouk led Cambodia to independence.
1960–70: Norodom Sihanouk became head of state in 1960 but, in 1970, was overthrown in a military coup backed by the USA. The country was renamed the Khmer Republic by its new right-wing leader, General Lon Nol.
1975–8: a communist guerrilla force, the Khmer Rouge, seized power. Cambodia was renamed Democratic Kampuchea in 1976, and was subjected to an extreme and brutal dictatorship led by Pol Pot.
1979: Vietnam occupied Cambodia, which was renamed the People's Republic of Kampuchea.
1989: Vietnamese troops left the country and the name of the State of Cambodia was restored.
1993: a new constitution was adopted, and the parliamentary monarchy was restored with Norodom Sihanouk as king.
1999: Cambodia was admitted to the Association of South-East Asian Nations (ASEAN).
2003: Cambodia was admitted to the World Trade Organization (WTO).

The People's Republic of China can be divided into two geographic regions. Western China is arid, desert-like and thinly populated, made up of vast plateaus and basins (the Tibetan and Mongolian plateaux, and the Tasidam and Tarim basins) surrounded by high mountain ranges including the Himalayas, Karakorum and Tien Shan. Lower-lying eastern China has a mixed relief that gradually descends towards the sea; plateaus, hills and plains are juxtaposed, and the climate, varying with altitude, creates a fundamental division between the north and south of the country, which are separated by the Qinling Range. Eastern China is almost completely within the monsoon zone, and receives summer rains that are far heavier in the south than in the north. Most of the country's population is concentrated in the east. Around forty cities have over one million inhabitants: Shanghai, Beijing and Hong Kong are among the world's largest cities.

Area: 9,596,961km²
Population (2002): 1,294,377,000
Capital: Beijing 10,836,000 (2001 e)
Government type and political system: republic with a socialist system
Head of state: (President of the Republic) Hu Jintao
Head of government: (Prime Minister) Wen Jiabao
Administrative structure: 22 provinces (not including Taiwan, which China regards as its 23rd province), 5 autonomous regions, 4 autonomous municipalities and 2 special administrative regions
Official language: Mandarin Chinese
Currency: renminbi (yuan)

DEMOGRAPHICS

Density: 133 inhab/km²
Percentage of population in urban areas (2001): 36.7%
Age structure of population (2000): 0–15 years: 24.8%, 15–65 years: 68.3%, over 65 years: 6.9%
Birth rate (2003): 14.5‰
Death rate (2003): 7‰
Infant mortality rate (2003): 36.6‰
Life expectancy at birth (2003): male: 68.9 years, female: 73.3 years

ECONOMY

GNP (2002): 1,234 billion US$
GNP per capita (2002): 960 US$
GNP per capita PPP (2001): 4,520 international dollars
HDI (2000): 0.726
GDP annual growth rate (2003): 9.1%
Annual inflation rate (2000): 0.26%
Labour force by occupation: n/a
GDP by sector (2000): agriculture: 15.9%, industry: 50.9%, services: 33.2%
Gross public debt: n/a
Unemployment rate (2002): 4%

Agriculture and fishing

Crops
citrus fruits (2002): 12,461,000t
pineapples (2001): 1,284,000t
groundnuts (2001): 14,553,000t
oats (2001): 650,000t
bananas (2001): 5,393,000t
wheat (2002): 90,290,000t
sugar cane (2001): 79,700,000t
rape (2001): 11,320,000t
honey (2001): 256,000t
millet (2001): 2,446,000t
hazelnuts (2001): 11,000t
barley (2002): 2,470,000t
sweet potatoes (2001): 115,122,000t
apples (2001): 21,559,000t
potatoes (2002): 66,573,000t
grapes (2001): 3,830,000t
rice (2002): 176,342,000t
soya beans (2002): 16,900,000t
tomatoes (2002): 26,151,000t
sunflowers (2002): 1,900,000t
Livestock farming and fishing
cattle (2002): 106,151,000 head
buffaloes (2001): 22,769,000 head
horses (2001): 8,768,000 head
sheep (2002): 136,972,000 head
pigs (2002): 464,695,000 head
chickens (2002): 3,919,000,000 head
fish (1999): 41,513,000t

Energy generation and mining

silver (2001): 1,800t
bauxite (2001): 9,500,000t
copper (2001): 588,000t
diamonds (2001): 1,185,000 carats

hydroelectricity (2001): 263,380 million kWh
total electricity (2001): 1,420,349 million kWh
tin (2001): 79,000t
iron (2001): 75,955,000t
natural gas (2002): 32,600 million m³
coal (2001): 1,032,201,000t
manganese (2001): 500,000t
molybdenum (2001): 28,200t
nickel (2001): 52,000t
gold (2001): 185,000kg
oil (2002): 168,900,000t
phosphate (2001): 21,000,000t
lead (2001): 600,000t
uranium (2001): 500t
zinc (2001): 1,600,000t

Industrial production

milk (2001): 13,370,000t
sugar (2002): 11,754,000t
wine (2002): 10,800,000hl
beer (2000): 227,379,000hl
meat (2001): 65,482,000t
palm oil (2001): 217,000t
steel (2003): 220,115,000t
cast iron (1998): 118,629,000t
aluminium (2001): 3,250,000t
copper (2001): 588,000t
tin (2001): 79,000t
lead (2001): 1,180,000t
zinc (2001): 2,080,000t
cars (2002): 1,091,000 units
commercial vehicles (1998): 1,043,000 units
cotton yarn (2001): 5,320,000t
jute (1997): 365,000t
wool (2001): 305,000t
sisal (2001): 36,800t
silk (2001): 62,001t
artificial textiles (1999): 472,000t
synthetic textiles (1999): 3,586,000t
synthetic rubber (2001): 1,052,000t
cement (2001): 626,500,000t
timber (2000): 96,421,000m³
paper (2000): 35,439,000t

Tourism

Tourism revenue (2001): 17,792 million US$

Foreign trade

Exports (2002): 325,651 million US$
Imports (2002): 281,484 million US$

Defence

Armed forces (2001): 2,270,000 people
Defence budget (2001): 1.45% of GDP

Standard of living

Inhabitants per doctor (1995): 1,062
Average daily calorie intake (2000): 3,029 (FAO minimum: 2,400)
Cars per 1,000 inhabitants (2000): 7
Televisions per 1,000 inhabitants (2001): 312

157

250 km

Legend:
- ● population over 5,000,000
- ● population 1,000,000 to 5,000,000
- • population 100,000 to 1,000,000
- · population less than 100,000
- ✈ airport
- ★ place of interest
- —— road
- —— railway line
- boundary of autonomous region or province
- Tianjin capital of autonomous region or province
- 200 1000 2000 4000 m

Countries and regions:
RUSSIAN FEDERATION, KAZAKHSTAN, KYRGYZSTAN, MONGOLIA, ULAANBAATAR (Ulan Bator), NORTH KOREA, PYONGYANG, SOUTH KOREA, SŎUL (Seoul), JAPAN, TŌKYŌ, TAIWAN, TAIPEI, PHILIPPINES, VIETNAM, HA NOI (Hanoi), LAOS, MYANMAR (BURMA), THAILAND, BANGLADESH, DHAKA (Dacca), INDIA, NEPAL, KATHMANDU, BHUTAN, THIMPHU, PAKISTAN, BISHKEK, VIANGCHAN (Vientiane)

Seas:
SEA OF JAPAN, YELLOW SEA, EAST CHINA SEA, SOUTH CHINA SEA, Bay of Bengal, Korea Bay, Bo Hai

Provinces / regions:
HEILONGJIANG, JILIN, LIAONING, NEI MONGOL ZIZHIQU (INNER MONGOLIA), XINJIANG UYGUR ZIZHIQU (SINKIANG), GANSU, QINGHAI, XIZANG ZIZHIQU (Plateau of Tibet), SICHUAN, YUNNAN, GUIZHOU, GUANGXI ZHUANGZU ZIZHIQU, GUANGDONG, HUNAN, JIANGXI, FUJIAN, ZHEJIANG, JIANGSU, ANHUI, HUBEI, HENAN, SHAANXI, SHANXI, HEBEI, SHANDONG, NINGXIA HUIZU ZIZHIQU, HAINAN

Cities:
BEIJING (Peking), Tianjin, Shanghai, Harbin, Changchun, Shenyang, Dalian (Luda), Qingdao, Jinan, Zhengzhou, Wuhan, Nanjing, Hangzhou, Chengdu, Chongqing, Kunming, Guangzhou (Canton), Hong Kong, Macau, Shenzhen, Xi'an, Lanzhou, Xining, Urumqi, Lhasa, Nanning, Guiyang, Changsha, Nanchang, Fuzhou, Xiamen, Taiyuan, Shijiazhuang, Hohhot, Baotou, Yinchuan, Qiqihar, Mudanjiang, Jiamusi, Jixi, Daqing, Hegang, Yichun, Heihe, Hailar, Haikou, Kashi, Korla, Hami, Kaohsiung

Physical features:
Gobi Desert, Tien Shan, Tarim Pendi, Taklimakan Shamo, Kunlun Shan, Altun Shan, Qilian Shan, Himalaya, Karakoram, Pamir, Altai Mts, Junggar Pendi, Qaidam Pendi, Qing Zang Gaoyuan (Plateau of Tibet), Mongolian Plateau, Da Hinggan Ling, Xiao Hinggan Ling, Manchuria, Hengduan Shan, Daxue Shan, Red Basin, Wuliang Shan, Huang He (Yellow River), Chang Jiang (Yangtze), Amur, Ussuri, Argun, Ertix, Brahmaputra, Ganges, Indus, Mekong, Salween, Tropic of Cancer, Lake Baikal, Ozero Balkhash, Nam Co, Qinghai Hu, Bosteng Hu

Mt Everest 8 846 m, K2 8 611 m, Muztag 7 723 m, Gongga Shan 7 590 m

HISTORY: KEY DATES

Archaeological evidence suggests that the Shang Dynasty (1766 BC–1122 BC) emerged from the legendary Xia (Hsia) Dynasty (c.2200 BC–1767 BC). The Bronze Age, which began during the Shang Dynasty, continued under the Zhou (Chou) Dynasty (1122 BC–256 BC).
5c BC–3c BC: a period of war between feudal states, during which Chinese culture and writing (notably the Confucian Classics) flourished.

Imperial China until the Mongol conquest
221 BC–206 BC: the Qin (Ch'in) Dynasty united the warring Chinese states.
206 BC–AD 220: the Han Dynasties expanded into Manchuria, Korea, Mongolia, Vietnam and Central Asia. This period saw the founding of the mandarinate, and Confucianism was the state orthodoxy. Control of trade links such as the silk route created an opening for foreign influences, particularly Buddhism.
AD 220–AD 581: the influence of Buddhism grew during a period of territorial divisions and wars. The Three Kingdoms period (AD 220–AD 280) was followed by the Western Jin, Eastern Jin and Southern dynasties (AD 266–AD 589).
AD 581–AD 618: the Sui Dynasty reunified the country.
618–907: the Tang (T'ang) Dynasty saw the emergence of the Chinese civil service system. China continued its expansion under Tang Taizong (627–649) and Tang Gaozong (650–683).
907–60: China was again divided into independent states during the tumultuous Five Dynasties and Ten Kingdoms period.
960–1279: the Song (Sung) Dynasty ruled over a far smaller territory than the Tang Dynasty after the 'Barbarians from

the North' created the Liao (947–1124) and Jin (1115–1234) empires. In 1279, Genghis Khan led the Mongol conquest of the territory.
1279–1368: the Mongol Yuan Dynasty was led by Zhu Yuanzhang (known as Hongwu), the founder of the Ming Dynasty.

China under the Ming and the Qing Dynasties
1368–1644: the emperors of the Ming Dynasty re-established national traditions, but introduced autocratic practices. Manchuria was conquered during this period.
1644–1911: the Qing (Ch'ing) Dynasty was founded by the invading Manchus. The Qing ruled over a larger territory than ever, including a protectorate over Tibet and parts of Mongolia and Central Asia.
1839–42 AND 1858–60: the Opium Wars ended in defeat for China.
1850–64: the Taiping Rebellion spread throughout southern China.
1875–1908: the Dowager Empress Cixi ruled the country. China lost Taiwan and Korea to Japan in the Sino–Japanese War (1894–5). Russia, Germany, the UK and France divided the country into areas of influence.
1898–1900: the Boxer Rebellion, a widespread revolt against foreign influence, took place.

The Republic of China
1911: the Republic of China was established.
1927: the Guomindang nationalists, led first by Sun Yixian (Sun Yat-sen) and then by Jiang Jieshi (Chiang Kai-shek), broke with the Communists.
1934–5: the Communists gained control of north-west China at the end of the

Long March.
1945–9: after the Japanese surrender, conflict between nationalists and Communists led to civil war.

The People's Republic of China
1949: the People's Republic of China was established under Mao Zedong (Mao Tse-tung), with Zhou Enlai (Chou En-lai) as its prime minister and foreign minister. The nationalists withdrew to Taiwan.
1956: in the face of resistance and economic difficulties, Mao launched the Hundred Flowers Campaign, during which the Communist Party authorities encouraged art, literature and debate.
1958: Mao imposed the Great Leap Forward programme, intended to achieve the collectivization of land and the creation of rural communes; this was an economic disaster.
1966: Mao launched the Great Proletarian Cultural Revolution, leading to ten years of unrest. China's relations with the USSR deteriorated.
1971: the People's Republic of China was admitted to the UN.
1976: Mao Zedong died. The 'Gang of Four' was arrested.
1977: China's new leader, Deng Xiaoping, introduced economic reforms and reversed many Maoist policies.
1989: the Soviet head of state Mikhail Gorbachev visited Beijing, confirming the normalization of China's relations with the USSR. Students and workers staged pro-democracy demonstrations which were violently suppressed; the killing of demonstrators in Tiananmen Square provoked international outrage.
1997: the UK returned the Crown Colony of Hong Kong to China.
1999: Portugal returned Macao to China.

The provinces

China comprises 22 provinces (not including Taiwan, which China regards as its 23rd province), 5 autonomous regions, 4 autonomous municipalities and 2 special administrative regions.

The provinces
Anhui (capital Hefei); **Fujian** (Fuzhou); **Gansu** (Lanzhou); **Guangdong** (Guangzhou); **Guizhou** (Guiyang); **Hainan** (Haikou); **Hebei** (Shijiazhuang); **Heilongjiang** (Harbin); **Henan** (Zhengzhou); **Hubei** (Wuhan); **Hunan** (Changsha); **Jiangsu** (Nanjing); **Jiangxi** (Nanchang); **Jilin** (Changchun); **Liaoning** (Shenyang); **Qinghai** (Xining); **Shaanxi** (Xi'an); **Shandong** (Jinan); **Shanxi** (Taiyuan); **Sichuan** (Chengdu); **Yunnan** (Kunming); **Zhejiang** (Hangzhou)

The special administrative regions
Hong Kong; **Macao**

The autonomous regions
Guangxi (capital Nanning); **Inner Mongolia** (Houhehot); **Ningxia** (Yinchuan); **Xinjiang** (Ürümqi); **Tibet** (Lhassa)

The autonomous municipalities
Beijing; **Chongqing**; **Shanghai**; **Tianjin**

CYPRUS

Situated close to the coasts of Turkey and Syria, the island republic of Cyprus is mainly mountainous. Its climate is Mediterranean.

Area: 9,251km²
Population (2002): 797,000
Capital: Nicosia 199,000 (2001 e)
Government type and political system: republic
Head of state and government: (President of the Republic) Tassos Papadopoulos; (Turkish Cypriot leader) Rauf Denktash
Administrative structure: 6 districts
Official languages: Greek and Turkish
Currency: Cyprus pound

DEMOGRAPHICS

Density: 85 inhab/km²
Percentage of population in urban areas (2001): 70.8%
Age structure of population (2000): 0–15 years: 23.1%, 15–65 years: 65.4%, over 65 years: 11.5%
Birth rate (2003): 13.2‰
Death rate (2003): 7.5‰
Infant mortality rate (2003): 7.7‰
Life expectancy at birth (2003): male: 76 years, female: 80.5 years

ECONOMY

GNP (2002): 9.37 billion US$
GNP per capita (2002): 12,370 US$
GNP per capita PPP (2000): 18,560 international dollars
HDI (2000): 0.883
GDP annual growth rate (2003): 2%
Annual inflation rate (2000): 4.14%
Labour force by occupation: n/a
GDP by sector (1999): agriculture: 4.2%, industry: 22.4%, services: 73.4%
Gross public debt (2002): 58.6% of GDP
Unemployment rate (2002): 3.3%

Agriculture

Crops
olives (2002): 17,500t
oranges (2002): 50,000t
barley (2002): 126,000t
grapefruits (2001): 35,000t
potatoes (2002): 142,000t
tomatoes (2002): 38,200t
Livestock farming
goats (2001): 379,000 head
sheep (2002): 297,000 head
pigs (2002): 445,000 head
chickens (2002): 3,400,000 head

Energy generation
total electricity (2001): 3,401 million kWh

Industrial production
wine (2002): 240,000hl
beer (2000): 369,000hl
cement (2001): 1,369,000t

Tourism
Tourism revenue (2001): 1,981 million US$

Foreign trade
Exports (2002): 843.6 million US$
Imports (2002): 3,702.7 million US$

Defence
Armed forces (2001): 10,000 people
Defence budget (2001): 3.59% of GDP

Standard of living
Inhabitants per doctor (1990): 556
Average daily calorie intake (2000): 3,259 (FAO minimum: 2,400)
Cars per 1,000 inhabitants (2000): 353
Televisions per 1,000 inhabitants (2001): 181

HISTORY: KEY DATES
1571: the island was conquered by the Turks.
1925: it was made a British Crown Colony.
1960: Cyprus became an independent republic.
1983: the Turkish community declared itself independent as the Turkish Republic of Northern Cyprus, which is recognized only by Turkey.
2004: Cyprus, as a divided island, became a member state of the European Union.

EAST TIMOR

Situated in the Timor Sea in South-East Asia, the Democratic Republic of Timor-Leste comprises part of the mountainous island of Timor as well as the islands of Pulau Atauro and Pulau Jaco.

Area: 14,874km²
Population (2002): 779,000
Capital: Dili 56,000 (2001 e)
Government type and political system: republic with a semi-presidential system
Head of state: (President of the Republic) Xanana Gusmão
Head of government: (Prime Minister) Mari Alkatiri
Administrative structure: 13 districts
Official languages: Tetum and Portuguese
Currency: US dollar

DEMOGRAPHICS

Density: 52 inhab/km²

Percentage of population in urban areas (2001): 7.5%
Age structure of population: n/a
Birth rate (2003): 23.8‰
Death rate (2003): 13.2‰
Infant mortality rate (2003): 123.7‰
Life expectancy at birth (2003): male: 48.7 years, female: 50.4 years

ECONOMY

GNP (2002): 0.42 billion US$
GNP per capita (2002): 520 US$
GNP per capita PPP: n/a
HDI: n/a
GDP annual growth rate (2003): −3.1%
Annual inflation rate: n/a
Labour force by occupation: n/a
GDP by sector: n/a
Gross public debt: n/a
Unemployment rate: n/a

Defence
Armed forces (2001): 636 people
Defence budget: n/a

HISTORY: KEY DATES
1970s–90s: Indonesia struggled with East Timorese pro-independence forces for control of the territory.
1999–2001: a large majority voted for independence from Indonesia. There followed a period of indiscriminate violence by pro-Indonesian forces. East Timor was then placed provisionally under UN administration and monitored by an international peacekeeping force.
2002: East Timor officially became an independent state and a member of the UN.

GEORGIA

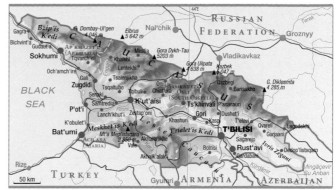

Georgia

▬ ▬	regional boundary
——	road
——	railway line

●	population over 1,000,000
●	population 100,000 to 1,000,000
●	population 30,000 to 100,000
•	population less than 30,000

200 500 1000 2000 m

Georgia is enclosed by the Greater Caucasus Mountains to the north and the Lesser Caucasus to the south. The Kolkhida lowlands, which open onto the Black Sea, are drained by the Rioni and Kura rivers. To the east are the Gori and Tbilisi basins. This relief leads to a great climatic diversity, and thus to a variety of environments and natural features.

Area: 69,700km²
Population (2002): 5,213,000
Capital: Tbilisi 1,406,000 (2001 e) including the suburbs
Government type and political system: republic with a presidential system
Head of state and government: (President of the Republic) Mikhail Saakashvili
Administrative structure: 9 regions, 9 cities and 2 autonomous republics
Official language: Georgian
Currency: lari

DEMOGRAPHICS

Density: 71 inhab/km²
Percentage of population in urban areas (2001): 56.5%
Age structure of population (2000): 0–15 years: 20.5%, 15–65 years: 66.6%, over 65 years: 12.9%
Birth rate (2003): 10.4‰
Death rate (2003): 9.9‰
Infant mortality rate (2003): 17.6‰
Life expectancy at birth (2003): male: 69.5 years, female: 77.6 years

ECONOMY

GNP (2002): 3.36 billion US$
GNP per capita (2002): 650 US$
GNP per capita PPP (2002): 2,270 international dollars
HDI (2000): 0.748
GDP annual growth rate (2003): 8.6%
Annual inflation rate (2000): 4.06%
Labour force by occupation (2001): agriculture: 52.7%, industry: 9.3%, services: 38%
GDP by sector (2000): agriculture: 32.1%,

industry: 13.2%, services: 54.7%
Gross public debt: n/a
Unemployment rate (2002): 12.3%

Agriculture

Crops
sugar beets (2002): 300t
wheat (2002): 200,000t
maize (2002): 400,000t
barley (2002): 58,000t
potatoes (2002): 414,000t
grapes (2002): 160,000t
tea (2001): 30,000t
sunflowers (2002): 16,000t
Livestock farming
cattle (2002): 1,180,000 head
sheep (2002): 568,000 head
pigs (2002): 445,000 head
chickens (2002): 8,900,000 head

Energy generation and mining
total electricity (2001): 7,270 million kWh
gold (2001): 2,000kg
oil (2002): 100,000t
zinc (2001): 200t

Industrial production
wine (2002): 812,000hl
beer (2002): 235,000hl
sugar (2002): 2,000t
steel (1999): 105,000t

Tourism
Tourism revenue (1999): 400 million US$

Foreign trade
Exports (2000): 459 million US$
Imports (2000): 970.5 million US$

Standard of living
Inhabitants per doctor (1996): 263
Average daily calorie intake (2000): 2,412

(FAO minimum: 2,400)
Cars per 1,000 inhabitants (2000): 46
Televisions per 1,000 inhabitants (2000): 474

HISTORY: KEY DATES

9c–13c: the independent kingdom of Georgia reached its peak under the rule of Queen Thamar (1184–1213), but was then devastated by the Mongols.
16c–18c: Georgia lost territories to Iran and the Ottoman Empire, and became a Russian protectorate (1783).
1801–4: Georgia became part of the Russian empire.
1918: an independent republic was proclaimed.
1921: the Red Army occupied the country and established a Soviet regime. Georgia was proclaimed a Soviet Socialist Republic.
1922: Georgia became a founder member of the USSR.
1991: Georgia declared its independence from the USSR.
1993: Georgia joined the Commonwealth of Independent States (CIS).
1995: a new constitution was adopted.
2001–2: the Russian government claimed that Georgia was harbouring Chechen rebels; a number of Chechens were eventually detained and extradited.
2004: the newly elected president, Mikhail Saakashvili, pledged to rein in the three secessionist provinces of Adzharia, Abkhazia and South Ossetia. Adzharia's leader capitulated in May, ending thirteen years of authoritarian rule in the province.

The Republic of India comprises three main geographical regions of varying size. It borders on the Himalayas in the north, but only a strip of this mountainous area belongs to India. The north of the country is drained or irrigated by the Ganges River and its tributaries; the Ganges plain is made fertile by summer monsoon rains, which are lighter in the south (beyond the Tropic of Cancer). To the south, the Deccan plateau, bordered by the Eastern and Western Ghats mountain ranges, is relatively dry.

Area: 3,287,263km²
Population (2002): 1,041,144,000
Capital: New Delhi 9,817,439 (2001 census), 12,987,000 (2001 e) including the suburbs
Government type and political system: republic with a parliamentary system
Head of state: (President of the Republic) A P J Abdul Kalam
Head of government: (Prime Minister) Manmohan Singh
Administrative structure: 28 states and 7 territories
Official language: Hindi, English and 17 others
Currency: Indian rupee

DEMOGRAPHICS

Density: 310 inhab/km²
Percentage of population in urban areas (2001): 27.9%
Age structure of population (2000): 0–15 years: 33.5%, 15–65 years: 61.5%, over 65 years: 5%
Birth rate (2003): 23.8‰
Death rate (2003): 8.5‰
Infant mortality rate (2003): 64.5‰
Life expectancy at birth (2000): male: 63.2 years, female: 64.6 years

ECONOMY

GNP (2002): 495 billion US$
GNP per capita (2002): 470 US$
GNP per capita PPP (2002): 2,650 international dollars
HDI (2000): 0.577
GDP annual growth rate (2003): 7.4%
Annual inflation rate (2000): 4.01%
Labour force by occupation: n/a
GDP by sector (2000): agriculture: 24.9%,

industry: 26.9%, services: 48.2%
Gross public debt: n/a
Unemployment rate: n/a

Agriculture and fishing
Crops
citrus fruits (2002): 4,580,000t
pineapples (2001): 1,100,000t
groundnuts (2001): 6,200,000t
bananas (2001): 16,000,000t
wheat (2002): 71,814,000t
coffee (2002): 317,000t
sugar cane (2001): 286,000,000t
rubber (2001): 630,000t
lemons (2002): 1,370,000t
rape (2001): 4,088,000t
copra (2001): 455,000t
cotton (2002): 4,750,000t
maize (2002): 11,110,000t
manioc (2001): 7,000,000t
millet (2001): 9,505,000t
walnuts (2001): 31,000t
cashew nuts (1998): 430,000t
oranges (2002): 2,980,000t
grapefruits (2001): 130,000t
sweet potatoes (2001): 1,200,000t
apples (2001): 1,500,000t
potatoes (2002): 24,082,000t
rice (2002): 113,580,000t
soya beans (2002): 4,270,000t
sorghum (2002): 6,920,000t
tobacco (2001): 530,000t
tea (2001): 855,000t

tomatoes (2002): 7,420,000t
Livestock farming and fishing
cattle (2002): 221,900,000 head
buffaloes (2001): 94,132,000 head
goats (2001): 123,500,000 head
camels (2001): 1,030,000 head
horses (2001): 800,000 head
sheep (2002): 58,800,000 head
pigs (2002): 18,000,000 head
chickens (2002): 737,000,000 head
fish (1999): 5,352,000t

Energy generation and mining
bauxite (2001): 8,387,000t
chromium (2001): 1,678,000t
nuclear electricity (2001): 18,235 million kWh
hydroelectricity (2001): 77,425 million kWh
total electricity (2001): 533,335 million kWh
iron (2001): 50,700,000t
natural gas (2002): 28,400 million m³
coal (2001) : 284,870,000 t.
lignite (2001): 22,255,000t
manganese (2001): 600,000t
oil (2002): 36,700,000t
phosphate (2001): 1,200,000t
lead (2001): 27,000t
uranium (2001): 200t
zinc (2001): 146,000t

HISTORY: KEY DATES

The origins of ancient India
2300 BC–1750 BC: the Indus Valley civilization (with important urban centres such as Mohenjo-daro) was in its heyday.
2000 BC–1000 BC: Indo-European tribes migrated from Central Asia to colonize northern India, which adopted their language (Sanskrit), their Vedic religion (the basis of Hinduism) and their social hierarchy (the Brahminic caste system).
c.327 BC–c.325 BC: Alexander the Great reached the Indus, and established Greek colonies there.
c.320 BC–c.185 BC: the Maurya Empire reached its peak under its ruler, Ashoka (around 269 BC), whose kingdom stretched from Afghanistan to the Deccan Plateau. He sent Buddhist missions to Southern India and Ceylon.
AD 1c: the Kushana empire flourished in northern India.
AD 320–AD 540: Hinduism was revived under the Gupta state system.
606–647: King Harsha reunited the country.
7c–12c: India was divided up again. Established in Southern India, the Pallava (8c–9c) and Chola (10c–12c) dynasties exported Indian civilization to South-East Asia. Sind was dominated by the Arabs (8c) and the Indus Valley fell into the hands of the Ghaznevids (11c).

Muslim India
1206–1414: the Sultanate of Delhi,

which extended from the Ganges Valley to the Deccan Plateau, was created. India was under Muslim hegemony during this period.
14c–16c: autonomous sultanates were created in Bengal, the Deccan region and Gujerat. The Vijayanagar empire, in the south, mobilized in political defence of Hinduism.
1497–8: the Portuguese explorer Vasco da Gama discovered a sea route to India.
1526–1857: the Mughal dynasty was founded, and came to dominate India thanks to its army, efficient administration and conciliatory attitude to the Hindu majority. After the successful reign of Akbar (1556–1605) and Shah Jahan (1628–58), Aurangzeb's reign (1658–1707) heralded a period of decline.
1600: the British East India Company was established.
1664: the French East India Company was established.
17c–18c: the Marathas, taking advantage of the Mughal decline, formed a Hindu kingdom and ruled India in the first half of the 18c.
1742–54: the Carnatic region and six provinces of the Deccan region came under French control.
1757: the East India Company, under Robert Clive, won the battle of Plassey against the Nawab of Bengal.
1763: the Treaty of Paris reduced India

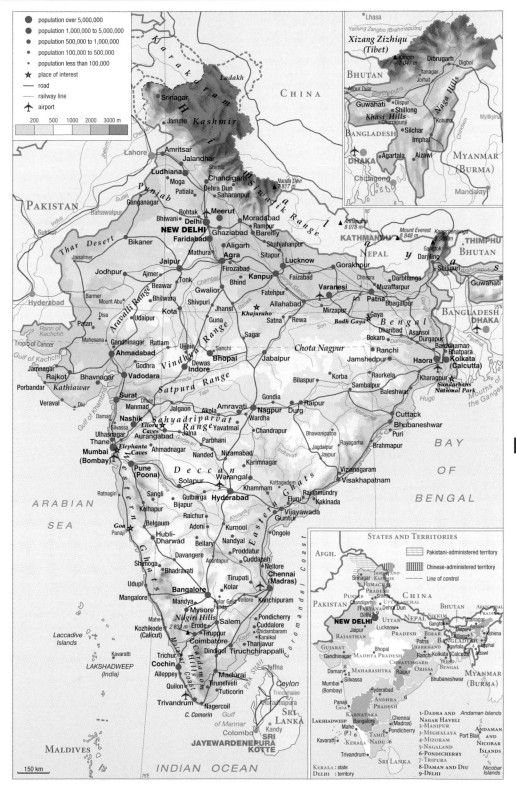

population over 5,000,000
population 1,000,000 to 5,000,000
population 500,000 to 1,000,000
population 100,000 to 500,000
population less than 100,000
★ place of interest
— road
— railway line
✈ airport

200 500 1000 2000 3000 m

STATES AND TERRITORIES

Pakistani-administered territory
Chinese-administered territory
Line of control

1-DADRA AND
  NAGAR HAVELI
2-MANIPUR
3-MEGHALAYA
4-MIZORAM
5-NAGALAND
6-PONDICHERRY
7-TRIPURA
8-DAMAN AND DIU
9-DELHI

Andaman Islands

Port Blair

ANDAMAN
AND
NICOBAR
ISLANDS

Nicobar
Islands

KERALA : state
DELHI : territory

163

150 km

INDIA

Industrial production
butter (2001): 2,250,000t
milk (2001): 83,970,000t
eggs (2001): 1,905,750t
honey (2001): 52,000t
sugar (2002): 20,475,000t
steel (2003): 31,779,000t
aluminium (2001): 630,000t
copper (2001): 30,900t
lead (2001): 94,000t
zinc (2001): 230,000t
cars (2002): 706,000 units
commercial vehicles (1998): 240,000 units
shipbuilding (2001): 6,000dwt
cotton yarn (2001): 1,750,000t
wool (2001): 47,600t
silk (2001): 15,197t
jute (1997): 1,720,000t
artificial textiles (1999): 247,700t
synthetic textiles (1999): 1,431,000t
cement (2001): 100,000,000t
timber (2000): 1,575,000m³

Tourism
Tourism revenue (2001): 3,042 million US$

Foreign trade
Exports (2002): 52,743 million US$
Imports (2002): 65,159 million US$

Defence
Armed forces (2001): 1,298,000 people
Defence budget (2001): 3.18% of GDP

Standard of living
Inhabitants per doctor (1993): 2,500
Average daily calorie intake (2000): 2,428
(FAO minimum: 2,400)
Cars per 1,000 inhabitants (1998): 5
Televisions per 1,000 inhabitants (2001): 83

⇨ HISTORY: KEY DATES

to five trading posts; the British kept Mumbai (Bombay), Chennai (Madras) and Bengal.

British rule
1772–85: Warren Hastings became Governor-General of Bengal and organized its colonization.
1799–1819: Great Britain conquered Southern India, the Ganges Valley and Delhi, and defeated the Marathas.
1849: Great Britain annexed the Sikh kingdom of the Punjab.
1857–8: the Great Rebellion of 1857 took place; its suppression led to direct British rule of India.
1876: Queen Victoria was crowned empress of India.
1885: the Indian National Congress was established.
1906: the Muslim League was established.
1920–22: Mahatma Gandhi launched a campaign of civil disobedience against Britain.
1929: Jawaharlal Nehru became president of the Congress Party.
1935: the Government of India Act made the provinces autonomous.

Independent India
1947: India became independent within the Commonwealth of Nations. It was divided into two states: the Indian Union, with a Hindu majority, and Pakistan, with a Muslim majority. This partition was accompanied by massacres of up to 500,000 people, and led to mass migration.
1947–64: Jawaharlal Nehru, as prime minister and president of the Congress, implemented a development programme and advocated non-alignment.
1947–8: war broke out between India and Pakistan over the control of Kashmir.
1948: Mahatma Gandhi was assassinated.
1950: a new constitution made India a federal, secular and parliamentary state, organized on ethnic and linguistic grounds.
1965: a second Indo-Pakistani war broke out over Kashmir. India drew closer to the USSR.
1966: Indira Gandhi, Nehru's daughter, came to power.
1971: a third Indo-Pakistani war led to the secession of Bangladesh.
1984: Indira Gandhi was assassinated by Sikh extremists.
1992: the destruction of the Ayodhya Mosque (Uttar Pradesh) by militant Hindu nationalists led to serious intercommunity conflict.
2000: India's population officially reached the 1 billion mark.
2002: India successfully tested a missile with nuclear capability.
2000–3: ongoing tension between India and Pakistan led to concern amongst international observers about the use of nuclear weapons technology by both countries.

164

INDIAN OCEAN MALDIVES

The Republic of Maldives is a coral archipelago in the Indian Ocean made up of 26 atolls, which contain over 1,000 small coral islands. 200 of the islands are inhabited. The Maldives, which has a tropical monsoon climate, is the lowest-lying country in the world, with an average altitude of 2m.

Area: 298km²
Population (2002): 309,000
Capital: Malé 84,000 (2001 e)
Government type and political system: republic with a semi-presidential system
Head of state and government: (President of the Republic) Maumoon Abdul Gayoom
Administrative structure: 1 municipality and 19 administrative atolls
Official language: Divehi
Currency: rufiyaa (Maldives rupee)

DEMOGRAPHICS

Density: 954 inhab/km²
Percentage of population in urban areas (2001): 28%
Age structure of population (2000): 0–15 years: 43.7%, 15–65 years: 52.8%, over 65 years: 3.5%
Birth rate (2003): 35.8‰
Death rate (2003): 6.1‰
Infant mortality rate (2003): 38.3‰
Life expectancy at birth (2003): male: 67.8 years, female: 67 years

ECONOMY

GNP (2002): 0.622 billion US$
GNP per capita (2002): 2,170 US$
GNP per capita PPP (2001): 4,520 international dollars
HDI (2000): 0.743
GDP annual growth rate (2003): 6.2%
Annual inflation rate (2000): −1.13%
Labour force by occupation (2000): agriculture: 13.7%, industry: 19%, services: 67.3%
GDP by sector (1998): agriculture: 16.4%, industry: n/a, services: n/a
Gross public debt: n/a
Unemployment rate: n/a

Agriculture and fishing
Crops
copra (2001): 1,420t
Fishing
fish (1999): 134,000t

Energy generation
total electricity (2001): 117 million kWh

Tourism
Tourism revenue (2001): 331 million US$

Foreign trade
Exports (2002): 133.6 million US$
Imports (2002): 344.7 million US$

Defence
Armed forces (1995): 700 people
Defence budget: n/a

Standard of living
Inhabitants per doctor (1990): 15 000
Average daily calorie intake (2000): 2,592
(FAO minimum: 2,400)
Cars per 1,000 inhabitants (1996): 4
Televisions per 1,000 inhabitants (2001): 120

HISTORY: KEY DATES
1887: after a century of British occupation, the Maldives became a self-governing British protectorate.
1965–8: the Maldives gained full independence, and became a republic.
2000–3: international observers raised concerns over allegations of political repression and human rights abuses.

The Republic of Indonesia is an island nation in South-East Asia with over 13,000 islands, less than half of which are inhabited. It extends over 5,000km from west to east and over 2,000km from north to south. Most of the islands are mountainous, some are volcanic, and any plains are very narrow. The latitude – near the equator – explains the constantly hot, tropical climate and almost permanent high humidity. These two factors have led to the proliferation of dense rainforests, which cover over 60% of the territory.

Area: 1,919,443km²
Population (2002): 217,535,000
Capital: Jakarta 11,429,000 (2001 e) including the suburbs
Government type and political system: republic
Head of state and government: (President of the Republic) Susilo Bambang Yudhoyono
Administrative structure: 27 provinces, 1 district and 2 regions
Official language: Bahasa Indonesian
Currency: Indonesian rupiah

DEMOGRAPHICS

Density: 112 inhab/km²
Percentage of population in urban areas (2001): 42%
Age structure of population (2000): 0–15 years: 30.8%, 15–65 years: 64.4%, over 65 years: 4.8%
Birth rate (2003): 20.7‰
Death rate (2003): 7.3‰
Infant mortality rate (2003): 41.6‰
Life expectancy at birth (2003): male: 64.8 years, female: 68.8 years

ECONOMY

GNP (2002): 150 billion US$
GNP per capita (2002): 710 US$
GNP per capita PPP (2001): 3,070 international dollars
HDI (2000): 0.684
GDP annual growth rate (2003): 4.1%
Annual inflation rate (2000): 3.72%
Labour force by occupation (1998): agriculture: 45%, industry: 16.3%, services: 38.7%
GDP by sector (2000): agriculture: 16.9%, industry: 47.3%, services: 35.8%
Gross public debt: n/a
Unemployment rate (2002): 9.1%

Agriculture and fishing

Crops
pineapples (2001): 300,000t
groundnuts (2001): 1,000,000t
bananas (2001): 3,600,000t
cocoa (2001): 340,000t
coffee (2002): 623,000t
sugar cane (2001): 23,500,000t
rubber (2001): 1,650,000t
copra (2001): 930,000t
maize (2002): 9,527,000t
manioc (2001): 16,158,000t
cashew nuts (1998): 69,027t
oil palms (2001): 1,760,000t
sweet potatoes (2001): 1,686,000t
rice (2002): 51,579,000t
soya beans (2002): 653,000t
tobacco (2001): 134,000t
tea (2001): 172,000t

Livestock farming and fishing
cattle (2002): 10,435,000 head
buffaloes (2001): 2,287,000 head
goats (2001): 12,456,000 head
horses (2001): 517,000 head
sheep (2002): 7,661,000 head
chickens (2002): 1,072,000,000 head
fish (1999): 4,797,000t

Energy generation and mining

silver (2001): 270t
bauxite (2001): 1,237,000t
copper (2001): 1,050,000t
hydroelectricity (2001): 10,080 million kWh
total electricity (2001): 95,780 million kWh
tin (2001): 51,000t
natural gas (2002): 70,600 million m³
coal (2001): 90,370,000t
nickel (2001): 102,000t
gold (2001): 130,000kg
oil (2002): 62,400,000t

Industrial production

sugar (2002): 1,963,000t
palm oil (2001): 7,135,000t
aluminium (2001): 180,000t
copper (2001): 1,050,000t
tin (2001): 51,000t
nickel (2001): 102,000t
cotton yarn (2001): 9,660t
jute (1997): 9,000t
artificial textiles (1999): 225,000t
synthetic textiles (1999): 1,250,400t
cars (2002): 24,000 units
commercial vehicles (1998): 163,000 units
paper (2000): 6,977,000t
timber (2000): 33,497,000m³

Tourism

Tourism revenue (2001): 5,411 million US$

Foreign trade

Exports (2002): 58,773 million US$
Imports (2002): 35,652 million US$

Indonesia

200 500 1000 m

— road
✈ airport
▲ volcano
★ place of interest

● population over 7,000,000
● population 1,000,000 to 7,000,000
● population 100 000 to 1,000,000
• population less than 100,000

300 km

INDONESIA

Defence
Armed forces **(2001)**: 297,000 people
Defence budget **(2001)**: 0.53% of GDP

Standard of living
Inhabitants per doctor **(1994)**: 5,000
Average daily calorie intake **(2000)**: 2,902
(FAO minimum: 2,400)
Cars per 1,000 inhabitants **(1998)**: 14
Televisions per 1,000 inhabitants **(2001)**:
153

HISTORY: KEY DATES

Early origins to the Dutch East Indies

7c–14c: Indonesia was part of the Buddhist Sri Vijaya kingdom and, later, the Hindu Majapahit kingdom.
13c–16c: the entire archipelago was gradually converted to Islam, except for Bali, which remained Hindu.
1511: the Portuguese took control of Malacca.
17c–18c: the Dutch East India Company exercised control over much of Indonesia.
1799: the company was liquidated, and its territory passed to the Dutch government.
19c: Indonesian guerrillas challenged the Dutch in a series of unsuccessful attacks against the colonists.
1942–5: Japan drove out the Dutch and occupied the Dutch East Indies until the end of World War II.

Independent Indonesia

1945: the independence leader Sukarno proclaimed Indonesia's independence.
1949: the Netherlands recognized Indonesia's status as an independent country.
1966–7: Sukarno was ousted, and handed over power to General Suharto. Regularly re-elected after 1968, Suharto implemented anti-Communist policies and improved relations with the West.
1969: West Papua was incorporated into Indonesia.
1975: the Indonesian occupation of East Timor led to a prolonged and bloody guerrilla war in which a large proportion of East Timor's population perished.
1980s: fundamentalist Islam spread over Indonesia.
1998: under pressure from opposition, exacerbated by the severe Asian economic crisis, Suharto resigned.
1999: East Timor voted for independence, leading to a period of human rights abuses in the country by pro-Indonesian militia.
2002: the independence of East Timor was proclaimed.
2004: Indonesia's first direct presidential elections were held.

Rubber

In South America, the Maya Indians and Aztecs used the secretions of the 'crying tree', rubber, to waterproof their moccasins and make toys and balls. Henry Wickham, a local planter working for the British government, harvested and exported 70,000 rubber tree seeds from Brazil to London in 1876. Of the 2,600 that germinated, only 22 seedlings survived. These seedlings were sent from Kew Gardens to Sri Lanka, and then to Singapore. This led to the spread of the rubber tree (*Hevea brasiliensis*) throughout South-East Asia, and to the development of all rubber plantations.

Natural rubber comes from the latex harvested from this tree, which is native to the Amazon rainforest. Latex is contained in a network of fine, interconnected ducts found in the tree's bark, immediately outside the cambium layer – the 'lactiferous layer'. Latex, in the form of a milky white liquid, will pour out of the bark for 2–4 hours after it has been cut, and can be collected in a container. It is a very unstable product which, if it is not stabilized with the correct chemicals (usually ammonia), will coagulate into a lump. After collection, the latex – in solid or liquid form – is taken to a factory where it is treated chemically, mechanically and thermally.

A one-hectare plantation of selected rubber trees can currently produce 2,000kg of latex per year (5–7kg per tree), depending on its age and density. Trees are ready to be exploited 5–7 years after they are planted, and can continue to be 'tapped' for up to 30 years.

Although natural rubber now has competitors in the form of synthetic elastomers, it remains in a privileged position thanks to its specific properties, which include high absorption of vibrations and noise, high resistance to tearing and being cut, and low internal heating when rolled (a useful quality for aeroplane tyres and heavy goods vehicles).

Situated between the Caspian Sea and the Indian Ocean, the Islamic Republic of Iran is a country made up of high plains, steppes and deserts, and has a climate of sharp contrasts (extremely hot in summer, cold in winter). Its large central plateau is surrounded in the north and west by rugged massifs and mountain ranges that lead down to narrow coastal lowlands. Earthquakes are frequent.

Area: 1,633,188km²
Population (2002): 72,376,000
Capital: Tehran 7,038,000 (2001 e)
Government type and political system: republic with a semi-presidential system
Supreme Leader of the Islamic Revolution: Ayatollah Sayed Ali Khamenei
Head of state and government: (President of the Republic) Mohammad Khatami
Administrative structure: 28 provinces
Official language: Farsi
Currency: Iranian rial

Iran

— motorway	★ place of interest	● population over 1,000,000
— road		● population 250,000 to 1,000,000
— railway line	oil field	● population 50,000 to 250,000
✈ airport	oil pipeline	• population less than 50,000

400 1000 2000 3000 m

DEMOGRAPHICS

Density: 41 inhab/km²
Percentage of population in urban areas (2001): 64.7%
Age structure of population (2000): 0–15 years: 37.4%, 15–65 years: 59.2%, over 65 years: 3.4%
Birth rate (2003): 20.3‰
Death rate (2003): 5.3‰
Infant mortality rate (2003): 33.3‰
Life expectancy at birth (2003): male: 68.9 years, female: 71.9 years

ECONOMY

GNP (2002): 113 billion US$
GNP per capita (2002): 1,720 US$
GNP per capita PPP (2001): 6,690 international dollars
HDI (2000): 0.721
GDP annual growth rate (2003): 5.9%
Annual inflation rate (2000): 14.48%
Labour force by occupation: n/a
GDP by sector (2000): agriculture: 18.9%, industry: 22.3%, services: 58.8%
Gross public debt: n/a
Unemployment rate (2002): 12.3%

Agriculture and fishing

Crops
citrus fruits (2002): 3,732,000t
almonds (2001): 87,000t
sugar beets (2002): 5,250,000t
wheat (2002): 12,500,000t
sugar cane (2001): 2,100,000t
lemons (2002): 1,040,000 t.
cotton (2002): 320,000t
dates (2001): 900,000t
mandarin oranges (1998): 684,000t
hazelnuts (2001): 11,000t
walnuts (2001): 138,000t
oranges (2002): 1,880,000t
barley (2002): 2,300,000t
peaches (2002): 385,000t
pistachios (2001): 120,000,000t
apples (2001): 1,900,000t
grapes (2002): 2,520,000t
rice (2002): 2,115,000t
tea (2001): 69,000t
tomatoes (2002): 3,000,000t

Livestock farming and fishing
cattle (2002): 8,738,000 head
goats (2001): 25,200,000 head
sheep (2002): 53,900,000 head
chickens (2002): 270,000,000 head
fish (1999): 419,000t

Energy generation and mining

bauxite (2001): 130,000t
chromium (2001): 105,000t
copper (2001): 140,000t
natural gas (2002): 64,500 million m³
hydroelectricity (2001): 3,615 million kWh
total electricity (2001): 124,582 million kWh
molybdenum (2001): 1,600t
oil (2002): 166,800,000t
lead (2001): 15,000t
zinc (2001): 85,000t

Industrial production

butter (2001): 119,697t
eggs (2001): 600,000t
sugar (2002): 1,041,000t
steel (2003): 7,869,000t
aluminium (2001): 140,000t
copper (2001): 140,000t
lead (2001): 50,000t
wool (2001): 73,907t
silk (2001): 900t
timber (2000): 1,060,000m³

Tourism

Tourism revenue (2001): 1,122 million US$

Foreign trade

Exports (2000): 28,345 million US$
Imports (2000): 15,207 million US$

Defence

Armed forces (2001): 520,000 people
Defence budget (2001): 5.82% of GDP

Standard of living

Inhabitants per doctor (1993): 3,333
Average daily calorie intake (2000): 2,913 (FAO minimum: 2,400)
Cars per 1,000 inhabitants (1996): 26
Televisions per 1,000 inhabitants (2001): 163

167

HISTORY: KEY DATES

Ancient Iran

2000 BC–1000 BC: the Aryans spread from the north-east to the west of present-day Iran.

9c BC: their descendants, the Medes and the Persians, reached the Zagros Mountains.

550 BC: the Achaemenid king Cyrus II founded the Persian empire, which ruled over the whole of Iran and part of Central Asia.

490 BC–479 BC: the Persian Wars ended in the defeat of the Achaemenid dynasty.

330 BC: after the death of Darius III, Alexander the Great controlled the Persian empire.

AD 224: the Sassanids took control of the region and established an empire of their own.

AD 224–AD 640: the Sassanid empire, which extended from the borders of India to those of Arabia, ruled until the Arab conquest.

Muslim Iran

641: the Arabs defeated the Sassanids at Nahavand.

7c: Iran became part of the Umayyad Muslim empire, and was converted to Islam.

11c–15c: Iran was conquered by the Turks and, later, by the Mongols.

1501–1722: the Safavid dynasty ruled Iran and established Shiite Islam as the state religion.

1722: the Safavids were overthrown by the Afghans.

1736: Nadir Shah expelled the Afghans and went on to assume control over Iran until his assassination in 1747.

Contemporary Iran

1794: the Qajar dynasty came to power.

1813–28: Iran lost control of the Caspian provinces to the Russian empire.

1906: a new constitution established a parliament and limited royal absolutism.

1907: an Anglo-Russian agreement divided Iran into two areas of influence.

1925: Iran's prime minister, Reza Khan, was crowned Shah.

1941: Soviet and British forces occupied part of Iran. The Shah abdicated in favour of his son, Mohammad Reza.

1963: the Shah launched a campaign to modernize and westernize Iran.

1979: political opposition forced the Shah and his family into exile. An Islamic republic was established, led by the then Ayatollah, Ruhollah Khomeini.

1980–88: the Iraqi invasion of Iran, which stemmed from a border dispute, led to the Iran–Iraq War.

1989: after the death of the Ayatollah Khomeini, Sayed Ali Khamenei succeeded him as the Supreme Leader of the Islamic Revolution.

1990: a major earthquake centred in northern Iran killed nearly 40,000 people.

1995: oil and trade sanctions were imposed against Iran by the USA.

1999: clashes occurred between the government and rioting pro-democracy demonstrators.

2002: relations with the USA deteriorated further after US President George W Bush described Iran as part of an 'axis of evil'.

2003: a major earthquake, centred on the city of Bam in south-eastern Iran, killed more than 40,000 people.

Persepolis

Persepolis (the Greek name for Parsa) was one of the residences of the Persian Achaemenid kings, situated not far from Shiraz in south-west Iran. Founded by Darius I (522 BC–486 BC) at the start of his reign, it was enlarged and embellished by his successors (Xerxes I and Ataxerxes I). Persepolis was destroyed by fire in 330 BC, during Alexander the Great's conquest. The site was thereafter uninhabited.

Persepolis is a grand palatial complex, probably the most perfect remaining example of Achaemenid architecture. Its buildings tower over a terrace that is partly artificial and partly cut into the mountain. Access to this terrace is via a monumental double spiral stairway leading to the Xerxes Gate. Beyond this are grand halls and palaces. The rest of the terrace is taken up with administrative buildings. Although many of the architectural elements were borrowed from those used in Greece's Asian territories (mouldings, capital volutes, etc), others show Egyptian or Mesopotamian influence. The same eclecticism is found in the sculptures of mythological scenes and bearers of offerings. This mixture of influences reflects the interconnection of different parts of the Eastern world, a phenomenon encouraged by the Achaemenid sovereigns.

Occupying most of Mesopotamia, between the Tigris and the Euphrates, the Republic of Iraq is a mainly flat semi-desert country, with extremely hot summers. To the west of the country is the eastern edge of the Syrian Desert and to the north, beyond the Djezireh Desert, are the Taurus Mountains, which lead on to the piedmont plain of the Zagros Mountains.

Area: 438,317km^2
Population (2002): 24,245,000
Capital: Baghdad 4,958,000 (2001 e) including the suburbs
Government type and political system: republic
Head of state and government: (Interim President) Ghazi Yawer; (Interim Prime Minister) Iyad Allawi
Administrative structure: 18 governorates
Official language: Arabic
Currency: Iraqi dinar

DEMOGRAPHICS

Density: 53 inhab/km^2
Percentage of population in urban areas (2001): 67.5%
Age structure of population (2000): 0–15 years: 41.6%, 15–65 years: 55.5%, over 65 years: 2.9%
Birth rate (2003): 35.1‰
Death rate (2003): 8.8‰
Infant mortality rate (2003): 83.3‰
Life expectancy at birth (2003): male: 59.2 years, female: 62.3 years

ECONOMY

GNP (1990): 48.66 billion US$
GNP per capita (1990): 2,170 US$
GNP per capita PPP: n/a
HDI (1999): 0.567
GDP annual growth rate (1989): 2.9%
Annual inflation rate: n/a
Labour force by occupation: n/a
GDP by sector (1991): agriculture: 23%, industry: 6%, services: 71%
Gross public debt: n/a
Unemployment rate: n/a

Agriculture and fishing

Crops
citrus fruits (2002): 321,000t
wheat (2002): 1,856,000t
sugar cane (2001): 65,000t

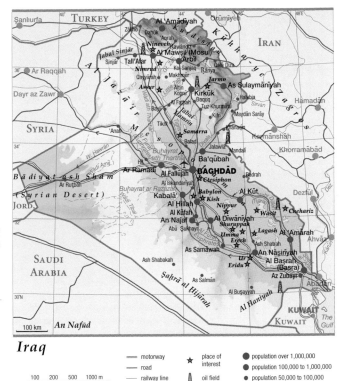

Iraq

━━ motorway	★ place of interest	● population over 1,000,000
━━ road		● population 100,000 to 1,000,000
━━ railway line	⛽ oil field	● population 50,000 to 100,000
✈ airport	⟶ oil pipeline	• population less than 50,000

dates (2001): 400,000t
maize (2002): 60,000t
barley (2002): 1,032,000t
potatoes (2002): 625,000t
grapes (2002): 265,000t
rice (2002): 150,000t
tobacco (2002): 2,250t

Livestock farming and fishing
cattle (2002): 1,400,000 head
buffaloes (2001): 65,000 head
goats (2001): 1,600,000 head

camels (2001): 7,600 head
horses (2001): 47,000 head
sheep (2002): 6,200,000 head
chickens (2002): 23,000,000 head
fish (1999): 26,800t

Energy generation and mining
total electricity (2001): 36,009 million kWh
oil (2002): 99,700,000t

Industrial production
wool (2001): 13,000t

169

HISTORY: KEY DATES

Antiquity to the Ottoman conquest
Present-day Iraq is made up of the ancient country of Mesopotamia, cradle of the Sumer, Akkad, Babylonian and Assyrian civilizations.
633–642: the Arabs conquered Mesopotamia.
750–1258: the Abbasid dynasty reigned over the Muslim empire.
762: the Abbasids established Baghdad as their capital.
1258: the Mongols sacked Baghdad.
1258–1515: Mongol and Turkmen dynasties controlled the country.
1401: Baghdad was sacked by the Tartar conqueror Timur.
1515–46: the Ottoman Turks incorporated Iraq into their empire, and

retained control of the country until World War I.

The Hashemite Kingdom
1914–18: Britain invaded and occupied the country.
1920: a nationalist revolt was suppressed, and Iraq was placed under British mandate by the League of Nations.
1921: the Hashemite Emir Faisal became the first king of Iraq.
1932: Iraq became independent after the termination of the British mandate.
1941: a pro-German, Arab nationalist regime seized power. Britain intervened to restore the king, and Iraq joined World War II alongside the Allies.

$\Rrightarrow$

IRAQ

sugar *(2002)*: 2,000t

Tourism
Tourism revenue (1998): 13 million US$

Foreign trade
Exports (1997): 2,309 million US$
Imports (1997): 765 million US$

Defence
Armed forces (2001): 389,000 people
Defence budget (2001): 9.33% of GDP

Standard of living
Inhabitants per doctor (1993): 1,667
Average daily calorie intake (2000): 2,197
(FAO minimum: 2,400)
Cars per 1,000 inhabitants (1996): 1
Televisions per 1,000 inhabitants (2000): 83

HISTORY: KEY DATES

The Iraqi Republic

1958: the Republic of Iraq was proclaimed following a military coup.
1961: a Kurdish rebellion broke out, leading to ongoing conflict between the Iraqi government and Kurdish rebel groups.
1968: the Ba'ath party took power in a bloodless coup.
1975: an agreement with Iran was signed with the intention of ending the ongoing border dispute between the two countries.
1979: Saddam Hussein became president of Iraq.
1980–88: the Iran–Iraq War.
1990–91: the Gulf War. Iraq invaded and then annexed Kuwait in August 1990, refusing to withdraw despite the UN's condemnation of its actions. A multinational, mainly US force attacked Iraq in January 1991 and liberated Kuwait the following month.
1998: Iraq's cessation of cooperation with UN weapons inspectors led to the launch of a bombing campaign by the US and UK military, intended to destroy Iraq's weapons programmes.
2003–4: the Iraqi regime collapsed. Iraq was provisionally placed under the civil administration of the USA, and an interim Iraqi governing council was established until the return of administrative control to Iraq. However, the stabilization of Iraq, due to extremely volatile conditions within the country, remained highly problematic.

The roots of civilization: Mesopotamia

Iraq is roughly coextensive with the territory of ancient Mesopotamia, where the first Western civilizations were born and the earliest known use of written symbols (around 3500 BC) took place.

In the fertile corridor formed by the valleys of the rivers Tigris and Euphrates, evidence has been discovered of human occupation from as early as the 9th millennium BC. The Sumerians, the Akkadians (founders of Babylon in the 3rd millennium BC), the Assyrians (founders of Niniva in the 2nd millennium BC) and the Elamites (established in Susa in 3500 BC) occupied this pivotal zone in the Middle East, which was successively invaded by peoples from Turkey (the Hittites) and Persia (the Medes and the Parthians) before being taken over by Armenia, Greece and finally the Roman Empire.

The State of Israel comprises four regions. Along the Mediterranean coastline is a fertile plain; inland is a mountainous region that includes the hills of Galilee and Judea. To the south is the semi-desert region of the Negev, which comprises over half of Israel's land area; to the east is the Jordan Valley, part of the Great Rift Valley.

ISRAEL

Area: 21,056km²
Population (2002): 6,303,000
Capital: Jerusalem 692,300 (2003 e) (*not recognized internationally as Israel's capital*); Tel Aviv-Jaffa 364,300 (2003 e)
Government type and political system: republic with a parliamentary system
Head of state: (President of the Republic) Moshe Katzav
Head of government: (Prime Minister) Ariel Sharon
Administrative structure: 6 districts
Official language: Hebrew and Arabic
Currency: Israeli shekel

PALESTINIAN AUTONOMOUS AREAS

Area: 6,231km² (including fully and partially autonomous areas)
Population (1997): 2,601,669 (*excluding Jewish settlers*)
Capital: East Jerusalem (*under Israeli occupation*); Gaza City
Government type and political system: republic with a parliamentary system
Head of state: (Acting Head of the Palestinian Authority) Rawhi Fattuh
Head of government: (Prime Minister) Ahmed Qurei
Administrative structure: n/a
Official language: Arabic
Currency: Jordanian dinar

DEMOGRAPHICS

Density: 296 inhab/km²
Percentage of population in urban areas (2001): 91.8%
Age structure of population (2000): 0–15 years: 28.3%, 15–65 years: 61.9%, over 65 years: 9.9%
Birth rate (2003): 19.8‰
Death rate (2003): 6‰
Infant mortality rate (2003): 5.9‰

Israel

- oil pipeline
- motorway
- road
- airport
- place of interest

district boundary
Hefa district capital

- population over 250,000
- pop. 100,000 to 250,000
- pop. 50,000 to 100,000
- pop. less than 50,000

0   200   500 m

Life expectancy at birth (2003): male: 77.1 years, female: 81 years

ECONOMY

GNP (2002): 105 billion US$
GNP per capita (2002): 16,020 US$
GNP per capita PPP (2002): 19,000 international dollars
HDI (2000): 0.896
GDP annual growth rate (2003): 1.3%
Annual inflation rate (2000): 1.12%
Labour force by occupation (2001): agriculture: 1.9%, industry: 23.4%, services: 74.7%
GDP by sector: n/a
Gross public debt: n/a
Unemployment rate (2002): 10.3%

Agriculture and fishing

Crops
citrus fruits (2002): 591,000t
bananas (2001): 108,000t
wheat (2002): 219,000t

cotton (2002): 43,000t
olives (2002): 180,000t
barley (2002): 33,700t
grapefruits (2001): 327,000t
potatoes (2002): 454,000t
grapes (2002): 114,000t

Livestock farming and fishing
cattle (2002): 1,162,000 head
goats (2001): 308,000 head
sheep (2001): 765,000 head
chickens (2002): 30,000,000 head
fish (1999): 28,300t

Energy generation and mining

total electricity (2001): 42,238 million kWh
natural gas (2001): 9.5 million m³
phosphate (2001): 3,511,000t

Industrial production

milk (2001): 1,329,000t
wine (2002): 60,000hl
cotton yarn (2001): 16,000t
wool (2001): 1,288t

Tourism

Tourism revenue (2001): 2,166 million US$

Foreign trade

Exports (2002): 27,653 million US$
Imports (2002): 31,212 million US$

Defence

Armed forces (2001): 161,500 people
Defence budget (2001): 9.18% of GDP

Standard of living

Inhabitants per doctor (1990): 350
Average daily calorie intake (2000): 3,562 (FAO minimum: 2,400)
Cars per 1,000 inhabitants (2000): 228
Televisions per 1,000 inhabitants (2000): 335

HISTORY: KEY DATES

1948: the State of Israel was created.
1948–9: Israel enlarged its territory after the first Arab–Israeli War.
1964: Arab governments established the Palestinian Liberation Organization.
1967: during the Six-Day War, Israel occupied the Sinai Peninsula as far as the Suez Canal, the Gaza Strip, the West Bank and the Golan Heights.
1973: the Yom Kippur War.
1981: Israel annexed the Golan Heights.
1982–3: Israel returned the Sinai Peninsula to Egypt. Later, Israel occupied Lebanon as far as Beirut, then withdrew from the south of the country.
FROM 1987: the occupied territories (the West Bank and the Gaza Strip) were the scene of a Palestinian uprising or intifada.
1993–4: an Israeli–Palestinian Agreement, the Declaration of Principles, was signed in Washington, DC. Israel withdrew from most of the Gaza Strip (excluding Jewish settlements) and Jericho.
1995: prime minister Yitzhak Rabin was assassinated.
2000: Israel withdrew its army from southern Lebanon.
2001–3: Ariel Sharon (Likud) became prime minister of Israel.

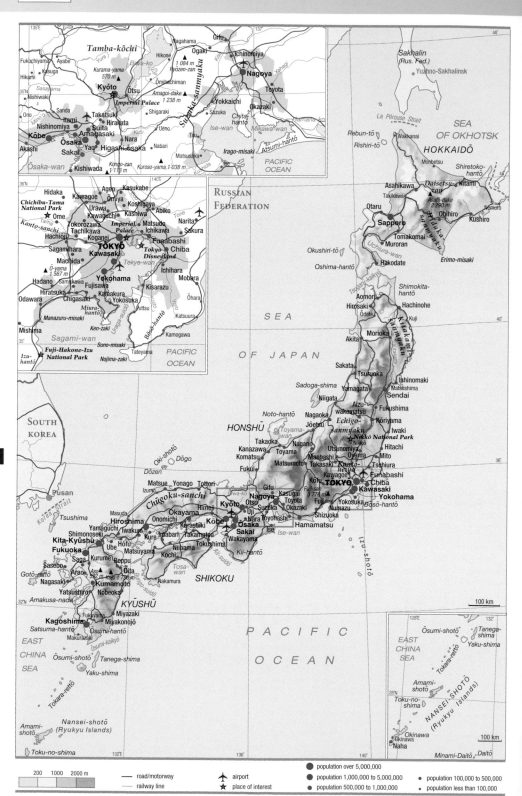

Japan is an island nation in north-east Asia comprising four large islands (Honshu, Hokkaido, Shikoku and Kyushu) and thousands of small islands. Although moderate in size, it is densely populated. The four main islands are mainly mountainous, with forests covering a large proportion of the territory and small, fertile plains along the coasts. Japan has many volcanoes, of which around 60 are active, and volcanic eruptions or earthquakes often produce destructive sea waves known as tsunami. Winters are cold and snowy in the north while most of the archipelago, which is situated in the monsoon zone, has hot, humid summers and mild winters.

Area: 377,829km[2]
Population (2002): 127,537,000
Capital: Tokyo 7,967,614 (1995 census), 26,546,000 (2001 e) including the suburbs
Government type and political system: constitutional monarchy with a parliamentary system
Head of state: (Emperor) Akihito
Head of government: (Prime Minister) Junichiro Koizumi
Administrative structure: 47 prefectures
Official language: Japanese
Currency: yen

DEMOGRAPHICS

Density: 340 inhab/km[2]
Percentage of population in urban areas (2001): 78.9%
Age structure of population (2000): 0–15 years: 14.7%, 15–65 years: 68.1%, over 65 years: 17.2%
Birth rate (2003): 9.2‰
Death rate (2003): 8.2‰
Infant mortality rate (2003): 3.2‰
Life expectancy at birth (2003): male: 77.9 years, female: 85.1 years

ECONOMY

GNP (2002): 4,324 billion US$
GNP per capita (2002): 34,010 US$
GNP per capita PPP (2002): 27,380 international dollars
HDI (2000): 0.933
GDP annual growth rate (2003): 2.7%
Annual inflation rate (2000): –0.67%
Labour force by occupation (2000): agriculture: 5.1%, industry: 31.2%, services: 63.7%
GDP by sector (2000): agriculture: 1.4%, industry: 32.1%, services: 66.6%
Gross public debt (2002): 147.3% of GDP
Unemployment rate (2002): 5.4%

Agriculture and fishing
Crops
citrus fruits (2002): 1,437,000t
sugar beets (2002): 4,098,000t
wheat (2002): 829,000t
sugar cane (2001): 1,482,000t
yams (2002): 180,000t
persimmons (2001): 281,800t
mandarin oranges (1998): 1,553,000t
sweet potatoes (2001): 1,073,000t
peaches (2002): 175,000t
apples (2001): 895,000t
potatoes (2002): 3,069,000t
rice (2002): 11,111,000t
tea (2001): 85,000t
Livestock farming and fishing
cattle (2002): 4,564,000 head
goats (2001): 31,000 head
sheep (2002): 11,000 head
pigs (2002): 9,612,000 head
chickens (2001): 287,000,000 head
fish (1999): 5,937,000t

Energy generation and mining
nuclear electricity (2001): 309,006 million kWh
hydroelectricity (2000): 86,956 million kWh
total electricity (2000): 1,036,798 million kWh
natural gas (2000): 2,587 million m[3]
coal (2000): 3,144,000t
oil (2002): 560,000t
zinc (2001): 44,500t

Industrial production
eggs (2001): 2,526,000t
meat (2001): 2,897,000t
sugar (2002): 945,000t
steel (2003): 110,510,000t
copper (2001): 744,000t
tin (2000): 683,937t
nickel (2001): 160,703t
zinc (2001): 683,937t
cars (2002): 8,619,000 units
commercial vehicles (1998): 2,289,000 units
shipbuilding (2001): 11,042,000dwt
cotton yarn (1998): 175,000t
silk (2001): 650t
artificial textiles (1999): 216,000t
synthetic textiles (1999): 1,222,800t
synthetic rubber (2001): 1,465,000t
cement (2001): 76,550,000t

Tourism
Tourism revenue (2001): 3,301 million US$

Foreign trade
Exports (2002): 395,580 million US$
Imports (2002): 301,750 million US$

Defence
Armed forces (2001): 239,900 people
Defence budget (2001): 0.97% of GDP

Standard of living
Inhabitants per doctor (1996): 555
Average daily calorie intake (2000): 2,762 (FAO minimum: 2,400)
Cars per 1,000 inhabitants (2000): 492
Televisions per 1,000 inhabitants (2001): 731

173

HISTORY: KEY DATES

The origins
9TH MILLENNIUM BC: Palaeolithic populations, who migrated from the northern part of continental Asia, inhabited present-day Japan.
6TH MILLENNIUM BC–3C BC: the culture of the Jomon period was named for the cord- or rope-like patterns on its pottery. As well as decorated pottery figures and vessels, it produced polished stone tools and mortars.
3C BC–AD 3C: the people of the Yayoi period cultivated rice, fashioned objects out of bronze and iron, wove textiles and produced pottery using a potter's wheel. During this period, populations from

Siberia – the Ainu – migrated to the extreme north of Japan.
AD 3C–AD 6C: in the Kofun period, keyhole-shaped burial mounds (kofun) and mural decorations depicting everyday life were produced, sometimes with accompanying terracotta funerary figures (haniwa – literally 'clay rings') made in the form of animals or warriors.

The ancient state
AD 5C–AD 6C: during the Yamamoto dynasty, Chinese influence reached Japan through Korean intermediaries.
c.538 AD: Buddhism was introduced from Korea.

600–22: the Regent Shotoku Taishi created the Horyu-ji Sanctuary.
645: the Nakatomi clan established a government imitating that of the Tang (T'ang) Dynasty in China.
710–94: during the Nara period, the Japanese Imperial Court was established at the capital, Nara.
794–1185: during the Heian period, a new capital was founded at Heiankyo (Kyoto).
858–12c: the Fujiwara family ruled the country.
1185: the Taira family were defeated by the Minamoto family in their struggle to take control of Japan.

↳

JAPAN

⟹

HISTORY: KEY DATES

The Shogunate
1192: the head of the Minamoto family, Yoritomo, was named chief military commander (*shogun*). He had a dual central role as emperor of the Imperial Court and shogun of the government.
1274–81: Japan repelled attempted Mongol invasions.
1338–1573: during the Muromachi period, the Ashikaga shogunate was established in Kyoto; civil conflict was ongoing between various groups and families. Portuguese merchants reached Japan in 1542.
1582: after nine years of fighting, the Ashikaga were eliminated.
1585–98: Toyotomi Hideyoshi, the emperor's prime minister, unified Japan.
1603–16: Tokugawa Ieyasu settled in Edo (Tokyo), declared himself the hereditary shogun and established a repressive but stable system of government.
1616–1867: the Edo or Tokugawa period. The country was closed to foreigners, apart from the Chinese and the Dutch, after the 1637 rebellion. A rigidly divided class system developed in Japan.
1854–64: Western military intervention forced Japan to open up to international trade.

Contemporary Japan
1867–8: the last shogun, Yoshinobu, resigned and the restoration of the emperor Meiji took place.
1868–1912: Western techniques and institutions were adopted in order to make Japan a great economic and political power. It was a period of external expansion: Japan acquired Formosa (present-day Taiwan) and established itself in Manchuria and Korea, which it annexed in 1910.
1912–26: during Yoshihito's reign, Japan entered World War I alongside the Allies.
1931: Japan occupied and renamed Manchuria.
1937–8: in a war with China, Japanese forces captured and committed atrocities in a number of cities.
1939–40: Japan signed a tripartite treaty with Germany and Italy.
1941: Japanese forces attacked the US Pacific fleet in Pearl Harbor, Hawaii. The USA and its main allies declared war on Japan the following day.
1942: Japan occupied most of South-East Asia and the Pacific.
1945: Japan capitulated after US planes dropped atomic bombs on Hiroshima and Nagasaki, causing massive destruction.
1947: a new constitution came into force, establishing a parliamentary system and granting universal suffrage.
1951–2: the San Francisco Peace Treaty was signed, and restored Japanese sovereignty.
1960–70: Japan signed a military alliance treaty with the USA, and went on to become one of the world's major economic powers.
1964: the city of Tokyo hosted the Olympic Games.
1989: Emperor Hirohito died, and was succeeded by his son Akihito.
1995: central Japan was struck by a major earthquake, in which thousands of people lost their lives. Two months later, religious extremists staged a nerve gas attack on the Tokyo underground railway system, killing twelve people and injuring thousands.
2004: Japan deployed non-combat troops to Iraq as part of the US-led military campaign.

Japan's principal islands

Name	Area	Number of inhabitants*	Main town(s)
Hokkaido	78 500 km²	5 683 062	Sapporo
Honshu	230 000 km²	106 479 000	Tokyo, Osaka, Yokohama, Kyoto and Kobe
Kyushu	42 000 km²	13 445 561	Kitakyushu and Fukuoka
Shikoku	18 800 km²	4 154 039	Matsuyama

*2000 census.

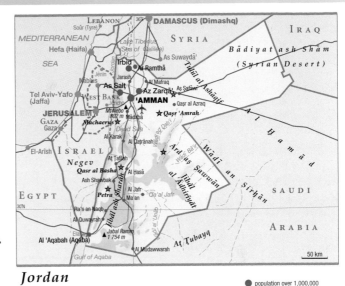

Jordan

★ place of interest

| 200 | 500 | 1000 m |

— road
--- railway line
✈ airport

● population over 1,000,000
● population 100,000 to 1,000,000
● population 50,000 to 100,000
• population less than 50,000

The Hashemite Kingdom of Jordan has a hot, arid desert climate. Summers are hot and winters are cold. The country's major geographical features are the Jordan Valley, also known as Al Ghor (part of the Great Rift Valley), which runs from north to south, the Transjordan Plateau and the surrounding highlands.

Area: 97,740km^2
Population (2002): 5,196,000
Capital: Amman 1,181,000 (2001 e)
Government type and political system: constitutional monarchy with a parliamentary system
Head of state: (King) Abdullah ibn Hussein II
Head of government: (Prime Minister) Faisal al-Fayez
Administrative structure: 12 governorates
Official language: Arabic
Currency: Jordan dinar

DEMOGRAPHICS

Density: 72 inhab/km^2
Percentage of population in urban areas (2000): 74.2%
Age structure of population (2000): 0–15 years: 40%, 15–65 years: 57.2%, over 65 years: 2.8%
Birth rate (2003): 28‰
Death rate (2003): 4.3‰
Infant mortality rate (2003): 23.9‰
Life expectancy at birth (2003): male: 69.7 years, female: 72.5 years

ECONOMY

GNP (2002): 9.09 billion US$
GNP per capita (2002): 1,760 US$
GNP per capita PPP (2002): 4,180 international dollars
HDI (2000): 0.717
GDP annual growth rate (2003): 3.2%
Annual inflation rate (2000): 0.67%
Labour force by occupation: n/a
GDP by sector (2000): agriculture: 2.2%, industry: 24.8%, services: 73%

Gross public debt: n/a
Unemployment rate (2000): 13.2%

Agriculture

Crops
citrus fruits (2002): 122,000t
bananas (2001): 30,000t
wheat (2002): 65,000t
olives (2002): 181,000t
barley (2002): 57,000t
grapes (2002): 34,800t
Livestock farming
cattle (2002): 68,000 head
goats (2001): 640,000 head
camels (2001): 18,000 head
sheep (2002): 1,458,000 head

Energy generation and mining
total electricity (2001): 7,091 million kWh
phosphate (2001): 5,843,000t

Industrial production
olive oil (2001): 14,800t

Tourism
Tourism revenue (2001): 700 million US$

Foreign trade
Exports (2002): 2,770 million US$
Imports (2002): 4,450.4 million US$

Defence
Armed forces (2001): 100,240 people
Defence budget (2001): 8.52% of GDP

Standard of living
Inhabitants per doctor (1994): 625
Average daily calorie intake (2000): 2,749 (FAO minimum: 2,400)
Cars per 1,000 inhabitants (1996): 48

Televisions per 1,000 inhabitants (2000): 84

HISTORY: KEY DATES

1946: the country became independent from Britain as the Hashemite Kingdom of Transjordan.
1949: the existing kingdom was united with the West Bank (which was part of the Arab state planned for the Partition Plan of Palestine in 1947) in an armistice. This left Jordan in control of the West Bank, and the West and East Banks were united within Jordan in 1951.
1952: Hussein ibn Talal became king of Jordan.
1967: during the Six-Day War, Israel occupied Jerusalem and the West Bank.
1970: government forces clashed with pro-independence Palestinian guerrillas. Many Palestinians fled to Lebanon and Syria.
1988: King Hussein formally relinquished Jordan's claim to the West Bank, and backed the Palestinians against Israel.
1994: Jordan signed a peace treaty with Israel.
1999: King Hussein died; his eldest son succeeded him as King Abdullah II.
2002–4: Jordan made plans for major construction projects to be undertaken jointly with Israel (a desert science centre) and Syria (the Wahdah Dam).

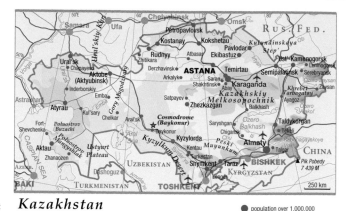

Kazakhstan

★ place of interest

| 0 | 200 | 500 | 1000 m |

— road
— railway line
✈ airport

● population over 1,000,000
● population 500,000 to 1,000,000
● population 100,000 to 500,000
• population less than 100,000

The Republic of Kazakhstan is the largest country in Central Asia, roughly equivalent in size to the whole of Western Europe. Kazakhstan's topography is very varied. The centre of the territory is formed by the arid, empty steppes of the Kazakh Melkosopochnik, a highly eroded plateau. In the north are high plains that extend as far as western Siberia, and there are semi-desert areas on the banks of the Aral Sea in the south-west. The Altai and Tien Shan mountain ranges are located in eastern Kazakhstan. The country's climate is arid, with extremely cold winters.

Area: 2,724,900km²
Population (2002): 16,026,000
Capital: Astana 287,000 (1993 e), 328,000 (2001 e) including the suburbs
Government type and political system: republic with a semi-presidential system
Head of state: (President of the Republic) Nursultan Nazarbayev
Head of government: (Prime Minister) Daniyal Akhmetov
Administrative structure: 14 regions and 3 municipalities
Official languages: Kazakh and Russian
Currency: tenge

DEMOGRAPHICS

Density: 6 inhab/km²
Percentage of population in urban areas (2001): 55.9%
Age structure of population (2000): 0–15 years: 27%, 15–65 years: 66.1%, over 65 years: 6.9%
Birth rate (2003): 16.2‰
Death rate (2003): 9.5‰
Infant mortality rate (2003): 51.7‰
Life expectancy at birth (2003): male: 60.9 years, female: 71.9 years

ECONOMY

GNP (2002): 22.6 billion US$
GNP per capita (2002): 1,520 US$
GNP per capita PPP (2002): 5,630 international dollars
HDI (2000): 0.75
GDP annual growth rate (2003): 9.5%

Annual inflation rate (2000): 13.17%
Labour force by occupation (1998): agriculture: n/a, industry: 18.6%, services: 58.5%
GDP by sector (2000): agriculture: 9.2%, industry: 42.9%, services: 47.9%
Gross public debt: n/a
Unemployment rate (2002): 2.6%

Agriculture and fishing

Crops
oats (2001): 254,000t
sugar beets (2002): 372,000t
wheat (2002): 12,700,000t
cotton (2002): 361,000t
maize (2002): 435,000t
millet (2001): 85,000t
barley (2002): 2,209,000t
potatoes (2002): 2,269,000t
grapes (2002): 26,300t
rice (2002): 199,000t
rye (2001): 67,000t
sunflowers (2002): 190,000t
Livestock farming and fishing
cattle (2002): 4,282,000 head
camels (2001): 99,000 head
horses (2001): 976,000 head
sheep (2002): 9,208,000 head
pigs (2002): 1,124,000 head
fish (1999): 27,000t

Energy generation and mining

silver (2001): 982t
bauxite (2001): 3,668,000t
chromium (2001): 2,046,000t
copper (2001): 470,000t
total electricity (2001): 52,425 million kWh
iron (2001): 8,000,000t
natural gas (2002): 12,300 million m³
coal (2001): 77,584,000t
manganese (2001): 350,000t.
molybdenum (2001): 200t
oil (2002): 47,200,000t
lead (2001): 37,700t
uranium (2001): 2,018t

zinc (2001): 344,000t

Industrial production

steel (2003): 4,880,000t
copper (2001): 470,000t
zinc (2001): 267,900t
cotton yarn (2001): 130,000t
timber (1996): 315,000m³

Tourism

Tourism revenue: n/a

Foreign trade

Exports (2002): 10,027.6 million US$
Imports (2002): 7,726.3 million US$

Defence

Armed forces (2001): 60,000 people
Defence budget (2001): 0.82% of GDP

Standard of living

Inhabitants per doctor (1996): 286
Average daily calorie intake (2000): 2,991 (FAO minimum: 2,400)
Cars per 1,000 inhabitants (1999): 65
Televisions per 1,000 inhabitants (2000): 241

HISTORY: KEY DATES

15c–18c: the Kazakh ethnic group occupied the region that is now Kazakhstan.
18c: the Russian empire began to take control of the territory.
1920: Kazakhstan became an autonomous republic of the Russian SFSR (Russian Soviet Federated Socialist Republic).
1936: Kazakhstan became a constituent republic of the USSR.
1991: the Supreme Soviet proclaimed the independence of Kazakhstan, which then became a member of the Commonwealth of Independent States (CIS).

Occupying the northern half of the Korean Peninsula, the Democratic People's Republic of Korea is a mountainous and heavily forested country. The climate is harsh, with extremely cold winters.

Area: 120,538km²
Population (2002): 22,586,000
Capital: Pyongyang 3,164,000 (2001 e)
Government type and political system: republic with a socialist system
Head of state: (Chairman, National Defence Commission) Kim Jong-il (Chairman, Presidium of the Supreme People's Assembly) Kim Yong-nam
Head of government: (Premier) Pak Pong-ju
Administrative structure: 9 provinces and 4 directly governed cities
Official language: Korean
Currency: North Korean won

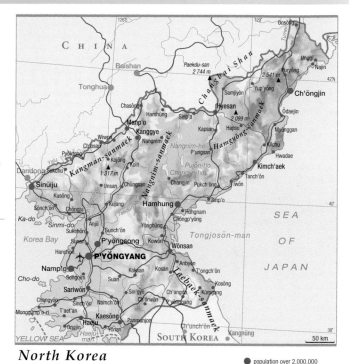

North Korea

500	1000	2000 m

— railway line
— road
✈ airport

● population over 2,000,000
● population 500,000 to 2,000,000
● population 100,000 to 500,000
• population less than 100,000

DEMOGRAPHICS

Density: 199 inhab/km²
Percentage of population in urban areas (2001): 60.5%
Age structure of population (2000): 0–15 years: 26.5%, 15–65 years: 67.6%, over 65 years: 5.9%
Birth rate (2003): 16.3‰
Death rate (2003): 11‰
Infant mortality rate (2003): 45.1‰
Life expectancy at birth (2003): male: 60.5 years, female: 66 years

ECONOMY

GNP: n/a
GNP per capita: n/a
GNP per capita PPP: n/a
HDI (1995): 0.766
GDP annual growth rate: n/a
Annual inflation rate: n/a
Labour force by occupation: n/a
GDP by sector: n/a
Gross public debt: n/a
Unemployment rate: n/a

Agriculture and fishing
Crops
maize (2002): 1,651,000t
potatoes (2002): 1,884,000t
rice (2002): 2,186,000t
soya beans (2002): 360,000t
Livestock farming and fishing
cattle (2002): 575,000 head
goats (2001): 2,300,000 head
pigs (2002): 3,152,000 head
fish (1999): 279,000t

Energy generation and mining
copper (2001): 13,000t
hydroelectricity (2001): 21,318 million kWh
total electricity (2001): 30,013 million kWh
iron (2001): 300,000t
coal (2001): 52,989,000t
lignite (2001): 67,561,000t
lead (2001): 70,000t
zinc (2001): 190,000t

Industrial production
silk (2001): 150t
copper (2001): 13,000t
zinc (2001): 180,000t
lead (2001): 78,000t

phosphate (2001): 350,000t
timber (2000): 1,500,000m³

Tourism
Tourism revenue: n/a

Foreign trade
Exports (1997): 907 million US$
Imports (1997): 1,686 million US$

Defence
Armed forces (2001): 1,082,000 people
Defence budget (2001): 7.22% of GDP

Standard of living
Inhabitants per doctor (1990): 370
Average daily calorie intake (2000): 2,185 (FAO minimum: 2,400)
Cars per 1,000 inhabitants: n/a
Televisions per 1,000 inhabitants (2001): 59

177

HISTORY: KEY DATES

AD 4c: Buddhism was introduced to the area that later became Korea.
10c: the Koryo dynasty was established.
1231: Mongol forces invaded from China.
1910: Japan formally annexed the country and made sweeping changes to its administration.
1945: Korea was occupied by Soviet troops in the north and US troops in the south.
1948: the country was partitioned

along the 38th Parallel with the Republic of Korea in the south and the Democratic People's Republic of Korea in the north.
1953: after the Korean War (1950–3), the country remained divided.
1991: both North and South Korea became members of the UN and signed a reconciliation agreement.
2002–4: North Korea's nuclear weapons programme caused tension in the international community.

KOREA, SOUTH

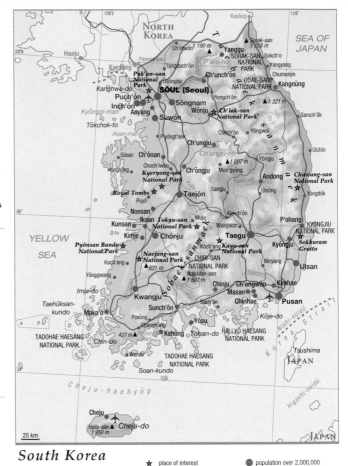

The Republic of Korea occupies the southern half of the Korean Peninsula, and is characterized by an extreme continental climate. It consists of the Taebaek Sanbaek mountain range in the east, with lower hills and coastal plains in the west.

Area: 99,268km²
Population (2002): 47,389,000
Capital: Seoul 9,862,000 (2001 e) including the suburbs
Government type and political system: republic with a semi-presidential system
Head of state: (President of the Republic) Roh Moo-hyun
Head of government: (Prime Minister) Lee Hae-chan
Administrative structure: 9 provinces and 7 metropolitan cities
Official language: Korean
Currency: South Korean won

DEMOGRAPHICS

Density: 473 inhab/km²
Percentage of population in urban areas (2001): 82.4%
Age structure of population (2000): 0–15 years: 20.8%, 15–65 years: 72.1%, over 65 years: 7.1%
Birth rate (2003): 11.9‰
Death rate (2003): 5.9‰
Infant mortality rate (2003): 5‰
Life expectancy at birth (2003): male: 71.8 years, female: 79.3 years

ECONOMY

GNP (2002): 473 billion US$
GNP per capita (2002): 9,930 US$
GNP per capita PPP (2002): 16,960 international dollars
HDI (2000): 0.882
GDP annual growth rate (2003): 3.1%
Annual inflation rate (2000): 2.26%
Labour force by occupation (2000): agriculture: 10.9%, industry: 28%, services: 61.1%
GDP by sector (2000): agriculture: 4.8%, industry: 44.4%, services: 50.8%
Gross public debt (1998): 11% of GDP
Unemployment rate (2002): 3.1%

Agriculture and fishing
Crops
mandarin oranges (1998): 649,000t
peaches (2002): 188,000t
rice (2002): 6,687,000t

soya beans (2002): 115,000 t
tobacco (2001): 56,000t
Livestock farming and fishing
cattle (2002): 1,954,000 head
pigs (2002): 8,974,000 head
chickens (2002): 102,000,000 head
fish (1999): 2,423,000t

Energy generation and mining
silver (2001): 600t
nuclear electricity (2001): 106,526 million kWh
total electricity (2001): 290,665 million kWh

Industrial production
meat (2001): 1,589,000t
steel (2003): 46,306,000t
cement (2001): 52,012,000t
cast iron (1998): 23,299,000t
cars (2002): 2,651,000 units
commercial vehicles (1998): 369,000 units
shipbuilding (2001): 11,882,000dwt

cotton yarn (1998): 275,000t
silk (2001): 10t
synthetic textiles (1999): 2,569,700t
timber (2000): 1,592,000m³

Tourism
Tourism revenue (2001): 6,283 million US$

Foreign trade
Exports (2002): 162,554 million US$
Imports (2002): 148,374 million US$

Defence
Armed forces (2001): 686,000 people
Defence budget (2001): 2.81% of GDP

Standard of living
Inhabitants per doctor (1996): 909
Average daily calorie intake (2000): 3,093 (FAO minimum: 2,400)
Cars per 1,000 inhabitants (1999): 168
Televisions per 1,000 inhabitants (2001): 363

South Korea

★ place of interest
— road
— railway line
✈ airport

● population over 2,000,000
● population 500,000 to 2,000,000
● population 100,000 to 500,000
• population less than 100,000

HISTORY: KEY DATES

AD 4c: Buddhism was introduced to the area that later became Korea.
10c: the Koryo dynasty was established.
1231: Mongol forces invaded from China. After thirty years of war, a Koryo-Mongol alliance was established.
1910: Japan formally annexed the country and made sweeping changes to its administration.
1945: Korea was occupied by Soviet troops in the north and US troops in the south.

1948: the country was partitioned along the 38th Parallel. The Republic of Korea was established in the south, and the Democratic People's Republic of Korea in the north.
1953: after the Korean War (1950–3), the partitioning of the country was maintained.
1987: a process of democratization began in South Korea, which had previously been ruled by an authoritarian regime.

1991: both North and South Korea became members of the UN and signed a reconciliation agreement.
2000: a historic summit was held in Pyongyang between North Korea's leader Kim Jong-il and the South Korean president, Kim Dae-jung. Kim Dae-jung received the Nobel Peace Prize.
2004: the USA proposed a significant reduction of its long-standing military presence in South Korea.

Ancient Korea

Legend has it that a man known as Tungun, the son of a she-bear who had changed into a woman, founded the ancient country of Choson (situated in the Taedong River basin in the north-west of the Korean Peninsula). Very early on, the Choson kingdom is said to have had contact with Chinese culture, according to accounts that attribute the founding of a new dynasty at Pyongyang in 1122 BC to Kija, a Chinese scholar and leader. The Chinese eventually established four colonies in the region. The most important of these, Luolang, was located near Pyongyang in the lower part of the Taedong River basin, whilst the three others (Zhenfan, Xuantu and Lindun) were located to the north, east and south of Luolang respectively.

These colonies were unable to withstand the pressure from local populations for long, and Luolang, despite being the most powerful of the four, disappeared at the beginning of the first century BC. It was at this time that territorial reorganizations took place, resulting in the creation of three separate kingdoms: the Koguryo kingdom, which stretched from north to south along the banks of the River Yalu and retained the old capital Pyongyang; the Paekche kingdom in the south-west, and the Silla kingdom in the south-east. These three states all occupied the Han River basin, a region rich in natural resources and a maritime gateway to China. Koguryo clashed with China and with the other kingdoms until, during the 7th century, the Silla kingdom prevailed. It formed an alliance with China, which, after suffering serious defeats at the beginning of the 7c, managed to destroy the Paekche kingdom's forces in 660 as well as those of the Paekche's Japanese allies. Whilst recognizing the Chinese suzerainty of the Tang (T'ang), the Silla kingdom gradually spread its influence over most of the Koguryo territory, finally unifying the Korean Peninsula under its hegemony in around 735. Buddhism, already present in the area, became dominant under Silla rule, and Korea was established as a prosperous country with a flourishing culture.

Situated on the north coast of the Persian Gulf, the State of Kuwait is made up of a desert plain scattered with occasional oases. Over half of the country's population is concentrated in the capital, Kuwait City.

Area: 17,818km²
Population (2002): 2,023,000
Capital: Kuwait City 888,000 (2001 e) including the suburbs
Government type and political system: monarchy
Head of state: (Emir) Sheikh Jaber al-Ahmad al-Jaber al-Sabah
Head of government: (Prime Minister) Sheikh Sabah al-Ahmad al-Jaber al-Sabah
Administrative structure: 5 governorates
Official language: Arabic
Currency: Kuwaiti dinar

DEMOGRAPHICS

Density: 111 inhab/km²
Percentage of population in urban areas (2001): 96.1%
Age structure of population (2000): 0–15 years: 31.3%, 15–65 years: 66.5%, over 65 years: 2.2%
Birth rate (2003): 20.2‰
Death rate (2003): 1.9‰
Infant mortality rate (2003): 10.8‰
Life expectancy at birth (2003): male: 74.9 years, female: 79 years

Kuwait

● population over 100,000
● population 50,000 to 100,000
● population less than 50,000

=== motorway
— road
✈ airport
🛢 oil field
⚓ oil-exporting port
→ pipeline

100   200 m

ECONOMY

GNP (2002): 38 billion US$
GNP per capita (2002): 16,340 US$
GNP per capita PPP (2002): 17,780 international dollars
HDI (2000): 0.813
GDP annual growth rate (2003): 9.9%
Annual inflation rate (2000): 1.8%
Labour force by occupation: n/a
GDP by sector (1995): agriculture: 0.4%, industry: 53.3%, services: 46.3%
Gross public debt: n/a
Unemployment rate (2001): 0.78%

Agriculture and fishing

Crops
dates (2001): 10,400t
tomatoes (2002): 35,100t
Livestock farming and fishing
cattle (2002): 20,000 head
goats (2001): 130,000 head
camels (2001): 9,000 head

sheep (2002): 800,000 head
chickens (2002): 32,500,000 head
fish (1999): 6,540t

Energy generation and mining
total electricity (2001): 31,492 million kWh
natural gas (2002): 8,700 million m³
oil (2002): 91,800,000t

Industrial production
milk (2001): 44,500t
eggs (2001): 22,500t

Tourism
Tourism revenue (1999): 243 million US$

Foreign trade
Exports (2002): 15,366 million US$
Imports (2002): 8,117 million US$

Defence
Armed forces (2001): 15,500 people
Defence budget (2001): 9.3% of GDP

Standard of living
Inhabitants per doctor (1990): 5,000
Average daily calorie intake (2000): 3,132 (FAO minimum: 2,400)
Cars per 1,000 inhabitants (1996): 359
Televisions per 1,000 inhabitants (2001): 482

HISTORY: KEY DATES

1756: Kuwait came under the control of the Al-Sabah family.
1961: Kuwait became independent after more than fifty years as a British protectorate.
1990–1: Iraq invaded Kuwait and occupied the country despite UN orders to withdraw. The Gulf War followed, ending in 1991 when Iraqi forces retreated.
2003: the Kuwait–Iraq border was a significant location in the US-led military campaign to oust Saddam Hussein from Iraq.

The oil kings

Despite its small size, Kuwait is an extremely powerful oil state. Some of its competitors in this industry are listed below.

Rank	Country	Value (millions of tonnes)	Rank	Country	Value (millions of tonnes)
1	Saudi Arabia	418 100	12	Iraq	99 700
2	Russia	379 600	13	Nigeria	98 600
3	United States	346 816	14	Kuwait	91 800
4	Mexico	177 999	15	Brazil	74 400
5	China	168 900	16	Algeria	70 200
6	Iran	166 800	17	Libya	64 700
7	Norway	156 381	18	Indonesia	62 400
8	Venezuela	151 400	19	Kazakhstan	47 200
9	Canada	123 347	20	Angola	44 600
10	United Kingdom	116 205	21	Oman	44 600
11	United Arab Emirates	105 600	22	Argentina	39 400

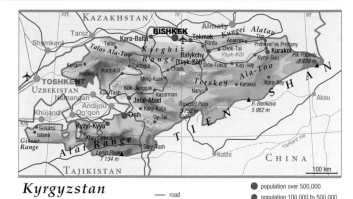

Kyrgyzstan

— road
— railway line
✈ airport

● population over 500,000
● population 100,000 to 500,000
● population 50,000 to 100,000
• population less than 50,000

1000 3000 5000 m

A landlocked and mainly mountainous country containing part of the Tien Shan mountain range, the Kyrgyz Republic has a continental climate with a wide range of temperatures.

Area: 199,900km²
Population (2002): 5,047,000
Capital: Bishkek 736,000 (2001 e)
Government type and political system: republic with a semi-presidential system
Head of state: (President of the Republic) Askar Akayev
Head of government: (Prime Minister) Nikolai Tanayev
Administrative structure: 7 provinces and 1 city
Official language: Kyrgyz
Currency: som

DEMOGRAPHICS
Density: 24 inhab/km²
Percentage of population in urban areas (2001): 34.4%
Age structure of population (2000): 0–15 years: 33.9%, 15–65 years: 60.1%, over 65 years: 6%
Birth rate (2003): 21.9‰
Death rate (2003): 7.1‰
Infant mortality rate (2003): 37‰
Life expectancy at birth (2003): male: 64.8 years, female: 72.3 years

ECONOMY
GNP (2002): 1.44 billion US$
GNP per capita (2002): 290 US$
GNP per capita PPP (2002): 1,560 international dollars
HDI (2000): 0.712

GDP annual growth rate (2003): 5.2%
Annual inflation rate (2000): 18.69%
Labour force by occupation (1999): agriculture: 52.4%, industry: 11.6%, services: 36%
GDP by sector (2000): agriculture: 39.4%, industry: 26.4%, services: 34.2%
Gross public debt: n/a
Unemployment rate: n/a

Agriculture
Crops
sugar beets (2002): 525,000t
wheat (2002): 1,163,000t
maize (2002): 428,000t
hazelnuts (2001): 1,650t
barley (2002): 166,000t
potatoes (2002): 1,244,000t
tobacco (2001): 24,000t
Livestock farming
cattle (2002): 970,000 head
horses (2001): 346,000 head
sheep (2002): 3,104,000 head
pigs (2002): 87,000 head

Energy generation and mining
total electricity (2001): 13,450 million kWh
hydroelectricity (2001): 12,425 million kWh
molybdenum (2001): 300t
gold (2001): 20,000kg

Industrial production
cotton yarn (2001): 28,300t
sugar (2002): 55,000t
silk (2001): 800t
timber (2000): 9,000m³

Tourism
Tourism revenue (1998): 8 million US$
Foreign trade
Exports (2002): 498.1 million US$
Imports (2002): 552 million US$
Defence
Armed forces (2001): 10,900 people
Defence budget (2001): 1.28% of GDP
Standard of living
Inhabitants per doctor (1995): 312
Average daily calorie intake (2000): 2,871 (FAO minimum: 2,400)
Cars per 1,000 inhabitants (1999): 39
Televisions per 1,000 inhabitants (2001): 49

181

HISTORY: KEY DATES
Kyrgyzstan was gradually conquered by Russia during the latter part of the 19th century.
1924: the area became known as the Kara-Kyrgyz Autonomous Region, within the Russian SFSR (Russian Soviet Federated Socialist Republic). It was renamed the Kyrgyz Autonomous Region in 1925, and became an autonomous republic in 1926.
1936: the country became a constituent republic of the USSR.
1991: the Supreme Soviet proclaimed the independence of Kyrgyzstan, which then became a member of the Commonwealth of Independent States (CIS).

LAOS

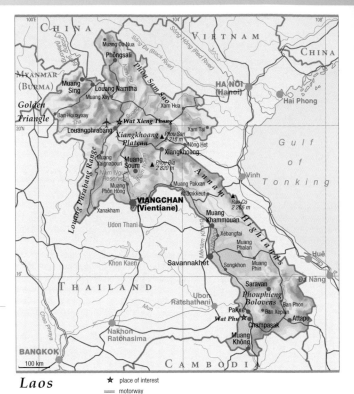

Lao People's Democratic Republic is a landlocked country in South-East Asia, situated between Vietnam and Thailand and made up of plateaux and mountains, which receive summer rains (monsoons). Forests and savannas cover most of the country. The River Mekong runs through Laos, and the majority of the population live in the Mekong valley.

Area: 236,800km²
Population (2002): 5,529,000
Capital: Vientiane 663,000 (2001 e)
Government type and political system: republic with a socialist system
Head of state: (President of the Republic) Khamtai Siphandon
Head of government: (Prime Minister) Boungnang Volachit
Administrative structure: 16 provinces, 1 municipality and 1 special zone
Official language: Lao
Currency: new kip

DEMOGRAPHICS

Density: 23 inhab/km²
Percentage of population in urban areas (2001): 19.7%
Age structure of population (2000): 0–15 years: 42.7%, 15–65 years: 53.8%, over 65 years: 3.5%
Birth rate (2003): 35.6‰
Death rate (2003): 12.6‰
Infant mortality rate (2003): 88 ‰
Life expectancy at birth (2003): male: 53.3 years, female: 55.8 years

ECONOMY

GNP (2002): 1.71 billion US$
GNP per capita (2002): 310 US$
GNP per capita PPP (2002): 1,660 international dollars
HDI (2000): 0.485
GDP annual growth rate (2003): 5.3%
Annual inflation rate (2000): 25.09%
Labour force by occupation: n/a
GDP by sector (2000): agriculture: 52.9%, industry: 22.8%, services: 24.3%
Gross public debt: n/a
Unemployment rate: n/a

Agriculture and fishing

Crops
citrus fruits (2002): 71,000t
pineapples (2001): 35,000t
bananas (2001): 23,000t
sugar cane (2001): 297,000t
maize (2002): 124,000t
manioc (2001): 71,000t
sweet potatoes (2001): 118,000t
potatoes (2002): 35,000t
rice (2002): 2,417,000t
Livestock farming and fishing
cattle (2002): 1,208,000 head
buffaloes (2001): 1,008,000 head
goats (2001): 240,000 head
pigs (2002): 1,416,000 head
fish (1999): 60,000t

Energy generation and mining
total electricity (2001): 1,317 million kWh
tin (2001): 400t

Industrial production
timber (2000): 567,000m³

Tourism
Tourism revenue (2001): 104 million US$

Foreign trade
Exports (2001): 311.1 million US$
Imports (2001): 527.9 million US$

Defence
Armed forces (2001): 29,100 people
Defence budget (2001): 0.76% of GDP

Standard of living
Inhabitants per doctor (1993): 4,450
Average daily calorie intake (2000): 2,266 (FAO minimum: 2,400)

Cars per 1,000 inhabitants (1996): 3
Televisions per 1,000 inhabitants (2001): 52

HISTORY: KEY DATES

18c: the country was divided into two rival kingdoms, Luang Phabang and Vientiane.
1778: Siam attempted to dominate both regions of Laos.
1893: Laos became a French protectorate and part of the federation of Indochina.
1949–54: Laos became semiautonomous within the French Union (1949), and then gained full sovereignty. Pathet Lao ('Land of Laos' – now the Lao People's Revolutionary Party, LPRP), an independence movement backed by the Vietminh Communists, occupied the north of the country.
1953–5: Laos gained full sovereignty and joined the UN.
1964–73: during the Vietnam War, Laos was heavily bombed by the USA.
1975: the Lao People's Democratic Republic was declared.
1990s: Laos moved towards a capitalist economy, and improved its relations with China and Thailand.

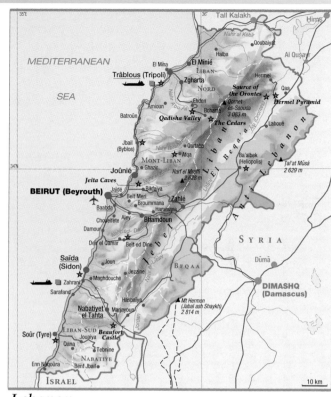

Lebanon

✈ international airport	— road
🚢 oil-exporting port	— railway
200 500 1000 2000 2500 m	

★ place of interest	
→ oil pipeline	● population over 1,000,000
■ oil refinery	● population 100,000 to 1,000,000
— governorate boundary	● population 10,000 to 100,000
Zahlé governorate admin. centre	• population less than 10,000

The territory of the Lebanese Republic is dominated by the limestone massifs of the Lebanon and Anti-Lebanon mountain ranges that frame the fertile Beqaa valley. To the west is a narrow, broken coastal plain where most of the country's population is concentrated, bordering on terraced, intensely developed plateaux. The climate is mild and humid on the coast and harsher and drier inland.

Area: 10,400km²
Population (2002): 3,613,000
Capital: Beirut 2,115,000 (2001 e) including the suburbs
Government type and political system: republic with a parliamentary system
Head of state: (President of the Republic) Emile Lahoud
Head of government: (Prime Minister-elect) Omar Karameh
Administrative structure: 6 governorates
Official language: Arabic
Currency: Lebanese pound

183

DEMOGRAPHICS

Density: 316 inhab/km²
Percentage of population in urban areas (2001): 90%
Age structure of population (2000): 0–15 years: 31.1%, 15–65 years: 62.8%, over 65 years: 6.1%
Birth rate (2003): 19.1‰
Death rate (2003): 5.4‰
Infant mortality rate (2003): 17.2‰
Life expectancy at birth (2000): male: 71.9 years, female: 75.1 years

ECONOMY

GNP (2002): 17.7 billion US$
GNP per capita (2002): 3,990 US$
GNP per capita PPP (2002): 4,600 international dollars
HDI (2000): 0.755
GDP annual growth rate (2003): 3%
Annual inflation rate (1994): 6.8%
Labour force by occupation: n/a
GDP by sector (2000): agriculture: 11.9%,
industry: 22%, services: 66.1%
Gross public debt: n/a
Unemployment rate: n/a

Agriculture and fishing

Crops
citrus fruits (2002): 317,000t
almonds (2001): 35,000t
bananas (2001): 110,000t
sugar beets (2002): 14,000t
wheat (2002): 119,000t
oranges (2001): 165,000t
grapefruits (2001): 58,000t
apples (2001): 120,000t
potatoes (2002): 397,000t
tomatoes (2002): 247,000t
Livestock farming and fishing
cattle (2002): 60,000 head
goats (2001): 445,000 head
sheep (2002): 350,000 head
chickens (2002): 33,000,000 head
fish (1999): 3,860t

Energy generation
total electricity (2001): 6,728 million kWh
Industrial production
olive oil (2001): 6,300t
wine (2002): 160,000hl
timber (2000): 7,150m³
cement (2001): 2,700,000t
Tourism
Tourism revenue (2001): 837 million US$
Foreign trade
Exports (1999): 677 million US$
Imports (1997): 7,456 million US$
Defence
Armed forces (2001): 71,830 people
Defence budget (2001): 3.54% of GDP
Standard of living
Inhabitants per doctor (1993): 526
Average daily calorie intake (2000): 3,155 (FAO minimum: 2,400)
Cars per 1,000 inhabitants (1996): 298
Televisions per 1,000 inhabitants (2001): 336

LEBANON

HISTORY: KEY DATES

Early origins to independence
3RD MILLENNIUM BC: the coast of Lebanon was occupied by the Canaanites and the Phoenicians, who founded the independent city-states of Byblos, Berytos (now Beirut), Sidon and Tyre.
1ST MILLENNIUM BC: the Phoenicians dominated Mediterranean trade.
7C BC–1C BC: the country was controlled by the Assyrians, the Egyptians, the Persians, the Babylonians and the Greeks in turn.
64 BC–AD 636: Lebanon was part of the Roman (and then Byzantine) Province of Syria. When the Roman Empire split into East and West, Syria became part of the Eastern or Byzantine Empire.
AD 636: Lebanon was conquered by the Arabs.
7C–11C: the coast and the mountains were used as a refuge by several Christian, Shiite and then Druze communities.
1516: Lebanon became part of the Ottoman Empire.
1858–60: conflict between the Muslim Druze and the Roman Catholic Maronite communities led to a massacre of the Maronites.
1861: France intervened and created the province of Mount Lebanon, which was granted a certain degree of autonomy.

1920–43: following World War II, Lebanon (as part of Syria) was placed under French mandate by the League of Nations.

The Lebanese Republic
1943: independence was declared. An unwritten agreement, known as the National Pact, instituted a political system under which power was divided between the Maronites, Sunnites, Shiites, Orthodox Greeks, Druze and Catholic Greeks.
1958: a civil war began, but was stopped by US intervention.
1970–6: clashes between Lebanese and Palestinian communities led to the beginning of another civil war. Syria intervened to resolve the conflict, and a ceasefire was eventually arranged.
1978: following a Palestinian attack, Israel invaded Lebanon and was requested by the UN to withdraw. The UN established an Interim Force in Lebanon (UNIFIL).
1982: Israel again invaded Lebanon and occupied West Beirut.
1983–5: the Israeli army withdrew from the whole of Lebanon except the south of the country, known as the 'security zone'. The war continued, complicated by internal fighting on each side, particularly between different Muslim

groups. In 1985, Shiite Hezbollah guerrillas began taking Western hostages (especially French and US nationals). This caused Syrian troops to return to West Beirut in 1987.
1988: two governments were established: one civil and Muslim, led by Selim Hoss in West Beirut; the other military and Christian, resistant to the Syrian presence and presided over by General Michel Aoun in East Beirut.
1990: the civil war came to an end.
1991: the disarming of the militia, and the deployment of the Lebanese army in Greater Beirut and the south of the country, marked the beginning of a restoration of state authority under Syrian supervision.
1996: Israel bombed Hezbollah bases in southern Lebanon and a UN base at Qana. A truce was negotiated by the USA, but the conflict between Israel and Hezbollah remained unresolved.
2000: the Israeli army withdrew from its security zone in southern Lebanon.
2002: Israel and Lebanon disagreed over proposed Lebanese plans to divert water from the river Wazzani.

Malaysia

200   500   1000 m

— road
--- railway line
✈ airport

● population over 1,000,000
● population 100,000 to 1,000,000
● population 50,000 to 100,000
• population less than 50,000

Malaysia is made up of two parts: West or Peninsular Malaysia (the former Federation of Malaya), and East Malaysia (the states of Sabah and Sarawak on the northern coast of Borneo, and the island of Labuan). Malaysia lies near the equator, is largely covered in forest, and has a hot and often humid climate. The population is concentrated on the alluvial plains and valleys surrounding or cutting into the mountainous region inland.

Area: 329,758km²
Population (2002): 23,036,000
Capital: Kuala Lumpur 1,297,526 (2000 census)
Capital: Putrajaya (administrative)
Government type and political system: constitutional monarchy with a parliamentary system
Head of state: (Yang di-Pertuan Agong or Supreme Ruler) Tuanku Syed Sirajuddin Syed Putra Jamalullail
Head of government: (Prime Minister) Datuk Seri Abdullah Ahmad Badawi
Administrative structure: 13 states and 3 federal territories
Official language: Malay
Currency: ringgit

DEMOGRAPHICS

Density: 67 inhab/km²
Percentage of population in urban areas (2001): 58.1%
Age structure of population (2003): 0–15 years: 34.1%, 15–65 years: 61.8%, over 65 years: 4.1%
Birth rate (2003): 22.6‰
Death rate (2003): 4.6‰
Infant mortality rate (2003): 10.1‰
Life expectancy at birth (2003): male: 70.8 years, female: 75.7 years

ECONOMY

GNP (2002): 8.65 billion US$
GNP per capita (2002): 3,540 US$
GNP per capita PPP (2002): 8,500 international dollars
HDI (2000): 0.782
GDP annual growth rate (2003): 5.2%
Annual inflation rate (2000): 1.53%
Labour force by occupation (2000): agriculture: 18.4%, industry: 32.2%, services: 49.4%

GDP by sector (2000): agriculture: 11.1%, industry: 45.4%, services: 43.5%
Gross public debt: n/a
Unemployment rate (2002): 3.8%

Agriculture and fishing

Crops
bananas (2001): 560,000t
cocoa (2001): 100,000t
sugar cane (2001): 1,600,000t
rubber (2001): 700,000t
copra (2001): 21,000t
manioc (2001): 370,000t
coconut (2001): 713,000t
cashew nuts (1998): 13,000t
oil palms (2001): 3,370,000t
rice (2002): 2,091,000t
tea (2001): 5,000t
Livestock farming and fishing
cattle (2002): 748,000 head
buffaloes (2001): 155,000 head
goats (2001): 232,000 head
sheep (2002): 118,000 head
pigs (2002): 1,824,000 head
chickens (2002): 161,000,000 head
fish (1999): 1,407,000t

Energy generation and mining

bauxite (2001): 64,000t
total electricity (2001): 68,335 million kWh
tin (2001): 4,973t
iron (2001): 241,000t
natural gas (2002): 50,300 million m³
gold (2001): 3,965kg
oil (2002): 37,000,000t

Industrial production

steel (2002): 2,430,000t
tin (2001): 4,973t
cars (2002): 380,000 units
commercial vehicles (1998): 42,000 units
shipbuilding (1998): 25,000dwt
cotton yarn (1998): 56,000t
synthetic textiles (1999): 355,000t
palm oil (2001): 11,660,000t
timber (2000):15,095,000m³
meat (2001): 1,106,374t

Tourism

Tourism revenue (2000): 4,563 million US$

Foreign trade

Export (2002): 93,383 million US$
Imports (2002): 75,248 million US$

Defence

Armed forces (2001): 100,000 people
Defence budget (2001): 2.71% of GDP

Standard of living

Inhabitants per doctor (1994): 2,500
Average daily calorie intake (2000): 2,919 (FAO minimum: 2,400)
Cars per 1,000 inhabitants (2000): 181
Televisions per 1,000 inhabitants (2001): 201

HISTORY: KEY DATES

Islam was introduced to the Malay Peninsula at the start of the 14c.
1511: Portuguese colonists settled in Malaysia.
1641: the Dutch drove the Portuguese out.
18c: a British presence in Malaysia was established.
1895: four states within Malaysia were grouped together, forming the Federated Malay States.
1942–5: Japan occupied the Malay Peninsula.
1948: the first Federation of Malaya was set up by the British.
1957: the Federation of Malaya became independent.
1963: the constitutional monarchy of the Federation of Malaysia was formed from continental Malaysia, Singapore and the former British colonies of Sarawak and Sabah. The new country became a member of the Commonwealth of Nations.
1965: Singapore withdrew from the Federation.
1969: tension between the Malay and ethnic Chinese communities led to anti-Chinese riots and the suspension of Parliament.
1979–89: large numbers of Vietnamese refugees sought asylum in Malaysia.
1999–2000: Malaysia's deputy prime minister Anwar Ibrahim was arrested, convicted of sodomy and imprisoned, despite condemnation of his trial by international observers.
2002–3: the Malaysian government introduced harsh new measures to curb illegal immigration.
2004: Anwar Ibrahim was freed after his conviction was overturned.

PAKISTAN

The north of the Islamic Republic of Pakistan consists primarily of mountains, some of which are over 7,000m in height. Most of the country's population and agricultural activity is concentrated along the alluvial plain of the Indus and its tributaries. The climate is mainly hot and dry.

Area: 796,095km²
Population (2002): 148,721,000
Capital: Islamabad 529,000 (1998 census), 636,000 (2001 e) including the suburbs
Government type and political system: republic with a parliamentary system
Head of state: (President of the Republic) General Pervez Musharraf
Head of government: (Prime Minister) Shaukat Aziz
Administrative structure: 4 provinces, 1 territory, 1 capital territory and 2 administered zones within the disputed Jammu and Kashmir region
Official language: Urdu
Currency: Pakistani rupee

DEMOGRAPHICS
Density: 195 inhab/km²
Percentage of population in urban areas (2001): 33.4%
Age structure of population (2000): 0–15 years: 41.8%, 15–65 years: 54.5%, over 65 years: 3.7%
Birth rate (2003): 35.9‰
Death rate (2003): 9.6‰
Infant mortality rate (2003): 86.5‰
Life expectancy at birth (2003): male: 61.2 years, female: 60.9 years

ECONOMY
GNP (2002): 61 billion US$
GNP per capita (2002): 420 US$
GNP per capita PPP (2002): 1,960 international dollars
HDI (2000): 0.499
GDP annual growth rate (2003): 5.5%
Annual inflation rate (2000): 4,37%
Labour force by occupation (2000): agriculture: 48.4%, industry:18.1%, services: 33.5%
GDP by sector (2000): agriculture: 26.3%, industry: 22.8%, services: 50.9%
Gross public debt: n/a
Unemployment rate (2000): 5.9%

Agriculture
Crops
almonds (2001): 32,000t
wheat (2002): 18,227,000t
sugar cane (2001): 43,606,000t
rape (2001): 262,000t
cotton (2002): 5,187,000t
dates (2001): 550,000t
maize (2002): 1,737,000t
walnuts (2001): 18,000t
oranges (2002): 1,400,000t
rice (2002): 6,718,000t
tobacco (2001): 85,000t
Livestock farming
cattle (2002): 22,857,000 head
buffaloes (2001): 23,300,000 head
goats (2001): 49,100,000 head
camels (2001): 800,000 head
sheep (2002): 24,398,000 head

Energy generation and mining
nuclear electricity (2001): 1,981 million kWh
hydroelectricity (2001): 18,880 million kWh
total electricity (2001): 66,961 million kWh
natural gas (2002): 20,900 million m³
coal (2001): 3,199,000t
oil (2002): 2,988,000t

Industrial production
milk (2001): 26,284,000t
cotton yarn (2001): 1,829,000t
wool (2001): 39,200t
butter (2001): 465,149t
sugar (2002): 3,507,000t
meat (2001): 1,782,000t
synthetic textiles (1999): 466,000t
cement (2001): 9,900,000t
timber (2000): 2,680,000m³

Tourism
Tourism revenue (2001): 92 million US$
Foreign trade
Exports (2002): 9,792 million US$
Imports (2002): 10,406 million US$
Defence
Armed forces (2001): 620,000 people
Defence budget (2001): 4.63% of GDP
Standard of living
Inhabitants per doctor (1993): 2,000
Average daily calorie intake (2000): 2,452 (FAO minimum: 2,400)
Cars per 1,000 inhabitants (1999): 5
Televisions per 1,000 inhabitants (2001): 148

HISTORY: KEY DATES
1947: the two provinces of East and West Pakistan were formed.
1948: India and Pakistan went to war over the disputed territory of Kashmir.
1956: a new constitution established the Islamic Republic of Pakistan, unifying the two provinces.
1965: the second Indo-Pakistani War took place.
1971: aided by Indian forces, East Pakistan seceded and became Bangladesh.
1999: a military coup ousted Pakistan's civilian government.
2000–3: tension between India and Pakistan led to concern about the use of nuclear weapons technology by both countries.

Pakistan
place of interest — road — railway line ✈ airport
● population over 1,000,000
● population 500,000 to 1,000,000
● population 100,00 to 500,000
● population less than 100,000

The Republic of the Philippines is a mountainous, volcanic archipelago within the tropical zone, made up of more than 7,000 islands.

Area: 300,000km²
Population (2002): 78,611,000
Capital: Manila 1,581,052 (2000 census), 10,069,000 (2001 e) including the suburbs
Government type and political system: republic with a presidential system
Head of state and government: (President of the Republic) Gloria Macapagal Arroyo
Administrative structure: 15 regions
Official languages: Filipino (Tagalog) and English
Currency: Philippine peso

DEMOGRAPHICS

Density: 253 inhab/km²
Percentage of population in urban areas (2001): 59.3%
Age structure of population (2000): 0–15 years: 37.5%, 15–65 years: 59%, over 65 years: 3.5%
Birth rate (2003): 25.3‰
Death rate (2003): 5.1‰
Infant mortality rate (2003): 29‰
Life expectancy at birth (2003): male: 68 years, female: 72 years

ECONOMY

GNP (2002): 82 billion US$
GNP per capita (2002): 1,030 US$
GNP per capita PPP (2002): 4,450 international dollars
HDI (2000): 0.754
GDP annual growth rate (2003): 4.5%
Annual inflation rate (2000): 4.36%
Labour force by occupation (2000): agriculture: 37.4%, industry: 16%, services: 46.6%
GDP by sector (2000): agriculture: 15.9%, industry: 31.2%, services: 52.9%
Gross public debt: n/a
Unemployment rate (2001): 9.8%

Agriculture and fishing

Crops
pineapples (2001): 1,572,000t
groundnuts (2001): 26,000t
bananas (2001): 5,061,000t
cocoa (2001): 6,610t
coffee (2002): 131,000t
sugar cane (2001): 28,238,000t
rubber (2001): 73,000t
copra (2001): 1,489,000t

Philippines

200	1000	2000 m

— motorway
— road
— railway line
✈ airport

● population over 1,000,000
● population 250,000 to 1,000,000
● population 100,000 to 250,000
• population less than 100,000

191

maize (2002): 4,319,000t
manioc (2001): 1,652,000t
sweet potatoes (2001): 545,000t
rice (2002): 13,271,000t
Livestock farming and fishing
cattle (2002): 2,548,000 head
buffaloes (2001): 3,066,000 head
goats (2001): 6,950,000 head
pigs (2002): 11,653,000 head
chickens (2002): 126,000,000 head
fish (1999): 2,199,000t

Energy generation and mining
total electricity (2000): 40,667 million kWh
coal (2001): 1,351,000t
nickel (2001): 27,400t
gold (2001): 30,000kg

Industrial production
palm oil (2001): 57,000t
sugar (2002): 1,922,000t
meat (2001): 1,976,000t
copper (2001): 20,300t
lead (2001): 24,000t
zinc (2001): 74,129t
timber (2000): 3,079,000m³

Tourism
Tourism revenue (2001): 1,723 million US$

Foreign trade
Exports (2002): 34,383 million US$
Imports (2002): 33,975 million US$

Defence
Armed forces (2001): 106,000 people
Defence budget (2001): 1.37% of GDP

Standard of living
Inhabitants per doctor (1990): 10,000
Average daily calorie intake (2000): 2,379 (FAO minimum: 2,400)
Cars per 1,000 inhabitants (1998): 10
Televisions per 1,000 inhabitants (2001): 173

HISTORY: KEY DATES

1521: Ferdinand Magellan claimed the archipelago for Spain.
19c: a nationalist movement began.
1898: the USA took control during the Spanish–American War.
1946: the islands became independent.
1972–86: the country remained under martial law (1972–81). Accusations of fraud, violence and corruption eventually forced President Ferdinand Marcos to flee.

SINGAPORE

QATAR→
ARABIAN PENINSULA

SAUDI ARABIA →
ARABIAN PENINSULA

The Republic of Singapore is a very densely populated city-state situated near the equator at the southern tip of the Malay Peninsula. It is made up of 55 tropical islands and islets, the largest of which – Singapore Island – is 42km long and linked to the peninsula by a road and rail causeway.

Area: 618km²
Population (2002): 4,189,000
Capital: Singapore 4,108,000 (2001 e)
Government type and political system: republic with a semi-presidential system
Head of state: (President of the Republic) S R Nathan
Head of government: (Prime Minister) Lee Hsien Loong
Administrative structure: no divisions
Official languages: English, Mandarin Chinese, Malay and Tamil
Currency: Singapore dollar

DEMOGRAPHICS

Density: 5,771 inhab/km²
Percentage of population in urban areas (2001): 100%
Age structure of population (2000): 0–15 years: 21.9%, 15–65 years: 70.9%, over 65 years: 7.2%
Birth rate (2003): 10.2‰
Death rate (2003): 5.2‰
Infant mortality rate (2003): 2.9‰
Life expectancy at birth (2003): male: 75.9

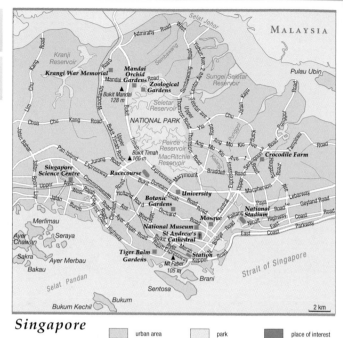

Singapore

urban area ☐   park ☐   place of interest ☐

192

years, female: 80.3 years

ECONOMY

GNP (2002): 86 billion US$
GNP per capita (2002): 20,690 US$
GNP per capita PPP (2002): 23,730 international dollars
HDI (2000): 0.885
GDP annual growth rate (2003): 1.1%
Annual inflation rate (2000): 1.36%
Labour force by occupation (1998): agriculture: 0.2%, industry: 29.2%, services: 70.6%
GDP by sector (2001): agriculture: 0.3%, industry: 25.4%, services: 74.3%
Gross public debt: n/a
Unemployment rate (2002): 5.2%

Agriculture and fishing
pigs (2002): 250,000 head
chickens (2002): 2,000,000 head
fish (1999): 9,080t

Energy generation
total electricity (2001): 30,480 million kWh

Industrial production
shipbuilding(2001): 65,000dwt

Tourism
Tourism revenue (2000): 6,370 million US$

Foreign trade
Exports (2002): 128,374 million US$
Imports (2002): 109,825 million US$

Defence
Armed forces (2001): 60,500 people
Defence budget (2001): 5.1% of GDP

Standard of living
Inhabitants per doctor (1995): 714
Average daily calorie intake (1995): 3,121 (FAO minimum: 2,400)
Cars per 1,000 inhabitants (1999): 97
Televisions per 1,000 inhabitants (2001): 300

HISTORY: KEY DATES

1819: a British trading post was established on Singapore Island.
1942–5: Singapore was invaded and occupied by Japan (and renamed Syonan) before returning to British control.
1963–5: Singapore spent two years as part of the Federation of Malaysia before becoming an independent republic.
2001: a number of long-running disputes between Singapore and Malaysia were resolved by mutual agreement.

The Democratic Socialist Republic of Sri Lanka is a pear-shaped tropical island off the south-east coast of India, made up of plateaux and hills surrounding a central mountainous massif. Nearly half of the island consists of forests or open woodlands.

Area: 65,610km²
Population (2002): 19,287,000
Capital (commercial): Colombo 681,000 (2001 e)
Capital (administrative): Sri Jayawardenepura Kotte
Government type and political system: republic
Head of state: (President of the Republic) Chandrika Bandaranaike Kumaratunga
Head of government: (Prime Minister) Mahinda Rajapakse
Administrative structure: 9 provinces
Official languages: Sinhala and Tamil
Currency: Sri Lankan rupee

DEMOGRAPHICS

Density: 285 inhab/km²
Percentage of population in urban areas (2001): 23.1%
Age structure of population (2000): 0–15 years: 26.3%, 15–65 years: 67.4%, over 65 years: 6.3%
Birth rate (2003): 16.4‰
Death rate (2003): 6.6‰
Infant mortality rate (2003): 20.1‰
Life expectancy at birth (2003): male: 69.9 years, female: 75.9 years

ECONOMY

GNP (2002): 16.1 billion US$
GNP per capita (2002): 850 US$
GNP per capita PPP (2002): 3,510 international dollars

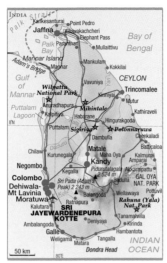

Sri Lanka

- ● population over 500,000
- ● population 100,000 to 500,000
- ● population 50,000 to 100,000
- • population less than 50,000
- ★ place of interest
- — road
- — railway line
- ✈ airport

200   500   1000   2000 m

HDI (2000): 0.741
GDP annual growth rate (2003): 5.5%
Annual inflation rate (2000): 6.18%
Labour force by occupation (1998): agriculture: 41.6%, industry: 22.5%, services: 35.9%
GDP by sector (2000): agriculture: 19.5%, industry: 27.5%, services: 53%
Gross public debt: n/a
Unemployment rate (2002): 8.7%

Agriculture and fishing

Crops
plantains (2001): 780,000t
cocoa (2001): 3,700t
sugar cane (2001): 1,066,000t
rubber (2001): 88,000t
copra (2001): 44,000t
manioc (2001): 249,000t
cashew nuts (1998): 15,000t
sweet potatoes (2001): 52,000t
rice (2002): 2,859,000t
tea (2001): 295,000t
Livestock farming and fishing
cattle (2002): 1,510,000 head
buffaloes (2001): 690,000 head
goats (2001): 500,000 head

pigs (2002): 73,000 head
fish (1999): 280,000t

Energy generation
total electricity (2001): 6,360 million kWh
hydroelectricity (2000): 3,070 million kWh

Industrial production
milk (2001): 295,000t
cotton yarn (1998): 14,000t
timber (2000): 676,000m³

Tourism
Tourism revenue (2001): 211 million US$

Foreign trade
Exports (2002): 4,699.2 million US$
Imports (2002): 6,105.6 million US$

Defence
Armed forces (2001): 157,900 people
Defence budget (2001): 4.03% of GDP

Standard of living
Inhabitants per doctor (1993): 10,000
Average daily calorie intake (2000): 2,405 (FAO minimum: 2,400)
Cars per 1,000 inhabitants (1999): 12
Televisions per 1,000 inhabitants (2001): 117

HISTORY: KEY DATES

10c: the region's existing Sinhalese monarchy, based in the Buddhist city of Anuradhapura, was overthrown by a king of the Chola dynasty.
1070: the island was recaptured by a Sinhalese prince.
14c–16c: the Sinhalese migrated southwards, whilst in the north the Tamil people established an independent kingdom.
16c: Portugal occupied the coast of the island.
1658: Dutch colonists drove out the Portuguese.
1796: Great Britain annexed the island, expelling the Dutch and becoming the first European power to gain control of the entire island.
1948: the island, known as Ceylon, became independent from Britain.
1972: the island was renamed Sri Lanka.
1970s–80s: ethnic tensions between the Tamil and Sinhalese communities increased until civil war broke out in the early 1980s.
2002–3: peace talks were held after nearly twenty years of civil war, but the Tamil Tigers guerrilla group suspended its participation shortly after the peace process had begun.

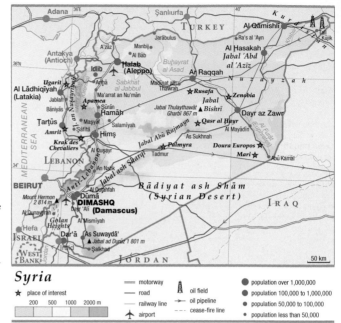

The Syrian Arab Republic is located in south-west Asia. A mountainous barrier, the Ansariyya range, extends south to the Anti-Lebanon and Hermon ranges, separating a narrow coastal plain from the desert plateaux in the east of the country.

Area: 185,180km²
Population (2002): 17,040,000
Capital: Damascus 2,195,000 (2001 e) including the suburbs
Government type and political system: republic with a parliamentary system
Head of state: (President of the Republic) Bashar al-Assad
Head of government: (Prime Minister) Muhammad Naji al-Otari
Administrative structure: 14 provinces
Official language: Arabic
Currency: Syrian pound

DEMOGRAPHICS

Density: 87 inhab/km²
Percentage of population in urban areas (2001): 51.8%
Age structure of population (2000): 0–15 years: 40.8%, 15–65 years: 56.1%, over 65 years: 3.1%
Birth rate (2003): 27.7‰
Death rate (2003): 3.9‰
Infant mortality rate (2003): 22.3‰
Life expectancy at birth (2003): male: 70.6 years, female: 73.1 years

ECONOMY

GNP (2002): 19.1 billion US$
GNP per capita (2002): 1,130 US$
GNP per capita PPP (2002): 3,470 international dollars
HDI (2000): 0.691
GDP annual growth rate (2003): 2.5%
Annual inflation rate (2000): −0.46%
Labour force by occupation: n/a
GDP by sector (2000): agriculture: 24.1%, industry: 30.2%, services: 45.7%
Gross public debt: n/a
Unemployment rate (2002): 11.7%

Agriculture and fishing

Crops
citrus fruits (2002): 756,000t
almonds (2001): 49,000t
sugar beets (2002): 1,481,000t
wheat (2002): 4,775,000t
cotton (2002): 802,000t

olives (2002): 999,000t
oranges (2002): 427,000t
barley (2002): 920,000t
pistachios (2001): 37,436,000t
grapes (2002): 369,000t
tobacco (2001): 28,900t
Livestock farming and fishing
cattle (2002): 867,000 head
goats (2001): 979,000 head
horses (2001): 30,000 head
sheep (2002): 13,497,000 head
fish (1999): 14,000t

Energy generation and mining

total electricity (2001): 23,256 million kWh
oil (2002): 28,600,000t
phosphate (2001): 2,043,000t

Industrial production

sugar (2002): 118,000t
olive oil (2001): 95,000t
cotton yarn (2001): 353,000t
wool (2001): 23.490t
timber (2000): 34,500m³

Syria

★ place of interest
200 500 1000 2000 m

═══ motorway
─── road
─── railway line
✈ airport

⛏ oil field
→ oil pipeline
--- cease-fire line

● population over 1,000,000
● population 100,000 to 1,000,000
● population 50,000 to 100,000
• population less than 50,000

50 km

HISTORY: KEY DATES

Ancient Syria

2ND MILLENNIUM BC: Syria was occupied by successive waves of Canaanites (including the Phoenecians), Amorites, Hurrians and Arameans (including the Hebrews).
539 BC: Syria became part of the Persian empire.
332 BC: Alexander the Great conquered Syria. The country became part of the Seleukid kingdom, whose capital, Antioch, was founded in 301 BC.
64 BC–63 BC: Syria became a Roman province.
AD 395: Syria became part of the Eastern Roman Empire.

Muslim Syria

636: the Arabs conquered the country.
661–750: the Umayyad caliphs made Damascus the capital of the Muslim empire.
8c: under the Abbasids, Baghdad became the capital of the empire.
1076–7: the Seljuk Turks captured

Damascus and most of Syria.
1193: Syria was overrun by Mongol invaders.
1260–91: the Mamluks defeated the Mongols, then governed the region until the Ottoman conquest of 1516.

Ottoman then French Syria

1516: Syria became part of the Ottoman Empire.
1858–60: conflict between the Muslim Druze and the Roman Catholic Maronite communities led to a massacre of the Maronites in Lebanon; France intervened to resolve the conflict.
1914–18: Syrian nationalists were encouraged by Britain to fight against the Ottoman Empire during World War I. In 1918, Ottoman control of Syria came to an end when Arab troops took Damascus.
1920–43: following World War I, France was granted a mandate over Syria by the League of Nations and established a ⇨

Tourism
Tourism revenue (2000): 474 million US$

Foreign trade
Exports (2000): 5,146 million US$
Imports (2000): 3,723 million US$

Defence
Armed forces (2001): 319,000 people
Defence budget (2001): 5.46% of GDP

Standard of living
Inhabitants per doctor (1990): 1,250
Average daily calorie intake (2000): 3,038 (FAO minimum: 2,400)
Cars per 1,000 inhabitants (1999): 9
Televisions per 1,000 inhabitants (2000): 67

☇ HISTORY: KEY DATES

Syrian Republic, an Alaouite Republic and a Druze state.

Independent Syria
1941: Syria was occupied by British and Free French troops. France proclaimed Syria's independence.
1946: the last French and British troops left Syria.
1958–61: Egypt, Yemen and Syria formed the United Arab Republic.
1967: the Six-Day War led to Israeli occupation of the Golan Heights region.
1976: Syrian troops intervened in Lebanon to resolve the ongoing conflict between Lebanese and Palestine forces.
1981: Israel announced its formal annexation of the Golan Heights region.
1990: Syria joined the US-led military campaign against Iraq.
2002: relations between Syria and the USA deteriorated; Syria was described as part of the 'axis of evil' identified by the US president George W Bush.
2004: relations between Syria and Turkey improved after a visit to Turkey by the Syrian president. The USA imposed economic sanctions on Syria.

Taiwan, formerly known as Formosa, is an island republic situated off the south-east coast of China. It is crossed by the Tropic of Cancer, and receives heavy rainfall during the summer monsoon. In the east there are high mountains and, in the west, hills and large alluvial plains.

Area: 36,000km²
Population (2002): 22,500,000
Capital: Taipei 2,624,257 (2000 census), 6,646,503 (2000 census) including the suburbs
Government type and political system: republic with a semi-presidential system
Head of state: (President of the Republic) Chen Shui-bian
Head of government: (Prime Minister) Yu Shyi-kun
Administrative structure: 2 special municipalities, 5 municipalities and 16 districts
Official language: Mandarin Chinese
Currency: New Taiwan dollar

DEMOGRAPHICS

Density: 611 inhab/km²
Percentage of population in urban areas (1991): 73%
Age structure of population (1993): 0–15 years: 26%, 15–65 years: 67%, over 65 years: 7 %
Birth rate (1995): 16‰
Death rate: n/a
Infant mortality rate (2000): 6‰
Life expectancy at birth (2000): male: 75 years, female: 78 years

ECONOMY

GNP: n/a
GNP per capita: n/a
GNP per capita PPP: n/a
HDI: n/a
GDP annual growth rate (2003): 3.2%
Annual inflation rate (1992): 4.5%
Labour force by occupation: n/a
GDP by sector (1989): agriculture: 5%, industry: 43%, services: 52%
Gross public debt: n/a
Unemployment rate: n/a

Agriculture and fishing

Crops
citrus fruits (2001): 463,000t
pineapples (2001): 389,000t
groundnuts (2001): 56,000t
bananas (2001): 205,000t
sugar cane (2001): 123,000t
maize (2001): 107,000t
rice (2001): 1,724,000t
soya beans (2001): 320t
tobacco (2001): 9,200t
Livestock farming and fishing
cattle (2001): 5,057,000 head
goats (2001): 7,219,000 head
pigs (2001): 1,166,000 head
chickens (2001): 376,196,000 head
fish (2001): 1,317,000t

Energy generation and mining
nuclear electricity (2001): 34,094 million kWh
hydroelectricity (2001): 9,108 million kWh
total electricity (2001): 151,114 million kWh
natural gas (2002): 868 million m³
coal (2000): 83,000t
lignite (2000): 83,000t
oil (2002): 40,000t

Industrial production
steel (2003): 18,903,000t
cars (2002): 245,000 units
commercial vehicles (1998): 108,000 units
artificial textiles (1999): 143,700t
synthetic textiles (1999): 2,915,000t
cotton yarn (1998): 364,000t
shipbuilding (2001): 279,000dwt
synthetic rubber (2001): 480,000t
timber (2001): 26,401,000m³

Tourism
Tourism revenue: n/a

Foreign trade
Exports (1991): 76,140 million US$
Imports (1991): 63,078 million US$

Defence
Armed forces (2001): 350,000 people
Defence budget (2001): 2.85% of GDP

Standard of living
Inhabitants per doctor: n/a
Average daily calorie intake (1995): 3,020 (FAO minimum: 2,400)
Cars per 1,000 inhabitants (1994): 216
Televisions per 1,000 inhabitants: n/a

HISTORY: KEY DATES

17c: Chinese, Dutch and Spanish settlers colonized Taiwan (then Formosa).
1895: the Shimonoseki Treaty ceded Taiwan to Japan.
1945: control of the island was restored to China.
1949: the Guomindang government, presided over by Jiang Jieshi (Chiang Kai-shek), fled to Taiwan.
1971: the Taiwanese government was given the seat normally reserved for China at the UN Security Council.
1991: Taiwan was officially recognized by the People's Republic of China for the first time in 40 years, thus ending its state of war with China.
2000: election victory by a pro-independence party led to the end of half a century of Guomindang rule.
2002: Taiwan became a member of the World Trade Organization (WTO).

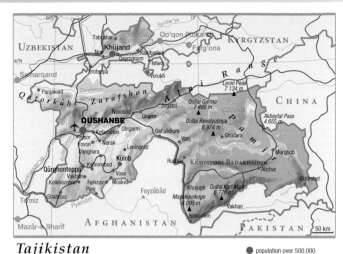

Tajikistan

500 1000 2000 4000 m

✈ airport
— road
— railway line

● population over 500,000
● population 100,000 to 500,000
● population 50,000 to 100,000
● population less than 50,000

The Republic of Tajikistan is a mountainous country in south-eastern Central Asia. In the east, the Pamir range, whose highest point is Peak Ismoili Somoni (formerly Communism Peak; 7,495m), forms the border with China. In the southeast is an arid plateau, and valleys occupy the north and southwest regions. The climate is continental, with cold winters and hot, dry summers.

Area: 143,100km²
Population (2002): 6,177,000
Capital: Dushanbe 522,000 (2001 e) including the suburbs
Government type and political system: republic
Head of state: (President of the Republic) Imamoli Sharipovich Rakhmanov
Head of government: (Prime Minister) Akil Ghaybulloyevich Akilov
Administrative structure: 2 provinces and 1 autonomous province
Official language: Tajik
Currency: Tajik somoni

DEMOGRAPHICS
Density: 43 inhab/km²
Percentage of population in urban areas (2001): 27.6%
Age structure of population (2000): 0–15 years: 39.4%, 15–65 years: 56%, over 65 years: 4.6%
Birth rate (2003): 24.5‰
Death rate (2003): 6‰
Infant mortality rate (2003): 50‰
Life expectancy at birth (2003): male: 66.2 years, female: 71.4 years

ECONOMY
GNP (2002): 1.12 billion US$
GNP per capita (2002): 180 US$
GNP per capita PPP (2002): 930 international dollars
HDI (2000): 0.667

GDP annual growth rate (2003): 10.2%
Annual inflation rate: n/a
Labour force by occupation (1997): agriculture: 49.8%, industry: 18.8%, services: 31.4%
GDP by sector (2000): agriculture: 19.4%, industry: 25.7%, services: 54.9%
Gross public debt: n/a
Unemployment rate (1997): 2.7%

Agriculture
Crops
wheat (2002): 361,000t
maize (2002): 35,000t
hazelnuts (2001): 1,100t
barley (2002): 15,000t
apples (2001): 60,000t
potatoes (2002): 357,000t
grapes (2002): 100,000t
tobacco (2001): 7,200t
tomatoes (2002): 202,000t
Livestock farming
cattle (2002): 1,091,000 head
goats (2001): 575,000 head
camels (2001): 42,000 head
sheep (2002): 1,490,000 head
pigs (2002): 700 head
chickens (2002): 1,320,000 head

Energy generation and mining
total electricity (2001): 14,180 million kWh
natural gas (2000): 40 million m³
coal (2001): 22,000t
oil (2000): 20,000t

Industrial production
aluminium (2001): 340,000t
cotton yarn (2001): 96,000t

silk (2001): 300t

Tourism
Tourism revenue: n/a

Foreign trade
Exports (2002): 699.2 million US$
Imports (2002): 822.9 million US$

Defence
Armed forces (2001): 6,000 people
Defence budget (2001): 0.17% of GDP

Standard of living
Inhabitants per doctor (1995): 423
Average daily calorie intake (2000): 1,720 (FAO minimum: 2,400)
Cars per 1,000 inhabitants: n/a
Televisions per 1,000 inhabitants (2000): 326

197

HISTORY: KEY DATES
1860–1900: Tajik lands came under the control of Tsarist Russia.
1924: the Autonomous Soviet Socialist Republic of Tajikistan (Tajik ASSR) was created.
1929: Tajikistan became a Soviet Socialist Republic of the USSR.
1991: Tajikistan became independent, and joined the Commonwealth of Independent States (CIS).
1992: civil war broke out between the government and the Islamist opposition.
1997: a UN-sponsored peace agreement ended the war, although fighting continued in some areas until 2000.

A central plain, drained by the Chao Phraya River, dominates the Kingdom of Thailand. To the north-east is the large, heavily-populated Khorat Plateau, and to the north a mountainous region. The south is a low-lying area of tropical rainforest.

Area: 513,115km²
Population (2002): 64,343,000
Capital: Bangkok 6,320,174 (2000 census), 7,527,000 (2001 e) including the suburbs
Government type and political system: constitutional monarchy with a parliamentary system
Head of state: (King) Bhumibol Adulyadej, officially known as King Rama IX the Great
Head of government: (Prime Minister) Thaksin Shinawatra
Administrative structure: 76 provinces
Official language: Thai
Currency: baht

DEMOGRAPHICS

Density: 119 inhab/km²
Percentage of population in urban areas (2001): 20%
Age structure of population (2000): 0–15 years: 26.7%, 15–65 years: 68.1%, over 65 years: 5.2%
Birth rate (2003): 17.3‰
Death rate (2003): 7.1‰
Infant mortality rate (2003): 19.8‰
Life expectancy at birth (2003): male: 65.3 years, female: 73.5 years

ECONOMY

GNP (2002): 123 billion US$
GNP per capita (2002): 2,000 US$
GNP per capita PPP (2002): 6,890 international dollars
HDI (2000): 0.762
GDP annual growth rate (2003): 6.7%
Annual inflation rate (2000): 1.55%
Labour force by occupation (2001): agriculture: 46%, industry: 18.8%, services: 35.2%
GDP by sector (2000): agriculture: 10.5%, industry: 40.1%, services: 49.5%
Gross public debt: n/a
Unemployment rate (2001): 2.6%

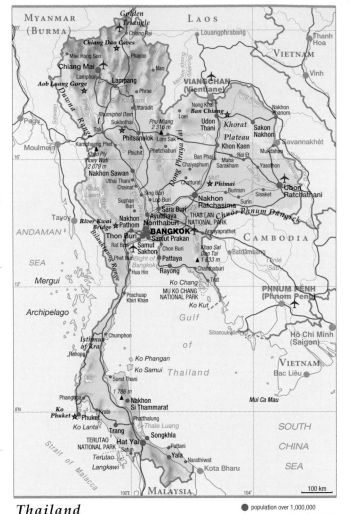

Thailand

200	500	1000 m

✈ airport
★ place of interest

═══ motorway
─── road
─── railway line

● population over 1,000,000
● population 100,000 to 1,000,000
● population 50,000 to 100,000
• population less than 50,000

100 km

Agriculture and fishing
Crops
pineapples (2001): 2,300,000t
bananas (2001): 1,720,000t
sugar cane (2001): 49,070,000t
rubber (2001): 2,380,000t
copra (2001): 55,000t
jute (1997): 110,000t
mandarin oranges (1998): 630,000t
manioc (2001): 18,283,000t
cashew nuts (1998): 20,000t
oil palms (2001): 118,000t
peaches (1999): 3,608,000t
rice (2002): 25,611,000t
soya beans (2002): 289,000t
sorghum (2002): 145,000t
tobacco (2001): 74,000t
Livestock farming and fishing
cattle (2002): 5,909,000 head

buffaloes (2001): 1,900,000 head
pigs (2002): 6,989,000 head
chickens (2002): 229,000,000 head
fish (1999): 3,608,000t

Energy generation and mining
total electricity (2001): 97,595 million kWh
tin (2001): 2,522t
natural gas (2002): 18,900 million m³
hydroelectricity (2001): 6,205 million kWh
lignite (2001): 19,603,000t
oil (2001): 7,900,000t

Industrial production
eggs (2001): 810,000t
steel (2000): 21,357t
zinc (2001): 74,129t
commercial vehicles (1998): 180,000 units

artificial textiles (1999): 65,000t
synthetic textiles (1999): 652,000t
palm oil (2001): 550,000t
silk (2001): 1,000t
sugar (2002): 5,947,000t
timber (2000): 6,262,000m^3

Tourism
Tourism revenue (2001): 6,731 million US$

Foreign trade
Exports (2002): 66,795 million US$
Imports (2002): 57,020 million US$

Defence
Armed forces (2001): 306,000 people
Defence budget (2001): 1.51% of GDP

Standard of living
Inhabitants per doctor (1993): 4,420
Average daily calorie intake (2000): 2,506
(FAO minimum: 2,400)
Cars per 1,000 inhabitants (1996): 27
Televisions per 1,000 inhabitants (2001): 300

HISTORY KEY DATES

11c–12c: present-day Thailand was part of the Khmer empire.

13c: the Siamese people captured the town of Sukhothai from the Khmers and made it the capital of a new kingdom.

16c–17c: Western traders and missionaries reached Siam, but the country remained independent. Resistance to colonization by foreign powers led to Siam being closed to foreigners for much of the 18c.

1782: King Rama I, the founder of the Chakri dynasty, was crowned in the new capital of Bangkok.

1782–1851: Siam resumed relations with the West, signing commercial treaties with Great Britain and the USA.

1893–1909: Siam's borders were officially established, reducing the size of the kingdom.

1932–5: a military coup led to the abdication of King Rama VII (1935).

1938: the country was renamed Thailand.

1941–4: Thailand formed an alliance with Japan.

1950: Bhumibol Adulyadej was crowned King Rama IX of Thailand.

1965: the USA was granted access to Thailand's military facilities during the Vietnam War.

1997: Thailand's economy was badly affected by a rapid drop in the value of its currency.

2003: a new and controversial anti-drugs policy was introduced.

2004: attacks on the authorities by suspected Islamic militants led to the imposition of martial law.

The Mekong

At around 4,200km, the Mekong is the longest river in South-East Asia and one of the world's major rivers. Its basin measures 800,000km^2, and its average annual rate of flow is around 17,000m^3 per second.

The river originates in Tibet at an altitude of over 5,000m and then flows through deep, rugged gorges. When it leaves the Yunnan (Kunming) province of China, it forms the border between Myanmar (Burma) and Laos, then flows through Laos and along the 820km border between Thailand and Laos. After this, it enters Cambodia and divides into several branches, one of which joins the Tônlé Sap River. The delta begins in Phnom Penh, and spreads into two main branches in Cambodia and Vietnam that open out into the South China Sea. The Mekong is fed by melting snow in its upper basin, as well as by monsoons farther downstream. It is navigable from Vientiane to Savannakhet before joining its main tributary, the Mun River, at the Laotian border.

Despite offering poor conditions for navigation – the large number of rapids make transport difficult – the Mekong, with its network of tributaries, has provided a link between the many regions and populations through which it flows. It has acted as a conduit between cultures and assisted the development of highly evolved civilizations in its area of influence, as well as contributing to the creation of organized states such as the Khmer empire.

The Republic of Turkey, which straddles
two continents, is mainly made up of
highlands. The Pontic mountains in the
north and the Taurus mountains in the
south surround the Anatolian plain, which
rises up gradually from the Aegean Sea and
gives way in the east to the volcanic
Armenian massif of which Mount Ararat is
a part. Except for the coastal regions, which
have a mainly Mediterranean climate,
winters in Turkey are extremely cold and
summers are generally hot and dry.

Area: 774,815km²
Population (2002): 68,569,000
Capital: Ankara 2,984,099 (1997
census), 3,208,000 (2001 e) including
the suburbs
Government type and political system:
republic with a parliamentary system
Head of state: (President of the
Republic) Ahmet Necdet Sezer
Head of government: (Prime Minister)
Recep Tayyip Erdogan
Administrative structure: 81 provinces
Official language: Turkish

Currency: Turkish lira

DEMOGRAPHICS
Density: 85 inhab/km²
**Percentage of population in urban areas
(2001):** 66.2%
Age structure of population (2000): 0–15
years: 30%, 15–65 years: 64.2%, over 65
years: 5.8%
Birth rate (2003): 20.9‰
Death rate (2003): 6‰
Infant mortality rate (2003): 39.5‰
Life expectancy at birth (2003): male: 68
years, female: 73.2 years

ECONOMY
GNP (2002): 173 billion US$
GNP per capita (2002): 2,490 US$
GNP per capita PPP (2002): 6,300
international dollars
HDI (2000): 0.742
GDP annual growth rate (2003): 5.8%
Annual inflation rate (2000): 54.92%
Labour force by occupation (2000):
agriculture: 34.9%, industry: 24.6%,
services: 40.5%
GDP by sector (2000): agriculture: 15.1%,
industry: 29.6%, services: 55.3%
Gross public debt (2002): 95% of GDP
Unemployment rate (2002): 10.3%

Agriculture and fishing
Crops
apricots (2001): 517,000t
citrus fruits (2002): 2,153,000t
almonds (2001): 45,000t
sugar beets (2002): 16,396,000t
butter (2001): 114,587t
wheat (2002): 19,500,000t
lemons (2002): 400,000t
cotton (2002): 2,240,000t
lentils (2001): 520,000t
mandarin oranges (1998): 410,000t
honey (2001): 71,000t

hazelnuts (2001): 630,000t
walnuts (2001): 136,000t
olives (2002): 1,500,000t
oranges (2002): 1,160,000t
barley (2002): 8,300,000t
grapefruits (2001): 140,000t
peaches (2002): 460,000t
pistachios (2001): 35,000,000t
apples (2001): 2,400,000t
potatoes (2002): 5,200,000t
grapes (2002): 3,650,000t
rye (2001): 250,000t
tobacco (2001): 145,000t
tea (2001): 143,000t
tomatoes (2002): 9,000,000t
sunflowers (2002): 850,000t

Livestock farming and fishing
cattle (2002): 10,548,000 head
sheep (2002): 26,972,000 head
chickens (2002): 218,000,000 head
fish (1999): 638,000t

Energy generation and mining
bauxite (2001): 242,000t
chromium (2001): 390,000t
hydroelectricity (2001): 23,770 million
kWh
total electricity (2001): 116,567 million
kWh
iron (2001): 2,400,000t
coal (2001): 2,357,000t
oil (2002): 2,420,000t

Industrial production
milk (2001): 9,676,000t
eggs (2001): 715,000t
sugar (2002): 2,110,000t
olive oil (2001): 185,000t
meat (2001): 1,319,000t
beer (2000): 6,904,000hl
steel (2003): 18,298,000t
cement (2001): 30,120,000t
synthetic rubber (2001): 43,000t
synthetic textiles (1999): 874,000t
wool (2001): 44,300t

Turkey

| | population over 1,000,000 |
| === motorway | ✈ airport | ● population over 1,000,000 |

200   1000   2000 m

=== motorway
— road
— railway line

✈ airport

★ place of
interest

● population over 1,000,000
● population 500,000 to 1,000,000
● population 100,000 to 500,000
• population less than 100,000

cotton yarn (2001): 876,000t
silk (2001): 22t
timber (2000): 10,429,000m³

Tourism
Tourism revenue (2001): 8,932 million US$

Foreign trade
Exports (2002): 39,818 million US$
Imports (2002): 48,130 million US$

Defence
Armed forces (2001): 514,850 people
Defence budget (2001): 3.86% of GDP

Standard of living
Inhabitants per doctor (1995): 976
Average daily calorie intake (2000): 3,416 (FAO minimum: 2,400)
Cars per 1,000 inhabitants (1999): 63
Televisions per 1,000 inhabitants (1999): 332

HISTORY: KEY DATES

Ancient Anatolia
Anatolia has been inhabited since prehistoric times, and contains the oldest known human urban agglomeration in the world (dating from 6500 BC–5500 BC).

c.3000 BC: city-states appeared and trade with the Mesopotamians and Syrians was established.

18c BC–12c BC: a number of kingdoms (Hittites, Hurrians and Louvites) and Greek settlements (Troy, Miletos) shared control of Anatolia.

1500 BC–1000 BC: the Greeks settled in Asia Minor.

c.283 BC–133 BC: the Attalids of Pergamon ruled Asia Minor.

From the Romans to the Byzantines
133 BC: the last king of Pergamon, Attalos III, left his kingdom to Rome, which established it as the Province of Asia (129 BC).

AD 324–AD 330: Constantine founded the city of Constantinople.

AD 395: when Theodosius died, his sons Arcadius and Honorius succeeded him as emperors of the east and west respectively, marking the beginning of the Byzantine empire.

867–1057: the empire flourished under the Macedonian dynasty.

1071: the Seljuk Turks beat the Byzantine army at Malazgirt (Manzikert). Turkish nomads spread over Asia Minor.

1243: the Mongols conquered Anatolia.

The Ottoman Empire
1299: Osman I Gazi became independent from the Seljuk Turks, and founded the Ottoman dynasty.

1326: Ohran Gazi (the son of Osman I) conquered Bursa, which he made into his capital.

1359–89: the Ottoman Empire extended its influence.

1402: the empire was attacked by the Tartar conqueror Timur.

1451–81: Mehmed II took Constantinople (1453), which he made into his capital, before taking control of Serbia (1459), the Trebizond empire (1461), Bosnia (1463) and Crimea (1475).

1514–7: Selim I conquered eastern Anatolia, Syria and Egypt.

1520–66: under Süleyman the Magnificent, the Ottoman Empire established its domination over Hungary, Algeria, Tunisia and Tripolitania.

1571: a coalition of Christian princes defeated the Ottomans at the Battle of Lepant.

1699: the Treaty of Karlowitz marked the end of the empire's expansion westwards into Europe, and the beginning of its disintegration.

1908: the Young Turks, a group of nationalists in favour of modernizing the State, came to power.

1912–3: after the Balkan Wars, the only possession the Ottoman Empire retained in Europe was eastern Thrace.

1918: the empire entered World War I alongside Germany.

Modern Turkey
1918–20: the empire was defeated and came to an end.

1923: the Lausanne Treaty fixed Turkey's borders. The republic was established, with Kemal Atatürk as its president. He initiated reforms intended modernize and westernize Turkey.

1928: Turkey became a secular state.

1945: Turkey became a member of the UN, and entered World War II on the side of the Allies.

1950: Adnan Menderes, leader of the opposition Democratic Party, was elected. He broke with the state-controlled planned economy and supported the return of Islamic traditions.

1952: Turkey became a member of the North Atlantic Treaty Organisation (NATO).

1960: General Cemal Gürsel came to power.

1961–71: coalition governments were formed by Ismet Inönü (1961–5) and Süleyman Demirel (1965–71).

1974: the Turkish military invaded Cyprus.

1980: internal conflict between Marxists, Muslim fundamentalists, and Kurd separatists grew worse. After a military coup, martial law was declared.

1983: after a new constitution came into force, political parties were legalized and a civil government came to power.

1983: in Cyprus, the Turkish community declared itself independent as the Turkish Republic of Northern Cyprus, recognized only by Turkey.

1984: Kurdish separatist guerrillas began a war against the Turkish government.

1995: Turkey invaded the Kurdish 'safe havens' in northern Iraq.

1999: an earthquake centred on north-west Turkey killed over 17,000 people.

2002–3: the Turkish government granted women legal equality with men. Other reforms designed to improve Turkey's chance of gaining European Union (EU) membership were also instituted.

TURKMENISTAN

Turkmenistan has a dry continental climate, characterized by a wide range of temperatures. The Kara Kum Desert occupies around 80 per cent of the country.

Turkmenistan

| 0 | 200 | 500 | 1000 m |

— road
-- railway line
✈ airport

● population over 1,000,000
● population 100,000 to 1,000,000
● population 50,000 to 100,000
• population less than 50,000

Area: 488,100km²
Population (2002): 4,930,000
Capital: Ashgabat 558,000 (2001 e) including the suburbs
Government type and political system: republic
Head of state and government: (President of the Republic) Saparmurad Atayevich Niyazov
Administrative structure: 5 administrative divisions
Official language: Turkmen
Currency: manat

DEMOGRAPHICS
Density: 9 inhab/km²
Percentage of population in urban areas (2001): 45%
Age structure of population (2000): 0–15 years: 37.6%, 15–65 years: 58.1%, over 65 years: 4.3%
Birth rate (2003): 22.2‰
Death rate (2003): 6.5‰
Infant mortality rate (2003): 48.6‰
Life expectancy at birth (2003): male: 63.9 years, female: 70.4 years

ECONOMY
GNP (2002): 5.14 billion US$
GNP per capita (2002): 1,090 US$
GNP per capita PPP (2002): 4,780 international dollars
HDI (2000): 0.741
GDP annual growth rate (2001): 20.5%
Annual inflation rate: n/a
Labour force by occupation: n/a
GDP by sector (2000): agriculture: 27.3%, industry: 50%, services: 22.7%

Gross public debt: n/a
Unemployment rate: n/a

Agriculture and fishing
Crops
wheat (2002): 2,200,000t
cotton (2002): 700,000t
maize (2002): 12,000t
barley (2002): 28,500t
potatoes (2002): 28,000t
grapes (2002): 130,000t
tobacco (2001): 3,000t
Livestock farming and fishing
cattle (2002): 860,000 head
sheep (2002): 6,000,000 head
pigs (2001): 45,000 head
chickens (2002): 4,800,000 head
fish (1999): 9,290t

Energy generation and mining
total electricity (2000): 9,256 million kWh
natural gas (2002): 49,900 million m³
oil (2002): 9,000,000t

Industrial production
cement (2001): 450,000t
cotton yarn (2001): 396,000t
silk (2001): 4,700t

Tourism
Tourism revenue: n/a

Foreign trade
Exports (1997): 549 million US$
Imports (1997): 1,201 million US$

Defence
Armed forces (2001): 17,500 people
Defence budget (2001): 2.33% of GDP

Standard of living
Inhabitants per doctor (1995): 305
Average daily calorie intake (2000): 2,675 (FAO minimum: 2,400)
Cars per 1,000 inhabitants: n/a
Televisions per 1,000 inhabitants (2000): 196

HISTORY: KEY DATES
1863–85: Russia took control of the territory around the eastern Caspian Sea.
1881: present-day Turkmenistan became part of Turkestan.
1925: Turkmenistan became part of the USSR.
1991: Turkmenistan became independent, and joined the Commonwealth of Independent States (CIS).
1990s: opposition parties were suppressed and a cult of personality developed around the country's president, Saparmurad Niyazov, who became president for life in 1999.

UNITED ARAB EMIRATES
➡ ARABIAN PENINSULA

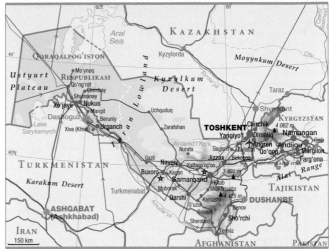

The Republic of Uzbekistan stretches from the Aral Sea to the Tien Shan and Pamir mountain ranges. The majority of the terrain is desert (notably the large Kyzyl Kum desert). The climate is continental and often arid.

Uzbekistan

200	500	1000	2000 m	

➤ oil pipeline — road
★ place of interest — railway line
✈ airport

● population over 2,000,000
● population 250,000 to 2,000,000
● population 100,000 to 250,000
• population less than 100,000

Area: 447,400km²
Population (2002): 25,618,000
Capital: Tashkent 2,157,000 (2001 e) including the suburbs
Government type and political system: republic
Head of state: (President of the Republic) Islam Abduganiyevich Karimov
Head of government: (Prime Minister) Shavkat Mirziyayev
Administrative structure: 12 provinces, 1 autonomous republic and 1 city
Official language: Uzbek
Currency: Uzbek som

DEMOGRAPHICS
Density: 54 inhab/km²
Percentage of population in urban areas (2001): 36.7%
Age structure of population (2000): 0–15 years: 36.3%, 15–65 years: 59%, over 65 years: 4.7%
Birth rate (2003): 21.7‰
Death rate (2003): 5.8‰
Infant mortality rate (2003): 36.7‰
Life expectancy at birth (2003): male: 66.8 years, female: 72.5 years

ECONOMY
GNP (2002): 7.85 billion US$
GNP per capita (2002): 310 US$
GNP per capita PPP (2002): 1,640 international dollars
HDI (2000): 0.727
GDP annual growth rate (2003): 0.3%
Annual inflation rate: n/a
Labour force by occupation (1999): agriculture: 38.5%, industry: 19.4%, services: 42.1%
GDP by sector (2000): agriculture: 34.9%, industry: 23%, services: 42.1%

Gross public debt: n/a
Unemployment rate (1995): 0.4%

Agriculture and fishing
Crops
wheat (2002): 4,956,000t
cotton (2002): 3,200,000t
maize (2002): 225,000t
barley (2002): 172,000t
potatoes (2002): 730,000t
grapes (2002): 570,000t
rice (2002): 143,000t
rye (2001): 4,500t
tobacco (2001): 19,000t
Livestock farming and fishing
cattle (2002): 5,400,000 head
goats (2001): 830,000 head
sheep (2002): 8,220,000 head
pigs (2002): 90,000 head
fish (1999): 8,540t

Energy generation and mining
copper (2001): 65,000t
hydroelectricity (2001): 5,247 million kWh
total electricity (2001): 44,487 million kWh
natural gas (2002): 53,800 million m³
lignite (2001): 2,599,000t
gold (2001): 87,000kg
oil (2002): 7,200,000t
uranium (2001): 2,400t
zinc (1993): 50,000t

Industrial production
milk (2001): 3,761,000t
sugar (2001): 11,000t
meat (2001): 512,000t
steel (2003): 500,000t
cotton yarn (2001): 1,200,000t

wool (2001): 16,000t
cement (2001): 4,000,000t
molybdenum (2001): 500t
zinc (2001): 20,000t
silk (2001): 1,200t
timber (2000): 6,000m³

Tourism
Tourism revenue (1998): 21 million US$

Foreign trade
Exports (1997): 2,893 million US$
Imports (1997): 4,842 million US$

Defence
Armed forces (2001): 50,000 people
Defence budget (2001): 5.31% of GDP

Standard of living
Inhabitants per doctor (1995): 303
Average daily calorie intake (2000): 2,371 (FAO minimum: 2,400)
Cars per 1,000 inhabitants: n/a
Televisions per 1,000 inhabitants (2000): 276

HISTORY: KEY DATES
19c: Tsarist Russia conquered the territory that now comprises Uzbekistan.
1924: the Autonomous Soviet Socialist Republic of Uzbekistan (Uzbek ASSR) was created, and became part of the USSR.
1991: Uzbekistan became independent, and joined the Commonwealth of Independent States (CIS).
1999–2004: a number of terrorist bomb attacks, blamed by the government on Islamic and foreign extremists, occurred in Uzbekistan.

The Socialist Republic of Vietnam stretches over 1,500km from north to south. A narrow strip of plateaux and mountains (the Truong Son range, formerly known as the Annam Highlands) separates the fertile and densely populated deltas of the Red River and the Mekong, and forms the backbone of the country. Vietnam has a tropical monsoon climate, and its coast is occasionally hit by typhoons.

Area: 331,689km²
Population (2002): 80,226,000
Capital: Hanoi 3,822,000 (2001 e)
Government type and political system: republic with a socialist system
Head of state: (President of the Republic) Tran Duc Luong
Head of government: (Prime Minister) Phan Van Khai; (Secretary-general of the Communist Party) Nong Duc Manh
Administrative structure: 58 provinces and 3 municipalities
Official language: Vietnamese
Currency: dong

DEMOGRAPHICS

Density: 238 inhab/km²
Percentage of population in urban areas (2001): 24.5%
Age structure of population (2000): 0–15 years: 33.4%, 15–65 years: 61.3%, over 65 years: 5.3%
Birth rate (2003): 20.2‰
Death rate (2003): 6.4‰
Infant mortality rate (2003): 33.6‰
Life expectancy at birth (2003): male: 66.9 years, female: 71.6 years

ECONOMY

GNP (2002): 34.8 billion US$
GNP per capita (2002): 430 US$
GNP per capita PPP (2002): 2, 300 international dollars
HDI (2000): 0.688
GDP annual growth rate (2003): 6%
Annual inflation rate (2000): –1.71%
Labour force by occupation: n/a
GDP by sector (2000): agriculture: 24.3%, industry: 36.6%, services: 39.1%
Gross public debt: n/a
Unemployment rate: n/a

Vietnam

★ place of interest
— road
— railway line
✈ airport

● population over 1,000,000
● population 100,000 to 1,000,000
● population 50,000 to 100,000
• population less than 50,000

200 500 1000 2000 m

Agriculture and fishing
Crops
pineapples (2001): 313,000t
groundnuts (2001): 375,000t
bananas (2001): 1,126,000t
coffee (2002): 689,000t
sugar cane (2001): 15,089,000t
rubber (2001): 305,000t
copra (2001): 148,000t
cotton (2002): 37,200t
jute (1997): 15,000t
maize (2002): 2,511,000t
manioc (2001): 2,050,000t
cashew nuts (1998): 53,251t
sweet potatoes (2001): 1,610,000t
rice (2002): 34,447,000t
tea (2001): 83,000t
Livestock farming and fishing
cattle (2001): 4,200,000 head
buffaloes (2001): 2,950,000 head
horses (2001): 190,000 head
pigs (2002): 23,170,000 head
fish (1999): 1,795,000t

Energy generation and mining
firewood (2001): 26,615,186 m³
chromium (2001): 60,000t
hydroelectricity (2001): 16,770 million kWh
total electricity (2001): 29,800 million kWh
tin (2001): 3,500t
coal (1998): 13,100,000
oil (2002): 17,300,000t

Industrial production
meat (2001): 2,004,000t
steel (2000): 306,000t
cement (2001): 14,000,000t
tin (2001): 3,500t
cotton yarn (2001): 6,990t
silk (2001): 900t
timber (2000): 4,183,000m³

Tourism revenue (1998): 86 million US$

Exports (2002): 16,076 million US$
Imports (2002): 17,760 million US$

Armed forces (2001): 484,000 people
Defence budget (2001): 0.49% of GDP

Inhabitants per doctor (1993): 2,300

Average daily calorie intake (2000): 2,583 (FAO minimum: 2,400)
Cars per 1,000 inhabitants: n/a
Televisions per 1,000 inhabitants (2001): 186

HISTORY: KEY DATES

Early origins to the Vietnamese empire
During the Neolithic period the Red River delta was populated by a mixture of Muong, Viet and Chinese ethnic groups, the ancestors of the Vietnamese people.

208 BC: the kingdom of Nam Viet was created.

111 BC: Nam Viet was invaded and annexed by the Chinese Han empire.

AD 2c: Buddhism was introduced to the country.

939: the Han rule ended when the Chinese were driven out by the Annamese people.

980–1471: the country, then known as Dai Viet or Great Viet, expanded towards the south, acquiring the kingdom of Champa.

1535: the Portuguese became the first Europeans to arrive in the country. The subsequent arrival of traders and missionaries led to the conversion of many Vietnamese people to Christianity.

1558–18c: the rival dynasties of Trinh and Nguyen controlled different parts of the country, based in Tonkin (present-day Hanoi) and Hue respectively.

1773–1802: rebellion against the Trinh and Nguyen families led to both dynasties being overthrown in the late 18c, and the country was reunited (with help from the French military) as the empire of Vietnam.

The Vietnamese empire and French rule
1858–84: France recaptured the southern region of Vietnam (Cochin China), which was made a colony, and established protectorates over the northern and central parts of the country.

1885–7: China recognized these conquests in the Treaty of Tianjin. France established the union of Indochina.

1885–96: a nationalist movement developed in the country.

1930: nationalist leader Ho Chi Minh founded the Indochinese Communist Party.

1941: a guerrilla organization, the League for the Independence of Vietnam (Viet Minh), was founded.

1945: the Japanese put an end to French rule, and the Viet Minh subsequently took over from the regime established by Japan. An independent republic was proclaimed.

1946–54: France contested the inclusion of Cochin China within the new state of Vietnam. War broke out between Vietnam and France.

1954: a Vietnamese victory at the battle of Dien Bien Phu led to peace talks in Geneva, which divided Vietnam into North and South along the 17th Parallel.

North and South Vietnam
1955: in the South, the emperor was deposed and the Republic of Vietnam was established in Saigon. In the North, the Democratic Republic of Vietnam was led by Ho Chi Minh from the capital at Hanoi.

1956–61: Communist insurgents in South Vietnam (the Viet Cong, part of the National Liberation Front) received support from the North. A significant area of South Vietnam fell under the control of the Viet Cong despite attempts from the USA to assist the government in suppressing them.

1963: a crisis arose in the South over the government's treatment of Buddhists, and mass popular protests occurred.

1964: the USA, determined to see South Vietnam resist Communist control, intervened directly against the North Vietnamese guerrillas.

1973–5: a ceasefire agreement was signed and US troops withdrew from the country, but the conflict continued.

1975: North Vietnamese troops seized Saigon and took control of South Vietnam.

Reunified Vietnam
1976: Vietnam was officially reunited as a socialist republic.

1978–9: armed conflict with China broke out after Vietnam invaded Cambodia to topple the regime of Pol Pot.

1980s: Vietnam strengthened its ties with the USSR.

1989: Vietnam withdrew from Cambodia, having established a new government there.

1992: a new constitution was adopted.

1994: the USA lifted the trade embargo it had imposed on Vietnam in 1975.

1995: Vietnam joined the Association of South-East Asian Nations (ASEAN).

2001: a trade agreement between Vietnam and the USA came into force.

YEMEN → ARABIAN PENINSULA

ALBANIA
ANDORRA
AUSTRIA
BELARUS
BELGIUM
BOSNIA AND
HERZEGOVINA
BULGARIA
CROATIA
CZECH REPUBLIC
DENMARK
ESTONIA
FINLAND
FRANCE
GERMANY

GREECE
HUNGARY
ICELAND
IRELAND
ITALY
LATVIA
LIECHTENSTEIN
LITHUANIA
LUXEMBOURG
MACEDONIA,
FORMER YUGOSLAV
REPUBLIC OF
MALTA
MOLDOVA
MONACO
THE NETHERLANDS

NORWAY
POLAND
PORTUGAL
ROMANIA
RUSSIA
SAN MARINO
SERBIA AND
MONTENEGRO
SLOVAKIA
SLOVENIA
SPAIN
SWEDEN
SWITZERLAND
UKRAINE
UNITED KINGDOM
VATICAN

Europe

200 500 1000 2000 4000 m

● population over 5,000,000
● population 1,000,000 to 5,000,000

● population 100,000 to 1,000,000
● population less than 100,000

EUROPE

EUROPE
10,500,000 km²
population 731 million
AFRICA
30,310,000 km²
population 842 million
THE AMERICAS
42,000,000 km²
population 880 million
ASIA
44,000,000 km²
population 3,826 million
OCEANIA
9,000,000 km²
population 33 million

ALBANIA

A series of mountain ranges runs from north-west to south-east through the Republic of Albania. In the north, a massive limestone extension of the Dinaric Alps reaches inland from neighbouring Montenegro. The centre of the country and the Adriatic coastline are made up of hills and fertile alluvial lowlands. The climate is Mediterranean on the narrow coastal plains and continental in the interior highlands.

Area: 28,748km²
Population (2002): 3,164,000
Capital: Tirana 299,000 (2001 e)
Government type and political system: republic with a parliamentary system
Head of state: (President of the Republic) Alfred Moisiu
Head of government: (Prime Minister) Fatos Nano
Administrative structure: 12 prefectures
Official language: Albanian
Currency: lek

DEMOGRAPHICS
Density: 107 inhab/km²
Percentage of population in urban areas (2001): 42.9%
Age structure of population (2000): 0–15 years: 30%, 15–65 years: 64.1%, over 65 years: 5.9%
Birth rate (2003): 18.2‰
Death rate (2003): 5.4‰
Infant mortality rate (2003): 25‰
Life expectancy at birth (2003): male: 70.9 years, female: 76.7 years

ECONOMY
GNP (2002): 4.58 billion US$
GNP per capita (2002): 1,450 US$
GNP per capita PPP (2002): 4,960 international dollars
HDI (2000): 0.735
GDP annual growth rate (2003): 6 %
Annual inflation rate (2000): 0.05%
Labour force by occupation: n/a
GDP by sector (2000): agriculture: 51%,

industry: 26.3%, services: 22.7%
Gross public debt: n/a
Unemployment rate (2002): 15.8%

Agriculture and fishing
Crops
sugar beets (2002): 39,200t
wheat (2002): 295,000t
maize (2002): 197,000t
olives (2002): 27,000t
potatoes (2002): 163,000t
grapes (2002): 83,000t
sunflowers (2002): 2,600t
Livestock farming and fishing
cattle (2002): 690,000 head
goats (2001): 1,120,000 head
sheep (2002): 1,844,000 head
fish (1999): 3060t

Energy generation and mining
chromium (2001): 130,000t
copper (2000): 900t
total electricity (2001): 5,289 million kWh
oil (2002): 300,000t

Industrial production
sugar (2002): 3,000t

wine (2002): 170,000hl
tobacco (2001): 4,100t
copper (2000): 350t
wool (2001): 3,500t
cement (2001): 110,000t

Tourism
Tourism revenue (1999): 211 million US$

Foreign trade
Exports (2002): 330.2 million US$
Imports (2002): 1,485.4 million US$

Defence
Armed forces (2001): 27,000 people
Defence Budget (2001): 1.03% of PIB

Standard of living
Inhabitants per doctor (1995): 714
Average daily calorie intake (2000): 2,823 (FAO minimum: 2,400)
Cars per 1,000 inhabitants (2000): 37
Televisions per 1,000 inhabitants (2000): 123

HISTORY: KEY DATES

Early origins to independence
Occupied in ancient times by Illyrian and Thracian peoples, Albania was then colonized by Greece (7c BC) and by Rome (2c BC). At the end of the 6c, the Slavs settled there in large numbers.
15c–19c: the country fell to the Ottoman Turks and, as part of the Ottoman Empire, was largely converted to Islam. Several attempted local rebellions failed, leading to the establishment of a national movement.

Independent Albania
1912: Albania became an independent principality.
1920: Albania joined the League of Nations.
1925–39: Ahmed Zogu led the newly proclaimed republic as president, and later as King Zog I.
1939: Albania was invaded by Italian troops.
1946: the Albanian People's Republic was declared. It severed its ties with the USSR (1961) and with China (1978).
1985–97: Albania emerged from its political and economic isolation and moved towards democratic reform; free elections were held in 1991.
1997: serious rioting destabilized the country after many Albanians lost their savings in an investment scandal.
1998–9: Albania was flooded with refugees from a crisis in neighbouring Kosovo.

Andorra

- ● population over 15,000
- ● 10,000 to 15,000
- ● 5,000 to 10,000
- ● less than 5,000

1000	1500	2000	2500 m

— road
— railway line

Situated on the southern slopes of the Pyrenees between France and Spain, the Principality of Andorra is a mountainous region (average altitude 1,800m) with a harsh climate, whose main source of income is tourism.

Area: 468km²
Population (2002): 64,000
Capital: Andorra la Vella 21,000 (2001 e)
Government type and political system: parliamentary system
Head of state: (co-princes) the president of France (Jacques Chirac) and the Bishop of Urgell, Spain (Joan Enric Vives i Sicília)
Head of government: (Prime Minister) Marc Forné Molné
Administrative structure: 7 parishes
Official language: Catalan
Currency: euro

DEMOGRAPHICS

Density: 168 inhab/km²

Percentage of population in urban areas (2001): 92.2%
Age structure of population: n/a
Birth rate (1990): 12.2‰
Death rate (1990): 3.7‰
Infant mortality rate (1997): 4.1‰
Life expectancy at birth (1990): male: 74 years; female: 81 years

ECONOMY

GNP: n/a
GNP per capita: n/a
GNP per capita PPP: n/a
HDI: n/a
GDP annual growth rate: n/a
Annual inflation rate: n/a
Labour force by occupation: n/a
GDP by sector: n/a
Gross public debt: n/a

Unemployment rate: n/a
Tourism
Tourism revenue: n/a
Foreign trade
Exports (1995): 49 million US$
Imports (1995): 1,069 million US$
Defence
Armed forces: n/a
Defence budget: n/a
Standard of living
Inhabitants per doctor: n/a
Average daily calorie intake (1995): 3,670 (FAO minimum: 2,400)
Cars per 1,000 inhabitants: n/a
Televisions per 1,000 inhabitants (2000): 462

HISTORY: KEY DATES

1278: Andorra was placed under the double suzerainty of French and Spanish co-princes. Its political, administrative and judicial organization was based on a feudal system.
1607: the French head of state and the Spanish Bishop of Urgell were established as co-princes of Andorra.
1982: an executive branch of government was established in Andorra, and a prime minister was elected by universal suffrage.
1993: a new constitution was adopted, establishing a parliamentary system. Andorra became a member of the United Nations.

The micro-states of Europe

E urope, like Oceania, contains several 'micro-states'. These states are listed in the table below according to their surface area, from the largest to the smallest. By way of comparison, the state that would be listed above Andorra in a complete classification table is Luxembourg, which, at 2,586km² and with 447,000 inhabitants, is five times as large.

Andorra, Liechtenstein and Monaco are ancient principalities, while San Marino has been a republic since the 13c. The most recently created micro-state is Malta, independent since 1964. The Vatican, the smallest state of all, was created in 1929 and is the only micro-state in Europe not to be a member of the United Nations.

states	area in km²	population
Andorra	468	64 000*
Malta	316	394 000*
Liechtenstein	160	30 000*
San Marino	61	27 000*
Monaco	2	30 000*
Vatican	0.44	524**

*estimate for 2002; **estimate for 2000

Most of the Republic of Austria is situated in the Alps, which culminate in the High Tauern range, cut through by deep valleys and basins where most of the population is concentrated. The north and east of the country are made up of fertile plains and hills.

Area: 83,859km²
Population (2002): 8,070,000
Capital: Vienna 1,539,848 (1991 census)
Government type and political system: republic with a semi-presidential system
Head of state: (Federal President) Heinz Fischer
Head of government: (Chancellor) Wolfgang Schüssel
Administrative structure: 9 states
Official language: German
Currency: euro

DEMOGRAPHICS
Density: 98 inhab/km²

Percentage of population in urban areas (2001): 67.4%
Age structure of population (2000): 0–15 years: 16.6%, 15–65 years: 67.8%, over 65 years: 15.6%
Birth rate (2003): 8.6‰
Death rate (2003): 9.9‰
Infant mortality rate (2003): 4.7‰
Life expectancy at birth (2003): male: 75.4 years, female: 81.5 years

ECONOMY
GNP (2002): 192 billion US$
GNP per capita (2002): 23,860 US$
GNP per capita PPP (2002): 28,910 international dollars
HDI (2000): 0.926
GDP annual growth rate (2003): 0.7%
Annual inflation rate (2000): 2.35%
Labour force by occupation (2000): agriculture: 5.8%, industry: 30.6%, services: 63.6%
GDP by sector (2000): agriculture: 2.2%, industry: 33.3%, services: 64.5%
Gross public debt (2002): 67.3% of GDP
Unemployment rate (2002): 4.3%

Agriculture
Crops
sugar beets (2002): 3,043,000t
wheat (2002): 1,434,000t
maize (2002): 1,956,000t
barley (2002): 861,000t
apples (2002): 684,000t
potatoes (2001): 695,000t
grapes (2002): 350,000t
Livestock farming
cattle (2002): 2,118,000 head
pigs (2002): 3,440,000 head

Energy generation and mining
total electricity (2001): 58,747 million kWh
iron (2001): 575,000t
natural gas (2002): 1,880 million m³
hydroelectricity (2001): 39,468 million kWh
lignite (2001): 1,206,000t
oil (2002): 1,041,000t

Industrial production
milk (2001): 3,364,000t
butter (2001): 37,129t
cheese (2001): 145,320t
steel (2003): 6,261,000t
aluminium (1996): 90,000t
copper (2000): 79,000t
lead (2001): 22,000t
cars (2002): 131,000 units
cotton yarn (1998): 16,000t
artificial textiles (1999): 154,900t
timber (2000): 10,416,000m³

Tourism
Tourism revenue (2001): 10,118 million US$

Foreign trade
Exports (2002): 73,667 million US$
Imports (2002): 70,096 million US$

Defence
Armed forces (2001): 34,800 people
Defence budget (2001): 0.79% of GDP

Standard of living
Inhabitants per doctor (1996): 357
Average daily calorie intake (2000): 3,757 (FAO minimum: 2,400)
Cars per 1,000 inhabitants (1999): 495
Televisions per 1,000 inhabitants (2001): 542

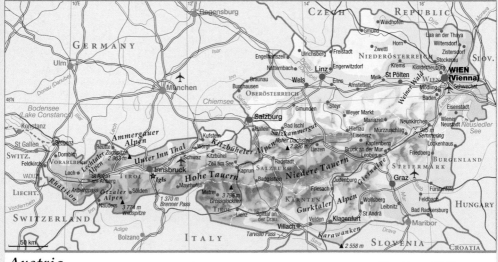

Austria

200 500 1000 2000 m

— motorway
— road
✈ airport
— railway line

★ place of interest
federal state boundary
Graz federal state capital

● population over 1,000,000
● population 100,000 to 1,000,000
● population 50,000 to 100,000
· population less than 50,000

HISTORY: KEY DATES

Early origins

The centre of the Hallstatt civilization in the 1st millennium BC, Austria was occupied by the Romans and then invaded by the Barbarians.

803: Charlemagne established an eastern outpost in the Danube Valley, west of Vienna, known as the Ostmark (Austria since 996).

1156: Austria became a hereditary duchy in the hands of the Babenberg family.

1282: the duchy passed to the Habsburg family.

The Habsburgs' Austria

After 1438, almost every head of the house of Habsburg was also king of Germany and Holy Roman Emperor.

1493–1519: Maximilian I expanded the Habsburg possessions, building the future empire of Charles V.

1521–6: Ferdinand I received the Austrian territories from his brother Charles V (emperor since 1519) and became king of Bohemia and Hungary.

16c–17c: Austria played a key part in Europe's resistance to the Ottoman Turks, and was the seat of the Catholic Reformation during the Thirty Years' War; however, it failed to avoid the political and religious disintegration of Germany (Peace of Westphalia, 1648).

18c: Austria suffered serious territorial losses during its long struggles against revolutionary France and against Napoleon I.

1804: Francis II became the emperor of Austria. Following the wishes of Napoleon I, he gave up the crown of the Holy Roman Empire, which was dissolved in 1806.

1814–48: the territories conquered by Napoleon I were returned to Austria by the Congress of Vienna. The influential statesman Metternich led Austria's dominance of European politics.

1866: Austria lost the Austro-Prussian War, defeated by Prussia at Sadowa.

1867: the Austro-Hungarian monarchy was established.

1879–82: Austria signed the Triple Alliance Agreement with Germany and Italy.

1914: the assassination of the Archduke Franz Ferdinand, heir to the Habsburg throne, triggered the outbreak of World War I.

1918: the Austro-Hungarian monarchy collapsed at the end of the war.

The Austrian Republic

1919: the borders of modern Austria were fixed in the Treaty of Saint-Germain.

1920: the Republic of Austria was declared and adopted a federal constitution.

1938–45: Austria was joined to Nazi Germany after Hitler's German Reich annexed it in 1938, and remained part of the Third Reich until 1945.

1955: after ten years of occupation by Allied forces, Austria became a neutral state.

1995: Austria became a member of the European Union (EU).

2000: the far-right Freedom Party, led by Joerg Haider, entered government.

2003: a coalition government (comprising the Freedom Party and the centre-right People's Party) introduced a number of restrictive asylum laws.

A E I O U

This list of the vowels in the English language is the same as the abbreviation of the Imperial House of Habsburg's motto. The motto can be read both in Latin (*Austriae est imperare orbi universo*: 'Austria is destined to rule the world') and in German (*Alles Erdreich is Österreich untertan*: 'It is Austria's responsibility to dominate the whole world'). Adopted by Frederick III in the 15c, it was a declaration of the Habsburgs' ambition as well as of the immensity of the empire over which they ruled.

The Republic of Belarus is a low-lying and mostly flat country, partially covered in forests and marshes and with a cool and humid climate. It still maintains important economic and cultural links with Russia. The population contains around 80% Belarusians and over 10% Russians.

Area: 207,600km²
Population (2002): 10,106,000
Capital: Minsk 1,664,000 (2001 e)
Government type and political system: republic with a semi-presidential system
Head of state: (President of the Republic) Alexander Lukashenko
Head of government: (Prime Minister) Sergei Sidorsky
Administrative structure: 6 districts
Official languages: Belarusian and Russian
Currency: Belarusian rouble

DEMOGRAPHICS

Density: 49 inhab/km²
Percentage of population in urban areas (2001): 69.6%
Age structure of population (2000): 0–15 years: 18.7%, 15–65 years: 68%, over 65 years: 13.3%
Birth rate (2003): 8.8‰
Death rate (2003): 13.2‰
Infant mortality rate (2000): 11.3‰
Life expectancy at birth (2000): male: 64.9 years, female: 75.3 years

ECONOMY

GNP (2002): 13.5 billion US$
GNP per capita (2002): 1,360 US$
GNP per capita PPP (2002): 5,500 international dollars
HDI (2000): 0.788
GDP annual growth rate (2003): 6.8%
Annual inflation rate (2000): 168.62%
Labour force by occupation: n/a
GDP by sector (2000): agriculture: 15.3%, industry: 37.4%, services: 47.3%
Gross public debt: n/a
Unemployment rate (2002): 3%

Agriculture

Crops
oats (2001): 600,000t
sugar beets (2002): 1,149,000t

Belarus

200 m	

regional boundary
Brest regional administrative centre

— road
--- railway line
✈ airport

● population over 1,000,000
● population 250,000 to 1,000,000
● population 100,000 to 250,000
● population less than 100,000

wheat (2002): 1,218,000t
barley (2002): 2,034,000t
potatoes (2002): 7,421,000t
Livestock farming
cattle (2002): 4,085,000 head
pigs (2002): 3,373,000 head

Energy generation and mining
total electricity (2001): 24,401 million kWh
natural gas (2002): 200 million m³
oil (2002): 1,700,000t

Industrial production
milk (2001): 4,300,000t
sugar (2002): 163,000t
meat (2001): 630,000t
steel (2003): 1,600,000t
cement (2001): 1,803,000t
flax (2001): 35,000t

Tourism
Tourism revenue (2000): 17 million US$

Foreign trade
Exports (2002): 7,964.7 million US$
Imports (2002): 8,879 million US$

Defence
Armed forces (2001): 79,800 people
Defence budget (2001): 1.01% of GDP

Standard of living
Inhabitants per doctor (1996): 233
Average daily calorie intake (2000): 2,902 (FAO minimum: 2,400)
Cars per 1,000 inhabitants (2000): 145
Televisions per 1,000 inhabitants (2000): 342

HISTORY: KEY DATES

9c–12c: present-day Belarus was part of the first East Slavic state, Kievan Rus.
13c–14c: known as White Russia, it became part of the Grand Duchy of Lithuania.
16c–17c: the duchy merged with Poland, and Polish influence became predominant.
1772–93: the Russian empire gained control of most of eastern Poland, including Belarus.
1919: the independent Belarusian Soviet Socialist Republic was declared.
1921: under the Treaty of Riga, Belarus was divided between Poland and Soviet Russia.
1922: the Belarusian Soviet Socialist Republic became a founding member of the USSR.
1945: the Belarusian SSR became a member of the United Nations.
1991: Belarus became independent, and Minsk became the headquarters of the Commonwealth of Independent States (CIS).
1994–2004: Belarus sought to form a 'union state' with Russia, strengthening economic, cultural and political ties between the two countries; however, no formal agreement was reached.

The Kingdom of Belgium is a small country, bounded to the north-west by the North Sea. It is made up of plains and low plateaux, with hills in the south-east (the Ardennes, whose highest point is the Signal de Botrange at 694m). Belgium's climate is cool and temperate, with strong maritime influences and regular rainfall.

Area: 30,528km²
Population (2002): 10,275,000
Capital: Brussels 136,730 (2002 e), 1,134,000 (2001 e) including the suburbs
Government type and political system: constitutional monarchy with a parliamentary system
Head of state: (King) Albert II
Head of government: (Prime Minister) Guy Verhofstadt
Administrative structure: 3 regions
Official languages: Dutch, French and German
Currency: euro

DEMOGRAPHICS
Density: 333 inhab/km²
Percentage of population in urban areas (2001): 97.4%
Age structure of population (2000): 0–15 years: 17.3%, 15–65 years: 65.7%, over 65 years: 17%
Birth rate (2003): 10.8‰
Death rate (2003): 10‰
Infant mortality rate (2003): 4.2‰
Life expectancy at birth (2003): male: 75.7 years, female: 81.9 years

ECONOMY
GDP (2002): 237 billion US$
GDP per capita (2002): 22,940 US$
GDP per capita PPP (2002): 28,130 international dollars
HDI (2000): 0.939
GDP annual growth rate (2003): 1.1%
Annual inflation rate (2000): 1.58%
Labour force by occupation (2000): agriculture: 2.2%, industry: 24%, services: 73.8%
GDP by sector (2000): agriculture: 1.4%, industry: 27.7%, services: 70.9%
Gross public debt (2002): 105.8% of GDP
Unemployment rate (2002): 7.3%

Agriculture
These data include Luxembourg's production.
Crops
oats (2001): 41,800t
sugar beets (2002): 6,537,000t
wheat (2002): 1,675,000t
barley (2001): 423,000t
potatoes (2002): 2,909,000t
Livestock farming
cattle (2002): 2,891,000 head
pigs (2002): 6,735,000 head

Energy generation
nuclear electricity (2001): 44,032 million kWh
total electricity (2001): 74,278 million kWh

Industrial production
milk (2001): 3,700,000t
cheese (2001): 65,000t
sugar (2002): 1,092,000t
beer (2000): 15,471,000hl
meat (2001): 1,803,000t
steel (2003): 11,128,000t
cast iron (1998): 8,618,000t
copper (2000): 423,000t
tin (2001): 8,000t
lead (2001): 96,000t
zinc (2001): 259,300t
cars (2002): 937,000 units
commercial vehicles (1998): 98,000 units
synthetic rubber (1998): 120,000t
cotton yarn (1998): 37,000t
flax (2001): 16,500t
artificial textiles (1991): 52,000t

Tourism
Tourism revenue (2001): 6,917 million US$

Foreign trade
Exports (2002): 160,731 million US$
Imports (2001): 159,790 million US$

Defence
Armed forces (2001): 39,260 people
Defence budget (2001): 0.97% of GDP

Standard of living
Inhabitants per doctor (1994): 270
Average daily calorie intake (2000): 3,701 (FAO minimum: 2,400)
Cars per 1,000 inhabitants (1999): 448
Televisions per 1,000 inhabitants (2001): 543

HISTORY: KEY DATES

Early origins to Austrian rule
57 BC–51 BC: Belgian Gaul, occupied by the Celts, was conquered by Julius Caesar.
AD 4c–AD 6c: the Franks invaded the north of the country.
9c–13c: the country was divided into a large number of principalities. During the 12c and the 13c, Flemish cloth manufacturing strengthened the economy of the towns.
14c–15c: the Netherlands or Low Countries, of which Belgium was a part, were united by the Dukes of Burgundy.
1477: through the marriage of Mary of Burgundy and Maximilian I of Austria, the Netherlands passed into the hands of the Habsburg family.

The Habsburgs' rule to independence
1515: Charles V increased the number of provinces in the Netherlands to 17.
1579: the northern provinces became independent and formed the United Provinces; those in the south, which make up present-day Belgium, were returned to Spain.
17c: Belgium's territorial framework was established after a number of European wars.
1713: under the Peace of Utrecht, Spain ceded its territories in the Netherlands to the Austrian Habsburgs.
1789–90: reforms imposed by Joseph II caused an uprising and led to the proclamation of the independent United States of Belgium.
1795–1815: France occupied the country.
1815: Belgium was given to the kingdom of the Netherlands (which was created at the Congress of Vienna).
1830: the Belgian provinces declared their independence from the Netherlands.

The kingdom of Belgium to the present day
1831: Belgium's independence was internationally recognized, and Leopold I became its first king.
1865–85: an industrial boom coincided with Belgian colonial expansion in Africa (notably in the Congo Free State). Leopold II acquired possession of this country, renaming it the Belgian Congo, in 1885.
1909–44: Germany occupied Belgium during World War I and World War II.
1944: the Allies liberated Belgium.
1958: Belgium, along with Luxembourg and the Netherlands, formed the Benelux Economic Union.
1960: the Belgian Congo (now the Democratic Republic of the Congo) became independent.
1962: Rwanda and Burundi, formerly controlled by Belgium, became independent.
1977–93: constitutional reform led to the establishment of three autonomous regions within Belgium (Brussels, Flanders and Wallonia).
2002: the Belgian franc was replaced by the euro as Belgium's currency.

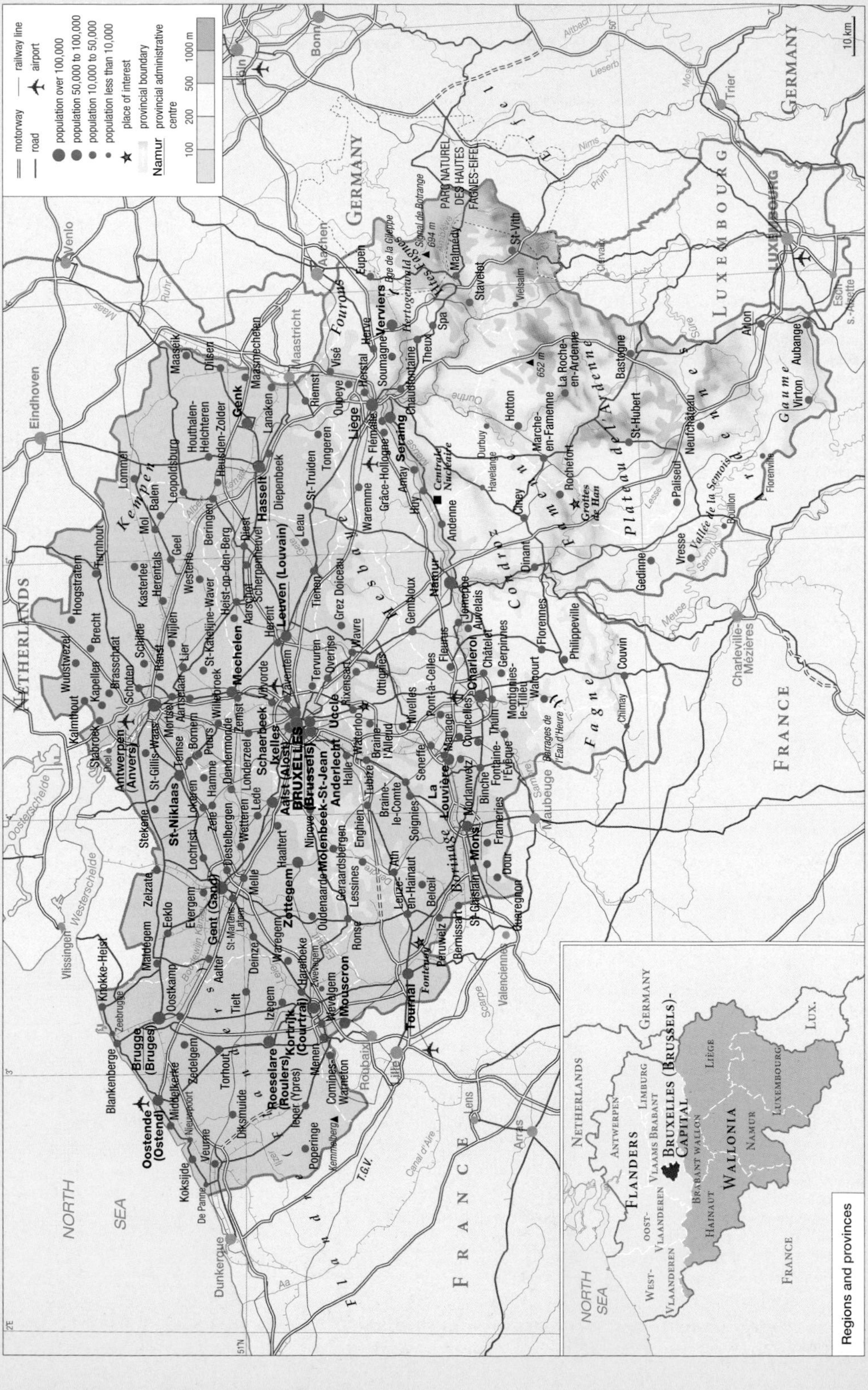

BELGIUM

Legend

- motorway
- road
- railway line
- airport
- population over 100,000
- population 50,000 to 100,000
- population 10,000 to 50,000
- population less than 10,000
- place of interest
- provincial boundary
- Namur provincial administrative centre

100 200 500 1000 m

10 km

214

NETHERLANDS

GERMANY

LUXEMBOURG

FRANCE

NORTH SEA

Eindhoven
Venlo
Maastricht
Aachen
Bonn
Trier

Brugge (Bruges)
Oostende (Ostend)
Blankenberge
Knokke-Heist
Gent (Gand)
Antwerpen (Anvers)
St-Niklaas
Mechelen
BRUXELLES (BRUSSELS)
Leuven (Louvain)
Hasselt
Genk
Maaseik
Liège
Verviers
Eupen
St-Vith
Malmédy
Stavelot
Spa
Namur
Charleroi
La Louvière
Mons
Tournai
Mouscron
Kortrijk (Courtrai)
Roeselare (Roulers)
Ieper (Ypres)
Seraing
Huy
Dinant
Bastogne
La Roche-en-Ardenne
Marche-en-Famenne
St-Hubert
Arlon
Virton
Bouillon

Regions and provinces

FLANDERS
WALLONIA
BRUXELLES (BRUSSELS)-CAPITAL

WEST-VLAANDEREN
OOST-VLAANDEREN
ANTWERPEN
LIMBURG
VLAAMS BRABANT
BRABANT WALLON
HAINAUT
NAMUR
LIÈGE
LUXEMBOURG

The Republic of Bosnia and Herzegovina is a mountainous, virtually landlocked country with a continental climate. From the valley of the River Sava to Dalmatia, the landscape is mainly made up of forests and pasturelands. The country's three main ethnic groups are the Bosnians, the Serbs and the Croats.

Area: 51,197km²
Population (2002): 4,127,000
Capital: Sarajevo 552,000 (2001 e)
Government type and political system: republic with a semi-presidential system
Head of state: (Chairman of the Presidency) Borislav Paravac (Serbian President); Dragan Čović (Croatian President); Sulejman Tihić (Muslim President) *Note: Tripartite presidency rotates every eight months; details given are correct at the time of going to press.*
Head of government: (Prime Minister) Adnan Terzic
Administrative structure: 2 regions (a Bosnian Muslim/Croat federation and a Bosnian Serb republic, Republica Srpska)
Official languages: Bosnian, Croatian and Serbian
Currency: convertible mark

DEMOGRAPHICS
Density: 78 inhab/km²
Percentage of population in urban areas (2001): 43.4%
Age structure of population (2000): 0–15 years: 18.9%, 15–65 years: 71.2%, over 65 years: 9.9%
Birth rate (2003): 9.7‰
Death rate (2003): 8.1‰
Infant mortality rate (2003): 13.5‰
Life expectancy at birth (2003): male: 71.3 years, female: 76.7 years

ECONOMY
GNP (2002): 5.4 billion US$
GNP per capita (2002): 1,310 US$
GNP per capita PPP (2002): 5,800 international dollars
HDI: n/a
GDP annual growth rate (2003): 3.5%
Annual inflation rate: n/a
Labour force by occupation: n/a
GDP by sector (2000): agriculture: 12.2%, industry: 26%, services: 61.8%
Gross public debt: n/a
Unemployment rate: n/a

Bosnia and Herzegovina

★ place of interest

| 200 | 500 | 1000 | 2000 m |

— road
— railway line
✈ airport
--- Dayton Accord Line 1996

● population over 500,000
● population 100,000 to 500,000
● population 30,000 to 100,000
● population less than 30,000

Agriculture
Crops
sugar beets (1997): 1,000t
wheat (2002): 272,000t
maize (2002): 903,000t
potatoes (2002): 404,000t
Livestock farming
cattle (2002): 440,000 head
sheep (2002): 670,000 head
pigs (2002): 300,000 head

Energy generation and mining
total electricity (2001): 9,979 million kWh
zinc (2001): 300t

Industrial production
wine (2002): 52,000hl

tobacco (2001): 3,440t

Tourism
Tourism revenue (2000): 17 million US$

Foreign trade
Exports (2002): 1,115 million US$
Imports (2002): 4,518.7 million US$

Defence
Armed forces (2001): 19,800 people
Defence budget (2001): 0.27% of GDP

Standard of living
Inhabitants per doctor (1990): 625
Average daily calorie intake (2000): 2,661 (FAO minimum: 2,400)
Cars per 1,000 inhabitants (1996): 23
Televisions per 1,000 inhabitants (2000): 111

215

HISTORY: KEY DATES
The region was conquered by the Ottomans in the late 15c. It was annexed by Austria–Hungary in 1908. It became part of the kingdom of the Serbs, Croats and Slovenes in 1918, and then one of the six republics within the Federal People's Republic of Yugoslavia (1945). ***1991–5:*** the Federal People's Republic of Yugoslavia collapsed as civil war broke out between the country's various ethnic groups. Ethnic cleansing and other atrocities were committed, despite the presence of UN troops in the region. ***1995:*** the Dayton Peace Accord, signed in the USA, proposed that a single Bosnian state should be divided up into

two self-governing provinces along ethnic and geographic lines: a Bosnian Serb Republic in the north and east, and a Muslim–Croat Republic in the west. A central multi-ethnic government was established. ***1996:*** the International Criminal Tribunal for the former Yugoslavia, based in The Hague, began to hear evidence about war crimes committed during the civil war. ***2004:*** reconstruction work was completed on Bosnia's historic Mostar Bridge, destroyed by Croat forces during the war.

The population of the Republic of Bulgaria is concentrated in the inland basins (Sofia) and plains (the Danube Valley and the Maritsa Valley), separated by the Balkan Mountains. The Rhodope Mountains are situated in the south-west of the country.

Bulgaria

★ place of interest

200 500 1000 2000 m

═══ motorway
─── road
─── railway line
✈ airport

● population over 1,000,000
● population 250,000 to 1,000,000
● population 100,000 to 250,000
• population 50,000 to 100,000
· population less than 50,000

Area: 110,912km^2
Population (2002): 7,790,000
Capital: Sofia 1,096,389 (2001 census)
Government type and political system: republic with a semi-presidential system
Head of state: (President of the Republic) Georgi Parvanov
Head of government: (Prime Minister) Simeon Saxe-Coburg Gotha (Simeon II)
Administrative structure: 28 districts
Official language: Bulgarian
Currency: Bulgarian lev

DEMOGRAPHICS

Density: 74 inhab/km^2
Percentage of population in urban areas (2001): 67.5%
Age structure of population (2000): 0–15 years: 15.7%, 15–65 years: 68.2%, over 65 years: 16.1%
Birth rate (2003): 7.9‰
Death rate (2003): 15.1‰
Infant mortality rate (2003): 15.2‰
Life expectancy at birth (2003): male: 67.4 years, female: 74.6 years

ECONOMY

GNP (2002): 14.1 billion US$
GNP per capita (2002): 1,770 US$
GNP per capita PPP (2002): 7,030 international dollars
HDI (2000): 0.779
GDP annual growth rate (2003): 4.3%
Annual inflation rate (2000): 10.32%
Labour force by occupation (2001): agriculture: 26.3%, industry: 27.7%, services: 46%
GDP by sector (2000): agriculture: 14,5%, industry: 27.8%, services: 57.7%
Gross public debt (2002): 53% of GDP
Unemployment rate (2002): 17.6%

Agriculture

Crops
wheat (2002): 4,123,000t
maize (2002): 1,288,000t
barley (2002): 1,211,000t
potatoes (2002): 627,000t

sunflowers (2002): 645,000t
Livestock farming
cattle (2002): 635,000 head
sheep (2002): 2,418,000 head
pigs (2002): 1,014,000 head

Energy generation and mining
copper (2001): 95,000t
nuclear electricity (2001): 18,238 million kWh
total electricity (2001): 41,381 million kWh
iron (2000): 178,000t
lead (2001): 11,000t
zinc (2001): 11,000t

Industrial production
sugar (2002): 3,000t
wine (2002): 2,300,000hl
tobacco (2001): 40,900t
steel (2001): 2,035,000t
copper (2001): 95,000t
lead (2001): 80,000t
zinc (2001): 85,000t
cotton yarn (2001): 2,800t
wool (2001): 8,000t

Tourism
Tourism revenue (2001): 1,201 million US$

Foreign trade
Exports (2002): 5,692.1 million US$
Imports (2002): 7,286.6 million US$

Defence
Armed forces (2001): 58,450 people
Defence budget (2001): 2.66% of GDP

Standard of living
Inhabitants per doctor (1995): 286
Average daily calorie intake (2000): 2,467 (FAO minimum: 2,400)
Cars per 1,000 inhabitants (2000): 234
Televisions per 1,000 inhabitants (2000): 449

HISTORY: KEY DATES

Early origins to Ottoman rule
The area that is now Bulgaria was conquered by the Romans in AD 1c. It later belonged to the Byzantine empire. Slavs and nomadic Bulgar tribes began to settle there in the 6c.
681: the first Bulgarian empire was established on the lower Danube.
1018: the Byzantines established their rule over Bulgaria.
1187: the second Bulgarian empire was founded.
14c: Bulgaria was divided into several principalities.
1396–1878: under Ottoman rule, Bulgaria was partially converted to Islam.

Independent Bulgaria
1908: Prince Ferdinand of Saxe-Coburg Gotha proclaimed Bulgaria's independence, with himself as czar.
1912–13: Bulgaria was defeated in the second Balkan War.
1915: Bulgaria aligned itself with Germany during World War I.
1943: the Bulgarian king, Boris III, died in mysterious circumstances following a meeting with Adolf Hitler. His six-year-old son Simeon II succeeded him.
1946: the monarchy was abolished in a referendum, and Bulgaria was pro-claimed a Socialist People's Republic.
1990s: several years of political instability and civil unrest followed the collapse of communism in Bulgaria.
2001: former king Simeon II was elected prime minister and pledged to introduce economic reforms.

Croatia

⭐ place of interest	
200　500　1000 m	

— motorway
— road
— railway line
✈ airport

● population over 500,000
● population 100,000 to 500,000
● population 30,000 to 100,000
• population less than 30,000

50 km

The Republic of Croatia stretches from the River Danube in the east to the Adriatic Sea in the west. It is mainly made up of hills and plains in the north and east, with higher mountains (the Dinaric Alps) in the west, dominating the coast of Dalmatia. The country's coastline (around Split and Dubrovnik) has a typical Mediterranean climate and is a major tourist destination.

Area: 56,538km²
Population (2002): 4,657,000
Capital: Zagreb 809,701 (2001 census), 1,081,000 (2001 e) including the suburbs
Government type and political system: republic with a semi-presidential system
Head of state: (President of the Republic) Stjepan Mesić, known as Stipe Mesić
Head of government: (Prime Minister) Ivo Sanader
Administrative structure: 20 counties and 1 city
Official language: Croatian
Currency: Crotaian kuna

DEMOGRAPHICS

Density: 79 inhab/km²
Percentage of population in urban areas (2001): 58.1%
Age structure of population (2000): 0–15 years: 18%, 15–65 years: 67.9%, over 65 years: 14.1%
Birth rate (2003): 11.1‰
Death rate (2003): 11.8‰
Infant mortality rate (2003): 8.1‰
Life expectancy at birth (2003): male: 70.3 years, female: 78.1 years

ECONOMY

GNP (2002): 20.3 billion US$
GNP per capita (2002): 4,540 US$
GNP per capita PPP (2002): 10,000 international dollars
HDI (2000): 0.809
GDP annual growth rate (2003): 4.4%
Annual inflation rate (2000): 5.42%
Labour force by occupation (2001): agriculture: 15.5%, industry: 30%, services: 54.5%
Structure du PIB (2000): agriculture: 9.5%, industry: 32.8%, services: 57.7%
Gross public debt: n/a
Unemployment rate (2002): 14.8%

Agriculture

Crops
sugar beets (2002): 1,183,000t

wheat (2002): 988,000t
maize (2002): 2,502,000t
olives (2002): 33,000t
potatoes (2002): 736,000t
Livestock farming
cattle (2002): 417,000 head
sheep (2002): 580,000 head
pigs (2002): 1,286,000 head

Energy generation and mining

total electricity (2001): 12,117 million kWh
natural gas (2002): 1,900 million m³
coal (1999): 15,000t
oil (2002): 1,000,000t

Industrial production

steel (2003): 40,000t
aluminium (2001): 15,000t

shipbuilding (1998): 443,000dwt

Tourism

Tourism revenue (2001): 3,335 million US$

Foreign trade

Exports (2002): 4,994.6 million US$
Imports (2002): 10,273.9 million US$

Defence

Armed forces (2001): 51,000 people
Defence budget (2001): 2.54% of GDP

Standard of living

Inhabitants per doctor (1994): 500
Average daily calorie intake (2000): 2,483 (FAO minimum: 2,400)
Cars per 1,000 inhabitants (2000): 257
Televisions per 1,000 inhabitants (2000): 293

HISTORY: KEY DATES

Occupied in ancient times by Illyrian peoples, Croatia became part of the Holy Roman Empire in the 9c.
1526–7: part of Croatia came under the control of the Ottoman empire; the rest fell into the hands of the Austrian Habsburg family.
1867–8: the Austro-Hungarian compromise placed Croatia under Hungarian rule.
1918–45: Croatia became part of the kingdom of the Serbs, Croats and Slovenes in 1918. The Croats were opposed to Serbian centralism.
1941–5: an independent Croat state was declared, led by the fascist regime of Ante Pavelić. The state came under first German and then Italian military control.
1945: Croatia became one of the six republics within the Federal People's Republic of Yugoslavia.
1991: Croatia declared its independence. Violent fighting broke out when Croatian Serbs in the east of the country, with the aid of the Yugoslav federal army, expelled Croats and seized control of the territory. The UN intervened to keep Croats and Serbs apart.
1992–5: Croatia lent its support to the Croat troops in the war in Bosnia-Herzegovina.
1996: diplomatic relations between Croatia and Yugoslavia were restored.

CZECH REPUBLIC

Czech Republic

200 500 1000 m

— railway line
✈ airport
★ place of interest

— motorway
— road

● population over 1,000,000
● population 100,000 to 1,000,000
● population 50,000 to 100,000
· population less than 50,000

50 km

The Czech Republic is a landlocked country in Eastern Europe. In Bohemia, the western part of the country, low mountains surround the fertile Polabí Plain. Moravia, in the east, consists of fertile lowlands as well as hilly country. The climate is continental.

Area: 78,866km²
Population (2002): 10,250,000
Capital: Prague 1,178,576 (2001 census)
Government type and political system: republic with a parliamentary system
Head of state: (President of the Republic) Václav Klaus
Head of government: (Prime Minister) Stanislav Gross
Administrative structure: 13 regions and 1 municipality
Official language: Czech
Currency: Czech koruna

DEMOGRAPHICS
Density: 130 inhab/km²
Percentage of population in urban areas (2001): 74.6%
Age structure of population (2000): 0–15 years: 16.4%, 15–65 years: 69.8%, over 65 years: 13.8%
Birth rate (2003): 8.8‰
Death rate (2003): 10.8‰
Infant mortality rate (2003): 5.6‰
Life expectancy at birth (2003): male: 72.1 years, female: 78.7 years

ECONOMY
GNP (2002): 56 billion US$
GNP per capita (2002): 5,480 US$
GNP per capita PPP (2002): 14,920 international dollars
HDI (2000): 0.849
GDP annual growth rate (2003): 2.9%
Annual inflation rate (2000): 3.9%
Labour force by occupation (2000): agriculture: 5.1%, industry: 40%, services: 54.9%
GDP by sector (2000): agriculture: 4.1%, industry: 41.4%, services: 54.5%
Gross public debt (2002): 27.1% of GDP
Unemployment rate (2002): 7.3%

Agriculture
Crops
sugar beets (2002): 3,832,000t
wheat (2002): 3,866,000t
rape (2001): 985,000t
barley (2002): 1,793,000t
potatoes (2002): 1,106,000t
Livestock farming
cattle (2002): 1,520,000 head

218

sheep (2002): 96,000 head
pigs (2002): 3,441,000 head
Energy generation and mining
hydroelectricity (2001): 2,033 million kWh
nuclear electricity (2001): 14,012 million kWh
total electricity (2001): 70,038 million kWh
natural gas (2002): 148 million m³
coal (2001): 65,640,000t
lignite (2001): 453,000t
oil (2002): 421,000t
Industrial production
milk (2001): 2,750,000t
butter (2001): 66,731t
sugar (2002): 574,000t
wine (2002): 480,000hl
beer (2000): 17,796,000hl
steel (2003): 6,790,000t
cast iron (1998): 4,982,000t
cars (2002): 441,000 units
commercial vehicles (1998): 70,000 units
cotton yarn (1998): 66,000t
wool (2001): 220t
flax (2001): 17,100t
artificial textiles (1999): 17,600t
synthetic textiles (1999): 17,400t
cement (2001): 3,550,000t
paper (2000): 804,000t
Tourism
Tourism revenue (2001): 2,979 million US$
Foreign trade
Exports (2002): 38,480 million US$
Imports (2002): 40,720 million US$
Defence
Armed forces (2001): 49,450 people
Defence budget (2001): 2.12% of GDP
Standard of living
Inhabitants per doctor (1996): 344
Average daily calorie intake (2000): 3,103 (FAO minimum: 2,400)
Cars per 1,000 inhabitants (2000): 335
Televisions per 1,000 inhabitants (2001): 534

HISTORY: KEY DATES
900–1306: Bohemia was a kingdom within the Holy Roman Empire.
1526–1648: Ferdinand of Austria, one of the Habsburg dynasty, was proclaimed king of Bohemia. This union with Austria was formalized by the 1627 constitution, which gave the crown of Bohemia to the Habsburgs as a hereditary title.
1618–48: a Bohemian rebellion (known as the Defenestration of Prague) led to the Thirty Years' War.
19c: the Czech peasantry was emancipated, and Czech nationalism grew.
1918: the Czechs became independent and, with the Slovaks, formed the Republic of Czechoslovakia.
1938: Czechoslovakia ceded the Sudetenland to Germany.
1939: Nazi forces occupied Bohemia-Moravia, making the area a German protectorate. Slovakia was proclaimed a separate state.
1945: Soviet troops liberated Prague.
1948: the Communist Party took power.
1968: the Communist leader Alexander Dubček initiated liberalizing reforms (known as the Prague Spring), leading to intervention and occupation by Soviet forces.
1969: Czechoslovakia became a federal state made up of the Czech and the Slovak republics.
1989: after a series of peaceful public demonstrations (known as the 'Velvet Revolution') the Communist authorities resigned. The dissident Václav Havel was elected president.
1991: all Soviet forces were withdrawn from the country.
1992–3: the Czech and Slovak governments negotiated the process of dividing Czechoslovakia into two independent states.

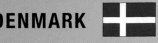

Made up of the Jutland Peninsula and over 500 islands, the Kingdom of Denmark is a country of plains and low plateaus (the highest point being 173m) with an oceanic and relatively humid climate. The United Kingdom of Denmark includes the Faroe Islands and Greenland, both of which are self-governing territories.

Area: 43,094km²
Population (2002): 5,342,000
Capital: Copenhagen 500,131 (2002 e), 1,332,000 (2001 e) including the suburbs
Government type and political system: constitutional monarchy with a parliamentary system
Head of state: (Queen) Margrethe II
Head of government: (Prime Minister) Anders Fogh Rasmussen
Administrative structure: 13 counties and 271 local authorities
Official language: Danish
Currency: krone

DEMOGRAPHICS
Density: 123 inhab/km²
Percentage of population in urban areas (2001): 85.1%
Age structure of population (2000): 0–15 years: 18.3%, 15–65 years: 66.7%, over 65 years: 15%
Birth rate (2003): 11.8‰
Death rate (2003): 11.3‰
Infant mortality rate (2003): 5.0‰
Life expectancy at birth (2003): male: 74.2 years, female: 79.1 years

ECONOMY
GNP (2002): 163 billion US$
GNP per capita (2002): 30,260 US$
GNP per capita PPP (2002): 30,600 international dollars

HDI (2000): 0.926
GDP annual growth rate (2003): 0.2%
Annual inflation rate (2000): 2.92%
Labour force by occupation (2000): agriculture: 3.3%, industry: 26.4%, services: 70.3%
GDP by sector (2000): agriculture: 2.6%, industry: 27.3%, services: 70.1%
Gross public debt (2002): 45.5% of GDP
Unemployment rate (2002): 4.6%

Agriculture and fishing
Crops
sugar beets (2002): 3,385,000t
wheat (2002): 4,059,000t
rape (2001): 350,000t
barley (2002): 4,121,000t
potatoes (2002): 1,506,000t
rye (2001): 350,000t
Livestock farming and fishing
cattle (2002): 1,796,000 head
sheep (2002): 131,000 head
pigs (2002): 12,732,000 head
fish (1999): 2,005,000t

Energy generation and mining
total electricity (2001): 35,469 million kWh
hydroelectricity (2001): 28 million kWh
natural gas (2002): 8,382 million m³
oil (2002): 18,183,000t

Industrial production
milk (2001): 4,660,000t
butter (2001): 50,000t
cheese (2001): 300,000t
sugar (2002): 566,000t
meat (2001): 2,090,000t
steel (2002): 392,000t
shipbuilding (1998): 508,000dwt

Tourism
Tourism revenue (2001): 3,923 million US$

Foreign trade
Exports (2002): 55,586 million US$
Imports (2002): 47,279 million US$

Defence
Armed forces (2001): 22,700 people
Defence budget (2001): 1.28% of GDP

Standard of living
Inhabitants per doctor (1996): 344
Average daily calorie intake (2000): 3,396 (FAO minimum: 2,400)
Cars per 1,000 inhabitants (2000): 357
Televisions per 1,000 inhabitants (2001): 857

219

HISTORY: KEY DATES

Early origins to the Christian Middle Ages
Inhabited since the Neolithic period, present-day Denmark had a very sophisticated culture during the Bronze Age.
9c: the Danish took part in Viking expeditions to the coasts of Western Europe.

10c: the Jutland dynasty unified Denmark, which was gradually converted to Christianity.
11c: Svein I (c.986–1014) gained control of England. His son Canute ruled England, Denmark and Norway.
1042: England gained independence from Denmark.
12c: a feudal regime became established

in Denmark, and the influence of the Roman Catholic Church grew.
1167: Archbishop Absalon (1128–1201) fortified the settlement of Copenhagen.
1157–1241: Denmark's medieval civilization flourished under Valdemar I and II.
14c: the Kalmar Union brought the three Scandinavian kingdoms of

DENMARK

HISTORY: KEY DATES

Denmark, Norway and Sweden together under Margrethe I and Erik of Pomerania.

The Reformation and the fight against Sweden

1523: the Kalmar Union was dissolved when Gustav I Vasa became king of Sweden.

1536: Lutheranism became Denmark's official religion.

17c: Denmark lost part of its territory to Sweden through the Thirty Years' War and several later wars.

1729: Greenland became a province of

Denmark.

1770–2: the mentally ill king Christian VII ceded power to the politician Johann Friedrich Struensee, who ruled as a dictator.

The 19c and the 20c

1814: under the Treaty of Kiel, Denmark ceded Norway to Sweden but kept possession of Greenland, the Faroe Islands and Iceland.

1849: Frederick VII introduced a democratic constitution and established a two-chamber parliament.

1864: Denmark fought against Prussia

and Austria, losing the territory of Schleswig-Holstein.

1940–5: Germany invaded and occupied Denmark.

1944: Iceland declared itself fully independent from Denmark.

1948: the Faroe Islands became a self-governing territory of Denmark.

1972: Margrethe II succeeded her father, Frederick IX.

1973: Denmark joined the European Economic Community (EEC).

1979: Greenland was granted home rule.

2001: a far-right coalition government was elected in Denmark.

The island of Greenland

Greenland is the largest island in the world, with a surface area of $2,186,000km^2$ (over fifty times the size of Denmark), and is almost completely covered in ice. Originally inhabited by Thule Eskimos, it was discovered around 985 by the Norseman known as Eric the Red, who gave the island its name in order to appeal to potential settlers. The early colonists eventually died out, but in the 16c the English navigator John Davis rediscovered Greenland.

After Denmark colonized it in 1721, the island became part of the Danish kingdom in 1953 and was granted home rule by the Danish parliament in 1979. Today a Danish–Greenlandic commission manages the country's natural resources and both countries are equal partners as far as energy resources are concerned, although the island's subsoil belongs to Denmark.

Greenland has over 55,000 inhabitants. The Greenlandic Inuit, made famous partly by the expeditions of the explorers Knud Rasmussen (1879–1933), Paul-Émile Victor (1907–95) and Jean Malaurie (born 1922), are the northernmost indigenous group of people on Earth.

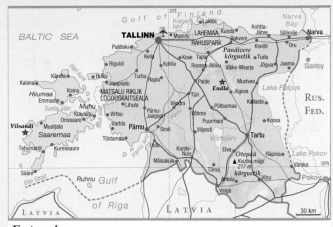

Estonia

★ place of interest

100   200 m

═══ motorway
─── road
─── railway line
✈ airport

● population over 300,000
● population 100,000 to 300,000
● population 50,000 to 100,000
• population less than 50,000

The Republic of Estonia is the smallest of the three Baltic States. It is a flat country, partially covered by forests and with a fairly mild climate. About two-thirds of the population consist of Estonians, while the remaining third come from other former Soviet republics (mainly Russia).

Area: 45,100km²
Population (2002): 1,360,000
Capital: Tallinn 404,000 (2000 census)
Government type and political system: republic with a parliamentary system
Head of state: (President of the Republic) Arnold Rüütel
Head of government: (Prime Minister) Juhan Parts
Administrative structure: 15 counties
Official language: Estonian
Currency: Estonian kroon

DEMOGRAPHICS

Density: 31 inhab/km²
Percentage of population in urban areas (2001): 69.4%
Age structure of population (2000): 0–15 years: 17.7%, 15–65 years: 67.9%, over 65 years: 14.4%
Birth rate (2003): 8.7‰
Death rate (2003): 13.6‰
Infant mortality rate (2003): 9.4‰
Life expectancy at birth (2003): male: 66.5 years, female: 76.8 years

ECONOMY

GNP (2002): 5.69 billion US$
GNP per capita (2002): 4,190 US$
GNP per capita PPP (2002): 11,630 international dollars
HDI (2000): 0.826
GDP annual growth rate (2003): 4.7%
Annual inflation rate (2000): 4.03%
Labour force by occupation (2001): agriculture: 6.9%, industry: 33%, services: 60.1%
GDP by sector (2000): agriculture: 6%, industry: 26.7%, services: 67.3%
Gross public debt (2002): 5.8% of GDP
Unemployment rate (2002): 10.3%

Agriculture and fishing

Crops
oats (2001): 84,000t
sugar beets (1998): 1,000t
wheat (2002): 148,000t
barley (2002): 249,000t
potatoes (2002): 286,000t
rye (2001): 40,800t
Livestock farming and fishing
cattle (2002): 261,000 head
sheep (2002): 28,800 head
pigs (2002): 345,000 head
fish (1999): 112,000t

Energy generation and mining

total electricity (2001): 7,937 million kWh

Industrial production

milk (2001): 687,000t
butter (2001): 10,800t
meat (2001): 57,000t
beer (2000): 950,000hl
timber (2000): 7,270,000m³

Tourism

Tourism revenue (2001): 507 million US$

Foreign trade

Exports (2002): 3,517.5 million US$
Imports (2002): 1,037.9 million US$

Defence

Armed forces (2001): 5,510 people
Defence budget (2001): 1.73% of GDP

Standard of living

Inhabitants per doctor (1996): 333
Average daily calorie intake (2000): 3,376 (FAO minimum: 2,400)
Cars per 1,000 inhabitants (2000): 339
Televisions per 1,000 inhabitants (2001): 629

HISTORY: KEY DATES

The original inhabitants of present-day Estonia were Finno-Ugric peoples. The country was occupied by Vikings (9c) and Russians (11c–12c).
1217: Estonia was conquered by an alliance of the Danes with the German crusading order of the Livonian Brothers of the Sword.
1561: possession of Estonia was divided between Sweden and Poland, before being granted entirely to Sweden.
1721: under the Treaty of Nystad, Estonia became part of the Russian empire.
1918: Estonia proclaimed its independence.
1920: a peace treaty was signed between Russia and Estonia; Russia formally recognized Estonia's independence.
1940: in accordance with the German–Soviet pact, Estonia was annexed by the USSR.
1941–4: Estonia was invaded and occupied by Germany.
1944: the country was re-annexed by the USSR.
1991: Estonia's independence was restored.
1994: Russian troops withdrew from Estonia.
2004: Estonia joined both the North Atlantic Treaty Organization (NATO) and the European Union (EU).

221

The Republic of Finland is a vast plateau made up of ancient rocks, and dotted with thousands of lakes and islands. Apart from the tundra zone in the north of the country, Finland's landscape is dominated by extensive conifer forests, which constitute the country's main natural resource.

Area: 338,145km²
Population (2002): 5,183,000
Capital: Helsinki 555,474 (2000 census), 936,000 (2001 e) including the suburbs
Government type and political system: republic with a parliamentary system
Head of state: (President of the Republic) Tarja Halonen
Head of government: (Prime Minister) Matti Vanhanen (since June 2003)
Administrative structure: 6 provinces
Official languages: Finnish and Swedish
Currency: euro

Finland

		motorway
100	200	500 m road
		railway line

● population over 500,000 ● population 50,000 to 100,000
● population 100,000 to 500,000 · population less than 50,000

DEMOGRAPHICS
Density: 15 inhab/km²
Percentage of population in urban areas (2001): 59%
Age structure of population (2000): 0–15 years: 18%, 15–65 years: 67.1%, over 65 years: 14.9%
Birth rate (2003): 10.8‰
Death rate (2003): 9.8‰
Infant mortality rate (2003): 4‰
Life expectancy at birth (2000): male: 74.4 years, female: 81.5 years

ECONOMY
GNP (2002): 130 billion US$
GNP per capita (2002): 23,890 US$
GNP per capita PPP (2002): 26,160 international dollars
HDI (2000): 0.93
GDP annual growth rate (2003): 1.9%
Annual inflation rate (2000): 3.37%
Labour force by occupation (2000): agriculture: 6.1%, industry: 27.6%, services: 66.3%
GDP by sector (2000): agriculture: 3.7%, industry: 34.2%, services: 62.1%
Gross public debt (2002): 42.7% of GDP
Unemployment rate (2002): 9.1%

Agriculture and fishing
Crops
oats (2001): 1,287,000t
sugar beets (2002): 1,066,000t
barley (2002): 1,739,000t
Livestock farming and fishing
cattle (2002): 1,025,000 head
pigs (2002): 1,315,000 head
fish (1999): 176,000t

Energy generation and mining
nuclear electricity (2001): 21,656 million kWh
total electricity (2001): 71,200 million kWh
hydroelectricity (2001): 13,342 million kWh
zinc (2001): 20,100t

Industrial production
milk (2001): 2,500,000t
butter (2001): 51,500t
cheese (2001): 106,000t
steel (2003): 4,766,000t
copper (2001): 11,500t
nickel (2001): 2,000t
zinc (2001): 248,800t
shipbuilding (1998): 42,000dwt
artificial textiles (1999): 52,600t
synthetic textiles (1997): 62,000t
timber (2001): 50,147,000m³
paper (2000): 13,509,000t

Tourism
Tourism revenue (2001): 1,441 million US$

Foreign trade
Exports (2002): 44,856 million US$
Imports (2002): 31,713 million US$

Defence
Armed forces (2001): 31,850 people
Defence budget (2001): 1.16% of GDP

Standard of living
Inhabitants per doctor (1996): 357

Average daily calorie intake (2000): 3,227 (FAO minimum: 2,400)
Cars per 1,000 inhabitants (1999): 403
Televisions per 1,000 inhabitants (2001): 678

HISTORY: KEY DATES
1150–1809: Finland was ruled by Sweden.
18c: recurring wars between Sweden and Russia wiped out nearly a third of Finland's population.
1809: Finland became a Grand Duchy of the Russian empire. During the reign of Alexander III and Nicholas II, the Russification of the country intensified, whilst national resistance grew.
1917: the Russian Revolution allowed Finland to declare its independence.
1939–44: following a battle against the Red Army, Finland lost approximately 10% of its territory to the USSR. Finland fought the USSR alongside the Third Reich from 1941 on.
1948: Finland signed a treaty of friendship and mutual assistance with the USSR. The treaty was renewed in 1970 and 1983, and declared null and void in 1992.
1995: Finland became a member of the European Union.

The French Republic is characterized by vast expanses of plains and low plateaux. The country's latitude and its proximity to the Atlantic give it a dominant oceanic climate with unstable weather patterns, small temperature ranges and abundant precipitation. Winters are harsher inland, and the south-east of France has a Mediterranean climate marked by hot, dry summers. Forests cover approximately a quarter of the country.

Area: 551,500km²
Population (2002): 61,411,000
Capital: Paris 2,147,857 (1999 census), 9,658,000 (2001 e) including the suburbs
Government type and political system: republic with a semi-presidential system
Head of state: (President of the Republic) Jacques Chirac
Head of government: (Prime Minister) Jean-Pierre Raffarin
Administrative structure: 26 regions, 100 departments, 4 overseas departments, 2 territorial collectivities, 4 overseas countries and territories
Official language: French
Currency: euro

DEMOGRAPHICS

Density: 110 inhab/km²
Percentage of population in urban areas (2001): 75.5%
Age structure of population (2000): 0–15 years: 18.7%, 15–65 years: 65.3%, over 65 years: 16%
Birth rate (2003): 12.8‰
Death rate (2003): 9.3‰
Infant mortality rate (2003): 5 ‰
Life expectancy at birth (2003): male: 75.2 years, female: 82.8 years

ECONOMY

GNP (2002): 1,362 billion US$
GNP per capita (2002): 22,240 US$
GNP per capita PPP (2002): 27,040 international dollars
HDI (2000): 0.928
GDP annual growth rate (2003): 0.2%
Annual inflation rate (2000): 1.7%
Labour force by occupation (2000): agriculture: 4%, industry: 24.5%, services: 71.5%
GDP by sector (2000): agriculture: 2.9%, industry: 26.2%, services: 70.9%
Gross public debt (2002): 59% of GDP
Unemployment rate (2002): 8.8%

Agriculture and fishing

Crops
bananas (2001): 431,964t
sugar beets (2002): 33,450,000t
wheat (2002): 38,934,000t
rape (2001): 2,906,000t
maize (2002): 16,460,000t
honey (2001): 18,251t
walnuts (2001): 28,000t
olives (2002): 20,700t
barley (2002): 10,988,000t
peaches (2002): 466,000t
apples (2001): 2,032,000t
potatoes (2002): 6,884,000t
grapes (2002): 6,782,000t
rice (2002): 130,000t
Livestock farming and fishing
cattle (2002): 20,552,000 head
horses (2001): 367,000 head
sheep (2002): 9,327,000 head
pigs (2002): 15,517,000 head
chickens (2002): 214,000,000 head
fish (1999): 899,000t

Energy generation and mining

bauxite (2001): 153,000t
nuclear electricity (2001): 400,900 million kWh
hydroelectricity (2001): 72,651 million kWh
total electricity (2001): 520,149 million kWh
iron (1998): 150,000t
natural gas (2002): 1,821 million m³
coal (2001): 1,809,000t
nickel (2001): 117,554t
oil (2002): 1,317,000t
uranium (2001): 124t

Industrial production

milk (2001): 25,629,000t
butter (2001): 445,000t
cheese (2001): 1,666,850t
meat (2001): 6,585,000t
sugar (2002): 5,425,000t
wine (2002): 51,999,000hl
tobacco (2001): 24,800t
steel (2003): 19,803,000t
cast iron (1998): 13,603,000t
aluminium (2001): 462,000t
lead (2001): 238,000t
zinc(2001): 347,000t
nickel (2000): 10,100t
synthetic rubber (1998): 606,000t
commercial vehicles (1997): 479,000 units
shipbuilding (1998): 13,000dwt
flax (2001): 75,000t
cotton yarn (1998): 94,000t
wool (2001): 22,000t
artificial textiles (1993): 2,000t
synthetic textiles (1999): 175,800t
paper (2000): 10,006,000t
timber (2000): 43,440,000m³

Tourism

Tourism revenue (2001): 29,979 million US$

Foreign trade

Exports (2002): 305,620 million US$
Imports (2002): 296,630 million US$

Defence

Armed forces (2001): 260,400 people
Defence budget (2001): 1.97% of GDP

Standard of living

Inhabitants per doctor (1996): 344
Average daily calorie intake (2000): 3,591 (FAO minimum: 2,400)
Cars per 1,000 inhabitants (2000): 476
Televisions per 1,000 inhabitants (2001): 632

HISTORY: KEY DATES

The first occupants of the territory of present-day France appeared around one million years ago. At the beginning of the first millennium BC, the Celts settled on Gallic soil.
58 BC–51 BC: Gaul was conquered by Julius Caesar's Roman legions.
AD 5c: as the Roman Empire declined, Germanic tribes including the Vandals and Visigoths invaded the country.

Franks and Merovingians

AD 486: Clovis, king of the Franks, conquered Gaul and founded the Merovingian dynasty.
AD 511: following the death of Clovis, his kingdom was divided amongst his descendents into three Merovingian kingdoms: Austrasia, Neustria and Burgundy. These three kingdoms fought each other.

The Carolingians

751: the Carolingian dynasty replaced the Merovingians when Pepin III, the Short became king of the Franks, uniting the three kingdoms.
800: the Frankish king Charlemagne was crowned Emperor of the West and reigned over most of Christian Europe (the Holy Roman Empire).
843: the Treaty of Verdun partitioned the empire into three kingdoms.

The Capetians

987: Hugh Capet became king and founded the Capetian Dynasty.
1226–70: Louis IX (Saint Louis) ruled France.
1337–1453: France fought against England in the Hundred Years' War. Following the victory of the English king, Henry V, at the battle of Agincourt (1415), England gained control of most of France. Charles VII

⇨

FRANCE

A map of France showing cities, geographical features, and places of interest.

Surrounding countries and regions:

UNITED KINGDOM · NETHERLANDS · BELGIUM · LUXEMBOURG · GERMANY · SWITZ. · ITALY · MONACO · ANDORRA · SPAIN

Bodies of water:

NORTH SEA · ENGLISH CHANNEL (LA MANCHE) · ATLANTIC OCEAN · MEDITERRANEAN SEA · Golfe de Gascogne · Golfe du Lion · Strait of Dover (Pas de Calais)

Selected cities (UK / Ireland area):

Birmingham · Cambridge · Oxford · Cardiff · Bristol · LONDON · Southend-on-Sea · Bournemouth · Southampton · Brighton · Plymouth · Portsmouth

Netherlands / Belgium / Germany:

'S-GRAVENHAGE · AMSTERDAM · Rotterdam · Antwerpen · BRUXELLES · Liège · LUXEMBOURG · Münster · Duisburg · Dortmund · Essen · Düsseldorf · Köln · Saarbrücken

French cities and places of interest:

Dunkerque (Dunkirk) · Calais · Boulogne-sur-Mer · Lille · Tourcoing · Roubaix · Villeneuve-d'Ascq · Valenciennes · Lens · Douai · Arras · Cambrai · Maubeuge · Amiens · Abbeville · Dieppe · Fécamp · Le Havre · Rouen · Beauvais · Compiègne · Laon · Charleville-Mézières · St-Quentin · Thionville · Verdun · Metz · Sarreguemines · Nancy · Strasbourg · Colmar · Mulhouse · Belfort · Épinal · Vittel · Chaumont · Troyes · Reims · Château-Thierry · Châlons-en-Champagne · Bar-le-Duc · St-Dizier · Langres · Vesoul · Montbéliard · Besançon · Dole · Lons-le-Saunier · PARIS · Versailles · Melun · Provins · Sens · Auxerre · Avallon · Dijon · Beaune · Chalon-s.-Saône · Mâcon · Bourg-en-Bresse · Autun · Nevers · Bourges · Vierzon · Orléans · Étampes · Chartres · Dreux · Évreux · Mantes · Évry · Bobigny · Créteil · Cergy · Nanterre · Boulogne-Billancourt

Cherbourg · C. de la Hague · Pte de Barfleur · B. de Seine · Deauville · Caen · Lisieux · St-Lô · Coutances · Avranches · Argentan · Alençon · Mont St-Michel · Granville · Golfe de St-Malo · St-Malo · Dinan · Dinard · St-Brieuc · Fougères · Lannion · Morlaix · Brest · Île d'Ouessant · Pte du Raz · Quimper · Pontivy · Lorient · Vannes · Belle-Île · Rennes · Laval · Le Mans · Châteaudun · Châteaubriant · St-Nazaire · Nantes · Angers · Cholet · Saumur · Tours · Blois · Chambord · Azay-le-Rideau · Chenonceaux · Loches · Châtellerault · Poitiers · Niort · Parthenay · Guéret · Châteauroux · Montluçon · Moulins · Vichy · Roanne

Île de Noirmoutier · Île d'Yeu · La Roche-sur-Yon · Les Sables-d'Olonne · Île de Ré · La Rochelle · Île d'Oléron · Rochefort · Saintes · Pointe de Grave · Angoulême · Limoges · Aubusson · Ussel · Tulle · Brive-la-Gaillarde · Périgueux · Bergerac · Lascaux Caves · Libourne · Pessac · Mérignac · Bordeaux · Langon · Agen · Montauban · Cahors · Figeac · Rodez · Millau · Albi · Castres · Toulouse · Carcassonne · Dax · Mont-de-Marsan · Auch · Pau · Tarbes · St-Gaudens · Foix · Limoux · Perpignan · Bayonne · Biarritz · P.N. des Pyrénées · Aneto 3 404 m

Clermont-Ferrand · Puy de Sancy 1 885 m · St-Flour · Aurillac · Le Puy-en-Velay · Mende · Florac · P.N. des Cévennes · Source of the Loire · St-Étienne · Privas · Valence · Aubenas · Montélimar · Die · Gorges du Tarn · Nîmes · Pont du Gard · Avignon · Alès · Montpellier · Béziers · Sète · Narbonne · Arles · Aix-en-Provence · Marseille · La Seyne-s.-Mer · Toulon · P.N. de Port-Cros · Îles d'Hyères · Brignoles · Digne-les-Bains · Grasse · Cannes · Antibes · Nice · MONACO · P.N. du Mercantour · P.N. des Écrins · Gap · Briançon · Grenoble · Vienne · Villeurbanne · Lyon · Mt Blanc 4 808 m · P.N. de la Vanoise · Chambéry · Annecy · Aosta · Torino · Thonon-les-Bains · Genève · Lausanne · Lac Léman · Sion · BERN

Regions:

HAUTE-NORMANDIE · BASSE-NORMANDIE · NORMANDIE (Normandy) · PICARDIE (PICARDY) · NORD-PAS-DE-CALAIS · ÎLE-DE-FRANCE · CHAMPAGNE-ARDENNE · LORRAINE · ALSACE · VOSGES · BRETAGNE (BRITTANY) · PAYS DE LA LOIRE · CENTRE · BOURGOGNE · FRANCHE-COMTÉ · JURA · ALPS (ALPES) · POITOU-CHARENTES · LIMOUSIN · AUVERGNE · RHÔNE · PROVENCE · CÔTE D'AZUR · AQUITAINE · LANDES · MIDI-PYRÉNÉES · MASSIF CENTRAL · LANGUEDOC-ROUSSILLON · Plateau de Millevaches · Plateau de Langres · Côte d'Azur · Bretagne · Carnac

Spain / Portugal:

Santander · Bilbao · Donostia-San Sebastián · Pamplona · Zaragoza · Burgos · MADRID · Barcelona · Tarragona · Lleida · SPAIN · Islas Baleares · Mallorca · Menorca · Cap de Creus

Inset:

CORSE (CORSICA) · C. Corse · Bastia · Calvi · Corte · Ajaccio · Sartène · Bonifacio · SARDEGNA (Italy)

Rivers / features labelled: Thames · Rhein (Rhin) · Rhône · Seine · Loire · Garonne · Dordogne · Duero · Ebro · Tajo (Tagus) · Gallego

224

France

Legend	
★	place of interest
	200 500 1000 2000 m
	motorway and expressway
	road
	railway line
✈	airport
	regional boundary
Tours	regional administrative centre
Chartres	departmental administrative centre
●	population over 1,000,000
●	population 500,000 to 1,000,000
●	population 100,000 to 500,000
•	population less than 100,000

50 km

∑»

HISTORY: KEY DATES

was aided by Joan of Arc, who led an army to break the English siege of Orleans in 1429. By 1453, the English were driven out of France.

1515–47: Francis I strengthened the powers of the monarchy and encouraged the development of the French Renaissance.

1572: at the height of the Wars of Religion that divided France, the Saint Bartholomew's Day Massacre – a widespread slaughter of Protestants – took place.

The Bourbons

1589–1610: Henry IV, who established the Bourbon Dynasty, ruled France.

1598: the Edict of Nantes guaranteed freedom of worship and civil equality, allowing Protestantism to become established throughout France.

1610–43: Louis XIII, with the close involvement of his minister Cardinal Richelieu, ruled France.

1643–1715: during the minority of Louis XIV, a class uprising threatened the royal authority. After the death of Cardinal Mazarin in 1661, Louis XIV ruled as an absolute monarch, revoking the Edict of Nantes in 1685 and persecuting the Huguenots.

1715–74: the reign of Louis XV, which began with the regency of Philip II of Orleans (1715–23), was marked by the disasters of the Seven Years' War and the loss of most of France's colonial empire to the Great Britain.

1774–89: Louis XVI was unable to resolve the social and economic crises of the 1780s.

The Revolution

1789: the Estates General combined its three houses into the National Assembly, abolishing feudal, aristocratic and clerical privileges.

1791–2: an attempt at the establishment of a constitutional monarchy under the Legislative Assembly failed, leading to the collapse of the monarchy.

1792–5: France was proclaimed a republic and a new national assembly, the National Convention, was established. The king, Louis XVI, was executed along with his queen, Marie Antoinette. A revolutionary government was instituted (June 1793–July 1794); the Jacobins instituted a dictatorship known as the Reign of Terror. The fall of its leader, Robespierre, led to the Thermidorian Reaction (July 1794–October 1795).

1795–9: the government of the Directory was established and retained power for four years.

The Consulate to the Second Empire

1799–1804: Napoleon Bonaparte came to power in the Brumaire Coup, which installed the Consulate.

1804–14: the First Empire. Napoleon Bonaparte crowned himself emperor of France, and was known as Napoleon I.

1814–15: the First Restoration. After the abdication of Napoleon Bonaparte, the Bourbons were restored. Louis XVIII granted a constitutional charter.

1815: Napoleon's attempt at a return to power during the Hundred Days ended when he was defeated at the Battle of Waterloo. He abdicated again.

1815–30: the Second Restoration. Charles X succeeded Louis XVIII in 1824.

1830–48: the July Monarchy. Louis-Philippe I became 'King of the French' or 'citizen king'.

1848–51: the Second Republic. Louis Napoleon Bonaparte was elected president on 10th December 1848. In 1851, after a coup ratified by a plebiscite, he instituted an authoritarian presidential regime.

1852–70: the Second Empire. Louis Napoleon Bonaparte became emperor under the name of Napoleon III.

The Third Republic to the present day

1870–1946: the Third Republic was proclaimed after the defeat of the empire during the Franco-German war. Its beginnings were marked by the revolutionary Paris Commune, and by the Dreyfus Affair.

1918: France emerged from World War I victorious, but very weak.

1936: the Popular Front coalition came to power in France and implemented major social reforms.

1939–45: in 1940, France was occupied by Germany. Marshal Philippe Pétain established the Vichy regime in the free zone. In 1944, the Allies landed on the Normandy beaches.

1946–58: the Fourth Republic. Wars with Indochina (1946–54) and Algeria (1954–62), and ministerial instability, undermined the regime.

1958: France became a member of the European Economic Community (EEC).

1958–95: the Fifth Republic was founded when Charles de Gaulle came to power, followed by Georges Pompidou in 1969, Valéry Giscard d'Estaing in 1974, François Mitterand in 1981 and Jacques Chirac in 1995.

GERMANY

The Federal Republic of Germany is one of the largest countries in western Europe, and is Europe's leading economic power. It is characterized by its complex geography. The north of the country consists mainly of plains, and is linked to Northern and in particular Central and Eastern Europe, while the south – which is more mountainous – borders on France, Switzerland and Austria.

Area: 357,022km²
Population (2002): 81,990,000
Capital: Berlin 3,319,000 (2001 e) including the suburbs
Government type and political system: republic with a parliamentary system
Head of state: (President of the Republic) Horst Köhler
Head of government: (Chancellor) Gerhard Schröder
Administrative structure: 16 Länder (federal states)
Official language: German
Currency: euro

DEMOGRAPHICS
Density: 230 inhab/km²
Percentage of population in urban areas (2001): 87.7%

Age structure of population (2000): 0–15 years: 15.5%, 15–65 years: 68.1%, over 65 years: 16.4%
Birth rate (2003): 8.7‰
Death rate (2003): 10.6‰
Infant mortality rate (2003): 4.5‰
Life expectancy at birth (2003): male: 75.2 years, female: 81.2 years

ECONOMY
GNP (2002): 1,876 billion US$
GNP per capita (2002): 22,740 US$
GNP per capita PPP (2002): 26,980 international dollars
HDI (2000): 0.925
GDP annual growth rate (2003): –0.1%
Annual inflation rate (2000): 1.95%
Labour force by occupation (2000): agriculture: 2.7%, industry: 33.4%, services: 63.9%
GDP by sector (2000): agriculture: 1.2%, industry: 31.5%, services: 67.3%
Gross public debt (2002): 60.8% of GDP
Unemployment rate (2002): 8.6%

Agriculture and fishing
Crops
oats (2001): 1,138,000t
sugar beets (2002): 26,794,000t
wheat (2002): 20,818,000t
rape (2001): 4,168,000t
barley (2002): 10,928,000t
apples (2001): 2,500,000t
potatoes (2002): 11,492,000t
grapes (2002): 1,425,000t
rye (2001): 5,158,000t
Livestock farming and fishing
cattle (2002): 14,227,000 head
horses (2001): 520,000 head
sheep (2002): 2,702,000 head
pigs (2002): 25,958,000 head
fish (1999): 312,000t

Energy generation and mining
nuclear electricity (2001): 162,640 million kWh
total electricity (2001): 544,828 million kWh
coal (2001): 26,583,000t
lignite (2001): 175,328,000t

Industrial production
milk (2001): 28,322,000t
butter (2001): 420,000t
meat (2001): 6,472,000t
sugar (2002): 4,380,000t
beer (2000): 103,257,000hl
wine (2002): 10,176,000hl
cast iron (1998): 30,215,000t
steel (2003): 44,841,000t
aluminium (2001): 652,000t
copper (2000): 710,000t
lead (2001): 374,000t
zinc (2001): 358,300t
cars (2002): 5,123,000 units
commercial vehicles (1998): 373,000 units
shipbuilding (1998): 1,204,000dwt
synthetic rubber (1998): 531,000t
cement (2001): 28,034,000t
cotton yarn (1998): 131,000t
artificial textiles (1999): 207,000t
synthetic textiles (1999): 763,400t
timber (2000): 51,088,000m³
paper (2000): 18,182,000t

Tourism
Tourism revenue (2001): 17,225 million US$

Foreign trade
Exports (2002): 615,020 million US$
Imports (2002): 492,840 million US$

Defence
Armed forces (2001): 296,000 people
Defence budget (2001): 1.17% of GDP

Standard of living
Inhabitants per doctor (1996): 294
Average daily calorie intake (2000): 3,451 (FAO minimum: 2,400)
Cars per 1,000 inhabitants (1999): 508
Televisions per 1,000 inhabitants (2001): 586

HISTORY: KEY DATES

Early origins
1ST MILLENNIUM BC: the Germanic peoples settled between the rivers Rhine and Vistula, displacing the Celts in Gaul. The expansion of the Roman Empire pushed them eastwards.
AD 5C–AD 6C: the Germanic Barbarians established a number of kingdoms, of which the Frankish kingdom was the most significant.
800: the Frankish king Charlemagne was crowned Emperor of the West and reigned over most of Christian Europe (the Holy Roman Empire).
843: the Treaty of Verdun partitioned the empire into three kingdoms: Louis the German received Francia Orientalis (the land east of the Rhine, now Germany).

The Holy Roman Empire of the German Nation
962: Otto I the Great founded the Holy Roman Empire of the German Nation.

1138–1250: the Swabian Dynasty (Hohenstaufen) with Frederick I Barbarossa and Frederick II, started a struggle between the Holy Roman Empire and the Papacy.
1273–1438: the imperial crown was passed on to the Habsburg dynasty, and then to the houses of Bavaria and Luxembourg.
1356: Charles IV of Luxembourg promulgated the Golden Bull, effectively the constitution of the Holy Roman Empire, which codified the procedures for imperial elections.
16c: the empire flourished under Maximilian I and Charles V. Martin Luther initiated the Protestant Reformation in 1517, leading to religious divisions and unrest within the country.
1618–48: the Thirty Years' War devastated Germany's population and economy, and was a significant setback

to attempts at unifying the country.
1648: the Peace of Westphalia confirmed how weak the imperial power had become.
18c: the kingdom of Prussia, ruled by the Hohenzollern, dominated Germany and became a major power under Frederick II.
1806: Napoleon I defeated Prussia at Jena and replaced the Holy Roman Empire with the Confederation of the Rhine, excluding Austria and Prussia.

German unity
1815: the Congress of Vienna created the German Confederation of 39 states, including Prussia and Austria.
1848–50: German national and liberal movements met with failure
1862–71: Otto von Bismarck, known as the Iron Chancellor, unified Germany. A German empire was proclaimed.

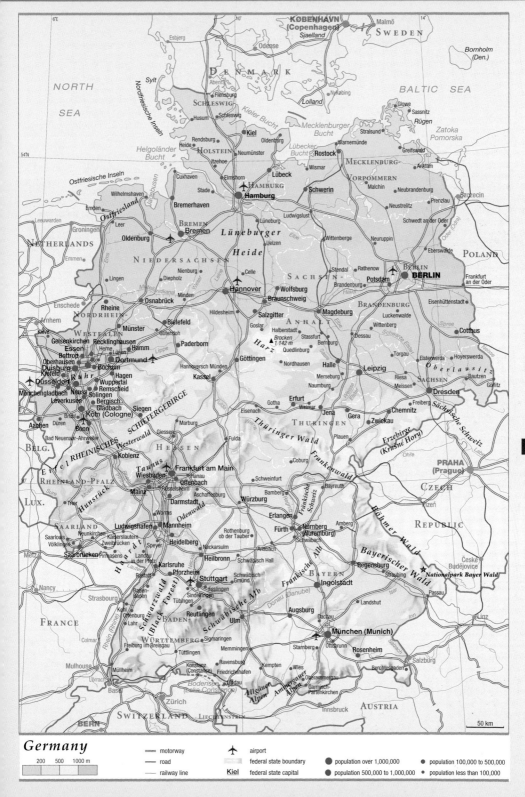

Germany

	200	500	1000 m		

═══	motorway	✈ airport
───	road	▦ federal state boundary
───	railway line	**Kiel** federal state capital

- ● population over 1,000,000
- ● population 500,000 to 1,000,000
- ● population 100,000 to 500,000
- · population less than 100,000

HISTORY: KEY DATES

1871–1914: great economic and political advances took place in Germany.
1918: World War I ended in defeat for Germany.

From Weimar to the Partition
1919–33: the democratic Weimar Republic crushed the Spartacists (a left-wing revolutionary faction). The humiliation caused by the Treaty of Versailles, the occupation of the Ruhr by France (1923–5) and the economic crisis combined to create favourable conditions for the rise of Nazism.
1933–4: Adolf Hitler, leader of the Nazi party, established a dictatorial and centralized state (the Third Reich).
1936: Hitler arranged the remilitarization of the Rhineland.
1938–9: Germany annexed Austria and part of Czechoslovakia, then attacked Poland; World War II began.
1945–9: after its defeat in World War II, Germany was occupied by Allied troops. Its border with Poland was marked in the east by the Oder–Neisse line.
1949: Germany was divided into the Federal Republic of Germany (the FRG, or West Germany) and, in the Soviet occupied zone, the German Democratic Republic (the GDR, or East Germany).

The Federal Republic of Germany
1949: the FRG, benefiting from American aid (the Marshall Plan), began a rapid economic recovery.
1955: the FRG became a member of the North Atlantic Treaty Organization (NATO).
1958: the FRG joined the European Economic Community (EEC).
1963: an Anglo-German Friendship and Co-operation Treaty was signed.
1969–74: having signed a treaty with the USSR and recognized the Oder–Neisse line as the Polish–German border (1970), the FRG signed the Basic Treaty with the GDR (1972), paving the way for the normalization of relations between the two German states.
1989: the FRG was faced with problems caused by a massive influx of East German refugees, and by changes that had occurred within the GDR.

The German Democratic Republic
The economic and political organization of the GDR was based on the Soviet model. It was governed by the Socialist Unity Party (SED).
1953: economic hardship led to a major uprising of workers in the GDR, starting in East Berlin and spreading through the country. Soviet intervention was required to suppress the revolt.
1955: the GDR joined the Warsaw Treaty Organization.
1961: the Berlin Wall was constructed between the eastern and western parts of the city, to reduce the numbers of East Germans emigrating to the FRG.
1972: the Basic Treaty was signed with the FRG, paving the way for the normalization of relations between the two German states.
1989: a mass exodus of East German citizens to the FRG, combined with significant demonstrations demanding the democratization of the East German regime, led to the resignation of the main SED leaders. The Berlin Wall was torn down, opening the border between the two German states.

Reunified Germany
1990: the economic and monetary unification of the FRG and the GDR occurred in July. In September, the Moscow Treaty (between East and West Germany, France, the UK, the USA and the USSR) established the borders of the united Germany, whose sovereignty was restored. The reunification of Germany was declared on 3 October 1990.

The Länder (Federal States)

The German word *Land* (plural *Länder*) is used to describe the 16 states that make up the Federal Republic of Germany.

state	area in km²	population*	capital
Baden-Württemberg	35 751	10 600 906	Stuttgart
Bayern	70 553	12 329 714	Munich
Berlin	889	3 388 434	Berlin
Brandenburg	29 059	2 593 040	Potsdam
Bremen	404	659 651	Bremen
Hamburg	753	1 726 363	Hamburg
Hessen	21 114	6 077 826	Wiesbaden
Mecklenburg-Vorpommern	23 838	1 759 877	Schwerin
Niedersachsen	47 344	7 956 416	Hannover
Nordrhein-Westfalen	34 070	18 052 092	Düsseldorf
Rheinland-Pfalz	19 847	4 049 066	Mainz
Saarland	2 568	1 066 470	Sarrbrücken
Sachsen	18 337	4 384 192	Dresden
Sachsen-Anhalt	20 445	2 580 626	Magdeburg
Schleswig-Holstein	15 727	2 804 249	Kiel
Thüringen	16 251	2 411 387	Erfurt

*2001 e

Greece – or the Hellenic Republic, as it is officially known – is a mountainous country, with Mount Olympus as its highest point (2,917m above sea level). Continental, peninsular (the Peloponnese) and insular (the Ionian Islands, Cyclades, Sporades, Dodecanese, Crete), it has a fragmented topography and limited expanses of plains and river basins. The climate is Mediterranean in the south, on the islands and in the coastal areas, but more continental in the north, where the winters can be harsh.

Area: 131,957km²
Population (2002): 10,631,000
Capital: Athens 772,072 (1991 census), 3,120,000 (2001 e) including the suburbs
Government type and political system: republic with a parliamentary regime.
Head of state: (President of the Republic) Constantine Stephanopoulos
Head of government: (Prime Minister) Kostas Karamanlis
Administrative structure: 13 administrative regions
Official language: Greek
Currency: euro

DEMOGRAPHICS
Density: 81 inhab/km²
Percentage of population in urban areas (2001): 60.4%
Age structure of population (2000): 0–15 years: 15.1%, 15–65 years: 67.3%, over 65 years: 17.6%
Birth rate (2003): 9.1‰
Death rate (2003): 10.5‰
Infant mortality rate (2003): 6.4‰
Life expectancy at birth (2003): male: 75.7 years, female: 80.9 years

ECONOMY
GNP (2002): 124 billion US$
GNP per capita (2002): 11,660 US$
GNP per capita PPP (2002): 18,770 international dollars
HDI (2000): 0.885
GDP annual growth rate (2003): 4.2%
Annual inflation rate (2000): 3.15%
Labour force by occupation (2000): agriculture: 17%, industry: 22.5%, services: 60.5%
GDP by sector (2000): agriculture: 7.6%, industry: 21.2%, services: 71.2%
Gross public debt (2002): 104.7% of GDP
Unemployment rate (2002): 10%

Agriculture and fishing
Crops
almonds (2001): 47,000t
wheat (2002): 2,076,000t
lemons (2002): 151,000t
maize (2002): 2,163,000t
honey (2001): 14,000t
hazelnuts (2001): 2,500t
walnuts (2001): 20,000t
olives (2002): 2,000,000t
oranges (2002): 1,165,000t
barley (2002): 273,000t
peaches (2002): 740,000t
grapes (2002): 1,000,000t
rice (2002): 169,000t
tomatoes (2002): 1,574,000t
Livestock farming and fishing
cattle (2002): 573,000 head
sheep (2002): 9,205,000 head
pigs (2002): 861,000 head
fish (1999): 216,000t

Energy generation and mining
bauxite (2001): 2,052,000t
total electricity (2001): 49,786 million kWh
hydroelectricity (2001): 1,906 million kWh
lignite (2001): 67,561,000t
nickel (2001): 20,800t
oil (2002): 189,000t
zinc (2001): 20,000t

Industrial production
cheese (2001): 236,200t
olive oil (2001): 422,000t
wine (2002): 5,000,000hl
tobacco (2001): 136,000t
steel (2003): 1,457,000t
aluminium (2001): 163,000t
nickel (2001): 20,800t
cotton yarn (2001): 442,000t
wool (2001): 9,600t

Tourism
Tourism revenue (2000): 9,221 million US$

Foreign trade
Exports (2002): 10,615 million US$
Imports (2002): 9,868 million US$

Defence
Armed forces (2001): 177,600 people
Defence budget (2001): 2.93% of GDP

Standard of living
Inhabitants per doctor (1994): 250
Average daily calorie intake (2000): 3,705 (FAO minimum: 2,400)
Cars per 1,000 inhabitants (1998): 254
Televisions per 1,000 inhabitants (2001): 519

HISTORY: KEY DATES

Ancient Greece
The earliest human settlements in the area that is now Greece date from the 7th millennium BC.
2000 BC–1500 BC: the Minoan civilization, centred on Crete, dominated the Aegean world.
c.1600 BC–c.1100 BC: the Mycenaean civilization succeeded the Minoans.
8c BC–6c BC: a system of city-states began to replace Greece's monarchic regime. Colonization progressed towards the West, the northern Aegean and the Black Sea.
490 BC–449 BC: the Greeks fought the Persians in the Persian Wars, forcing them to retreat to Asia Minor.
431 BC–404 BC: in the Peloponnesian War, Athens was defeated by Sparta.
371 BC–362 BC: the city-state of Thebes defeated Sparta and established its hegemony over continental Greece.
359 BC–336 BC: Philip II of Macedonia extended his rule over the Greek city-states.
336 BC–323 BC: Alexander the Great, ruler of Greece, conquered the Persian Empire.
323 BC–168 BC: after the division of Alexander's empire, Greece was given to the Antigonid kings of Macedonia, who were fighting against Rome.
146 BC: Greece became a Roman province.

Byzantine Greece
AD 395: Greece became part of the Byzantine empire.
1204–61: the fourth crusade ended in the temporary disintegration of the Byzantine empire, which was restored in 1261.
14c–15c: the Venetians, Genoese and Catalans fought over possession of Greece, while the Ottoman Turks occupied Thracia, Thessalia and Macedonia.
1456: the Ottomans conquered Athens and the Peloponnese.

Modern Greece
18c: a nationalist movement developed in Greece.
1827–30: Britain, France and Russia supported Greece in a war of independence against the Ottomans. An autonomous Greek state was created and recognized by Turkey under the Treaty of Adrianople.
1912–13: after the Balkan Wars, Greece obtained most of Macedonia, the south of Epirus, Crete and the islands of Samos, Chio, Mytilene and Lemnos.
1917: Greece joined World War I alongside the Allies.
1921–2: the Greco-Turkish War ended in defeat for Greece.
1924: a Greek republic was proclaimed; a period of economic and political instability followed.

➩

GREECE

230

The Republic of Hungary is a landlocked state that lies in the Danube basin between the Alps and the Carpathian Mountains. The Danube separates the Great Plain in the east – the Nagyalföld – from the western part of the country, Transdanubia, which is hillier, with the Bakony Mountains rising to the north of Lake Balaton. Hungary has a continental climate.

Hungary

100 200 500 m

★ place of interest
═══ motorway
── road
── railway line

● population over 1,000,000
● population 100,000 to 1,000,000
● population 50,000 to 100,000
• population less than 50,000

Area: 93,032km²
Population (2002): 9,867,000
Capital: Budapest 1,812,000 (2001 e)
Government type and political system: republic with a parliamentary system
Head of state: (President of the Republic) Ferenc Mádl
Head of government: (Prime Minister) Ferenc Gyurcsany
Administrative structure: 19 counties, 20 urban counties and the capital city
Official language: Hungarian
Currency: forint

DEMOGRAPHICS

Density: 108 inhab/km²
Percentage of population in urban areas (2001): 64.8%
Age structure of population (2000): 0–15 years: 16.9%, 15–65 years: 68.5%, over 65 years: 14.6%
Birth rate (2003): 8.8‰
Death rate (2003): 13.5‰
Infant mortality rate (2003): 8.8‰
Life expectancy at birth (2003): male: 67.7 years, female: 76 years

ECONOMY

GNP (2002): 54 billion US$
GNP per capita (2002): 5,290 US$
GNP per capita PPP (2002): 13,070 international dollars
HDI (2000): 0.835
GDP annual growth rate (2003): 2.9%
Annual inflation rate (2000): 9.79%
Labour force by occupation (2000): agriculture: 6.7%, industry: 34.5%, services: 58.8%
GDP by sector (2000): agriculture: 4.4%, industry: 34.2%, services: 61.4%
Gross public debt (2002): 56.3% of GDP
Unemployment rate (2002): 5.6%

Agriculture and fishing

Crops
sugar beets (2002): 2,274,000t
wheat (2002): 3,910,000t
maize (2002): 6,121,000t

barley (2002): 1,046,000t
potatoes (2002): 752,000t
Livestock farming and fishing
cattle (2002): 783,000 head
sheep (2002): 1,136,000 head
pigs (2002): 4,822,000 head
fish (1999): 19,500t

Energy generation and mining

bauxite (2001): 1,000,000t
nuclear electricity (2001): 13,420 million kWh
total electricity (2001): 34,385 million kWh
natural gas (2002): 3,106 million m³
oil (2002): 1,641,000t
uranium (1999): 10t

Industrial production

milk (2001): 2,184,000t
cheese (2001): 89,240t
sugar (2002): 378,000t
wine (2002): 3,800,000hl

steel (2003): 1,989,000t
cast iron (1998): 1,259,000t
aluminium (2001): 35,000t
cement (2001): 3,500,000t
cotton yarn (1998): 220,000t
synthetic textiles (1996): 25,000t

Tourism

Tourism revenue (2001): 3,933 million US$

Foreign trade

Exports (2002): 34,792 million US$
Imports (2002): 36,911 million US$

Defence

Armed forces (2001): 33,400 people
Defence budget (2001): 1.59% of GDP

Standard of living

Inhabitants per doctor (1995): 270
Average daily calorie intake (2000): 3,458 (FAO minimum: 2,400)
Cars per 1,000 inhabitants (1999): 238
Televisions per 1,000 inhabitants (2000): 437

231

HISTORY: KEY DATES

Early origins to Béla III

c.500 BC: present-day Hungary was inhabited by the Illyrians and the Thracians.
35 BC–AD 9: the country was conquered by Rome.
AD 4c–6c: a series of nomadic groups including the Huns, Ostrogoths, Lombards and Avars settled in the region.
896: under the leadership of their chief, Árpád, the Magyars conquered most of Hungary.

The Habsburgs

1526: the Habsburg monarch Ferdinand of Austria claimed the Hungarian throne.
1699: the Peace of Kalowitz granted most of Hungary to Austria.
1703–11: following a Hungarian rebellion against the Habsburgs, Austria recognized Hungarian autonomy.

Hungary since 1918

1918: Mihály Károlyi proclaimed Hungary's independence.
1941–5: Hungary joined World War II alongside the Axis powers. It was occupied by the Soviet army.
1949: Matyas Rákosi proclaimed the Hungarian People's Republic and imposed a Stalinist regime.
1956–8: a national uprising against the Stalinist regime took place; it was violently suppressed by Soviet troops.
1989: the Hungarian Socialist Workers' Party ceased to control the country, and the Communist party congress was dissolved.
1999: Hungary became a member of the North Atlantic Treaty Organization (NATO).
2004: Hungary became a member of the European Union (EU).

ICELAND

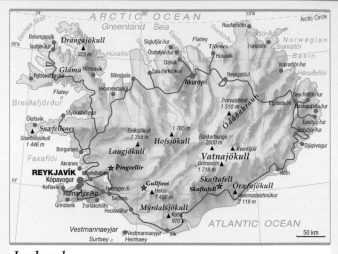

Iceland

glacier	200	600	1000 m	— road	⬤ population over 100,000
				★ place of interest	⬤ population 10,000 to 100,000
					⬤ population less than 10,000

The Republic of Iceland is an island state lying between the northern Atlantic Ocean and the Arctic Ocean. Located on a geological 'hot spot' on the Mid-Atlantic Ridge, Iceland is a country of glaciers (which cover one-tenth of the island) and has many active volcanoes. Although most of the country lies just south of the Arctic Circle, the climate is relatively warm due to the influence of the Gulf Stream. Over half of the island's population lives in the capital, Reykjavik.

Area: 103,000km²
Population (2002): 283,000
Capital: Reykjavik 175,000 (2001 e) including the suburbs
Government type and political system: republic with a semi-presidential system
Head of state: (President of the Republic) Ólafur Ragnar Grímsson
Head of government: (Prime Minister) Halldor Asgrimsson
Administrative structure: 9 regions
Official language: Icelandic
Currency: króna

DEMOGRAPHICS

Density: 3 inhab/km²
Percentage of population in urban areas (2001): 92.6%
Age structure of population (2000): 0–15 years: 23.3%, 15–65 years: 65%, over 65 years: 11.7%
Birth rate (2003): 14.1‰
Death rate (2003): 6.9‰
Infant mortality rate (2003): 3.4‰
Life expectancy at birth (2003): male: 77.6 years, female: 81.9 years

ECONOMY

GNP (2002): 7.94 billion US$
GNP per capita (2002): 27,960 US$
GNP per capita PPP (2002): 29,240 international dollars
HDI (2000): 0.936
GDP annual growth rate (2003): 4%
Annual inflation rate (2000): 5.16%
Labour force by occupation (2000): agriculture: 8.3%, industry: 23%, services: 68.7%
GDP by sector (1997): agriculture: 9.4%, industry: 28.2%, services: 62.4%
Gross public debt (2002): 44.8% of GDP
Unemployment rate (2002): 3.3%

Agriculture and fishing

Crops
potatoes (2002): 8,800t
Livestock farming and fishing
cattle (2002): 67,000 head
horses (2001): 78,000 head
sheep (2002): 469,000 head
pigs (2002): 44,000 head
fish (1999): 1,740,000t

Energy generation

total electricity (2001): 7,894 million kWh
hydroelectricity (2001): 6,512 million kWh

Industrial production

milk (2001): 108,000t
butter (2001): 1,600t
cheese (2001): 4,860t
aluminium (2001): 243,000t
wool (2001): 1,000t
cement (2001): 155,000t

Tourism

Tourism revenue (2001): 335 million US$

Foreign trade

Exports (2002): 2,229 million US$
Imports (2002): 2,095 million US$

Defence

Armed forces (2001): 5,330 people
Defence budget (2001): 0.25% of GDP

Standard of living

Inhabitants per doctor (1994): 333
Average daily calorie intake (2000): 3,342 (FAO minimum: 2,400)
Cars per 1,000 inhabitants (2000): 568
Televisions per 1,000 inhabitants (2000): 509

HISTORY: KEY DATES

c.870: Norse settlers began to colonize Iceland.
930: the Althing, or 'assembly of free men', thought to be the world's oldest parliament, was established in Iceland.
1000: Christianity was introduced to the country.
12c–13c: Iceland developed as a feudal state, and was divided by civil wars. Norwegian intervention led to a period of rule by King Haakon IV of Norway.
1380: Both Iceland and Norway came under Danish rule.
1550: the Lutheran Reformation, led by

Christian III, imposed Lutheranism by force throughout Iceland.
1602: Denmark established a private trading company with a monopoly over all Icelandic trade, to the detriment of the Icelandic economy.
18c: volcanic eruptions, disease and famine decimated Iceland's population.
1874: the island was granted limited autonomy by Denmark.
1918: Iceland became fully independent under a treaty of union with Denmark, which retained control only over the island's foreign affairs.

1944: the Republic of Iceland was proclaimed, and all ties with Denmark were cut.
1949: Iceland became a member of the North Atlantic Treaty Organization (NATO).
1958–61 AND 1975–6: the 'Cod Wars', a series of disputes over fishing rights, took place between Iceland and Great Britain.
2001: Iceland announced its intention to resume commercial whale hunting after a gap of more than ten years, despite an International Whaling Commission (IWC) moratorium.

IRELAND

Ireland has a mild, damp climate. High hills and moderately high mountains line its coasts, and in the centre of the country is a vast peaty plain, dotted with lakes and drained by the River Shannon.

Area: 70,273km²
Population (2002): 3,878,000
Capital: Dublin 481,854 (1996 census), 993,000 (2001 e) including the suburbs
Government type and political system: republic with a semi-presidential system
Head of state: (President of the Republic) Mary McAleese
Head of government: (Prime Minister) Bertie Ahern
Administrative structure: 4 provinces
Official languages: English and Irish Gaelic
Currency: euro

DEMOGRAPHICS

Density: 53 inhab/km²
Percentage of population in urban areas (2001): 59.3%
Age structure of population (2000): 0–15 years: 21.6%, 15–65 years: 67.1%, over 65 years: 11.3%
Birth rate (2003): 14.4‰
Death rate (2003): 8.3‰
Infant mortality rate (2003): 5.8‰
Life expectancy at birth (2003): male: 74.4 years, female: 79.6 years

ECONOMY

GNP (2002): 90 billion US$
GNP per capita (2002): 23,030 US$
GNP per capita PPP (2002): 29,570 international dollars
HDI (2000): 0.925
GDP annual growth rate (2003): 1.4%
Annual inflation rate (2000): 5.56%
Labour force by occupation (2000): agriculture: 7.9%, industry: 28.6%, services: 63.5%
GDP by sector (2000): agriculture: 3.6%, industry: 41.4%, services: 55%
Gross public debt (2002): 32.2% of GDP

Ireland

★ place of interest	— road
	─ railway line
✈ airport	
	provincial boundary

100   200 m

- population over 500,000
- population 100,000 to 500,000
- population 50,000 to 100,000
- population less than 50,000

30 km

Unemployment rate (2002): 4.3%

Agriculture and fishing

Crops
oats (2001): 121,000t
sugar beets (2002): 1,313,000t
wheat (2002): 867,000t
barley (2002): 963,000t
potatoes (2002): 519,000t
Livestock farming and fishing
cattle (2002): 6,408,000 head
horses (2001): 70,000 head
sheep (2002): 4,807,000 head
pigs (2002): 1,763,000 head
fish (1999): 330,000t

Energy generation and mining
total electricity (2001): 23,525 million kWh
natural gas (2002): 801 million m³
hydroelectricity (2001): 550 million kWh
lead (2001): 44,500t
zinc (2001): 225,000t

Industrial production
milk (2001): 5,416,000t
butter (2001): 129,300t

cheese (2001): 93,750t
sugar (2002): 215,000t
meat (2001): 1,013,000t
steel (2001): 150,000t
lead (2000): 12,000t
cotton yarn (1998): 21,000t
wool (2001): 12,000t
synthetic textiles (1999): 109,700t

Tourism
Tourism revenue (2001): 3,547 million US$

Foreign trade
Exports (2002): 85,830 million US$
Imports (2002): 50,931 million US$

Defence
Armed forces (2001): 10,460 people
Defence budget (2001): 0.61% of GDP

Standard of living
Inhabitants per doctor (1996): 476
Average daily calorie intake (2000): 3,613 (FAO minimum: 2,400)
Cars per 1,000 inhabitants (1998): 296
Televisions per 1,000 inhabitants (2000): 399

233

IRELAND

HISTORY: KEY DATES

Early origins

4c BC: a Celtic population, the Gaels, settled on Irish soil. The numerous small kingdoms that were founded joined together in five large political units.

AD 2c: the kings of Connacht asserted their pre-eminence.

AD 432–AD 461: Saint Patrick evangelized Ireland.

6c–7c: Irish monks established major abbeys and monasteries in Ireland as well as in England, Scotland and Wales.

7c–11c: Ireland was occupied by the Scandinavians.

1014: Ireland's king, Brian Boru (who won the Battle of Clontarf), halted the expansion of the Scandinavians.

English rule

1175: the English king Henry II established his sovereignty over Ireland.

1541: Henry VIII became king of Ireland. When the Irish rebelled against his religious reforms, he redistributed Irish territory amongst English people. These seizures continued under Edward VI and Elizabeth I.

17c–18c: Irish rebellions against England became more frequent, and were supported by the Spanish and the French.

1649: Oliver Cromwell led the Drogheda Massacre, a bloody repression of the Irish which was followed by a general despoliation of Irish land.

1690: James II was defeated at the Battle of the Boyne by William III. Ireland was then completely dominated by the English aristocracy.

1796–8: the Irish rebelled, influenced by the American and French revolutions.

1800: William Pitt the Younger proclaimed the union of Ireland and England.

1829: the great Irish statesman Daniel O'Connell, known as 'the Liberator', headed a political movement to force the British to pass the Irish Emancipation Act, which allowed Catholics to serve in the British parliament.

1846–8: the Great Irish Famine led to mass emigration (notably to the USA) and depopulated the country.

1902: Arthur Griffith, a journalist, founded a movement called Sinn Féin, meaning 'ourselves alone', advocating self-government for Ireland.

1916: a national uprising was harshly repressed.

Independent Ireland

1921: the Anglo-Irish Treaty gave Ireland independent dominion status as the Irish Free State, with full internal self-government rights. The treaty partitioned the north-east of the country from the rest of the island. This area (Northern Ireland) remained part of the United Kingdom.

1922: a civil war began between the provisional Irish government and those who opposed the partitioning of the country.

1937: a new constitution was adopted, and Ireland adopted the Gaelic name of Éire.

1948: Éire became the Republic of Ireland and withdrew from the Commonwealth of Nations.

1973: Ireland became a member of the European Economic Community (EEC).

1985: an Anglo-Irish agreement on the management of Northern Irish affairs was signed, giving the Republic of Ireland a consultative role in the government of Northern Ireland.

1993–4: the Northern Ireland peace process was relaunched.

1999: in accordance with an agreement signed in 1998, a regional assembly was established in Northern Ireland.

ITALY

The Italian Republic stretches over more than 10° of latitude between the Alps and the Mediterranean Sea and thus has very varied landscapes, with a predominance of hills (42% of the country) over mountains (35%) and plains (23%). Italy has three distinct geographical regions. In the north, the southern slopes of the Alps tower over the great plain of the River Po valley (50,000 km²), which stretches from Turin to Venice towards the Adriatic Sea. In the south of Italy, from Liguria to Calabria, the Appennines form the backbone of the country. In central Italy, mountains are surrounded by hills, plateaux and alluvial plains. The climate is only truly Mediterranean in central and southern Italy (including the islands), since the climate is harsher in the Alps and more continental in the plain of the River Po valley.

Area: 301,318km²
Population (2002): 57,450,000
Capital: Rome 2,655,970 (2000 e)
Government type and political system: republic with a parliamentary system
Head of state: (President of the Republic) Carlo Azeglio Ciampi
Head of government: (Prime Minister) Silvio Berlusconi
Administrative structure: 20 regions
Official language: Italian
Currency: euro

DEMOGRAPHICS
Density: 190 inhab/km²
Percentage of population in urban areas (2001): 67.1%
Age structure of population (2000): 0–15 years: 14.3%, 15–65 years: 67.6%, over 65 years: 18.1%
Birth rate (2003): 8.8‰
Death rate (2003): 10.9‰
Infant mortality rate (2003): 5.4‰
Life expectancy at birth (2003): male: 75.5 years, female: 81.9 years

ECONOMY
GNP (2002): 1,101 billion US$
GNP per capita (2002): 19,080 US$
GNP per capita PPP (2002): 26,170 international dollars
HDI (2000): 0.913
GDP annual growth rate (2003): 0.3%
Annual inflation rate (2000): 2.54%
Labour force by occupation (2000): agriculture: 5.4%, industry: 32.4%, services: 62.2%
GDP by sector (2000): agriculture: 2.9%, industry: 29.2%, services: 67.9%
Gross public debt (2002): 106.7% of GDP
Unemployment rate (2002): 9%

Agriculture and fishing
Crops
sugar beets (2002): 12,726,000t
wheat (2002): 7,529,000t
lemons (2002): 486,000t
maize (2002): 10,824,000t
mandarin oranges (1998): 505,000t
hazelnuts (2001): 120,000t
olives (2002): 2,732,000t
oranges (2002): 1,724,000t
peaches (2002): 1,587,000t
apples (2001): 2,255,000t
potatoes (2002): 2,075,000t
grapes (2002): 7,394,000t
rice (2002): 1,371,000t
soya beans (2002): 566,000t
tomatoes (2002): 5,748,000t
Livestock farming and fishing
cattle (2002): 7,395,000 head
goats (2001): 1,375,000 head
sheep (2002): 10,952,000 head
pigs (2002): 8,410,000 head
fish (1999): 541,000t

Energy generation and mining
total electricity (2001): 258,841 million kWh
natural gas (2002): 15,050 million m³
hydroelectricity (2000): 47,691 million kWh
oil (2002): 4,517,000t

Industrial production
milk (2001): 13,048,000t
cheese (2001): 1,020,712t
olive oil (2001): 558,000t
sugar (2002): 1,532,000t
tobacco (2001): 130,000t
meat (2001): 4,163,000t
wine (2002): 44,604,000hl
steel (2003): 26,740,000t
aluminium (2001): 187,000t
cast iron (1998): 10,704,000t
lead (2001): 203,000t
zinc (2001): 177,800t
cars (2002): 1,126,000 units
commercial vehicles (1998): 272,000 units
shipbuilding (1998): 284,000dwt
cotton yarn (1998): 230,000t
wool (2001): 10,504t
artificial textiles (1999): 25,900t
synthetic textiles (1999): 582,900t
cement (2001): 39,804,000t
synthetic rubber (1991): 300,000t
paper (2000): 9,129,000t

Tourism
Tourism revenue (2001): 25,787 million US$

Foreign trade
Exports (2002): 253,680 million US$
Imports (2002): 237,147 million US$

Defence
Armed forces (2001): 216,800 people
Defence budget (2001): 1.45% of GDP

Standard of living
Inhabitants per doctor (1996): 181
Average daily calorie intake (2000): 3,661 (FAO minimum: 2,400)
Cars per 1,000 inhabitants (1999): 545
Televisions per 1,000 inhabitants (2000): 494

235

HISTORY: KEY DATES

Antiquity
Italy has been inhabited since the 3rd millennium BC.
8c BC: the Etruscans settled between the River Po and the Campania. The Greeks set up trading posts on the southern coasts.
4c BC: the Celts occupied the plain of the River Po Valley.
4c BC–2c BC: Rome (founded by Romulus and Remus in 753 BC, according to legend) benefited from the divisions between the different peoples who progressively tried to conquer the whole peninsula. After Rome's victory over Carthage, it dominated the whole of the western Mediterranean.
58 BC–51 BC: under Julius Caesar, Italy conquered Gaul.

42 BC: Octavian (who later became known as Augustus) incorporated Cisalpine Gaul into Italy.
27 BC–AD 5c: after Octavian, Italy was the centre of a vast empire. Christianity, introduced in the 1c and persecuted for many years, triumphed in the 4c when Rome became the seat of the papacy.

The Middle Ages
AD 5c: barbarian invasions reduced the Western Roman Empire to Italy, which was itself not spared (Sacks of Rome, 410 and 476).
6c: Italy developed around three centres: Milan, centre of the Lombard Kingdom, Ravenna, under Byzantine rule, and the pontifical territory around Rome.
8c: the Pope sought aid from the Franks

to halt the Lombards' advances. The Frankish king Charlemagne became king of the Lombards in 774, before being crowned Holy Roman Emperor in 800.
10c: Italy became part of the Holy Roman Empire.
1075–1122: the Investiture Conflict ended in the Papacy's victory over the Holy Roman Empire.
1122–1250: when the conflict between Rome and the Empire was revived, disputes arose in the cities between the guelfs (supporters of the Pope) and the Ghibellines (supporters of the emperor).
1309–76: the papacy was forced to leave Rome and move to Avignon.
1378–1417: the papacy was weakened by the Great Western Schism.

↘

GERMANY

FRANCE

SLOVAKIA

Bratislava

WIEN (Vienna)

BUDAPEST

AUSTRIA

HUNGARY

München

Salzburg

Bodensee

Basel

Zürich

VADUZ

LIECHTENSTEIN

BERN

SWITZ.

Innsbruck

Brenner Pass

Pécs

Balaton

SLOVENIA

LJUBLJANA

ZAGREB

CROATIA

Passo dello Stelvio

Merano

Bolzano

Cortina d'Ampezzo

TRENTINO ALTO ADIGE

Belluno

Feltre

FRIULI VENEZIA GIULIA

Tarvisio Pass

Udine

Gorizia

Trieste

Gulf of Trieste

Rijeka

Istra

BOSNIA-HERZEGOVINA

SARAJEVO

Great St Bernard Pass

Simplon Tunnel

Mt Blanc 4 808 m

Mte Cervin 4 478 m

C. du Pt St. Bernard

Gran Paradiso 4 061 m

Fréjus Tunnel

Mte Viso 3 841 m

Lago Maggiore

Verbania

Varese

Como

Lecco

Sondrio

LOMBARDIA

Bergamo

Brescia

VENETO

Trento

Vicenza

Verona

Padova (Padua)

Mestre

Treviso

Venezia (Venice)

Gulf of Venice

FR.

MONACO

Aosta

D'AOSTA

Biella

Ivrea

Novara

Milano (Milan)

Monza

Gorgonzola

Bardolino

Stresa

Vercelli

Vigevano

Pavia

Lodi

Cremona

Sesto S. Giovanni

Villafranca di Verona

Este

Rovigo

Chioggia

Adige

Po Delta

Susa

Pinerolo

Torino (Turin)

Moncalieri

Casale Monferrato

Alessandria

Piacenza

Mantova (Mantua)

Ferrara

Valli di Comacchio

Saluzzo

C. de Larche

Cuneo

Savona

Novi Ligure

Parma

Reggio nell'Emilia

Modena

Bologna

Imola

Ravenna

EMILIA ROMAGNA

Rapallo

Riviera di Levante

Massa

La Spezia

Pistoia

Prato

Faenza

Forlì

Cesena

Rimini

SAN MARINO

ADRIATIC SEA

Imperia

San Remo

Bordighera

Ventimiglia

LIGURIAN SEA

Golfo di Genova

Riviera di Ponente

Genova (Genoa)

LIGURIA

Viareggio

Lucca

Pisa

Livorno

Firenze (Florence)

Fiesole

Urbino

Pesaro

Fano

Senigallia

Ancona

Jesi

Macerata

Loreto

MARCHE

S. Benedetto del Tronto

Split

Zadar

Dalmacija

Dubrovnik

Corse

Ajaccio

Bastia

Arcipelago Toscano

Isola di Montecristo

Isola d'Elba

Piombino

Portoferraio

Colline Metallifere

Mte Amiata 1 734 m

Grosseto

San Gimignano

Volterra

Siena

Chiusi

Gubbio

Assisi

Perugia

TOSCANA

UMBRIA

Foligno

Orvieto

Terni

Spoleto

Rieti

Ascoli Piceno

Teramo

Pescara

ABRUZZO

Isole Tremiti

Lago di Lesina

Lago di Varano

Gargano

S. Severo

Manfredonia

Golfo di Manfredonia

Isola Asinara

Golfo dell'Asinara

Porto Torres

Sassari

Olbia

Costa Smeralda

Isola Caprera

Tarquinia

Civitavecchia

Cerveteri

Necropolis

VATICAN CITY

ROMA (Rome)

Fiumicino

Ostia

Mentana

Tivoli

Subiaco

Anagni

Frosinone

LAZIO

L'Aquila

Avezzano

Parco Nazionale d'Abruzzo

Gran Sasso d'Italia

Chieti

Vasto

MOLISE

Isernia

Campobasso

Foggia

Barletta

Andria

Molfetta

Bari

Bitonto

Monopoli

Martina Franca

PUGLIA

Potenza

Matera

Brindisi

Lecce

Salentino

Otranto

Alghero

SARDEGNA (SARDINIA)

Nuoro

Gennargentu 1 834 m

Oristano

Golfo di Oristano

Isola di San Pietro

Cagliari

Golfo di Cagliari

Isola di Sant'Antioco

C. Spartivento

TYRRHENIAN SEA

Anzio

Latina

Gaeta

Golfo di Gaeta

Capua

Caserta

Benevento

Avellino

Hercolaneum

Pompei

Salerno

Portici

Napoli (Naples)

Golfo di Salerno

Amalfi

Paestum

CAMPANIA

Isole Ponziane

Isola d'Ischia

Torre del Greco

Torre Annunziata

Capri

Sorrento

Vesuvio 1 281 m

Mte Cassino

Pozzuoli

Golfo di Policastro

BASILICATA

Mte Pollino 2 271 m

Golfo di Taranto

Taranto

Sybaris Copia

Rossano

C. Santa Maria di Leuca

Cosenza

CALABRIA

La Sila 1 929 m

Crotone

IONIAN SEA

Nicastro

Golfo di Santa Eufemia

Catanzaro

Golfo di Squillace

Vibo Valentia

Appennino

Stromboli

Isole Lipari

Isola di Ustica

Palermo

Cefalù

Isola Vulcano

Messina

Stretta di Messina

Aspromonte 1 956 m

Reggio di Calabria

Taormina

Acireale

Catania

Augusta

Trapani

Erice

Isola Favignana

Monreale

Segesta

Marsala

Mazara del Vallo

SICILIA (SICILY)

Selinonte

Caltanissetta

Enna

Piazza Armerina

Gela

Etna 3 345 m

Siracusa (Syracuse)

Agrigento

Licata

Ragusa

Modica

Avola

Pantelleria

C. Passero

Malta Strait

MALTA

VALLETTA

MEDITERRANEAN SEA

Bizerte

C. Bon

TUNIS

TUNISIA

Annaba

ALGERIA

50 km

Legend

▲ volcano

200 400 1000 2000 m

motorway

road

railway line

✈ airport

★ place of interest

provincial boundary

Bari regional capital

Lecce provincial admin. centre

● population over 1,000,000

● pop. 500,000 to 1,000,000

● pop. 100,000 to 500,000

• pop. less than 100,000

HISTORY: KEY DATES

15c: a new power, the Duchy of Savoy, emerged in the north. The Italian Renaissance reached its height in the cities.

The decline of the 16c to the Risorgimento
1494–1559: the Wars of Italy led to the establishment of Spanish rule over the peninsula.
1713: Italy was ruled by the Habsburgs of Austria.
1792–9: France annexed Savoy and Nice, and occupied the Republic of Genoa.
1802–4: Napoleon Bonaparte conquered the whole peninsula, and proclaimed an 'Italian Republic' in the north.
1805–14: the republic, which eventually became the kingdom of Italy, was ruled by Napoleon, who was crowned king of Italy; the kingdom of Naples was occupied in 1806.

1846–9: an upsurge of liberalism and nationalism, the Risorgimento, was suppressed by Austria. However, the Piedmont region, with Victor Emmanuel II and his minister Cavour, obtained support from France.
1860: Savoy and Nice were returned to France. Revolutionary movements in central Italy and in Naples ended in union with the Piedmont region.
1861: the kingdom of Italy was proclaimed, with Victor Emmanuel II of Sardinia as its sovereign.
1866: Venice became part of the kingdom.

The kingdom of Italy to the present day
1900: Victor Emmanuel III came to the throne.
1915–18: Italy took part in World War I alongside the Allies.

1922: Benito Mussolini came to Rome and established a fascist regime.
1929: the Lateran Treaty between Italy and the Vatican created the Vatican State.
1935–6: Italy conquered Abyssinia (Ethiopia), which became an Italian colony and, along with Eritrea and Somalia, formed the Italian African Empire.
1943: Mussolini, having aligned his forces with those of Germany in 1940, took refuge in the north, where he constituted the Republic of Salo. He was arrested and shot in 1945.
1944: Victor Emmanuel III abdicated.
1946: the Italian Republic was proclaimed.
1958: Italy became a member of the European Economic Community (EEC).

237

The regions of Italy

region	area (in km²)	population*	capital or adm. centre	provinces
Abruzzo	10 798	1 243 690	L'Aquila	4 (L'Aquila, Chieti, Pescara and Teramo)
Basilicata	9 992	605 940	Potenza	2 (Matera and Potenza)
Calabria	15 080	2 037 686	Catanzaro	5 (Catanzaro, Cosenza, Crotone, Reggio di Calabria and Vibo Valentia)
Campania	13 595	5 589 587	Naples	5 (Avellino, Benevento, Caserta, Napoli and Salerno)
Emilia-Romagna	22 124	3 899 170	Bologna	9 (Bologna, Ferrara, Forli-Cesena, Modena, Parma, Piacenza, Ravenna, Reggio nell'Emilia and Rimini)
Friuli-Venezia Giulia	7 855	1 193 520	Trieste	4 (Gorizia, Trieste, Udine and Pordenone)
Lazio	17 203	5 031 230	Rome	5 (Frosinone, Latina, Rieti, Roma and Viterbo)
Liguria	5 421	1 668 078	Genoa	4 (Genova, Imperia, Savona and La Spezia)
Lombardy	23 850	8 882 000	Milan	11 (Bergamo, Brescia, Como, Cremona, Lecco, Lodi, Mantova, Milano, Pavia, Sondrio and Varese)
Marche	9 694	1 427 666	Ancona	4 (Pesaro e Urbino, Ancona, Macerata and Ascoli Piceno)
Molise	4 438	327 893	Campobasso	2 (Campobasso and Isernia)
Piedmont	25 399	4 290 412	Turin	8 (Alessandria, Biella Asti, Cuneo, Novara, Turin, Verbano-Cusio-Ossola and Vercelli)
Puglia	19 362	3 986 430	Bari	5 (Bari, Brindisi, Foggia, Lecce and Taranto)
Sardinia	24 090	1 637 705	Cagliari	4 (Cagliari, Nuoro, Oristano and Sassari)
Sicily	25 708	4 961 383	Palermo	9 (Agrigento, Caltanisetta, Catania, Enna, Messina, Palermo, Ragusa, Siracusa and Trapani)
Tuscany	22 997	3 510 114	Florence	10 (Arezzo, Firenze, Grosseto, Livorno, Lucca, Massa Carrara, Pisa, Pistoia Prato and Siena)
Trentino-Alto Adige	13 607	886 914	Trento	2 (Trento and Bolzano)
Umbria	8 456	804 054	Perugia	2 (Perugia and Terni)
Valle d'Aosta	3 263	115 397	Aosta	1 (Aosta)
Veneto	18 391	4 363 157	Venice	7 (Belluno, Padova, Rovigo, Treviso, Venice, Verona and Vicenza)

*2000 e

The Republic of Lithuania is the largest of the Baltic States and the one with the highest number of inhabitants. Unlike its neighbours, Lithuania has always maintained strong links with the rest of Europe. It lies in a region of hills covered in moraine (ice-worn rocks), and is largely made up of farmland and forest dotted with lakes and small plains.

Lithuania

⭐ place of interest	— motorway
100 200 m	— road
	— railway line
	✈ airport

● population over 500,000
● population 100,000 to 500,000
● population 50,000 to 100,000
• population less than 50,000

Area: 65,200km²
Population (2002): 3,681,000
Capital: Vilnius 554,800 (2001 census)
Government type and political system: republic with a semi-presidential system
Head of state: (President of the Republic) Valdas Adamkus
Head of government: (Prime Minister) Algirdas Brazauskas
Administrative structure: 10 counties
Official language: Lithuanian
Currency: Lithuanian litas

DEMOGRAPHICS

Density: 56 inhab/km²
Percentage of population in urban areas (2001): 68.7%
Age structure of population (2000): 0–15 years: 19.5%, 15–65 years: 67.1%, over 65 years: 13.4%
Birth rate (2003): 8.7‰
Death rate (2003): 11.6‰
Infant mortality rate (2003): 8.7‰
Life expectancy at birth (2003): male: 67.5 years, female: 77.6 years

ECONOMY

GNP (2002): 12.7 billion US$
GNP per capita (2002): 3,670 US$
GNP per capita PPP (2002): 10,190 international dollars
HDI (2000): 0.808
GDP annual growth rate (2003): 9%
Annual inflation rate (2000): 1.01%
Labour force by occupation (2001): agriculture: 16.3%, industry: 27.6%, services: 56.1%
GDP by sector (2000): agriculture: 7.6%, industry: 32.9%, services: 59.5%
Gross public debt (2002): 22.7% of GDP
Unemployment rate (2002): 13.8%

Agriculture and fishing
Crops
sugar beets (2002): 1,052,000t
wheat (2002): 1,218,000t
barley (2002): 871,000t

potatoes (2002): 1,531,000t
rye (2001): 260,000t
Livestock farming and fishing
cattle (2002): 752,000 head
sheep (2002): 12,300 head
chickens (2002): 6,580,000 head
pigs (2002): 1,011,000 head
fish (1999): 35,200t

Energy generation
nuclear electricity (2001): 11,362 million kWh
total electricity (2001): 14,617 million kWh

Industrial production
sugar (2002): 150,000t
flax (2001): 7,200t

Tourism
Tourism revenue (2001): 384 million US$

Foreign trade
Exports (2002): 6,028.4 million US$
Imports (2002): 7,343.3 million US$

Defence
Armed forces (2001): 13,510 people
Defence budget (2001): 1.4% of GDP

Standard of living
Inhabitants per doctor (1996): 250
Average daily calorie intake (2000): 3,040 (FAO minimum: 2.400)
Cars per 1,000 inhabitants (2000): 334
Televisions per 1,000 inhabitants (2000): 422

HISTORY: KEY DATES

c.5c AD: Balto-Slavic tribes in the region were united by their resistance to Scandinavian invasion.
c.1240: Mindaugas founded the Grand Duchy of Lithuania.
1385–6: Lithuania formed an alliance with Poland; the Grand Duke of Jagellon became the king of Poland under the name of Ladislas II.
1392–1430: under Vytautas (who reigned over the Grand Duchy under the suzerainty of his cousin Ladislas II), Lithuania extended its territory as far as the Black Sea.
1569: the Union of Lublin created a Polish–Lithuanian state.
1795: the Russian empire annexed most of the country.
1915–18: Lithuania was occupied by Germany.

1918: Lithuania proclaimed its independence.
1920: Soviet Russia recognized Lithuania's independence.
1940: in accordance with a German–Soviet pact, Lithuania was annexed by the USSR.
1941–4: Lithuania was occupied by Germany.
1944: Lithuania became a Soviet Republic again.
1991: Lithuania's independence, proclaimed in 1990, was recognized by the international community.
1993: the last remaining Russian (Soviet) troops left Lithuania.
2004: Lithuania joined both the North Atlantic Treaty Organization (NATO) and the European Union (EU).

Ösling, the northern region of the Grand Duchy of Luxembourg, is part of the Ardennes Plateau, which is mainly covered with forests and cut through by steep-sided valleys (Sûre). It has been largely left undeveloped because of the unfavourable natural conditions. In the southern part of the country (Gutland), which is a prolong-ation of the French region, Lorraine, the fertility of the soils and the milder climate have favoured a boom in various types of agriculture and cattle farming.

Area: 2,586km²
Population (2002): 447,000
Capital: Luxembourg 76,687 (2000 census)
Government type and political system: constitutional monarchy with a parliamentary system
Head of state: (Grand Duke) Henri
Head of government: (Prime Minister) Jean-Claude Juncker
Administrative structure: 3 administrative districts
Official languages: French, German, Lëtzebuergesch
Currency: euro

DEMOGRAPHICS

Density: 167 inhab/km²
Percentage of population in urban areas (2001): 91.8%
Age structure of population (2000): 0–15 years: 18.7%, 15–65 years: 66.9%, over 65 years: 14.4%
Birth rate (2003): 12.6‰
Death rate (2003): 8.2‰
Infant mortality rate (2003): 5.4‰
Life expectancy at birth (2003): male: 75.1 years, female: 81.4 years

ECONOMY

GNP (2002): 17.5 billion US$
GNP per capita (2002): 39,470 US$
GNP per capita PPP (2002): 53,290 international dollars
HDI (2000): 0.925
GDP annual growth rate (2003): 1.2%
Annual inflation rate (2000): 3.15%
Labour force by occupation (2000): agriculture: 1.9%, industry: 23.9%, services: 74.2%
GDP by sector (2000): agriculture: 0.7%, industry: 20.8%, services: 78.5%
Gross public debt (2002): 5.7% of GDP
Unemployment rate (2002): 2.8%

Luxembourg

	district boundary
Diekirch	district capital
motorway	railway line
road	airport
●	population over 50,000
●	population 10,000 to 50,000
•	population less than 10,000

200 500 m · 10 km

Agriculture and fishing
The data for Luxembourg are included in those given for Belgium.

Energy generation
total electricity (2001): 457 million kWh

Industrial production
steel (2003): 2,670,000t
cement (2001): 750,000t

Tourism
Tourism revenue (1998): 309 million US$

Foreign trade
Exports (2002): 9,609 million US$

Imports (2002): 11,772 million US$

Defence
Armed forces (2001): 900 people
Defence budget (2001): 0.77% of GDP

Standard of living
Inhabitants per doctor (1993): 455
Average daily calorie intake (2000): 3,701 (FAO minimum: 2,400)
Cars per 1,000 inhabitants (2000): 602
Televisions per 1,000 inhabitants (2001): 663

241

HISTORY: KEY DATES

963: the County of Luxembourg was created in the heart of the Holy Roman Empire as a result of the partitioning of Lotharingia.
1354: Charles IV of Luxembourg elevated the county to a duchy.
1441: Philip the Good, the Duke of Burgundy, ruled Luxembourg.
1506: Luxembourg became a possession of the Habsburgs of Spain.
1714: under the Treaty of Rastatt, Luxembourg was ceded to Austria.
1795: France annexed Luxembourg.
1815: the Congress of Vienna made Luxembourg a grand duchy, personally linked to the king of the Netherlands, and a member of the German Confederation.
1831: the western half of the Grand Duchy of Luxembourg became Belgian (the Province of Luxembourg).
1867: the Treaty of London made

Luxembourg a neutral, independent state, guaranteed by major world powers.
1890: the crown passed to the Nassau family.
1912: following the repeal of the Salic Law, Marie-Adélaïde became Grand Duchess.
1914–18: Luxembourg was occupied by Germany.
1919: Charlotte of Nassau became Grand Duchess and established a democratic constitution.
1940–4: Germany occupied Luxembourg again.
1958: Luxembourg became a member of the European Economic Community (EEC).
1964: Jean became Grand Duke of Luxembourg.
2000: Jean abdicated in favour of his son, Henri.

MACEDONIA (FYROM)

Macedonia (FYROM)

—	road
—	railway line
★	place of interest

●	population over 400,000
●	population 50,000 to 400,000
●	population 30,000 to 50,000
•	population less than 30,000

200 500 1000 2000 m

The Former Yugoslav Republic of Macedonia is a landlocked, mountainous country. River basins or valleys (such as the Vardar valley) cut through its hills and mountains. Arable land accounts for around 24% of the country. The fact that Macedonia is landlocked has caused the country economic problems, since its nearest and most accessible port is Thessaloniki in Greece. A two-year Greek trade blockade from 1994–5 forced Macedonia to obtain oil for fuel through Bulgaria by truck, leading to serious fuel shortages in Macedonia that crippled the economy.

Area: 25,713km²
Population (2002): 2,051,000
Capital: Skopje 437,000 (2001 e) including the suburbs
Government type and political system: republic with a semi-presidential system
Head of state: (President of the Republic) Branko Crvenkovski
Head of government: (Prime Minister) Hari Kostov
Administrative structure: 123 municipalities
Official languages: Macedonian and Albanian
Currency: Macedonian denar

DEMOGRAPHICS
Density: 79 inhab/km²
Percentage of population in urban areas (2001): 59.5%
Age structure of population (2000): 0–15 years: 22.6%, 15–65 years: 67.4%, over 65 years: 10%
Birth rate (2003): 14.5‰
Death rate (2003): 8.4‰
Infant mortality rate (2003): 16‰
Life expectancy at birth (2003): male: 71.4 years, female: 75.8 years

ECONOMY
GNP (2002): 3.49 billion US$
GNP per capita (2002): 1,710 US$
GNP per capita PPP (2002): 6,420 international dollars
HDI (2000): 0.772
GDP annual growth rate (2003): 3.1%
Annual inflation rate (1999): −1.26%
Labour force by occupation: n/a
GDP by sector (2000): agriculture: 11.8%, industry: 33.1%, services: 55.1%
Gross public debt: n/a

Unemployment rate (2002): 31.9%

Agriculture
Crops
sugar beets (2002): 43,800t
wheat (2002): 267,000t
maize (2002): 140,000t
barley (2002): 128,000t
potatoes (2002): 183,000t
grapes (2002): 119,000t
Livestock farming
cattle (2002): 259,000 head
sheep (2002): 1,234,000 head
pigs (2002): 196,000 head
chickens (2002): 2,900,000 head

Energy generation
copper (2001): 10,000t
total electricity (2001): 6,465 million kWh
lead (2001): 20,000t
zinc (2001): 65,000t

Industrial production
wine (2002): 447,000hl
sugar (2002): 4,600t
lead (2001): 25,000t
zinc (2001): 12,000t

Tourism
Tourism revenue (2001): 23 million US$

Foreign trade
Exports (2002): 1,110.5 million US$
Imports (2002): 1,878.1 million US$

Defence
Armed forces (2001): 12,300 people
Defence budget (2001): 2.48% of GDP

Standard of living
Inhabitants per doctor (1995): 435
Average daily calorie intake (2000): 3,006 (FAO minimum: 2,400)
Cars per 1,000 inhabitants (1996): 142
Televisions per 1,000 inhabitants (2000): 282

HISTORY: KEY DATES
356 BC–336 BC: Philip II led the Macedonian kingdom to its peak, and imposed his hegemony over Greece.
336 BC–323 BC: Alexander the Great conquered Egypt and the East.
323 BC–276 BC: after the death of Alexander the Great, his generals (the Diadochi) fought over Macedonia.
276 BC–168 BC: the Antigonids ruled the country.
168 BC: the Roman victory at the Battle of Pydna put an end to Macedonian independence.
148 BC: Macedonia became a Roman province.
AD 4c: Macedonia became part of the Eastern Roman Empire.
7c: the Slavs occupied the region.
9c–14c: the Byzantines, Bulgarians and Serbians fought over the country.
1371–1912: Macedonia was part of the Ottoman Empire.
1912–13: the first Balkan War liberated Macedonia from the Turks.
1913: Serbia, Greece and Bulgaria disputed the division of their joint conquests in Macedonia during the second Balkan War.
1915–18: the Allies carried out a campaign in Macedonia against Austrian–German–Bulgarian forces.
1945: the Republic of Macedonia was created within the Federal Republic of Yugoslavia.
1991: Macedonia became independent.
1993: Macedonia became a member of the North Atlantic Treaty Organization (NATO), and was renamed the Former Yugoslav Republic of Macedonia.

MALTA

Malta

★ place of interest
200   500 m

— road
✈ airport

● population over 10,000
● population less than 10,000

Strategically situated in the centre of the Mediterranean between Europe and North Africa, the Republic of Malta is an archipelago that comprises two main islands, Malta and Gozo, a smaller island, Comino, and two tiny islets. The island of Malta is made up of rocky, low-lying limestone plateaux. The country has a mild climate with winter rains, allowing a wide variety of crops to flourish.

Area: 316km²
Population (2002): 394,000
Capital: Valletta 82,000 (2001 e) including the suburbs
Government type and political system: republic with a parliamentary system
Head of state: (President of the Republic) Edward Fenech Adami (known as Eddie Fenech Adami)
Head of government: (Prime Minister) Lawrence Gonzi
Administrative structure: no divisions
Official languages: English, Maltese
Currency: Maltese lira

DEMOGRAPHICS
Density: 1,230 inhab/km²
Percentage of population in urban areas (2001): 91.2%
Age structure of population (2000): 0–15 years: 20.2%, 15–65 years: 67.4%, over 65 years: 12.4%
Birth rate (2003): 11.8‰
Death rate (2003): 7.9‰

Infant mortality rate (2003): 7.1%
Life expectancy at birth (2003): male: 75.9 years, female: 80.7 years

ECONOMY
GNP (2002): 3.68 billion US$
GNP per capita (2002): 9,260 US$
GNP per capita PPP (2002): 17,710 international dollars
HDI (2000): 0.875
GDP annual growth rate (2003): 1.3%
Annual inflation rate (2000): 2.37%
Labour force by occupation (2001): agriculture: 2.2%, industry: 31.8%, services: 66%
GDP by sector (1993): agriculture: 3.2%, industry: 34.9%, services: 61.9%
Gross public debt (2002): 66.4
Unemployment rate (2002): 6.8%

Agriculture and fishing
Crops
potatoes (2002): 27,500t
grapes (2002): 1,200t
Livestock farming and fishing
cattle (2002): 18,000 head
sheep (2002): 6,600 head
pigs (2002): 79,000 head
chickens (2002): 1,000,000 head
fish (1999): 3,040t

Energy generation
total electricity (2001): 1,768 million kWh

Tourism
Tourism revenue (2001): 580 million US$
Foreign trade
Exports (2002): 2,243.8 million US$
Imports (2002): 2,653 million US$
Defence
Armed forces (2001): 2,140 people
Defence budget (2001): 0.72% of GDP
Standard of living
Inhabitants per doctor (1993): 400
Average daily calorie intake (2000): 3,543 (FAO minimum: 2,400)
Cars per 1,000 inhabitants (2000): 485
Televisions per 1,000 inhabitants (2001): 566

HISTORY: KEY DATES
4TH MILLENNIUM BC–2ND MILLENNIUM BC: Malta was the centre of a Megalithic civilization.
9c BC: Malta became a Phoenician trading post. It was then occupied by the Greeks (8c) and the Carthaginians (6c).
218 BC: the Romans annexed Malta.
870: the Arabs occupied the island.
1090: Roger I of Sicily took control of Malta, establishing a link with the kingdom of Sicily that lasted until the 16c.
1530: Charles V ceded the island to the Knights Hospitaller on the condition that they resisted the Ottoman invasion.
1798: Napoleon Bonaparte occupied Malta.
1800–15: captured by the British during the Napoleonic Wars, Malta became a strategic base and, in 1815, a British Crown Colony.
1940–3: Malta played a decisive role in the Mediterranean during World War II.
1964: Malta became independent within the framework of the Commonwealth of Nations.
1974: Malta became a republic.
2004: Malta became a member of the European Union (EU).

243

The Knights Hospitaller

The full official name of this order is the Sovereign Military Order of St John of Jerusalem of Rhodes and of Malta, but it is also known as the Order of Malta, the Knights of Malta or the Knights of Rhodes. It began as a Benedictine nursing order from the St John Hospital in Jerusalem, which was founded around 1070.

When the Crusades reached Jerusalem in 1099, the Knights Hospitaller constituted a religious order whose rules served as a model to other hospitaller orders. After Acre was captured, the order settled in Cyprus (1191), Rhodes (1309) and then Malta (1530), where it remained until the island was taken by Napoleon Bonaparte in 1798. Divided into eight languages (or nations), the order was then placed under the rule of a great elected master on whom around 600 commanderies depended. He settled in Rome in 1834 and established a new constitution, approved by the Holy See. Today, the 10,000 members of this Catholic lay order mainly carry out charitable work in leper hospitals, general hospitals, health centres and ambulances. Non-Catholic branches exist in Germany, Scandinavia and the Netherlands.

MOLDOVA

The Republic of Moldova is a landlocked, hilly country in Eastern Europe that has extremely fertile alluvial plains, a mild humid climate, sufficient water for irrigation and environmental conditions that are favourable for agriculture.

Area: 33,851km²
Population (2002): 4,273,000
Capital: Chişinău 662,000 (2001 e)
Government type and political system: republic with a semi-presidential system
Head of state: (President of the Republic) Vladimir Voronin
Head of government: (Prime Minister) Vasile Tarlev
Administrative structure: 10 districts, 1 autonomous territory and 1 municipality
Official language: Moldovan (Romanian)
Currency: Moldovan leu

DEMOGRAPHICS

Density: 129 inhab/km²
Percentage of population in urban areas (2001): 41.7%
Age structure of population (2000): 0–15 years: 23.1%, 15–65 years: 67.6%, over 65 years: 9.3%
Birth rate (2003): 11.5‰
Death rate (2003): 10.7‰
Infant mortality rate (2003): 18.1‰
Life expectancy at birth (2003): male: 65.5 years, female: 72.2 years

ECONOMY

GNP (2002): 1.68 billion US$
GNP per capita (2002): 460 US$
GNP per capita PPP (2002): 1,600 international dollars

Moldova

— road
-- railway line
✈ airport
200 m

● population over 500,000
● population 100,000 to 500,000
● population 50,000 to 100,000
• population less than 50,000

HDI (2000): 0.701
GDP annual growth rate (2003): 6.3%
Annual inflation rate (2000): 31.29%
Labour force by occupation (2001): agriculture: 51%, industry: 13.9%, services: 35.1%
GDP by sector (2000): agriculture: 28%, industry: 20%, services: 52%
Gross public debt: n/a
Unemployment rate (2002): 6.8%

Agriculture

Crops
oats (2001): 3,200t
sugar beets (2002): 1,116,000t
wheat (2002): 1,122,000t
maize (2002): 1,193,000t
hazelnuts (2001): 850t
barley (2002): 220,000t
potatoes (2002): 325,000t
grapes (2002): 660,000t
tobacco (2001): 15,100t

Energy generation
total electricity (2001): 3,394 million kWh

Industrial production
sugar (2002): 115,000t

wine (2002): 2,100,000hl
tobacco (2001): 15,100t
steel (2003): 875,000t

Tourism
Tourism revenue (2001): 46 million US$

Foreign trade
Exports (2002): 659.8 million US$
Imports (2002): 1,038.1 million US$

Defence
Armed forces (2001): 7,210 people
Defence budget (2001): 0.4% of GDP

Standard of living
Inhabitants per doctor (1996): 278
Average daily calorie intake (2000): 2,763 (FAO minimum: 2,400)
Cars per 1,000 inhabitants (1999): 54
Televisions per 1,000 inhabitants (2001): 296

HISTORY: KEY DATES

1538: Bessarabia, which made up most of Moldova, was annexed by the Ottoman Empire.
1812: Bessarabia was ceded to Russia.
1918: following the Bolshevik Revolution, Bessarabia declared its independence from Russia and united with Romania.
1924: the Soviets created the Moldavan Autonomous Soviet Socialist Republic on the east bank of the River Dniester within Ukraine.
1940: the Soviets annexed Bessarabia, the southern part of which was part of Ukraine. The rest of Bessarabia and part of the Moldovian Autonomous Soviet Socialist Republic formed the Moldovian Soviet Socialist Republic within the USSR.
1941–4: the Moldavian Soviet Socialist Republic was occupied by Romania, which was allied to Germany.
1991: Moldova declared its independence and became a member of the Commonwealth of Independent States (CIS).
1994: the possibility of uniting Moldova and Romania was rejected by a referendum. A new constitution granted special autonomy status to Transdniester and the Gagauz region, and declared Moldovan to be the country's official language.

244

Comprising four 'quartiers' or districts (Fontvieille, La Condamine, Monaco-Ville and Monte-Carlo), the Principality of Monaco is a microstate whose steep, rocky terrain does not permit any kind of agricultural use.

Area: 2km²
Population (2002): 30,000
Government type and political system: constitutional monarchy
Head of state: (Prince) Rainier III
Head of government: (Minister of State) Patrick Leclercq
Administrative structure: no divisions
Official language: French
Currency: euro

DEMOGRAPHICS

Density: 16,798 inhab/km²
Percentage of population in urban areas (2001): 100%
Age structure of population: n/a
Birth rate: n/a
Death rate: n/a
Infant mortality rate: n/a
Life expectancy at birth: n/a

ECONOMY

GNP: n/a
GNP per capita: n/a
GNP per capita PPP: n/a
HDI: n/a
GDP annual growth rate: n/a
Annual inflation rate: n/a
Labour force by occupation: n/a
GDP by sector: n/a
Gross public debt: n/a
Unemployment rate: n/a
Tourism
Tourism revenue: n/a
Foreign trade
Exports: n/a
Imports: n/a
Defence
Armed forces: n/a
Defence budget: n/a

Monaco

| | built-up area | | green space | | building |

Standard of living
Inhabitants per doctor: n/a
Average daily calorie intake: n/a

Cars per 1,000 inhabitants (1996): 528
Televisions per 1,000 inhabitants (1995): 750

HISTORY: KEY DATES

A Phoenician colony in antiquity, Monaco was then ruled by the Greek colony of Marseilles. It was known as Monoikos, and later (to the Romans) as Monoecus.
1297: the Grimaldi family won control of the city of Monaco. Control of the city was a contentious issue, and the Grimaldis did not secure full possession of Monaco until 1419.
1512: France recognized Monaco's independence.
1542–1641: Monaco was under Spanish protection.
1641–1793: Monaco was under French

protection.
1793: France formally annexed Monaco.
1815: Monaco became a protectorate of the kingdom of Sardinia.
1861: Monaco became a French protectorate.
1911: a liberal regime replaced the absolutist regime.
1949: Rainier III became prince of Monaco.
1962: Prince Rainier III liberalized the constitution.
1993: Monaco became a member of the United Nations.

Situated on the North Sea, the Kingdom of the Netherlands is a mainly flat country. Around 20% of its total area – the polders (reclaimed land) – is situated below sea level, and is separated from the sea by an extensive system of dykes. The climate is oceanic, mild and humid for its relatively high latitude, with a high level of precipitation (700–800mm on average per annum) throughout the year, creating favourable conditions for agriculture.

Area: 41,526 km²
Population (2002): 15,990,000
Capital: Amsterdam 734,594 (2001 e), 1,105,000 (2001 e) including the suburbs
Government type and political system: constitutional monarchy with a parliamentary system
Head of state: (Queen) Beatrix
Head of government: (Prime Minister) Jan Peter Balkenende
Administrative structure: 12 provinces
Official language: Dutch
Currency: euro

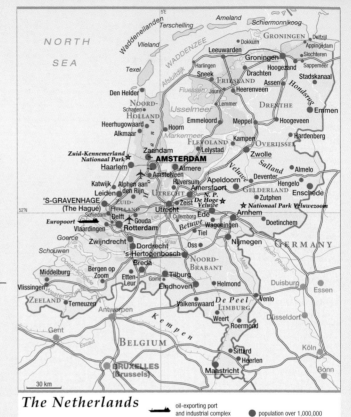

The Netherlands

✈ airport	oil-exporting port and industrial complex	● population over 1,000,000
▬ motorway	★ place of interest	● population 100,000 to 1,000,000
0 m	▬ road	● population 30,000 to 100,000
	▬ railway line	Zwolle provincial capital	● population less than 30,000

— provincial boundary

246

DEMOGRAPHICS

Density: 464 inhab/km²
Percentage of population in urban areas (2001): 89.6%
Age structure of population (2000): 0–15 years: 18.3%, 15–65 years: 68.1%, over 65 years: 13.6%
Birth rate (2003): 12.1‰
Death rate (2003): 8.9‰
Infant mortality rate (2003): 4.5‰
Life expectancy at birth (2003): male: 75.6 years, female: 81 years

ECONOMY

GNP (2002): 378 billion US$
GNP per capita (2002): 23,390 US$
GNP per capita PPP (2002): 28,350 international dollars
HDI (2000): 0.935
GDP annual growth rate (2003): –0.8%
Annual inflation rate (2000): 2.52%
Labour force by occupation (2000): agriculture: 3.3%, industry: 21.3%, services: 75.4%
GDP by sector (2000): agriculture: 2.7%, industry: 27.2%, services: 70.1%
Gross public debt (2002): 52.4% of GDP

Unemployment rate (2002): 2.7%

Agriculture and fishing
Crops
sugar beets (2002): 6,250,000t
wheat (2002): 1,057,000t
flax (2001): 25,600t
barley (2002): 315,000t
potatoes (2002): 7,363,000t
Livestock farming and fishing
cattle (2002): 3,858,000 head
sheep (2002): 1,186,000 head
pigs (2002): 11,648,000 head
chickens (2002): 101,000,000 head
fish (1999): 624,000t

Energy generation
nuclear electricity (2001): 3,777 million kWh
total electricity (2001): 88,315 million kWh
natural gas (2002): 75,555 million m³
oil (2002): 3,073,000t

Industrial production
butter (2001): 125,000t
milk (2001): 10,500,000t
cheese (2001): 660,000t

beer (2000): 20,143,000hl
steel (2003): 6,587,000t
aluminium (2001): 294,000t
zinc (2001): 204,800t
cars (2002): 182,000 units
commercial vehicles (1998): 40,000 units
shipbuilding (2001): 164,000dwt
cotton yarn (1996): 3,000t
synthetic rubber (2001): 188,000t

Tourism
Tourism revenue (2001): 6,722 million US$

Foreign trade
Exports (2001): 202,947 million US$
Imports (2001): 204,507 million US$

Defence
Armed forces (2001): 49,580 people
Defence budget (2001): 1.49% of GDP

Standard of living
Inhabitants per doctor (1991): 398
Average daily calorie intake (2000): 3,294 (FAO minimum: 2,400)
Cars per 1,000 inhabitants (1999): 383
Televisions per 1,000 inhabitants (2001): 553

HISTORY: KEY DATES

Early origins to the Spanish period

Megalithic monuments and Bronze Age burial mounds provide proof of a prehistoric human presence in the area of the Netherlands.

57 BC: Julius Caesar conquered the country, which was inhabited by Celtic and Germanic tribes.

15 BC: the province of Belgian Gaul (the Roman region of Gallia Belgica) occupied the territory that would later become the Netherlands.

AD 4c: Saxon invaders settled in the east of the country, while Franks occupied the southern territories.

10c–12c: weakened in the 9c by Norman invasions and territorial divisions (Treaty of Verdun, 843), the country was divided into a large number of feudal principalities.

15c: through purchases, marriages and inheritances, the Dukes of Burgundy gradually united all of the Low Countries (the present-day Netherlands and Belgium).

1477: following the death of Charles the Bold, the last Duke of Burgundy, and the marriage of his daughter to Maximilian of Austria, the country became a possession of the Habsburg dynasty.

1515: Charles V increased the number of provinces to seventeen and annexed them all to the Burgundian Circle of the Empire (1548). The ideas of the Reformation spread across the country.

The Netherlands from the 16c to the 18c

1566: the politics of the absolutist Philip II, who was hostile to Protestants, led to uprisings in Flanders, Hainaut and the northern provinces.

1568–73: a rebellion in Holland and Zeeland, led by William of Orange, was soon followed by similar uprisings in other provinces.

1579: the southern provinces, mainly Catholic, came under Spanish rule and formed the Union of Arras. The northern provinces, mainly Calvinist, proclaimed the Union of Utrecht, which laid the foundations for the United Provinces of the Netherlands.

1648: the independence of the United Provinces of the Netherlands was recognized by Spain, who nevertheless kept control of the southern provinces.

1714: Austria gained control of the Spanish Netherlands.

1795: France annexed the Spanish Netherlands; the United Provinces of the Netherlands became the Batavian Republic.

The kingdom of the Netherlands to the present day

1815: the Congress of Vienna reunited all the provinces in the kingdom of the United Netherlands. William I became king.

1839: William I recognized Belgium's independence, which was proclaimed in 1830.

1890: Queen Wilhelmina acceded to the Dutch throne.

1914–18: the Dutch remained neutral during World War I.

1940–5: Germany occupied the Netherlands.

1948: Wilhelmina abdicated in favour of her daughter, Juliana.

1949: Indonesia became independent from the Netherlands.

1958: the Netherlands became a member of the European Economic Union (EEC).

1980: Queen Beatrix acceded to the throne.

The Delta Plan

The Delta Plan's gigantic hydraulic engineering works were carried out from 1958–86 in order to link the islands of South Holland (Voorne, Overflakkee) with those of Zeeland (Schouwen, Noord-Beveland and Walcheren) by dykes. Conceived after a disastrous tidal wave in 1953, the Delta Plan's most important aim was to prevent flooding. It has allowed for the creation of freshwater reserves, the improvement of road links, the development of inland navigation between the river Escaut and the Rhine, the growth of regional tourist potential and, to a certain extent, the creation of new polders.

Occupying the western part of the Scandinavian Peninsula, the Kingdom of Norway stretches over 1,500km from north to south. It is a rugged, mountainous country (except in the north, where plateaus predominate) and is covered with forests. The coastline is jagged, cut by long, narrow, steep-sided fjords on which Norway's main cities, Oslo, Bergen, Trondheim and Stavanger, are located.

Area: 323,877km²
Population (2002): 4,506,000
Capital: Oslo 512,589 (2002 e), 787,000 (2001 e) including the suburbs
Government type and political system: constitutional monarchy with a parliamentary system
Head of state: (King) Harald V
Head of government: (Prime Minister) Kjell Magne Bondevik
Administrative structure: 19 counties and 2 metropolitan regions
Official language: Norwegian
Currency: Norwegian krone

DEMOGRAPHICS

Density: 14 inhab/km²
Percentage of population in urban areas (2001): 75%
Age structure of population (2000): 0–15 years: 19.8%, 15–65 years: 64.8%, over 65 years: 15.4%
Birth rate (2003): 12‰
Death rate (2003): 9.9‰
Infant mortality rate (2003): 4.5‰
Life expectancy at birth (2003): male: 76 years, female: 81.9 years

ECONOMY

GNP (2002): 176 billion US$
GNP per capita (2002): 38,730 US$
GNP per capita PPP (2002): 36,690 international dollars
HDI (2000): 0.942
GDP annual growth rate (2003): 0.2%
Annual inflation rate (2000): 3.09%
Labour force by occupation (2000): agriculture: 4.2%, industry: 21.9%, services: 73.9%
GDP by sector (2000): agriculture: 1.9%, industry: 43%, services: 55.1%
Gross public debt (2000): 27.1% of GDP
Unemployment rate (2002): 3.9%

Agriculture and fishing

Crops
oats (2001): 389,000t
wheat (2002): 268,000t
barley (2002): 601,000t
potatoes (2002): 343,000t
Livestock farming and fishing
cattle (2002): 938,000 head
sheep (2002): 2,396,000 head
pigs (2002): 451,000 head
fish (1999): 3,086,000t

Energy generation and mining
total electricity (2001): 120,100 million kWh
hydroelectricity (2001): 119,213 million kWh
iron (2001): 340,000t
natural gas (2002): 67,627 million m³
coal (2001): 1,508,000t
nickel (2001): 2,500t
oil (2002): 156,381,000t
zinc (1999): 12,000t
copper (1998): 3,000t

Industrial production
milk (2001): 1,690,000t
butter (2001): 13,500t
cheese (2001): 81,700t
steel (2003): 698,000t
aluminium (2001): 1,068,000t
copper (2000): 2,700t
nickel (2001): 2,500t
zinc (1999): 12,000t
shipbuilding (2001): 71,000dwt
wool (2001): 5,250t
timber (2000): 7,478,000m³
paper (2000): 2,300,000t

Tourism
Tourism revenue (2001): 2,042 million US$

Foreign trade
Exports (2002): 60,064 million US$
Imports (2002): 35,693 million US$

Defence
Armed forces (2001): 26,600 people
Defence budget (2001): 1.84% of GDP

Standard of living
Inhabitants per doctor (1996): 357
Average daily calorie intake (2000): 3,414 (FAO minimum: 2,400)
Cars per 1,000 inhabitants (2000): 412
Televisions per 1,000 inhabitants (2001): 883

Norway

★ place of interest

200 400 1000 1500 m

════ motorway
──── road
──── railway line
✈ airport

● population over 500,000
● population 100,000 to 500,000
● population 50,000 to 100,000
• population less than 50,000

HISTORY: KEY DATES

Early origins to the Middle Ages
9c: Harald I Hårfagre (Fair Hair) unified Norway.
995–1000: King Olaf I Tryggvesson attempted to convert his subjects to Christianity.
1016–30: his work was continued by Olaf II Haraldsson, or Saint Olaf.
12c: dynastic disputes weakened the Norwegian monarchy.
1163: Magnus V Erlingsson became the Holy King of Norway. The church thus conferred a spiritual authority on the Norwegian monarch.
1223–63: Haakon IV Haakonsson established his authority over the Faroe, Orkney and Shetland Islands, as well as over Iceland and Greenland.
1263–80: his son, Magnus VI Lagaböte, improved Norway's legislation and its administration.
13c: the merchants of the Hanseatic League established their economic supremacy over the country.
1319: Magnus VII Eriksson united Norway and Sweden.

1363: his son, Haakon VI Magnusson, married Margrethe, daughter of Valdemar IV Atterdag, king of Denmark.
1380: Margrethe I became regent after the death of her husband, and governed Denmark and Norway. Taking advantage of a rebellion by the Swedes against their king, she proclaimed herself queen of Sweden in 1388.

The Union to independence
1397: the Kalmar Union brought the three Scandinavian kingdoms of Denmark, Norway and Sweden together under Margrethe I and her cousin and heir, Erik of Pomerania.
1523: Sweden became independent again, and the kings of Denmark ruled Norway for three centuries. Denmark imposed the Lutheran religion and the Danish language on the inhabitants of Norway.
17c: Denmark, dragged into European conflicts, was forced to cede its territories to Sweden.

1814: under the Treaty of Kiel, Denmark ceded Norway to Sweden but kept possession of Greenland, the Faroe Islands and Iceland. Norway obtained its own constitution, with an assembly, or Storting.
1884: the leader of the national resistance, Johan Sverdrup (1816–92) established a parliamentary system by forcing the king to adopt the practice of appointing ministers from the party with the majority in parliament.

Independent Norway
1905: after a plebiscite decided by the Storting, Norway broke away from Sweden. Norway chose a Danish prince, who became king under the name of Haakon VII.
1925: Svalbard was incorporated into Norway.
1940–5: Germany occupied Norway during World War II.
1957: Olaf V became king.
1991: Olaf V died and was succeeded by his son, Harald V.

Vikings, Normans, Varangians

The Norwegian, Danish and Swedish Vikings were known as Normans in the Carolingian period, when, driven by overpopulation and the search for commercial outlets and booty, they began to spread across Europe (8c). Under the name of Varangians, the Swedish began in the mid-9c to occupy the upper valley of the Dnieper River, and even reached Constantinople. They acted as intermediaries between Byzantium and the West, between Muslims and Christians. They discovered Iceland (around 860) and Greenland (10c). The Norwegians colonized the north of Scotland and Ireland. The Danish settled in north-east England (11c). In the Carolingian empire after Charlemagne's death, the Normans frequently carried out acts of piracy.

Organized in small groups and embarked on flotillas of snekkja (longships) or drakkar ('serpents', usually the largest ships in a Viking king's fleet), they sailed up rivers and carried out devastating raids inland. On more than one occasion, Charles II, the Bald had to pay them to retreat. From 885–6, the Normans laid siege to Paris, which was courageously defended by Count Eudes and Bishop Gozlin. Charles III, the Fat paid them an enormous ransom and authorized them to pillage Burgundy. In 911, under the treaty of Saint-Clair-sur-Epte, Charles III, the Simple left the region today known as Normandy to the Norman leader Rollon. The Normans then left the country in the 11c to conquer England. Rollon and his subjects were baptized and recognized Charles III, the Simple as their suzerain. In the 11c and 12c, the Normans also founded principalities in southern Italy and on Sicily.

POLAND

Situated on the Baltic Sea, the Republic of Poland is first and foremost a country of plains and plateaux, with a mountainous region in the south. Young mountains in the east (the Carpathians) contrast with ancient massifs in the south (Holy Cross Mountains) and the south-west (Sudety Mountains). The climate is continental, winters are harsh – often accompanied by snow – and summers are relatively hot and humid.

Area: 323,250km²
Population (2002): 38,543,000
Capital: Warsaw 1,615,369 (1999 e), 2,282,000 (2001 e) including the suburbs
Government type and political system: republic with a semi-presidential system
Head of state: (President of the Republic) Aleksander Kwaśniewski
Head of government: (Prime Minister) Marek Belka
Administrative structure: 16 provinces
Official language: Polish
Currency: złoty

DEMOGRAPHICS

Density: 124 inhab/km²
Percentage of population in urban areas (2001): 62.6%
Age structure of population (2000): 0–15 years: 19.2%, 15–65 years: 68.7%, over 65 years: 12.1%
Birth rate (2003): 9.6‰
Death rate (2003): 10‰
Infant mortality rate (2003): 9.1‰
Life expectancy at birth (2003): male: 69.8 years, female: 78 years

ECONOMY

GNP (2002): 177 billion US$
GNP per capita (2002): 4,570 US$
GNP per capita PPP (2002): 10,450 international dollars
HDI (2000): 0.833
GDP annual growth rate (2003): 3.7%
Annual inflation rate (2000): 10.13%
Labour force by occupation (2000): agriculture: 18.8%, industry: 30.8%, services: 50.4%
GDP by sector (2000): agriculture: 3.8%, industry: 35%, services: 61.2%

Poland

★ place of interest
200 500 1000 m

═══ motorway
─── road
─── railway line
✈ airport

● population over 1,000,000
● population 500,000 to 1,000,000
● population 100,000 to 500,000
• population less than 100,000

50 km

Gross public debt (2002): 41.8%
Unemployment rate (2002): 19.8%

Agriculture and fishing

Crops
oats (2001): 1,331,000t
sugar beets (2002): 13,434,000t
wheat (2002): 9,304,000t
rape (2001): 1,073,000t
barley (2002): 3,370,000t
apples (2001): 2,224,000t
potatoes (2002): 15,524,000t
rye (2001): 4,921,000t
Livestock farming and fishing
cattle (2002): 5,501,000 head
horses (2001): 550,000 head
sheep (2002): 333,000 head
pigs (2002): 18,707,000 head
fish (1999): 269,000t

Energy generation and mining

silver (2001): 1,100t
copper (2001): 474,000t
total electricity (2001): 134,963 million kWh
natural gas (2002): 5,562 million m³
coal (2001): 102,490,000t
lignite (2001): 59,540,000t
oil (2002): 814,000t
lead (2001): 60,000t
zinc (2001): 151,000t

Industrial production

butter (2001): 163,000t

milk (2001): 12,031,000t
cheese (2001): 460,100t
meat (2001): 2,924,000t
steel (2003): 9,047,000t
cast iron (1998): 6,178,000t
aluminium (2001): 55,000t
copper (2001): 474,000t
lead (2001): 45,000t
zinc (2001): 175,000t
cotton yarn (1998): 110,000t
wool (2001): 1,350t
artificial textiles (1999): 2,300t
synthetic textiles (1999): 83,400t
synthetic rubber (2001): 90,000t
cement (2001): 11,918,000t
timber (2000): 24,489,000m³

Tourism

Tourism revenue (2001): 4,815 million US$

Foreign trade

Exports (2002): 46,742 million US$
Imports (2002): 53,991 million US$

Defence

Armed forces (2001): 163,000 people
Defence budget (2001): 1.94% of GDP

Standard of living

Inhabitants per doctor (1996): 416
Average daily calorie intake (2000): 3,376 (FAO minimum: 2,400)
Cars per 1,000 inhabitants (2000): 259
Televisions per 1,000 inhabitants (2000): 400

POLAND

HISTORY: KEY DATES

Early origins and the Piast Dynasty

AD 5c–6c: the Slavs settled between the rivers Oder and Elbe.

7c–10c: the Polish ethnic group emerged from the Western Slav community, which had settled between the basins of the rivers Oder and the Vistula.

966: Duke Mieszko I (c.960–992), the founder of the Piast Dynasty, was baptized.

1025: Bolesław I Chrobry (Boleslaus I the Brave) was crowned king.

12c: the country was plagued by German incursions and weakened by its division into territories.

1226–1309: to drive back the pagan Prussians, Konrad of Mazovia called in the Teutonic Knights, who conquered Prussia (1230–83), then Eastern Pomerania (1308–9).

1320–33: Władysław I Łokietek restored the unity of the country, which remained cut off from Silesia and Pomerania.

1330–70: Kasimierz III the Great, son of Łokietek, expanded Poland towards the east (Ruthenia, Volhynia), and founded the University of Kraków (1364).

1370: the crown was passed to Louis I the Great, the king of Hungary.

The Jagiellonians and the Republic of Nobles

1385–6: the Union of Krewo established a personal link between Lithuania and Poland. Jagiełło, the Grand Duke of Lithuania, King of Poland under the name of Władysław II (1386–1434) founded the Jagiellonian Dynasty.

1506–72: the reigns of Sigismund I, the Old (1506–48) and Sigismund II Augustus (1548–72) were marked by the spread of humanism and religious tolerance, and by economic prosperity.

1569: the Union of Lublin ensured Poland's union with Lithuanian in a 'republic' governed by a single diet and a common sovereign. The Sejm (Noble Parliament) moved to Warsaw, which was chosen as the capital of this new commonwealth.

1587–1632: Sigismund III Vasa engaged in ruinous wars against Russia, Sweden and the Ottoman Empire.

1648–60: Russia conquered Belarus and Lithuania, while Sweden occupied almost all of Poland.

18c: the interference of foreign powers in Poland's domestic affairs led to the War of the Polish Succession.

The three partitions of Poland and foreign rule

1772: Russia, Austria and Prussia carried out the first partition of Poland.

1788–91: the patriots brought together the Grand Diet and introduced widespread reform through a new constitution (known as the May Constitution).

1793: Russia and Prussia carried out the second partition of Poland.

1794: the Kościuszko Uprising was crushed.

1795: the third partition of Poland removed the country's name.

1807–13: Napoleon Bonaparte established the Grand Duchy of Warsaw.

1815: after the Congress of Vienna, Poland became a semi-independent state called the Congress Kingdom of Poland and was incorporated into the Russian empire.

1830–1918: following uprisings in 1830 and 1864, the Prussian and the Russian parts of Poland were subjected to an assimilation policy.

Independent Poland

1918: Marshal Józef Piłsudski proclaimed the independent republic of Poland in Warsaw.

1920–1: after the Polish-Soviet War, at the Peace Treaty of Riga, Poland's border was extended to 200km east of the Curzon line.

1926–35: Piłsudski, who had resigned in 1922, returned to power and remained in control of the country until his death in 1935. Poland signed non-aggression pacts with the USSR (1932) and Germany (1934).

1939: German and then Soviet troops invaded Poland. Germany and the Soviet Union divided Poland between them in accordance with the German–Soviet Pact. Polish citizens, particularly the Jewish population, were brutally treated by the invaders.

1940: a government in exile, led by Władysław Sikorski, was established in London.

1943: an uprising by Jews in the Warsaw ghetto lasted nearly four weeks before the ghetto was destroyed by the Nazis.

1945: Soviet troops captured Warsaw and established the Lublin Committee, which became a provisional government. Poland's borders were established at the Yalta and Potsdam conferences.

Poland since 1945

1948: Władysław Gomułka, the leader of the Polish Communists and proponent of a Polish approach to socialism, was replaced by Bolesław Bierut, who adhered to the Soviet model.

1956: Gomułka returned to power after the workers' riots in Poznań.

1970: Edward Gierek attempted to modernize Poland's economy with assistance from the West.

1978: Karol Wojtyła, Bishop of Kraków, was elected Pope (under the name of John Paul II).

1980: the independent trade union known as Solidarity (Solidarność) was established, with Lech Wałęsa as its leader.

1981–3: General Wojciech Jaruzelski imposed martial law.

1989: negotiations between the government and the opposition ended in the restoration of trade union pluralism and in the democratization of many institutions.

1990: Wałęsa was elected President of the Republic.

1991: following the first completely free legislative elections, around thirty parties were represented in the Diet.

1997: a new constitution was adopted.

1999: Poland became a member of the North Atlantic Treaty Organization (NATO).

2004: Poland joined the European Union (EU).

The Portuguese Republic is situated on the western side of the Iberian Peninsula, bounded to the north and east by Spain and to the west and south by the Atlantic Ocean. Portugal's climate is hot and dry in the south, and cooler in the north. The land rises from the coastal plains towards the western edge of an enormous plateau, la Meseta, which occupies most of the Iberian Peninsula. Portugal's highest points are found in the north, reaching almost 2,000m in the Lousã and da Estrela ranges. Only the lower reaches of Portugal's three main rivers – the Douro, the Tagus and the Guadiana – flow through the country.

Area: 91,982km²
Population (2002): 10,048,000
Capital: Lisbon 559,248 (2001 census), 3,942,000 (2001 e) including the suburbs
Government type and political system: republic with a semi-presidential system
Head of state: (President of the Republic) Jorge Fernando Branco de Sampaio
Head of government: (Prime Minister) Pedro Santana Lopes
Administrative structure: 18 districts and 2 autonomous regions
Official language: Portuguese
Currency: euro

DEMOGRAPHICS

Density: 107 inhab/km²
Percentage of population in urban areas (2001): 65.6%
Age structure of population (2000): 0–15 years: 16.7%, 15–65 years: 67.7%, over 65 years: 15.6%
Birth rate (2003): 11‰
Death rate (2003): 10.8‰
Infant mortality rate (2003): 6.1‰
Life expectancy at birth (2003): male: 72.6 years, female: 79.6 years

ECONOMY

GNP (2002): 109 billion US$
GNP per capita (2002): 10,720 US$
GNP per capita PPP (2002): 17,820 international dollars
HDI (2000): 0.88
GDP annual growth rate (2003): −1.3%
Annual inflation rate (2000): 2.87%
Labour force by occupation (2000): agriculture: 12.6%, industry: 35.3%,

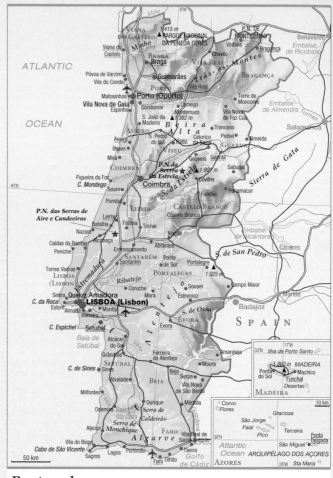

Portugal

★	place of interest
✈	airport
	200 500 1000 1500 m

═══	motorway
───	road
───	railway line
	regional boundary
Braga	regional capital

●	population over 500,000
●	population 100,000 to 500,000
●	population 50,000 to 100,000
·	population less than 50,000

services: 52.1%
GDP by sector (2000): agriculture: 3.7%, industry: 30.6%; services: 65.7%
Gross public debt (2002): 58.1% of GDP
Unemployment rate (2002): 5.1%

Agriculture and fishing
Crops
oats (2001): 45,000t
wheat (2002): 434,000t
lemons (2002): 11,200t
maize (2002): 790,000t
mandarin oranges (1998): 36,000t
hazelnuts (2001): 800t
olives (2002): 240,000t
oranges (2002): 278,000t
barley (2002): 20,000t
potatoes (2002): 1,250,000t
grapes (2002): 1,039,000t
rice (2002): 146,000t
Livestock farming and fishing

cattle (2002): 1,404,000 head
sheep (2002): 5,478,000 head
pigs (2002): 2,389,000 head
fish (1999): 215,000t

Energy generation and mining
copper (2001): 83,000t
total electricity (2001): 44,322 million kWh
tin (2001): 1,200t
coal (1990): 280,000t
hydroelectricity (2001): 13,894 million kWh
uranium (1999): 10t

Industrial production
butter (2001): 24,000t
cheese (2002): 72,800t
wine (2002): 7,789,000hl
olive oil (2001): 41,400t
steel (2003): 722,000t
shipbuilding (2001): 17,000dwt

PORTUGAL

cotton yarn (1998): 119,000t
wool (2001): 8,500t
synthetic textiles (1998): 73,000t
cement (2001): 10,300,000t
timber (2000): 10,231,000m³

Tourism
Tourism revenue (2001): 5,479 million US$

Foreign trade
Exports (2002): 27,009 million US$
Imports (2002): 39,124 million US$

Defence
Armed forces (2001): 43,600 people
Defence budget (2001): 1.42% of GDP

Standard of living
Inhabitants per doctor (1996): 333
Average daily calorie intake (2000): 3,716
(FAO minimum: 2,400)
Cars per 1,000 inhabitants (1998): 321
Televisions per 1,000 inhabitants (2001): 415

HISTORY: KEY DATES

The formation of the nation
The country was occupied by a succession of peoples including Phoenicians, Carthaginians and Greeks.
2c BC: the west of the Iberian peninsula was conquered by the Romans.
AD 5c: the province of Lusitania was invaded by the Suevi and the Alani, and then by the Visigoths.
711: the Muslims conquered the country.
866–910: Alfonso II, king of Asturias, regained control of the Porto region.
1064: Ferdinand I, king of Castile and León, liberated the region situated between the rivers Douro and Mondego.
1097: Alfonso VI, king of Castile and León, entrusted Portugal to his son-in-law, Henry of Burgundy, the founder of the house of Burgundy.
1139–85: Henry of Burgundy's son, Alfonso Henriques, became king of Portugal after his victory over the Moors at the Battle of Ourique (1139), and proclaimed Portugal's independence.
1249: Alfonso III (1248–79) occupied the Algarve.
1385: John I (1385–1433) founded the Aviz dynasty and defeated the Castilians at the Battle of Aljubarrota.

The Golden Age
15c–16c: Portugal launched many significant voyages of discovery and exploration, encouraged by Prince Henry the Navigator.
1488: Bartolomeu Dias rounded the Cape of Good Hope and entered the Indian Ocean.
1494: the Treaty of Tordesillas established a north-south line of demarcation 370 leagues west of the Cape Verde Islands, between Spain and Portugal's possessions outside of Europe.
1497: Vasco da Gama discovered the sea route to India.
1500: Pedro Cabral claimed Brazil for Portugal.

The crises and the decline
1580: Philip II of Spain incorporated Portugal into the Spanish crown. Portugal was ruled by Spain from 1580–1640.
1640: Portugal regained its independence from Spain and proclaimed the Duke of Bragança, John IV (1640–56) king of Portugal.
1668: Spain recognized Portugal's independence.
17c: resigned to the collapse of its positions in Asia and its withdrawal from Africa, Portugal devoted itself to exploiting the resources of Brazil.
1750–77: Joseph I called on the Marquis of Pombal, who became Portugal's de facto ruler and rebuilt Lisbon after a devastating earthquake in 1755.
1807: John VI fled to Brazil while the Anglo-Portuguese, led by the regent Beresford, fought until 1811 against French invaders.
1822: John VI (1816–26) returned to Lisbon. His son, Peter I, proclaimed himself emperor of Brazil, whose independence was recognized in 1825.
1826: on the death of John VI, a dynastic conflict arose between Peter I, who had become king of Portugal under the name of Peter IV, his daughter Marie II and his brother Miguel, who had proclaimed himself king under the name of Michael I.
1852–1908: under Peter V, King Louis I and King Charles I, Portugal had a real parliamentary regime and attempts were made to reconstruct a colonial empire around Angola and Mozambique.

The Republic
1910: the republic of Portugal was proclaimed.
1933–68: Antonio de Oliveira Salazar established the 'New State' (Estado Novo), which was corporatist and nationalist.
1974: a group of military officers seized power in a coup known as the Captain's Revolution.
1975: the former Portuguese colonies became independent.
1986: Portugal became a member of the European Economic Community (EEC).
1999: Portugal's last overseas territory, Macau, was handed back to China.
2004: the Portuguese prime minister, Jose Manuel Durao Barroso, resigned to take up a new role as president of the European Commission.

253

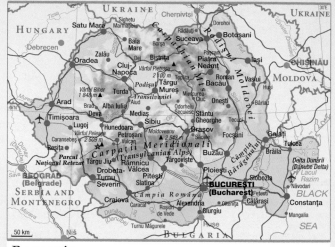

Situated in south-eastern Europe, Romania is dominated by the Carpathian Mountains, which form a crescent shape around the plateaus of Transylvania, where the Apuseni Mountains are located. The edges of this central, mountainous area are made up of plateaux and plains. Romania's climate is continental.

Area: 238,391km²
Population (2002): 22,332,000
Capital: Bucharest 1,998,000 (2001 e)
Government type and political system: republic with a semi-presidential system
Head of state: (President of the Republic) Ion Iliescu
Head of government: (Prime Minister) Adrian Nastase
Administrative structure: 40 districts and 1 municipality
Official language: Romanian
Currency: leu

DEMOGRAPHICS

Density: 94 inhab/km²
Percentage of population in urban areas (2001): 55.3%
Age structure of population (2000): 0–15 years: 18.3%, 15–65 years: 68.4%, over 65 years: 13.3%
Birth rate (2003): 10.4‰
Death rate (2003): 12.5‰
Infant mortality rate (2003): 20‰
Life expectancy at birth (2003): male: 67 years, female: 74.2 years

ECONOMY

GNP (2002): 41.7 billion US$
GNP per capita (2002): 1,870 US$
GNP per capita PPP (2002): 6,490 international dollars
HDI (2000): 0.775
GDP annual growth rate (2003): 4.9%
Annual inflation rate (2000): 45.67%
Labour force by occupation (2001): agriculture: 42.3%, industry: 26.2%, services: 31.5%
GDP by sector (2000): agriculture: 12.8%, industry: 36.3%, services: 50.9%
Gross public debt (2002): 22.7% of GDP
Unemployment rate (2002): 8.1%

Agriculture

Crops
oats (2001): 520,000t
wheat (2002): 4,421,000t
flax (2001): 3,000t
maize (2002): 8,400,000t
walnuts (2001): 30,000t
barley (2002): 691,000t

potatoes (2002): 4,000,000t
grapes (2002): 1,077,000t
soya beans (2002): 146,000t
sunflowers (2002): 1,003,000t
Livestock farming
cattle (2002): 2,800,000 head
horses (2001): 858,000 head
sheep (2002): 7,251,000 head
pigs (2002): 4,447,000 head
chickens (2002): 71,000,000 head

Energy generation and mining

bauxite (1998): 162,000t
total electricity (2001): 50,858 million kWh
iron (2000): 55,000t
natural gas (2002): 10,800 million m³
coal (2001): 310,000t
hydroelectricity (2001): 14,021 million kWh
lignite (2001): 29,694,000t
oil (2002): 6,100,000t
uranium (2001): 115t

Industrial production

wine (2002): 5,461,000hl
sugar (2002): 73,000t
steel (2003): 5,776,000t
cast iron (1998): 4,525,000t

aluminium (2001): 175,000t
cars (2002): 65,000 units
commercial vehicles (1996): 23,000 units
shipbuilding (2001): 96,000dwt
cotton yarn (2001): 6t
wool (2001): 22,000t
silk (2001) : 130t
artificial textiles (1999): 6,100t
synthetic textiles (1999): 27,900t
synthetic rubber (2001): 23,200t
cement (2001): 5,668,000t
timber (2000): 10,116,000m³

Tourism

Tourism revenue (2001): 362 million US$

Foreign trade

Exports (2002): 13,876 million US$
Imports (2002): 16,487 million US$

Defence

Armed forces (2001): 99,200 people
Defence budget (2001): 2.49% of GDP

Standard of living

Inhabitants per doctor (1996): 556
Average daily calorie intake (2000): 3,274 (FAO minimum: 2,400)
Cars per 1,000 inhabitants (1999): 133
Televisions per 1,000 inhabitants (2000): 381

HISTORY: KEY DATES

6c: the Slavs settled in the region.
11c: the Hungarians conquered Transylvania.
14c–19c: Wallachia and Moldavia were states of the Ottoman Empire.
1878: the independence of Romania was recognized.
1919–20: after World War I, Bukovina, Transylvania, Bessarabia and part of the Banat were granted to Romania.
1944: the dictator Antonescu, who in 1941 had engaged Romania in World War II alongside Hitler, was overthrown.

1947: the People's Republic of Romania was proclaimed.
1974: Nicolae Ceauşescu, head of state and president of the State Council since 1967, became president of the republic.
1989: an uprising toppled Ceauşescu, who attempted to flee the country but was captured and executed by firing squad on Christmas Day. The National Salvation Front took power.
1990: Romania's first free elections were won by the National Salvation Front.
2004: Romania joined the North Atlantic Treaty Organization (NATO).

The Russian Federation is by far the largest country in the world, stretching across some 10,000km from the Baltic to the Pacific and crossing eleven time zones. It is mainly made up of plains and plateaus, with mountains in the south (the Caucasus, and the ranges that border on Mongolia and China) and the east (on the edge of the Pacific Ocean). The Ural Mountains constitute the traditional frontier between European Russia in the west and Asian Russia, or Siberia, in the east. The latitude, but more especially the distance from the ocean and the topography, explain the wide temperature range of the climate, which is characterized by very harsh winters in the east, as well as by the zonal distribution of the vegetation. Moving from north to south, one can find tundra, taiga, deciduous forests and grassy steppes.

Area: 17,075,400km²
Population (2002): 143,752,000
Capital: Moscow 8,316,000 (2001 e) including the suburbs
Government type and political system: republic with a semi-presidential system
Head of state: (President of the Republic) Vladimir Vladimirovich Putin
Head of government: (Prime Minister) Mikhail Fradkov
Administrative structure: 49 oblasts, 21 republics, 10 autonomous okrugs, 6 krays, 2 federal cities and 1 autonomous oblast
Official language: Russian
Currency: rouble

DEMOGRAPHICS

Density: 9 inhab/km²
Percentage of population in urban areas (2001): 72.9%

Age structure of population (2000): 0–15 years: 18%, 15–65 years: 69.5%, over 65 years: 12.5%
Birth rate (2003): 8.6‰
Death rate (2003): 14.6‰
Infant mortality rate (2003): 15.9‰
Life expectancy at birth (2003): male: 60.8 years, female: 73.1 years

ECONOMY

GNP (2002): 307 billion US$
GNP per capita (2002): 2,130 US$
GNP per capita PPP (2002): 8,080 international dollars
HDI (2000): 0.781
GDP annual growth rate (2003): 7.3%
Annual inflation rate (2000): 20.75%
Labour force by occupation: n/a
GDP by sector (2000): agriculture: 7.1%, industry: 38.7%, services: 54.2%
Gross public debt: n/a
Unemployment rate (2000): 11.4%

Agriculture and fishing

Crops
oats (2001): 8,010,000t
sugar beets (2002): 15,665,000t
wheat (2002): 50,609,000t
maize (2002): 1,541,000t
millet (2001): 1,315,000t
hazelnuts (2001): 2,000t
barley (2002): 18,739,000t
peaches (2002): 35,000t
apples (2001): 1,800,000t
potatoes (2002): 32,871,000t
rice (2002): 483,000t
rye (2001): 6,000,000t
soya beans (2002): 423,000t
tomatoes (2002): 1,980,000t
sunflowers (2002): 3,684,000t
Livestock farming and fishing
cattle (2002): 27,107,000 head
goats (2001): 1,700,000 head
horses (2001): 1,750,000 head
sheep (2002): 13,035,000 head
pigs (2002): 16,047,000 head
chickens (2002): 330,000,000 head
fish (1999): 4,210,000t

Energy generation and mining

silver (2000): 380t
bauxite (2001): 4,000,000t
chromium (2001): 70,000t
copper (2001): 620,000t
diamond (2001): 23,200,000 carats
hydroelectricity (2001): 173,450 million kWh
nuclear electricity (2001): 125,360 million kWh

total electricity (2001): 846,455 million kWh
tin (2001): 4,500t
iron (2000): 51,000,000t
natural gas (2002): 554,900 million m³
coal (2001): 155,689,000t
lignite (2001): 100,080,000t
molybdenum (2001): 2,600t
nickel (2000): 270,000t
gold (2001): 152,000kg
oil (2002): 379,600,000t
phosphate (2001): 10,500,000t
iron (2001): 12,300t
uranium (2001): 2,000t
zinc (2001): 124,000t

Industrial production

butter (2001): 269,000t
cheese (2001): 433,000t
milk (2001): 32,285,000t
honey (2001): 50,000t
sugar (2002): 1,742,000t
wine (2002): 4,060,000hl
eggs (2001): 1,956,000t
meat (2001): 4,474,000t
steel (2003): 61,325,000t
cast iron (1998): 34,736,000t
aluminium (2001): 3.300,000t
copper (2001): 620,000t
nickel (2000): 270,000t
lead (2001): 67,500t
zinc (2001): 237,000t
cars (2002): 981,000 units
commercial vehicles (1998): 117,000 units
cotton yarn (1998): 156,000t
jute (1997): 45,000t
wool (2001): 38,000t
flax (2001): 48,000t
synthetic rubber (2001): 920,000t
timber (2000): 105,800,000m³
paper (2000): 5,310,000t

Tourism

Tourism revenue (1999): 7,510 million US$

Foreign trade

Exports (2002): 107,247 million US$
Imports (2002): 60,966 million US$

Defence

Armed forces (2001): 988,100 people
Defence budget (2001): 2.41% of GDP

Standard of living

Inhabitants per doctor (1995): 263
Average daily calorie intake (2000): 2,917 (FAO minimum: 2,400)
Cars per 1,000 inhabitants (2000): 140
Televisions per 1,000 inhabitants (1999): 421

255

HISTORY: KEY DATES

Early origins and the medieval principalities

AD 5c: the Eastern Slavs moved towards the south-east, where they inherited the vestiges of the Scythian and Sarmat civilizations.
8c–9c: the Vikings (Varangians) dominated the two trade routes between the Baltic Sea and the Black Sea – between the Dniepr and the Volga rivers. They founded principalities whose leaders are semi-legendary (Askold at Kiev and Rurik at Novgorod).
8c–9c: Rurik's successor Oleg established the state of Kievan Rus, with Kiev as its capital.
989: Vladimir I imposed the official act of public baptism on his subjects, and converted Russia to Christianity.
1019–54: under Yaroslav the Wise, the state of Kievan Rus flourished, reaching its political and cultural zenith.
1169: the town of Vladimir was chosen as the capital of the second Russian state, the Principality of Vladimir-Suzdal.
1238–40: the Mongols conquered almost all of Russia.

Σ»

RUSSIA

BERING SEA

Kuril'skiye Ostrova
(Kuril Islands)

JAPAN

Komandorskiye
Ostrova

Ostrov Karaginskiy

Sopka Klyuchevskaya
4 750 m

Petropavlovsk-
Kamchatskiy

Yuzhno-
Sakhalinsk

Hokkaido

JAPAN

Koryakskiy Khrebet

Severnaya
Zemlya

Anadyrskiy Zaliv

Uelen

Chukotskiy
Poluostrov

CHUKCHI SEA

Sakhalin

SEA
OF

Nikhodka

Vladivostok

NORTH

Sikhote-Alin'

Palana

Anadyr'

Kamchatka

Markovo

Evensk

Magadan

Khrebet Kolymskiy

OKHOTSKOYE MORE
(SEA OF OKHOTSK)

Tartarskiy Proliv

Komsomol'sk-
na-Amure

Khabarovsk

Birobidzhan

CHINA

Harbin

Changchun

Ostrov Vrangelya
(Wrangel Island)

VOSTOCHNO-
SIBIRSKOYE MORE
(EAST SIBERIAN SEA)

Ostrov
Novaya Sibir'

Lyakhovskiye
Ostrova

Ostrov
Kotel'nyy

Sredne-
Kolymsk

Cherskiy

Chokurdakh

Indigirka

Srednekolymsk

Khrebet Cherskogo

Verkhoyansk

Ust'-Ilimsk

Aldan

Yakutsk

Khrebet Dzhugdzhur

Svobodny

Stanovoy Khrebet

Blagoveshchensk

Ussuri

Birakan

Ostrov Bol'shevik

Severnaya Zemlya
(North Land)

Zemlya Frantsa-Iosifa
(Franz Josef Land)

Ostrov
Oktyabr'skoy
Revolyutsii

Ostrov
Komsomolets

Khatanga

Olenek

Severo-Sibirskaya Nizmennost'

Severo-Sibirskaya Nizmennost'

Tura

Sredne-
Sibirskoye
Ploskogor'ye
(Central Siberian
Plateau)

Lena

Olekminsk

Lensk

Bratsk

Ust'-Ilimsk

Chita

Ulan-Ude

Angarsk

Yakutsk

Yablonovyy Khrebet

MONGOLIA

ULAANBAATAR

ARCTIC OCEAN

Poluostrov Taymyr

Gory Byrranga

Poluostrov
Taymyr

Noril'sk

Gory
Putorana

Dudinka

Igarka

Yenisey

Turukhansk

Kyzyl

Gorno-Altaysk

Abakan

Kansk

Krasnoyarsk

Achinsk

Biysk

Belukha
4 506 m

Altay Mts.

KARSKOYE MORE
(KARA SEA)

Novaya Zemlya

Dikson

Ob'

Salekhard

Nadym

Vorkuta

Nar'yan-Mar

Noviy Port

Poluostrov
Yamal

Zapadno-
Sibirskaya
Ravnina
(West Siberian Plain)

Nizhnevartovsk

Surgut

Tomsk

Kemerovo

Novosibirsk

Leninsk-Kuznetskiy

Novokuznetsk

Prokop'yevsk

Barnaul

Rubtsovsk

Omsk

Petropavlovsk

KAZAKHSTAN

Karaganda

ASTANA

BARENTS SEA

Svalbard
(Norw.)

NORDKAPP

NORWEGIAN
SEA

Nordkapp

Poluostrov
Kanin

Pechenga

Murmansk

Monchegorsk

Kol'skiy
Poluostrov

Severodvinsk

Arkhangel'sk

Kotlas

Pechora

Ukhta

Ural'skiy Khrebet
(Ural Mountains)

Syktyvkar

Berezniki

Solikamsk

Perm'

Nizhniy Tagil

Krasnoturinsk

Yekaterinburg (Sverdlovsk)

Nizhnevartovsk

Kamensk-Ural'skiy

Chelyabinsk

Kurgan

Tyumen'

Magnitogorsk

Orsk

Orenburg

Ob'

Ishim

LAPPLAND

Lappland

FINLAND

HELSINKI

SWEDEN

STOCKHOLM

Arctic Circle

Gulf of Bothnia

NORWAY

Kirov

Glazov

Izhevsk

Kazan'

Naberezhnye Chelny

Ufa

Nab. Chelny

Sterlitamak

Ul'yanovsk

Tol'yatti

Samara

Saratov

Balakovo

Syzran'

Penza

Saransk

MOSKVA (Moscow)

Nizhniy Novgorod (Gor'kiy)

Cheboksary

Yoshkar-Ola

Vladimir

Ivanovo

Kostroma

Yaroslavl'

Vologda

Rybinsk

Tver'

Sankt-Peterburg
(St Petersburg)

Velikiy Novgorod

Pskov

Velikiye Luki

Smolensk

Bryansk

Orel

Kursk

Belgorod

Lipetsk

Voronezh

Tambov

Ryazan'

Tula

Kaluga

Ostrov

ESTONIA

TALLINN

RIGA

LATVIA

LITHUANIA

VILNIUS

Kaliningrad

POLAND

WARSZAWA

BERLIN

DENMARK

KØBENHAVN

BALTIC SEA

MINSK

BELARUS

KYIV

UKRAINE

Odesa

Kharkiv

Donets'k

Rostov-na-Donu

Taganrog

Shakhty

Novocherkassk

Volgograd (Stalingrad)

Kamyshin

Engel's

Volzhskiy

Astrakhan'

CASPIAN SEA

Makhachkala

Groznyy

Nal'chik

Vladikavkaz

El'brus
5 642 m

Kazbek
5 033 m

Stavropol'

Armavir

Krasnodar

Sochi

Novorossiysk

Maykop

BLACK SEA

SEA OF AZOV

GEORGIA

TBILISI

YEREVAN

BAKI

AZERBAIJAN

ARMENIA

TURKEY

Trabzon

UZB.

Aral'skoye More

MOSKVA (Moscow) inset

MOSKVA (Moscow)

Tver'

Vologda

Rybinsk

Yaroslavl'

Sergiyev Posad

Kostroma

Kineshma

Ivanovo

Nizhniy Novgorod (Gor'kiy)

Dzerzhinsk

Suzdal'

Vladimir

Kovrov

Lyubertsy

Elektrostal'

Kolomna

Ryazan'

Tula

Novomoskovsk

Serpukhov

Podol'sk

Kaluga

Orel

150 km

Legend

● population over 5,000,000
● population 1,000,000 to 5,000,000
● population 100,000 to 1,000,000
• population less than 100,000

✈ airport

── road
── railway line
─ republic boundary

2000 m
1000
500
200
0

300 km

Republics

1 - Adygeya Rep
2 - Altay Rep
3 - Bashkortostan Rep
4 - Buryat Rep
5 - Chechen Rep
6 - Chuvash Rep
7 - Dagestan Rep
8 - Rep of Ingushetia
9 - Kabardino-Balkaria Rep
10 - Kalmykia Rep
11 - Karachay-Cherkessia Rep
12 - Rep of Karelia
13 - Khakassia Rep
14 - Komi Rep
15 - Mariy El Rep
16 - Rep of Mordovia
17 - Rep of North Ossetia-Alania
18 - Sakha Rep (or Yakutia)
19 - Tatarstan Rep
20 - Tuva Rep
21 - Rep of Udmurtia

⊅»

HISTORY: KEY DATES

Muscovy
14c: the principality of Moscow gained supremacy over the other Russian principalities.
1380: Dmitri Donskoi defeated the Mongols at the Battle of Kulikovo.
1462–1505: Ivan III, the Great organized a powerful, centralized state, ended the Mongol suzerainty and proclaimed himself 'Sovereign of all Russia' (1480).
1533–84: Ivan IV, the Terrible, who took the title of Tsar in 1547, began to conquer Siberia.
1605–13: after the reign of Boris Gudonov, Russia suffered from political and social problems, and was invaded by Sweden and Poland. The period came to be known as the Time of Troubles.
1649: serfdom became a legal institution in Russia.
1666–7: the condemnation of the Old Believers or Old Ritualists by the Russian Orthodox Church led to a schism.

The Russian empire to the middle of the 19c
1682–1725: Peter I the Great began to westernize the country, and established the Russian empire (1721).
1762–96: Catherine II the Great pursued policies of prestige and expansion. In 1774, Russia gained access to the Black Sea, and after the three partitions of Poland, Russia acquired Belarus, western Ukraine and Lithuania.
1801–25: Alexander I ruled Russia. Defeated by Napoleon Bonaparte, he then formed an alliance with him (Tilsit, 1807), and went on to play an active role in his downfall during the Russian campaign of 1812. In 1815, Alexander I took part in the Congress of Vienna and, along with Francis I of Austria and Frederick William III of Prussia, formed the Holy Alliance.
1825–35: Tsar Nicholas I pursued authoritarian policies, suppressing the Decembrist Conspiracy (1825) and the Polish Rebellion (1831).
1854–6: Russia was defeated by France and Great Britain during the Crimean War.

Modernizing and maintaining the autocracy
1860–97: Russia annexed the region adjacent to the Amur and Ussuri rivers and the Pacific Ocean, and then conquered Central Asia.

1861–4: Alexander II freed the serfs.
1881–94: Alexander III restricted the application of the previous reign's reforms. Russia underwent a rapid industrialization process at the end of the 1880s.
1904–5: the Russo-Japanese War was disastrous for Russia and created favourable conditions for the revolution of 1905. After introducing a democratic constitution and establishing a parliament, Tsar Nicholas II returned to an autocratic style of government, leading to widespread discontent. During this period, Russia strengthened its ties with Great Britain, and the two countries, along with France, formed the Triple Entente.
1915: during World War I, Russia suffered heavy losses in the Austro-German offensives in Poland, Galicia and Lithuania.
1917: the February Revolution brought down the Tsarist regime and abolished the monarchy; the October Revolution gave power to the Bolsheviks.

The USSR
1918–20: the Russian Soviet Federated Socialist Republic (SFSR) was proclaimed. Germany imposed the Peace Treaty of Brest-Litovsk on Russia. Civil war broke out between the Red Army and the White Russians, or anti-Communists, who were aided by Great Britain, France and the USA.
1920: Soviet Russia recognized the independence of the Baltic States. The Red Army occupied Armenia.
1922: Stalin became secretary-general of the Communist Party. Russia united with Transcaucasia, Ukraine and Belarus in the Union of Soviet Socialist Republics (USSR).
1936: a Constitution specified the organization of the USSR into 11 federated republics: Russia, Ukraine, Belarus, Kazakhstan, Kyrgyzstan, Uzbekistan, Tajikistan, Turkmenistan, Armenia, Azerbaijan and Georgia.
1939: the German–Soviet pact was concluded.
1939–40: the USSR annexed eastern Poland, the Baltic States, Karelia, Bessarabia and northern Bukovina.
1941: Germany invaded Russia.
1943: the Red Army won the Battle of Stalingrad.
1944–5: Soviet forces advanced through eastern Europe and, in accordance with the Yalta Conference (February 1945) agreements, occupied

eastern Germany.
1947–9: Cominform (the Communist Information Bureau) was created in 1947. The Cold War developed.
1955: the USSR signed the Warsaw Pact (the Warsaw Treaty of Friendship, Cooperation and Mutual Assistance) with Albania, Bulgaria, Czechoslovakia, East Germany, Hungary, Poland and Romania.
1956: the Soviet Army violently suppressed a national uprising in Hungary.
1962: the installation of Soviet nuclear missile bases in Cuba led to international incidents that became known as the Cuban Missile Crisis.
1968: following a period of reform in Czechoslovakia known as the Prague Spring, Soviet troops invaded and occupied the country.
1979: Soviet troops occupied Afghanistan to support the Afghan government against the Mujahidin (Muslim guerrillas).
1985–7: Mikhail Sergeevich Gorbachev implemented perestroika (the process of 'reconstructing' the Soviet economy and society).
1989: the USSR fully withdrew its troops from Afghanistan. The first multiparty elections took place, and nationalist demands grew.
1990: the party leadership role was abolished and a presidential system was introduced. The USSR, by signing the Moscow Treaty, accepted the reunification of Germany.

The Russian Federation
1991: the restoration of the independence of the Baltic States was followed by the collapse of the USSR. Russia, Ukraine, Belarus, Moldova and the republics of Central Asia and the Caucasus (except for Georgia), who had proclaimed their independence, formed the Community of Independent States (CIS). Russia adopted the official name of the Russian Federation.
1994: Russian troops invaded the breakaway republic of Chechnya. Protest attacks by Chechen rebel groups, who often claimed provocation by Russian forces, became increasingly frequent over the following decade.
2002: Russia and the USA agreed a treaty for the strategic reduction of the number of nuclear weapons held by the two countries.

Surrounded by Italy, the landlocked Republic of San Marino is perched 749m above sea level on the slopes of Mount Titano in the Italian Apennines. San Marino is the oldest surviving republic in Europe.

San Marino

— road

200	300	500 m

● pop. over 4,000
● less than 4,000

Area: 61km²
Population (2002): 27,000
Capital: San Marino 5,000 (2001 e) including the suburbs
Government type and political system: republic
Heads of state and government: (captains-regent) Elected by the Great General Council on a rotating basis every six months
Administrative structure: 9 municipalities and the capital
Official language: Italian
Currency: euro

DEMOGRAPHICS

Density: 435 inhab/km²
Percentage of population in urban areas

(2001): 90.4%
Age structure of population (1993): 0–15 years: 16%, 15–65 years: 70%, over 65 years: 14%
Birth rate: n/a
Death rate: n/a
Infant mortality rate: n/a
Life expectancy at birth: n/a

ECONOMY

GNP (1995): 0.4 billion US$
GNP per capita (1995): 17,000 US$
GNP per capita PPP: n/a
HDI: n/a
GDP annual growth rate: n/a

Annual inflation rate: n/a
Labour force by occupation (1999): agriculture: 1.3%, industry: 40.2%, services: 58.5%
GDP by sector: n/a
Gross public debt: n/a
Unemployment rate (2002): 3.6%

Tourism

Tourism revenue: n/a

Foreign trade

Exports: n/a
Imports: n/a

Defence

Armed forces: n/a
Defence budget: n/a

Standard of living

Inhabitants per doctor: n/a
Average daily calorie intake (1995): 3,561 (FAO minimum: 2,400)
Cars per 1,000 inhabitants: n/a
Televisions per 1,000 inhabitants (1995): 360

HISTORY: KEY DATES

According to tradition, San Marino was founded in the 4c by Marinus, a Christian stonemason who came to Mount Titano seeking refuge from religious persecution. His reputation as a saint attracted a small community, which gradually grew and became secular.
9c: the town of San Marino became autonomous.
13c: San Marino became a republic.
1992: San Marino became a member of the United Nations.

A different republic

O riginally a medieval commune established on Italian soil, the Republic of San Marino escaped the Italian unification. This sovereign state is governed by a constitution dating back to 1600, making it the oldest constitution still in use today. The executive power is in the hands of two captains-regent (*capitani reggenti*), who are elected every six months. They preside over a Great General Council, whose 60 members are elected by direct universal suffrage for five-year periods. In no other country is the head of state renewed so frequently. Moreover, this function is carried out collectively in San Marino. The two captains-regent are assisted by a Congress of State, made up of ten Secretaries of State. Legislative power is exercised by the Great General Council. San Marino is divided into nine local municipalities, each of which has its own local council.

Stretching southwards from the Danube to the Adriatic, Serbia and Montenegro is a federation of the last two republics that were left in the former Yugoslav Federation. In March 2002, they agreed to create a new, looser union of Serbia and Montenegro. The northern part of the country is made up of low-lying, heavily cultivated terrain, while the southern part, which belongs to the Dinaric Alps, is hillier, larger and still mainly covered with forests and pasturelands.

Area: 102,173km²
Population (2002): 10,523,000
Capital: Belgrade 1,687,000 (2001 e) including the suburbs
Government type and political system: republic with a parliamentary system
Head of state: (President of the Republic) Svetozar Marović;
Head of government: (Prime Minister, Serbia) Vojislav Kostunica; (Prime Minister, Montenegro) Milo Djukanovic
Administrative structure: 2 republics
Official language: Serbo-Croat
Currency: Serbian dinar (in Serbia), euro (in Montenegro and Kosovo)

Serbia and Montenegro

★ place of interest
200 500 1500 m

— motorway
— road
-- railway line
✈ airport

— federal state boundary
-·- regional boundary

● population over 1,000,000
● population 100,000 to 1,000,000
● population 50,000 to 100,000
· population less than 50,000

DEMOGRAPHICS

Density: 104 inhab/km²
Percentage of population in urban areas (2001): 51.7%
Age structure of population (2000): 0–15 years: 20 %, 15–65 years: 66.9%, over 65 years: 13.1%
Birth rate (2003): 11.7‰
Death rate (2003): 10.6‰
Infant mortality rate (2003): 13‰
Life expectancy at birth (2003): male: 70.9 years, female: 75.6 years

ECONOMY

GNP (2002): 11.6 billion US$
GNP per capita (2002): 1,400 US$
GNP per capita PPP: n/a
HDI: n/a
GDP annual growth rate (2003): 3%
Annual inflation rate: n/a
Labour force by occupation: n/a
GDP by sector (1999): agriculture: 22%, industry: 38.8%, services: 39.2%
Gross public debt: n/a

Unemployment rate (2002): 13.8% of GDP

Agriculture and fishing

Crops
sugar beets (2002): 2,098,000t
wheat (2002): 2,245,000t
maize (2002): 5,597,000t
walnuts (2001): 23,776t
barley (2002): 355,000t
potatoes (2002): 1,030,000t
soya beans (2002): 244,000t
sunflowers (2002): 280,000t
Livestock farming and fishing
cattle (2002): 1,355,000 head
goats (2001): 241,000 head
sheep (2002): 1,691,000 head
pigs (2002): 3,608,000 head
fish (1999): 9,940t

Energy generation and mining

bauxite (2001): 610,000t
copper (2001): 22,000t
total electricity (2001): 31,710 million kWh
lignite (2001): 35,750,000t
oil (2002): 800,000t

lead (2001): 15,000t
zinc (2001): 1,200t

Industrial production

sugar (2002): 271,000t
wine (2002): 1,470,000hl
aluminium (2001): 70,000t
copper (2001): 22,000t
zinc (2001): 13,467t
cars (2002): 10,300 units
wool (2001): 2,968t
cement (2001): 2,418,000t

Tourism

Tourism revenue (2001): 40 million US$

Foreign trade

Exports (1997): 1,088 million US$
Imports (1997): 2,527 million US$

Defence

Armed forces (2001): 74,500 people
Defence budget (2001): 4.89% of GDP

Standard of living

Inhabitants per doctor (1995): 500
Average daily calorie intake (2000): 2,570 (FAO minimum: 2,400)
Cars per 1,000 inhabitants (1999): 150
Televisions per 1,000 inhabitants (2000): 282

SERBIA AND MONTENEGRO

HISTORY: KEY DATES

The formation of the Yugoslav state
2c BC: the region, which was inhabited by Illyrians, Thracians and then Celts, was incorporated into the Roman Empire.
6c–7c: the Slavs invaded the region.
9c: the Serbs, influenced by Byzantium, were converted to Christianity.
11c: present-day Montenegro became the centre of a state.
c.1170–c.1196: Stephen Nemanja liberated Serbian lands from Byzantium.
1217: his son, Stephen I Nemanjić (c.1196–1227) became king of Serbia and established an independent Serbian church.
1360: the kingdom of Zeta, which had been included in the kingdom of Serbia from the 13c–14c, regained its independence.
1389–1830: the Serbs were defeated by the Turks at Kosovo, and were incorporated into the Ottoman Empire. Montenegro was also under Ottoman rule from 1479–1878.
1804–1813: the Serbs revolted under the leadership of Karageorge.
1830: Michael Obrenović, having been recognized as prince of Serbia by the Ottomans since 1815, obtained absolute autonomy.
1878: Montenegro and Serbia gained their independence.
1912–13: Serbia took part in the two

Balkan Wars and obtained the majority of Macedonia.
1914: after a Serbian nationalist assassinated the Archduke Franz Ferdinand, heir to the Habsburg throne, Austria declared war on Serbia, thereby triggering the outbreak of World War I.
1918: the kingdom of the Serbs, Croats and Slovenes was established under the authority of Peter I Karageorgević, the king of Serbia.
1919–20: several post-war treaties established the country's borders.
1921: a centralist constitution and parliament were established.
1929: the country adopted the name of Yugoslavia.
1941: two main resistance groups were organized – one by Draš Mihailović, a Serbian soldier with royalist and centralist tendencies, and another by the Communist Croat, Josip Broz Tito. Peter II sought refuge in London.

The Federal People's Republic of Yugoslavia under Tito
1945–6: the Federal People's Republic of Yugoslavia was created, made up of six republics: Bosnia-Herzegovina, Croatia, Macedonia, Montenegro, Serbia and Slovenia. Tito headed an authoritarian regime.
1948–9: Stalin excluded Yugoslavia from Cominform (the Communist Information Bureau).

1950: self-rule was established.
1963: the country became the Socialist Federal Republic of Yugoslavia (SFRY).
1974: a new constitution was introduced.
1980: after the death of Tito, a collective leadership was established.

The collapse of the Yugoslav Federation
1980s: tensions between different ethnic communities grew (especially in Kosovo) while economic, political and social conditions deteriorated.
1991: Croatia and Slovenia proclaimed their independence. After armed clashes, the federal army retreated from Slovenia; fierce fighting broke out between the Croats, the federal army and the Croatian Serbs. Macedonia proclaimed its independence.
1992: the international community recognized the independence of Croatia, Slovenia and Bosnia-Herzegovina. Serbia and Montenegro formed the Federal Republic of Yugoslavia.
1999: in response to ethnic violence in the province of Kosovo, the North Atlantic Treaty Organization (NATO) launched air strikes in Yugoslavia. Kosovo was provisionally placed under UN administration.
2003: the Federal Republic of Yugoslavia was renamed Serbia and Montenegro.

The Balkans – a turbulent peninsula

The northern boundary of the Balkan Peninsula (or the Balkans) is generally defined as the line formed by the rivers Sava and Danube. The Peninsula includes Albania, Bosnia-Herzegovina, Bulgaria, Croatia, Greece, Macedonia, European Turkey and Serbia and Montenegro. This region is a melting pot of different ethnic groups and has long been plagued by great political instability.

At the end of the 14c, the Balkan Peninsula was ruled by the Ottomans or Turks. Christian Europe, and the houses of Austria and Russia in particular, started to conquer the area in the 18c. The struggle between the inhabitants of the Balkans against Ottoman domination, religious dissent between Orthodox Christians, Catholics and Muslims, and rivalry between the major world powers has given rise to many conflicts: the Russo–Turkish Wars (1877–8), the Greco–Turkish War (1897), the Balkan Wars (1912–13), the campaigns of the Dardanelles, Serbia and Macedonia during World War I and the Balkans campaign (1940–1). Problems with national minorities and state boundaries arose when Yugoslavia broke up in 1991–2, leading to the wars in Croatia (1991–2) and Bosnia-Herzegovina (1992–5) and the Kosovo conflict (1999).

Slovakia

★ place of interest

200 500 1000 2000 m

━━━ motorway
━━━ road
┄┄┄ railway line
✈ airport

● population over 100,000
● population 50,000 to 100,000
● population 10,000 to 50,000
• population less than 10,000

The Slovak Republic is a landlocked country situated at the north-western end of the Carpathian Mountains in central Europe. Slovakia is a mainly mountainous country with a continental climate. The highest peaks are found in the north of the country, in the High Tatra Mountains, which are separated from the Low Tatra Mountains by the upper reaches of the River Váh. In the north, the Beskid range forms borders with Poland and the Czech Republic.

Area: 49,012km²
Population (2002): 5,408,000
Capital: Bratislava 464,000 (2001 e) including the suburbs
Government type and political system: republic with a parliamentary system
Head of state: (President of the Republic) Ivan Gasparovic
Head of government: (Prime Minister) Mikuláš Dzurinda
Administrative structure: 8 regions
Official language: Slovak
Currency: koruna

DEMOGRAPHICS
Density: 110 inhab/km²
Percentage of population in urban areas (2001): 57.6%
Age structure of population (2000): 0–15 years: 19.5%, 15–65 years: 69.1%, over 65 years: 11.4%
Birth rate (2003): 10.2‰
Death rate (2003): 9.8‰
Infant mortality rate (2003): 8‰
Life expectancy at birth (2003): male: 69.8 years, female: 77.6 years

ECONOMY
GNP (2002): 21.3 billion US$
GNP per capita (2002): 3,970 US$
GNP per capita PPP (2002): 12,590 international dollars
HDI (2000): 0.835
GDP annual growth rate (2003): 4.2%
Annual inflation rate (2000): 12.04%
Labour force by occupation (2001): agriculture: 6.1%, industry: 37.6%, services: 56.3%
GDP by sector (2000): agriculture: 4.6%, industry: 34.6%, services: 60.8%
Gross public debt (2002): 42.6
Unemployment rate (2002): 18.7%

Agriculture and fishing
Crops
sugar beets (2002): 1,340,000t
wheat (2002): 1,554,000t
maize (2002): 754,000t
barley (2002): 695,000t
potatoes (2002): 484,000t
rye (2001): 119,000t
Livestock farming and fishing
cattle (2002): 645,000 head
horses (2001): 10,000 head
sheep (2002): 358,000 head
pigs (2002): 1,469,000 head
chickens (2002): 5,840,000 head
fish (1999): 2,260t

Energy generation and mining
total electricity (2001): 30,293 million kWh
natural gas (2002): 200 million m³
coal (1993): 2,286,000t
lignite (2001): 3,423,000t

Industrial production
sugar (2002): 200,000t
wine (2002): 316,000hl
steel (2003): 4,588,000t
cars (2002): 225,000 units
cotton yarn (1997): 17,000t
flax (2001): 2,000t
cement (2001): 3,123,000t
timber (2000): 5,046,000m³
paper (2000): 925,000t

Tourism
Tourism revenue (2001): 639 million US$

Foreign trade
Exports (2000): 11,896 million US$
Imports (2000): 12,791 million US$

Defence
Armed forces (2001): 26,200 people
Defence budget (2001): 1.66% of PIB

Standard of living
Inhabitants per doctor (1995): 333
Average daily calorie intake (2000): 3,133 (FAO minimum: 2,400
Cars per 1,000 inhabitants (1999): 229
Televisions per 1,000 inhabitants (2001): 407

HISTORY: KEY DATES

10c: the Magyars (Hungarians) destroyed Great Moravia and annexed Slovakia, which then constituted Upper Hungary.
1526: the area was united with the rest of Hungary in the Habsburg empire.
1540: the Ottomans occupied the Hungarian Plain. The Hungarian government was established in Pressburg (today's Bratislava), where it remained until 1848.
19c: the Slovak national movement developed.
1918: Slovakia became part of Czechoslovakia.
1939: a separate Slovak state, a protectorate of Germany, was created.
1945–8: Slovakia was reincorporated into Czechoslovakia.
1948–53: Czechoslovakia's communist leader Klement Gottwald strengthened the country's ties with the USSR.
1968: the Communist leader Alexander

Dubček initiated liberalizing reforms (known as the Prague Spring), leading to intervention and occupation by Soviet forces.
1969: Czechoslovakia became a federal state made up of the Czech and the Slovak republics.
1989: after a series of peaceful public demonstrations (known as the 'Velvet Revolution') the Communist authorities resigned. The role of party leader was abolished, and the dissident Václav Havel was elected president.
1990: the Slovak deputies renamed Czechoslovakia the Czech and Slovak Federative Republic.
1992–3: the Czech and Slovak governments negotiated the process of dividing Czechoslovakia into two independent states.
2004: Slovakia became a member of the North Atlantic Treaty Organization (NATO) and the European Union (EU).

Slovenia

200 1000 2000 3000 m

═══ motorway
─── road
─── railway line

✈ airport
★ place of interest

● population over 250,000
● population 100,000 to 250,000
● population 30,000 to 100,000
• population less than 30,000

The Republic of Slovenia is a mountainous country in central Europe. Forests cover approximately half of the country, and the the Drava and Sava river valleys cut through its mountains. Slovenia can be divided into three main regions: the Slovenian Alps (2,853m at their highest peak, Mount Triglav), the Karst plateau and Mediterranean coast in the south-west, which is humid and forested, and the fertile Pannonian Plain in the east and north-east of the country, where vineyards grow in the hillier areas.

Area: 20,256km²
Population (2002): 1,984,000
Capital: Ljubljana 250,000 (2001 e) including the suburbs
Government type and political system: republic with a semi-presidential system
Head of state: (President of the Republic) Janez Drnovšek
Head of government: (Prime Minister) Janez Janša
Administrative structure: 12 regions
Official language: Slovene
Currency: tolar

DEMOGRAPHICS
Density: 98 inhab/km²
Percentage of population in urban areas (2001): 49.2%
Age structure of population (2000): 0–15 years: 15.9%, 15–65 years: 70.2%, over 65 years: 13.9%
Birth rate (2003): 8.3‰
Death rate (2003): 9.8‰
Infant mortality rate (2003): 5.5‰
Life expectancy at birth (2003): male: 72.6 years, female: 79.8 years

ECONOMY
GNP (2002): 20.4 billion US$
GNP per capita (2002): 10,370 US$
GNP per capita PPP (2002): 18,480 international dollars
HDI (2000): 0.879
GDP annual growth rate (2003): 2.3%
Annual inflation rate (2000): 10.85%
Labour force by occupation (2001): agriculture: 9.9%, industry: 38.1%, services: 52%
GDP by sector (2000): agriculture: 3.3%, industry: 38.3%, services: 58.4%
Gross public debt (2002): 28.3% of GDP
Unemployment rate (2002): 5.9%

Agriculture and fishing
Crops
sugar beets (2002): 232,000t
wheat (2002): 175,000t
maize (2002): 371,000t
apples (2001): 130,000t
potatoes (2002): 166,000t
grapes (2002): 123,000t
Livestock farming and fishing
cattle (2002): 477,000 head
sheep (2002): 94,000 head
pigs (2002): 600,000 head
fish (1999): 3,220t

Energy generation
total electricity (2001): 13,692 million kWh

Industrial production
sugar (2002): 25,000t
wine (2002): 480,000hl
beer (2000): 1,490,000hl
meat (2001): 171,000t
steel (2003): 543,000t
aluminium (2001): 100,000t
cement (2001): 1,300,000t

Tourism
Tourism revenue (2001): 996 million US$

Foreign trade
Exports (2002): 10,472.6 million US$
Imports (2002): 10,715.7 million US$

Defence
Armed forces (2001): 9,000 people
Defence budget (2001): 1.48% of GDP

Standard of living
Inhabitants per doctor (1995): 476
Average daily calorie intake (2000): 3,168 (FAO minimum: 2,400)
Cars per 1,000 inhabitants (2000): 426
Televisions per 1,000 inhabitants (2000): 368

HISTORY: KEY DATES
6c: Slav tribes (Slovenians) settled in the region, establishing the state of Samo.
788: Samo became part of Charlemagne's empire.
1335: the Habsburg family took control of the region, which eventually became part of Austria.
16c–17c: Turkish invasions weakened the country.
19c: serfdom was abolished following rebellions among the peasant population.
1918: Slovenia became part of the kingdom of the Serbs, Croats and Slovenes.
1929: the kingdom adopted the name Yugoslavia.
1941–5: Yugoslavia was divided up between Germany, Italy and Hungary.
1945: Slovenia became one of the six republics within the Federal People's Republic of Yugoslavia.
1990: the democratic opposition won the country's first free elections.
1991: Slovenia proclaimed its independence.
2004: Slovenia became a member of the North Atlantic Treaty Organization (NATO) and the European Union (EU).

The Kingdom of Spain is a country in south-western Europe, bordering on the Atlantic Ocean in the north and south-west, and the Mediterranean in the south and east. Spain shares land boundaries with France and Andorra in the Pyrenees in the north-east, and Portugal in the west. The country is made up of a vast inland plateau (la Meseta) and has a dry climate, hot in summer and cold in winter. The plateau is bisected by the Sistema Central and cut through by the valleys of the Tajo (Tagus) and Duero rivers. There are ranges of high mountains such as the Cordillera Cantábrica and the Cordillera Ibérica in the north and the Sierra Morena in the south. Other ranges include the Pyrenees in the north-east and the Sistemas Béticos in the south-east. Most of Spain's major rivers rise in the mountains around the Sistema Central and flow westwards through Portugal towards the Atlantic Ocean. The River Ebro is an exception; it rises in the Cordillera Cantábrica in northern Spain, and flows in a south-easterly direction.

Area: 505,992km²
Population (2002): 39,924,000
Capital: Madrid 2,938,723 (2001 census), 5,423,384 (2001 census including the suburbs)
Government type and political system: constitutional monarchy with a parliamentary system
Head of state: (King) Juan Carlos of Bourbon
Head of government: (Prime Minister) José Luis Rodríguez Zapatero
Administrative structure: 17 autonomous communities and 2 autonomous cities
Official languages: Spanish (Castilian); Basque (Euskera), Catalan and Galician (Gallego) are co-official in their respective autonomous communities.
Currency: euro

DEMOGRAPHICS

Density: 78 inhab/km²
Percentage of population in urban areas (2001): 77.8%
Age structure of population (2000): 0–15 years: 14.7%, 15–65 years: 68.3%, over 65 years: 17%
Birth rate (2003): 9.3‰
Death rate (2003): 9.1‰
Infant mortality rate (2003): 5.1‰
Life expectancy at birth (2003): male: 75.9 years, female: 82.8 years

ECONOMY

GNP (2002): 596 billion US$
GNP per capita (2002): 14,580 US$
GNP per capita PPP (2001): 21,210 international dollars
HDI (2000): 0.913
GDP annual growth rate (2003): 2.4%
Annual inflation rate (2000): 3.43%
Labour force by occupation (2000): agriculture: 6.8%, industry: 31%, services: 62.2%
GDP by sector (2000): agriculture: 3.6%, industry: 30.5%, services: 65.9%
Gross public debt (2002): 53.8% of GDP
Unemployment rate (2002): 11.3%

Agriculture and fishing

Crops
sugar beets (2002): 8,040,000t
wheat (2002): 6,783,000t
lemons (2002): 909,000t
maize (2002): 4,463,000t
mandarin oranges (1998): 1,737,000t
olives (2002): 4,279,000t
oranges (2002): 2,866,000t
barley (2002): 8,333,000t
peaches (2002): 1,247,000t
potatoes (2002): 3,099,000t
grapes (2002): 5,875,000t
rice (2002): 816,000t
tomatoes (2002): 3,878,000t
sunflowers (2002): 757,000t
Livestock farming and fishing
cattle (2002): 6,411,000 head
sheep (2002): 24,301,000 head
pigs (2002): 23,858,000 head
chickens (2002): 128,000,000 head
fish (1999): 1,485,000t

Energy generation and mining

copper (2001): 9,700t
hydroelectricity (2001): 40,592 million kWh
nuclear electricity (2001): 60,523 million kWh
total electricity (2001): 222,545 million kWh
iron (2001): 1,965,000t
natural gas (2002): 539 million m³
coal (2001): 10,134,000t
oil (2002): 316,000t
lead (2001): 49,500t
uranium (2001): 30t
zinc (2001): 183,000t

Industrial production

sugar (2002): 1,317,000t
olive oil (2001): 1,072,000t
wine (2002): 36,419,000hl
beer (2000): 25,000,000hl
meat (2001): 5,049,000t
steel (2003): 16,129,000t
aluminium (2001): 376,000t
copper (2001): 9,700t
lead (2001): 98,000t
zinc (2001): 340,000t
cars (2002): 2,267,000 units
commercial vehicles (1998): 596,000 units
shipbuilding (1998): 660,000dwt
synthetic rubber (1998): 104,000t
cotton yarn (2001): 104,000t
wool (2001) : 30 800 t.
artificial textiles (1999): 30,300t
synthetic textiles (1999): 314,600t
timber (2000): 13,160,000m³
paper pulp (2001): 5,131,000t

Tourism

Tourism revenue (2001): 32,873 million US$

Foreign trade

Exports (2002): 125,795 million US$
Imports (2002): 158,893 million US$

Defence

Armed forces (2001): 177,950 people
Defence budget (2001): 1.2% of GDP

Standard of living

Inhabitants per doctor (1996): 238
Average daily calorie intake (2000): 3,352 (FAO minimum: 2,400)
Cars per 1,000 inhabitants (1998): 404
Televisions per 1,000 inhabitants (2000): 591

HISTORY: KEY DATES

Prehistoric times

Spain has been inhabited since the Palaeolithic period. The earliest known inhabitants included the Iberians. At the end of the 2nd millennium BC, the Phoenicians and Greeks established trading posts on the country's coasts.
6c BC: the Celts merged with the Iberians to form the Celtiberians.
3c BC–2c BC: the Punic Wars took place. Spain was ruled by Carthage, then Rome.

AD 5c: the Vandals were the first Germanic group to invade Spain.
AD 419: the Visigoths established a kingdom in Spain.

Islam and the Reconquista

711: the Arab conquest of the area began.
756: Spain became a Muslim state, and remained so for several hundred years. The Reconquista (Christian Reconquest) then began in the north of the country, where Christian areas still remained, including Castile, León, and Aragon still remained.
1085: Alfonso VI of Castile took Toledo back from the Moors.
1212: the Arabs were defeated at the battle of Las Navas de Tolosa.
1248: Ferdinand III of Castile captured Sevilla from the Arabs. By the mid-13c the Muslims had been driven back into the south, and only retained control of the kingdom of Grenada.

$\Rightarrow$

SPAIN

264

Madrid · Barcelona · Valencia · Sevilla · Zaragoza · Bilbao · Málaga · Portugal · France · Mediterranean Sea · Atlantic Ocean · Islas Canarias (Canary Islands)

HISTORY: KEY DATES

1492: the Catholic rulers Ferdinand of Aragon and Isabella I expelled all Arabs and Jews from Spain.

The Golden Age
16c: in addition to his colonial conquests in America, Charles of Spain, who became Emperor Charles V in 1519, added the Habsburgs' Austrian territories to his possessions. Philip II inherited Portugal in 1580, and his reign began the golden age of the arts in Spain. However, the defeat of the Armada by England in 1588 was a prelude to Spain's decline.

The decline
1640: the Union of Spain and Portugal ended.
1700–14: the end of the Habsburg dynasty after Charles II (the last Habsburg Spanish king) allowed Philip of Bourbon, the grandson of Louis XIV, to become king of Spain. The War of the Spanish Succession lasted from 1701 to 1714.
1759–88: Charles III, an enlightened despot, tried to put the country back on its feet.
1808: Napoleon I placed his brother Joseph on the throne. In a bloody uprising (known as the *Dos de Mayo*, Second of May), the Spaniards revolted

against Joseph Bonaparte. They were then suppressed when French troops fired on a crowd in Madrid the following day (*Tres de Mayo*). This marked the beginning of the War of Independence.
1814–33: Ferdinand VII established an absolutist monarchy, and lost Spain's colonies in America.

Fratricidal wars
1833–68: Queen Isabella II was defeated in war with the Carlists, supporters of her uncle Don Carlos, and was overthrown in the 1868 Revolution.
1874: the Bourbons returned to power after the short-lived First Republic, and Alfonso XII was proclaimed king.
1885–1931: the regency of María Cristina (until 1902) and the reign of Alfonso XIII were marked by unrest. Following a war with the USA, Spain lost Cuba, the Philippines and Puerto Rico. Domestic anarchy led to the emergence of the Basque and Catalan nationalist movements.
1923–30: Miguel Primo de Rivera established a dictatorship.
1931: Alfonso XIII left Spain and the Second Republic was established.
1936: in February, the Popular Front

won elections. In July, General Franco's military coup marked the beginning of the Spanish Civil War.

General Franco's dictatorship
1939–75: General Franco, head of state for life, led an authoritarian regime. Legislative power was devolved to the Cortes, a non-elected assembly (1942). During World War II, although Spain was sympathetic to the Axis Powers, it refused either to join the Axis Alliance or to fight alongside the Allies.
1950s and 60s: Spain became a member of the United Nations (UN).
1969: Franco chose Juan Carlos as his successor.

Democratic Spain
1975: after the death of Franco, Juan Carlos became king of Spain and attempted to introduce democratic reforms.
1978: a new constitution re-established the country's democratic institutions, and created autonomous governments in the seventeen regions.
1982: Spain became a member of the North Atlantic Treaty Organization (NATO).
1986: Spain became a member of the European Economic Community (EEC).

The Autonomous Communities

autonomous communities	area in km²	population*	name of inhabitants	capital	number of provinces
Andalucia	87 268	7 357 558	Andalucian	Seville	8
Aragon	47 650	1 204 215	Aragonese	Zaragoza	3
Asturias	10 565	1 062 998	Asturian	Oviedo	1
Balearic Islands	5 014	841 669	Balearic	Palma de Mallorca	1
Canary Islands	7 300	1 694 477	Canary Islander	Las Palmas	2
Cantabria	5 289	535 131	Cantabrian	Santander	1
Castilla-La Mancha	79 500	1 760 516		Toledo	5
Castilla y Leon	94 200	2 456 474		Valladolid	9
Cataluna	32 100	6 343 110	Catalan	Barcelona	4
Euskadi/Pais Vasco	7 254	2 082 587	Basque	Vitoria-Gasteiz	3
Extremadura	41 602	1 058 503	Extremaduran	Mérida	2
Galicia	29 734	2 695 880	Galician	Santiago de Compostela	4
La Rioja	5 034	276 702		Logroño	1
Madrid	8 028	5 423 384		Madrid	1
Murcia	11 317	1 197 646	Murcian	Murcia	1
Navarre	10 421	555 829		Pamplona	1
Valencia	23 305	4 162 776	Valencian	Valencia	3

autonomous cities	population*
Ceuta and Melilla	137 916

*2001 census

The Kingdom of Sweden is the largest country in Scandinavia, bounded to the west by Norway and to the east by Finland, the Gulf of Bothnia and the Baltic Sea. The northern region, Norrland, has a harsh climate (average temperatures in February vary between –6°C and 12°C) and contrasts with southern Sweden, which is crossed by a depression filled with several large lakes. Now linked by the Göta Canal, these lakes connect the Skagerrak in the west with the Baltic Sea in the east. Off the south-east coast of Sweden, where temperatures are milder, lie the islands of Gotland and Öland, where lakes alternate with forests.

Area: 449,964km²
Population (2002): 8,823,000
Capital: Stockholm 755,619 (2001 e), 1,626,000 (2001 e) including the suburbs
Government type and political system: constitutional monarchy with a parliamentary system
Head of state: (King) Karl XVI Gustav
Head of government: (Prime Minister) Göran Persson
Administrative structure: 21 counties
Official language: Swedish
Currency: krona

Sweden

★ place of interest
200 400 1000 1500 m

═══ motorway
─── road
─── railway line
✈ airport

● population over 500,000
● population 100,000 to 500,000
● population 50 000 to 100,000
• population less than 50,000

DEMOGRAPHICS
Density: 20 inhab/km²
Percentage of population in urban areas (2001): 83.3%
Age structure of population (2000): 0–15 years: 18.2%, 15–65 years: 64.4%, over 65 years: 17.4%
Birth rate (2003): 10.3‰
Death rate (2003): 10.6‰
Infant mortality rate (2003): 3.4‰
Life expectancy at birth (2003): male: 77.6 years, female: 82.6 years

ECONOMY
GNP (2002): 232 billion US$
GNP per capita (2002): 25,970 US$
GNP per capita PPP (2001): 25,820 international dollars
HDI (2000): 0.941
GDP annual growth rate (2003): 1.6%
Annual inflation rate (2000): 1%
Labour force by occupation (2000): agriculture: 2.4%, industry: 24.6%, services: 73%
GDP by sector (2000): agriculture: 1.8%,

industry: 28%, services: 70.2%
Gross public debt (2002): 52.7% of GDP
Unemployment rate (2002): 4.9%

Agriculture
Crops
oats (2001): 961,000t
sugar beets (2002): 2,664,000t
wheat (2002): 2,113,000t
rape (2001): 106,000t
barley (2002): 1,778,000t
potatoes (2002): 914,000t
Livestock farming
cattle (2002): 1,638,000 head
sheep (2002): 427,000 head
pigs (2002): 1,882,000 head

Energy generation and mining
silver (2001): 295t
copper (2001): 79,000t
hydroelectricity (2001): 77,622 million kWh
nuclear electricity (2001): 65,750 million kWh
total electricity (2001): 152,913 million kWh
iron (2001): 12,811,000t

lead (2001): 95,000t
zinc (2001): 161,000t

Industrial production
milk (2001): 3,300,000t
butter (2001): 50,000t
cheese (2001): 132,000t
sugar (2002): 470,000t
cast iron (1998): 3,370,000t
aluminium (2001): 102,000t
copper (2001): 79,000t
lead (2001): 81,800t
cars (2002): 238,000 units
commercial vehicles (1998): 119,000 units
artificial textiles (1999): 22,200t
cement (2001): 2,700,000t
timber (2000): 58,920,000m³
paper (2000): 10,786,000t

Tourism
Tourism revenue (2001): 4,162 million US$

Foreign trade
Exports (2002): 81,538 million US$
Imports (2002): 66,069 million US$

SWEDEN

Defence	Standard of living	(FAO minimum: 2,400)
Armed forces (2001): 33,900 people	Inhabitants per doctor (1996): 322	Cars per 1,000 inhabitants (2000): 451
Defence budget (2001): 1.94% of GDP	Average daily calorie intake (2000): 3,109	Televisions per 1,000 inhabitants (2001): 965

HISTORY: KEY DATES

Early origins to the formation of the Swedish nation

9c–11c: the inhabitants of Sweden, known as Varangians, traded mainly with Russia. Christianity advanced after the baptism of the king, Olof Skötkonung, in 1008.

c.1157: Eric IX, the Saint, led a crusade against Finland.

1250–66: Birger Jarl, the founder of the Folkung dynasty, established his capital in Stockholm and reinforced the unity of the country.

1319: Magnus VII Eriksson united Norway and Sweden.

1380: Margrethe I became regent after the death of her husband, and governed Denmark and Norway. Taking advantage of a rebellion by the Swedes against their king, she proclaimed herself queen of Sweden in 1388.

1397: the Kalmar Union brought the three Scandinavian kingdoms of Denmark, Norway and Sweden together under Margrethe I and her cousin and heir, Erik of Pomerania.

1440–1520: the Swedish national opposition rallied around the Sture family.

The golden era

1523–60: Gustav I Vasa, who conquered the Danish, became king. He restored Sweden's independence and established Lutheranism as the state religion.

1568–92: Johan III Vasa began to build a Swedish empire in the Baltic region.

1611–32: Gustav II Adolf was victorious in the Thirty Years' War.

1632–54: Queen Christina (under the regency of Count Axel Oxenstierna until 1644), came to the throne. The Peace of Westphalia (1648) gave a number of territories to Sweden.

1654–60: Karl X Gustav defeated the Danish.

1697–1721: under Karl XII, Sweden suffered heavy losses in the Northern War.

The Age of Liberty to the present day

18c: opposition between the pacifist 'Cap' party and the militaristic, pro-French 'Hat' party marked the politics of this era, which was known as the Age of Liberty.

1771–92: Gustav III reigned, restoring absolutism.

1808: Gustav IV Adolf ceded Finland to Russia.

1810: Karl XIII adopted the French Marshal Jean-Baptiste Jules Bernadotte as his successor. Bernadotte formed alliances with Great Britain and Russia against Napoleon Bonaparte.

1814: under the Treaty of Kiel, Denmark ceded Norway to Sweden.

1818–44: Bernadotte became king of Sweden and Norway under the name of Karl XIV Johan.

1905: Norway seceded from Sweden.

1907–50: under the reign of Gustav V, Sweden remained neutral during the two world wars.

1973: Karl XVI Gustav succeeded Gustav VI Adolf as king.

1995: Sweden became a member of the European Union (EU).

Marshal Bernadotte, king of Sweden

Jean-Baptiste Jules Bernadotte was born the son of a lawyer in Pau, France in 1763. He joined the French army in 1780 and fought his way up to become marshal in 1804. In 1799 he became Minister of War, and for his conduct at the Battle of Austerlitz (1805) was named Prince of Pontecorvo. In 1810, after fighting in several Napoleonic campaigns, he was made heir to the Swedish throne by a group of Swedes who had been impressed by his conduct and wished to please Napoleon, then at the height of his power. On coming to Sweden, Bernadotte was received into the Lutheran faith and adopted the name Karl Johan. He took control of his adopted country's foreign policy, steering it away from France. He concluded an alliance with Russia and took command of the allied forces in northern Germany in the final campaigns, forcing France's ally, Denmark, to surrender Norway to Sweden at the Treaty of Kiel (1814). His autocratic rule after his accession, and his alliance with Russia, caused opposition to him in the 1830s. He died in Stockholm and was succeeded by his son, Oscar I.

Legend:
- motorway
- road
- railway line
- ✈ airport
- ● population over 100,000
- ● population 50,000 to 100,000
- • population 10,000 to 50,000
- · population less than 10,000
- canton boundary
- ● canton administrative centre
- ● semi-canton admin. centre
- Chur — canton administrative centre
- Stans — semi-canton admin. centre

500 1000 1500 2000 m

10 km

GERMANY

AUSTRIA

LIECHTENSTEIN

VADUZ

ITALY

FRANCE

VOSGES

Lake Constance (Bodensee)

Schaffhausen · Stein · Diessenhofen · Kreuzlingen · Konstanz · Frauenfeld · Romanshorn · Arbon · St Gallen · Rorschach · Altstätten · Buchs · Gossau · Herisau · Wil · Winterthur · Bülach · Kloten · Wetzikon · Uster · Dietikon · Schlieren · Zürich · Wädenswil · Thalwil · Horgen · Zug · Baar · Einsiedeln · Schwyz · Brunnen · Altdorf · Glarus · Linthal · Chur · Bad Ragaz · Davos · Scuol · Müstair

AARGAU · BASELLAND · SOLOTHURN · LUZERN · ZUG · SCHWYZ · URI · GLARUS · SANKT GALLEN · APPENZELL AUSSER RHODEN · APPENZELL INNER RHODEN · THURGAU · ZÜRICH · GRAUBÜNDEN · TICINO · VALAIS · BERN · FRIBOURG · NEUCHÂTEL · VAUD · GENÈVE · JURA

Basle (Basel) · Riehen · Liestal · Pratteln · Aarau · Olten · Zofingen · Langenthal · Burgdorf · Solothurn · Grenchen · Biel · Delémont · Moutier · BERN · Köniz · Thun · Spiez · Interlaken · Brig · Visp · Zermatt · Sierre · Sion · Martigny · Monthey · Montreux · Vevey · Lausanne · Morges · Nyon · Genève (Geneva) · Meyrin · Lancy

Neuchâtel · La Chaux-de-Fonds · Le Locle · Yverdon · Fribourg · Bulle · Payerne

Monte Rosa · Mont Blanc 4,808 m · Great St Bernard Pass 2,469 m · Simplon Pass 2,005 m · Passo del San Gottardo · Aletsch · Alpi Pennine · Berner Alpen (Bernese Alps) · Glarner Alpen · Albula Alpen · Silvretta Gruppe · Ober Engadin · Lago di Como · Lago di Lugano · Lago Maggiore · Lugano · Bellinzona · Locarno · Domodossola

Lac Léman (Lake Geneva) · Lac de Neuchâtel · Lac de la Gruyère · Thuner See · Brienzer See · Zürichsee · Zuger See · Vierwaldstätter See

The Swiss Confederation is a landlocked republic in Western Europe. It is a mountainous country that can be divided into three main regions: the Jura Mountains, the Swiss Plateau (or Mittelland) and the Alps, which tower above the valleys of the rivers Rhône and Rhine, as well as the plain of the River Po. The Swiss Plateau, situated between the Alps and the Jura Mountains, is made up of hills and valleys which decrease in size towards the south.

Area: 41,284km²
Population (2002): 7,168,000
Capital: Bern 122,469 (2001 e), 316,000 (2001 e) including the suburbs
Government type and political system: republic
Head of state and government: (President of the Swiss Confederation) Joseph Deiss
Administrative structure: 23 cantons and 3 semi-cantons
Official languages: German, French, Italian and Romansch
Currency: Swiss franc

DEMOGRAPHICS

Density: 179 inhab/km²
Percentage of population in urban areas (2001): 67.5%
Age structure of population (2000): 0–15 years: 16.7%, 15–65 years: 67.3%, over 65 years: 16%
Birth rate (2003): 8.7‰
Death rate (2003): 9.8‰
Infant mortality rate (2003): 4.8‰
Life expectancy at birth (2003): male: 75.9 years, female: 82.3 years

ECONOMY

GNP (2002): 264 billion US$
GNP per capita (2002): 36,170 US$
GNP per capita PPP (2002): 31,840 international dollars
HDI (2000): 0.928
GDP annual growth rate (2001): 0.9%
Annual inflation rate (2000): 1.58%
Labour force by occupation (2000): agriculture: 4.5%, industry: 26.4%, services: 69.1%
GDP by sector (1998): agriculture: 2.6%, industry: 33.5%, services: 63.9%
Gross public debt: n/a
Unemployment rate (2002): 3.2%

Agriculture

Crops
sugar beets (2002): 1,408,000t
wheat (2002): 550,000t
maize (2002): 195,000t
barley (2002): 254,000t
apples (2001): 170,000t
potatoes (2002): 526,000t
Livestock farming
cattle (2002): 1,594,000 head
sheep (2002): 441,000 head
pigs (2002): 1,557,000 head

Energy generation

hydroelectricity (2001): 40,894 million kWh
nuclear electricity (2001): 25,470 million kWh
total electricity (2001): 68,682 million kWh

Industrial production

milk (2001): 3,927,000t
butter (2001): 37,400t
cheese (2001): 162,300t
meat (2001): 433,000t

sugar (2002): 241,000t
wine (2002): 1,190,000hl
aluminium (2001): 35,000t
cotton yarn (1998): 26,000t
synthetic textiles (1999): 90,500t
cement (2001): 3,950,000t
timber (2000): 7,612,000m³
paper (2000): 1,616,000t

Tourism

Tourism revenue (2001): 7,618 million US$

Foreign trade

Exports (2002): 100,475 million US$
Imports (2002): 94,043 million US$

Defence

Armed forces (2001): 3,500 people
Defence budget (2001): 1.13% of GDP

Standard of living

Inhabitants per doctor (1996): 312
Average daily calorie intake (2000): 3,293 (FAO minimum: 2,400)
Cars per 1,000 inhabitants (2000): 494
Televisions per 1,000 inhabitants (2001): 554

HISTORY: KEY DATES

Early origins and the Confederation

58 BC: the Romans conquered Switzerland's early inhabitants, the Helvetii.
AD 5c: the Burgundii and the Alemanni invaded Switzerland and Germanized the north and centre of the country.
7c–9c: the country was converted to Christianity.
1033: Switzerland was united as part of the Holy Roman Empire.
11c–13c: the Habsburg dynasty gained control of most of the Swiss territory.
13c: the Swiss cantons fought Austria to defend their freedom.
1291: the three forest cantons (Uri, Schwyz and Unterwalden) formed a defensive league and signed a perpetual covenant, declaring their freedom and promising mutual support. This marked the start of the Swiss confederation.
14c: Lucerne, Zürich, Glarus, Zug and Bern joined the confederation. After the victories of Sempach (1386) and Näfels (1388), the confederation was recognized as a significant military power.
1499: Maximilian I signed the Peace Treaty of Basle, making Switzerland virtually independent.
1481–1513: Solothurn, Fribourg, Basle, Schaffhausen and Appenzell joined the confederation.
1516: Switzerland signed a perpetual alliance with France after being defeated at the battle of Marignano.
16c: Huldreich Zwingli and John Calvin preached the Reformation in

Zürich and Geneva respectively. Religious differences divided Switzerland.
1648: the Peace of Westphalia recognized the independence of the confederation.

Contemporary Switzerland

1798: the French Revolutionary government (the Directory) established the short-lived Helvetic Republic.
1803: Napoleon Bonaparte ratified an Act of Mediation, restoring the confederation.
1813: the Act of Mediation was abrogated.
1815: a new pact between twenty-three cantons was ratified by the Congress of Vienna, which recognized Switzerland's neutrality.
1845–7: the seven Catholic cantons formed a separate league (the Sonderbund) to protect Catholic interests.
1848: a new constitution established a federal state, with Bern as its centre of government.
1914–8, 1939–45: Switzerland maintained armed neutrality throughout World War I and World War II.
1979: a new canton, Jura, was created.
1998: international pressure led Swiss banks to compensate the families of Holocaust victims whose stolen assets had been deposited there by Nazis.
1999: a new constitution was adopted.
2002: Switzerland voted in favour of joining the United Nations.

UKRAINE

Ukraine is the second largest republic in Europe (after Russia). It has a continental climate with cold winters and hot, humid summers. Most of the country is covered by steppes, with high elevations in the west, south and south-east. There are forests in northern Ukraine, and more arid terrain around the Black Sea.

Area: 603,700km²
Population (2002): 48,652,000
Capital: Kiev 2,488,000 (2001 e)
Government type and political system: republic with a semi-presidential system
Head of state: (President of the Republic – outgoing) Leonid Kuchma
Head of government: (Prime Minister – outgoing) Viktor Yanukovich
Administrative structure: 24 regions, 2 municipalities and 1 autonomous republic
Official language: Ukrainian
Currency: hryvnia

DEMOGRAPHICS
Density: 84 inhab/km²
Percentage of population in urban areas (2001): 68%
Age structure of population (2000): 0–15 years: 17.8%, 15–65 years: 68.4%, over 65 years: 13.8%
Birth rate (2003): 8.4‰
Death rate (2003): 14.2‰
Infant mortality rate (2003): 13.8‰
Life expectancy at birth (2003): male: 64.7 years, female: 74.7 years

ECONOMY
GNP (2002): 37.9 billion US$
GNP per capita (2002): 780 US$
GNP per capita PPP (2002): 4,800 international dollars
HDI (2000): 0.748
GDP annual growth rate (2003): 9.3%
Annual inflation rate (1997): 15.9%
Labour force by occupation (1998): agriculture: 26.1%, industry: 27.4%, services: 46.5%
GDP by sector (2000): agriculture: 13.8%, industry: 38.5%, services: 47.7%
Gross public debt: n/a
Unemployment rate (2002): 10.1%

Agriculture and fishing
Crops
oats (2001): 1,100,000t
sugar beets (2002): 14,453,000t
wheat (2002): 20,556,000t
maize (2002): 4,180,000t
millet (2001): 600,000t
walnuts (2001): 52,000t
barley (2002): 10,364,000t
apples (2001): 750,000t
potatoes (2002): 16,620,000t
rye (2001): 1,500,000t
tomatoes (2002): 1,038,000t
sunflowers (2002): 3,271,000t
Livestock farming and fishing
cattle (2002): 9,421,000 head
horses (2001): 675,000 head
sheep (2002): 1,111,000 head
pigs (2002): 8,370,000 head
fish (1999): 442,000t

Energy generation and mining
hydroelectricity (2001): 12,973 million kWh
nuclear electricity (2001): 71,667 million kWh
total electricity (2001): 164,690 million kWh
iron (1998): 29,100,000t
natural gas (2002): 17,200 million m³
coal (2001): 62,987,000t
manganese (2001): 930,000t
oil (2002): 3,900,000t
uranium (2001): 500t

Ukraine

200   500   1000 m

★ place of interest   ✈ airport

— road
— railway line

● population over 1,000,000
● population 500,000 to 1 000,000
● population 100,000 to 500,000
• population less than 100,000

100 km

Industrial production

milk (2001): 13,405,000t
butter (2001): 160,000t
sugar (2002): 1,554,000t
honey (2001): 52,000t
wine (2002): 1,953,000hl
steel (2003): 36,707,000t
cast iron (1998): 20,777,000t
aluminium (2001): 122,000t
lead (2001): 12,000t

shipbuilding (2001): 12,000dwt
cotton yarn (1997): 12,000t
flax (2001): 10,000t

Tourism

Tourism revenue (2001): 2,725 million US$

Foreign trade

Exports (2002): 18,669 million US$
Imports (2002): 17,959 million US$

Defence

Armed forces (2001): 302,300 people
Defence budget (2001): 1.59% of GDP

Standard of living

Inhabitants per doctor (1995): 222
Average daily calorie intake (2000): 2,871 (FAO minimum: 2,400)
Cars per 1,000 inhabitants (1999): 104
Televisions per 1,000 inhabitants (2000): 456

HISTORY: KEY DATES

9c–12c: present-day Ukraine was part of the first East Slavic state, Kievan Rus.
1238–40: the Mongols conquered the region.
13c–14c: Lithuania and Poland annexed all the regions where the Ukrainian civilization developed, except for Subcarpathian Ruthenia, which was under Hungarian rule.
15c–16c: Cossack communities were established along the Don and Dniepr rivers.
1654: the Russian tsar agreed to give his protection to the Cossack rebel Bohdan Khmelnitsky, who led a rebellion against Polish rule.
1667: under the Treaty of Andrusovo, Ukraine was divided between Poland and Russia.
1709: the Russian tsar Peter I, the Great, defeated the Cossack hetman (leader) Mazeppa at the battle of Poltava.
1918: Ukraine proclaimed itself an independent republic after the Bolshevik Revolution.
1921: the Ukrainian Soviet Socialist Republic was declared.
1939–40: the USSR annexed the Polish territories inhabited by Ukrainians, as well as northern Bukovina and Bessarabia.
1941–4: during the Nazi occupation of Ukraine, millions of civilians and soldiers (including most of Ukraine's 1.5 million Jews) were massacred.
1945: Subcarpathian Ruthenia was incorporated into the Ukrainian Soviet Socialist Republic.
1954: Crimea was incorporated into the Ukrainian Soviet Socialist Republic.
1991: Ukraine declared its independence and became a member of the Commonwealth of Independent States (CIS).

Seas of many colours

The Black Sea, an inland sea bordered by Ukraine, Russia, Georgia, Turkey, Bulgaria and Romania, is not the only sea in the world to bear the name of a colour. The White Sea (or Beloye More) in north-west Russia is an arm of the Barents Sea that almost constitutes a landlocked extension of the Arctic Ocean. The Yellow Sea, a large inlet of the western Pacific Ocean, lies north of the East China Sea between northern China and the Korean Peninsula. The best-known 'coloured' expanse of water is the Red Sea, a long arm of the Indian Ocean situated between Africa and the Arabian Peninsula.

There is also a Blue Sea – not a body of water, but a province in China, situated to the north-east of Tibet where the Huang He (Yellow River), the Yangtze and the Mekong rivers rise. The province takes its name from a salt lake, Qinghai Hu ('blue sea' in Chinese and Mongolian). There is no Green Sea, although there are two Green Bays in Canada; however, there is an Emerald Sea at the entrance to Antsiranana Bay in Madagascar, and an Emerald Coast in France (a popular tourist destination between Dinard and Saint-Malo). Finally, the Kenyan soda lake, Lake Turkana, is commonly known as the Jade Sea. The lake owes its lovely name to algae particles that give its water a beautiful jade colour.

The United Kingdom is a union of four countries: England, Scotland and Wales (which form Great Britain) and Northern Ireland. The United Kingdom combined with the Irish Republic and several small islands around Britain constitute the British Isles. The nation's past prosperity was not a result of its natural environment (except perhaps its insularity): the total surface area is quite modest and the landscape is a mixture of lowlands, uplands and mountainous areas. The climate is wet and cool, and is often more favourable for livestock farming than for crops.

Area: 242,900km²
Population (2002): 59,657,000
Capital: London 2,765,975 (2001 census), 7,172,000 (2001 census) including the suburbs
Government type and political system: constitutional monarchy with a parliamentary system
Head of state: (Queen) Elizabeth II
Head of government: (Prime Minister) Tony Blair
Administrative structure: 4 nations
Official language: English
Currency: pound sterling

DEMOGRAPHICS
Density: 233 inhab/km²

Percentage of population in urban areas (2001): 89.5%
Age structure of population (2000): 0–15 years: 19%, 15–65 years: 65.2%, over 65: 15.8%
Birth rate (2003): 11‰
Death rate (2003): 10.4‰
Infant mortality rate (2003): 5.4‰
Life expectancy at birth (2003): male: 75.7 years, female: 80.7 years

ECONOMY
GNP (2002): 1,511 billion US$
GNP per capita (2002): 25,510 US$
GNP per capita PPP (2002): 26,580 international dollars
HDI (2000): 0.928
GDP annual growth rate (2003): 2.3%
Annual inflation rate (2000): 2.93%
Labour force by occupation (2000): agriculture: 1.5%, industry: 25.4%, services: 73.1%
GDP sector (2000): agriculture: 1.1%, industry: 28.7%, services: 70.2%
Gross public debt (2002): 38.5% of GDP
Unemployment rate (2002): 5.1%

Agriculture and fishing
Crops
oats (2001): 615,000t
sugar beets (2002): 9,435,000t
wheat (2002): 16,053,000t
rape (2001): 1,159,000t
barley (2002): 6,192,000t
potatoes (2002): 6,376,000t
Livestock farming and fishing
cattle (2002): 10,343,000 head
sheep (2002): 35,832,000 head
pigs (2002): 5,588,000 head
chickens (2002): 156,000,000 head
fish (1999): 1,041,000t

Energy generation and mining
hydroelectricity (2001): 3,184 million kWh
nuclear electricity (2001): 85,607 million kWh
total electricity (2001): 360,926 million

kWh
natural gas (2002): 108,435 million m³
coal (2001): 28,903,000t
oil (2002): 116,205,000t

Industrial production
milk (2001): 14,722,000t
butter (2001): 126,000t
cheese (2001): 382,000t
sugar (2002): 1,548,000t
meat (2001): 3,270,000t
beer (2001): 55,279,000hl
steel (2003): 12,949,000t
cast iron (1998): 13,215,000t
aluminium (2001): 341,000t
copper (2000): 50,000t
lead (2001): 366,000t
zinc (2001): 100,000t
cars (2002): 1,628,000 units
commercial vehicles (1998): 238,000 units
shipbuilding (1998): 74,000dwt
synthetic rubber (1998): 254,000t
wool (2001): 49,339t
artificial textiles (1999): 88,000t
synthetic textiles (1999): 205,400t
paper (2000): 6,868,000t

Tourism
Tourism revenue (2001): 16,283 million US$

Foreign trade
Exports (2002): 279,330 million US$
Imports (2002): 332,380 million US$

Defence
Armed forces (2001): 210,450 people
Defence budget (2001): 2.37% of the GDP

Standard of living
Inhabitants per doctor (1993): 667
Average daily calorie intake (2000): 3,334 (FAO minimum: 2,400)

Cars per 1,000 inhabitants (1999): 389
Televisions per 1,000 inhabitants (2001): 950

HISTORY: KEY DATES

Early origins to the United Kingdom
Inhabited since the 3rd millennium BC, Britain and Ireland were occupied by the Celts around 650 BC.
AD 1c: the country was invaded by Rome and became a province of the Roman Empire, named Brittania after a Romano-Celtic goddess.
5c: Germanic tribes (Angles, Jutes and Saxons) invaded Britain, driving the Celts out of what is now England into Ireland, Scotland and Wales.
9c–11c: the Danes invaded and their king, Canute, became king of England.
1066: after defeating his Anglo-Saxon rival Harold at the battle of Hastings, William of Normandy (William the Conqueror) was crowned king of England.

1154: King Henry II founded the Plantagenet dynasty in England.
1215: the Magna Carta, a written charter of traditional freedoms that marked the beginning of the nation's constitutional development, was granted by King John of England.
1327–1453: rivalry and dynastic disputes between England and France led to the Hundred Years War.
1455–1485 the Wars of the Roses, a series of civil wars between rival branches of the Plantagenets, led to the House of Tudor becoming the ruling family of England. Henry VII became the first Tudor king.
1534: King Henry VIII severed relations with the Catholic Church in Rome and proclaimed himself the sole

head of the Church of England.
1558–1603: the reign of Elizabeth I, whose victory over Spain in 1588 prefigured the future power of the English navy.
1603: King James VI of Scotland became king of England and Ireland under the name of James I, thereby uniting the crowns of the two kingdoms.
1688: William of Orange landed in England and dethroned King James VII and II. After ratifying the Declaration of Rights, he was proclaimed king in 1689, with his wife Mary as queen.
1707: the Act of Union united the kingdoms of England and Scotland.
1714: the Hanovers succeeded the

⇨

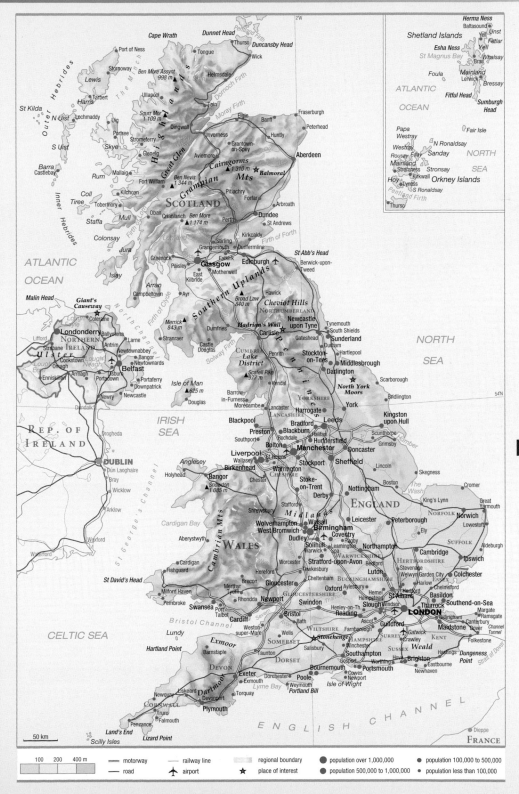

Shetland Islands

Herma Ness
Baltasound
Yell Unst
Esha Ness Fetlar
Whalsay
Foula Mainland
Lerwick Bressay
ATLANTIC
OCEAN
Fitful Head
Sumburgh
Head

Papa
Westray Fair Isle
Westray N Ronaldsay
Rousay Eday Sanday NORTH
Mainland Stronsay SEA
Stromness
Hoy Kirkwall Orkney Islands
Lyness S Ronaldsay
Thurso

Scotland

Cape Wrath
Dunnet Head
Port of Ness
Thurso Duncansby Head
Tongue Wick
Ben More Assynt Helmsdale
998 m
Stornoway
Lewis
Harris Tarbert
Ullapool
Dornoch Firth
St Kilda
N Uist Lochmaddy Uig Tain
Skye Portree Dingwall Elgin Fraserburgh
Sgurr Mor Inverness Moray Firth
1 109 m Stromeferry Grantown- Huntly Peterhead
S Uist Glenelg on-Spey Banff
Barra Aviemore Aberdeen
Castlebay Cairngorms
Rum Fort Willtam 1 310 m Balmoral
Ben Nevis Grampian
Kilchoan 1 344 m Mts Pitlochry
Coll Tobermory Forfar
Tiree Oban Ben More Perth Arbroath
Mull Crianlarich 1 174 m St Andrews Dundee
Staffa Stirling
Colonsay Grangemouth Kirkcaldy Firth of Forth
Jura Falkirk Dunfermline
Greenock Edinburgh St Abb's Head
Paisley Glasgow Berwick-upon-
Islay Arran East Motherwell Tweed
Campbeltown Kilbride
Ayr Southern Uplands Hawick
Malin Head Broad Law Cheviot Hills
Giant's Merrick 840 m NORTHUMBERLAND
Causeway 843 m Dumfries Newcastle
Londonderry Coleraine Hadrian's Wall upon Tyne
NORTHERN Ballymena Carlisle Tynemouth
Ulster Antrim Stranraer Gateshead South Shields
Strabane IRELAND Larne Castle Penrith Durham Sunderland
Omagh Newtownabbey Douglas CUMBRIA Hartlepool
Cookstown Bangor Lake Stockton- Middlesbrough
Enniskillen Armagh Belfast Newtownards District on-Tees
Portadown Lisburn Scafell Pike Darlington
Newry Portaferry 977 m Kendal Scarborough
Downpatrick North York
Newcastle Isle of Man Moors Bridlington
625 m Barrow- Yorkshire York
in-Furness Morecambe Lancaster
Dundalk Blackpool Lancashire Harrogate Kingston
Drogheda Preston Bradford Leeds upon Hull
REP. OF Blackburn Scunthorpe
IRELAND Southport Rochdale Halifax Huddersfield Grimsby
Bolton Doncaster Lincoln
Liverpool Manchester Sheffield
DUBLIN Wallasey St Helens Stockport Skegness
Dún Laoghaire Anglesey Birkenhead Warrington The Wash
Bray Holyhead Chester CHESHIRE Boston Cromer
Wicklow Bangor Stoke- Nottingham
Snowdon on-Trent Derby King's Lynn Great
Arklow 1 085 m Stafford Yarmouth
Shrewsbury ENGLAND NORFOLK Norwich
Wexford Midlands Leicester Peterborough Lowestoft
Cambrian Mts Wolverhampton Walsall Ely SUFFOLK
Waterford Aberystwyth West Bromwich Birmingham Coventry Northampton Aldeburgh
Dudley Rugby Cambridge
Cardigan Bay WALES Solihull Leamington WARWICKSHIRE Ipswich
Warwick Bedford HERTFORDSHIRE
Cardigan Worcester Stratford-upon-Avon Stevenage Colchester
Fishguard Hereford Cheltenham BUCKINGHAMSHIRE Welwyn Garden City
Merthyr Gloucester Oxford Aylesbury Hemel Harlow Chelmsford
St David's Head Milford Haven Tydfil Brecon Hempstead Hertford
Pembroke Rhondda Newport Swindon Henley-on-Th. Slough St Albans Basildon
Swansea Bristol Reading Windsor Thurrock Southend-on-Sea
Port Bath Ascot Margate
Talbot Cardiff WILTSHIRE Farnborough Guildford LONDON Billingham Ramsgate
Bristol Channel Weston- Gatwick SURREY Canterbury
super-Mare Wells HAMPSHIRE Crawley Maidstone Dover
Lundy SOMERSET Salisbury Stonehenge Winchester SUSSEX KENT Channel
Exmoor DORSET Gosport Weald Folkestone
Hartland Point Barnstaple Taunton Southampton Worthing Hastings
Portsmouth Brighton Dungeness
DEVON Bournemouth Eastbourne Point
Exeter Dorchester Poole Cowes Newhaven
Dartmoor Exmouth Weymouth Isle of Wight
Newquay Liskeard Torquay Lyme Bay Portland Bill
Devonport
CORNWALL Truro Plymouth
Penzance Falmouth ENGLISH CHANNEL
Land's End
Scilly Isles Lizard Point FRANCE
Dieppe

Water bodies and regions

ATLANTIC OCEAN
Outer Hebrides
The Minch
Inner Hebrides
Firth of Lorn
Firth of Clyde
North Channel
Lough Foyle
Lough Neagh
Lough Erne
IRISH SEA
Solway Firth
St George's Channel
CELTIC SEA
PENNINES
HUMBER
NORTH SEA
Strait of Dover

2W

54N

⥱

HISTORY: KEY DATES

Stuarts as monarchs of England and Scotland.

1756–63: following the Seven Years War, Britain obtained a number of new territories (including Canada and India) under the Treaty of Paris.

1760–1820: the first industrial revolution made Britain the world's leading economic power.

1775–83: ongoing tension between Britain and the colonists led to the American Revolution (or War of Independence), which resulted in the independence of the thirteen American colonies.

1793–1815: Britain was victorious over Napoleon's revolutionary France.

1800: the union of Great Britain and Ireland created the United Kingdom.

The British hegemony

1829: the Catholic Emancipation Act.

1837: Queen Victoria succeeded her uncle, William IV.

1876: Victoria was proclaimed Empress of India.

1895: the government's imperialist policies led to a large number of international disputes, including the Fashoda Crisis and the Boer War.

1904: the Entente Cordiale between Britain and France was formally established.

1910: George V became king.

From one war to another

1914–18: Britain participated actively in World War I.

1921: the Anglo-Irish Treaty gave Ireland independent dominion status as the Irish Free State, with full internal self-government rights. The treaty partitioned the six northern counties of Ireland from the rest, and this area (Northern Ireland) remained part of the United Kingdom of Great Britain and Northern Ireland.

1931: the Commonwealth of Nations was established.

1936: Edward VIII succeeded George V, but abdicated almost immediately in favour of his brother, George VI.

1939–45: during World War II, Great Britain, led by Winston Churchill, successfully resisted the German invasion.

The UK post-1945

1945–51: Great Britain joined the North Atlantic Treaty Organization (NATO) in 1949.

1952: Elizabeth II became queen.

1973: Great Britain joined the Common Market.

1982: following Argentina's invasion and occupation of the Falkland Islands, Great Britain despatched a task force to re-establish British control.

1985: an Anglo-Irish agreement on the management of Northern Irish affairs was signed, giving the Republic of Ireland a consultative role in the government of Northern Ireland.

1991: Great Britain took part in the military operations in the Gulf War.

1993: the Maastricht Treaty, creating the European Union (EU), was ratified. The peace process in Northern Ireland was relaunched.

1997: devolved legislative assemblies were established in Scotland and Wales. The UK restored the former British Crown Colony of Hong Kong to the People's Republic of China.

1999: in accordance with an agreement signed in 1998, a regional assembly was established in Northern Ireland.

2001: the UK provided military support for a US campaign against international terrorism.

2003: the UK joined a US-led military campaign against Iraq.

The European Monarchies

Several European countries have a form of government known as a constitutional monarchy, in which the sovereign has very little or no political power. The executive authority is vested in an elected head of government.

country	monarch	dynasty/house
Belgium	King Albert II	Saxe-Coburg-Gotha
Denmark	Queen Margrethe II	Schleswig-Holstein-Sonderburg-Glücksburg
Netherlands	Queen Beatrix	Orange-Nassau
Norway	King Harald V	Norway (Schleswig-Holstein-Sonderburg-Glücksburg)
Spain	King Juan Carlos	Bourbon
Sweden	King Karl XVI Gustav	Bernadotte
United Kingdom	Queen Elizabeth II	Windsor (Hanover-Saxe-Coburg-Gotha)

The three European principalities (Andorra, Liechtenstein and Monaco) and the Grand Duchy of Luxembourg, which are all neither republics nor monarchies, should also be mentioned.

country	title	name	dynasty / house
Andorra	Co-princes	the Bishop of Urgell the President of the French Republic	
Liechtenstein	Prince	Hans Adam II	Liechtenstein
Luxembourg	Grand Duke	Henri of Luxembourg	Luxembourg (Nassau-Weilburg)
Monaco	Prince	Rainier III	Grimaldi

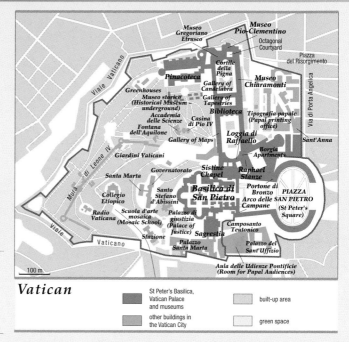

Vatican

| | St Peter's Basilica, Vatican Palace and museums | | | built-up area |
| | other buildings in the Vatican City | | | green space |

The Vatican, also known as the Holy See, is an independent papal sovereign state entirely surrounded by Italy. The world's smallest independent nation, it includes St Peter's Basilica, the Vatican Palace and Museum, the Vatican garden, several buildings in Rome and the Pope's summer villa at Castel Gandolfo.

Area: 0.44km²
Population (2000): 524
Head of state and government: (Pope) John Paul II
Administrative structure: no divisions
Official language: Latin
Currency: euro

DEMOGRAPHICS
Density: 1,194 inhab/km²

HISTORY: KEY DATES

AD 5c–1377: the Vatican was a papal residence until the return of the papacy to Rome.
1870: Rome became the capital of the newly united kingdom of Italy. The Pope, who had previously resided in the Quirinal Palace (which was now the royal palace of the kings of Italy), withdrew in protest to the Vatican, where he considered himself a prisoner, and refused to leave the area.
1929: the Lateran Treaty, signed by Pope Pius XI and Mussolini, recognized the sovereignty of the Vatican in return for papal recognition of the kingdom of Italy.

The election of the Pope and the Conclave

For many years the election of the Pope was only carried out by the Roman clergy, and frequently led to intense rivalries. Nicholas II decreed in 1059 that henceforth only cardinal bishops of the Holy Roman Church could elect the Roman Pontiff. In 1179, the third Treaty of Lateran extended this prerogative to all cardinals; however, the ambitions of the cardinal bishops and their protectors impeded the process. At the second Council of Lyon in 1274, Pope Gregory X decided that cardinals should meet within ten days of a pope's death and that they should be kept in strict seclusion, with no contact with the outside world, until a pope was chosen. This is the origin of the word 'conclave' (derived from the classical Latin term *cum clave* – literally 'with a key'), a word that is used to describe both the room in which the cardinals are locked up whilst choosing a new pope, and the group of cardinals themselves. In 1967, Pope Paul VI decreed that the cardinals electing the pope had to be under 80 years old and further simplified the conclave ritual (which takes place in a special area of the Vatican palaces) and the voting in the Sistine Chapel. When a pope has been selected, the ballot papers are burned and the resulting white smoke indicates to observers that there is a new pontiff and that the conclave is over. Traditionally, the chosen candidate had to obtain two-thirds of the votes plus one, but this rule was changed by Pope John Paul II in 1996. He stated that if no candidate had been chosen after 12 or 13 days, the conclave could select a pope by absolute majority.

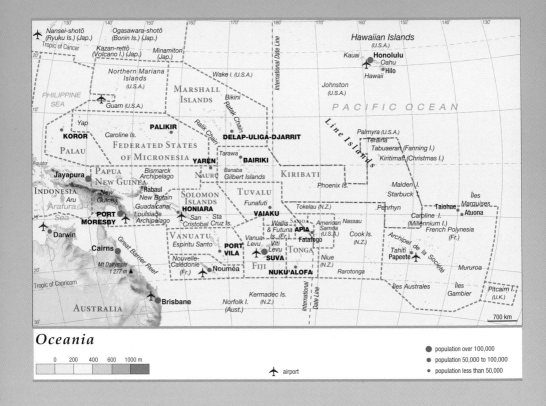

Oceania

0 200 400 600 1000 m	✈ airport

● population over 100,000
● population 50,000 to 100,000
● population less than 50,000

700 km

Nansei-shotō (Ryuku Is.) (Jap.)
Tropic of Cancer
Ogasawara-shotō (Bonin Is.) (Jap.)
Kazan-rettō (Volcano I.) (Jap.)
Minamitori (Jap.)
Hawaiian Islands (U.S.A.)
Kauai
Oahu
Honolulu
Hilo
Hawaii
Northern Mariana Islands (U.S.A.)
Wake I. (U.S.A.)
Johnston (U.S.A.)
PACIFIC OCEAN
PHILIPPINE SEA
MARSHALL ISLANDS
Bikini
Ratak Chain
International Date Line
Line Islands
Palmyra (U.S.A.)
Teraina
Tabuaeran (Fanning I.)
Kiritimati (Christmas I.)
Guam (U.S.A.)
Yap
KOROR
PALIKIR
Caroline Is.
Ralik Chain
DELAP-ULIGA-DJARRIT
Tarawa
PALAU
FEDERATED STATES OF MICRONESIA
YAREN
BAIRIKI
Equator
Jayapura
PAPUA NEW GUINEA
Bismarck Archipelago
New Guinea
Banaba
NAURU
Gilbert Islands
KIRIBATI
Malden I.
Starbuck I.
Îles Marquises
Taiohae
Atuana
INDONESIA
Aru
Arafura Sea
Darwin
Rabaul
New Britain
Guadalcanal
SOLOMON ISLANDS
HONIARA
Funafuti
TUVALU
Phoenix Is.
Penrhyn
Caroline I. (Millennium I.)
French Polynesia (Fr.)
PORT MORESBY
Louisiade Archipelago
San Cristobal
Sta Cruz Is.
VAIAKU
Vanua Levu
Wallis & Futuna Is. (Fr.)
SAMOA
APIA
Fatatogo
American Samoa (U.S.A.)
Tokelau (N.Z.)
Nassau
Cook Is. (N.Z.)
Archipel de la Société
Tahiti
Papeete
Cairns
Great Barrier Reef
VANUATU
Espiritu Santo
Nouvelle-Calédonie (Fr.)
PORT VILA
Viti Levu
SUVA
Tonga
NUKU'ALOFA
Niue (N.Z.)
Mururoa
Mt Dalrymple 1 277 m
Fiji
Rarotonga
Îles Australes
Îles Gambier
Pitcairn I. (U.K.)
Tropic of Capricorn
Noumèa
Kermadec Is. (N.Z.)
Norfolk I. (Aust.)
International Date Line
AUSTRALIA
Brisbane

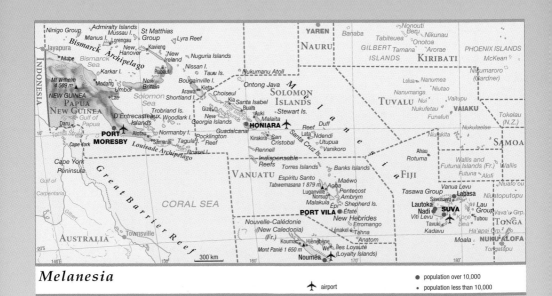

Melanesia

✈ airport

● population over 10,000
● population less than 10,000

300 km

Ninigo Group
Admiralty Islands
Mussau I.
St Matthias Group
Lyra Reef
YAREN
Banaba
Nonouti
Beru
Nikunau
NAURU
Tabiteuea
Onotoa
Arorae
PHOENIX ISLANDS
Jayapura
Manus I.
Lorengau
Kavieng
Nuguria Islands
GILBERT ISLANDS
Tamana
KIRIBATI
McKean
Bismarck Archipelago
New Hanover
New Ireland
Nissan I.
Nukumanu Atoll
Nikumaroro (Gardner)
INDONESIA
Aitape
Bismarck Sea
Karkar I.
Rabaul
Tauu Is.
Bougainville I.
Kieta
Ontong Java
Lolua
Nanumea
Niutao
Nanumanga
Nikumaroro
Mt Wilhelm 4 509 m
Madang
Umbol
New Britain
Arawa
Choiseul
Kia
Santa Isabel
SOLOMON ISLANDS
Nui
Vaitupu
TUVALU
NEW GUINEA
PAPUA NEW GUINEA
Lae
Solomon Sea
Trobriand Is.
D'Entrecasteaux Islands
Woodlark I.
Shortland I.
Gizo
New Georgia Islands
Malaita
Buala
Auki
Stewart Is.
Duff
Nukufetau
Funafuti
Nukulaelae
Tokelau (N.Z.)
Daru
Gulf of Papua
PORT MORESBY
Torres Strait
Alotau
Samarai
Tagula I.
Normanby I.
Pocklington Reef
Rossel I.
Louisiade Archipelago
Kirakira
HONIARA
Guadalcanal
San Cristobal
Lata
Ndendi
Reef
Santa Cruz Is.
Utupua
Vanikoro
Niulakita
Ahau
Rotuma
SAMOA
Cape York
Rennell
Indispensable Reefs
Torres Islands
Banks Islands
Wallis and Futuna Islands (Fr.)
Futuna
Alofi
Wallis
Niutao'ou
Cape York Peninsula
VANUATU
Espiritu Santo
Tabwemasana 1 879 m
Maéwo
Aoba
Pentecost
Tasawa Group
Savusavu
Vanua Levu
Labasa
N'utoputoņu
Gulf of Carpentaria
Gilbert
CORAL SEA
Luganville
Norsup
Ambrym
Malakula
Épi
Shepherd Is.
Lautoka
Nadi
Viti Levu
SUVA
Lau Group
Tubou
Vava'u Grp.
TONGA
Great Barrier Reef
Nouvelle-Calédonie (New Caledonia) (Fr.)
PORT VILA
New Hebrides
Erromango
Tanna
Éfaté
Tavuki
Kadavu
Kore Sea
Ha'apai Grp.
NUKU'ALOFA
AUSTRALIA
Townsville
Koumac
Hienghéne
Mont Panié 1 650 m
Anatom
Iles Loyauté (Loyalty Islands)
Lénakel
Moala
Tongatapu
Noumèa

OCEANIA

AUSTRALIA

NEW ZEALAND

PACIFIC ISLANDS

FIJI

KIRIBATI

MARSHALL ISLANDS

MICRONESIA,
FEDERATED STATES OF

NAURU

PALAU

SAMOA

SOLOMON ISLANDS

TONGA

TUVALU

VANUATU

PAPUA NEW GUINEA

OCEANIA	
9,000,000 km^2	
population 33 million	
AFRICA	
30,310,000 km^2	
population 842 million	
THE AMERICAS	
42,000,000 km^2	
population 880 million	
ASIA	
44,000,000 km^2	
population 3,826 million	
EUROPE	
10,500,000 km^2	
population 731 million	

AUSTRALIA

Although it is the world's sixth largest country and smallest continent, the Commonwealth of Australia is very sparsely populated. It is primarily a country of plains and plateaux apart from its mountainous eastern coastline, which stretches from north to south and crosses the Tropic of Capricorn. Australia's climate is mainly arid in the interior, tropical in the north-east, temperate in the south-east and Mediterranean in the south-west.

Area: 7,741,220km²
Population (2002): 19,536,000
Capital: Canberra 298,847 (1996 census)
Government type and political system: constitutional monarchy with a parliamentary system
Head of state: (Queen) Elizabeth II represented by the Governor-General Michael Jeffery
Head of government: (Prime Minister) John Howard
Administrative structure: 6 states and 2 territories
Official language: English
Currency: Australian dollar

DEMOGRAPHICS

Density: 2 inhab/km²
Percentage of population in urban areas (2001): 91.1%
Age structure of population (2000): 0–15 years: 20.5%, 15–65 years: 67.2%, over 65 years: 12.3%
Birth rate (2003): 12.3‰

Death rate (2003): 7.4‰
Infant mortality rate (2003): 5.5‰
Life expectancy at birth (2003): male: 76.4 years, female: 82 years

ECONOMY

GNP (2002): 384 billion US$
GNP per capita (2002): 19,530 US$
GNP per capita PPP (2002): 27,440 international dollars
HDI (2000): 0.939
GDP annual growth rate (2003): 3%
Annual inflation rate (2000): 4.5%
Labour force by occupation (2000): agriculture: 4.9%, industry: 22%, services: 73.1%
GDP by sector (2000): agriculture: 3.5%, industry: 26.1%, services: 70.4%
Gross public debt (1998): 33.6% of GDP
Unemployment rate (2002): 6.3%

Agriculture and fishing

Crops
almonds (2001): 18,000t
oats (2001): 1,300,000t
butter (2001): 166,000t
wheat (2002): 10,059,000t

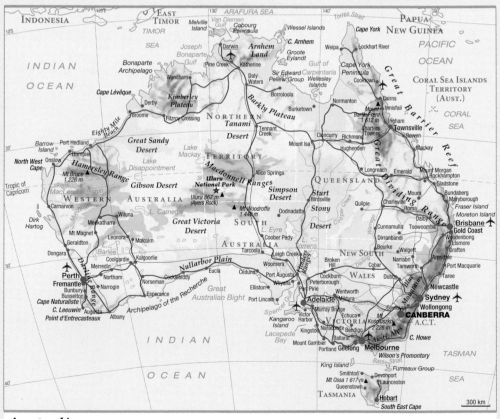

Australia

200 500 1000 m

— road
— railway line
✈ airport

★ place of interest
▦ provincial boundary
Perth provincial capital

● population over 2,000,000
● population 1,000,000 to 2,000,000
● population 100,000 to 1,000,000
• population less than 100,000

300 km

sugar cane (2001): 31,039,000t
rape (2001): 1,900,000t
cotton (2002): 822,000t
oranges (2002): 439,000t
barley (2002): 3,268,000t
apples (2001): 310,000t
potatoes (2002): 1,260,000t
timber (2000): 24,042,000m³
grapes (2002): 1,754,000t
rice (2002): 1,275,000t
sorghum (2002): 204,000t
tomatoes (2002): 400,000t
Livestock farming and fishing:
cattle (2002): 27,870,000 head
horses (2001): 220,000 head
sheep (2002): 106,200,000 head
pigs (2002): 2,912,000 head
chickens (2002): 93,000,000 head
fish (1999): 250,000t

Energy generation and mining
silver (2001): 2,100t
bauxite (2001): 53,285,000t
chromium (2001): 11,800t
copper (2001): 869,000t

diamonds (2001): 23,800,000 carats
total electricity (2001): 198,248 million kWh
tin (2001): 9,602t
iron (2001): 120,250,000t
natural gas (2002): 32,607 million m³
lignite (2001): 66,402,000t
manganese (2001): 948,000t
nickel (2001): 197,000t
gold (2001): 285,030kg
oil (2002): 31,121,000t
phosphate (2001): 1,893,000t
lead (2001): 714,000t
uranium (2001): 7,720t
zinc (2001): 1,519,000t

Industrial production
cheese (2001): 444,000t
honey (2001): 18,852t
meat (2001): 3,890,000t
sugar (2002): 4,987,000t
wine (2002): 12,204,000hl
aluminium (2001): 1,798,000t
cast iron (1998): 7,723,000t
copper (2001): 869,000t

tin (2001): 9,602t
nickel (2001): 197,000t
lead (2001): 303,000t
zinc (2001): 564,000t
cars (2002): 307,000 units
commercial vehicles (1998): 27,000 units
cotton yarn (2001): 755,000t
wool (2001): 700,000t
cement (2001): 7,500,000t

Tourism
Tourism revenue (2000): 8,442 million US$

Foreign trade
Exports (2002): 65,099 million US$
Imports (2002): 70,503 million US$

Defence
Armed forces (2001): 50,920 people
Defence budget (2001): 1.9% of GDB

Standard of living
Inhabitants per doctor (1996): 400
Average daily calorie intake (2000): 3,176 (FAO minimum: 2,400)
Cars per 1,000 inhabitants (1998): 510
Televisions per 1,000 inhabitants (2001): 731

HISTORY: KEY DATES

Australia is thought to have been inhabited since the Aboriginals arrived from present-day South-East Asia, more than 40,000 years ago.
17c: Dutch explorers visited Australia, naming it New Holland.
1770: Captain James Cook explored the southern coast of Australia and claimed it for Britain.
1788: the British colonization of New South Wales began with the establishment of a penal colony in Port Jackson (present-day Sydney).
19c: the discovery of gold and the ensuing gold rushes led to an increase in immigration, and the rest of Australia began to be colonized. Railway lines were constructed, and sheep and grain farming became widespread.
1901: the Commonwealth of Australia was created, incorporating the six colonies of New South Wales, Western Australia, South Australia, Queensland, Tasmania and Victoria.
1911: the Northern Territory joined the Commonwealth.
1914–18 AND 1939–45: Australia fought alongside the Allies during World War I and World War II.
1945 ONWARDS: Australia increased its level of participation in world affairs, and developed its economic ties with Japan, South Korea, China and the Association of South-East Asian Nations (ASEAN).

New Zealand is situated in the Pacific Ocean about 2,000km south-east of Australia, and is almost entirely located in the temperate zone of the southern hemisphere. The country is made up of two large islands and several smaller ones. Around 70% of the population live on North Island – where the two main cities, Auckland and Wellington, are located – which constitutes 42% of the country's total surface area. The terrain on South Island is more rugged and is dominated by the Southern Alps.

Area: 270,534km²
Population (2002): 3,837,000
Capital: Wellington 167,190 (2001 census), 345,000 (2001 e) including the suburbs
Government type and political system: constitutional monarchy with a parliamentary system
Head of state: (Queen) Elizabeth II represented by the Governor-General Dame Silvia Cartwright
Head of government: (Prime Minister) Helen Clark
Administrative structure: 22 regions, 2 self-governing territories and 2 non-self-governing territories
Official languages: English and Maori
Currency: New Zealand dollar

DEMOGRAPHICS
Density: 14 inhab/km²
Percentage of population in urban areas (2001): 85.9%
Age structure of population (2000): 0–15 years: 22.9%, 15–65 years: 65.3%, over 65 years: 11.8%
Birth rate (2003): 14‰
Death rate (2003): 7.6‰
Infant mortality rate (2003): 5.8‰
Life expectancy at birth (2003): male: 75.8 years, female: 80.7 years

ECONOMY
GNP (2002): 52 billion US$
GNP per capita (2002): 13,260 US$
GNP per capita PPP (2002): 20,550 international dollars
HDI (2000): 0.917
GDP annual growth rate (2003): 3.5%
Annual inflation rate (2000): 2.6%
Labour force by occupation (2000): agriculture: 8.7%, industry: 23.2%, services: 68.1%
GDP by sector (1996): agriculture: 7.8%, industry: 27.7%, services: 64.5%

New Zealand

★ place of interest
road
railway line
✈ airport
500 1000 2000 m

● population over 500,000
● population 100,000 to 500,000
● population 50,000 to 100,000
• population less than 50,000

Gross public debt: n/a
Unemployment rate (2002): 5.2%

Agriculture and fishing
Crops
wheat (2002): 355,000t
apples (2001): 485,000t
potatoes (2002): 500,000t
Livestock farming and fishing
cattle (2002): 9,633,000 head
sheep (2002): 39,546,000 head
pigs (2002): 341,000 head
fish (1999): 687,000t

Energy generation and mining
total electricity (2001): 37,505 million kWh
natural gas (2002): 6,090 million m³
coal (2001): 2,986,000t
gold (2001): 8,600kg
oil (2002): 1,599,000t

Industrial production
milk (2001): 13,162,000t

butter (2001): 352,000t
cheese (2001): 280,615t
meat (2001): 1,349,000t
aluminium (2001): 322,000t
cars (1999): 481,000 units
wool (2001): 250,100t

Tourism
Tourism revenue (2001): 2,252 million US$

Foreign trade
Exports (2001): 13,920 million US$
Imports (1999): 13,028 million US$

Defence
Armed forces (2001): 8,710 people
Defence budget (2001): 1.43% of GDP

Standard of living
Inhabitants per doctor (1996): 476
Average daily calorie intake (2000): 3,252 (FAO minimum: 2,400)
Cars per 1,000 inhabitants (2000): 580
Televisions per 1,000 inhabitants (2001): 557

HISTORY: KEY DATES

1642: the Dutch explorer Abel Tasman reached the archipelago, which was then inhabited by the Maori.

1769–70: Captain James Cook explored the coastline of New Zealand.

1814: Catholic and Protestant missionaries began to evangelize the country.

1841: a British governor was installed. Britain's colonial expansion policies led to wars between the colonists and the Maori, which were known as the Maori Wars (1843–7, 1860–70).

1852: a constitution came into force, granting the colony a great deal of autonomy.

1870: the country grew more prosperous as a result of the earlier discovery of gold.

1893: New Zealand became the first country to grant women the right to vote.

1898: the government introduced a system of old-age pensions.

1907: New Zealand became the self-governing Dominion of New Zealand within the British Empire.

1914–18 AND *1939–45*: New Zealand fought alongside the Allies during World War I and World War II.

1945: New Zealand became a full partner of the South-East Asian and Pacific nations.

1951: New Zealand signed the ANZUS (Australia, New Zealand, United States) security treaty.

1965–71: New Zealand supported the USA by sending troops to Korea and Vietnam.

1986: New Zealand's participation in ANZUS was suspended.

1999: New Zealand sent troops to join the UN peacekeeping force in East Timor.

The Maori

The Polynesian peoples known as the Maori arrived in New Zealand in two main waves (c.800 and c.1300). They initially settled on the coasts, where they hunted large birds known as Moas. Archaeologists therefore refer to this phase of Maori prehistoric culture as the Moa Hunter period. During the Classical period (c.1300) the Maori, organized in tribes or clans around sophisticated villages, colonized the mountainous interior of the islands and farmed the land. From around 1840, early British colonization of the country was strongly resisted by the Maori, who refused to sell their land to the colonists. After a truce (the Treaty of Waitangi) the Maori resistance was organized, but was unsuccessful in preventing the best Maori lands from falling into the hands of colonists. The Maori population was then decimated by illness, dropping to around 40,000.

The Maori were granted the right to vote in 1876. During the 20c (particularly after 1950) their population increased due to a high birth rate, and they received specific aid for agriculture, health and education. Today the Maori population numbers almost 430,000.

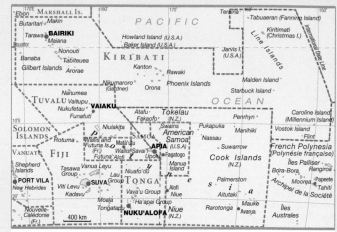

The Republic of the Fiji Islands is made up of an archipelago comprising over 800 volcanic and coral islands. The country's population resides mostly on the two main islands, Viti Levu and Vanua Levu.

Area: 18,274km²
Population (2002): 832,000
Capital: Suva 203,000 (2001 e)
Government type and political system: republic with a parliamentary system
Head of state: (President of the Republic) Ratu Josefa Iloilo
Head of government: (Prime Minister) Laisenia Qarase
Administrative structure: 4 divisions and 1 dependency
Official languages: English, Fijian and Hindi
Currency: Fijian dollar

Pacific Islands

BAIRIKI capital

● population over 10,000
● population less than 10,000

DEMOGRAPHICS
Density: 45 inhab/km²
Percentage of population in urban areas (2001): 50.2%
Age structure of population (2000): 0–15 years: 33.3%, 15–65 years: 63.3%, over 65 years: 3.4%
Birth rate (2003): 23.6‰
Death rate (2003): 5.5‰
Infant mortality rate (2003): 17.8‰
Life expectancy at birth (2003): male: 68.1 years, female: 71.5 years

ECONOMY
GNP (2002): 1.75 billion US$
GNP per capita (2002): 2,130 US$
GNP per capita PPP (2002): 5,330 international dollars

HDI (2000): 0.758
GDP annual growth rate (2003): 5.2%
Annual inflation rate (2001): 2.3%
Labour force by occupation: n/a
GDP by sector (2000): agriculture: 17.7%, industry: 29.3%, services: 53%
Gross public debt: n/a
Unemployment rate (1995): 5.4%

Agriculture and fishing
Crops
sugar cane (2001): 3,500,000t
manioc (2001): 32,600t
rice (2002): 12,900t
Livestock farming and fishing
cattle (2002): 320,000 head
goats (2001): 246,000 head
pigs (2002): 138,000 head
chickens (2002): 3,800,000 head
fish (1999): 38,500t

Energy generation and mining
total electricity (2001): 520 million kWh
silver (2001): 2t
gold (2001): 3,858kg

Industrial production
milk (2001): 52,000t
butter (2001): 1,800t

meat (2001): 21,700t
sugar (2002): 317,000t

Tourism
Tourism revenue (2001): 226 million US$

Foreign trade
Exports (1999): 537.7 million US$
Imports (1999): 653.3 million US$

Defence
Armed forces (2001): 3,500 people
Defence budget (2001): 1.67% of GDP

Standard of living
Inhabitants per doctor (1990): 2,030
Average daily calorie intake (2000): 2,861 (FAO minimum: 2,400)
Cars per 1,000 inhabitants (1996): 37
Televisions per 1,000 inhabitants (2001): 116

HISTORY: KEY DATES
1874: the Fiji Islands were annexed by Great Britain and became a British Crown Colony.
1970: the country became independent within the Commonwealth of Nations.

The Republic of Kiribati is an island nation in the Pacific Ocean that comprises three main groups of coral atolls (33 islands in total). Kiribati lay on either side of the international dateline until 1995, when the government adjusted the line eastwards to beyond the easternmost island, Caroline Island, thus ensuring that the date was the same across the whole country.

Area: 726km²
Population (2002): 77,000
Capital: Tarawa 32,000 (2001 e)
Government type and political system: republic with a semi-presidential system
Head of state and government: (President) Anote Tong
Administrative structure: 3 island groups

Official language: English
Currency: Australian dollar

DEMOGRAPHICS

Density: 93 inhab/km²
Percentage of population in urban areas (2001): 38.6%
Age structure of population: n/a
Birth rate (1999): 30.28‰
Death rate (1999): 7.74‰
Infant mortality rate (1998): 58‰
Life expectancy at birth: n/a

ECONOMY

GNP (2002): 0.091 billion US$
GNP per capita (2002): 960 US$
GNP per capita PPP (1999): 3,186 international dollars
HDI: n/a
GDP annual growth rate (2003): 2.5%
Annual inflation rate (2001): 7.7%
Labour force by occupation: n/a
GDP by sector (1998): agriculture: 20.7%, industry: 6.1%, services: 73.2%
Gross public debt: n/a
Unemployment rate: n/a

Agriculture and fishing
Crops
bananas (2001): 4,500t
coconuts (2001): 96,000t
Livestock farming and fishing

pigs (2002): 12,000 head
chickens (2002): 450,000 head
fish (1999): 48,200t

Energy generation and mining
total electricity (2001): 7 million kWh

Industrial production
meat (2001): 1,210t
copra (2001): 3,770t

Tourism
Tourism revenue (1999): 2 million US$

Foreign trade
Exports (1997): 11 million US$
Imports (1997): 93 million US$

Defence
Armed forces: n/a
Defence budget: n/a

Standard of living
Inhabitants per doctor: n/a
Average daily calorie intake (2000): 2,957 (FAO minimum: 2,400)
Cars per 1,000 inhabitants: n/a
Televisions per 1,000 inhabitants (2001): 35

HISTORY: KEY DATES

1979: Kiribati, formerly known as the Gilbert Islands, became independent within the Commonwealth of Nations.
1999: Kiribati became a member of the UN.

The Republic of the Marshall Islands is an archipelago made up of two island groups, the Ratak Chain and the Ralik Chain (meaning the 'Sunrise' and 'Sunset' chains respectively). The main atolls are Jaluit, Kwajalein, Eniwetok and Bikini.

Area: 181km²
Population (2002): 63,000
Capital: Majuro 25 000 (2001 e) including the suburbs
Government type and political system: republic
Head of state and government: (President of the Republic) Kessai Note
Administrative structure: 2 island groups
Official language: English
Currency: US dollar

DEMOGRAPHICS

Density: 355 inhab/km²
Percentage of population in urban areas (2001): 66%
Age structure of population (1993): 0–15 years: 51%, 15–65 years: 46%, over 65 years: 3%
Birth rate (1993): 43‰
Mortality rate: n/a
Infant mortality rate (1996): 26‰
Life expectancy at birth (2000): male: 59.1 years, female: 63 years

ECONOMY

GNP (2002): 0.126 billion US$
GNP per capita (2002): 2,380 US$
GNP per capita PPP: n/a
HDI: n/a
GDP annual growth rate (2000): 0.5%
Annual inflation rate: n/a
Labour force by occupation: n/a
GDP by sector (2000): agriculture: 12.5%, industry: 15.8%, services: 71.7%
Gross public debt: n/a
Unemployment rate: n/a

Agriculture and fishing
Crops
coconuts (2001): 15,000t
Fishing
fish (1999): 400t

Energy generation
total electricity: n/a

Tourism
Tourism revenue (1999): 4 million US$

Foreign trade
Exports (1995): 17 million US$
Imports (1995): 74 million US$

Defence
Armed forces: n/a
Defence budget: n/a

Standard of living
Inhabitants per doctor: n/a
Average daily calorie intake: n/a
Cars per 1,000 inhabitants: n/a
Televisions per 1,000 inhabitants: n/a

HISTORY: KEY DATES

1885–1914: the Marshall Islands were part of the protectorate of German New Guinea.
1920–44: the islands were conquered by Japan in World War I, and administered by Japan after the war.
1947: the United Nations made the Marshall Islands a UN Trust Territory, administered by the USA.
1991: the Marshall Islands became fully independent and were admitted to the UN.

The Federated States of Micronesia is a group of islands in the western Pacific Ocean, which consists of over 600 islands divided up into four states: Yap, Kosrae, Chuuk and Pohnpei. Micronesia includes most of the islands and islets in the Caroline Islands archipelago.

Area: 702km²
Population (2002): 106,000
Capital: Palikir 6,000 (2001 e)
Government type and political system: republic
Head of state and government: (President of the Republic) Joseph Urusemal
Administrative structure: 4 states
Official language: English
Currency: US dollar

DEMOGRAPHICS

Density: 168 inhab/km²
Percentage of population in urban areas (2001): 28.7%
Age structure of population: n/a
Birth rate (2003): 28‰
Death rate (2003): 5.9‰
Infant mortality rate (2003): 33.9‰

Life expectancy at birth (2003): male: 68 years, female: 69.1 years

ECONOMY

GNP (2002): 0.24 billion US$
GNP per capita (2002): 1,970 US$
GNP per capita PPP: n/a
HDI: n/a
GDP annual growth rate (2000): 3%
Annual inflation rate: n/a
Labour force by occupation: n/a
GDP by sector: n/a
Gross public debt: n/a
Unemployment rate: n/a

Agriculture and fishing

Crops
bananas (2001): 2,000t
maize (2002): 40t
manioc (2001): 11,800t
sweet potatoes (2001): 3,000t
rice (2002): 90t
Livestock farming and fishing
cattle (2002): 13,900 head
pigs (2002): 32,000 head
fish (1999): 11,900t

Energy generation
total electricity (1996): 40 million kWh
Tourism
Tourism revenue (1997): 2,128 million US$
Foreign trade
Exports (1995): 70 million US$
Imports (1995): 164 million US$
Defence
Armed forces: n/a
Defence budget: n/a
Standard of living
Inhabitants per doctor: n/a
Average daily calorie intake: n/a
Cars per 1,000 inhabitants: n/a
Televisions per 1,000 inhabitants (2001): 20

HISTORY: KEY DATES

1947: the United Nations placed the archipelago under US administration, as part of the UN Trust Territory of the Pacific Islands.
1991: Micronesia was admitted to the UN.

Federated States of Micronesia

state boundary   Kolonia state capital   ● pop. over 10,000
YAP name of state   ✈ airport   ● pop. less than 10,000

284

The world's smallest republic, the Republic of Nauru is situated in the southern Pacific Ocean near the Equator. It consists of one small phosphate atoll, which lies south of the Marshall Islands.

Area: 21km²
Population (2002): 10,000
Capital: Yaren 13,000 (2001 e) including the suburbs
Government type and political system: republic with a parliamentary system
Head of state and government: (President of the Republic) Ludwig Scotty
Administrative structure: 14 districts
Official languages: Nauruan and English

Currency: Australian dollar

DEMOGRAPHICS

Density: 549 inhab/km²
Percentage of population in urban areas (1995): 100%
Age structure of population: n/a

ECONOMY

GNP (1993): 0.11 billion US$
GNP per capita (1993): 12,000 US$
GNP per capita PPP: n/a
HDI: n/a
GDP annual growth rate: n/a
Annual inflation rate: n/a

Labour force by occupation: n/a
GDP by sector: n/a
Gross public debt: n/a
Unemployment rate: n/a

Agriculture and fishing

Crops
coconuts (2001): 1,600t
Livestock farming and fishing
pigs (2002): 2,800 head
chickens (2002): 5,000 head
fish (1999): 250t

Energy generation and mining
total electricity (2001): 30 million kWh
phosphate (2001): 266,000t

Tourism
Tourism revenue: n/a
Foreign trade
Exports: n/a
Imports: n/a
Defence
Armed forces: n/a

Defence budget: n/a
Standard of living
Inhabitants per doctor: n/a
Average daily calorie intake (1995): 3,202 (FAO minimum: 2,400)
Cars per 1,000 inhabitants: n/a
Televisions per 1,000 inhabitants: n/a

HISTORY: KEY DATES
1968: the state of Nauru became independent within the Commonwealth of Nations.
1999: Nauru was admitted to the UN.

PACIFIC ISLANDS PALAU

The Republic of Palau is an archipelago made up of around 350 islands and atolls, over half of which are inhabited.

Area: 459km²
Population (2002): 20,000
Capital: Koror 14,000 (2001 e)
Government type and political system: republic
Head of state and government: (President of the Republic) Tommy Remengesau
Administrative structure: 16 regions
Official languages: Palauan and English
Currency: US dollar

DEMOGRAPHICS
Density: 40 inhab/km²
Percentage of population in urban areas (2001): 69.5%
Age structure of population (2000): 0–15 years: 26.8%, 15–65 years: 68.6%, over 65 years: 4.6%

Birth rate (2000): 19.32%
Death rate (2000): 7.11%
Infant mortality rate (1998): 16.21%
Life expectancy at birth (2000): male: 65 years, female: 69 years

ECONOMY
GNP (2002): 0.136 billion US$
GNP per capita (2002): 6,820 US$
GNP per capita PPP: n/a
HDI: n/a
GDP annual growth rate (2000): 5.4%
Annual inflation rate: n/a
Labour force by occupation: n/a
GDP by sector: n/a
Gross public debt: n/a
Unemployment rate: n/a
Fishing
fish (1999): 1,800t
Energy generation
total electricity: n/a

Tourism
Tourism revenue: n/a
Foreign trade
Exports (1995): 12 million US$
Imports (1995): 63 million US$
Defence
Armed forces: n/a
Defence budget: n/a
Standard of living
Inhabitants per doctor: n/a
Average daily calorie intake: n/a
Cars per 1,000 inhabitants: n/a
Televisions per 1,000 inhabitants: n/a

HISTORY: KEY DATES
1947: the United Nations made Palau a UN Trust Territory, administered by the USA.
1994: Palau became independent and was admitted to the UN.

PACIFIC ISLANDS SAMOA

The Independent State of Samoa comprises two large volcanic islands, Savaii and Upolu, and several smaller islets. It is a mountainous, volcanic archipelago covered by dense forests.

Area: 2,831km²
Population (2002): 159,000
Capital: Apia 35,000 (2001 e) including the suburbs
Government type and political system: monarchy
Head of state: (President) Malietoa Tanumafili II
Head of government: (Prime Minister) Tuila'epa Sailele Malielegaoi
Administrative structure: 11 districts
Official languages: Samoan and English
Currency: tala

DEMOGRAPHICS
Density: 63 inhab/km²
Percentage of population in urban areas (2001): 22.3%
Age structure of population (2000): 0–15 years: 40.6%, 15–65 years: 55%, over 65 years: 4.3%
Birth rate (2003): 28.8‰
Death rate (2003): 5.5‰
Infant mortality rate (2003): 26.1‰

Life expectancy at birth (2003): male: 66.9 years, female: 73.4 years

ECONOMY
GNP (2002): 0.251 billion US$
GNP per capita (2002): 1,430 US$
GNP per capita PPP (2002): 5,570 international dollars
HDI (2000): 0.715
GDP annual growth rate (2003): 3.1%
Annual inflation rate (2001): 4%
Labour force by occupation: n/a
GDP by sector (2000): agriculture: 16.6%, industry: 26.6%, services: 56.8%
Gross public debt: n/a
Unemployment rate: n/a
Agriculture and fishing
Crops
pineapples (2001): 5,700t
bananas (2001): 20,000t
mangoes (2001): 2,500t
coconuts (2001): 140,000t
Livestock farming and fishing
cattle (2002): 28,000 head
pigs (2002): 201,000 head
chickens (2002): 450,000 head
fish (1999): 9,750t
Energy generation and mining
total electricity (2001): 105 million kWh

Industrial production
meat (2001): 5,140t
timber (2000): 61,000m³
Tourism
Tourism revenue (2001): 39 million US$
Foreign trade
Exports (2002): 5.12 million US$
Imports (2000): 25.13 million US$
Defence
Armed forces: n/a
Defence budget: n/a
Standard of living
Inhabitants per doctor (1990): 3,570
Average daily calorie intake (1995): 2,828 (FAO minimum: 2,400)
Cars per 1,000 inhabitants: n/a
Televisions per 1,000 inhabitants (2000): 61

HISTORY: KEY DATES
1722: Dutch explorers visited Samoa.
1962: the country, then known as Western Samoa, became independent. It joined the Commonwealth of Nations in 1970.
1997: the legislative assembly voted to change the country's name to Samoa.

The Solomon Islands is an independent country in the south-west Pacific Ocean that consists of an archipelago of several hundred islands and islets. Rainfall is very abundant, and dense forests cover most of the land.

Area: 28,896km²
Population (2002): 479,000
Capital: Honiara 78,000 (2001 e)
Government type and political system: constitutional monarchy with a parliamentary system
Head of state: (Queen) Elizabeth II represented by the Governor-General Nathaniel Waena
Head of government: (Prime Minister) Sir Allan Kemakeza
Administrative structure: 1 capital territory and 7 provinces
Official language: English
Currency: Solomon Islands dollar

DEMOGRAPHICS
Density: 15 inhab/km²

Percentage of population in urban areas (2001): 20.2%
Age structure of population (2000): 0–15 years: 43.4%, 15–65 years: 53.9%, over 65 years: 2.7%
Birth rate (2003): 33.3‰
Death rate (2003): 4.6‰
Infant mortality rate (2003): 20.7‰
Life expectancy at birth (2003): male: 67.9 years, female: 70.7 years

ECONOMY
GNP (2002): 0.256 billion US$
GNP per capita (2002): 580 US$
GNP per capita PPP (2002): 1,590 international dollars
HDI (2000): 0.622
GDP annual growth rate (2003): 5.6%
Annual inflation rate (2001): 7%
Labour force by occupation: n/a
GDP by sector (1991): agriculture: 49%, industry: 9%, services: 42%
Gross public debt: n/a
Unemployment rate: n/a

Agriculture and fishing
Crops
bananas (2001): 290t
yams (2002): 28,500t
manioc (2001): 2,300t
sweet potatoes (2001): 79,000t
Livestock farming and fishing
cattle (2002): 13,000 head
pigs (2002): 68,000 head
fish (1999): 82,000t

Energy generation and mining
total electricity (2001): 32 million kWh
gold (2001): 300kg

Industrial production
palm oil (2001): 30,000t
oil palms (2001): 8,000t
copra (2001): 11,000t

Tourism
Tourism revenue (1999): 6 million US$

Foreign trade
Exports (1999): 164.57 million US$
Imports (1999): 110.04 million US$

Defence
Armed forces: n/a
Defence budget: n/a

Standard of living
Inhabitants per doctor (1990): 7,420
Average daily calorie intake (2000): 2,277 (FAO minimum: 2,400)
Cars per 1,000 inhabitants: n/a
Televisions per 1,000 inhabitants (2000): 23

HISTORY: KEY DATES
1893–9: the Southern Solomon Islands became a British protectorate in 1893 and the Northern Solomon Islands (Bougainville and Buka) were ceded to Great Britain by Germany in 1899.
1942–5: Japanese forces occupied the Solomon Islands.
1920–75: Bougainville and Buka were placed under Australian administration by a League of Nations mandate in 1920. In 1975, they became part of Papua New Guinea.
1978: the Southern Solomon Islands (now the Solomon Islands), became independent within the Commonwealth of Nations.

The Kingdom of Tonga, also known as the Friendly Islands, is an archipelago of 171 islands and islets in the south-west Pacific, mainly made up of raised coral plateaux. Over two-thirds of Tonga's inhabitants live on the Island of Tongatapu, where the capital is situated.

Area: 747km²
Population (2002): 98,000
Capital: Nuku'alofa 33,000 (2001 e) including the suburbs
Government type and political system: monarchy
Head of state: (King) Taufa'ahau Tupou IV
Head of government: (Prime Minister) Prince 'Ulukalala Lavaka Ata
Administrative structure: 3 island groups
Official languages: Tongan and English
Currency: pa'anga

DEMOGRAPHICS
Density: 141 inhab/km²
Percentage of population in urban areas (2001): 33%
Age structure of population (2000): 0–15 years: 37.5%, 15–65 years: 57%, over 65 years: 5.5%
Birth rate (2003): 26.5‰
Death rate (2003): 7.2‰
Infant mortality rate (2003): 33.9‰
Life expectancy at birth (2003): male: 68 years, female: 69.1 years

ECONOMY
GNP (2002): 0.146 billion US$
GNP per capita (2002): 1,440 US$
GNP per capita PPP (2002): 6,820 international dollars
HDI: n/a
GDP annual growth rate (2003): 2.5%
Annual inflation rate (2001): 7%
Labour force by occupation: n/a
GDP by sector (2000): agriculture: 28.5%, industry: 15.1%, services: 56.4%
Gross public debt: n/a
Unemployment rate: n/a

Agriculture and fishing
Crops
bananas (2001): 700t
lemons (2002): 2,500t
yams (2002): 4,400t
manioc (2001): 9,070t
coconuts (2001): 57,685t
sweet potatoes (2001): 5,500t
Livestock farming and fishing
cattle (2002): 11,300 head
goats (2001): 12,500 head
horses (2001): 11,400 head
pigs (2002): 81,000 head
chickens (2002): 300,000 head
fish (1999): 3,660t

Energy generation
total electricity (2001): 27 million kWh

Industrial production
milk (2001): 370t
meat (2001): 2,180t
eggs (2001): 28t

Tourism
Tourism revenue (2000): 9 million US$

Foreign trade
Exports (2001): 6.7 million US$
Imports (2001): 63.7 million US$

HISTORY: KEY DATES
1970: Tonga became independent within the Commonwealth of Nations.
1999: Tonga was admitted to the UN.

Defence
Armed forces (1991): 300 people
Defence budget: n/a

Standard of living
Inhabitants per doctor (1991): 2,000
Average daily calorie intake (1995): 2,946

(FAO minimum: 2,400)
Cars per 1,000 inhabitants (1996): 10
Televisions per 1,000 inhabitants (2000): 66

PACIFIC ISLANDS TUVALU

Tuvalu is a small archipelago in the south-west Pacific Ocean, made up of nine coral atolls.

Area: 26km²
Population (2002): 9,000
Capital: Fongafale (on Funafuti)

Government type and political system: constitutional monarchy with a parliamentary system
Head of state: (Queen) Elizabeth II represented by the Governor-General Faimala Luka
Head of government: (Prime Minister) Maatia Toafa
Administrative structure: 9 atolls
Official languages: English and Tuvaluan
Currency: Tuvaluan dollar or Australian dollar

DEMOGRAPHICS
Density: 488 inhab/km²
Percentage of population in urban areas (1995): 46%
Age structure of population: n/a
Birth rate (1990): 30‰
Death rate (1990): 10‰

Infant mortality rate: n/a
Life expectancy at birth (1990): male: 60 years, female: 63 years

ECONOMY
Agriculture and fishing
Crops
bananas (2001): 250t
Livestock farming and fishing
pigs (2002): 13,200 head
fish (1999): 400t
Industrial production
meat (2001): 130t

HISTORY: KEY DATES
1978: the archipelago became independent within the Commonwealth of Nations.
2000: Tuvalu became a member of the UN.

PACIFIC ISLANDS VANUATU

The Republic of Vanuatu is an archipelago made up of over 80 islands, around 60 of which are inhabited. The climate is humid and tropical. Extensive forests cover around 75% of the country, and the islands contain three active volcanoes.

Area: 12,189km²
Population (2002): 207,000
Capital: Port-Vila 31,000 (2001 e) including the suburbs
Government type and political system: republic with a parliamentary system
Head of state: (President of the Republic) Kalkot Mataskelekele
Head of government: (Prime Minister) Serge Vohor
Administrative structure: 6 provinces
Official languages: Bislama, English and French
Currency: vatu

DEMOGRAPHICS
Density: 16 inhab/km²
Percentage of the population in urban areas (2001): 22.1%
Age structure of population (2000): 0–15 years: 42%, 15–65 years: 54.8%, over 65 years: 3.2%
Birth rate (2003): 30.5‰
Death rate (2003): 5.4‰
Infant mortality rate (2003): 28.5‰
Life expectancy at birth (2003): male: 67.5 years, female: 70.5 years

ECONOMY
GNP (2002): 0.212 billion US$
GNP per capita (2002): 1,050 US$
GNP per capita PPP (2002): 2,850 international dollars
HDI (2000): 0.542
GDP annual growth rate (2003): 1%
Annual inflation rate (2001): 2%
Labour force by occupation (2000): agriculture: 65%, industry: 30%, services: 5%
GDP by sector (2000): agriculture: 20.2%, industry: 9.9%, services: 69.9%
Gross public debt: n/a
Unemployment rate: n/a
Agriculture and fishing
Crops
ground nuts (2001): 1,800t
bananas (2001): 13,000t
maize (2002): 700t
Livestock farming and fishing
cattle (2002): 130,000 head

pigs (2002): 62,000 head
chickens (2002): 340,000 head
fish (1999): 95,000t
Energy generation
total electricity (2001): 43 million kWh
Industrial production
milk (2001): 3,100t
meat (2001): 9,140t
Tourism
Tourism revenue (2001): 46 million US$
Foreign trade
Exports (2001): 19.89 million US$
Imports (2001): 77.96 million US$
Defence
Armed forces: n/a
Defence budget: n/a
Standard of living
Inhabitants per doctor (1991): 10,000
Average daily calorie intake (2000): 2,587
(FAO minimum: 2,400)
Cars per 1,000 inhabitants (1996): 22
Televisions per 1,000 inhabitants (2001): 12

287

HISTORY: KEY DATES
1606: Portuguese explorers visited the archipelago.
1906: France and Britain agreed to establish a jointly administered condominium on the New Hebrides, as the islands were then called.
1980: the archipelago took the name of Vanuatu and became independent from France and Britain.

Ha Nôi (Hanoi), 204
Ha Tinh, 204
Haaltert, 214
Ha'apai Group, 282
Haapajärvi, 222
Haapsalu, 221
Ha'Arava ('Arabeh, Wadi al), 171
Haardt, 227
Haarlem, 246
Haast, 280
Habarane, 193
Habiganj, 153
Hachinohe, 172
Hachiôji, 172
Hadano, 172
Hadarom, 171
Hadd, Ra's al, 147
Hadejia [river], 79
Hadejia [town], 79
Hadera, 177
Haderslev, 219
Hadramawt, 147
Haedo, Cuchilla de, 142
Haeju, 177
Haeju-man, 177
Hafnarfjörður, 232
Hagen, 227
Hague, Cap de la, 224
Hague, The = 's-Gravenhage, 246
Hahotoé, 90
Hai Duong, 204
Hai Phong, 204
Haicheng, 158
Haifa = Hefa, 171
Haikou, 158
Hâ'il, 147
Hailar, 158
Hainan, 158
Haiti, 122
Hajdúböszörmény, 231
Hakodate, 172
Halab (Aleppo), 194
Halabja, 169
Halaib, 87
Halāniyāt, Juzur al, 147
Halawa, 138-9
Halba, 183
Halberstadt, 227
Half Assini, 61
Halfmoon Bay, 280
Halifax [Canada], 106
Halifax [U.K.], 273
Halkadiki, 230
Hall Islands, 284
Halla-san, 178
Halle [Belgium], 214
Halle [Germany], 227
Hallein, 210
Halmahera, 165
Halmstad, 266
Haltia, 222, 248
Hamadān, 167
Hamāh, 194
Hamamatsu, 172
Hamana-ko, 172
Hamâta, Gebel, 54
Hambantota, 193
Hamburg [region], 227
Hamburg [town], 227
Hämeenlinna, 222
Hamerkaz, 171
Hamersley Range, 278
Hamgyŏng-sanmaek, 177
Hamhŭng, 177
Hamhŭng, 177
Hami, 158
Hamilton [Canada], 106
Hamilton [N.Z.], 280
Hamim, Wadi al-, 70
Hamm, 227
Hammamet, 91
Hammamet, Golfe de, 91
Hammana, 183
Hamme, 214
Hammerfest, 248
Hamoyet, Jebel, 87
Hampshire, 273
Hamrîn, Jabal, 169
Hamrun, 243
Han, 178

Han Shui, 158
Hanalei, 138-9
Hanau, 227
Hanchon, 177
Handan, 158
Handeni, 89
Hangayn Nuruu, 186
Hangzhou, 158
Hanko, 222
Hannover, 227
Hannoversch Münden, 227
Hanoi = Ha Nôi, 204
Hanover, 124
Hanson Bay, 280
Haora, 163
Haouach, Ouadi, 48
Haouz, 74
Happy Valley-Goose Bay, 106
Hapsu, 177
Haradh, 147
Haradok, 212
Harare, 95
Harāsis, Jiddat al, 147
Harat, 57
Harazé-Mangueigne, 48
Harbel, 69
Harbin, 158
Hardenberg, 246
Harelbeke, 214
Härer, 58
Harf el Mreffi, 183
Hargeysa, 84
Hari kurk, 221
Hari Rūd, 146
Haringhat, 153
Harlingen, 246
Harlow, 273
Harmil, 57
Harney Basin, 138-9
Härnösand, 266
Harper, 69
Harris, 273
Harrisburg, 138-9
Harrismith, 85
Harstad, 248
Hartford [Liberia], 69
Hartford [U.S.A.], 138-9
Hartland Point, 273
Hartlepool, 273
Harts, 85
Haryana, 163
Harz, 227
Hasbaïya, 183
Hasselt, 214
Hassi Messaoud, 39
Hassi Rmel, 39
Hastings [N.Z.], 280
Hastings [U.K.], 273
Hat Yai, 198
Hatansuudal, 186
Hatgal, 186
Hato Mayor, 116
Hatteras, Cape, 138-9
Hatvan, 231
Haugesund, 248
Hauraki Gulf, 280
Haut Atlas, 74
Haute-Normandie, 224
Hautes Fagnes, 214
Hauts Plateaux, 39
Havana = La Habana, 114
Havel, 227
Havelange, 214
Havířov, 218
Havlíčkův Brod, 218
Havre, 138-9
Havre Rock, 280
Havre-St-Pierre, 106
Hawaii [island], 138-9
Hawaii [state], 138-9
Hawaiian Islands, 138-9
Hawalli, 180
Hawera, 280
Hawi, 138-9
Hawick, 273
Hawke Bay, 280
Hawrân, Wâdî, 169
Hay River, 106
Hazafon, 171

Hazar, Küh-e, 167
Hazarajat, 146
Hearst, 106
Hebei, 158
Heerenveen, 246
Heerhugowaard, 246
Heerlen, 246
Hefa (Haifa) [region], 171
Hefa (Haifa) [town], 171
Hefei, 158
Hegang, 158
Heide, 227
Heidelberg, 227
Heihe, 158
Heilbronn, 227
Heilongjiang, 158
Heimaey, 232
Heist-op-den-Berg, 214
Hekla, 232
Helan Shan, 158
Helena, 138-9
Helgoländer Bucht, 227
Heliopolis = Ba'albek, 183
Helleh, 167
Helmand, 146
Helmond, 246
Helmsdale, 273
Helsingborg, 266
Helsingør, 219
Helsinki, 222
Helwân, 54
Hemel Hempstead, 273
Hemlemle, Mount, 88
Henan, 158
Hendrik Top, 137
Hengduan Shan, 158, 187
Hengelo, 246
Hengyang, 158
Henley-on-Thames, 273
Henzada, 187
Héraðsflói, 232
Herät, 146
Hérault, 224
Heredia [region], 113
Heredia [town], 113
Hereford, 273
Herent, 214
Herentals, 214
Herisau, 268
Herma Ness, 273
Hermel, 183
Hermon, Mount (Shaykh, Jabal ash), 183, 194
Hermosillo, 130
Hernandarias, 134
Herne, 227
Herning, 219
Herstal, 214
Hertford, 273
Hertfordshire, 273
Hertogenwald, 214
Herve, 214
Hesbaye, 214
Hespérange, 241
Heusden-Zolder, 214
Hhohho, 88
Hian, 61
Hidaka, 172
Hidaka-sanmyaku, 172
Hidalgo del Paral, 130
Hieflau, 210
Hienghène, 276
Higashi-ōsaka, 172
Higashi-suidō, 178
High Veld, 88
Highgate, 124
Highlands (Lesotho), 68
Highlands [U.K.], 273
Higüey, 116
Hiiumaa, 221
Hijârah, Sahrâ al, 169
Hijaz, 147
Hikami, 172
Hikone, 172
Hildesheim, 227
Hillaby, Mount, 125

Hilo, 138-9
Hilversum, 246
Himachal Pradesh, 163
Himalayas, 154, 158, 163, 190
Himarë, 208
Himeji, 172
Hims, 194
Hînceşti, 244
Hinche, 122
Hinda, 50
Hindu Kush, 146, 190
Hingurakgoda, 193
Hinterrhein, 268
Hirakata, 172
Hiratsuka, 172
Hirosaki, 172
Hiroshima, 172
Hirtshals, 219
Hisor, 197
Hït, 169
Hitachi, 172
Hjørring, 219
Hkakabo Razi, 187
Hlatikulu, 88
Hlotse, 68
Hluti, 88
Hlybokaye, 212
Ho, 61
Hô Chi Minh (Saigon), 204
Hoa Binh, 204
Hoang Liên Son, 204
Hobart, 278
Hobro, 219
Hobyo, 84
Höd, 73
Hodda, 84
Hódmezővásárhely, 231
Hodna, Chott el, 39
Hodonín, 218
Höfn, 232
Hofsjökull, 232
Hôfu, 172
Hoggar, 39
Hoggar, Tassili du, 39
Hoh Xil Shan, 158
Hohe Tauern, 210
Hoher Dachstein, 210
Hohoe, 61
Hôi An, 204
Hoima, 93
Hokitika, 280
Hokkaidō, 172
Hoktemberyan, 151
Hola, 67
Holguín, 114
Holíč, 261
Holland, 246
Hólmavík, 232
Holohory, 270
Holon, 171
Holstebro, 219
Holyhead, 273
Hombori, Mont, 72
Homyel' [Gomel], 212
Hondarribia, 264
Hondo, 102
Hondsrug, 246
Honduras, 123
Honduras, Gulf of, 123
Hông Gai, 204
Hông, Sông (Red River), 204
Hongchŏn, 178
Hongor, 186
Hongsŏng, 178
Honiara, 276
Honokaa, 138-9
Honolulu, 138-9
Honshū, 172
Hoogeveen, 246
Hoogezand, 246
Hoogstraten, 214
Hoolehua, 138-9
Hoorn, 246
Hope Bay, 124
Hopedale, 106
Horadiz, 152
Horconcitos, 133
Horgen, 268
Horki, 212
Horlivka, 270

Hormuz, Strait of, 147, 167
Horn, 210
Horn, Cape = Hornos, Cabo de, 99, 109
Hornos, Cabo de (Horn, Cape), 99, 109
Horombe, 64
Horqueta, 134
Horsens, 219
Horw, 268
Horyn, 212
Hosingen, 241
Hoste, Isla, 109
Hotan, 158
Hotazel, 85
Hotte, Massif de la, 122
Hotton, 214
Houmt Souk, 91
Houndé, 43
Houston, 138-9
Houthalen-Helchteren, 214
Hovd, 186
Hove, 273
Hövsan, 152
Hövsgöl Nuur, 186
Howa, Ouadi, 48
Howakil Island, 57
Howe, Cape, 278
Howland Island, 282
Hoy, 273
Hoyerswerda, 227
Hradec Králové, 218
Hrasnica, 215
Hrazdan, 151
Hrodna (Grodno), 212
Hron, 261
Hsifo, 196
Hsinchu, 196
Hsinchuang, 196
Hsintien, 196
Hsinying, 196
Hsüeh Shan, 196
Hua Hin, 198
Huacho, 135
Huai He, 158
Huainan, 158
Hualien, 196
Huallaga, 135
Huamachuco, 135
Huancané, 135
Huancavelica, 135
Huancayo, 135
Huang He (Yellow River), 158
Huánuco, 135
Huanuni, 103
Huapi, Montañas de, 132
Huaral, 135
Huaráz, 135
Huarmey, 135
Huascarán, 135
Huasco, 109
Hubei, 158
Hubli-Dharwad, 163
Huddersfield, 273
Hudson Bay, 106
Hudson Strait, 106
Huê, 204
Huehuetenango, 120
Huelva, 264
Huércal-Overa, 264
Huesca, 264
Hughenden, 278
Hugli, 163
Huhhot, 158
Huib-Hoch Plateau, 77
Hula, 288
Hulayfah, 147
Hullo, 221
Humaitá [Brazil], 105
Humaitá [Paraguay], 134
Humansdorp, 85
Humber, 273
Humenné, 261
Húnaflói, 232
Hunan, 158
Hunedoara, 254
Hüngnam, 177
Hunsrück, 227
Huntington Beach, 138-9

Huntly, 273
Huntsville, 138-9
Hunza, 190
Huon Gulf, 288
Huon Peninsula, 288
Hurghada, 54
Huron, Lake, 106, 138-9
Hurup, 219
Húsavík, 232
Huşi, 254
Husum, 227
Hutag, 186
Huttwil, 268
Huy, 214
Huzhou, 158
Hvammstangi, 232
Hvannadalshnúkur, 232
Hvar, 217
Hveragerði, 232
Hvitá, 232
Hvolsvöllur, 232
Hwadae, 177
Hwange, 95
Hwedza, 95
Hyargas Nuur, 186
Hyderabad [India], 163
Hyderabad [Pakistan], 190
Hydra = Ýdra, 230
Hyères, Îles d', 224
Hyesan, 177
Hyoman, 212
Hyrynsalmi, 222
Hyvinkää, 222

I

Ialomita, 254
Ialpug, 244
Iargara, 244
Iaşi, 254
Ibadan, 79
Ibagué, 111
Ibar, 259
Ibarra, 117
Ibb, 147
Ibba, 87
Ibenga, 50
Iberian Range, 264
Ibicuy, 99
Ibiza = Eivissa, 264
Iboundji, Mont, 59
Ibrã, 147
Ibrahim, Nahr, 183
Ica, 135
Içá, 105
Içana, 105
Içel (Mersin), 200
Iceland, 232
Ichihara, 172
Ichikawa, 172
Ichinomiya, 172
Idah, 79
Idaho, 138-9
Idaho Falls, 138-9
Idfu, 54
Idi, 230
Idiofa, 51
Idjil, Kedia d', 73
Idku, 54
Idlib, 194
Idrija, 262
Ieper (Ypres), 214
Ierapetra, 230
Ifakara, 89
Ifalik, 284
Ife, 79
Iferouâne, 78
Ifrane, 74
Igalula, 89
Iganga, 93
Igarka, 256
Igatimi, 134
Igombe, 89
Igoumbi, Mont, 59
Igoumenitsa, 230
Iguaçu, 105
Iguaçu Falls, 99, 105
Igualada, 264
Iguéla, 59
Iguidi, Erg, 39, 73
Iharaña, 64
Ihema, Lake, 80

301

O

314

319

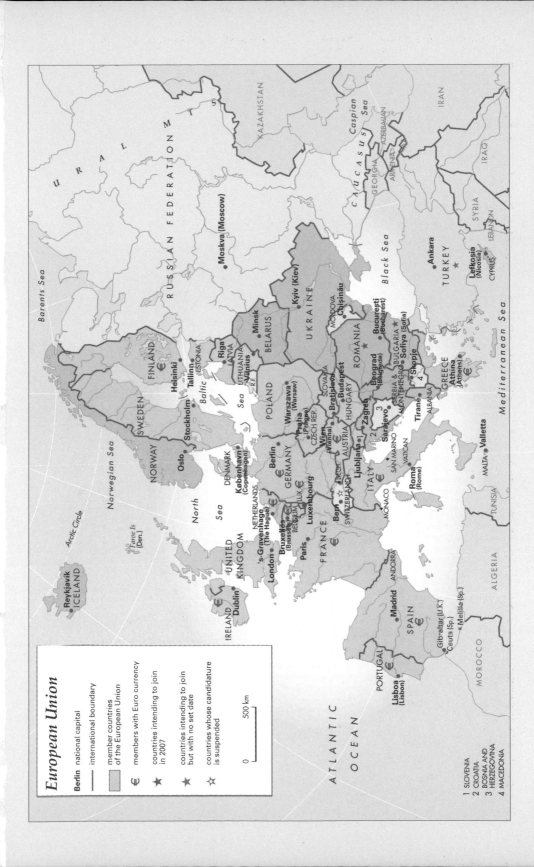

European Union

Berlin national capital

international boundary

member countries
of the European Union

€ members with Euro currency

★ countries intending to join
in 2007

★ countries intending to join
but with no set date

☆ countries whose candidature
is suspended

0   500 km

1 SLOVENIA
2 CROATIA
3 BOSNIA AND
  HERZEGOVINA
4 MACEDONIA

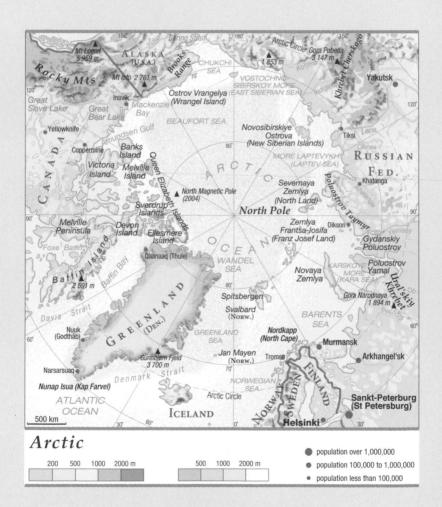

Arctic

Land elevation (colour scale 1): 200   500   1000   2000 m

Sea depth (colour scale 2): 500   1000   2000 m

- ● population over 1,000,000
- ● population 100,000 to 1,000,000
- • population less than 100,000

Map labels

Mt Logan 5 959 m
ALASKA (U.S.A.)
Brooks Range
Yukon
Bering Strait
Arctic Circle
Gora Pobeda 3 147 m
Khrebet Cherskogo
1 853 m
Kolyma
Rocky Mts
Mt Isto 2 761 m
CHUKCHI SEA
VOSTOCHNO-SIBIRSKOY MORE (EAST SIBERIAN SEA)
Indigirka
Yakutsk
Inuvik
Mackenzie Bay
Ostrov Vrangelya (Wrangel Island)
120°
Great Slave Lake
Great Bear Lake
Amundsen Gulf
BEAUFORT SEA
Novosibirskiye Ostrova (New Siberian Islands)
Lena
Tiksi
Olenek
Yellowknife
80°
A R C T I C
MORE LAPTEVYKH (LAPTEV SEA)
RUSSIAN FED.
Coppermine
Banks Island
Severnaya Zemlya (North Land)
Khatanga
Khatanga
Victoria Island
Melville Island
Queen Elizabeth Islands
North Magnetic Pole (2004)
Poluostrov Taymyr
CANADA
Sverdrup Islands
North Pole
Zemlya Frantsa-Josifa (Franz Josef Land)
Dikson
Yenisey
90°
Melville Peninsula
Devon Island
Ellesmere Island
O C E A N
Gydanskiy Poluostrov
Foxe Basin
Qaanaaq (Thule)
WANDEL SEA
Poluostrov Yamal
90°
Baffin Island
2 591 m
Baffin Bay
80°
Novaya Zemlya
KARSKOYE MORE (KARA SEA)
Ural'skiy Khrebet
Ob
Davis Strait
Spitsbergen
Gora Narodnaya 1 894 m
Pechora
Nuuk (Godthåb)
GREENLAND (DEN.)
Svalbard (NORW.)
BARENTS SEA
60°
60°
GREENLAND SEA
Nordkapp (North Cape)
Murmansk
Narsarsuaq
Gunnbjørn Fjeld 3 700 m
Jan Mayen (NORW.)
Tromsø
Arkhangel'sk
Nunap Isua (Kap Farvel)
Denmark Strait
NORWAY SWEDEN FINLAND
ATLANTIC OCEAN
Arctic Circle
NORWEGIAN SEA
Sankt-Peterburg (St Petersburg)
ICELAND
Helsinki
500 km